WHERE WILL WE BE IN 1995?

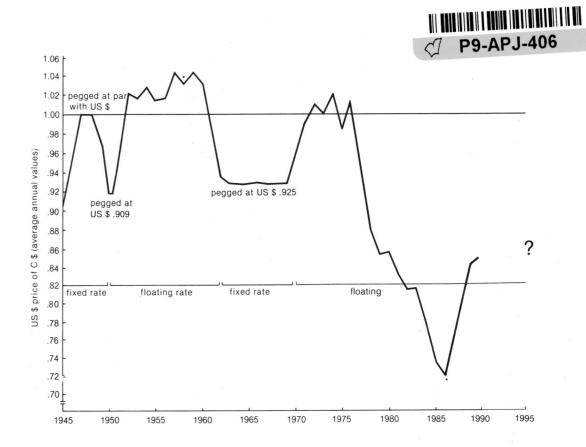

Canadian Dollar Exchange Rate in Terms of the American Dollar

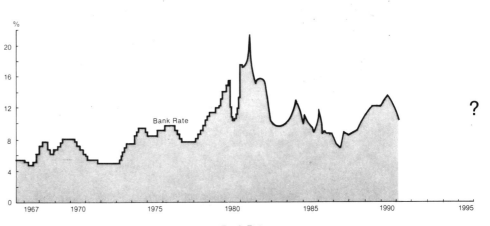

Bank Rate

Economic Analysis

& CANADIAN POLICY

Seventh Edition

Economic Analysis

Analysis

& CANADIAN POLICY

Seventh Edition

David Stager
University of Toronto

Butterworths
Toronto and Vancouver

Economic Analysis and Canadian Policy
© Butterworths Canada 1992

Printed and bound in Canada

Canadian Cataloguing in Publication Data

Stager, David, 1937-
Economic analysis & Canadian policy

7th ed.
Includes bibliographical references and index.
ISBN 0-409-89941-0

1. Economics.   2. Canada - Economic policy.
I. Title.   II. Title: Economic analysis and
Canadian policy.

HB171.5.S7 1991   330   C91-095415-1

Sponsoring Editor: Craig Laudrum
Development Editor: Edward O'Connor
Editor: Julia Keeler
Cover Design: Brant Cowie
Production: Kevin Skinner
Cover Photograph: Freeman Patterson/Masterfile

The Butterworth Group of Companies

Canada
Butterworths Canada Ltd., 75 Clegg Road, MARKHAM, Ont. L6G 1A1 and
409 Granville Street, Suite 1455, VANCOUVER, B.C. V6C 1T2

Australia
Butterworths Pty Ltd., SYDNEY, MELBOURNE, BRISBANE, ADELAIDE,
PERTH, CANBERRA and HOBART

Ireland
Butterworth (Ireland) Ltd., DUBLIN

New Zealand
Butterworths of New Zealand Ltd., WELLINGTON and AUCKLAND

Puerto Rico
Equity de Puerto Rico, Inc., HATO REY

Singapore
Malayan Law Journal Pte. Ltd., SINGAPORE

United Kingdom
Butterworth & Co. (Publishers) Ltd., LONDON and EDINBURGH

United States
Butterworth Legal Publishers, AUSTIN, Texas; BOSTON, Massachusetts;
CLEARWATER, Florida (D & S Publishers); ORFORD, New Hampshire
(Equity Publishing); ST. PAUL, Minnesota; and SEATTLE, Washington.

Preface

The objective of this seventh edition remains the same as that of previous editions—to present a concise introduction to economics and to Canadian economic policy for a wide range of readers. That the preceding editions have been used by universities, community colleges, and institutions of technology suggests that students and instructors have found this text useful in a variety of courses.

The primary goal of most introductory courses is to guide students in using economic concepts and reasoning in making decisions from day to day, in reading newspaper accounts of economic issues with a critical sense, and in recognizing the economic components of contemporary social problems.

Many of the difficulties that students encounter in economics courses arise from the presentation rather than from the nature of economic analysis. The lengthy exposition and complex organization of many elementary economic texts can obscure the basic simplicity of economics and its application to common economic problems. A more concise approach to each topic should help students to see the logical development and the use of economic concepts in various problem areas. Each general topic in the text is therefore presented according to the same pattern: an explanation of the objectives or goals, followed by the theoretical framework for analyzing the economic activity concerned, and finally the related policy in terms of historical experience, current legislation, or alternative actions.

This book is intended to serve primarily as a core text for a two-semester course, but it is organized so that it can also be used for a sequence of two complete one-semester courses. The length has been deliberately constrained to avoid overwhelming students, and so that each instructor can add the most appropriate supplementary material for specific courses or programs.

The major revision in this seventh edition occurs in the development of the real sector model for the macroeconomy. Previous editions had presented the simple Keynesian model with constant prices, followed in the fiscal policy section by a discussion of the contemporary problem of simultaneous inflation and unemployment. The macroeconomic equilibrium, traditionally represented in the *IS-LM* diagram, was reserved for an appendix to the chapters on monetary theory. In this revision, it has been possible to retain the original concise treatment, yet present a more contemporary model based on aggregate expenditures in a real sector with constant prices, followed by aggregate demand and aggregate supply when prices are allowed to vary.

Students have found certain features particularly helpful in reviewing the main topics of each chapter. The captions accompanying the diagrams explain the main points illustrated by the diagram, often rephrasing the explanation offered in the text. The review of the main points at the end of each chapter is intended to be a short, precise review that includes important details. Students have also found this feature to be a useful introduction to the main ideas of the chapter. Greater use is made of subheads in recent editions to identify each point relating to the topic, and to provide a roadmap of each chapter as it is approached or reviewed.

A study guide is available to accompany the textbook. For each chapter it includes multiple-choice and true-false questions, problems, and discussion questions. These are specially designed to retrace the derivation of basic economic principles, and to extend the analysis to further applications.

I owe a considerable debt to the instructors who have taken time to write with comments on the previous editions and to offer useful suggestions; as well, students in my introductory economics courses have contributed more than they realized by questioning difficult or ambiguous passages.

I am especially grateful to several instructors who commented in detail on individual chapters of the sixth edition prior to the revision of this edition; they are: Torben Anderson, Red Deer College; Gordon Boreham, University of Ottawa; Robert Jeacock, Malaspina College; Jane Kryzanowski, St. Peter's College; Chantale LaCasse, Brock University; Mark Lovewell, Ryerson Polytechnical Institute; Mollie O'Neill, Seneca College; Clayton Petrick, Confederation College; Stephen Rakoczy, Humber College; Cal Shaw, George Brown College; Fazley Siddiq, Dalhousie University; William Sinkevitch, St. Clair College; James White, Seneca College.

Contents

PART ONE

Economics and The Market Place

1 Economics: The Analysis of Choice

What Is Economics?

"What is Economics?" is a question that cannot be answered in a few words. This chapter provides a partial answer by examining basic economic problems and the way societies are organized to deal with these problems. Only after economics is considered in these ways can simple definitions of economics be read with some understanding. Nonetheless, it is useful to have such definitions as guideposts to what is to come.

Definitions of economics offered by prominent economists have included:

Economics is the science which studies human behaviour as a relationship between ends and scarce means which have alternative uses.

— *Lionel Robbins*

Economics comes in whenever more of one thing means less of another.

— *Fritz Machlup*

The theory of economics . . . is a method rather than a doctrine, an apparatus of the mind, a technique of thinking, which helps its possessor to draw correct conclusions.

— *John Maynard Keynes*

These definitions emphasize that economics involves both individual and social decisions; that the means for satisfying human wants are limited; that this scarcity requires giving up something to gain something else; and that the study of economics provides a method for thinking about economic problems, rather than settled conclusions.

Economists are applying basic economic analysis—or the technique for economic thinking—to an increasing number of problem areas.

Studies of the economics of crime, education, health, discrimination, housing, poverty, disarmament, and pollution have all been added to economic literature in recent years.

Economic problems arise from the need to make decisions or choices about an endless number of alternatives: alternative uses for the output of economic activity, alternative methods for producing this output, and alternative ways of distributing this output among individuals.

Basic Vocabulary

Many economic terms are also common words in our everyday language, but more specific meanings are given to them in economics. New terms are defined as they are introduced in successive chapters of this book, but some of the basic ones can be mentioned here.

Each economy has a variety of resources or *factors of production*, including the *natural resources* of land and water, *human resources* consisting of the population's mental and physical skills, and *man-made or capital resources* such as buildings, machinery, roads, and railways. These productive factors can be combined in various ways with *raw materials* such as minerals, timber, animals, and fish, to produce *commodities* that are useful and ultimately provide satisfaction to consumers.

All commodities can be described as either *goods* or *services*. Goods are tangible commodities such as bread, automobiles, and sweaters; services are intangible commodities like baby-sitting, legal advice, and bus rides. *Intermediate goods* are those that are partly finished, such as bread flour, and require further processing before they are useful. When they have passed through all stages of production, they are *final goods*. Consumer goods and services are those that individuals value because they provide direct satisfaction of various kinds, either physiological or psychological. Such satisfaction usually derives not from possessing these goods but from using them. This use of commodities to provide satisfaction is *consumption*. The satisfaction that consumers realize from commodities is also called *utility*.

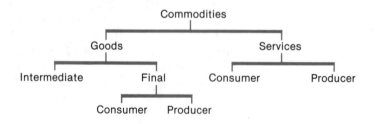

Producer goods and services are those that do not provide satisfaction directly, but are used in the production of other goods and services. *Production* is the creation of utility or satisfaction through the transformation of raw materials — by using productive factors — into commodities that ultimately yield satisfaction to consumers.

Production may be a matter of *form*: making a milkshake or producing a concert; it may be a matter of *time*: providing storage so that consumers may enjoy a properly aged wine, or fresh apples in February; or it may be a matter of *place*: transporting goods such as new automobiles or fresh lobsters to consumers who are some distance from the origin of these goods.

The study of economics is concerned not only with production and consumption, which have just been defined, but also with *distribution*. This concerns the actual pattern of consumption by various groups in the economy — namely, who gets how much of which goods and services.

Scarcity and Choice

Goods can be described as either *economic goods* or *free goods*.

Scarcity Economic goods are those that are *scarce* — there is not enough of the particular good to provide as much as all consumers would like if the good were free. A free good is one that exists in sufficient abundance to satisfy everyone's wants, even when no price is charged.

Drinking water is often regarded as a free good, apart from the municipal service charge for pumping and piping, but in areas of some countries even drinking water is not a free good, since it can be bought only in bottled form.

The fact that goods are scarce is a result of the *limited availability of productive resources to meet unlimited human wants*. The emphasis here is not on *needs* (items necessary to maintain life) but on *wants*. The basic needs of people in many parts of the world have not yet been met, but there may be some hope of doing so. Indeed, calculations have shown that a redistribution of the world's current output would solve this problem, provided that the redistribution would not lead to an increase in the population. But the wants of individuals, whether rich or poor, seem endless.

Choices The scarcity of resources to meet these unlimited wants forces individuals and societies to make *choices*. Choices have to be made between alternative commodities that could be produced, alternative means for producing them, and alternative distributions among individuals of the commodities produced.

Making choices entails giving up or forgoing something if something else is to be enjoyed. This is the common experience of most consumers; purchasing a new house may mean that a family must put off purchasing a new car for a few years. Self-employed professionals face a similar problem: taking an extended holiday requires giving up the income that would have been earned during that period. Students, too, forgo potential earnings to continue their education, as well as forgoing the satisfaction derived from other things that would have been bought with money spent for books and tuition fees.

Opportunity Cost

The satisfaction or output that would have been derived from the best alternative use of resources is termed the *opportunity cost* of the choice actually made.

Opportunity cost is an important concept in everyday life because it describes the total cost entailed in making a specific choice. Without looking at a potential choice in terms of all that must be given up, one might, for example, measure the cost of a vacation only in terms of actual expenditures and omit either forgone earnings or the enjoyment that might be gained from the given amount of time. Furthermore, opportunity cost emphasizes the real goods or services that are forfeited, rather than the monetary value of the item in question.

Societies face the same kind of choices involving the consideration of opportunity costs, especially in decisions about dividing resources between the production of privately consumed goods and services like food and clothes and public goods and services such as defence, education, health, and so on. This problem is illustrated in Figure 1.1.

Production-Possibilities Boundary   If all the economy's productive resources are fully utilized and the most efficient technology is used in producing only private goods, the maximum output per year would be C_3 units.[1] On the other hand, allocating all resources to public goods would yield P_3 units. Thus there are limits to what the economy can produce, namely C_3 or P_3 units, even if all the resources are concentrated on one type of good. The economy, however, will probably want some combination of these.

The *production-possibilities boundary* represented by the curved line between C_3 and P_3 shows the range of maximum possible combinations of public and private goods that can be produced with the given resources used in the most efficient manner. Suppose an economy is at point A, enjoying C_2 units of private goods and P_1 units of public goods.

[1] Students who have not been working with graphs recently may find it useful to review the Appendix to this chapter.

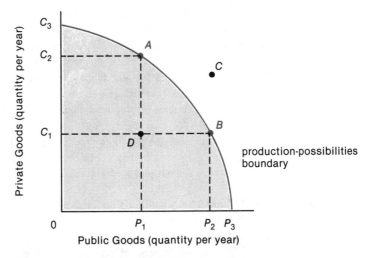

Figure 1.1   Production-Possibilities Boundary
Any point on the production-possibilities boundary or frontier indicates one of numerous combinations of maximum output that can be obtained by the use of available resources and the most efficient technology. Moving from *A* to *B* requires giving up some private goods to obtain more public goods. *C* represents an unattainable combination and *D* represents a combination that does not make full or efficient use of resources. Any other two commodities could be portrayed on a similar curve. The concavity of the curve reflects diminishing returns as more resources are allocated to producing a given commodity.

If it wants to increase its output of public goods to P_2 units, the production-possibilities boundary shows that individuals must then forgo the difference between C_2 and C_1 units of private goods. This reduction in private goods is the opportunity cost of the increase in public goods. The new combination would be C_1 and P_2 units, represented by point B.

The economy would be able to increase its output of public goods without reducing private goods only if the economy were not at its *production-possibilities frontier* or *boundary*. If productive resources are not being fully utilized or are being used inefficiently, the economy will be inside this boundary, perhaps at point D. In this case, output of public goods could be increased from P_1 to P_2 by improving the use of resources, without reducing private consumption, and thus without incurring an opportunity cost. All combinations within the production-possibilities boundary are possible combinations, but only combinations on the curve represent maximum combinations of output. Point C lies beyond the curve, representing a combination of public and private goods unattainable with the given quantity of productive resources and the existing state of technology.

Diminishing Productivity   When the production-possibilities boundary is concave (or bowed outward) as in Figure 1.1, this indicates *diminishing productivity* of resources with increasing output of the good in question. This would occur if the productive resources were allocated first to the goods for which they are most effective and then were transferred to the production of the other good as its output was being increased. For example, land that is best suited for growing grain will be used first for producing grain crops. Only when grain output is to be greatly increased will the rougher, less fertile lands be used for these crops. A straight-line boundary would indicate that productive resources were equally effective in producing either good.

Shifting the Boundary   It would be possible to attain combination C if there were a sufficient increase in *productive resources*, in the form of more arable land, a bigger or better-educated labour force, or more factories. If such increases are in proportion to the existing stock of resources there would be a parallel outward shift of the production-possibilities boundary, as shown in Figure 1.2a. Alternatively, if there should be an *improvement in technology*, such as a new productive process or the discovery of

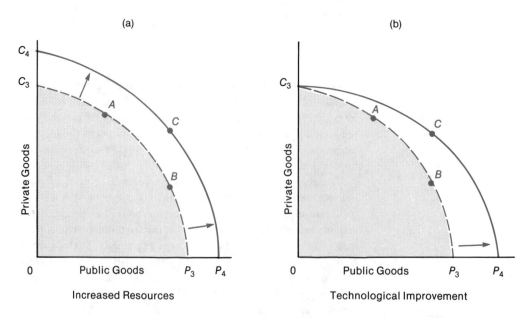

Figure 1.2   Outward Shifts in Production-Possibilities Boundaries
Combination C becomes attainable if there is an outward shift of the production-possibilities boundary due either to increased productive resources, as in (a), or a technological improvement in the production of one of the commodities, as in (b).

better sources of raw materials, this would increase the maximum output attainable for the commodity affected by the technological changes. This would shift the production-possibilities boundary outward along the axis representing the commodity in question, as shown in Figure 1.2b. It becomes possible to consume more of both commodities because the more efficient use of resources due to improved technology for producing one commodity releases some resources to produce more of the other commodity. Some technological changes do increase the output of all products—as in the case of new energy sources—but most changes are specific to a few products.

The production-possibilities boundary is an important concept because it shows the basic economic problems: scarcity is defined by the limited output available with given resources; choice is evident in the range of possible combinations from which an economy must choose; and the cost of each choice is given by the change in coordinates defining the boundary.

Basic Economic Decisions

The basic economic decisions facing all economies are the same: What is to be produced? How will these items be produced? Who will receive what is produced?

What Is to Be Produced?

An economy can produce thousands of different commodities, and in a wide range of quantities of each. Thus decisions must be made not only about the kinds of commodities but also about the quantity of each that should be produced. In most cases, this total collection will include some producer goods both to maintain existing productive capacity and to incorporate advancing technology in new equipment. This requires a further decision about the opportunity cost, in terms of forgone satisfaction from current consumption, that should be incurred to gain increased future output. In other words, what resources should be released from the production of consumer goods to increase the production of producer goods?

This decision is illustrated in Figure 1.3 using a *consumption-possibilities curve*. Note the similarity of this curve with the production-possibilities boundary of Figure 1.1. If all existing productive resources are allocated to current consumption, C_1 units can be enjoyed now. But if the same resources, except those required to sustain life, are used for producer goods to increase the output of consumer goods in the future, F_1 units of consumer goods can be enjoyed in the future. Note that F_1 is

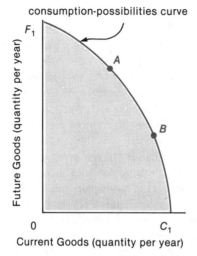

consumption-possibilities curve

F₁

Future Goods (quantity per year)

A

B

0   C₁

Current Goods (quantity per year)

Figure 1.3   A Consumption-Possibilities Curve
Productive resources can be used to produce alternative combinations of
consumer goods and producer goods. Choice of combination A rather than
B implies a higher rate of economic growth, because more resources are
directed to producer goods now to increase output of consumer goods in
the future. A higher proportion of producer goods increases the quantity of
consumer goods available in the future, represented by a movement from
B to A.

greater than C_1. Of course, some resources must be used to produce
commodities for current consumption and some for at least maintaining
current productive capacity. The actual combination chosen will lie
somewhere along the consumption-possibilities curve, perhaps at either
point A or point B. An economy that chooses combination B over A is
said to have a higher *rate of time preference*, because its preference for
current goods over future goods is stronger than that exhibited by an
economy that chooses combination A.

How Will the Commodities Be Produced?

Almost every commodity can be produced using different techniques.
Roads can be built using people working with shovels and picks, or
using fewer workers and some light machinery, or using very few
workers and huge earth-moving and paving machines designed specifically for road-building. Similarly, most consumer goods can be produced using mainly manual labour, or with little labour and much
machinery.

The production methods chosen will depend on the state of technology in the economy and the relative availability of capital, or producer

goods, and labour of various skill levels. Technology—the knowledge of alternative processes, raw materials, and sources of raw materials for producing specific commodities—is generally available to any economy, although some effort may be required to adapt technology to the needs of a particular economy. Thus the major conditions influencing the choice of production methods are the amount of labour and capital available and the willingness to forgo current consumption in order to develop capital goods and to improve the skills of the labour force.

Who Will Get How Much?

An economy must also decide who will receive how much of each of the commodities produced. Although production problems received much of the economists' attention for many years, distribution problems have received increasing attention. Some have even suggested that production problems have been solved, in the sense that the world's existing resources and technology are capable of producing at least a minimum standard of living for the world's population, and that only the distribution problem remains. It is in this area that political and social considerations enter most strongly, and therefore it is here that the type of decision-making mechanism or organization is most important.

Other Economic Decisions

The preceding three sets of questions are the basic ones facing any economy. They are often stated succinctly as *How? What? For Whom?* Other decisions can be drawn from these for special attention. They include questions about the rate of economic growth, the level of resources used in the economy, and how to provide flexibility in response to economic and other changes.

The desired rate of economic growth is one aspect of the resource allocation decision. Economic growth can be illustrated, as in Figure 1.4, as an outward shift of the production-possibilities boundary. In Figure 1.1, combination *C* was unattainable because sufficient resources were not available to produce this combination of commodities. However, if the economy decides to allocate more of its resources to producer goods to expand its productive capacity, the boundary may shift outward over time, as shown by the outer curve in Figure 1.4. Combination *C* becomes attainable, indicating that more of both public goods and private goods can be made available.

The level of resources available to the economy has been taken as fixed at any given time. While this is so, the quantity of resources actually used, and particularly labour services, can be changed fairly quickly. This involves decisions about the quantity of labour service to

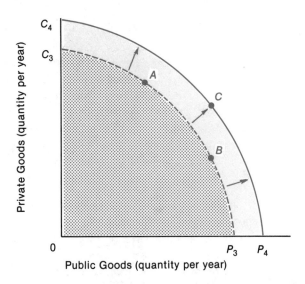

Figure 1.4   Outward Shift of Production-Possibilities Boundary
Choosing a higher proportion of producer goods (reflecting a higher
preference for future consumer goods) leads to greater economic growth,
with an outward shift of the production-possibilities boundary due to the
increase in resources. Full use of available resources produces a larger
total output of both public and private goods—such as at C—than the
maximum combinations shown in Figure 1.1.

be made available, that is, the number of hours per week and weeks per
year that persons will work in paid employment, and who will be available for employment. The decision about the quantity of labour actually used determines whether everyone who wants to work will be able to
find employment—that is, whether the economy will decide that full
employment has a high priority, or that other considerations are more
important. This raises specific questions about whether retirement
should be mandatory at a certain age, whether other employment discrimination will be permitted, and whether child-care facilities will be
available for working parents.

How to provide for flexibility in response to changing conditions is a
question that arises when the three basic questions are considered over
a period of time. Each of the What? How? and For Whom? questions
may be answered differently as available resources, technology,
consumer preferences, and political values change. Part of the answer
to each of the basic questions must therefore include a means for
responding to such changes.

Economic Systems

Every economy faces the same basic economic questions, but each has a different way of deciding the answers. An economy can therefore be classified in terms of the method used to make its basic economic decisions. Each of the wide variety of *economic systems* in existence uses a combination of decision-making arrangements. To understand their operation more fully, it is useful to consider the pure forms of economic systems. Although such pure forms do not exist in the real world, some of their characteristics occur in varying degrees in each of the world's economies. The three basic types of economic systems are: traditional economy, planned economy, and market economy.

Traditional Economy

The *traditional economy* is based on small units, such as families or villages, each producing everything it consumes, with little need for specialization of labour and exchange of goods. Everyone joins in to help with harvesting crops and building new homes, and a few persons become skilled in the production of clothing and equipment.

Decisions about the allocation of resources for producing various commodities are rather simple in a traditional economy. Food, clothing, buildings, and tools are the same as have been produced as long as the members of the economic unit can remember.

Tradition not only dictates what commodities are to be produced and how much is required to maintain the unit, but also how these commodities are produced and distributed. Tradition also determines who will make any remaining decisions. A few centuries ago, this was the dominant form of economic organization, but colonization, political independence, and worldwide emphasis on economic development have transformed almost all of the earlier examples of traditional economies.

Planned Economy

The essential feature of a *planned economy* is that a central authority makes all the important economic decisions. In practice, this method is often used by a totalitarian form of government and thus is sometimes called a *command economy*. Furthermore, the central authority usually, but not necessarily, owns the productive resources of land and physical capital.

The economy is operated on the basis of a series of plans that specify the total output of each commodity, how much each production unit will produce, and how much of the economy's productive resources will be made available to each unit. Within this framework, labourers and consumers are free to realize the greatest satisfaction possible. They are constrained to the extent that only certain jobs will be available in specific areas, and only certain consumer goods and services will be available and at specified prices.

The central authorities thus decide what will be produced and in what quantity, what production methods will be used and, by setting wages and prices, how the output will be distributed. The major problems of a planned economy are to provide sufficient consumer goods and services to maintain the confidence and support of the population, to utilize resources efficiently, and to take account of all the detailed decisions required to make the plan operational. Authorities must also maintain the structure of the plan while remaining sufficiently flexible to deal with unforeseen events such as droughts, wars, and new technology.

Pure planned economies do not exist, but the major characteristics of a planned economy dominated the economies of the U.S.S.R. and most Eastern European countries until the 1990s, when greater use was made of the market system.

Market Economy and the Price Mechanism

The main feature of the *market economy* is that prices are determined in a separate market for each commodity, with these prices in turn determining the answers to each of the basic economic questions. *A market is the organized collection of potential buyers and sellers for a specific commodity.* Markets for different commodities are interdependent because buyers have alternative products and productive resources available to them, and suppliers can use their resources to provide alternative commodities. As the prices of various products and productive resources change, both buyers and suppliers may change their decisions about what to buy and to produce, such that changes in the prices and quantities in several markets may follow from a change in any given market.

Various terms have been associated with this form of economic organization. The term *price mechanism* stresses that prices are central to the decision-making in a market economy; *free enterprise economy* appropriately describes only one aspect of the pure form, whereby any individual is free to produce any commodity in any quantity and by any method; and *capitalist economy* emphasizes that individuals may own physical capital, thereby realizing larger incomes than if they offered only their labour services. These latter two terms, however, have political connotations that can detract from an understanding of the essential elements of the market economy.

Prices, and particularly differences between prices, determine what will be produced and in what quantity, because producers will supply those commodities that can be sold for at least the cost of producing them. The prices of productive resources determine what production methods will be used. As the price of labour increases relative to the cost of machinery, more of the latter will be substituted for labour. The distribution of consumer goods and services is determined by the prices that individuals receive for their labour services and for the use of their physical capital and land.

Mixed Economies

All economies are more appropriately described as *mixed economies*. This term is not very informative; rather, its value lies in emphasizing that elements of each of the pure forms can be found in any existing economy. In the Canadian economy, for example, the market system is dominant, but there are also features of the planned and traditional economies. Formal education, for example, is provided mainly through a planning mechanism, with authorities at different levels of government deciding who shall go to school (under the compulsory attendance legislation), where schools shall be built, and what shall be taught. Elements of the traditional economy may be found in Canada in some Inuit and Indian communities.

There are at least two criteria for choosing which of these systems should be followed, or how dominant each system should be in a mixed economy. One is economic performance — achieving maximum output per person — and the other is the freedom of choice available to producers and consumers.

The conflicts between these two criteria are found in any economy, but they are particularly evident in some countries in Asia and Africa that have substantial elements of central economic planning but also maintain many of the freedoms of a market system.

Review of the Main Points

1. Because human wants are unlimited, resources used in producing goods and services to satisfy these wants are scarce. This scarcity requires that choices be made about the use of available resources and the distribution of the commodities produced. Such choices involve opportunity costs — the forgone satisfaction or output that would have been derived from the next best alternative use of resources.

2. A production-possibilities boundary shows the maximum possible combinations of two commodities (or two types of commodities) that can be produced with the resources and technology available, and illustrates the choice that must be made between alternative combinations. A greater output of goods and services could be obtained either by increasing the quantity of resources or by improving the technology, or by making both of these changes.

3. The basic economic decisions are: (a) what commodities should be produced in what quantities—including decisions about private and public goods, and current and future goods—such that the total combination of commodities provides the maximum satisfaction possible with the given resources; (b) how these commodities will be produced, given the state of technology and the relative availability of labour and physical capital, to make the most efficient use of productive resources; and (c) how the commodities will be distributed among the population to accord with generally held views about social justice.

4. Three types of economic systems can be defined according to the way the basic economic decisions are made: these are the traditional economy, the planned economy, and the market economy.

5. The traditional economy consists of small self-sufficient units of families or villages, with decisions made according to traditional practices. The planned economy is directed by planning authorities who decide how these basic questions will be answered. The market economy is directed by the set of prices determined in markets for each commodity.

6. Pure forms of these economic systems do not exist; each economy combines features from each pure system and thus should be described as a "mixed economy". Nevertheless, economies are often classified according to the most dominant features; thus the U.S.S.R. was predominantly a planned economy prior to 1990, and Japan, a market economy.

Key Concepts and Topics

economics	utility
economic resources	production
factors of production	scarcity
commodity	opportunity cost
intermediate vs. final goods	production-possibilities boundary
producer vs. consumer goods	consumption-possibilities curve
economic vs. free goods	economic decisions or problems
services	technology
consumption	economic growth

economic systems
traditional economy
planned economy
market economy

price system
market
mixed economies

Questions for Review and Discussion

1. Do you think it is valid to assume that not all wants can ever be satisfied? Why?
2. Canada is sometimes described as an affluent society, yet economists continue to base their analyses on the fact of scarcity. Can these two situations—affluence and scarcity—be reconciled? Explain carefully what scarcity means in this context.
3. Why is water sometimes an economic good and sometimes a free good?
4. If there were no parking meters and parking was permitted on any street, could on-street parking be considered a free good in Canadian cities? Why, or why not?
5. Why is the opportunity cost concept so important in economic analysis and economic decisions?
6. Calculate your opportunity cost for attending school or college this year.
7. What is meant by an "economic system"? What is the difference between an economic system and a political system?
8. Assume you are the chief planner in a planned economy. How will you decide what to produce, how much to produce of each commodity, and how much will be distributed to various members of the population?
9. The chapter gives a short definition for "market", but what is the meaning of the full term "market *system*"?
10. Could there ever be a pure market economy? Explain.
11. A distinction is made between "wants" and "needs" in describing the problem of scarcity. Can you think of some goods or services for which this sharp distinction cannot be made? Why is there some doubt about the category in which such goods or services should be placed?

Sources and Selected Readings

Ebenstein, Wm. *Today's Isms*, 9th ed. Englewood Cliffs, N.J.: Prentice-Hall, 1985.

Grossman, Gregory. *Economic Systems*, 2nd ed. Englewood Cliffs, N.J.: Prentice-Hall, 1974.

Heilbroner, Robert L. *The Making of Economic Society*, 6th ed. Englewood Cliffs, N.J.: Prentice-Hall, 1980.

Marr, Wm. L., and B. Raj, eds. *How Economists Explain: A Reader in Methodology*. Lanham, Md.: University Press of America, 1983.

Nove, Alec. *The Soviet Economic System*, 3rd ed. London: Allan and Unwin, 1986.

Appendix: Economics and the Use of Graphs

Much of economics is concerned with the quantitative relationships between different events or actions. The relationships can be described verbally, but verbal presentations have a disadvantage: they usually require a lengthy discussion of a topic that might be stated concisely in mathematical terms.

Geometry has been used in economics because of its pictorial aspect; often one diagram can explain clearly what would take several pages of prose to describe. Although geometry limits the analysis to two or three variables or dimensions, geometrical presentations are satisfactory for an exposition of basic economic principles and their applications. Graphs are therefore used at many points in this text to illustrate economic relationships. However, students who have no training in geometry, or who have forgotten the fundamentals of geometry, should have little difficulty in working with graphs following this brief review.

A graph consists of 2 coordinates, or straight lines, intersecting each other at an angle of 90 degrees at a point called the origin. Figure 1.5 shows a coordinate graph dividing space into 4 quadrants. The vertical coordinate is labelled y and the horizontal one, x. Positive values of y are measured above the origin and negative values below. Positive values of x are measured to the right of the origin and negative values to the left. The upper right-hand quadrant thus contains positive values of both x and y. Frequently only this quadrant is used because the values of the variables concerned are often both positive.

In specific cases, the coordinates or axes are labelled according to the variables involved. Figure 1.6 is an example of a graph depicting the relationship between annual personal income and consumption expenditures. Consumption is on the vertical or y axis; annual personal income is on the horizontal or x axis. (Consumption expenditures are positive even when income is zero, since some expenditures are necessary for survival; the individual is assumed to borrow or draw on savings to provide this amount.) Consumption expenditures are assumed to be a

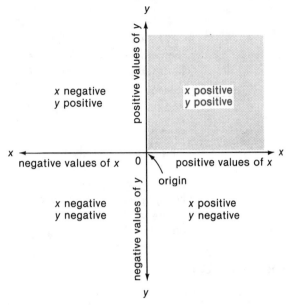

Figure 1.5 A Coordinate Graph
A coordinate graph divides space into four quadrants. Relationships
between two variables are specified by plotting the value of one variable on
the horizontal x axis and the value of a second variable on the vertical y
axis. Since economics is usually concerned with variables having positive
values, the quadrant most often used is the one where both x and y are
positive.

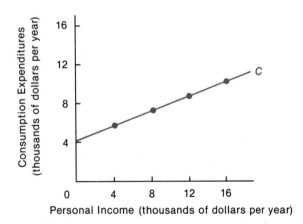

Figure 1.6 Hypothetical Consumption Curve
Consumer expenditures are a function of, or are dependent on, the level of
personal income. Consumption expenditures observed at each level
of income are plotted on a coordinate graph to illustrate the relationship
between consumption and personal income as consumption curve C.

function of income; that is, the amount of these expenditures will *depend* on the level of income.

The dependent variable (consumption) is conventionally shown on the vertical axis and the independent variable (income) is shown on the horizontal axis. An important exception to this convention occurs in supply and demand analysis. There the independent variable, price, is on the vertical axis and the dependent variable, quantity demanded or supplied, is on the horizontal axis.

The line representing the consumption function in Figure 1.6 happens to be a straight line, but functions more often are non-linear or curved. In fact, the functions plotted on a graph are generally referred to as curves even when they are straight lines. Curves are described as being upward-sloping, or downward-sloping, to the right. A curve that is upward-sloping to the right has a positive slope; a negative slope is represented by a curve sloping downward to the right.

Key Concepts and Topics

coordinate graph
dependent variable
independent variable

2 Economic Analysis and Economic Policy

Economists often disagree on the results of economic analysis, the conclusions to be drawn from these results, or the appropriate prescriptions for individual decisions or for social policies. Some of the disagreement stems from problems with analytical techniques and inadequate statistics. But more often the disagreement stems from differences in political or social judgments about what should be done in response to economic problems.

Normative and Positive Economics

These two types of disagreement reflect different aspects of economics: *economic analysis* and *economic policy*.

A policy is a course of action that is expected to bring about some specific objective or goal.

An economic policy thus includes a statement of what the goals should be, as well as the means for attaining such goals. It is at this point that the role of the economist is sharply questioned; that is, should his or her studies be confined to analysis or *positive economics*, or should these deal in policy or *normative economics* as well?

Positive economics is concerned with describing and analyzing the way things are. Normative economics emphasizes the way things should or ought to be.

Positive economics would, for example, be interested in the effects of a change in the price of milk, without being concerned about whether this price was "good" or "bad". Normative economics, however, would make a judgment about the price of milk, perhaps that it was so high that some children received too little milk, or so low that dairy farmers received an inadequate income.

Disputes in positive economics can be settled by appealing to the relevant facts and the analytical techniques. If there is agreement on what the facts are and how they should be analyzed, there is no reason for further dispute. Because economists have been concerned with developing analytical techniques, they are equipped to handle problems in positive economics. However, they have no similar tools for dealing with disagreements about the *value judgments* made in normative economics. When people hold different basic political views, these often cannot be reconciled; they may attempt persuasion, or they may hold a vote, or they may simply agree to differ. For this reason many economists and other social scientists have traditionally declared that they should restrict their work to positive studies, leaving value judgments to politicians and their electorates.

Although this distinction can be made clearly in abstract discussions, it cannot be drawn so clearly in specific economic studies. The categories established for collecting and analyzing data, assumptions made to simplify the analysis, and the particular type of analysis used can reflect the values or personal concerns of the researcher. Moreover, what is left out of the analysis can be as important in determining the results as what is included. Thus conclusions drawn from similar economic studies can vary, depending somewhat on the views of persons doing the studies. The reasons for such differences can usually be determined, however, by examining the data and techniques used. Articles in economic journals often appear to be quite technical, because it is as important to know how an economist arrived at the conclusion as it is to know what conclusions were reached.

The problem areas selected for economic analysis also reflect value judgment, to the extent that some problems are considered more important than others. Several factors influence an economist's choice of topics for analysis: availability of data, previous work done in the field, interest of other economists in the same topic, and adequate financial assistance.

Distinguishing Normative and Positive Economics

The distinction between normative and positive economics is made more difficult because intelligent normative statements involve an element of positive analysis. The statement that the legal minimum wage should be raised, as one means for dealing with poverty, requires an accurate knowledge of the consequences. A higher minimum wage may result in more unemployment but also in higher total wage payments to the low-income groups that remain employed. It is also possible that both employment and total wage payments would be reduced.[1] A judg-

[1] The possible consequences of minimum wage legislation are discussed in Chapter 4.

ment about minimum wage legislation therefore requires both an understanding of its various effects, and a further judgment about whether the number of persons employed is more important or less important than the total wages paid to the lowest income group.

Despite these various difficulties in distinguishing normative and positive economics, it is usually possible to determine at least which statements can be settled by agreeing on the analysis used and which statements can be settled only by agreeing on value judgments.

Since policy is a statement of actions to be taken to achieve certain objectives, the designing of economic policy requires both a clear understanding of the objectives and a knowledge of economic analysis. Each major section of this book is therefore arranged in a sequence that reflects the development of economic policy: first, a discussion of goals and the measurement concepts related to these goals; second, an outline of theory explaining the behaviour of economic factors concerned; and finally, the policy actions that could be considered, together with a brief review of Canada's experience with specific policies.

Scientific Method in Economics

The social sciences, including economics, are based on the same scientific method used in physics, chemistry, and biology, but experimentation is more difficult than in the physical or natural sciences.

The scientific method requires examining questions by referring to actual evidence rather than to intuition, judgment, or personal experience.

Evidence or facts must be gathered and analyzed to arrive at conclusions. Suitable evidence, however, usually must be drawn from controlled experiments. This involves controlling or manipulating the relevant variables so that the effects of particular actions can be isolated from the effects of all other actions. Physical scientists are able to do this by controlling temperature, light, moisture, or whatever other variables might affect the results. Biological scientists can control their experiments by, for example, adding a particular nutrient to one group of plants or animals but not to another group that is similar in all other respects. The results obtained in each case are then compared and conclusions are drawn.

Are There Economic Laws?

The scientific method also involves the development of laws or principles through repetition of such experiments until it can be concluded that there is a very high probability that the matter under examination will behave in a certain way when specific conditions exist.

The bodies of knowledge represented by different sciences are based, for example, on laws concerning heat, sound, gravity, or genetics. Occasionally the question is raised whether a social science is even possible; that is, whether laws can be determined for human behaviour, since humans have free will to decide how they will behave under various circumstances.

Long and continued observation of human behaviour has shown, however, that while the actions of a particular individual may be unpredictable, the behaviour of groups of individuals in response to specific situations can be predicted. The more precisely the situations can be defined or described, the more accurate the predictions can be. Many studies have found, for example, that a smaller quantity of a good will be sold when the price of the good increases. There may be some situations, however, in which this does not occur. The prediction about what will happen when the price increases can be made more accurately if information is also available about other important factors such as whether incomes are also rising, whether the good is being advertised, and whether the prices of similar goods are also increasing. When large groups of individuals are seen to behave similarly in well-defined situations after repeated observations, economic laws can be stated that have at least considerable predictive power in economic analysis, if not the universal validity of the laws of physical sciences.

Theories, Models, and the Real World

Behavioural laws provide the basis for *predictions* of what will happen in certain circumstances. They do not, however, *explain* why these things happen. If one knows the reason why certain events occur, then it may be possible to alter the circumstances so that they will not happen, or alternatively, so that they will happen more frequently. A theory about why such things happen will provide the basis for a policy or a set of actions to be taken to achieve the desired ends. *A theory is an explanation of the relationships between situations and events*. It is more powerful than a law, in that it provides both an explanation and a basis for predictions.

A theory also provides the framework for observation of events in the real world. Observation of "facts" is meaningful only when what is observed has some relationship to other items of interest. One could, for example, collect information on the prices of sugar in every grocery store and supermarket in the country. The information would be meaningless unless one had some theory about why such prices should be the same or different in different types of stores, different regions of the country, or in cities and towns of various sizes. A theory therefore assists in defining the data to be collected for economic analysis.

A theory has three component parts: a set of *definitions of terms* used in the theory; a set of *assumptions defining the conditions* in which the theory is applicable; and *hypotheses concerning the relationships* among the situations and events the theory is intended to explain.

Definitions   Each of these components will limit the applicability of the theory. The definitions may be so restrictive as to exclude significant aspects of the situation. A definition of labour services, for example, may treat labour as undifferentiated with respect to skills, whereas everyone knows that there is a wide variation in skills among members of the labour force. Whether this kind of definition imposes a serious limitation on the theory's validity depends on what the theory is intended to explain. Thus the definitions used in a theory must be examined to see how they influence the conclusions reached.

Assumptions   Similarly, assumptions may be made that initially seem inappropriate or contrary to what one knows to be true. In a theory explaining the effects of price changes, for example, it may be assumed that consumers' incomes are constant, even though it is known that incomes have been rising. Assumptions of this kind are made as substitutes for the regulation of variables in controlled experiments. By assuming first that incomes are constant and then that incomes are rising, a theory can be used to explain the specific effect that increasing incomes have on prices.

Such limitations only point out the respects in which a theory is inadequately specified, rather than the need to discard it. Too often, one hears such statements as, "That's too theoretical", or, "That's all right in theory but not in practice". Sometimes these statements reflect a person's dislike for a complex explanation of events, but more often they stem from the view that a theory is too simple to take account of specific cases or complicated situations. In this case, one can reply that a simple theory can at least explain the general relationships and, furthermore, form the basis for more complex theories that take into account greater variation in the circumstances or observed outcomes.

Hypotheses   The validity of an hypothesis and therefore of a theory is tested by comparing its predictions with evidence drawn from actual experience; such evidence must of course be classified according to the definitions used in the theory.

If actual experience coincides with the predictions, a valid theory has been devised and only needs to be tested from time to time to recertify its validity. If experience differs from the predictions, two alternatives are available: either to abandon the theory for another existing theory that would have predicted the actual outcome more accurately; or to modify and improve the initial theory. In this latter case, an initial, imperfect theory at least provides a framework for interpreting the new evidence.

Economic Models

Economists have taken the scientific method as applied to economics one step further than the development of theories. By combining theories they have been able to construct models of the operation of segments or the whole of the economy. The terms "model" and "theory" are sometimes used interchangeably; one may talk about either a model or a theory of national income determination, but generally a model represents a more detailed and complex set of relationships than does a theory.

Economic models are constructed by *abstracting* from real-world situations. Abstraction involves, as it did in developing theories, identifying the important features or variables such as income levels, unemployment and inflation rates, and tax rate structures, and stating the expected relationships among these. The model is next tested against the evidence by using data from previous years to determine whether the model would have predicted the actual outcome. When the model is correctly specified in this sense, it can then be used for experimentation. Tariff rates on imported goods could be varied, for example, to determine the effects of these changes on other variables such as employment and prices of domestic commodities. This information can then provide guidance for designing the federal government's tariff policy. If policies based on experimental results are actually implemented, the real-world results can be compared with the model's predictions. Any important discrepancies will indicate how the model should be modified for future experimentation and policy development.

Such models provide a means by which experiments can be conducted to provide predictions of the economic performance, under alternative conditions, of firms, industries, or the entire economy. Models of an economy require much time and effort to construct and maintain, and thus reflect the cooperative effort of many economists. Such models of the Canadian economy have been developed at the Bank of Canada and the Economic Council of Canada, and are used to ascertain both what would happen if certain policies were introduced and what can be expected to happen because of policy actions already taken. Several economic models representing various countries have been joined through an international "Project LINK" so that the impact of major events, such as oil price increases, can be studied on a worldwide basis.

Box 2.1   What Is an Economic Model?

The Economic Council of Canada has described its model—called CANDIDE—as follows:

> Basically, a model is a system of mathematical equations that represents the operation of a part of the economy or the national economy as a whole. The equations express relationships between economic variables that are based on established economic theory and estimated from historical data. Since theory does not cover all relationships, it is necessary to call upon judgment and experience when formulating them. . . . If analysis depends so much on judgment, what then is the advantage of using a complex model instead of simpler analytical methods? The main advantage is the ability to formulate the relationships between the major variables in the economic system, and to specify the way in which the variables interact, so that they will form a consistent pattern no matter how many there are. When a great number of variables, perhaps hundreds at a time, interact simultaneously, we can be sure of their mutual consistency only by deriving them within a well-defined framework—that is, within a model.

Source: Economic Council of Canada, *Ninth Annual Review: The Years to 1980*. Reproduced with the permission of the Chairman of the Economic Council of Canada, 1991.

Difficulties with Measurement

Development of economics as a science requires that observations be expressed in quantitative terms, if theories and models are to be tested and ultimately judged valid. Some of the concepts used in economics, however, cannot be measured easily, if at all. This does not mean that such concepts must be discarded. In fact, some economic relationships can be explained only by drawing on concepts that can be described qualitatively, but that cannot be measured. The satisfaction or enjoyment provided by clothing, food, or entertainment cannot be measured precisely because individuals can only say, for example, that they like beef better than fish. Yet the concept of satisfaction or utility is used extensively in economics.

Another measurement problem follows from the need to rely on samples when it is not possible to examine the entire population of the group in question, usually due to the extreme expense of collecting information on the complete group. A chemist can work with any sample of pure sulphur dioxide, knowing that every other sample would have the same properties. An economist, however, must be certain that the sample accurately represents the population, at least with respect to the characteristics under study. Furthermore, conclusions drawn from one sample may be valid only for a limited time, requiring that subsequent studies be undertaken whenever it is thought that the circumstances affecting the sample might have changed.

Some Basic Concepts

Some basic concepts are introduced here because they are frequently used in economic analysis and thus appear at many points throughout this book.

Rationality   A basic assumption in economic analysis is that individuals behave rationally. At one time, this assumption was incorporated in the concept of *economic man*. Individuals were assumed to be primarily interested in increasing their material well-being. If someone were offered a higher wage or a higher price for his or her output, it was expected that this would be readily accepted. The emphasis then shifted from the assumption that *all* individuals are *always* seeking to improve their material well-being to the assumption that *most* individuals will *usually* behave in this way. The more general meaning of rationality is, however, that individuals will behave or take such actions as are necessary to achieve their objectives, whatever these may be.

"Other Things Being Equal"   The phrase "other things being equal"—or its Latin equivalent, *ceteris paribus*—is used to compensate for the inability to control particular variables in the real world. Economists *assume* that other things are equal or unchanged, that is, they reason *as if* this is the case. A common example is the statement: "As the price of a good increases, fewer units of the good will be purchased, *other things being equal*". Because factors influencing the purchase of goods, other than the price, do not remain unchanged, the specific effect of a price change can be isolated only by making this assumption. Moreover, the assumptions can be changed gradually to allow each of the other factors to change separately so that their specific effects can also be determined.

Stocks and Flows   Much of economics is concerned with total quantities involved at a point in time and with changes in quantities over a period of time. This distinction can be made by reference to stocks and flows. *A stock is the quantity that exists at any particular point in time*. To describe a stock requires a statement of both the quantity and the time at which it is measured. Thus the Canadian labour force can be stated as a stock: there were 14.1 million persons in the labour force in August 1990.

A flow is the change in the quantity occurring during a period of time. To describe a flow requires a statement of both the quantity and the length of time involved. Thus the net change in the Canadian labour force is stated as a flow: 157,000 persons were added to the labour force during the 12 months prior to August 1990.

Microeconomics and Macroeconomics

The study of economics can be divided into two major areas: microeconomics and macroeconomics. "Micro" is derived from a Greek word meaning "small": *microeconomics is concerned with small or specific segments of the economy*, such as the behaviour of individual consumers and firms, of labour groups, and of groups of firms in industries. The branches of economic analysis falling within microeconomics include the theory of consumer behaviour, the theory of the firm, the theory of price and wage determination, the theory of income distribution, and most aspects of international trade theory.

"Macro" is derived from the Greek word for "large": *macroeconomics deals with large segments, or with the whole economy*. Emphasis is on the broad aggregates of total employment, total output and incomes, total money supply, and so on. The major objectives of macroeconomic studies are an understanding of the problems of unemployment, inflation, stability in national and international economic relations, and economic growth.

Some topics are difficult to classify as either microeconomics or macroeconomics because they involve elements of theory drawn from both areas. An analysis of the government or public sector, for example, involves microeconomic studies of specific programs but macroeconomic studies of the overall effects of government taxation and expenditures.

Review of the Main Points

1. Positive economics deals with an analysis of the way things are; normative economics is concerned with the way things should be. The latter involves making value judgments about economic goals or objectives and thus is not properly included in a science of economics. But assumptions and classifications used in economic analysis reflect value judgments that can cause disagreements about the results of economic analysis.
2. The scientific method consists of gathering information or facts, and analyzing these to arrive at conclusions. Economists usually cannot perform controlled experiments and thus must make numerous observations to identify the laws or principles of economic behaviour.

3. Laws state what will happen in particular situations but do not explain why. Theories provide this explanation, as well as predictions, and a framework for collecting information. A theory includes definitions of terms, assumptions defining conditions for its applicability, and hypotheses about the relationships between the events or conditions the theory is intended to explain. The validity of a theory is tested by comparing its predictions with evidence drawn from actual experience. Any discrepancy requires that the theory be modified to provide more accurate predictions.

4. A model of economic behaviour is usually a combination of theories representing large segments or the whole of the economy, but its construction involves the same process used for theories. Models are used to experiment with policy alternatives or to predict the effects of actual policies.

5. In some cases economics is imprecise, or involves only qualitative statements, because some concepts such as consumer satisfaction are immeasurable or because only samples of a total population can be analyzed.

6. Some basic concepts used in economic analysis include: rationality, the assumption that individuals will act to achieve their objectives; "other things being equal", the assumption that all other factors influencing a particular condition remain constant; and stocks and flows, a distinction made between the quantity existing at one time and the change in quantity occurring during a period of time.

7. Economics is often divided into microeconomics and macroeconomics; the former deals with specific segments of the economy while the latter deals with the whole economy.

Key Concepts and Topics

economic analysis
economic policy
positive vs. normative economics
value judgments
scientific method
laws of behaviour
theory

economic model
rational behaviour
"other things being equal"
stock vs. flow
microeconomics
macroeconomics

Questions for Review and Discussion

1. Many House of Commons debates focus on economic issues. Should there therefore be a large proportion of economists among the MPs elected to Parliament? Why?

2. Why is it so much more difficult to decide whether governments are acting rationally than to decide whether the behaviour of consumers and producers is rational?
3. Think of three statements you have recently heard about the Canadian economy. Decide whether they are positive or normative statements, and indicate how you decided which category was most appropriate.
4. Is it still necessary for economists to make explicit the assumption of rational behaviour?

Sources and Selected Readings

Boulding, Kenneth E. *Economics as a Science*. Lanham, Md.: University Press of America, 1988.

Browne, M. N., and John H. Hoag. *Understanding Economic Analysis*. Boston: Allyn and Bacon, 1983.

Marr, Wm. L., and B. Raj, eds. *How Economists Explain: A Reader in Methodology*. Lanham, Md.: University Press of America, 1983.

Smith, D. C., ed. *Economic Policy Advising in Canada*. Montreal: C. D. Howe Research Institute, 1981.

3 Demand, Supply, and Market Prices

Scarcity requires choices to be made in the use of limited productive resources. In virtually all modern economies these choices are based on prices. Most prices are determined by the forces of supply and demand, but certain prices, such as college tuition fees, are determined by planners' decisions or by government decree. It is important to understand how consumers and producers react to changes in prices and, conversely, how consumers and producers can influence the level of prices. These relationships are examined by supply and demand analysis.

Forces influencing the market for each commodity could be grouped or categorized in several ways. The most obvious groupings, however, consist of all the forces affecting buyers and all those affecting sellers. Separating the demand and supply sides of markets in this way emphasizes that these two sets of forces act independently of each other. This independence of buyers and sellers cannot be stressed too often.[1]

Demand for Consumer Goods and Services

Although "demand" is used in several ways in everyday language, it has one specific meaning in economics:

The demand for a commodity is the set of quantities that would be purchased at various alternative prices, given (or holding constant) all the other conditions that influence purchases of the commodity.

Only one price-quantity combination will be observed for any commodity in a given market at a particular point in time; the quantities that would be purchased at other prices are hypothetical. How then can one establish how much would be purchased at prices other than the

---

[1] The analysis in this chapter is based on the assumption that there are many buyers and sellers for each commodity. Chapters 17 and 18, dealing with competitive supply and imperfect competition, extend this analysis.

prevailing price? One could ask individuals how much they would be willing to buy at a variety of possible prices or, in some cases, one could determine the demand for a commodity by examining the amounts purchased at different times in the past as the price of the commodity changed. But this *historical approach* is unreliable if other factors affecting purchases have changed along with the price of the commodity.

Because these other factors do change quite frequently, an alternative, *survey approach* is sometimes considered more dependable. However, this approach has obvious limitations, since people are simply asked what they *would* do. Although most people find it difficult to answer with certainty what quantity they would purchase at each of various alternative prices, the concept of demand is a useful tool for analyzing the effects of a wide variety of forces influencing the market for any commodity.

Demand Schedules

The relationship between prices and the quantity purchased at each price can be shown as a *demand schedule*, as in Table 3.1. Suppose that an individual has been asked about her demand for cups of coffee to be provided by an office "coffee-pool". Her answers as presented in Table 3.1 indicate that if the price were $1.00 per cup she would buy no coffee. At $.80, however, she would buy one cup each day. As the price dropped further, she would buy more coffee throughout the day. At $.10 per cup, for example, she would buy five cups. Note that even if the coffee were provided at zero price (free), she would take a total of only seven cups; there is a biological limit to her consumption of beverages.

Table 3.1

Individual's Demand Schedule for Coffee

Price ($ per cup)	Quantity demanded (cups per day)
1.00	0
.80	1
.60	2
.40	3
.20	4
.10	5
.00	7

Demand Curves

The information provided in a demand schedule can be plotted on a graph as a *demand curve*. The conventional practice is to show prices per unit on the vertical axis and quantities purchased in a given period of time on the horizontal axis. The individual's demand schedule for coffee is shown as a demand curve in Figure 3.1. The separate combinations of quantity and price (zero cups at $1.00, one cup at $.80, etc.) have been plotted at the appropriate points on the graph. These points are then joined by a smooth line to determine the continuous demand curve, *D*.

Law of Demand

The demand curve illustrates the effect of a basic economic principle or law:

The law of demand states that as the price of a commodity falls, the quantity purchased will increase, all other things being equal; or alternatively, that the quantity purchased will decrease as the price rises.

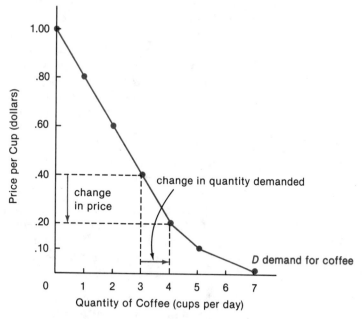

Figure 3.1 Individual's Demand Curve for Coffee
The individual's demand schedule for coffee is plotted as demand curve *D*. The downward-sloping curve shows that price and quantity are inversely related: the quantity demanded increases as the price decreases. This is true for almost all commodities, and hence provides a basic economic principle, the law of demand.

Within limited price ranges there occasionally can occur what appear to be exceptions to the law of demand. One such case is related to the difficulty in determining quality differences among similar commodities. Some people tend to judge the quality of a good by its price: a manufacturer of plastic garbage bags, for example, may find that it sells less of its product at a low price than it would if it introduced the bags at a higher price.

Another apparent exception occurs when the satisfaction derived from some good is directly dependent on its price. To the extent that diamonds are a source of satisfaction for some people mainly *because* they are expensive, fewer diamonds would be purchased at lower prices. If a good can be stored for future use, an increase in price may lead to a greater quantity purchased if consumers *expect* that the price will rise again in the near future.

Change in Quantity Demanded versus Shift in Demand

Demand has been defined as a schedule of the quantities of a commodity that would be purchased at various prices, when other factors are held constant. The quantity that will be bought at a specific price is referred to as the *quantity demanded*. It is difficult to talk about, for example, the "demand for coffee" because this involves a description of the entire demand schedule or curve. Rather, when people talk about the "demand" for a commodity, they are usually referring instead to the *quantity demanded*, or purchased, at the prevailing price. When this price increases, people may also tend to say that the "demand has fallen", when in fact they are referring to a *change in the quantity demanded*. Refer again to Figure 3.1. The change in quantity demanded as the price of a cup of coffee drops from $.40 to $.20 is the increase from three to four cups. If all other factors are unchanged, a change in price *must* result in a change in the quantity demanded or purchased.[2]

The law of demand included the words "all other things being equal". There are many factors that determine a person's demand for a commodity, or that explain, for example, why the coffee drinker would buy four cups at a price of $.20 per cup instead of either three or five cups. These factors fall into three major groups:

- the price of related commodities;
- the consumer's income level;
- the consumer's taste or preference for the commodity relative to other commodities.

[2] One exception to this is the rare case where demand is perfectly inelastic, as explained in the next major section, which deals with elasticity.

**Relative Prices of
Related Commodities**

Substitutes   Consider each of these factors in relation to the coffee consumer's demand for coffee. If the prices of tea, milk, and soft drinks
should fall, the quantity of coffee purchased at each of the various
prices would likely decline. But if the price of each of these beverages
should rise, the quantity of coffee purchased would likely increase. This
indicates that if the price of a commodity (tea) that is a *substitute* for
the good in question (coffee) should increase, there would be an
increase in demand for the good in question (coffee). This would be
represented by a *shift in demand*, or a shift of the demand curve to the
right and upward. This is illustrated in Figure 3.2, where the original
demand for coffee is shown as D. The new demand curve resulting from
the shift in demand is D_1. The shift is described as being both upward
and to the right because more of the commodity is bought at the *same
price* (a rightward shift), or, alternatively, the *same quantity* would be
purchased at a higher price (an upward shift).

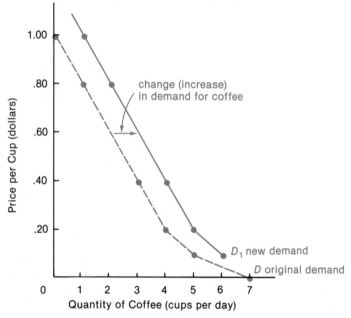

Figure 3.2   A Shift in Demand
A change in price leads to a change in the quantity demanded, but a
change in other factors produces a shift in demand: the entire demand
curve shifts to a new position on the graph. An outward shift, or an
increase in demand to D_1, means that a greater quantity would be
purchased at any given price. This would follow from an increase in the
consumer's income, an increase in the price of close substitutes for
the product, or the consumer's increased preference for the product.

Complements   There is a shift or change in demand with a change in the price of *complementary goods*, as well as with the price of *substitutes*. It may be obvious that the demand for coffee depends on the relative prices of substitutes such as tea and milk. Perhaps it is less obvious that the demand for a commodity also depends on the prices of *complements—commodities that are usually used along with the particular commodity*. If the coffee drinker could not possibly take her coffee without cream and sugar, and if the supplier now charged $.25 for each of these, the demand for coffee would fall, and the demand curve for coffee would be to the left of and lower than the *D* curve shown in Figure 3.1.

An increase in the price of complements will decrease the demand for the good in question, while an increase in the price of substitutes will increase the demand for that good.

Consumer Income   The second major determinant of demand is the *consumer's income level*. Assume now that the coffee drinker's income is much greater than it was when the demand schedule in Table 3.1 was determined. Since she now has a higher level of income, with more to spend on all items, she probably will also spend more to satisfy her desire for coffee. At a price of $.80 she might now be willing to buy two cups instead of one. An increase in the quantity purchased could also be anticipated for each price level. Thus an increase in income usually leads to an increase, or rightward shift, in demand; a decrease in income would lead to a decrease, or leftward shift, in demand.[3]

Consumer Preferences   A third factor, the consumer's *set of preferences or tastes* for all commodities, will also influence the demand for any given commodity. Such tastes usually change slowly, being altered by increasing age or changing lifestyle, or by experience with different commodities. Preferences among brands of soft drinks, for example, may also be modified by advertising campaigns. In fact, the primary purpose of advertising is to shift outward the demand curve for the advertised product. Rather abrupt changes in tastes may occur, however, with specific circumstances. The information that cigarette-smoking causes cancer has rapidly changed at least some individuals' preference for cigarettes relative to, for example, their preference for pipe tobacco, or other commodities.

Another factor that is included in more complex analyses of demand is the consumer's *expectation* about future prices. For example, a slight increase in price may lead a consumer to purchase more—rather than

---

[3] If the quantity purchased decreases with an increase in income, the commodity is termed an *inferior good*. This is discussed more fully in the following section.

less—if the consumer expects that the price will increase still further. For this introductory analysis, however, the assumption is that prices are expected to remain stable.

Total Market Demand

So far the discussion of demand has been concerned only with the individual. Practical interest in demand, however, is usually directed to the *total market demand* for a particular product.

The market demand for a commodity is derived by adding the demand curves or schedules of all individuals.

Adding the demand schedules requires that the quantities that all persons would buy *at a given price* and at a given time be totalled. The relevant market in the coffee example might be the total group of employees in the office building. If each employee were asked about his or her demand for coffee, it might be found that a total of 30 cups would be sold at $.60, 75 cups at $.40, 150 cups at $.20, and so on. The adding of demand curves requires that the curves for each individual be added *horizontally*, as shown in Figure 3.3.

Since the market demand curve is a summation of individuals' demand curves, the special features of the individual demand curves are also applicable to the market demand. Shifts in market demand and changes in the quantity demanded by the market are defined in the same manner as for individuals. But moving to the market level intro-

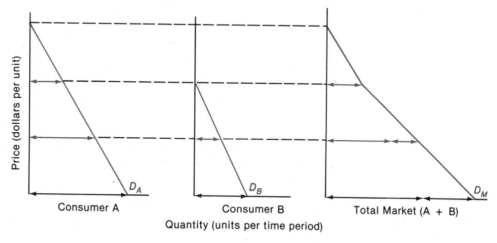

Figure 3.3 Adding Individuals' Demand Provides Market Demand
The market demand curve, D_M, is derived by adding horizontally the individual demand curves for all consumers in the market.

duces further factors causing shifts in demand, namely an increase in the population and its greater total income, as well as the distribution of that income. The greater total income will usually increase demand, but the effect on different commodities will depend on how the income is distributed.

Elasticity: Sensitivity to Price Changes

That the quantity demanded will increase as the price of a good falls, all other things being equal, usually comes as no surprise to anyone. It is more important to know how sensitive consumers are, or how strongly they react, to a price change. The concept of *elasticity* is used to measure this quantitative relationship between the price change and the resulting change in quantity demanded.

The general concept of elasticity is defined as the percentage change in one variable resulting from a given percentage change in another variable.

Price Elasticity of Demand

The measure of the relationship of price and quantity demanded is termed *price elasticity of demand*. Applying the general definition given above to this specific context yields the following definition of the price elasticity of demand:

$$E_D = - \frac{\text{percentage change in } Q_X}{\text{percentage change in } P_X}$$

where E_D is the coefficient or measure of elasticity, Q_X is the quantity demanded of product X, and P_X is the price of X.

Note that there is a minus sign in the above formula. There is normally an inverse relationship between a change in price and the quantity demanded: a decrease in price will result in an increase in quantity, and vice versa. The elasticity coefficient would therefore be negative, but including the additional minus sign ensures that the measure will be positive—a simple convenience now generally adopted. Alternatively, some economics textbooks simply drop the minus sign in the calculation.

Point versus Arc Elasticity   Elasticity, or the degree of responsiveness of consumers to price changes, is usually different for each price level. Elasticity is therefore ideally measured at a particular price, or at a particular point on the demand curve. This is called *point elasticity*. But changes in price and quantity of such small dimensions that they can be referred to as points are not measurable except with calculus.[4]

An alternative measure, *arc elasticity*, can be used to approximate the value of the point elasticity. This measures the responsiveness of consumers over a short segment of a demand curve, rather than at a particular point. The example in Box 3.1 shows how this calculation is made.

The formula for arc elasticity is:

$$E_D = -\frac{\Delta Q}{\Delta P} \times \frac{P_1 + P_2}{Q_1 + Q_2}$$

where ΔQ is $(Q_2 - Q_1)$ and ΔP is $(P_2 - P_1)$. (The Δ sign is the Greek letter *delta* and means *change in*.)

Although there are many instances when it is necessary to know the precise value of the elasticity measure, more often it is sufficient to discuss the elasticity of demand in general terms. *Five elasticity categories* can be used for this purpose. In the example in Box 3.1, the quantity demanded changed proportionately less than the change in price: a 67 per cent change in price led to a 29 per cent change in quantity demanded. The elasticity measure, E_D, was therefore less than one; in this case the demand is said to be *inelastic*. If quantity demanded had changed proportionately more than price, E_D would have been greater than one, and the demand would be described as *elastic*. If E_D had been exactly equal to one — the percentage change in quantity demanded the same as the percentage change in price — the condition would have been one of *unitary elasticity*. Summarizing briefly:

when $E_D < 1$, demand is inelastic;
when $E_D = 1$, demand is of unitary elasticity;
when $E_D > 1$, demand is elastic.

The other two cases are the extreme limits of elasticity. When there is no change in the quantity demanded as price changes, demand is *perfectly inelastic* and $E_D = 0$. But if there is an infinitely large change in quantity demanded with the most minute change in price, the demand is *perfectly elastic* and $E_D = \infty$ (infinity). These are illustrated in Figure 3.4.

[4] Readers who are familiar with calculus will recognize that the change in quantity with respect to a change in price is the derivative dq/dp. Point elasticity is defined as $e = dq/dp \times p/q$. This is the definition more frequently used in economic analysis when it is possible to estimate the demand equation.

The approximate degree of elasticity can sometimes be estimated from the nature of the product in question.

Box 3.1   Calculating Elasticity

Calculation of elasticity can be illustrated using the coffee drinker's demand schedule in Table 3.1. If the price of coffee falls from \$.40 to \$.20, she would increase the quantity demanded by one cup, going from three to four cups per day. The percentage price decrease is calculated by dividing the change in price by the *average* of the old and new prices and multiplying by 100. It is this averaging of prices that permits the approximation of elasticity at a point, since one must be able to calculate the effect of a change in price regardless of whether there is an increase or a decrease. The percentage *price* change is

$$\frac{\Delta P}{\frac{P_1 + P_2}{2}} \times 100 = \frac{-20}{\frac{20 + 40}{2}} \times 100 = -67\%$$

The Δ sign is the Greek letter *delta* and means *change in*, and is calculated as $P_2 - P_1$. The value of ΔP is negative because the price decreased.

Similarly, the percentage change in *quantity demanded* would be calculated by the formula:

$$\frac{\Delta Q}{\frac{Q_1 + Q_2}{2}} \times 100 = \frac{1}{\frac{3 + 4}{2}} \times 100 = 29\%$$

The price elasticity of demand for coffee, *over the price range from \$.20 to \$.40*, is therefore:

$$E_D = -\frac{29}{-67} = .43$$

Recall that this coefficient means that for each 10 per cent increase (or decrease) in price there will be a 4.3 per cent decrease (or increase) in quantity demanded, within the price range in question.

The complete formula by which this coefficient was obtained is:

$$E_D = -\frac{\Delta Q}{\frac{Q_1 + Q_2}{2}} \times 100 \div \frac{\Delta P}{\frac{P_1 + P_2}{2}} \times 100$$

This is simplified to:

$$E_D = -\frac{\Delta Q}{\Delta P} \times \frac{P_1 + P_2}{Q_1 + Q_2}$$

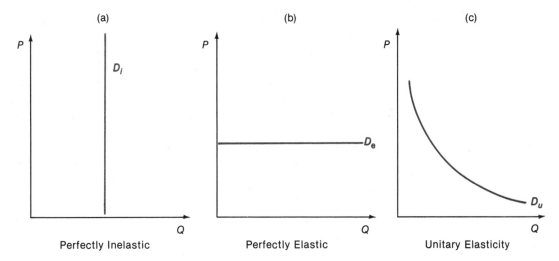

Figure 3.4 Special Cases of Demand Elasticity
When a price change produces no change in quantity demanded, demand
is perfectly inelastic. When the percentage change in quantity is equal to
the percentage change in price, demand is of unitary elasticity. (This is
shown by a rectangular hyperbola, or a curve where $P \times Q = k$.) When
even a small change in price would reduce quantity demanded to zero, the
demand is perfectly elastic—a straight horizontal line.

*The demand for goods and services will tend to be more elastic or less
inelastic:*

1. If there are *close substitutes* for the product. As the price of a good
   rises, consumers will switch to other goods if these are close
   substitutes.
2. If the good is a *luxury item*. When consumers can easily do without a particular good, they will be readier to forgo its purchase as
   its price increases.
3. If the good is a *significant item in the consumer's budget*. If a consumer usually buys a large quantity of beef each year, she will be
   more likely to reduce her beef consumption as its price increases
   relative to the price of other meats, than if beef is a minor item in
   her budget.

Conversely, *the demand for goods and services will tend to be more
inelastic or less elastic:*

1. If there are *few close substitutes*. Since there are apparently no
   close substitutes for milk in the diet of small children, there will be
   little change in quantity demanded as the price of milk rises.
2. If the good is a *necessity*. A specific good, such as salt, that is con-

sidered a necessity will be purchased in the necessary quantity regardless of its price.

3. If the good represents an *insignificant part of the consumer's budget*. A person who buys one package of tulip bulbs each year probably will not be very responsive to increasing bulb prices, but a city parks department that has spent large amounts for tulip bulbs in the past may switch part of its budget to other bulbs or plants.

Further cases of demand elasticity are described in the appendix to this chapter. In particular, the responses of consumers in the purchase of substitutes and complements, when the price of a given good changes, are analyzed in terms of *cross elasticity*. Further conclusions about the changes of elasticity for a given good are also presented.

Price Effects on Total Revenue

Elasticity can also be defined in terms of the effect of price changes on the total revenue received from the sale of a commodity, or on the total amount paid by the consumer. If the coffee drinker found the price to be $.20, she would buy three cups of coffee for a total expenditure of $.60. At a price of $.10 per cup, her purchase of four cups would require a total expenditure of $.40. The decrease in price would result in decreased total revenue or total expenditure for coffee. Thus one can conclude that

> if a price decrease results in a decreased total revenue, the demand is inelastic. Alternatively, if a price decrease increases the total revenue, the demand is elastic. When the total revenue remains unchanged with changes in price, there is unitary elasticity of demand.

This alternative definition suggests why the elasticity of demand for any product is of considerable interest to producers and governments. Although a producer will usually sell more units if the price of the product falls, the total revenue may fall if the demand is inelastic. Similarly, a government seeking more revenue will want to increase sales taxes on products for which the demand is inelastic, so that there is relatively little reduction in the quantities purchased after the tax is imposed, and so that total revenues, including the tax revenues, are increased.

Pricing of telephone service provides another example of elasticity considerations. Telephone companies such as Bell Canada favour higher prices for local calls because the demand is inelastic; but prices for long-distance calls—especially outside business hours—have actually decreased due to the elastic demand resulting from alternatives such as letters and telegrams.

Income Elasticity

The effect of a change in income on the quantity demanded of a specific commodity can also be described in terms of the general elasticity concept.

Income elasticity is the percentage change in quantity demanded divided by the percentage change in income.

The formula for calculating income elasticity can be derived from this definition in the same way that the price elasticity was derived. Hence, income elasticity is calculated as follows:

$$E_Y = \frac{\Delta Q}{\Delta Y} \times \frac{Y_1 + Y_2}{Q_1 + Q_2}$$

where E_Y is the coefficient of income elasticity, ΔY is the difference between the two income levels, Y_1 and Y_2, and ΔQ is the difference between the two quantity levels, Q_1 and Q_2.

For most commodities, the quantity demanded increases as income increases. The income-elasticity coefficient will therefore be positive, since the direction of change is the same for both the quantity demanded and income.

Normal Goods   Commodities for which the income-elasticity coefficient is positive are termed *normal goods* because consumers purchase a greater quantity of these, or spend more for these goods, as their incomes rise. Common examples of goods with a high income elasticity include filet mignon, theatre box-seats, and rare wines.

Inferior Goods   Where income elasticity is negative, the goods in question are described as *inferior goods*. These are goods for which the quantity purchased declines as income increases; they probably include the cheaper meat cuts and lower quality wines.[5]

Supply of Consumer Goods and Services

It is now time to turn to the sellers' side of the market. This discussion of supply can be shorter than the section on demand because there are several similarities in the way the two sides of the market are analyzed. Care must be taken of course to note the important differences. Just as

---

[5] One study has found that the income elasticity for lamb was .68, for beef, .51, and for pork, .13. Eggs and skim milk powder had an income elasticity of zero, while lard was an inferior good with an elasticity of -.10. See Z.A. Hassan and S.R. Johnson, "The Demand for Major Foods in Canada", *Canadian Farm Economics*, Vol. 12, No. 2.

"demand" was given a specific definition to distinguish it from the everyday usage of the word, so "supply" is given a special meaning.

The supply of a commodity is the quantity that would be offered for sale at each of various alternative prices, given (or holding constant) all the other conditions that influence a producer's willingness to supply that commodity.

As in the case of demand, there can be only one price-quantity combination for any commodity in a given market at a particular time. Any other prices and related quantities are hypothetical. Again, the complete supply schedule or curve would be determined by interviewing potential suppliers, or possibly by examining data on previous prices and quantities offered at these prices. The *market* supply schedule would be derived by adding the supply schedules for all of the suppliers in a market.

Supply Slopes Upward   The supply curve, as illustrated in Figure 3.5, usually slopes upward to the right: the quantity that would be supplied increases with higher prices. The reasons for this are examined more fully in Chapter 17. For the present discussion, the assumption—which is generally valid—of an upward-sloping supply curve is sufficient. As prices rise, existing producers are tempted to produce more, and new producers will be attracted into the market, so that a larger quantity will be offered at each increase in price. But as more producers enter the market, and more units of the good are produced, the prices of the inputs used in producing the good will be bid up. As production costs per unit rise with increasing output, suppliers will be willing to offer a greater quantity only if the price increases still further.

Change in Quantity Supplied versus Shift in Supply

Provided that "all other things are equal", or that there is no change in the factors influencing the suppliers' decisions, the actual quantity supplied will change only with a change in price. Or alternatively, *whenever there is a change in price, there usually is a change in the quantity supplied.* Figure 3.5 shows that a change in price, from P_1 to P_2, results in a change in the quantity supplied, from Q_1 to Q_2.

A change in supply or a shift of the supply curve will occur when any of the factors change that were previously assumed to be held constant. These are quite different factors from the ones that caused the consumer's demand curve to shift to the left or right.

Because different factors influence supply than influence demand, supply and demand are said to be independent.

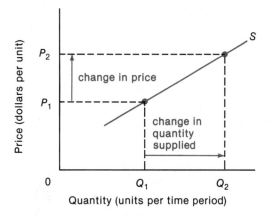

Figure 3.5 Individual Producer's Supply Curve
The producer's supply curve, *S*, shows the quantity that would be offered at each price. An increase in price would result in an increase in quantity supplied, because producers could then cover the higher costs per unit associated with a larger output. Note that the supply curve would not intersect the quantity (*Q*) axis, but likely would intersect the price (*P*) axis, because the supplier must receive at least a price greater than zero before any quantity would be offered to the market.

Factors Causing Supply Changes

The factors causing a shift in the supply curve are related to the suppliers' production costs. Such factors can be placed in three categories:

1. the prices of the inputs or factors of production;
2. changes in technology related to the production of the specific good;
3. time available to adjust to changes in the commodity's price.[6]

If the price of labour, raw materials, electrical power, or manufacturing equipment should increase, manufacturers would find that the production cost per unit would also increase and they would be willing to offer fewer units at any given price. This situation is represented by a leftward or inward shift of the supply curve, as illustrated in Figure 3.6.

Technological changes, however, may lead to quite substantial outward shifts of the supply curve. Economists give "technology" a very broad definition. A change in technology would include a new source of raw materials or other inputs, new kinds of inputs, new transportation methods for either the inputs or the products, as well as new combinations of inputs or a new technique for combining the inputs used previ-

---

[6] Time periods are given detailed examination in Chapter 16, where production costs and competitive supply are fully discussed.

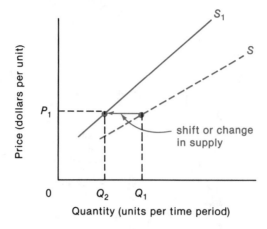

Figure 3.6 A Shift in Supply
An increase in the price of productive factors, such as labour, increases the producer's cost per unit. Thus, a lower quantity, Q_2, will be offered at the same price, P_1. Since the cost per unit is higher at any output quantity, the entire supply curve shifts to S_1. Technological changes that reduce the producer's cost per unit would shift the supply curve to the right or below S.

ously. Given this wide interpretation of technology, there are obviously many potential ways for reducing the production cost per unit for any particular good, and thus for shifting its supply curve outward.

Supply Elasticity

Just as demand elasticity measures the responsiveness of consumers to changes in product prices, supply elasticity measures the responsiveness of producers to changes in product prices. *The elasticity of supply with respect to price is the percentage change in the quantity supplied divided by the percentage change in the price.* This can be represented by the formula:

$$E_S = \frac{\Delta Q}{\Delta P} \times \frac{P_1 + P_2}{Q_1 + Q_2}$$

Note that a minus sign is not added to the right-hand side of the equation as it was for demand elasticity. This is because a positive change in price is assumed to result in a positive change in quantity supplied; the coefficient or measure of supply elasticity will therefore be positive.

The general categories of supply elasticity are the same as those used for demand elasticity:

when $E_S = 0$, supply is perfectly inelastic;
when $E_S < 1$, supply is inelastic;

when $E_S = 1$, supply is of unitary elasticity;
when $E_S > 1$, supply is elastic;
when $E_S = \infty$, supply is perfectly elastic.

Note that the definition of demand elasticity that is based on the effect of a price change on total revenue is *not* applicable to supply elasticity, since any increase in price will increase total revenue. That is, in the case of supply, total revenue will increase *whenever* price increases, but in the case of demand the total revenue may either rise or fall, depending on elasticity.

Unitary Elasticity   Another difference between supply and demand elasticities concerns the special case of unitary elasticity. Figure 3.4 showed that a demand curve of unitary elasticity throughout its length would take the special shape described as a rectangular hyperbola. In the case of supply, however, *any* straight line through the origin of the graph will be of constant unitary elasticity. This is because the constant slope of the straight line assures that the value of $\Delta Q/\Delta P$ is always equal to $(Q_1 + Q_2)/(P_1 + P_2)$ at any price level, and therefore $(\Delta Q/\Delta P) \times (P_1 + P_2)/(Q_1 + Q_2)$ will always equal one. This is shown in Figure 3.7.

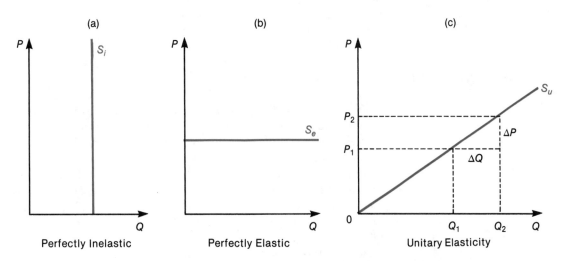

Figure 3.7   Special Cases of Supply Elasticity
Cases of perfectly inelastic and perfectly elastic supply, as shown in (a) and (b) are the same as those for the extreme demand elasticities. Unitary supply elasticity, however, is quite different from the unitary demand case. Any straight-line supply curve passing through the origin will be of unitary elasticity throughout the price range, since $\Delta Q/\Delta P$ will always be equal to the reciprocal of P/Q or $(P_1 + P_2)/(Q_1 + Q_2)$. The coefficient will therefore always be one.

Why Elasticity Differs   Supply elasticity varies for different products because of two main factors:

- the *availability of inputs* to produce the commodity in question;
- the *time* required to adjust production to the new price level.

The *availability of inputs* can be illustrated by the case of residential housing. The price of housing may increase, for example, but there will be little increase in the number of new houses offered for sale in a specific area if the land zoned for residential housing has been exhausted. Supply would be almost perfectly inelastic if such an important input were unavailable. In the case of a commodity like bread, however, the supply would be much more elastic, assuming there were no difficulty in obtaining more bread flour and semiskilled labourers, and in operating the bakery for longer hours.

Time is an important determinant of supply elasticity, because most inputs that are not immediately available can be produced over longer periods of time; more land can be annexed and zoned for housing, or more flour can be milled, in the examples cited above. Furthermore, a significant price increase may induce producers to change production techniques or their productive capacity over a longer period of time. But these changes would also depend on the producers' *expectations*. If they expect that the price rise is temporary, no such change in productive capacity or techniques is likely.

Price Determined by Supply and Demand

Treating demand and supply separately emphasizes their independence and shows the separate responses of consumers and producers to price changes. The preceding sections took different prices as given; now it is time to see how demand and supply interact to *determine* the price of any commodity. Figure 3.8 shows the market demand and supply curves for coffee on the same graph. The demand curve indicates that *if* the price is $.90 per cup, 50 cups will be purchased each day, but producers will supply 150 cups per day. There will be a *surplus* or *excess supply* of 100 cups per day.

This condition causes producers to lower the price of coffee to assure that they will not be left with a surplus on future days. As the price falls, consumers will be willing to buy more, but producers will supply less. The process of adjusting to the excess supply, and the resulting pressure on prices, thus involves the consumers as well as the producers.

Suppose producers become impatient with this adjustment process and decide that they will be able to dispose of all their coffee only when

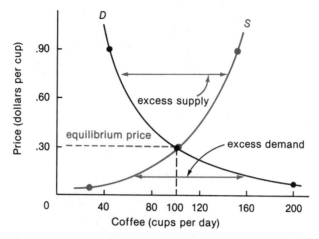

Figure 3.8 Equilibrium Price Determined By Market Demand and Supply
The equilibrium price of $.30 per cup is determined by the intersection of the market demand curve, *D*, and the market supply curve, *S*. At a price above $.30 per cup, suppliers would offer more than consumers are willing to purchase: there would be an excess supply. Similarly, at a price below $.30, there would be an excess demand. At $.30, however, the quantity supplied, 100 cups per day, exactly equals the quantity demanded.

the price is as low as $.05. (Producers are assumed to have done no market research and do not have the advantage of examining Figure 3.8.) At $.05 per cup, producers are willing to provide only 25 cups per day, but customers want to buy 200 cups per day. Producers find that their coffee is sold quickly, and many disappointed customers are still in the lineup to buy coffee for $.05. In fact, they would like to buy another 175 cups, the amount of the shortage or excess demand.

Through this trial-and-error procedure, the price might just happen to be set at $.30. At this price, 100 cups per day are offered by suppliers and exactly the same number are purchased by the customers.

This price is the equilibrium price, namely the price at which the quantity demanded is equal to the quantity supplied.

When the price was $.60, the excess supply or surplus was a downward pressure on the price. At $.05, the excess demand exerted an upward pressure. Since at $.30 there is neither excess demand nor excess supply, there are no such pressures and the market is in equilibrium.

Change in the Equilibrium Price

"Equilibrium" is used to describe a price-quantity combination at which the forces acting on demand and supply are in balance, or exactly offset each other. There is no suggestion that these are necessarily ideal or desirable prices and quantities, or that they will remain at these levels for any length of time. In fact, since the given demand and supply curves are not necessarily valid for more than one point in time, an excess of demand or supply may easily arise at what had previously been the equilibrium price. A new equilibrium price for the product may emerge as the forces influencing either supply or demand change.

Supply and demand analysis can be used to explain both why the price of a product might have changed in the past, and what will happen to the price if demand and/or supply are changed in the future.

Consider the coffee market again. Suppose that the equilibrium price of a cup of coffee had been $.20 in the past. A coffee drinker returns to this particular office after an absence of some months to find that the price is now $.25. Why has the price increased? Can she make some informed guesses, using her knowledge of supply and demand in the coffee market?

One possible set of reasons for the price increase is suggested by Figure 3.9a. If the quantity sold has increased along with the price, there has been an increase in demand, or an outward shift of the demand curve. This may have been due to a recent pay increase received by the office personnel or to a substantial rise in the price of tea and milk, or even to the (improbable) medical discovery that coffee was the key to longevity. Note there has been an increase in the *quantity supplied*, as the demand curve shifted upward along the existing supply curve.

Alternatively, the curious coffee drinker may find that the increased coffee price has been accompanied by a decrease in the quantity sold. This implies that there has been a decrease in supply, or an upward shift of the supply curve, as illustrated in Figure 3.9b. The shift of the supply curve upward along the existing demand curve may have been due to an increase in the price of coffee beans or in the wages paid to the producers' employees. In this case there has been a shift in supply and a decrease in the quantity demanded, but no change in the demand for coffee.

Finally, the coffee drinker may find that there has been no change in the quantity sold, even though the price has increased. As Figure 3.9c suggests, this would occur only if there was a shift in both supply and demand. The demand curve has shifted outward, and the supply curve inward, just enough to leave the quantity sold unchanged.

The coffee drinker who did not have the benefit of Figure 3.9 could deduce only that if the quantity sold has increased, demand has increased by more than supply has decreased. Conversely, if the quantity sold has decreased, supply has decreased by more than the increase in demand.

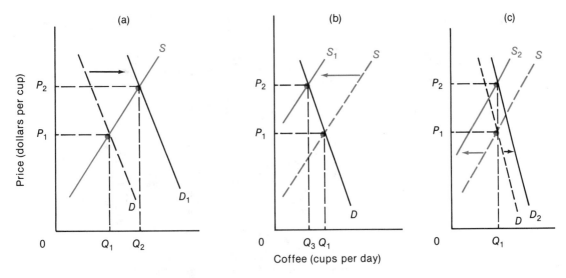

Figure 3.9   Shifts in Supply or Demand Affect Equilibrium Price
A higher equilibrium price, P_2, could be the result of either an outward shift in demand (to D_1), or an inward shift in supply (to S_1), or some combination of these shifts in both demand and supply. In the last case, the equilibrium quantity may be unchanged despite an increase in price.

Interdependence of Markets

The equilibrium price and quantity in each market is dependent on changes occurring in other markets. The example of coffee drinkers and suppliers examined only one market. It was suggested however that one possible reason for the outward shift of the coffee demand curve with the resulting price increase was an increase in the price of milk. That is, what happens in the coffee market is partly dependent on what happens in the milk market. But why would the price of milk increase? Perhaps this was due to a leftward shift of the milk supply curve caused by an increase in the price of feed for dairy cattle, which in turn was due to an increased demand for feed for beef cattle, due to an increase in demand for steaks, due to an increase in wages of automobile workers, due to an increase in the demand for automobiles, and so on and on.

Although this example of related markets gives the impression of a chain of effects, the interdependence of markets is more appropriately seen as a network. Increased wages for automobile workers, for example, might increase the demand not only for steaks but for many other consumer goods and services as well. The market for each of these would in turn directly influence several other markets.

Box 3.2

Rise in beef prices is linked to dollar

Spokesmen for major supermarket chains said yesterday the price of beef in Ontario will take a marked jump this week, mostly because of the drop in value of the Canadian dollar, now worth about 87 U.S. cents.

Allen Jackson, executive vice-president of Dominion, said beef prices will go up 10 to 30 cents a pound. He said the wholesale cost to stores has gone up to $1.03 a pound this week from 85 cents in February.

Loblaws president David Nichol said the recent plunge in value of the Canadian dollar has made beef more attractive to U.S. buyers who can get about 13 per cent more for their dollar.

"What's happening is that there's a great deal of beef going into the United States and there's probably no change in sight at least until the fall,"said Mr. Nichol.

Spokesmen for A and P. Steinberg's Miracle Mart chain and Food City all agreed that prices will increase this week.

Last week, spokesmen for the Canadian meat industry said that pork prices will likely be higher than anticipated because the U.S. supply is less than expected.

W. F. McLean, president of Canadian Packers Ltd., said that profit margins in the industry have been tight in the last 12 to 18 months because of a large increase in worldwide meat production. — CP

Source: *The Globe and Mail*, 26 April 1978

One example of the interdependence of markets is shown in the above news item. The falling value of the Canadian dollar meant that Canadian beef would be cheaper for American buyers, who would then increase their quantity demanded. This would reduce the supply of beef in Canada, and hence increase its price. At the same time, the decline in the supply of U.S. pork in Canada would increase pork prices, thus reinforcing the pork price increase that would have resulted as Canadian consumers switched to pork from the high-priced beef.

General Equilibrium

For some purposes, it may be sufficient to know the effect of increased wages on only one market, but for other purposes it may be necessary to know the effect on what is termed the *general equilibrium* of the economy. A market is in equilibrium at the price where the quantity demanded exactly equals the quantity supplied. The economy is in equilibrium when *each* market has reached this equilibrium state.

Such a condition is not likely to occur. Manufacturers often find that a product can be produced more efficiently by using more equipment and less labour. This shift will have effects on both the equipment market and the labour market, with further consequences working their way through all other markets. Similarly, consumers may decide they would be happier if they attended more movies and bought fewer clothes. Again the consequences would ripple through a succession of markets. Thus, the concept of general equilibrium is of more practical significance in its explanation of the *adjustment process* of interdependent markets and for its prediction of the *direction* in which the economy will move than for the determination of prices and quantities that will actually exist at any time.

Review of the Main Points

1. Many factors influence the price of a commodity. These factors act either on the demand side or on the supply side of the market, and are independent of each other.

2. Demand is the set of quantities of a commodity that would be purchased at various alternative prices, holding constant all other conditions that influence purchases of the commodity. The list of these price-quantity combinations is a demand schedule; plotting this schedule on a graph yields a demand curve.

3. The law of demand states that as the price of a commodity falls, the quantity demanded will increase, all other things being equal, or alternatively, that the quantity demanded decreases as the price rises. A change in quantity demanded is the result of a change in price with all other factors held constant; a change in demand is the result of a change in one or more other factors that influence consumers' purchases. "Other factors" are the prices of related commodities, the consumers' income level, and the consumers' set of tastes or preferences.

4. The total market demand for a commodity is found by adding the quantity demanded at each price by each consumer in the market.

5. The elasticity of demand for a good, with respect to price, is defined as the percentage change in quantity demanded divided by the percentage change in price. When $E_D < 1$, demand is inelastic; when $E_D > 1$, demand is elastic; and when $E_D = 1$, demand is of unitary elasticity. When total revenue increases as price increases, the demand is inelastic; but if total revenue falls, the demand is elastic. When total revenue is unchanged as price changes, demand is of unitary elasticity.

6. Income elasticity is the percentage change in quantity demanded divided by the percentage change in income. If the quantity demanded increases as income increases, or if the income elasticity is positive, the commodity is a normal good. Negative income elasticity indicates an inferior good.

7. The supply of a commodity is the quantity that would be offered for sale at each of various alternative prices, holding constant all other conditions that influence a producer's willingness to supply the commodity. The supply curve usually slopes upward to the right.

8. A change in the quantity supplied results from a change in price, but a shift in supply is the result of changes in other factors. These are the cost of inputs used to produce the good and the technology related to the production of this good.

9. The elasticity of supply with respect to price measures the responsiveness of suppliers to changes in product prices, and is defined as the percentage change in the quantity supplied divided by the percentage change in price. When $E_s < 1$, supply is inelastic; when $E_s > 1$, supply is elastic; and when $E_s = 1$, supply is of unitary elasticity.

10. The elasticity of supply with respect to price depends on the availability of inputs within a given production period, the time required to adjust production to the new price level, and whether the supplier expects the price change to be only temporary.

11. A product market is in equilibrium at the price where the quantity supplied is equal to the quantity demanded. At a price above equilibrium price, the pressure of excess supply leads to a lower price; at a price below the equilibrium price, the pressure of excess demand leads to a higher price. The equilibrium of a product market will be disturbed, leading to a new equilibrium price and quantity, when there is a shift either in demand or in supply. It is possible that a shift of both demand and supply will leave *either* price *or* quantity unchanged, but not both.

12. The equilibrium price and quantity in each market are dependent on changes occurring in other markets. When all markets are in equilibrium, the economy is in general equilibrium; all products are being produced as efficiently as possible and all individuals are realizing as much satisfaction as possible, given the state of technology and the level and distribution of incomes. The concept of general equilibrium is most useful in explaining the process whereby markets adjust to changes and in predicting the direction of changes in each market.

Key Concepts and Topics

independence of supply and
    demand
demand
demand schedule
demand curve

law of demand
quantity demanded
relative prices
shift or change in demand
substitute goods

complementary goods
consumer tastes or preferences
market demand
elasticity
price elasticity of demand
point elasticity
arc elasticity
total revenue
income elasticity
normal goods
inferior goods

supply
quantity supplied
shift or change in supply
technological change
elasticity of supply
excess supply
excess demand
equilibrium price
interdependence of markets
general equilibrium

Questions for Review and Discussion

1. (a) Why are economists so interested in the equilibrium price of a commodity when the actual or observed price is often different from the equilibrium price?

   (b) What forces are at work to move the price of a commodity toward its equilibrium price?

2. List five commodities for which you think the demand is inelastic, and five for which the demand is elastic, over the range of prices usually observed for these commodities. Explain why the demand would be inelastic or elastic in each case.

3. Why is it incorrect to say that the demand for luxuries is elastic and the demand for necessities is inelastic? (Note that the chapter says "will tend to be more elastic or less inelastic", and question 2 above says "over the range of prices usually observed".)

4. List five pairs of commodities that are very close substitutes. Can you think of any *perfect* substitutes? If two commodities are perfect substitutes, are they in fact different commodities? List five pairs of commodities that are complementary goods. Are there any *perfect* complements?

5. Why is the price of salt so low even though it is so important for our physical health?

6. Use a supply and demand diagram to explain the probable changes in price and quantity purchased if the sale of marijuana were to be legalized and conducted without government controls.

Sources and Selected Readings

Eckert, R.D., and R.H. Leftwich. *The Price System and Resource Allocation*, 10th ed. Hinsdale, Ill.: Dryden Press, 1988.

Stigler, George L. *The Theory of Price*, 4th ed. New York: Macmillan, 1987.

Appendix: Further Elasticity Cases

Elasticity Changes with Price Level

For any given demand curve, the elasticity of demand will usually be different at each price level. The reason for this can be seen by looking at the elasticity formula again in terms of geometry. Note that $\Delta Q/\Delta P$ is the reciprocal of the slope of the demand curve. (Recall that the slope is defined as rise/run, or $\Delta P/\Delta Q$.) A straight-line demand curve, such as the one shown in Figure 3.10, has a constant slope and thus its reciprocal, the value of $\Delta Q/\Delta P$, is constant for all price levels. However, the other part of the elasticity formula $(P_1 + P_2/Q_1 + Q_2)$ changes for each segment of the demand curve as the price-quantity combinations change. At high prices this ratio takes a very high value because the quantity demanded is low. Thus demand becomes more elastic at higher prices and more inelastic at lower prices. When the price is so high that the quantity demanded approaches zero, the elasticity approaches infinity. Alternatively, as the price approaches zero the elasticity also approaches zero.

Elasticity Changes with Demand Change

Using this same geometrical approach, it can be seen that the demand elasticity at any given price level will change with a parallel shift in the demand curve. For example, if the demand shown in Figure 3.10 were to increase such that there was a parallel outward shift in the demand curve, the slope (and $\Delta Q/\Delta P$) would be unchanged, but the value of $Q_1 + Q_2$ would be greater for any given price range (or $P_1 + P_2$). The value of $(P_1 + P_2/Q_1 + Q_2)$ would be less at each price level and therefore demand would be less elastic (or more inelastic).

Cross Elasticity of Demand

The quantity demanded of a given good will depend not only on its own price, but also on the price of related goods. Earlier in this chapter, goods were described as substitutes if an increase in the price of one good led to an increase in the quantity demanded of the other good. The reverse was the case of complementary goods: an increase in the price of one led to a decrease in the quantity demanded of the other.

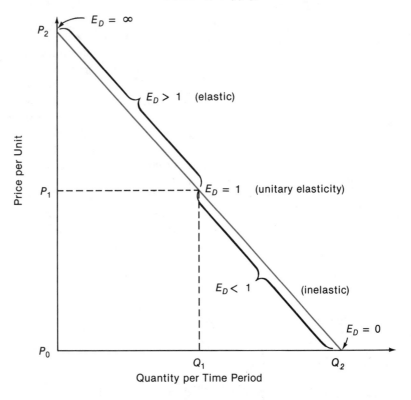

Figure 3.10 Elasticity Changes Even When Slope Is Constant
Elasticity changes over the length of a linear demand curve (with constant slope = $\Delta P/\Delta Q$) from a coefficient of zero at zero price to infinity at zero quantity. The elasticity is unitary at the price where quantity demanded, Q_1, is one-half the quantity demanded at zero price.

This relationship can now be measured by another application of the elasticity concept, namely *cross elasticity of demand*.

Cross elasticity is the percentage change in the quantity demanded of one good resulting from a given percentage change in the price of a different good.

Cross elasticity is calculated as:

$$E_{XY} = \frac{\Delta Q_X}{\Delta P_Y} \times \frac{(P_1 + P_2)_Y}{(Q_1 + Q_2)_X}$$

where E_{XY} is the coefficient of cross elasticity, and X and Y are two different commodities. (Note that there is no minus sign following the equal sign.)

Substitutes   If X and Y are substitutes, the quantity demanded of X will increase when the price of Y increases; therefore the elasticity coefficient will be positive for substitutes. The greater the value of the coefficient, the greater the degree of substitutability. Commodities that are very close substitutes, such as "Large" eggs and "Medium" eggs, would have a very high coefficient of cross elasticity.

Complements   If X and Y are complements, the quantity demanded of X will decrease when the price of Y increases; therefore the elasticity coefficient will be negative for complements. Again the increasing magnitude of the negative coefficient is a measure of the increasing degree of complementarity.

It should now be apparent that if the cross elasticity coefficient is zero, the goods are unrelated. They are neither complements nor substitutes, since a zero coefficient means that a change in the price of one good has no effect on the quantity demanded of the other. Summarizing briefly:

when $E_{XY} < 0$, the commodities are complements;
when $E_{XY} = 0$, the commodities are unrelated;
when $E_{XY} > 0$, the commodities are substitutes.

Key Concepts and Topics

cross elasticity

4 Government in the Market Economy

The market system, with its price mechanism for allocating resources and distributing finished products, is said by its supporters to provide the most efficient use of resources and the greatest possible satisfaction for consumers. The case made for the market system two centuries ago by Adam Smith, in his book *The Wealth of Nations*, has often been quoted to demonstrate the merits of a market economy. Smith argued that individuals would try to achieve their own greatest economic gain and, in doing so, would promote the most efficient use of resources.

Box 4.1   **The Invisible Hand**

Every individual endeavours to employ his capital so that its produce may be of greatest value. He generally neither intends to promote the public interest, nor knows how much he is promoting it. He intends only his own security, only his own gain. And he is in this led by an *invisible hand* to promote an end which was no part of his intention. By pursuing his own interest he frequently promotes that of society more effectually than when he really intends to promote it.

Source: Adam Smith, *The Wealth of Nations*

The "invisible hand" described by Adam Smith was the price mechanism at work, allocating or guiding resources to the most efficient production of commodities most desired by consumers. All of this was done without restricting individuals' freedom to determine their own role in the economy.

Limitations of the Market System

But Smith was writing at a time (1776) when the prevailing concept of individual freedom included freedom from a collective will—such as big government—as well as from a dictator's authoritarian command.

Furthermore, the economic organization Smith observed in England and Scotland, and particularly in his home city of Glasgow, was quite different from what he would see today in Canada, or in the United States, Japan, and Western Europe. Although the many small shop-keepers such as butchers and bakers that formed the core of Smith's economy are still evident, they are overshadowed by giant multinational corporations and international labour unions. All of these reduce the freedom and flexibility of individuals, whether they be workers, producers, or consumers.

Nevertheless, Adam Smith recognized that the "invisible hand" would not provide a satisfactory answer in every case, even in an economy with considerable individual freedom. He argued, for example, that parents would not always recognize the advantages of providing an education for their children. Even if they did recognize the advantages, they either would not or could not pay for the education, and at best would not provide as much education as would be in the general public interest. That is, the total economy would benefit from higher levels of education and skills leading to lower-cost output and a greater variety of goods, as well as from the sociocultural benefits of a better-educated population.

Inadequacies in market solutions to economic problems are commonly described as instances of *market failure: the failure of the market to produce an outcome that provides maximum social benefit and that agrees with the currently prevailing notion of social justice.*

In this context, social justice is defined simply as the results that the people of an economy would like to achieve. It may be expressed through the voting mechanism, as a complement to the economy's price mechanism. There are two groups of reasons for market failure: imperfect competition and the existence of non-market problems.

Imperfect Competition

Economies such as Canada's are not organized to meet all the requirements for the price mechanism to achieve the most efficient use of productive resources. Instead of perfectly competitive markets, where there are many producers of each commodity and where new firms can easily be established to produce these commodities, there are frequently only a few large firms, each powerful enough for various reasons to keep out any potential competition.

There are a number of reasons for imperfectly competitive markets. These include inadequate information, adjustment lags, monopolistic pressures, and market barriers.

Inadequate Information

One of the most serious difficulties in the market system is that buyers and sellers alike often lack satisfactory information concerning prices and qualities of products and productive factors. Consumers acquire information about food and clothing (if only by experience) fairly easily, by comparison with the difficulties they have in informing themselves about the quality of items such as cameras and radios, and intangibles like legal and medical services. Workers, too, have limited information about potential employment, wages paid in other jobs and locations, and working conditions.

Adjustment Lags

Part of the explanation for unemployment and other market failures is that the market system may be slow to adjust to changes in consumer tastes and technology. Labour mobility is far from perfect. Workers often cannot make occupational, industrial, and geographical shifts quickly enough to take advantage of wage differences. Retraining is costly in human effort and time, and moving to another locality imposes many social costs.

Increased mechanization and scale of production has "locked in" producers to particular commodities, techniques, and plant size, for longer periods of time. Financial resources are often unavailable for new projects because lenders take a "wait-and-see" attitude.

Tendency to Monopolistic Power

The market system has also tended to encourage the development of monopolistic power in many markets. The rapid adjustment implied in the price mechanism requires competition among many producers. Producers, however, would prefer to avoid such adjustments and hence they strive to gain more control of their markets. There are several consequences of monopolistic control: potential competitors are excluded, output is restricted, and prices are higher than when no producer has such control.

Although competition may spur technological change, this in turn can foster monopolistic control. Modern technology generally can be implemented most successfully when firms are assured of large markets and have access to large-scale financing, specialized management, and dependable sources of raw materials. Thus producers will strive to control the factor markets from which they obtain their productive resources, as well as the markets in which they sell their products. Monopoly power can, however, also lead to slower rather than faster technological change, especially if profit can be realized only in the much longer run. Producers will generally seek a prompt return on their investment, particularly in an era of rapid technological change.

One response to the monopolistic power of producers has been the emergence of large unions. This development of "countervailing power" of labour against management improves the position of workers, but may lead the market system further from its most efficient allocation of resources, because changes in labour resources must be in accordance with union rules as well as market conditions.

Barriers to Markets   Monopolistic power of producers and unions bars other firms from entering some product markets and other workers from some labour markets. Other factors, especially personal and social prejudices, also bar individuals from product markets and from labour markets. Prejudices such as these are now overruled by legislation, but enforcement tends to be slow and expensive. Specific commissions have therefore been established, for example, to promote human rights and employment equity.

Non-Market Problems

There are an increasing number of questions requiring a collective or social decision: questions, for example, of equitable income distribution, conservation of resources, and abatement of pollution. The market is not capable of providing a satisfactory solution to such questions. Rather, social questions require public intervention in private markets.

Equitable Income Distribution   The price mechanism allocates consumer products according to individuals' ability to pay for them. This in turn is determined by prices established for the productive resources that individuals offer to factor markets. Workers therefore are able to purchase goods and services in proportion to the total time they work and the hourly or monthly wage they receive. The market system, it is argued, is an inadequate means for determining how commodities should be distributed because some individuals are able to accumulate more physical capital and land than is considered just or fair, especially if these are accumulated through successive inheritances. As a result the market system allocates more resources to producing luxury goods for the wealthy and fewer resources to producing necessities for the poor.

Even if incomes were not realized from inheritances—or from simple good luck, as in winning a lottery—a normative or ethical question would remain. Should an individual's enjoyment of goods and services be related directly to his or her *economic* role in society, or should some other standard be used for distributing income or goods and services? Although there appears to be wide agreement that the market system fails to distribute income equitably, there is much disagreement on what would be fair or just, and on alternative criteria and systems.

Controversial Consumer Wants

One aspect of the individual freedom associated with the market system is *consumer sovereignty*: the power that consumers have to determine what shall be produced by directing their expenditures to the products they want most. Although consumer sovereignty has been diminished by monopolistic producers, the market system still responds by offering what consumers will buy. In fact, there is a constant search by enterprising individuals to create products that do not exist, but that consumers would be prepared to buy—such as the skateboard and the Walkman radio.

But the market makes no value judgment about what should be produced. Thus some goods and services become the focus of social and political controversy—alcohol, tobacco, marijuana, heroin, prostitution, pornography, betting shops, lotteries, and guns have all been subjects of continuing debate about their proper control. The political system is used to correct what are regarded as failures or undesirable consequences of the market system: alcohol is sold by government agencies, tobacco advertising is banned, prostitution is made illegal, lotteries are licensed, books and films are censored, safety standards are imposed for automobiles, and so on. The legislation that governs the production and sale of these items at any time and in each country or province reflects—or so one assumes—the consensus of society about these items.

Unmet Public Needs

The market may also fail to provide public needs or *public goods. These are items that, if not purchased collectively, will not be produced at all.* This is because they would be equally available to everyone due to the difficulty in excluding those who would not pay. Strictly speaking, many public goods and services could be purchased individually, but their effectiveness is far greater when purchased collectively: imagine, for example, an economy in which individuals made their own arrangements for police and fire protection, and even for weather forecasts. Everyone's health is improved if chest X-rays and vaccinations are provided to all in the community, rather than to the few who choose to purchase them individually. Public action through governments is required to make such collective decisions, which would not occur if the market system were left to make these choices on the basis of individual preferences.

Externalities Ignored

Externalities are economic effects that are not taken into account by buyers and sellers of a commodity; such effects are external to market transactions. An individual who improves the appearance of his or her home usually provides the neighbours with an external economy or

---

**Box 4.2   Moore Park resident cuts his tree and
upsets his neighbors**

By Peter Whelan

It might have become the battle of Moore Park but the neighborhood was too civilized.

At 7 a.m. yesterday the chain saw roared to life and bit into the weeping willow in Nicholas Kilburn's back yard on Clifton Road. Limb by limb, the tree disappeared.

Back-fence neighbors John Pemberton and Anthony Paine of Cornish Road were shocked.

It was not just any old tree. Eighty-five feet tall and 75 years old, it was there before the 60-year-old houses around it. It dominated the burgeoning maples. Its canopy shaded all the yards.

There was a sense of "our tree" and of outrage. People take their trees seriously in this green enclave of Toronto. . . .

At the end of the Paines' garden, the chain saw growled through another limb. Tree remover John Roberto and his two helpers were working steadily.

Enter the owners. Mr. Kilburn was at rehearsal—he plays bassoon in the Toronto Symphony—and his wife Susan was mourning for her tree . . . .

As the day and the cutting went on, there finally was a neighborly meeting. They talked among the fallen branches of the willow and the tensions eased with the sharing of regrets for the tree . . . .

In the yard next door, where Dr. J. William Balfe will become a new neighbor next month, is a huge dying poplar. They all share its shade, too. When it goes, the sun will pour in.

Perhaps, with Dr. Balfe, they will form a little tree co-operative and pay jointly for the best trees to shade them all.

In law, the willow was the property and responsibility of the Kilburns alone. Mrs. Pemberton seemed to mourn it the most.

She thinks the time must come when esthetics shared by a neighborhood—especially a green one like Moore Park—become a protected right of all the neighbors.

Source: *The Globe and Mail*, 23 May 1972

Externalities—even those as intangible as the shade of a tree on a neighbour's lawn—can be internalized when everyone who benefits contributes to the provision of the good or service in question.

---

benefit, if only because they can realize a higher price for their own homes due to the improved appearance of the neighbourhood. Conversely, a factory that pollutes a river, making it unsuitable for swimming, imposes an external diseconomy or cost on a downstream holiday resort, which can no longer provide a swimming area as one of its attractions.

Externalities are quite common in everyday experience, but the market system ignores them. If people who improved the appearance of their homes could collect the value of the benefits realized by their neighbours, homeowners would allocate more resources to such activity because there would be a greater monetary return from the costs they incur. If resort owners who were harmed by a factory's pollutants could collect full compensation for the harm caused, factories probably would change their techniques or disposal systems in response. In each case, resource allocation would come closer to maximizing society's satisfaction than occurs under an unregulated or free market system. Other means must be found, therefore, either to "internalize" these effects so that individuals will take them into account, or to offset the effects by other actions.

Government in the Market Economy

Examining the workings of the market system makes it easier to understand the role of government in a market economy. More public action is required than the traditional views of writers on liberal democracy would suggest. Not only must governments provide the legal foundation for a market economy, including laws of property, contracts, and incorporation, as well as police protection and national defence; they must also give the market economy some social direction or objectives.

The major failures of the market system stem from the fact that in its pure form it has no function other than to provide efficiently the commodities demanded by individuals who control the productive resources. This does not mean that the market system must be rejected if social objectives or wants are to be satisfied. Rather, the market system can be adapted as an instrument for effecting social or public policy.

Society can make normative decisions about desirable outcomes of the market and alter the market forces to achieve these outcomes. It may be necessary, for example, to transfer income to some groups by taxing it from others, but the recipients of income transfers can then spend these as they wish. Governments can direct producers to take external costs into account by taxing pollution or specifying installation of non-polluting equipment. Producers of external benefits can be subsidized by taxing persons who enjoy the benefits.

If the market system is to provide the results assumed for its purely competitive form, government intervention is also required to bring some stability to the fluctuations of individual decisions, hasten adjustments to changing conditions, and restrain monopolistic tendencies and private control of unique resources.

The economic roles of governments in a market system can be grouped into three categories: allocation, distribution, and stabilization.

Allocation   *Allocation* activities include purchasing or providing public goods; making externalities explicit in individuals' decisions by taxation, subsidy, or regulation; and regulating the structure of markets to obtain more competitive conditions. This function probably accounts for the largest portion of governments' involvement in economies. A more detailed discussion of these activities is presented in the next section of this chapter.

Distribution   The *distribution* function is largely a matter of arranging direct income transfers by taxing higher-income persons and making grants to lower-income persons in the form of welfare payments, unemployment compensation, pensions, and other financial assistance. However, almost all government spending has some redistributive effect because the incomes of persons receiving government goods or services usually differs from the incomes of taxpayers supporting the expenditures. Government regulations can also have a redistributive impact: anti-pollution legislation reduces the profit of the polluting factory, reduces the real income of its customers by increasing the price of the product, but increases the profit of the downstream resort owner and the enjoyment of recreation facilities by the vacationers.

Stabilization   *Stabilization* is pursued mainly by varying the government's expenditure and taxation program, although monetary and foreign trade policies are also designed to stabilize economic activity. Since these policies may include government actions to improve resource allocation or income distribution, the latter activities can also have stabilizing or destabilizing effects. For example, under certain conditions, increasing income transfers to low-income groups can send the economy off on an inflationary spiral. Governments therefore need not only to determine the appropriate extent of their involvement in each economic activity, they must also set their priorities where there are potential conflicts in the goals they pursue through the market system.

Caution!   Descriptions of market failures and government intervention to set things right again can leave the impression that these problems are easily resolved. As the proportion of government activity in the economy increases, however, it is increasingly important that society be alert to government decisions that have the same faults as were noted for markets. Public highway projects, for example, may be planned with little regard for the external costs they impose through environmental damage. The political goal of "citizen participation" can become a matter of "citizen protest", unless governments avoid elements of monopolistic control, external costs, adjustment lags, and so on, in their own economic actions.

Government's Responsibility for Resource Allocation

Governments have taken greater responsibility in the past several years, not only for economic stabilization and income distribution, but also for assuring that the economy's productive resources are used efficiently and are used to provide the goods and services desired by the public.

Regulation   Although direct government control over the use of resources through expenditures on goods and services has been shown to be substantial and growing steadily, governmental influence on resource allocation is even more significant through its regulation of the private sector. The maintenance of competition involves legal restraints on monopoly practices such as mergers, price fixing, and market sharing.

Public Goods   The second major rationale for government control of resource allocation concerns what are called public goods, or collective consumption goods. Since confusion can arise about the use of terms in this area of economics, it is necessary to specify further that this section deals with pure public goods, while the next section examines quasi-public goods. One of the earliest economic functions of government was to provide pure public goods: goods — or more often, services — that one person can use or enjoy without diminishing the use of that good or service by anyone else.

The chief distinguishing characteristic of a public good is that it is impossible to exclude anyone from using or benefiting directly from that good.

It is this "exclusion principle" that dictates that some services, if they are to be available at all, must be made available through collective action, since they would be equally available to everyone once they were produced.

National defence is the most obvious public good. No one living within the country concerned can be excluded from the general effects of a defence program. If a few individuals were to establish an effective defence program, everyone else would benefit as much as the persons who paid for the program. In such a situation, it is likely that each person would refrain from providing defence — or other similar services —

for himself, knowing that he could derive the benefits at no cost to himself, if only someone else would take action. Everyone would wait for "someone else" to do it, and nothing would happen. Hence the only way that such services can be provided is for individuals to agree that governments should tax each of them and provide the services collectively.

Quasi-Public Goods   Pure public goods account for only a minor part of governments' expenditures. Why then, do governments undertake the rest of their expenditure programs? Prices could be charged for items such as highways, education, health care, and parks. Individuals unwilling to pay the price could be excluded. These services could therefore be provided by the private sector — and indeed, each of these has been or is available from private producers.

Collection Costs   In some cases, *the cost of collecting the price charged* would be too great for the private entrepreneur to realize a profit on the activity. It was possible to collect tolls, for example, when there were only a few roads: early photographs of some Canadian cities show toll booths at the main intersections. But the proliferation of roads, with the spread of residential areas and increase in the numbers of vehicles, led to the collective action of paying property taxes and gasoline taxes to provide a system of public streets and highways.

Economies of Scale   Another, more important, reason for the collective provision of some services is that there are *economies of scale* in the production of these services. Several producers could provide postal, transportation, or communications services — and they have. But it was realized, for example, that the transportation services provided by several private companies in Toronto's suburbs could be provided more efficiently by combining these operations, hence the Toronto Transportation Commission was formed. Similarly, many of the early telephone companies were combined to form the Bell Telephone System, and a number of the railroads were combined to form the Canadian National Railway. These latter two examples illustrate alternative methods of government control: Bell Canada remains a private firm with its rates set by a government board, whereas the CNR is government-owned.

Externalities   *Externalities* constitute the third and most important reason for governments to provide services such as education, health, and science research. Externalities are the economic effects of actions of producers and consumers for which no compensation is paid, or economic effects that are not considered in decisions about market transactions. Environmental pollution is a common form of externality. Factories emitting sulphur dioxide, noisy trucks passing through residential communities, and boats discharging sewage into lakes all impose a "cost" on people adversely affected by these actions. If no compensation is charged against the offender, the effects are *external diseconomies*, or external costs.

Box 4.3   Environmental Externalities

The family which takes its mauve and cerise, air-conditioned, power-steered, and power-braked automobile out for a tour passes through cities that are badly paved, made hideous by litter, blighted buildings, billboards, and posts for wires that long since should have been put underground. They pass into a countryside that has been rendered largely invisible by commercial art. . . . They picnic on exquisitely packaged food from a portable icebox by a polluted stream and go on to spend the night at a park which is a menace to public health and morals. Just before dozing off on an air mattress, beneath a nylon tent, amid the stench of decaying refuse, they may reflect vaguely on the curious unevenness of their blessings.

Source: John Kenneth Galbraith, *The Affluent Society*, 1st edition, 1958, p. 253. Copyright 1958, 1969, 1976, 1984 by author. Reprinted by permission of Houghton Mifflin Company.

Alternatively, there can be positive effects or benefits for which the person affected is not required to compensate the producer of the effects. Examples of such *external economies*, or external benefits, range from the enjoyment of shade from a neighbour's tree to the improvement in one's own health when everyone has had inoculations against contagious diseases.

If these external effects are not taken into account by collective action, resources will not be allocated in what, from the whole economy's point of view, is the most efficient manner.

When the producers of external diseconomies are not required to pay the cost of preventing pollution or to compensate those adversely affected, more of their goods will be produced than should be, because the full cost is not considered in their production decisions. The result is an inefficient use of resources. Similarly, external benefits enjoyed by other individuals are not taken into account in private decisions, for example, about health and education expenditures. Unless activities like education or disease prevention are subsidized, individuals underestimate the full benefits associated with the costs of particular activities and thus too few resources are allocated to these activities. Governments are therefore expected to try to assess externalities and to regulate or tax those who cause external diseconomies, while subsidizing the producers of external economies.

Alternative Ways to Provide Public Goods

Direct Production   Governments can provide public goods and services, and can represent the public interest in the private sector, through a number of alternative techniques. The most obvious one is *direct production by government-owned firms or through various government departments*. Governments can become direct producers by employing labour and purchasing other supplies to provide many types of public services. The Department of National Defence, for example, hires and trains personnel and purchases equipment to provide defence services. Similarly, land is purchased and persons hired to provide the services of national parks. Police services are "produced" directly by federal, provincial, and municipal governments.

There is considerable disagreement on how many and what types of goods and services should be produced directly by governments. One part of this debate focuses on the question of "nationalizing" some industries such as petroleum, steel, and banking to produce more efficiently the goods and services supplied by these industries. Another part of the debate is concerned with the extent to which governments should control publishing and broadcasting, for example, and whether these industries would have any independence under government ownership. Recently, more attention is paid to whether governments should be direct producers of all the many services already under their control.

A major argument favouring government production is that where one producer can provide the output required more efficiently than could several firms, the government should be that single producer, in order to provide any specific quantity at the lowest possible price.

Another argument is that governments need to have direct control over vital services such as defence, and police and fire protection. These have been government functions for so long that it is impossible for some people to imagine them being arranged privately. Yet fire protection was provided privately in some parts of Canada during the last century by the fire insurance companies, and some aspects of police service are available privately through firms providing security guards and private detectives. There are, in fact, a number of alternative arrangements open to governments for the provision of most services now appearing in public budgets.

Purchases   Another alternative is to purchase the goods or services from the private sector or from other governments, instead of producing them directly. The federal government, for example, currently buys student places in educational institutions to provide further training for people who qualify under the National Training Act. Under a previous technical training act, the federal government participated jointly with the provinces to produce technical training. Thus, governments must regularly confront this "make-or-buy" decision.

Regulations　The simplest, and often least expensive, alternative is the use of legislation and regulations to control the private sector. Monopolies such as Bell Canada are allowed to exist in the private sector because governments can regulate the prices they charge for their services.

Subsidies　Yet another alternative is to increase the production of some goods and services, notably those with associated external economies, by direct subsidies to private producers. For example, most universities in Canada are legally private institutions but they receive substantial grants from governments so that they can offer services (instruction) at prices (tuition fees) lower than their full cost.

Taxes　Although taxation is discussed in the second part of this chapter, it must be noted here that taxes can be used to achieve the opposite effect of a subsidy. Taxes can be imposed on private firms so that fewer goods are produced and at higher prices. It has been argued, for example, that pollution could be controlled more effectively by taxing pollution rather than by using legislation to forbid it. A sufficiently high tax on pollution might reduce pollution further and at less direct cost to the government than through the difficult and costly process of prosecuting every apprehended case of pollution.

Using the Price Mechanism for Public Policies

Governments can attempt to correct the perceived failures of the market system in several ways. One common method is through the price mechanism. Examples are the setting of maximum or minimum prices and the taxing or subsidizing of particular commodities. Some existing or proposed public policies are examined here to illustrate the effects of government intervention and the significance of supply and demand elasticities in designing a policy that will have the desired results.

Rent Controls: An Example of Ceiling Prices

A common proposal for increasing the real incomes of persons living in rented apartments is to set maximum rental rates, thus leaving these persons a larger portion of their incomes to spend on other goods and services. The general consequences of such a policy are illustrated by Figure 4.1. Suppose that only high-rise apartments are covered by the

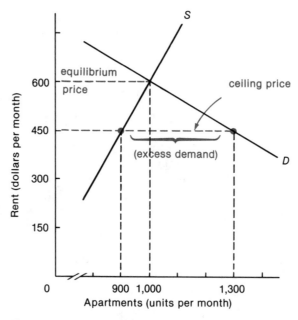

Figure 4.1 Ceiling Prices Create an Excess Demand
Setting the maximum apartment rent at $450 per month, below the
equilibrium price of $600 per month, increases the quantity demanded to
1,300 units but reduces the quantity supplied to 900 units. The difference,
400 units, is an excess demand, which results in illegal, black-market
transactions and possibly in government allocation or rationing of the 900
units supplied.

policy, and not other housing alternatives such as flats and rooms in
houses, duplexes, and townhouses.

Over the relevant price range, demand is neither very inelastic,
because housing alternatives are available, nor very elastic, because
some form of housing is necessary and for some people the alternatives
to high-rise apartments may not be very good substitutes. Supply is
fairly inelastic because (it is assumed) costs of labour, land, and
materials all increase sharply as more apartment buildings are constructed and because other buildings cannot be readily converted to
apartments.

The equilibrium price is $600 per month and the quantity rented in
this local market is 1,000 units. Assume that the maximum rent is set at
$450 per month. The quantity demanded will increase, as a result of the
price decrease, to 1,300 units per month. People who have been living
in other types of accommodation or who have been sharing other accommodation will want to rent units at this lower price. But the quantity
supplied will decrease to 900 units per month, perhaps because apartment owners can convert housing units to offices for doctors, dentists, or

other professionals. *The result is an excess demand or shortage of 400 units.*

The rent control policy has created *disequilibrium* in the housing market. The excess demand created will be greater the more elastic are the supply and the demand between the equilibrium price and the ceiling price.

Note however that there is no change in the *equilibrium* price, because there is no change in demand or supply. That is, there is no shifting of these curves. Furthermore, if the maximum rent is set at $600 per month or more (at or above the equilibrium price), this policy will have no effect on the market unless supply decreases (the supply curve shifts leftward), or demand increases (the demand curve shifts rightward).

When the price mechanism is working freely, it allocates or rations the available goods or services among potential buyers. But when a constraint is placed on the price mechanism in the form of a ceiling price, some other means must be found for allocating the 900 units among the 1,300 customers willing to pay the price of $450. In this case, the 900 units will probably be made available to the tenants who were fortunate enough not to be in apartments withdrawn from that market (that is, the tenants remaining in the 900 units will be allowed to stay). Some of the 900 units will be vacated by persons moving from the area or to other accommodation, and these apartments will be eagerly sought.

Apartment superintendents may lease these apartments to the first-comers, but more likely will practise some discrimination, such as selecting persons who are likely to give the superintendents the least trouble, or persons who are highly recommended by current tenants. Alternatively, the superintendent may accept or insist on payments or gifts and, in effect, auction the apartments to the highest bidder. *When price controls are in effect, suppliers are able to do what they cannot do in a free market: exercise some discrimination among potential buyers.* This often results in political pressure to allocate the available units through a method that is acknowledged to be fairer or more just than allowing individual suppliers to decide. The responsible government department or agency might, for example, establish a means test or other standards for considering applications.

Despite the appearance of a "fair" allocation system for the 900 units, there remain 400 unsatisfied prospective tenants. The pressure for more apartments created by their frequent enquiries about vacancies is likely to stimulate the development of a *black market: the buying and selling of a commodity at prices above the maximum legal price.* Apartment owners may offer a "business office", for example, that is actually a housing unit, at a higher price than $450 per month. Apartment superintendents may insist on an additional payment of up to $150 per month, threatening harassment if the bribe is not paid. Or there may be additional charges, for keys, use of kitchen appliances and other furniture, or parking, to raise the full price of the apartment substantially above the legal price. To the extent that this occurs, more apartments will be provided, and the number demanded will decrease, until the market equilibrium is re-established at $600 per month for 1,000 units.

**Box 4.4   Cash under table buys key to door
for Metro renters**

By Sean Fine, Robert MacLeod and
Carol McDowell

When Josie Morris of Toronto went to look at an apartment near Leslie Street and York Mills Avenue, she was told it would cost her an extra $4,500 to move in.

"They advertised the rent as $400," said Ms Morris, . . . "But you had to buy drapes and broadloom for $4,500."

Another apartment at Yonge Street and Lawrence Avenue was available only if she paid the outgoing tenant $1,500.

"It's disgusting," she said. . . . "The sad part is, people are willing to pay key money—so you can't get an apartment."

Key money, long a part of apartment renting in New York, has turned up in Metro Toronto, where the apartment vacancy rate is a stifling 0.1 per cent—for every 1,000 units, there is only one vacancy.

(In comparison, Calgary enjoys a 4.4 per cent vacancy rate, Montreal stands at 1.8 per cent and the Halifax rate is 2.6 per cent. Vancouver registers a 0.9 per cent vacancy rate; Kitchener ranks close to Toronto, at 0.2 per cent.)

Charging key money has been illegal since the provincial [Ontario] Residential Rent Regulation Act came into effect on Jan. 1, but so far there have been no prosecutions.

However, a spokesman for the Ministry of Housing indicated that the province has chosen three Toronto neighborhoods for a crackdown. . . .

Key money is often disguised as a payment for draperies, carpeting and painting. . . .

Alex Bell, communications officer with the Ministry of Housing, said: "It's all key money, there's no way around it. In some cases it's disguised, but it's still key money and it's illegal." . . .

The new law sets a maximum fine of $25,000 for a corporation and $2,000 for an individual for charging key money.

Source: *The Globe and Mail*, 3 April 1987.

"Key money" represents at least part of the amount that is required to restore the equilibrium price in a market where there are price controls. This situation is typical under rent controls, but it also occurs, for example, when price controls are placed on strategic goods—such as gasoline—during wartime or other national emergencies.

Alternative Policies   Other policies have been proposed as alternatives to rent controls. These include increasing the quantity of land zoned and serviced for residential construction, subsidies for housing construction, and providing additional income supplements or housing grants for low-income families and individuals. *Increasing residential land* would shift the supply curve outward, lower the equilibrium price, and increase the quantity of apartments. If the costs of *subsidies* were met from income tax revenues, everyone would benefit from the lower rents (and lower house prices), but the middle- and higher-income groups would bear most of the cost. *Housing grants* for persons with lower incomes would help them pay their rents. Although the additional income would also be expected to increase demand for housing and increase the equilibrium price slightly, this increase would be less than the amount of the housing grant.

Price controls are frequently used in wartime to restrain the rapid inflation that would otherwise occur in consumer goods, as resources are shifted to defence production. *Rationing* of the inadequate quantity supplied is usually done by issuing *ration coupons*. In this situation, a potential consumer needs both money and ration coupons to buy one unit of a good. Only enough coupons are issued to buy the quantity available at the legal price. Since the demand for rationed commodities is influenced by individuals' levels of "coupon income" as well as money income, a limited distribution of coupons is intended to shift the demand curve leftward to the point where it intersects the supply curve at the controlled price. When price controls are used in peacetime, governments attempt to offset the excess demand by trying to stimulate an increase in the supply of commodities covered by the controls.

Minimum Wages: An Example of Floor Prices

Minimum wage laws and guaranteed floor prices for selected agricultural products are two common examples of minimum price setting by governments. All provincial governments and the federal government have minimum wage legislation enabling them to specify the minimum hourly wage that can be paid in certain areas, occupations, or industries. When new minimum levels are announced, most employees are at a wage rate above that level; only some categories of unskilled labour are affected.

Suppose the market for unskilled labour in a particular area is represented by the supply and demand curves shown in Figure 4.2. The equilibrium hourly wage is $4.50 at a quantity of 20,000 hours per week. A legal minimum wage of $4.50 or less per hour will have no effect on the market. Assume, however, that the minimum wage is set at $5.00 per hour. The result is that employers want only 16,000 hours per week, but

24,000 hours are offered. Those who remain employed receive a higher wage, but (assuming a 40-hour week) 100 persons lose their jobs, since the quantity demanded drops from 20,000 to 16,000 hours. But the unemployed now include not only the 100 persons who have lost their jobs, but also a further 100 persons who would like to work at a higher wage and who were not in the labour market at the previous wage of $4.50 per hour.

This unemployment might be reduced if the higher wage for those remaining in employment leads to increased consumer expenditures and hence to an outward shift in the demand for labour and more persons employed at the minimum wage or above. But if the demand for unskilled labour is elastic, a wage increase will reduce the total wages paid (recall the relationship between price and total revenue from Chapter 3), reduce the level of consumer spending, thereby reducing the demand for labour, and increasing unemployment.

It is often argued, however, that one result of minimum wage legislation is that employers are stimulated to make better use of their unskilled labour so that their existing employees will be worth more to

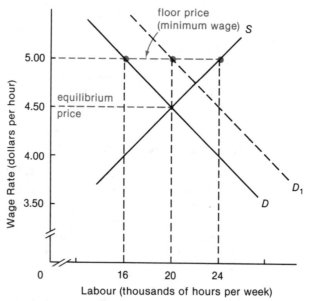

Figure 4.2 Floor Prices Create an Excess Supply
Setting the minimum wage rate at $5.00 per hour, above the equilibrium rate of $4.50 per hour, increases the quantity of labour supplied and reduces the quantity demanded. The excess supply, or unemployment of labour, would be 8,000 hours per week. Even if employers can shift their demand curve to D_1 by making more efficient use of their existing employees, new entrants to the labour market, at the higher wage, will not be employed.

them, hence justifying a higher wage. This is in effect an outward shift of the labour demand curve to D_1. Should this occur, the existing employees would not lose their jobs, but the additional 4,000 hours per week offered to this market would find no employers. There would still be unemployment resulting from the new wage legislation.

The actual effects of minimum wages remain the subject of much controversy. Empirical studies are hampered by the problem of isolating other changes occurring in the economy at the same time. Frequently, the minimum wage has been increased in a period of economic prosperity, when the labour demand curve is shifting outward faster than the supply curve, with the result that actual unemployment has been slight or negligible. There is general agreement, however, that minimum wage legislation has been a primary cause of the current high levels of unemployment among young people.

Black markets do not emerge under minimum wage legislation as they do when price ceilings are imposed. However, employers may find prospective workers pressing them for employment at a wage below the legal minimum, or workers may offer to work more hours than they would be paid for. The government therefore appoints employment inspectors to guard against such violations when minimum wage legislation is implemented.

Sales Taxes to Reduce Consumption

The effect of a government's intervention in a market can be seen most clearly in the case of sales taxes. A general sales tax of 5 per cent, for example, on the value of all purchases except necessities like food, is levied primarily as a source of government revenue. Taxes on specific commodities, however, are sometimes intended to reduce the consumption of those items. One common proposal, for example, is that governments should impose a much higher sales tax on cigarettes, if they wish to reduce smoking, rather than requiring a health warning to be printed on the package or banning cigarette advertising. Similarly, it has been proposed that marijuana be legalized but taxed heavily. Opponents of automobile exhaust pollution who are sceptical about emission control devices argue that increasing the gasoline tax is the most effective means of reducing such pollution. Controversy on such proposals often centres on whether the quantity purchased would be substantially reduced.

Consider the case of automobile gasoline. Assume the existing supply and demand are as shown in Figure 4.3a. At an equilibrium price of $.50 per litre, 500 litres are sold each hour in a specific market area. Assume further that the provincial government increases the gasoline tax by $.05 per litre. If gas stations were to continue to supply 500 litres, they would need to receive $.55 per litre to meet their own costs and pay the higher taxes. In fact, to provide any given quantity after the new tax is in effect, suppliers will require $.05 per litre more than they did before the tax. *This is reflected in an upward shift of the supply curve to S_1 by a vertical distance equal to $.05.*

Specific versus Percentage Tax   *A specific tax*, one that states an absolute amount to be paid on each unit, results in a parallel vertical shift of the supply curve. If the new tax had been an *ad valorem tax*, stated as a *percentage* of the selling price, the new supply curve would have had a *steeper slope*, because the absolute amount of the tax per unit would be greater as the selling price increased.

Figure 4.3a shows that the effect of the increased tax is to raise the *equilibrium* price to $.53 per litre, but gasoline consumption is reduced by only 25 litres per hour since this portion of the demand curve is inelastic. (Calculate the elasticity over the range of the price change.)

But what would the effect be if the demand for gasoline were quite elastic, as in Figure 4.3b? This situation would occur if there were close substitutes for gasoline or automobile transportation, such as public transit. The price would increase only slightly, from $.50 to $.51, but the quantity sold would fall to 425 litres per hour. (Calculate the elasticity of demand in this case.)

Effects of a Sales Tax   This comparison of two cases of demand elasticity illustrates some conclusions that can be drawn about the effects of a sales tax:

- provided that the demand is not perfectly elastic, a sales tax will increase the price paid by consumers, but by less than the full amount of the tax;
- the more *inelastic* is the *demand* for a commodity, the higher is the new market price;
- the more *inelastic* is the *supply* of a commodity, the lower is the new market price;
- except when either demand or supply are perfectly inelastic, a sales tax will reduce the quantity exchanged. The more elastic are both demand and supply, the greater is this reduction in quantity.

The example considered above assumed that the purpose of the tax was to reduce consumption. A government is also interested in the revenue realized from a sales tax; this will also differ depending on the elasticity of demand and supply. The more inelastic is demand or supply, the less the quantity bought and sold is reduced by the tax, and hence the higher is the tax revenue. Governments therefore will find sales taxes more effective in reducing consumption the more elastic is demand or supply for the commodity concerned, but more effective in raising revenue the more inelastic is demand or supply for the commodities to be taxed.

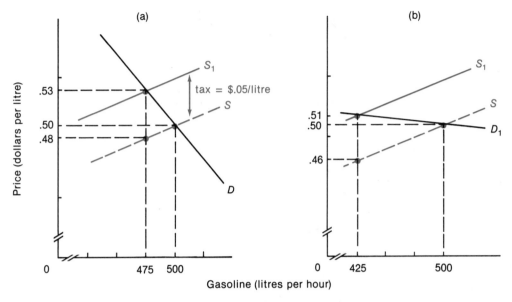

Figure 4.3   **Effect of a Sales Tax Depends on Elasticities of Supply and Demand**
Imposing a gasoline sales tax of $.05 per litre shifts the market supply curve upward, to S_1, by the amount of the tax. The increase in the equilibrium price, however, is less than the tax: the more elastic the demand (compare D_1 and D), the less the price increase but the greater the reduction in quantity purchased.

Subsidies to Increase Consumption

A subsidy is a payment to a producer to offset part of the production costs. The payment may be either a fixed sum or a sum that varies directly with the quantity produced. Subsidies are paid when a government wants to increase the output of a particular item, without being directly involved in its production and distribution.

It has often been proposed, for example, that the federal government increase its financial assistance to Canadian publishing firms so that Canadians will be encouraged to read more works by Canadian authors. To determine the effects of implementing this proposal, consider an example that makes some simplifying assumptions. Suppose the demand for Canadian paperback books can be represented by demand curve D as shown in Figure 4.4. Since for the general reader there are many close substitutes, ranging from foreign books to Canadian magazines, the demand is assumed to be quite elastic. Supply is also assumed to be elastic because the costs of labour and materials probably do not rise very quickly with increased output. The current equilibrium price is $13.90 per book; 10,000 books are sold at this price each month.

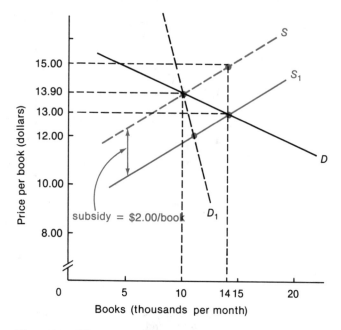

Figure 4.4   Effect of a Subsidy Depends on Supply and Demand Elasticities
A government subsidy of $2.00 per book shifts the market supply curve
downward to S_1 by the amount of the subsidy. However, the equilibrium
price falls by less than the full subsidy: the more elastic the demand curve,
the less the price falls but the more quantity is increased. The broken-line
demand curve can be used to visualize the subsidy's effect on price and
quantity when demand is more inelastic.

Next assume the government offers Canadian publishers a subsidy of
$2.00 per paperback book.[1] Since publishers are currently willing to
supply 10,000 books per month at a market price of $13.90, they should
be willing to supply the same 10,000 books at a market price of $11.90
when the government pays a $2.00 subsidy. *Thus the effect of the sub-
sidy will be to shift the supply curve downward by the amount of the
subsidy.* The new supply curve, S_1, intersects the demand curve at a
lower price and higher quantity. The new market price is $13.00, and
14,000 books are sold each month. The subsidy in this case does substantially increase the consumption of Canadian books.

Effects of a Subsidy   As in the case of a sales tax, however, the elasticity of demand and of
supply have a significant effect on the results of a subsidy. An alterna-
tive, inelastic demand curve (the broken line, D_1) is also shown in

[1] This is the case of a *per unit* subsidy. The effect of a *lump sum* subsidy can be
determined using the theory of the firm, as developed in Chapters 17 and 18 on
competition and monopoly.

Figure 4.4. to make it easier to compare the influence of different demand elasticities on the price and quantity effects of a subsidy. In the inelastic demand case, the subsidy would lead to a greater reduction in price but the increase in quantity would be less.

Some general conclusions can be drawn from this comparison:

- provided that the demand is not perfectly elastic, a subsidy will reduce the price paid by consumers by less than the full amount of the subsidy;
- the more *inelastic* is the *demand* for a commodity, the *lower* is the new market price and the greater is the benefit of the subsidy to consumers in terms of a price reduction;
- the more *elastic* is the *supply* of a commodity, the *lower* is the new market price;
- except when either demand or supply are perfectly inelastic, a subsidy will increase the quantity bought and sold. The more elastic are both demand and supply, the greater is this increase in quantity.

Review of the Main Points

1. Markets provide some results that are inefficient or contradict the prevailing notion of social justice. Market failure is due in part to imperfect competition resulting from inadequate information, adjustment lags, a tendency to monopoly power, and barriers preventing some persons from having access to all markets.

2. Furthermore, a market system makes no judgments about income distribution and consumer wants; does not provide public goods and services such as national defence; may not provide enough quasi-public goods such as education and health; and ignores external benefits and costs.

3. The rationale for government involvement in a market system is to correct the results of market failure, through legislation and direct participation in specific markets.

4. Economic functions of government include stabilization of aggregate economic activity, redistribution of income in an equitable manner, and reallocation of productive resources to more efficient uses.

5. Reallocation of resources involves both regulation of private sector production and direct production of goods and services within the public sector. Public goods and services such as defence are those that would not be produced except through collective action. Quasi-public goods such as highways, education, and health care

are produced collectively due to high costs of excluding non-contributors, economies of scale, or external benefits.

6. Public and quasi-public goods and services may be provided through direct production by government departments or agencies, by purchasing the goods or services from the private sector, by regulating private monopolies, by subsidizing producers, or by imposing taxes on activities that are contrary to the public interest.

7. Governments can use the price mechanism to achieve certain results, for example, by imposing price ceilings or price floors and by levying sales taxes or offering subsidies; but governments need to be aware of the consequences of these actions.

8. A price ceiling such as rent control creates an excess demand or shortage; rationing may therefore be used to reduce effective demand. A black market is also likely to arise.

9. A price floor such as a legal minimum wage creates a surplus or excess supply (unemployment). Employers may effectively increase the demand for labour by improving the utilization of labour. There is also an incentive for potential employees to offer their labour services, illegally, below the minimum wage.

10. A sales tax shifts the supply curve upward by the amount of the tax per unit and hence increases the equilibrium price and reduces the quantity sold. The more inelastic the demand and the more elastic the supply, the higher is the new price. The more elastic are both demand and supply, the greater is the reduction in quantity.

11. A subsidy shifts the supply curve downward by the amount per unit of the subsidy, reduces the equilibrium price, and increases the quantity sold. The more inelastic the demand and the more elastic the supply, the lower is the new price and the greater the benefit realized by the consumer.

Key Concepts and Topics

"invisible hand"
market failure
imperfect competition
adjustment lags
barriers to markets
equitable income distribution
consumer sovereignty
floor prices
externalities
allocation
distribution

stabilization
public goods
exclusion principle
quasi-public goods
ceiling prices
black market
price controls
ad valorem tax
specific tax
subsidy

Questions for Review and Discussion

1. What did Adam Smith mean by "an invisible hand" and how was this expected to bring about the beneficial effects Smith mentions?

2. Outline the basic conditions that must exist for the market system to be of maximum benefit to consumers, that is, if the market is to be described as "perfect." Would there still remain a problem of "market failure"?

3. List as many instances as you can of external costs and of external benefits you have experienced today. What legislative or other changes might be made to bring these effects within the decision-making of persons who produced these effects?

4. Describe several examples of current government intervention in the market system in Canada that produce better or worse results than you would expect to be produced in a pure market system. Think particularly of the basic economic decisions that were discussed in Chapter 1.

5. What conflicts are there among the three basic economic functions of government: allocation, distribution, and stabilization? Which of these functions should receive highest priority? Why?

6. Explain carefully why a government, rather than a private firm, might provide each of the following: traffic signals, weather forecasts, chest X-ray clinics, postal services.

7. Describe one example of each case where government uses taxes and subsidies to reallocate productive resources, and suggest reasons why such reallocations are thought to be socially desirable.

8. Do you agree with the book that ". . . the market system still responds by offering whatever consumers will buy"? Explain fully why you agree or disagree.

9. To what extent does "consumer sovereignty" have an effect on the automobile market? Consider specific changes in the product—such as size, comfort, safety, range of choice, and quality of materials—and indicate the areas where consumers have influenced the suppliers as individual buyers, as associations, through government intervention, or not at all. Why has the consumer's influence been expressed in such diverse forms, again considering specific changes separately?

10. Suppose that effective rent-ceiling legislation were introduced, but that any rental housing constructed in the following five years would be exempt. Use a supply-demand diagram to explain how this legislation would differ in its effect on prices and quantities from rent controls *without* such an exemption.

Sources and Selected Readings

Galbraith, John Kenneth. *The Affluent Society*, 4th ed. Boston: Houghton Mifflin, 1984.

Hayek, F.A., et al. *Rent Control: A Popular Paradox*. Vancouver: Fraser Institute, 1975.

Eckert, R.D., and R.H. Leftwich. *The Price System and Resource Allocation*, 10th ed. Hinsdale, Ill.: Dryden Press, 1988.

Stigler, George L. *The Theory of Price*, 4th ed. New York: Macmillan, 1987.

West, E.G., and M. McKee. *Minimum Wages: The New Issues in Theory, Evidence, Policy and Politics*. Ottawa: Economic Council of Canada and the Institute for Research on Public Policy, 1980.

PART TWO

The Canadian Economy

5 Measuring Canada's Economic Performance

Canada's Economic Goals

Canada's economic goals were stated explicitly by the Economic Council of Canada almost three decades ago in its *First Annual Review* and, with some variation, have been repeated in its subsequent *Reviews*. The Council has recognized five basic economic goals:

- Reasonable price stability;
- Full employment;
- A high rate of economic growth;
- A viable balance of payments;
- An equitable distribution of rising incomes.

But the various goals are not always compatible with each other. The Council went on to emphasize:

> Policies designed to accomplish a particular aim such as full employment or a rapid rate of growth may be in conflict with the policies needed to avoid inflation or to maintain a viable balance of payments. There is always the overriding requirement to reconcile conflicting tendencies and to achieve consistency.[1]

The following chapters in Part Two examine the structure and operation of the economy and consider the policies that might be pursued to achieve the first four of these goals. Policies directed toward improving income distribution are considered in Part Four.

[1] Economic Council of Canada, *First Annual Review: Economic Goals for Canada to 1970*. Ottawa: Queen's Printer, 1964, p. 2.

In order to determine whether progress is being made toward achieving Canada's economic goals, some method is required for measuring the economy's performance. The measures currently used to assess this performance are described in this chapter. The combination of these various measures forms the framework for the overall assessment of the government's economic policies.

Inflation and Price Stability

What Is Inflation?

Inflation is *an increase in the general price level of consumer goods and services.* Prices of intermediate goods or producer goods may rise, but if producers are able to take some offsetting action, such as accelerated productivity increases or narrower profit margins, so that prices of consumer goods and services are unchanged, most of the undesirable effects of inflation will not be realized. Governments do watch the prices of intermediate goods, especially of important products like steel, because they know that an increase in prices of raw or semi-finished products or in wholesale prices often leads to an increase in the price of consumer goods.

Problems of Inflation

Inflation is of public concern because it has different effects on the incomes or purchasing power of different groups of people, and because it can adversely affect Canada's competitive position in world markets. If everyone could anticipate precisely the annual price increase and could adjust his or her income and financial assets or debts accordingly, the disadvantages of inflation would be sharply reduced. Although there has been some improvement in this direction, for example, through the introduction of cost-of-living adjustments in some wage contracts and pension plans, the effects of inflation remain severe for some groups. Persons on unadjusted pensions and other fixed incomes experience a reduction in their purchasing power as prices rise.

Creditors may also be disadvantaged by inflation because $500 repaid after ten years will buy fewer goods and services than would $500 when the loan was made. Creditors try to estimate future inflation and include this in the interest rate charged on loans. But forecasting the rate of inflation for several years hence is a difficult art. Creditors may overestimate the extent of inflation, thus imposing an unnecessary burden on borrowers. This also contributes to further inflation, for example, through higher rents and higher mortgage costs for home-owners.

In general, inflation has the effect of shifting purchasing power from the older to the younger generations, because older generations tend to include a larger number of creditors and persons living on fixed incomes.

If the rate of inflation is higher in Canada than in other countries, Canada's foreign trade position may be adversely affected. As the prices of Canadian products rise relative to the prices in the other countries, Canadians increase their purchases of imported goods and sell fewer goods abroad. Consequently, exporters and related industries are made worse off, and importers and their related industries derive the benefit of inflation.

Causes of Inflation

Several explanations for inflation have emerged from the theoretical analysis and empirical research of the past three decades, but these can be grouped within two major categories: *demand-pull* and *cost-push*.

Demand-Pull Inflation
The traditional explanation for inflation has been that there is excess demand: the quantity of goods and services desired by consumers and producers at the prevailing price level exceeds the quantity of goods and services available. This demand-pull explanation—expressed popularly as "too many dollars chasing too few goods"—assumes that prices of factors and products are flexible enough to move upward under the pressure of increased demand.

Cost-Push Inflation
Cost-push inflation, or "sellers' inflation", is so named to emphasize that the inflationary pressure arises on the supply side of product markets or factor markets. In the case of labour markets, this has been described as a "wage-price spiral". However, the wage-push aspect of cost-push inflation depends on a number of critical assumptions:

- that workers can obtain wage increases proportionately greater than any increase in labour productivity;
- that the wage increase leads to an increase in the labour cost per unit;
- that this necessarily increases the total production cost per unit;
- that producers increase selling prices whenever production costs rise.

For this process to occur, labour must have strong bargaining power—usually in the form of strong unions—and producers need some monopolistic power in product markets to pass on the price increases. Cost-push inflation is therefore more likely to occur in industries where there are strong unions and only a few producers. It can also occur at high levels of unemployment, especially when this is concentrated in other industries or regions. Although the cost-push explanation has tended to emphasize the role of labour unions, suppliers of any materials or productive factors who can exercise some market power— or some direct control over their selling prices—can contribute to cost-push inflation.

Inflation can also be caused by an increase in prices that are strongly influenced by government actions—or what are termed collectively "regulated prices". These include three broad groups of commodities. First, there are the goods and services that government agencies produce and price themselves. Postage stamps, local bus transportation, and municipal water services are priced by governments, indirectly through an agency or crown corporation. A second, larger category covers those items produced in the private sector but whose prices are (or have been) regulated by governments: telephone services, air transporation, milk, and so on. Finally, some goods are so heavily taxed— such as alcohol and tobacco products—that price changes are due mainly to changes in the sales and excise taxes.

Measuring Inflation: Consumer Price Index

The Consumer Price Index (the CPI) measures changes in prices of commonly purchased consumer goods and services, and thus indirectly the change in the purchasing power of consumers' incomes. Each month the federal government's statistics bureau, Statistics Canada, announces changes in the Consumer Price Index from the previous month and from the same month one year ago. If consumers' incomes are unchanged from the previous year, but prices of consumer goods and services have increased by 9 per cent, the consumers' purchasing power has fallen by 9 per cent.

Base Year   The CPI is calculated by comparing current prices of commodities generally purchased by consumers with the price of the same commodities in an earlier, *base year*. Current prices of goods and services are expressed as a percentage of the base year prices. Thus, if the base year price of a light bulb was $1.50 and the current price is $1.80, the price index for light bulbs would be 120, since (1.80/1.50) × 100 = 120. Since the CPI is expressed as an index, or percentage of the base year prices, calculation of the annual inflation rate requires a comparison of index values for each year. For example, the CPI in 1989 was 114.0, or 5 per cent higher than the 1988 CPI of 108.6.

Weights   The relative importance of each commodity included in the CPI is indicated by a weight that reflects the proportion of the consumers' total expenditures directed to this item. Housing and food, for example, have large weights in the CPI; recreational items have a much lower weight. The CPI therefore reflects both the average prices paid and the relative quantities purchased by the average Canadian consumer.[2] These weights and price increases for each component are shown in Table 5.1.

Persons who divide their personal budgets differently from the weights used in the CPI, perhaps spending unusually large amounts on fashionable clothing or recreation, will find that the CPI is not a satisfactory measure for changes in the purchasing power of their own incomes if the prices of these items move differently from prices of most other goods.

Because the base year quantity weights remain constant while the actual distribution of the consumer's budget may change over time, the CPI may not be an accurate reflection of changes in purchasing power. The base year is therefore revised occasionally to keep abreast of these changes. The CPI will slightly overstate the inflationary effect actually experienced by consumers, since they will tend to reduce their expenditures on those items whose prices are increasing most quickly. Revision of the base year also overcomes problems associated with the changing quality of the commodity concerned. For example, changes in automobile styles and features make price comparisons difficult over a range of more than a few years.

Finally, the CPI deals only with retail prices of consumer items. The Industrial Product Price Index measures changes in wholesale prices, and other indexes measure changes in prices of raw materials, including oil, gas, and coal.

Table 5.1

Consumer Price Index Components

Component	Weights (percentage of total expenditure[1])	Price Change, 1990 over 1989 (percentage)
Food	18.1	4.1
Housing	36.3	4.5
Clothing	8.7	2.8
Transportation	18.3	5.6
Health and personal care	4.2	4.9
Recreation, reading, and education	8.8	4.4
Tobacco and alcohol	5.6	8.8
Total (All Items)	100.0	4.8

Source: Statistics Canada, *The Consumer Price Index.*
[1] Total expenditure for all goods and services by consumers in Canada, 1986, as reported by the Family Expenditure Survey.

[2] Specifically, the CPI is based on the relative quantities of about 400 items purchased by individuals and families living in urban areas with a population over 30,000.

The Economic Council of Canada defined "reasonable price stability" in 1964 as the average annual rates of change in prices and costs in the preceding decade, or about 2 per cent annually. Strictly speaking, price stability should be defined as *no change* in prices. However, the Council was reflecting the common view that, since some inflation seems inevitable, price stability can be defined as a low, steady increase in the price index. The Council raised the target inflation rate to 3 per cent in 1972, but in 1973, an absolute target was abandoned. The Council instead proposed that there should be zero difference between the CPI in Canada and the weighted index of consumer prices in countries that are Canada's major trading partners: United States, United Kingdom, West Germany, Japan, France, and Italy.

Inflation rate targets returned briefly during an anti-inflation program in 1975–78, but subsequently, the Council based its targets on alternative forecasts of the economy's performance, and spoke in terms of ranges, rather than specific values.

In 1989–90, however, the Bank of Canada advocated and pursued an objective of zero inflation; but in the 1991 federal government budget, target inflation rates were set at 3 per cent for the end of 1992 and 2 per cent by year-end 1995.

Figure 5.1 illustrates Canada's experience with inflation since 1954. Prices rose at an average of about 2 per cent annually through the late 1950s and early 1960s. By the mid-1960s inflation was about 4 to 5 per cent. This was soon followed by the extreme price increases that occurred in 1974–75, and again in 1980–82. Inflation declined sharply in 1983, following a recession in 1982–83, and remained at about 4.5 for the rest of the decade.

The relative inflation rates in Canada and the United States are also shown in Figure 5.1. For more than half of the period shown, Canada has experienced higher annual inflation than the United States and thus has been handicapped by inflation in its trade in goods and services with the Americans.

Unemployment and Full Employment

When the Economic Council first attempted to define "what would be a reasonable employment target for the Canadian economy", it stated candidly:

The concept of full employment varies considerably from country to country. Nowhere does it mean 100 per cent of the labour force. In any

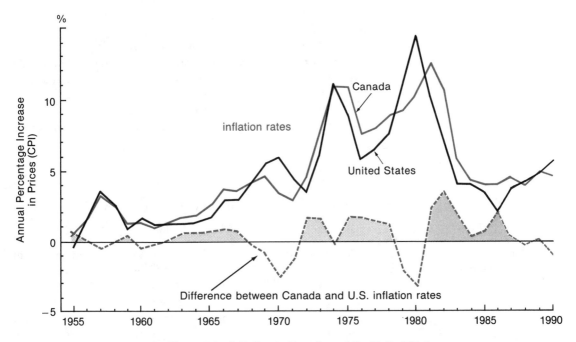

Figure 5.1 Inflation in Canada and the United States
The inflation rate in Canada from 1954 to 1962 averaged less than 2 per
cent annually, but was above 3 per cent during 1965–70. Inflation exceeded
10 per cent in 1974 and 1975 and again in 1980 to 1982. Inflation in
the United States has generally been below the Canadian level, with the
exception of the late 1960s (due to the Vietnam War), 1979–1980, and 1988
and 1990. The shaded areas indicate years when inflation was higher in
Canada than in the United States.

Source: Statistics Canada, *The Consumer Price Index*; and United States
Government Printing Office, *Statistical Abstract of the United States*.

free society—even in countries experiencing an intense labour shortage—
there will always be a certain minimum amount of voluntary or
unavoidable unemployment as workers move from one job to another.[3]

Full Employment

Full employment usually refers to the labour resources of an economy,
but a broader interpretation of full employment includes the full utilization of all productive resources—the productive plant and equipment
and land—as well as the labour force. This definition is used less often
in measuring economic activity because arbitrary decisions are required
to determine when a plant is working at full capacity. Is it 10 hours per
day for five days per week? or for two 8-hour shifts? or for three 8-hour
shifts? "Full capacity" however, can be applied to such plants as

[3] Economic Council of Canada, *op. cit.*, pp. 37-38.

steel mills, which are normally in continuous operation, and to other manufacturing plants.[4]

Unemployment of labour represents a serious social problem as well as an underutilization of economic resources. The common definition of full employment, however, is concerned with whether a person has a job, and not with the number of working hours per week that are either possible or desirable. *Full employment is defined as the situation in which everyone aged 15 or over who is willing and able to work for pay has a job.*

Causes of Unemployment

The many causes of unemployment can be grouped in four major categories: *inadequate demand, frictional, seasonal, and structural.*

Inadequate-Demand Unemployment

The opposite of excess-demand inflation is inadequate-demand unemployment. It results when demand is insufficient to produce employment for all labour offered at the prevailing wage level. It has also been termed *cyclical* unemployment, because it corresponds with the fluctuations in demand for labour over the course of the business cycle.

Inadequate demand tends to be more variable in its effect on different industries than is the effect of excess demand on product prices. When labour is employed under two- or three-year contracts, for example, a decrease in demand can have less effect than when contracts cover shorter periods, or unions have less influence on temporary laying off of workers. Decreased demand will also have less effect on skilled and technical employees, who are retained during slack periods so that employers will not have to compete for special skills when demand begins to rise again.

Frictional Unemployment

At any time, there will be some people looking for work who have just left a job or who are just entering or re-entering the labour force. This is frictional unemployment and is generally regarded as the least serious form of unemployment. In fact, frictional unemployment is likely to be highest when demand and output are rising quickly and workers believe there is a good possibility of finding a better job. Conversely, frictional unemployment usually declines during slack periods because workers are less venturesome in leaving their current jobs to look for others and relatively fewer people are attracted into the labour market.

[4] It has been estimated that the utilization of the physical plant in Canadian manufacturing averaged about 85 per cent of capacity over the period 1967 to 1990, but utilization was only 80 per cent in the early and late 1980s, having dropped to a low of 72 per cent in the recession of 1982. (See Statistics Canada, *Capacity Utilization Rates in Canadian Manufacturing.*)

Frictional unemployment could become more serious, however, if the *duration* of this unemployment increased due to increased difficulty in locating suitable work.

Seasonal Unemployment

The seasonal fluctuations of some work, especially in temperate countries like Canada, lead to substantial seasonal unemployment. Construction, agriculture, forestry, fishing, and some parts of the retail and recreation industries have a fluctuating demand for labour due to climatic restrictions on their work or climatic influences on the demand for goods and services. A broader view of seasonality includes fluctuations in the demand for labour over the course of one year, due, for example, to layoffs during retooling for new models in the automobile industry.

Seasonal unemployment, especially due to climatic conditions, is diminishing since a smaller percentage of the labour force is engaged in agriculture and other primary industries. Changes in construction technology also make outdoor work possible year-round, and winter sports have stabilized the demand for recreational equipment and facilities.

Structural Unemployment

The unusually high unemployment rates of the early 1960s provoked much debate about whether the unemployment was due to inadequate demand or to structural changes in the demand for labour. Changes in the composition of demand for goods and services and improvements in technology were expected to produce *structural unemployment* in some goods-producing industries, among unskilled workers displaced by technological changes.

Structural unemployment is also described as long-duration unemployment, because workers displaced by structural changes may not be able to find work again in the same occupation, industry, or locality. A change in occupation or a move to another area may be postponed for some time until all other prospects have been exhausted.

But these four simple categories of causes of unemployment do not directly suggest the most appropriate corrective policies. People may lose their jobs due to declining consumer demand for the product of a particular industry; or the demand for their type of skills may have declined only temporarily, for seasonal or aggregate demand reasons; or it may have declined permanently, due to technological change. A different policy would be required in each case.

Unemployment Rate

The unemployment rate is calculated each month by Statistics Canada. It is based on the monthly Labour Force Survey of about 48,000 Canadian households. *Employed persons* include those who, during the survey week:

- worked for one hour or more as paid employees, or were self-employed; or
- worked without pay for a family farm or business; or
- who did not actually work but were only temporarily absent from their jobs due to weather, illness, industrial disputes (strikes and lockouts), or vacations.

Unemployed persons include those who were not at work during the survey week but who were able to work and had actively looked for work. The *labour force* is defined as the total of employed and unemployed persons. The *unemployment rate* can then be calculated simply: the number of persons unemployed as a percentage of the total labour force.

Definition Problems   These definitions of the labour force raise a number of problems concerning the measurement of unemployment. First, it should be clear that "the unemployed" do not include all those who are not earning income. Large groups of people are considered to be outside the active labour force: housewives who are not at work outside the home, full-time students who do not have part-time jobs, all persons under 15 years of age, and most retired people. Another important group not in the labour force includes those who have been employed, have moved into the unemployed group, have become discouraged by the lack of employment opportunities, and are no longer actively seeking work.

Mismatching   One may wonder why there are so many unemployed people while so many job vacancies exist. Part of the explanation is that some people are not able to find work for which they are trained and at the wage level they expect. They may have decided that it pays to spend some time looking for the proper job rather than to accept the first one available. Second, job vacancies may occur in one area of the country, while the unemployed persons are living in a different area. Again, it may be more rational for an unemployed person to seek work close to home rather than bear the cost of moving.

Underemployment   Another problem is that the current definition of unemployment does not include *disguised unemployment* or *underemployment*. This occurs when people have jobs, but are not working at jobs that would fully utilize their specific skills. An unemployed chemical engineer may decide to drive a taxi or work on a construction site until he can find work in his field. He would not be counted as unemployed in the labour force survey; nevertheless, he may be actively seeking some other employment.

Persons working fewer hours per week than they prefer, such as a waiter restricted to working in the peak hours, are also underemployed. Some people are able to "moonlight" — take a second job — but it is often difficult to find two jobs that can be held conveniently at the same time. Surveys conducted by Statistics Canada during the past two decades have found that only 2 to 4 per cent of the employed labour force held more than one job.

Duration   The unemployment rate reflects only the number of persons unemployed; it does not measure directly the average duration of unemployment. Unemployment is obviously more serious if persons have been out of work for three or four months rather than for a week or so.[5]

Seasonal Adjustment   Finally, a problem may arise in understanding monthly reports on unemployment rates, because the monthly rates cited are usually those that are *seasonally adjusted*. Changes in the rates may be caused by regular seasonal events such as climate changes, crop cycles, holidays, and vacation periods. This requires that the rate calculated from the monthly Labour Force Survey be adjusted to take account of the fact that the unemployment rate is usually higher in the winter and lower in the summer. If a review of recent years shows the unemployment rate as usually 1.5 times greater in January than for the 12-month average, the actual rate for January will be divided by 1.5 to obtain the *seasonally adjusted rate*. This adjustment makes it possible to see the underlying long-term trend as the monthly data move through their usual seasonal variation.

Employment Targets

The Economic Council concluded in the 1960s that a 3 per cent rate of unemployment represented a reasonable employment target for Canada. However, the Council recognized in 1972 that this was an ambitious target, when taken together with its inflation target of less than 2 per cent, and noted that "Not once during the last fifteen years has the Canadian economy even approached both goals simultaneously". A new unemployment rate target was set at 4.5 per cent. After proposing targets of 4 to 6 per cent in the mid-1970s, the Council virtually abandoned specific targets in 1977. Instead, the Council estimated the levels of unemployment that might be associated with alternative government policies.

The upward trend of the unemployment rate in recent years is shown in Figure 5.2. The most troublesome feature of this development has been that it has occurred along with an increase in the rate of infla-

---

[5] The average duration of unemployment in Canada during the past decade was in the range of 20 to 25 weeks.

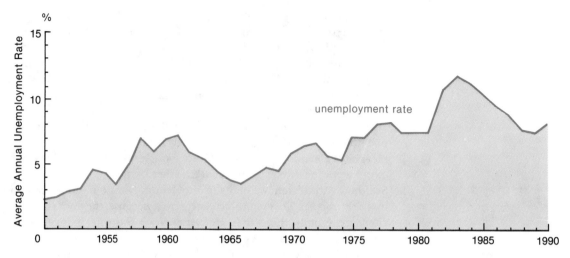

Figure 5.2   Unemployment in Canada
The unemployment rate had tended to be high when the inflation rate was low, but in the late 1960s and the late 1970s inflation and unemployment increased at the same time. The inverse relationship seems to have been restored by the mid-1980s. There has, however, been a substantial increase in unemployment over the long run. Note particularly the long-run increase in unemployment since 1965.

Source: Statistics Canada, *Canadian Statistical Review.*

tion in certain years. Much more will be said about this compounded problem in Chapter 9 on economic stabilization policies.

Differences in unemployment rates between different groups and in different regions of Canada are shown in Table 5.2. Young people have a higher unemployment rate for several reasons: the survey may have found them when they were entering the labour force for the first time and had not yet found a job; they are often the first to be laid off due to lack of seniority; or they may lack the experience many employers are seeking. Reasons for the variation in unemployment rates among the provinces are examined in Part Four.

Economic Growth and National Income

Two Approaches Economic growth can be measured using two approaches: one focuses on the increase in *actual output* of goods and services, while the other refers to an increase in the economy's productivity or its increased *ability* to produce goods and services.

The latter approach is based on either *total-factor productivity*—value of output divided by total value of all productive factors—or

Table 5.2

Annual Uemployment Rates by Age, Sex, and Province, Canada, 1990

Age and Sex	Unemployment Rate	Province	Unemployment Rate
Males		Newfoundland	17.1
15–24	14.0	Prince Edward Island	14.9
25 and over	6.8	Nova Scotia	10.5
		New Brunswick	12.1
Total	8.1	Quebec	10.1
		Ontario	6.3
Females		Manitoba	7.2
15–24	11.4	Saskatchewan	7.0
25 and over	7.3	Alberta	7.0
Total	8.1	British Columbia	8.3
Total	8.1		

Source: Statistics Canada, *Historical Labour Force Statistics.*

labour productivity—the value of the economy's total output divided by the number of persons employed. Labour productivity depends on the technology and physical plant with which labour is combined, as well as the quality of labour in terms of its education and skills.

Labour productivity in Canada increased at a long-run average rate of about 2.5 per cent annually until the late 1970s, when it began to decline. (See Figure 5.3.) This decline in productivity presents a serious problem for economic policy, which is considered further in Chapter 12 on economic growth and productivity.

Another common definition of economic growth is the *rate of increase in real Gross Domestic Product per capita.* This definition requires more complex measurements than were used for either price stability or full employment. Before turning to the meaning of "real" or "per capita", it will be necessary to focus on Gross Domestic Product (GDP) and other related measures of national income.

Why Measure Growth?

Economic growth is one of Canada's basic economic goals because an annual increase in goods and services available to each consumer is a major step toward improving the population's well-being—although economists recognize that well-being also depends on several other, non-economic conditions.

One reason for measuring this growth is to determine how well the Canadian economy is being managed. On the basis of past experience

Figure 5.3   Labour Productivity in Canada
Labour productivity is the real value of Gross Domestic Product divided by the annual level of employment. Productivity showed a long-run improvement from 1958 to 1973, but the rate of growth in productivity was slow and uneven during the 1970s and 1980s.

Source: Statistics Canada, *Canadian Statistical Review.*

with this and other economies, economists can estimate what would be produced if all available physical and human resources were fully employed (albeit according to some arbitrary definition of full employment). If the actual output falls below the estimated potential level, the economy is not performing at full capacity. Changes should then be made in the organization of the economy and the economic policies of governments.

Comparisons of economic performance from year to year provide a measure of how successful economic policies have been, and whether other policies or programs will be required. Past rates of economic growth also provide a basis for forecasting future growth rates, and thus for estimating what the level of output will be several years hence. These estimates can aid governments, for example, in determining whether existing tax structures will yield sufficient revenues to finance planned expenditure programs. Firms can also estimate whether consumer incomes will increase enough to justify expansion of productive capacity.

Circular Flow of Payments

Each of the many goods and services produced every year must be classified in such a way that none is omitted or counted twice. A classification system that traces the flows of payments through the economy must separate two basic flows of economic activity: the flow of goods and services, and the flow of payments made for these goods and services. The latter is used, because this provides the required monetary measure.

In a simple economy, payments flow in only two directions. Producers or firms pay individuals or households for the use of their labour, land, and capital—in the form of wages, rent, and interest. Households pay the firms for the goods or services produced.

The flow of payments in a more complex economy is illustrated in Figure 5.4. This economy has four parts or sectors: households, firms, governments, and trade with foreign countries. Households pay firms for consumer goods and services and receive payments from firms in the form of wages, interest, rent, and dividends. Some firms buy the products of other firms, but these goods and services are used in producing the final products for consumers or households.

Governments add another dimension to the flow of payments since they receive tax payments from both households and firms. Government payments are made to households for labour and other productive services, and to firms for the goods and services purchased by governments. Payments also flow out of the economy to purchase the products and the productive services of other countries, which also purchase products and productive services from this economy.

This description of the circular flow of payments illustrates two approaches to measuring an economy's productive activity. *Payments*

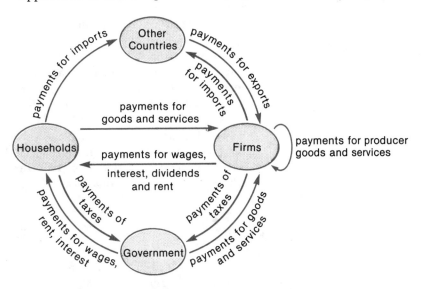

Figure 5.4   The Economy's Circular Flow of Payments
The simplified basic flow of payments in the economy consists of payments made by firms (producers) to households (of one or more individuals) for the use of productive factors—labour, land, and capital—and payments from households to firms for final goods and services. Firms also make payments to other firms for producer goods and services. Governments receive payments as taxes, and make payments to buy final products from firms and productive services from households. Trade with other countries requires payments for imports and returns payments for exports.

for productive services—wages, interest, rent, and dividends—can be aggregated to determine total incomes, while *payments for goods and services* purchased by consumers, governments, firms, and foreign countries can be added to determine the total output. Payments to foreign countries must be subtracted from payments received from foreign countries to obtain the net increase (or decrease) in incomes or products of the Canadian economy.

Value Added

These two approaches to measuring economic activity are reflected in two sets of accounts: the *national income* accounts and the *national expenditure* accounts. It is relatively easy to keep track of all income payments, but expenditures for firms' goods and services present a serious problem. Which expenditures are for products used by consumers and which are for products to be used by other firms? If all sales by all firms were totalled, the economy's total output could be greatly increased simply by dividing the existing firms into many smaller units. Totalling all sales made by all firms involves counting, for example, the value of iron ore and steel several times, whereas the additional value added to the economy by these products is reflected in the value of a final product such as an automobile.

Avoiding Double Counting   The solution to the problem of double counting is to measure only the value added to the final product by each stage in the production process. The method for calculating the value added is illustrated in Table 5.3. A rancher sells a steer to a cattle buyer for $800. The buyer transports the steer to a central yard and feeds it for a short time until it is sold to a meat packer for $1,000. The packer takes the steer to the plant where it is killed, cleaned, quartered, and sold to a supermarket for $1,300. Finally, the supermarket's butcher divides the quarters into the desired cuts, trims the fat, and packages the meat, for a final price of $1,700.

The value added at each stage of the process is calculated by subtracting the purchases from firms or suppliers from the selling price of the item at that stage.

The value added to the final product by the meat packer, for example, is the selling price of $1,300 minus the $1,000 paid to the cattle buyer. The total value added by the complete process is the total value for all sales, $4,800, minus the $3,100 paid in purchases from other firms, or $1,700. This is equal to the selling price of the final consumer goods at the supermarket. By subtracting the value of purchases from other firms, one can isolate the intermediate goods from the final goods. (Recall from Chapter 1 that intermediate goods are those that will be

Table 5.3
Value Added: Three Calculation Methods

	Purchases from Other Firms	Payments to Productive Factors			Value of Sales
		Wages	Interest and Rent	Profits	
Rancher	$ 0	$ 670	$ 80	$ 50	$ 800
Cattle Buyer	800	100	40	60	1,000
Meat Packer	1,000	140	60	100	1,300
Supermarket	1,300	200	100	100	1,700
Totals	$3,100	$1,110	$280	$310	$4,800

Value Added =

1. Payments to Productive Factors = $1,110 + 280 + 310   = 1,700
   or
2. Value of Finished Product (Supermarket sales in this case)   = 1,700
   or
3. Total Sales minus Purchases from Other Firms = $4,800 − 3,100 = 1,700

processed further, while final goods are used either as producer goods or consumer goods.)

It is not a coincidence that the total payments made through the entire process for wages, interest, rent, and profits, equal the value added as calculated above. The price paid by the household or firm is the total payment for all the productive services required to provide the final product, including the profits paid to entrepreneurs at each stage. Since profit is calculated as a residual (or by subtraction), the payments to factors must logically equal the total selling price.

Thus the value of all incomes received in the economy must equal the value of all final goods and services produced.

Economic activity or value added can be measured therefore in terms of either total income or total expenditure for final products.

National Income and Expenditure Accounts

The national income and expenditure accounts have been developed as a comprehensive, consistent set of accounts to measure various components in the growth of economic activity. The preceding simple illustration of value added calculations showed that such measures could be based on two approaches, payments to productive factors and expenditures for goods and services. This section examines the structure and rationale of the major accounts and their interrelationships, first for the income or factor payments side and then for the expenditures side. The following discussion of each acccount will be more readily understood if one makes frequent reference to Table 5.4 and Figure 5.5.

Gross Domestic Product (GDP) has replaced GNP as the primary measure of Canada's output. This is because GNP includes the income from Canadian-owned investment in other countries but omits the income earned by foreign-owned investment in Canada. This understates the true annual output of the Canadian economy by about 3 to 5 per cent, because foreign investment in Canada is substantially greater than Canadian investment abroad.

GDP is equal to GNP plus investment income paid to non-residents minus investment income received from non-residents.

Table 5.4

National Income and Expenditure, Canada, 1990
(in billions of dollars)

Incomes		*Expenditures*		
Wages and salaries[1]	$383	Consumption (*C*)		$402
Corporation profits before taxes[2]	45	personal expenditure on consumer		
Interest and other investment income	58	goods and services		
Net income of farm and non-farm				
unincorporated businesses[3]	40	Gross investment (*I*)		136
		government investment[4]	17	
Net Domestic Income	526	residential construction	45	
		non-residential construction	36	
Indirect taxes less subsidies	76	machinery and equipment	43	
Depreciation, or capital consumption		change in inventories	−3	
allowances	77			
Statistical discrepancy	−2	Government purchases (*G*)		132
		government current expenditures on		
		goods and services		
Gross Domestic Product	$678	Exports less imports (*E − M*)		3
(income based)		exports	168	
		imports	165	
		Statistical discrepancy		2
		Gross Domestic Product		$678
		(expenditure based)		

Source: Statistics Canada, *National Income and Expenditure Accounts.*

Note: Detailed items may not add to totals due to rounding.

[1] Includes other labour income, and military pay and allowances
[2] less inventory valuation adjustments ($2.5 billion)
[3] includes net income of independent professional practitioners (such as doctors and lawyers), farmers, and other self-employed persons
[4] includes outlay on new durable assets such as building and highway construction by governments other than government business enterprises.

The GDP approach is also used to calculate annual output for separate industries and provinces, and it is also used by most other countries (except the United States) to measure their output.

Box 5.1 **Goodbye GNP! Hello GDP**

By Catherine Harris

Canada's output is higher than we all think.

Up to now, Statistics Canada, economists and the media have been focusing on the concept of gross national product. However, the data keepers at StatCan will be switching to gross domestic product [GDP] as the prime measure of Canada's output when they publish figures on the economy's first-quarter performance around the end of this month [June, 1986] . . . .

It's important to note, however, that the level of GDP has outrun GNP every year since 1926, the first year for which StatCan has numbers. When it comes to growth rates, it doesn't matter much which series you look at—GNP or GDP . . . .

The pattern of growth—the booming years of the late 1960s, the slowdown in the mid-1970s and the deep recession of 1981-82—remains the same whichever measure you use.

The key difference between GNP and GDP is this: Gross national product measures production that is "owned" by residents of Canada—whether that production is taking place in Canada or abroad; Gross domestic product measures production taking place in Canada (i.e. domestic output), regardless of who owns the factories—Canadians or foreigners.

Since so much of our economy is foreign owned and we don't own a lot of companies in other countries, the level of GNP always comes in lower than GDP. Here's how the numbers worked in 1985:

	$billion
Gross national product	453.7
Subtract: Investment income received from nonresidents	− 6.3
Add: Investment income paid to nonresidents	+ 22.4
Equals: Gross domestic product	469.8

The move to GDP from GNP will put us at odds with the U.S., but we'll be in line with others. Most countries outside of the U.S. tend to focus on GDP rather than GNP. And the Organization for Economic Co-operation & Development uses GDP for its international comparisons . . . .

Both the GDP and GNP measures have their uses. However, an important advantage of using GDP in Canada is that it ties in better with other series in the economy—jobs and productivity in particular. Employment, after all, is tied to what production is actually taking place within our borders. And productivity is a measure of the output in Canada per employed person.

Also, StatCan's provincial economic output numbers are prepared on a GDP basis, which means the provincial totals will now add to the national one. The industry output totals also add to GDP . . . .

Source: *The Financial Post*, 7 June 1986.

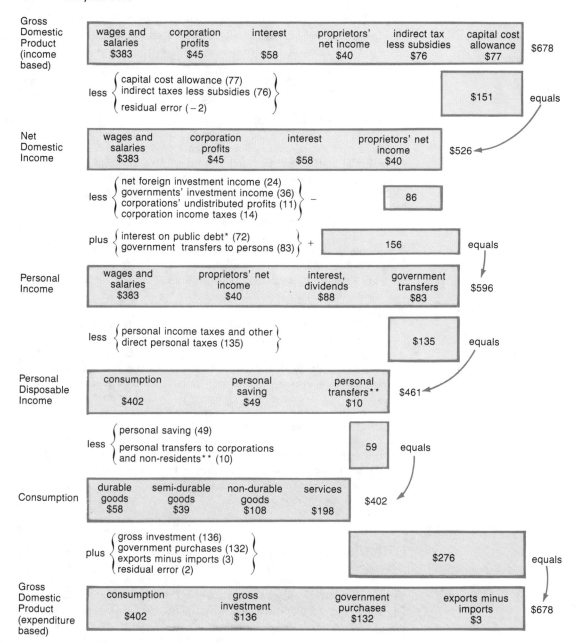

Figure 5.5   National Income and Expenditure Accounts, Canada, 1990 (in billions of dollars)

Source: Statistics Canada, *National Income and Expenditure Accounts*.

* includes interest on consumer debt
** includes interest paid by consumers to corporations and private transfers to non-residents

Note: Items may not add to totals due to rounding.

Net Domestic Income

The term "national income" is often used as a generic term to describe the general level of economic activity without specifying one of the several concepts or accounts outlined in this section. The most precise meaning of national income is *Net Domestic Income: the total of all incomes earned by the economy's productive factors*. Net Domestic Income is the sum of wages and salaries, interest and other investment income, corporation profits before taxes, and the net income of unincorporated enterprises. These items are shown in Table 5.4 on the incomes side, and in the second horizontal bar of Figure 5.5.

1. *Wages and salaries*, plus any supplementary income or bonuses paid to employees, are calculated as gross pay before deductions by employers for taxes, union dues, pension contributions, and similar payments.

2. *Interest and other investment income* includes the returns to investments held by individuals. Dividends are not included in this item, because they are paid out of the corporations' profits; but dividends are included in Personal Income, as shown below. Investment income received by corporations is included in corporation profits and rental income of individuals is in the income of self-employed persons.

3. *Corporation profits* (before taxes) are adjusted for price changes affecting the value of their inventories during the year.

4. Incomes of self-employed persons appear as *net income of farm and non-farm unincorporated businesses*, or "proprietors' net income" in Figure 5.5. Included are the incomes of self-employed professionals as well as thousands of farms and small businesses, after deducting the expenses incurred in operating the business. Also included is the estimated net rental value of owner-occupied homes. This estimated or imputed value of the use of housing avoids the misleading increase in GDP that would occur if an unusually large number of people suddenly decided to rent rather than buy homes.

Table 5.5 shows the relationships among corporations' profits, income taxes, dividends, and retained earnings (or undistributed profits).

Gross Domestic Product: Incomes Approach

Gross Domestic Product measures the market value of all final goods and services produced in the current year by Canadian factors of production, by making necessary adjustments to the value of Net Domestic Income. Gross Domestic Product is equal to Net Domestic Income plus indirect taxes less subsidies plus depreciation (or capital consumption allowances).

Table 5.5

Disposition of Corporations' Gross Profits, Canada, 1990
(in billions of dollars)

			percentage
Corporations' profits before taxes[1]		$40.6	100
less Corporations' income taxes		−14.4	35
Corporations' profits after taxes		26.2	
less Dividends:			
to non-residents	6.4	−13.0	32
to Canadian residents	6.6		
less bad debts and charitable donations		−0.7	2
Undistributed corporate profits[1]		$12.4	31

Source: Statistics Canada, *National Income and Expenditure Accounts.*

Note: Items may not add to totals due to rounding.

[1]Before inventory valuation adjustments. Net of international investment income flows.

1. *Indirect taxes* (sales and excise taxes) paid by businesses are not a cost of production; they are included in GDP since these taxes are included in the selling price of finished products. *Subsidies* to producers must be subtracted. Although these form part of the payments to productive factors, the selling prices of the goods do not need to cover all costs since part of these is met by the subsidy. Another way to view these adjustments is to recall that a sales tax increases the market price and a subsidy decreases the price. These effects must be included with factor payments to arrive at the market value for GDP.

2. *Depreciation,* or *capital consumption allowance*, is not a direct payment to productive factors but does represent a cost—namely, the allowance or reserve fund to replace worn-out or obsolete plant and machinery.

The last item in the GDP account, the *statistical discrepancy*, is the correction required to equate total income with total expenditure for final products. Since some entries in both sets of accounts are estimated, the totals may differ slightly. Half the difference is subtracted from the higher total and added to the lower total so that income will equal expenditure.

Personal Income   Some of the income included in Net Domestic Income does not go directly, or even eventually, to individuals. An adjustment must be made for the net amount of investment income paid to foreigners and received by Canadian residents from abroad. (This "net foreign investment income" is the adjustment that was described earlier to derive GNP from GDP.) The investment income received by governments must also be subtracted from Net Domestic Income to obtain Personal Income. Corporations pay part of their profits to governments as corporate income tax, another part takes the form of shareholders' dividends, and the balance — retained earnings or undistributed corporate profits — is held by the corporations. This balance may be held in the form of stocks or bonds, or used to expand the business, or loaned to other firms. These components are shown in Table 5.5.

Personal incomes are increased by the transfer payments made by governments to individuals. *Transfer payments* are those for which no goods or services are provided in exchange, such as family allowances, pensions, and welfare assistance. Interest on government bonds is also a transfer payment, because it is a transfer from taxpayers to bondholders, and does not represent new economic output. Private transfer payments — another term for gifts — are not included in these adjustment calculations, since they redistribute, rather than increase, total personal income.

Personal Disposable Income   Individuals are free to decide how to dispose of only a part of their incomes. Personal income taxes must be subtracted from Personal Income to determine Personal Disposable Income, which people can use however they wish. Although there are thousands of spending decisions open to each individual, the basic decision concerns the portion of one's income to be spent on goods and services now, and the portion to be saved for the enjoyment of goods and services in the future. Disposable Income therefore includes *current consumption*, and postponed consumption represented by *saving*.[6] Consumer goods may be grouped according to their durability — from non-durables such as food to durables like automobiles, furniture, and household appliances.

Gross Domestic Product: Expenditures Approach

Gross Domestic Product (GDP) is the sum of expenditures for all final goods and services in the economy during the year. The components of GDP included in the incomes approach were categorized in terms of the factors of production; components of GDP included in the expenditures approach are grouped according to the users of the final products. These are consumers, businesses, governments, and other countries.

---

[6] There are two minor qualifications to this statement. Small amounts of disposable income are paid as private transfers (or gifts) to residents of other countries, and as interest payments to corporations. Personal savings in the 1980s represented about 10 to 16 per cent of personal disposable income. (See Figure 6.9 in Chapter 6.) Personal savings take the form of pension contributions, repayment of mortgages, as well as bank deposits and other financial assets.

Purchases by governments and by other countries are itemized separately so that changes in the importance of the public sector and the foreign trade sector can be measured easily in the national accounts.

Gross Domestic Product (Expenditure) includes personal expenditures on consumer goods and services, governments' current expenditures for goods and services (excluding transfer payments), gross investment, net exports of goods and services, and the statistical discrepancy.

Gross investment includes both government investment (such as schools and highways) and business investment in:

- new residential construction (housing);
- new non-residential construction and equipment;
- change in the value of inventories.

The last item is included because semi-finished goods and finished goods that have not been sold have required income payments to productive factors, which were included in GDP.

Net Investment

Gross Domestic Product is the market value of the total output of final goods and services of an economy. It is not the most suitable measure of the year-to-year net increase in goods and services, however, because some goods are used just to maintain the economy at its previous productive capacity. Some producer goods, such as cement and paint, are used to repair roads, schools, houses, and other buildings; other producer goods replace worn-out machinery. It is virtually impossible to determine how much of the gross investment, or total output of producer goods, is used to maintain the existing capital stock and how much represents net additions to housing or productive capacity. Instead, depreciation, or capital consumption allowance, is estimated and subtracted from gross investment. The difference is *net investment*.

What Is Measured in the National Accounts

Although the thousands of different goods and services produced each year can be aggregated only by using the Canadian dollar as a common unit, there is a disadvantage in using a money measure: only goods and services that are bought and sold will have an explicit price. Although an artist may be able to estimate the market value of his or her painting, for example, no one can determine its price precisely until it is sold. Thus, only the goods and services that are exchanged for money can be included in the measure of economic growth. (One important exception is the estimated rental value of owner-occupied housing.) Work around the house such as cleaning, cooking, caring for children, carpentry, automobile repairs, and painting is not included unless someone has been paid for this work. Illegal activities such as drug-trafficking, prostitution, and bootlegging are also economic activities but are omitted from the measured output of the economy because it is difficult to estimate the total economic value of these activities.

The Underground Economy   In addition to these illegal activities, there exists considerable other economic activity that is not measured in the national income accounts because it is not reported in the income tax system. Work may be paid for by currency rather than by cheques, or there may be an exchange agreement whereby, for example, a plumber and a dentist, or a carpenter and a lawyer, do work of equal value for each other so that no cash payments are made. Such practices result in an underestimation of the true level of national income and output.

Various estimates have been made of the magnitude of these unreported activities. One approach, for example, assumes that with an increase in the use of currency for payments there will be an increase in the ratio of currency in circulation to total chequing deposits. Such estimates lead to the conclusion that the *underground economy* may equal 10 to 20 per cent of the official GDP statistics. And this excludes the do-it-yourself work around the home. In addition to understating the true level of income and output, the omission of this work results in an overestimate of unemployment. Persons who are receiving unemployment insurance payments are unlikely to report such jobs, or even to think of them when interviewed in the monthly labour force survey.

Real Income per Capita

A major use of the national income accounts is to measure the change in output and incomes from year to year, but such comparisons require further adjustments of GDP. The GDP for a given year may be greater than the GDP in the previous year, but if all of the increase was due to price increases, physical output was no greater than the previous year. Values calculated in the national accounts must therefore be adjusted for inflation if comparisons of GDP over time are to show changes in real or tangible output, rather than in the nominal or monetary value of the output. When the effect of price change is removed from nominal GDP, the result is termed "real" GDP.

GDP Deflator

This adjustment for inflation requires a price index that is based on all components of GDP. The Consumer Price Index is unsuitable for

Table 5.6

Real Gross Domestic Product per Capita

Year	Nominal GDP (in current prices) (millions)	GDP Implicit Price Index (1986 = 100)	Real GDP (in 1986 prices) (millions)	Canada's Population on June 1 (thousands)	Real GDP per Capita
1971	$97,290	33.3	$292,162	21,569	$13,545
1981	355,994	79.5	447,791	24,342	18,396
1986	505,227	100.0	505,227	25,612	19,726
1990	677,900	118.8	570,743	26,512	21,528

Source: Statistics Canada, *Canadian Statistical Review* and *Canadian Economic Observer.*

this purpose, since GDP includes other goods and services as well as consumer items. A GDP Price Index has been developed to take account of price changes and the relative weights in the major expenditure categories included in Gross Domestic Product. Real GDP is obtained by dividing the nominal GDP, measured in current prices, by the GDP Price Index. The latter is sometimes referred to as the "GDP deflator" because the continuous rise in prices means that current GDP is being deflated rather than inflated.

Conversion of GDP in current dollars to GDP in constant (1986) dollars — or from nominal GDP to real GDP — is shown in Table 5.6. GDP as measured by the current prices for each year increased 266 per cent from 1971 to 1981, but the increase in real GDP during the same period was only 53 per cent. The difference is explained by the 139 per cent increase in prices, as indicated by the change in the GDP Price Index. The annual rate of increase in real GDP over recent decades is shown in Figure 5.6.

Real GDP may rise, for example, 5 per cent each year, but this does not necessarily mean that individuals' real incomes will also rise by 5 per cent. Increases in the real output per person will also depend on the rate of increase in population. Table 5.6 shows that although real GDP grew by 53 per cent between 1971 and 1981, the real GDP per capita rose by only 36 per cent between 1971 and 1981 because Canada's population increased by 13 per cent during this period. Note that GDP is the measure of final goods and services produced over the period of one year, and that the population by which it is to be divided changes daily during the year; the mid-year population estimate is therefore used to represent the population when GDP per capita is calculated.

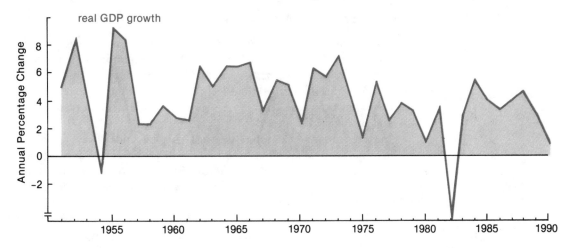

Figure 5.6   Real Growth in Gross Domestic Product
The annual growth in total real GDP averaged about 4.8 per cent in Canada over the period 1951 to 1980, but averaged only 2.6 per cent annually in the 1980s. Such growth, however, has been quite uneven. Figure 5.6 shows clearly the recession of 1954 followed by a boom in 1955, slow growth from 1957 to 1961, the sustained growth of 1962 to 1966, and recent recessions of 1975, 1980, and especially 1982.

Source: Statistics Canada, *National Income and Expenditure Accounts.*

National Income at Full Employment

National income accounts can also indicate by how much the economy fell short of its potential output. Full employment is one of the basic economic goals, but apart from counting the number of persons who are looking for work at any given time, there are few measures of the extent to which an economy is utilizing its productive resources. It was noted previously that persons may be employed in part-time jobs or in jobs that do not make full use of their skills. Plant and equipment may also be operating at less than full capacity. By subtracting the total output achieved under these conditions from the estimated potential output, the extent of underutilization of productive resources can be obtained. This estimate of "the GDP gap" is at the same time a clear statement of the cost of underutilization in terms of the additional goods and services that could have been produced and the additional incomes that could have been earned. The Economic Council has estimated the potential output for Canada in recent years by forecasting GDP growth based on various assumptions. The resulting differences between the worst and best scenarios show that the GDP gap has varied between 0.5 per cent and 2 per cent.

Innovations in Measures of Economic Performance

The national income accounts have served as the main measure of economic progress in Canada. Definitions have been improved, data collection techniques have been revised almost continuously, and historical data have been modified to reflect revised definitions. But at their best, the national income accounts measure only the level of marketed output and monetary incomes.

Imputed Items Considerable work is now under way to improve national income accounting so that it will provide more accurate measures of output and income, and the distribution of these. Some economists are attempting to estimate, for example, the value of items not in the accounts — such as students' time spent in educational institutions and persons' work at home — as well as expenditures that are required simply to avoid a decline in social progress. As an example of the latter case, it can be argued that:

> Programs designed to reduce environmental deterioration — investment in pollution control, for example — are quite apt to show up as increased real output, as indeed they should if the benefits from the program exceed the costs. However, the level of output would still be overstated relative to the level in past years when there was no need for pollution control because there was less pollution.[7]

Social Indicators A second major proposal for improving measurement of progress toward social and economic goals is a set of *social indicators*. The national accounts, even if revised to take account of expenditures required to maintain the social and physical environment and unmarketed labour services, cannot indicate how well output has been utilized to achieve other national goals. Social scientists have therefore begun to develop a system of social accounts or social indicators to monitor progress in such areas as health, education, crime prevention, and housing.

Progress toward methods of measuring social progress, however, is bound to be exceedingly slow. The Economic Council of Canada has stated quite plainly that "the search for a unique all-inclusive measure or index of human well-being does not seem very promising except in the longest of long runs".[8] Such a measure depends on the almost impossible task of measuring individual satisfaction, and then of aggregating such measures for the whole population.

Moreover, most people increasingly recognize that the methods used to achieve economic growth have serious consequences for their total well-being. Smelters and pulp mills, automobiles and pop-cans may contribute to their enjoyment, but may also contribute to an unpleasant

[7] National Bureau of Economic Research, *Economics — A Half Century of Research, 1920-1970*. New York: National Bureau of Economic Research, 1970, p. 10 fn.

[8] Economic Council of Canada, *Eighth Annual Review, Design for Decision-Making*. Ottawa: Information Canada, 1971, p. 24.

environment. Technological improvements can increase the incomes of many persons, but put others out of work, perhaps permanently. Alternatively, these improvements may lead to a shorter work week, leaving employees with both higher pay and more leisure time. Ideally, these and many similar effects should be included in any measure of collective and individual well-being. But until better measures are developed, it is useful to use increases in the total output of the economy as an indicator of improving consumer satisfaction.

Review of the Main Points

1. Canada's basic economic goals are: reasonable price stability, full employment, a high rate of economic growth, a viable balance of payments, and an equitable distribution of rising incomes.

2. Inflation is an increase in the general price level of consumer goods and services. Price changes in consumer goods and services are measured by the Consumer Price Index (CPI); price changes for all final goods and services are measured by the GDP Price Index. The CPI is calculated by comparing current prices of consumer commodities with the prices of the same collection of commodities in the base year. Changes in the quality of commodities and in the combination of commodities produced or consumed make it necessary to change the base year every five to ten years.

3. Inflation reduces the purchasing power or the real income of persons living on fixed incomes such as pensions, reduces the real value of repayments of debts to creditors, and may increase the prices of a country's exports relative to those of other countries.

4. For policy and analysis purposes, two types of inflation are identified: demand-pull and cost-push. The first is caused by excess demand, the second by increases in production costs per unit of output.

5. Full employment of all productive resources is difficult to measure because it is almost impossible to define the full utilization of all factors. "Full employment" is therefore usually related only to the labour force and is defined as the situation in which everyone aged 15 or over who wants to work, and is able to do so, has employment. The full employment goal, however, is often expressed in terms of an acceptable or target rate of unemployment.

6. Four types of unemployment are identified: inadequate demand, frictional, seasonal, and structural. The first is caused by inadequate demand, the second by persons leaving one job to look for another, the third by seasonal fluctuation in the demand for labour, and the fourth by changes in the composition of demand for final goods and by changes in production technology.

7. The labour force consists of everyone who is at work and persons who are unemployed but who are looking for work. However, the

current measure of unemployment does not take account of under-employment or underutilization of the labour force due to persons working at jobs not making full use of their skills or time.

8. Economic growth is measured by changes in productivity or by the rate of increase in real Gross Domestic Product per capita. Total factor productivity is total output divided by total input; labour productivity is total output divided by employment.

9. The circular flow of payments for productive factors and payments for finished goods and services means that the economy's performance can be measured either in terms of incomes received by productive factors or in terms of the market values of the finished products.

10. In order to avoid double counting of commodities, the values added at each stage of a productive process are summed to determine the total value added throughout the process. The value added at each stage is calculated by subtracting the purchases from other firms from the total receipts from the sale of the product of any given firm.

11. The GDP accounts are supplemented by other accounts that provide measures of income or output for more specific purposes. Net Domestic Income includes only the payments to factors of production; Personal Income includes both factor income and transfer payments received by individuals; Personal Disposable Income is the balance of Personal Income remaining after deducting personal income taxes; Net Investment is Gross Investment minus depreciation and thus measures the net addition to goods and services after allowing for replacement of obsolete or worn-out plant, equipment, and housing.

12. Real increases in income and output are distinguished from the monetary value of income and output by adjusting the current value of GDP for the price changes (usually increases) occurring during the year. Such price changes are reflected in the GDP Price Index, commonly called the "GDP deflator". A similar adjustment must be made for the annual increase in population, if current per capita output is being compared with that for previous years.

13. The national accounts of income and expenditures provide a measure of the economic activity of a country, but are only a proxy measure of the well-being of its population. An attempt is therefore being made to develop other social accounts or indicators to measure progress toward the achievement of national goals.

Key Concepts and Topics

economic goals

inflation

demand-pull inflation

cost-push inflation

consumer price index (CPI)

base year

full employment	Gross Domestic Product
unemployment	Gross National Product
unemployment rate	Net Domestic Income
inadequate-demand unemployment	indirect taxes
frictional unemployment	depreciation
seasonal unemployment	Personal Income
structural unemployment	transfer payments
underemployment	Personal Disposable Income
labour force	investment (gross and net)
seasonal adjustment	real income
economic growth	GDP Price Index
labour productivity	GDP gap (or national income gap)
households	social indicators
firms	underground economy
value added	

Questions for Review and Discussion

1. Explain why comparisons of GDP over time or among countries should be regarded only as imprecise estimates.

2. In the national income accounts, should the expenditures for a college education be treated as consumption or investment? Why?

3. "Inflation is a much more serious problem than unemployment because inflation affects everyone while unemployment is a problem only for those out of work." Do you agree? Why?

4. Would you regard the high unemployment rate for young people (aged 19 to 24) to be due mainly to frictional, seasonal, cyclical, or structural unemployment? Why?

5. Which of the five basic economic goals do you think should receive highest priority in the federal government's economic policy? Why?

6. Why are real estate assets said to be a "hedge against inflation"?

7. What is the difference between "income" and "wealth"? (Explain in terms of stocks and flows.)

8. Why is it necessary to remove government transfer payments from total government expenditures before estimating GDP? Why do private transfer payments (or gifts) not appear as a separate item in the national income accounts?

9. What is the difference between net investment and net foreign investment?

10. When is a bag of flour an intermediate good, and when is it a final good, for purposes of national income accounting? Why does this difference exist?

11. "Although the nominal GDP rose by 10 per cent last year this does not mean that Canadians are 10 per cent better off". Give specific reasons why you agree or disagree.

12. Why would GDP not provide an adequate comparison of the standard of living in different countries? Explain how you would interpret "standard of living". How would you modify the national income accounts to provide better international comparisons of standards of living?

Sources and Selected Readings

Dornbush, R., S. Fisher, and G. Sparks. *Macroeconomics*, 3rd ed. Toronto: McGraw-Hill Ryerson, 1989.

Economic Council of Canada. *First Annual Review: Economic Goals for Canada to 1970*. Ottawa: Queen's Printer, 1964. Also, *Annual Review* for subsequent years.

Feige, E.L., ed. *The Underground Economies*. New York: Cambridge University Press, 1988.

Mishan, E.J. "GNP—Measurement or Mirage?" *National Westminster Bank Quarterly Review* (November 1984): 2–13.

Paquet, Gilles. "The Underground Economy". *Policy Options* 10, no. 1 (1989).

Parkin, Michael, and Robin Bade. *Modern Macroeconomics*, 2nd ed. Toronto: Prentice-Hall, 1986.

Selody, J. *The Goal of Price Stability: A Review of the Issues*. Ottawa: Bank of Canada, 1990.

Statistics Canada. *Canada Year Book*. Ottawa: Supply and Services Canada, annual.

——. *Historical Statistics of Canada*, 2nd ed. Ottawa: Supply and Services Canada, 1983.

——. *National Income and Expenditure Accounts*. Ottawa: Supply and Services Canada, quarterly.

——. *Prices and Price Indexes*. Ottawa: Supply and Services Canada, annual.

——. *The Labour Force*. Ottawa: Supply and Services Canada, monthly.

Wilton, David, and David M. Prescott. *Macroeconomics: Theory and Policy in Canada*, 2nd ed. Toronto: Addison-Wesley, 1987.

6 Aggregate Expenditure and National Income

Although the national accounts provide a reasonably accurate measure of changes in national income, economists continue to try to explain why these changes occur, why there are unemployed resources, and what action is required to achieve full employment and stable prices. Explanations for fluctuations in national income and employment are described as the *theory of national income determination*. The original version of this theory was developed during the Depression of the 1930s by John Maynard Keynes, who showed how it was possible for the economy to become stuck at high levels of unemployment. Prior to that period, any unemployment was expected to last only a short time. The natural tendency in any economy was thought to be toward full employment of all productive resources. Widespread and persistent unemployment during the Depression, however, was evidence that some assumptions and conclusions of earlier economic theory were incorrect.

Full Employment in Classical Economics

Many economists preceding Keynes had argued that the economy would function effectively if market forces were allowed to follow a natural course. This *laissez-faire* view that there was no need for government intervention at the aggregative or national levels of economic activity was based on the assumption that wages, prices, and interest rates were quite flexible, and would move up and down freely with changing economic conditions.

Say's Law The classical or traditional view of aggregate economic activity that preceded Keynes' work was stated most simply by a French economist, Jean-Baptist Say (1767-1832). According to Say's Law, "supply creates its own demand". This has become a simplified statement for Say's more elaborate explanation of the automatic forces keeping an economy at, or close to, the full-employment level. The incomes of workers and their employers would be equal to the value of the goods and services they produced. They would, in turn, spend their earnings on goods and services produced by other workers. If all incomes were spent, the total purchases would be just equal to the total output of the economy, since the total purchasing power of all incomes was exactly equal to the value of all goods and services produced.

Although economic growth received only minor attention until the nineteenth century, growth could be taken into account in Say's model. As technological change enabled the factors of production to increase their outputs, wages and other earnings would be increased proportionately. Additional income would thus be available to purchase the increased output.

Flexibility of Wages, Prices, and Interest Rate   The possibility of some temporary unemployment was conceded in classical theory, but it was assumed that flexibility in wage rates would return the economy to full employment. If, for example, demand for a certain good had fallen and workers were unemployed, the general level of wages would fall as some workers offered to work for less while others left the labour force. Lower wages would then encourage other employers to hire more labour, bringing the economy back to full employment.

Similar flexibility was assumed with respect to product prices. A decrease in demand for goods and services, and the competition among producers to dispose of all output, would result in lower prices. Consumers could therefore buy a greater quantity of goods and services with their existing incomes, and markets would be cleared of potential surpluses.

The simplest version of the classical model assumed that workers would spend all of their earnings, and without delay. But what would happen if this were not the case? If individuals decided to save some of their incomes, there would be more funds available as loans to investors. The rate of interest would fall, making possible an expansion of production facilities, so businesses would increase their purchases of investment goods, demand would be maintained, and with it the validity of Say's Law.

But Say's Law and the whole neoclassical theory of employment and output were to be challenged by John Maynard Keynes. In turn, Keynes' work has been revised and extended by economists who have attempted to explain more recent economic conditions.

Theory of National Income Determination

An important landmark in the development of our understanding of the economic environment was John Maynard Keynes' book *The Gen-*

eral Theory of Employment, Interest, and Money,[1] published in 1936. The "Keynesian revolution" consisted of a detailed attack on the classical economists' explanation for the level of employment and output, and the conclusion that government intervention rather than *laissez-faire* was required to move the economy to the full-employment level.

The foundation stone of the Keynesian model or explanation of the operation of the economy is aggregate expenditure.

Aggregate expenditure is the total spending of all consumers, businesses, governments, and foreign buyers for the final goods and services produced *within the economy concerned*. The spending for imports is excluded because these are not produced within the economy and therefore do not directly influence the level of employment and output. Say's Law had stated that the total spending for goods and services would be just equal to the total output. Keynes disputed this. He argued that individuals might choose to save some of their incomes, and that there was no logical reason for foreigners or businesses to buy precisely the amount that would offset this shortfall in aggregate spending. It was thus left to governments either to encourage more consumer and business spending by reducing taxes or to increase government spending directly. Moreover, Keynes argued that prices and wages were less flexible (especially downward) than classical economists had assumed and that declining demand for goods and services could therefore lead to persistent unemployment.

Aggregate Expenditure

Aggregate expenditure is essentially the same concept as Gross Domestic Product in the national income accounts. Both terms refer to the total expenditure for goods and services produced within an economy in a given period of time. There is an important difference, however: GDP refers to actual spending, whereas aggregate expenditure, in this theoretical treatment, refers to planned or intended spending. Planned (or "intended" or "desired") aggregate expenditure is the spending that each of the four basic groups (consumers, businesses, governments, and foreigners) plan or intend to spend at any given level of national income. As noted above, however, there is no logical reason why the spending plans of these four independent groups should always exactly

[1] In a letter written to George Bernard Shaw on January 1, 1935, Keynes stated: "I believe myself to be writing a book on economic theory which will largely revolutionize—not, I suppose, at once but in the course of the next ten years—the way the world thinks about economic problems."

equal the value of the economy's output; in fact, actual aggregate expenditure is likely to be different from planned aggregate expenditure (as will be shown later in this chapter).

A first step in developing a model for the operation and management of the economy is to examine the factors influencing each of the four separate components of aggregate expenditure: consumption, investment, government spending, and exports. The most simplified model of an economy would include only two sectors—consumption and investment; adding a government sector introduces taxes and expenditures, which are the means for a government's fiscal policy; and adding the export sector changes the model from a "closed economy" to an "open economy". These components are expressed collectively as:

$$AE = C + I + G + (X - M)$$

where AE is aggregate expenditure, C is consumption, I is investment, G is government spending for goods and services, X is exports, and M is the imports component included in each of the other groups. $(X - M)$ is also termed net exports.

By examining the factors that cause changes in the separate components of aggregate expenditure, and therefore changes in the planned or desired level of total spending in the economy, it will be possible to see why changes can occur in total employment and national income. At this stage, it is assumed that prices are constant (there is no inflation) and that there is no change in the money supply (or the amount of money circulating in the economy). Later, the theory of national income determination will be modified to take account of changes in the price level and the money supply.

Consumption Spending

The largest component—about three-fifths—of aggregate expenditure is consumption.

Consumption, in the model presented here, includes all current spending for consumer goods and services. Consumer goods and services are those for final use by individuals or households.

The consumption category in national income accounting, as presented in Chapter 5, included spending for imported consumer goods and services because this could not easily be separated from consumption spending for domestically produced goods and services. These imports were excluded indirectly by subtracting them from total exports. In the theoretical model, consumer spending should include only domestically produced goods and services, but this continues to be represented by excluding imports in the expression $(X - M)$.

The total income of an economy can be used in only four ways: for consumption of domestically produced goods and services, for saving, for purchases of imports (goods and services produced in other economies), and for tax payments. That is,

$$Y = C + S + M + T$$

where Y is national income (GDP), C is consumption, S is saving, M is imports, and T is taxes. To simplify the model, it is assumed that saving is done only by households and not by business firms.

Saving

Saving is defined as postponed consumption because it represents future purchasing power, or the ability to buy goods and services in the future.

One must distinguish between "savings", used to refer to a *stock* — the total value of savings at a point in time — and "saving", used to refer to a *flow* — the act of saving, that is, abstaining from consumption, that is done over a period of time. The latter is the concept used in the national income model.

Some initial difficulty in understanding this distinction may result from the narrow, everyday use of the word "savings", for example, in reference to bank savings deposits. But this is only one form in which savings can be held. The future purchasing power represented by savings can also be held in bonds, stocks, real estate, or other forms of financial assets.

Since saving represents the postponement of consumption, people try to hold their savings in a form that will preserve the real value of this postponed enjoyment of goods and services, and that may even increase this value. Such financial assets are widely described as "investments", but economists usually use "investment" as it is in national income accounting, to include housing, non-residential buildings, equipment, and additions to inventories.

Consumption

The major influence on the level of consumption is the level of current income.

Individuals are strongly governed in their spending decisions by their income, and particularly by the income available to them after income taxes are deducted. From the perspective of the overall economy, however, the level of consumption can be said to be determined by the level of the national income, as represented by Gross Domestic Product.

In more complex models, individuals' consumption decisions would also be related to their average annual incomes over the long run (generally termed "permanent income"), to take account of the year-to-year fluctuations in incomes of, for example, salespersons, entertainers, and farmers. The size of one's wealth (or accumulated assets) also has some influence on consumption, since one can draw on wealth to finance major purchases such as automobiles and furniture. Financial assets, however, have their major effect on consumption through the annual income they yield in the form of interest, dividends, and rents.

Propensity to Consume

Individuals must decide how much of their annual incomes they will spend immediately and how much they will save. Families with lower incomes may find it necessary to spend all of their incomes; some may even spend more than their current incomes by borrowing against anticipated increases in future incomes. A few may be able to consume more than their current incomes by drawing on the savings from incomes in previous years.

High-income families consume more than low-income families, but they also save more. Usually, the higher the family income, the lower is the proportion of income consumed and the higher the proportion saved. *The proportion of income going to consumption is described as the propensity to consume.* As noted previously, "income" for the purpose of the model presented here is being defined as the GDP. However, the simple concept of the propensity to consume can be more readily illustrated by reference to hypothetical families and their annual disposable, or after-tax, incomes. This is done in Table 6.1. As family incomes rise, the share or proportion of the income going to consumption falls, that is, the propensity to consume declines. The remaining portion of the income goes to savings and imports; this proportion therefore tends to rise with higher incomes.

The information in Table 6.1 is shown in graphic form in Figure 6.1. Since the scale on each axis is the same, any point along the line drawn at a 45° angle to each axis represents equal values for consumption and disposable income. That is, if a family's entire disposable income were spent for consumption at each income level, the consumption curve or function would appear as the 45° line marked $C = DI$ in Figure 6.1a. Comparing this "equality line" with the consumption curve marked C reveals that the percentage of income consumed declines with increasing income levels. One can also identify the income level at which all the annual income—but only that amount—goes to consumption, namely,

Table 6.1

Marginal Propensities to Consume, Save, and Import: Some Hypothetical Examples

							Marginal Propensities		
Disposable Income per Family	Con-sumption	Saving	Imports	Additional Consumption	Additional Saving	Additional Imports	To Consume	To Save	To Import
$40,000	$40,400	$−400	$ 0						
				3,600	400	0	.9	.10	.00
44,000	44,000	0	0						
				3,200	600	200	.8	.15	.05
48,000	47,200	600	200						
				2,800	800	400	.7	.20	.10
52,000	50,000	1,400	600						
				2,400	1,000	600	.6	.25	.15
56,000	52,400	2,400	1,200						

$44,000. At lower incomes, families are "dissaving": they are borrowing against future income or drawing on previous savings, to finance current consumption.

Since disposable income can only be spent for domestic consumption, or for imports, or be saved, the vertical distance between the equality line and the consumption curve shows the amount used for imports and saved (or dissaved) at each income level. Import spending and saving can be plotted against income levels in Figure 6.1b to obtain the saving and imports curve marked $S + M$.

Average Propensity to Consume   These diagrams also illustrate both the average and marginal propensities to consume. The *average propensity to consume, APC*, is the proportion of total disposable income, *DI*, used for current consumption of goods and services, *C*, and is calculated by the simple formula:

$$APC = \frac{C}{DI}$$

Similarly, the *average propensity to save, APS*, is the proportion of disposable income that is saved and is calculated as $APS = S/DI$. The average propensity to import is $APM = M/DI$.

Marginal Propensity to Consume   Even more important than knowing the proportion of total income that households allocate to consumption, is knowing how consumption changes with any change in income.

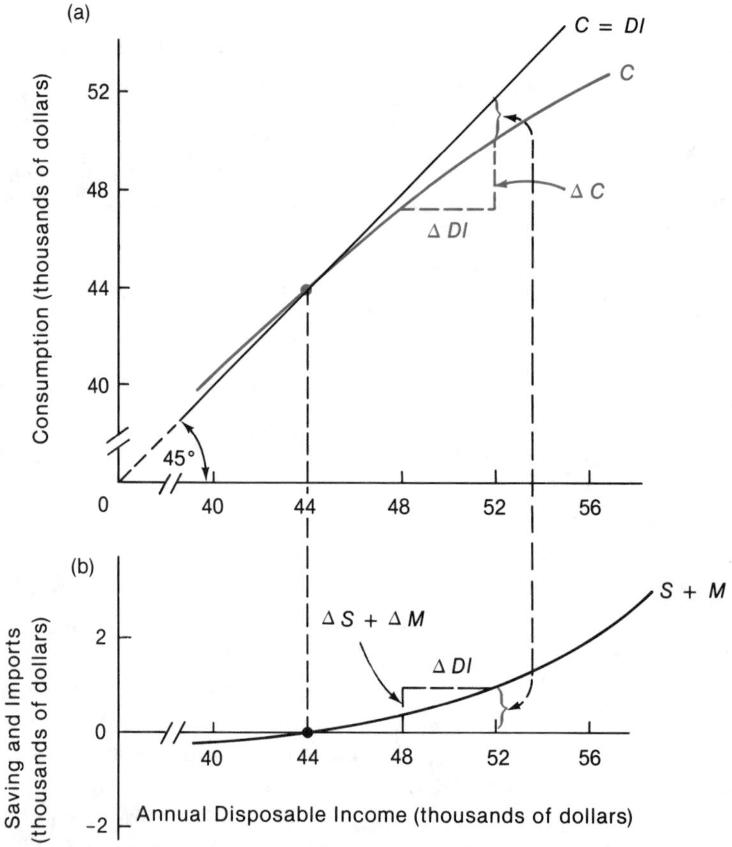

Figure 6.1   Consumption, Saving, and Import Spending Depend on Disposable Income
As a family's disposable income rises, it tends to spend a lower percentage on consumption of domestic goods and services, and to increase the percentage saved and the percentage spent for imported goods. Data provided in Table 6.1 are plotted to obtain the family's consumption curve, C, and its saving and imports curve, S + M. At income levels below $44,000, the family spends more than its current income on domestic consumer goods and services. The marginal propensity to consume, MPC, is the increase in consumption, ΔC, associated with a given increase in income, ΔDI; the combined marginal propensities to save and to import, MPS + MPM, are calculated from the increase in saving and imports, ΔS + ΔM, associated with an increase in income, ΔDI.

The marginal propensity to consume, MPC, in this example, is the change in consumption associated with a change in the family's disposable income. That is,

$$MPC = \frac{\Delta C}{\Delta DI}$$

where Δ is interpreted as "marginal" or "incremental".

Table 6.1 shows that when the family that has had an income of $44,000 receives an additional or extra income of $4,000, the additional consumption is $3,200. The *MPC* between $44,000 and $48,000 is 3,200 ÷ 4,000, or 0.8.

The values for ΔC and ΔDI are shown on Figure 6.1a between the $48,000 and $52,000 income level. Note that these amounts also represent the "rise" and the "run" for this section of the consumption curve, and hence:

$$\frac{\Delta C}{\Delta DI} = \text{the slope of the curve.}$$

Thus the *MPC* is equal to the slope of the consumption curve. The gradual flattening of the consumption curve, or its decreasing slope, reflects the decrease in *MPC* as income rises, as shown in Table 6.1. Similarly, the marginal propensity to save, *MPS*, is equal to the slope of the savings curve, and *increases* with income.

The Whole Equals Its Parts   Note that *the total of the values for MPC, MPS, and MPM at each income level equals 1*. This follows from the condition that families can only consume, save, or import with their disposable incomes, and therefore the total changes in these three categories must equal the change in income. Thus for any change in disposable income it will always be the case that:

$$MPC + MPS + MPM = 1$$

Although savings can be calculated by subtracting consumption and imports from disposable income, one should not assume that the amount saved is simply the residual effect of a decision to spend a certain amount for consumption. Usually saving and spending decisions are made together: a family may want a new car now but it wants even more an expensive trip during the summer vacation next year. Families and individuals vary greatly in their saving goals and habits. Some may have specific reasons for their savings, while others simply try to save an increasing amount as their incomes rise.

Changes in MPC   A family or individual at a given level of income may have a different *MPS* or *MPC* under different conditions. The $48,000 family, for example, may have a higher *MPS* when inflation and interest rates are high, both because prices of some goods are so high that purchases are postponed and because high interest rates provide an incentive to accumulate savings.

These changing conditions and decisions would be reflected in *shifts* of the consumption curve upward in low inflation times and downward in high inflation times—accompanied by shifts in the savings curve in the opposite direction. When inflation is higher at home than abroad, the imports curve is also likely to shift upward, because imports become relatively less expensive. Many other conditions that affect consumers' tastes and expectations can also cause a shift in these curves.

Be careful to distinguish between a *movement along* the consumption curve and a *shift* of the whole curve. As noted earlier, consumption tends to increase with increased income, although less than proportionately. These changes occur as individuals and economies move along the consumption curve. An upward *shift* in the consumption curve results from a decision to save and/or to import less *at a given level of income*.

Since most economies have experienced continuously rising levels of income, it may be difficult to imagine changed spending patterns at a given level of income. One might more readily understand these shifts occurring at the same time national income is increasing. To cite an extreme example, the removal of all tariffs next year would lead to a sharp increase in imports, far greater than the slight increase that might have been expected with no change in tariffs and a small increase in consumers' incomes. The M_1 curve in Figure 6.2 indicates that when disposable income is $60 billion in year 1, the value of imports is $6 billion. If DI rose to $65 billion in year 2, imports would rise to $7 billion. The removal of tariffs in year 2, however, results in imports of $10 billion: one-quarter of the $4 billion increase is due to the increased DI, but the balance is due to the upward shift of the import curve, from M_1 to M_2. The consumption curve would shift downward by the same amount, unless the savings curve also shifted downward.

Propensity to Consume and the GDP

The propensity to consume concept was introduced in terms of families and their disposable incomes because these are more readily visualized and understood. However, this concept must now be redefined in terms of the spending decisions of the total economy and the national income or GDP. The marginal propensity to consume becomes the change in consumption associated with a change in national income; and hence

$$MPC = \frac{\Delta C}{\Delta Y}$$

where Y is the GDP or national income. Similarly, $MPS = \Delta S/\Delta Y$ and $MPM = \Delta M/\Delta Y$.

The shift from disposable income to GDP requires that income taxes be returned to the discussion. This introduces a further concept, the marginal propensity to make tax payments, which reflects the percentage of additional income that is paid as taxes. The marginal pro-

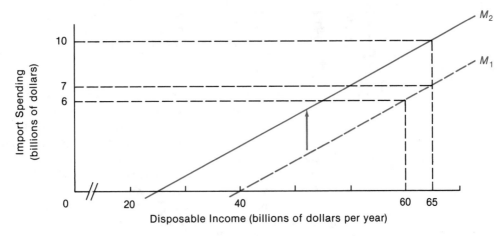

Figure 6.2   A Shift in the Propensity to Import
A distinction must be made between a movement along a planned spending curve and a shift of the entire curve. The propensity to import curve, M_1, indicates that an increase in disposable income from $60 to $65 billion increases import spending to $7 billion. An upward shift in the propensity to import, to M_2, increases import spending by a further $3 billion, at the same level of disposable income.

pensity to pay taxes is the change in income tax payments associated with a change in GDP. Hence,

$$MPT = \frac{\Delta T}{\Delta Y}$$

In the simple model being developed here, this can be treated as the marginal rate of taxation.[2]

Other Spending Components

Investment

The second major component of aggregate expenditure is gross investment.

Gross investment is defined as purchases of new plant and equipment, new residential construction, and additions to inventories.

Gross investment rather than net investment is included in aggregate expenditure, since some investment spending is for replacement of

[2] See Chapter 14 for a description of marginal tax rates, especially Table 14.2.

depreciated and obsolete items. Gross investment includes, for example, all new equipment purchased. Net investment is the net addition to equipment after allowing for the replacement of obsolete and worn-out equipment.

Expected Yield   Investment expenditures are expected to result in a profit. The rate of return or the yield rate is the annual profit earned, expressed as a percentage of the investment expenditure. The firm or individual who decides to invest in new plant and equipment is influenced not so much by the current level of national income as by the *expected yield rate on the planned investment* compared with the *rate of interest charged on funds to be borrowed* for the investment. If the expected yield rate is greater than the interest rate, the project is expected to realize a net profit and thus can reasonably be undertaken.

The expected yield rate on plant and equipment is calculated by comparing the expected annual after-tax profits with the total value of the plant and equipment. The rate of return on housing owned by apartment developers is the net profit compared with the cost of the housing project. For owner-occupants, the yield is based on the implicit rental value of housing.

As an increasing amount is invested in the economy, the expected yield on each *additional* investment project is likely to be less than on preceding projects. This follows from the assumption that rational investors will undertake the highest-yielding projects first. The yield or rate of return on additional or marginal investment is termed the *marginal efficiency of investment*, or *MEI*. This is shown in Figure 6.3. Since the expected yield declines with increasing levels of investment, the *MEI* curve is downward-sloping to the right. This curve also represents the demand for investment goods, since the declining *MEI* means that there will be increases in investment spending only at lower interest rates. (Even if a firm uses its own funds to finance investment spending, the interest rate represents the opportunity cost in using these funds.)

Inventories   Inventories are considered a necessary component of production—and are therefore included in investment—since inventories (or the available stock of any given good) must be large enough to fill customers' orders quickly or, in the case of raw and semifinished materials, to assure continued production. The larger the inventories, the greater are the potential sales and profits, but it is the additional *profit* associated with additional inventories that represents the marginal yield on that form of investment. This profit must be weighed against the cost of holding inventories. Firms must finance the wages and other costs

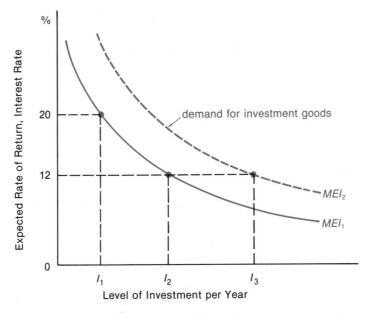

Figure 6.3   The Marginal Efficiency of Investment
The marginal efficiency of investment (*MEI*) is the expected yield or rate of return on additional or marginal investment. This is expected to decline as investment increases, on the assumption that investment projects with the highest profit or yield rates will be undertaken first. Investment is also expected to continue until the yield rate falls to the prevailing interest rate level. At an interest rate of 20 per cent, for example, investment would continue only to level I_1, but with the interest rate at 12 per cent investment would continue to I_2. If the *MEI* curve shifted outward, for example due to a reduction in the tax rate on corporate profits, to a level such as MEI_2, there would be a greater level of investment at a given interest rate. The *MEI* curve also represents the demand curve for investment goods.

entailed in unsold products, either from their own funds or with short-term loans.

Induced and Autonomous Investment   Profit expectations depend partly on the current level of technology, and partly on the level of national income, since higher consumer spending means a potentially larger market for the firm's products. But in this initial formulation of the national income model, investment is assumed to be unrelated to income levels. Such investment is termed *autonomous investment*. The investment associated with increases in national income is termed *induced investment*, and can be added later in the development of the model.

Finally, it should be noted that, for the purpose of examining aggregate expenditure, investment is defined here as including only the investment goods produced domestically, just as consumption was restricted to consumer goods and services produced domestically. Imported investment goods are also excluded in the $(X - M)$ expression.

Government Spending

The third component of aggregate expenditure is government spending for domestically produced goods and services.[3] Each level of government—federal, provincial, and municipal—is included. This category excludes *government transfer payments*, which are not payments for goods or services but are transfers of income from one group (taxpayers) to another group (recipients of payments such as family allowances, government pensions, unemployment insurance).

Transfer payments are excluded from government spending because they become part of consumers' disposable income, and thus are included in consumption, saving, or imports.

Governments' purchases of goods and services may be used directly in administration, or for provision of public services and facilities such as defence forces, highways, and parks. The level of government spending at any income level depends on current attitudes about the appropriate role for governments, especially in the fields of health, education, and social assistance, and hence depends on population growth and urbanization. Generally, total government expenditures rise as national income increases, but government spending may also rise abruptly in wartime and decrease thereafter. But again, for the simplified version of the national income model, it is assumed that government spending is independent from national income.

Exports

The final component of aggregate expenditure is exports. Since demand for exports comes from outside the country concerned, there are many factors influencing export sales that do not directly affect the other components of aggregate expenditure, from weather conditions in other countries to changes in their governments. Generally, however, it is the levels of incomes and prices in other countries that determine their demand for an economy's exports. Consequently, the spending for exports is assumed to be independent of the level of national income in the given economy.

[3] Note that these expenditures are for current-use goods and services only. Governments' investment expenditures are included in the investment component— both in this chapter and in the national income accounts section of the previous chapter.

Note that exports in the context of the national income model include both goods and services. Note also that by including exports this model represents an "open economy", by comparison with a "closed economy" model, in which no provision is made for international trade.

Toward Equilibrium National Income

The separate components of aggregate expenditure can now be combined. At this initial stage of the development of the national income model, the simple assumption is made that the respective levels of investment, government spending, and exports, are all autonomous, or independent, of the level of national income. This independence is reflected in the horizontal I, G, and $X - M$ curves in Figure 6.4.

The vertical axes in Figure 6.4 are labelled "planned spending". This refers to the distinction between planned or intended spending and actual spending. The distinct sectors representing investment, government spending, and foreign trade have independent plans to spend certain amounts for the existing output of goods and services. The total of these intended purchases—together with consumption—may be more than, less than, or equal to the actual level of output.[4]

The horizontal (income) axis is now labelled *GDP* rather than *DI* as in Figure 6.1, because governments, businesses, and foreign buyers are now included in the analysis. The consumption curve is plotted first (Figure 6.4a), then the $6 billion for I, $10 billion for G, and $4 billion for $X - M$ are added successively. Since these amounts do not vary as income changes, the addition of each item produces a parallel upward shift of the total spending curve.

Domestic Output   *Domestic output* can be represented by the 45° angle or equality line shown in Figure 6.4e. This line shows the value of total output at each level of national income.

The domestic output curve appears as an equality line, when the scales on each axis are the same, because the value of the output at any level of national income is *necessarily* equal to the national income.

This is because the national income was earned by producing the total output that is shown for each income level. For example, at national income or GDP of $60 billion, the domestic output is $60 billion because the GDP represents the total factor payments included in producing a total output valued at $60 billion.

---

[4] This use of "planned" does not refer to the decisions of a planned economy; rather, the reference is to the plans or intentions of individual businesses, governments, and foreign buyers.

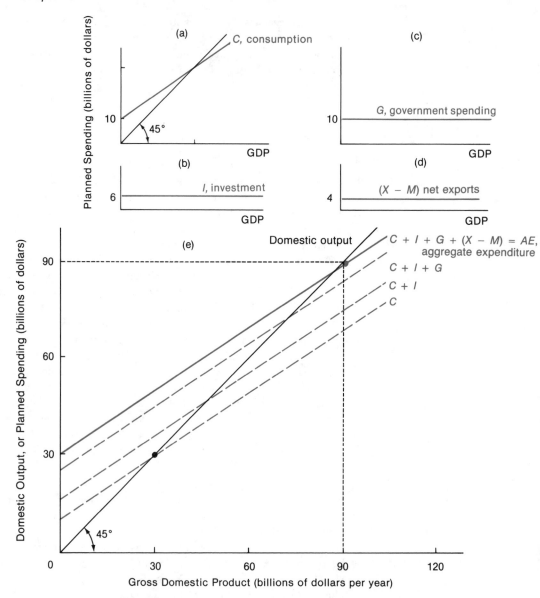

Figure 6.4   Aggregate Expenditure and Domestic Output Determine Equilibrium National Income
Planned aggregate expenditure for domestically produced goods and services consists of planned spending for consumption, investment, government goods and services, and exports. Initially, the latter three components are assumed to be unaffected by the level of GDP. Thus, I, G, and $(X - M)$ are constant, while C increases with increasing income. The aggregate expenditure, AE, is plotted by adding vertically the values for C, I, G, and $(X - M)$ at each income level. When planned aggregate spending equals domestic output, the economy is at its equilibrium level of GDP, namely, $90 billion.

Equilibrium Level Defined

The equilibrium level of national income is the level at which national income will remain unless some forces are operating to move it to a higher or lower level. If all of the factors influencing national income remain unchanged, or if forces acting in opposite directions exactly offset each other, national income will be unchanged.

Any economy is said to be at its equilibrium level of national income when the level of planned aggregate spending is equal to the actual domestic output at that level of income.

In other words, the total amount that consumers, investors, governments, and foreign purchasers of exports plan to spend for domestic goods and services is just equal to the amount produced.[5]

The equilibrium level of national income is not necessarily the desirable level. In fact, Keynes recognized that the major economies during the Depression of the 1930s were more or less in equilibrium—or were stuck—at undesirably low levels of national income. By examining the forces that could move the economies away from this low equilibrium level, Keynes was able to suggest ways of moving to higher levels of income and employment.

Inventory Adjustment   It is not enough to know that when planned aggregate spending is equal to domestic output, the economy is at equilibrium national income. One needs to look further for the process that brings about this equilibrium. If at any given level of GDP, the planned aggregate spending is less than the value of actual output, there will be unpurchased goods left in the stores and warehouses of the economy. These unpurchased goods represent an *undesired or unplanned inventory* of goods, from the producers' point of view.

Desired Inventories   Businesses want to hold some goods as inventories, but only the *desired or planned level of inventories* that was included in the investment component of planned aggregate spending. A firm's total inventory (particularly in manufacturing) includes raw materials, semifinished goods, and finished goods. Each of these is necessary so that the firm can continue producing and shipping without delays. Firms are able to determine a desirable inventory level—namely sufficient inventory in each category so that the firm does not need to

---

[5] This equilibrium condition of the model can also be expressed in algebraic terms: planned $AE = C + I + G + (X - M)$. When $MPC = \frac{2}{3}$ (or 0.67), C = 10 + 0.67Y, $I = 6$, $G = 10$, $(X - M) = 4$, and $Y = $ *domestic output*. In equilibrium planned $AE = $ *domestic output* $= Y$. Therefore $Y = 10 + 0.67Y + 6 + 10 + 4$, or $Y = 90$ in equilibrium.

wait for raw materials or disappoint its customers—only on the basis of assumptions about future economic conditions such as the level of national income. When these assumptions are not realized, firms' inventories will be above or below the desired level.

Excess Inventories   Excess inventories are undesirable because businesses do not have the cash income from those potential sales to pay for the labour and other inputs used to produce the excess goods and services. It may be necessary to borrow this extra money. The interest payments then add to the producers' costs and reduce their expected

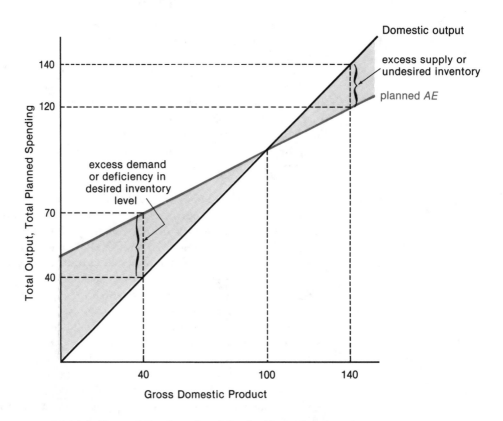

Figure 6.5   Actual and Desired Inventory Levels
At the GDP level of 100, where the economy is at equilibrium income, the actual inventory is also equal to the desired level. At higher levels of GDP, planned or desired aggregate expenditure is less than the actual output. Since the desired level of aggregate expenditure includes the desired level of inventories, the excess supply represents undesired inventories. Similarly, at GDP levels below 100, where desired aggregate expenditure is greater than output, inventories will be below their desired or intended level.

profits. Producers respond to this situation by deciding to produce less in the following period, both to get rid of the undesired inventories and to prevent the same thing from happening again. The unplanned inventories are shown in Figure 6.5 as the vertical difference between planned aggregate expenditure and domestic output at, for example, a GDP of $140 billion. The economy is *not* at the equilibrium level of national income, because the undesired inventory level and producers' revised decisions prevent the economy from remaining at this level.

Achieving Equilibrium   Suppose that producers react to undesired or excess inventories by cutting their output back to a level represented by a GDP of $80 billion. Employees are laid off, purchases of other input services and raw materials fall, and incomes fall to the $80 billion level. The economy is again out of equilibrium, but this time it is the level of planned aggregate expenditure that exceeds domestic output. Although aggregate expenditure has been reduced somewhat due to the effect of declining incomes on consumers' spending, there is still such a demand for goods and services that inventories fall below the level planned or desired by producers. Shelves are emptied and warehouse stocks are depleted. The next response is to increase output. Employees are rehired, more raw materials are purchased, and incomes rise. If producers have estimated correctly, the level of GDP might rise to $100 billion, where planned aggregate expenditure will be just sufficient to purchase the domestic output. The equilibrium level of national income has been reached.

There can be only one level of national income at which *planned* aggregate expenditure is equal to domestic output: this is the equilibrium level of national income.

Since the value of unplanned inventories is the difference between domestic output and planned aggregate expenditure, unplanned inventories is the item that makes *actual* aggregate expenditure necessarily equal to domestic output. Actual aggregate expenditure and output will always be equal regardless of the level of national income because unplanned inventories are included with investment in calculating actual expenditure.

The level of inventories in Canada averaged about 92 per cent of the level of sales in the 1970s, and about 86 per cent in the 1980s, but fluctuated between 82 and 98 per cent. A low inventory level in 1981 did not lead to strong economic growth because the high interest rates resulted in a high cost of holding inventories. Normally, however, such a sharp decline in inventories would produce a surge in output the following year.

Alternative Definition of Equilibrium

It is possible—although rather unlikely—that the various shifts in the components of aggregate spending may continue to offset each other, with the net result that planned aggregate spending will remain equal to domestic output at the equilibrium level of national income. If the forces that tend to push the economy out of equilibrium do not counterbalance each other exactly, the economy will move toward a new equilibrium level of national income.

Injections and Withdrawals
These forces or factors can be categorized as *injections* and *withdrawals*. Injections are additions to planned aggregate spending on domestic goods and services at a given level of national income. Withdrawals are reductions in planned aggregate spending on domestic goods and services at a given level of national income.

Withdrawals result from saving, taxes, and imports. Increases in each of these components reduce the amount of spending, from a given level of income, for purchases of domestic goods and services. Injections include additions to investment spending, to government spending, and to exports. Consumption is not included in this list, because changes in domestic consumption from a given level of income are already reflected indirectly in the changes in saving, imports, and personal income taxes.

It should now be apparent that the economy will remain at its equilibrium level of national income if the injections equal the withdrawals, or if

$$I + G + X = S + M + T$$

where I = Investment   and S = Saving
G = Government spending M = Imports
X = Exports T = Taxes.

Thus there are two approaches to a definition of the equilibrium level of income: (1) the income at which planned aggregate spending equals domestic output, and (2) the income at which planned injections, $I + G + X$, equal planned withdrawals, $S + M + T$.

Note that *some* of the withdrawals may be used to provide *some* of the spending for the injections, but that there is no reason to expect that planned withdrawals will necessarily equal planned injections. Savings will be used to finance some of the investment spending, but some savings may be held in the form of foreign bank deposits or foreign real estate holdings. Similarly, investment may be financed partly by foreign creditors or shareholders. In some years, government spending may exceed taxes, with the difference financed partly by foreign borrowing; in other years tax revenues may exceed government expenditures, with

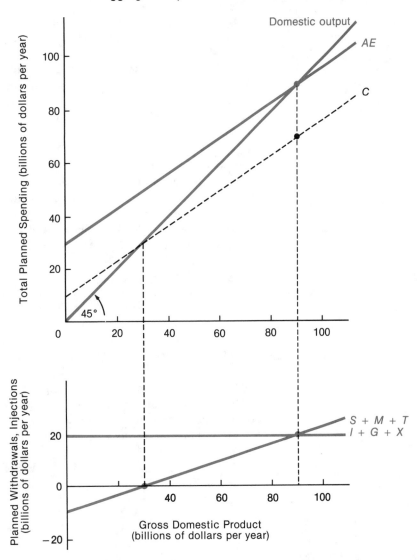

Figure 6.6   Alternative Approaches to Equilibrium National Income
The economy is at its equilibrium level of GDP, $90 billion, when planned
aggregate expenditure, *AE*, is equal to the total domestic output of final
goods and services. This condition occurs when planned injections of
spending for investment, government goods and services, and exports
(*I* + *G* + *X*) are equal to withdrawals for saving, imports, and taxes
(*S* + *M* + *T*). Injections equal the vertical distances between *C* and *AE*,
while withdrawals equal the vertical distances between *C* and Domestic
output.

the surplus used to retire government bonds held by foreigners. Similarly, the value of exports is seldom exactly equal to the value of imports.

The two definitions of equilibrium national income are illustrated in Figure 6.6 The domestic output and aggregate expenditure curves are the same curves shown in Figure 6.4e. The injections curve $I + G + X$ is equal to the difference between C and AE, and appears as a horizontal line because injections are assumed at this stage to be independent of the level of income.

The withdrawals curve $S + M + T$ is obtained from the difference between the consumption and domestic output curves. Since the gross income paid to the factors for the production of the domestic output can be used only for consumption, taxes, savings, or imports, the difference between domestic output and consumption must equal withdrawals. Thus, at the income level where C = Domestic output, the withdrawals are zero and the $S + M + T$ curve intersects the horizontal axis. The upward slope of the $S + M + T$ curve indicates that saving, imports, and taxes are assumed to increase with higher levels of income.

Moving the Equilibrium Level

Imagine the planned aggregate expenditure curve shifting up or down from the position it takes in Figure 6.4e. Wherever it shifted, it would still intersect the domestic output curve at some point. Any point along the 45° line represents a potential equilibrium level of GDP. By examining the separate components of aggregate expenditure to determine why each of these may change, it is possible to see why aggregate expenditure shifts and how the equilibrium level of national income can be changed.

Consumption   A change in consumption may result either directly from decisions about spending on domestic goods and services, or indirectly from decisions about saving and importing. It may also result from changes in the level of disposable income at any given level of national income.

One major reason for a downward shift in the consumption curve is an increase in personal income taxes at each income level. This would reduce disposable income. Similarly, a reduction in income taxes would increase disposable income and would likely shift the consumption curve upward.

An upward shift may also occur if consumers expect their incomes to rise fairly quickly. Anticipation of rising income may lead them to spend more now, saving less for a "rainy day" or for extended holidays, which they believe can be financed directly from their higher future incomes. The consumption curve may continue to shift upward over time as consumers' choice widens and as they experience more ways to spend their incomes. Easier and faster air travel for vacations and growing concern about health care are only two of many such possibilities.

An increase in the price of imported goods relative to prices of domestic goods would also shift the consumption curve upward, as consumers switched to purchases of domestic goods.

The consumption curve may shift downward if the yield on financial assets improves sharply. A substantial increase in interest paid on bank savings deposits and savings bonds is comparable to an increase in the price of current goods relative to the price of future goods, and will encourage consumers to increase their saving or postpone consumption.

Investment   The investment spending curve will shift with changes in profit expectations, that is, with shifts in the *MEI* or investment demand curve, or with changes in the interest rate that result in a movement *along* the *MEI* curve. Profit expectations depend on many factors, from advances in technology to political conditions in Canada and abroad. If producers become pessimistic about the effects of foreign trade barriers on their ability to export their products, for example, the *MEI* curve and thus the investment spending curve may shift downward. A reduction in corporate income tax rates would improve profits and thus would shift the *MEI* and investment spending curves upward.

Government Expenditures   Shifts in government expenditures play an especially important role in aggregate spending because governments can attempt to offset any undesirable changes in the other components of aggregate expenditure. Government budgets may be designed to provide substantial increases in spending if, for example, it appears that the investment spending curve is shifting downward. In severe wartime situations, the government may have less freedom to decide whether spending will be increased or not. Even in these conditions, spending on government programs other than military activities can be reduced if necessary to achieve the desired level of national income.

Exports   Changes in the foreign spending for exports also occur for a wide range of reasons. In the Canadian case, these shifts may be the outcome of special agreements or arrangements such as the Canada-U.S. Free Trade Agreement or the sale of unusually large quantities of wheat to foreign countries. An unusually sharp increase in prices of Canadian goods will reduce export sales if similar price increases have not occurred elsewhere. A depreciation of the value of the Canadian dollar, relative to other major currencies, will have an upward effect on the exports curve since Canadian goods will become less expensive for foreigners.

Expenditure Multiplier

The preceding sections have been concerned with how equilibrium GDP is attained and what causes the equilibrium level to change. This section explains the *multiplier effect*, through which small changes in aggregate expenditure may result in much larger changes in the level of national income. Like the wind, the multiplier cannot be observed directly; one can only examine its effects. Assume that in Figure 6.7 aggregate spending initially consists only of consumption spending. The equilibrium national income would then be $30 billion. By a net addition of $20 billion to planned aggregate spending, equilibrium income is increased by $60 billion, to the $90 billion level. The final increase in national income is *three times* the initial increase in spending.

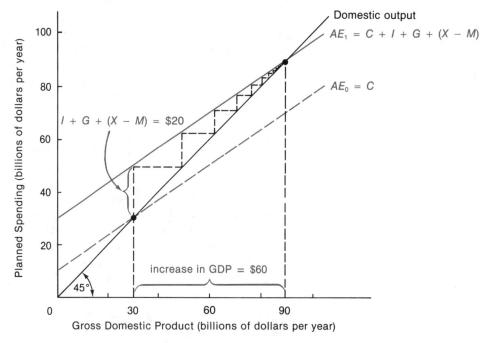

Figure 6.7   Multiplier Effect of Increased Spending
Injections of spending ($I + G + (X - M)$), additions to these components, or increases in planned consumption have a final effect on GDP that is greater than the initial change. With $MPC = 2/3$, the addition of $20 billion for $I + G + (X - M)$ increases equilibrium GDP by $60 billion. The larger the value of the multiplier, the larger the final change in GDP.

The multiplier is the factor by which initial changes in spending change the level of national income.

Further inspection of Figure 6.7 will suggest that if the consumption curve rose less steeply, the addition of the same total amount for $I + G + (X - M)$ would produce an aggregate expenditure curve with a flatter slope, and that AE_1 and Domestic output would be in equilibrium at a lower income level. One can conclude from this that the multiplier is related to the slope of the consumption curve. Moreover, it should be recalled that the slope of the consumption curve is equal to the marginal propensity to consume. A high marginal propensity to consume is represented by the steeply sloped consumption curve that led to a high multiplier effect.

In order to find an explanation for this effect, it is necessary to recall some of the initial discussion of consumption in this chapter. When families or individuals received an addition to their incomes, part of this was spent on domestic consumer goods, some was spent on imports, some was saved, and some was required for income taxes. The fraction consumed was termed the marginal propensity to consume, MPC[6]. Now suppose for the sake of simplicity that $MPC = {}^2/_3$ for every family and individual in the economy, where MPC is defined as $\Delta C / \Delta GDP$.

Assume that a firm decided to build a new plant. It might first employ an architect, paying a fee of $10,000. The architect would spend two-thirds of this amount; one-third would go to savings, imports, and taxes. The $6,667 for consumption would go to many other persons and firms in the economy, each of which would also consume two-thirds of the additional income, for a further increase in consumption spending of $4,445. The next round of consumption spending would amount to $2,963. This process would continue until the successive amounts of consumption spending became infinitely small. By that time, the total additional spending, including the original $10,000, would amount to $30,000.[7]

---

[6] Recall throughout this discussion of the multiplier that consumption, C, is defined as consumption of domestically produced goods and services. Purchases of imported goods and services are designated as M.

[7] The final effect on national income of the initial increase in spending can be determined from the formula for the sum of a geometric progression. The values for the successive rounds of spending were calculated by multiplying the previous spending times the MPC, or ${}^2/_3 \, \Delta I + ({}^2/_3)^2 \, \Delta I + ({}^2/_3)^3 \, \Delta I + \ldots + ({}^2/_3)^{n+1} \, \Delta I$, where ΔI is the initial increase in investment spending.

The formula for the sum of a geometric progression is $\Sigma \infty = a[1/(1-r)]$ where a is the initial change (ΔI in this case) and r is the value by which it is multiplied in series. Thus $[1/(1-r)] = [1/(1 - {}^2/_3)] = 3$.

When the *MPC* is $\frac{2}{3}$, the effect of the original spending will be a threefold increase in the level of national income. If the *MPC* had been $\frac{3}{4}$, each round of spending would have been larger and the final effect would have been a fourfold increase in national income for any given increase in spending. The value of the multiplier, k, is defined as

$$k = \frac{1}{1 - MPC}$$

Since $1 - MPC = MPS + MPM + MPT$, this can also be written as

$$k = \frac{1}{MPS + MPM + MPT} \text{ or } k = \frac{1}{MPW}$$

where *MPW* is the marginal propensity to withdraw, or the total of the three withdrawal factors.

This is an extremely useful conclusion, indicating that the higher the marginal propensity to consume, the greater will be the effect of increased spending on the level of national income. The importance of this effect can be recognized by letting $MPC = 1$. Since there would then be no withdrawal from spending, the value of the multiplier would be infinitely large; an increase in spending of only one dollar (or even less) would be sufficient to keep the national income increasing indefinitely!

The multiplier has the same effect on withdrawals as on injections, but in the opposite direction. If someone decides to increase the amount saved by $1,000, this reduces consumption by the same amount. That spending *would have* generated more spending, but now incomes are reduced for each of the potential recipients in what would have been successive spending rounds. The total decline in spending and national income is equal to the original decrease times the multiplier of 3 (when $MPC = \frac{2}{3}$), or $3,000.

The multiplier can be defined as the value or number by which an autonomous change in spending (such as investment) is multiplied to determine the total change in national income resulting from the initial, autonomous change in spending.

Special Cases of the Multiplier

There are two special cases of the multiplier, one related to foreign trade, and the other to government spending and taxes. The *foreign trade multiplier* shows that an economy that attempts to expand its exports in order to bolster aggregate expenditure must be prepared to take one step back for each few steps forward. An autonomous increase in exports of $1,000 represents an increase in spending and in incomes, but part of this increased income will be saved and part will be spent on imports. When $MPC = \frac{2}{3}$, $MPS = \frac{1}{6}$, $MPM = \frac{1}{6}$ (and $MPT = 0$ for simplicity), an increase in export sales of $1,000 results in increased national income of $3,000, but one-sixth or $500 of this is spent on imports. The *net* income in foreign trade is equal to the increase in exports less the increase in imports of $500.

The *balanced budget multiplier* refers to the particular case of a balanced change in a government's budget. One might expect that when tax revenues and government spending are each increased by the same amount, there will be no change in national income. To determine what *does* happen, consider the following example.

Assume again that $MPC = \frac{2}{3}$ and that $(MPS + MPM + MPT) = \frac{1}{3}$. Suppose that there is an autonomous increase in government spending of $3 billion and that this is balanced by an increase in tax revenues of $3 billion. The multiplier effect on new government spending alone would result in an increase in national income of $9 billion. But the $3 billion increase in tax revenues reduces incomes initially by $3 billion. Consumption is reduced, however, by only two-thirds of this amount (since $MPC = \Delta C/\Delta Y = \frac{2}{3}$), or by $2 billion. Therefore the multiplier effect of the reduced consumption spending is to reduce national income by three times this amount, or $6 billion. The effect of a $3 billion increase in taxes is a $6 billion decline in national income. The net effect of the balanced or equal increase in taxes and in government spending is a $3 billion increase in national income.

Try a similar case using a balanced increase of, say, $10 billion. One should find that the net effect is a $10 billion increase in national income. In fact, *the balanced budget multiplier will always have a net effect on national income equal to the initial change in taxes and in government spending, provided that these amounts are equal.* The value of the balanced budget multiplier therefore will always be equal to one.

There is an expansionary effect of government spending in spite of the balanced increase in taxes, because some of the new tax revenues would have gone into savings or imports, but the government is now directing these into expenditure for domestic goods and services. Because a change in government spending has a greater effect on national income than an equal change in taxes, government spending is said to be a more powerful weapon in influencing national income than is a change in taxes.

Estimated Multipliers The value of the multiplier used in these examples was derived from hypothetical assumptions about marginal propensities. Empirical studies of the Canadian economy have found that the value of the multiplier for a change in government expenditure is in the range of 1.0 to 2.0.[8] The low multiplier values reflect the strong influence in Canada of import spending, a high marginal propensity to save, and the progressive income tax rates. Together, these factors form a large withdrawal component.

Paradox of Thrift

The practice of saving some part of one's income has generally been regarded as a prudent habit. Not only would one be in a better position to meet financial emergencies, but well-managed savings could be expected to increase future income through interest and dividends on financial assets. It may seem paradoxical therefore that an increase in the desire to save can have a deterrent effect on national income, and will likely even lead to a lower level of actual saving.

Up to this point, the components of aggregate expenditure other than consumption have been assumed to be unaffected by the level of national income. It is more likely of course that investment and government spending will rise with increasing national income. That is, there will be spending induced by rising income, as well as autonomous spending. Exports are less likely to be related to national income levels, although some increase in exports may be expected with higher levels of output if, for example, this leads to more competitive prices for exports due to specialization and economies of scale.

Autonomous investment combined with investment induced by increases in the level of national income is shown by the upward slope of the $I + G + X$ curve in Figure 6.8. The $S + M + T$ curve reflects the initial relationship between planned savings, imports, and taxes, at the given level of GDP. If persons should decide that at this level of national income they would like to save more, with no change in planned imports or taxes, the change in desired saving would shift the $S + M + T$ curve up to $S_1 + M + T$ as in Figure 6.8.

The increase in desired saving has two important effects. The increase in planned withdrawals from spending is not matched by a change in planned injections of $I + G + X$. Reduced consumption results in excess inventories, which in turn lead to reduced employment

---

[8] Bank of Canada Technical Report 3, "Responses of various econometric models to selected policy shocks" (1983).

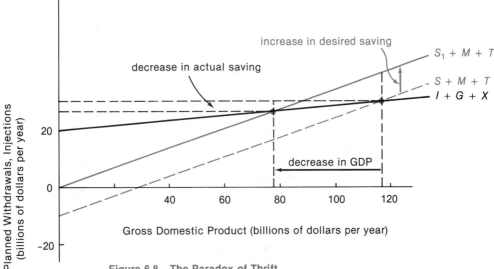

Figure 6.8   The Paradox of Thrift
With planned withdrawals at $S + M + T$, the economy is in equilibrium at a GDP of $117 billion. If, at this GDP level, households decide to increase saving, the equilibrium level of GDP falls to about $78 billion because increased saving reduces consumption, which then increases inventories beyond the desired level. Employment and output are reduced until the economy returns to equilibrium at the lower GDP. Actual saving when GDP is $78 billion is less than the actual saving when GDP was $117 billion: the attempt to save more finally led households to save less.

and output. The economy therefore is being forced away from the initial equilibrium level of national income. The multiplier increases the effect of the initial increase in saving (and decrease in spending) such that total decline in spending is somewhat greater than the initial increase in saving. National income reaches an equilibrium level at a much lower level than the initial equilibrium point.

As the level of national income falls, the average income of families and individuals falls and the absolute level of saving will also fall. The *paradox of thrift is that the intended increase in saving has led to a decrease in actual saving.*

The paradox of thrift would be less likely to occur, however, when there was a high rate of inflation, with the economy at full employment. In that case, an increase in personal saving and a decrease in consumer spending would cause a shift of resources from consumer goods to producer goods. Thus there could be true saving without a decline in real income.

Box 6.1   **Saving habit turns into major restraint on economy**

By Peter Cook

At a time when the federal Government is launching its annual Canada Savings Bond drive, economists are becoming increasingly alarmed at the preference Canadians have developed for saving rather than spending.

Plainly, a high rate of national savings has beneficial consequences; it creates a pool of capital that can be used for investment. Canadians traditionally have been zealous savers, much better at salting away their money than, for example, Americans.

But under current conditions, with the economy mired in recession, the saving habit is becoming as much a hindrance as a help.

"If you could persuade people to go out and spend next year instead of saving, you could have an economic boom on your hands," said James Webber, deputy chief economist at the Toronto-Dominion Bank. "And it would be a non-inflationary boom just because the economy is so depressed and capacity rates in industry are so low."

. . . In a time of recession, a lower level of purchasing by consumers — the main source of growth for the economy — can be a serious drain. Moreover, economists are aware that they know little about what motivates people to increase or reduce their savings.

Obviously, feelings of economic insecurity play a part. And so do incentives in the form of high returns on savings accounts. But rates of personal savings are now in uncharted territory and it is difficult to forecast when normal patterns of spending will resume.

. . . If a high savings rate does persist for a number of years, it will create an extremely poorly performing economy. In such circumstances, with income growth being held down by restraint programs, it is difficult to envisage any recovery in the economy that would have much strength to it.

. . . Any projection of what could happen to the savings rate remains essentially theoretical. But most economists do not see the rate coming down much. And as a result, they are pessimistic about prospects for the economy in the period ahead.

Mr. Webber describes the outlook for the personal savings rate in the next year or so as "the $64,000 question for economists."

Source: *The Globe and Mail*, 12 October 1982.

Actual Saving Rates

For the past several years, the personal saving rate in Canada has been above its long-term average. Through the 1960s, the saving rate — measured as the percentage of personal disposable income going to saving (including pension funds) — was about 6 per cent. But with the introduction of registered retirement savings plans in the early 1970s, followed by high interest rates in the later 1970s and early 1980s, the

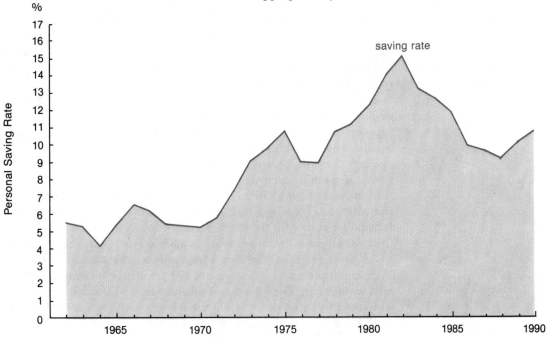

Figure 6.9   Personal Saving Rate for Canada
The personal saving rate for Canada (personal saving as a percentage of disposable income) had been about 5 to 6 per cent, and about 2 points below the saving rate in the United States, until 1972. Introduction of tax incentives to increase saving and higher interest rates pushed the Canadian saving rate to a record high of 16 per cent in 1982. At the same time the American saving rate fell to 4 or 5 per cent. The high Canadian saving rate had a strong restraining effect on the economy as it emerged from the 1982 recession.

Source: Department of Finance, *Quarterly Economic Review*.

saving rate rose sharply to reach a peak of 16 per cent in 1982. This reinforced the serious recession that had begun in 1981. (See Box 6.1.) The saving rate then dropped to 10 per cent by 1987, as shown in Figure 6.9, and has risen only slightly since then. (By contrast, the personal saving rate in the United States has been about 4 per cent in recent years.) Economic forecasts tend to show that a 1 percentage point decline in the personal saving rate in Canada is accompanied by a 0.5 percentage point increase in economic growth.

Acceleration Principle

One of the most important factors causing changes in the level of aggregate expenditure and national income is the acceleration principle. This principle, often referred to simply as the *accelerator*, describes the effect of a change in consumption, through the effect on investment, on the level of national income. The accelerator refers to the fact that an increase in spending for consumer goods can lead to an even greater percentage increase in the factors of production required to produce those goods.

A simple arithmetic example may illustrate this relationship and the assumptions underlying the acceleration principle. Table 6.2 presents hypothetical data for a firm producing fibreglass skis (both cross-country and downhill). Assume that for every 10,000 skis produced annually the firm requires one machine, and that the firm replaces one worn-out machine each year.

In the years prior to 1982, the firm was selling a constant 50,000 skis annually; thus there was no change from year to year in the level of demand for skis or for the machines used in their manufacture. But in 1982, ski sales rose by 20 per cent. In addition to purchasing the usual replacement machine, the firm added another machine to its capital stock; this represented an increase of 100 per cent in its annual level of gross investment. The next year brought a boom in ski sales: ski consumption rose by 67 per cent while machine purchases rose by 150 per cent. Although the 1984 sales held steady at the 1983 level, the firm was able to reduce its purchases of machines to the one machine required annually as a replacement for old equipment. The annual level of gross investment fell by 80 per cent. In 1985, the level of investment again increased sharply, but then fell back just as quickly in 1987.

There was no *fixed* numerical relationship between the percentage changes in consumption and in investment; the 20 per cent increase in consumption in 1982 *accelerated* investment to a 100 per cent increase, but to maintain the doubling of investment realized in 1985, consumption would have had to increase in 1986 by 27 per cent.

Table 6.2

Accelerator Effects on Investment: Example of a Hypothetical Firm

Year	Consumption (skis per year in thousands)	Machines Required	Investment — Additional	Replace-ment	Total	Investment Change %	Consumption Change %
			(number of machines)				
1981	50	5	0	1	1	0	0
1982	60	6	1	1	2	100	20
1983	100	10	4	1	5	150	67
1984	100	10	0	1	1	−80	0
1985	110	11	1	1	2	100	10
1986	120	12	1	1	2	0	9
1987	120	12	0	1	1	−50	0

Assumptions   Important assumptions underlie the acceleration principle. One (not illustrated in the example), is that when consumption falls, *firms do not dispose of unused machinery*. However, if ski sales had dropped to 50,000 units in 1984, the firm *might* have sold its unused machines to firms using such machines for another product, if the firm expected sales to remain at the new low level for some time. If firms could and would dispose of unneeded machinery when sales fell in one area, an increase in sales in another area would not have so strong an effect on investment, because productive capacity would be transferred to where it was required.

It is also assumed that *firms are operating at full capacity*. If the ski firm had been operating at only five-sixths of its capacity when sales were at 50,000 units, the increased sales of 1982 could have been produced without adding to productive capacity and without any change in the usual level of annual investment.

The acceleration principle also assumes that *firms expect annual sales to remain at the new higher level*; it would be unprofitable to purchase a new machine only for short-term use.

Finally, it is assumed that there is a high elasticity of supply of investment goods, that is, *firms supplying the investment goods (or machines) can respond immediately* to meet the accelerated demand for this equipment.

Although none of these assumptions is universally valid, the effects of the acceleration principle are nevertheless evident and have been shown to account for some of the wide swings in economic activity.

Accelerator-Multiplier Interaction   Since the multiplier amplifies the effects on national income of a change in planned investment, the multiplier also interacts with the accelerator to reinforce the effects on national income of a change in consumption and investment. The increased investment means higher output and incomes in the machine industry. This higher income is then multiplied through successive rounds of spending to result in higher national income. Similarly, sharp declines in investment due to the accelerator effect are also multiplied, leading to even sharper drops in national income.

National Income at Full Employment

Two of Canada's basic economic goals, as outlined in the preceding chapter, are full employment and price stability. A desirable level of national income would be the level at which these two goals could be achieved. The economy's objective therefore is to realize an equilibrium level of national income at full employment and without inflation.

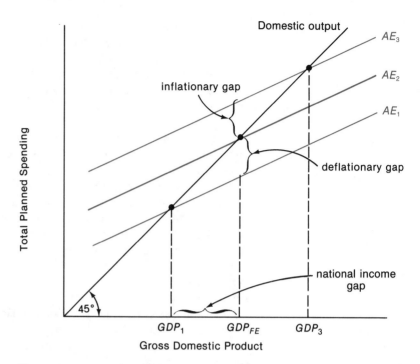

Figure 6.10   Inflationary and Deflationary Gaps
AE_2 shows the level of aggregate expenditure required at various levels of
GDP to move the economy to the full-employment level of GDP_{FE}. The
deflationary gap is the increase in planned spending required for
equilibrium at the full-employment level. Similarly, the inflationary gap is the
required decrease in planned spending.

The estimated potential output when the economy is operating at
full employment is shown in Figure 6.10 as GDP_{FE}. If planned aggregate expenditure were at AE_2, the economy would be in equilibrium
exactly at the full-employment level of national income, because
planned spending would be just sufficient for the full employment of
the economy's resources. But because the total of planned spending is
dependent on many diverse factors, there is no reason to expect that
aggregate expenditure will necessarily be at AE_2, or that it would
remain at this level for any length of time.

Deflationary Gap   If planned aggregate expenditure is at AE_1, spending will not be sufficient to maintain full employment. The *additional*
spending required to bring the economy to the full-employment level
of national income is referred to as the *deflationary gap*, because the
inadequacy of spending has a deflating or depressing effect on the
economy.

Note that the size of the deflationary gap shown in Figure 6.10 is less
than the GDP gap, or the national income gap — the difference

between GDP_{FE} and GDP_1, or between national income at full employment and the national income resulting from the lower aggregate expenditure. The deflationary gap illustrates the potential effect of the multiplier. If an initial injection of spending equal to the deflationary gap can be realized when the economy is at GDP_1 the multiplier will act on this spending to raise the national income by more than the initial expenditure.

Inflationary Gap   What happens if planned aggregate expenditure is greater than full-employment output, as at AE_3? In this case the economy is in equilibrium where the total value of output or national income *exceeds* the full-employment level. Such an equilibrium level of national income above the full-employment level can be achieved only through an increase in prices. There would be no increase in *real* output—since the economy is already at full employment—but the increase in prices would increase the *monetary value* of the full-employment level of output. The amount by which planned spending exceeds the spending required for full employment in this case is termed the *inflationary gap*, since it is this excess spending that is causing inflation.

Aggregate Demand

The emphasis in the theory of national income determination, up to this point, has been on total spending—or aggregate expenditure—for final goods and services that would be planned or desired at each level of national income (or GDP). The general level of prices was assumed to be constant: there was neither inflation nor deflation. Shifts in the aggregate expenditure curve at a given level of national income were caused by conditions other than a change in prices; consumption spending, for example, likely would increase if there were a decrease in personal income taxes; and investment spending would fall if the interest rate rose. In this next stage, however, the general level of prices is no longer held constant, and the total spending that would provide an equilibrium level of national income at each price level is termed *aggregate demand* in order to distinguish it from aggregate expenditure. (In each case, the components of total spending are the same—consumption, investment, government, and net exports.)

The aggregate demand curve represents the equilibrium level of national income—where planned aggregate expenditure is equal to actual domestic output—that would occur at each price level.

The derivation of the aggregate demand curve is illustrated in Figure 6.11a. Suppose that planned aggregate expenditure in an economy is at AE_2, and that the equilibrium level of national income (real GDP) is $40 billion. Assume also that the price level, as measured by the GDP implicit price index (or GDP deflator), is at 100. If prices then rise, the purchasing power of consumers' financial assets—including currency, bank deposits, and savings bonds—will decline and there will be a drop in consumer spending. Net export spending would also fall because expenditures for exports likely would decline as prices rose, and spending for imports would likely rise. Moreover, the resulting drop in planned aggregate expenditures would occur at any level of national income. This is represented as a downward shift in the aggregate expenditure curve to AE_1.

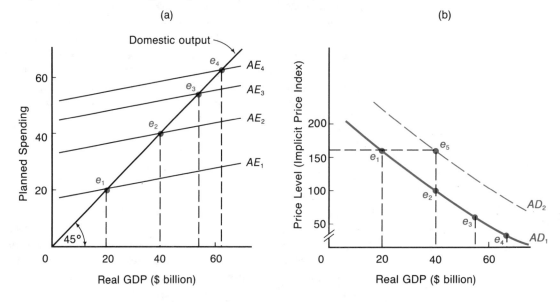

Figure 6.11   Aggregate Expenditure and Aggregate Demand
The aggregate expenditure curve AE_4 represents total planned spending at a low price level. As prices rise, the AE curve shifts downward toward AE_1. Consequently, there is a different equilibrium level of national income for each price level, shown by e_1 to e_4.
  When these equilibrium levels of national income are plotted against the price levels with which they are associated, the plotted points e_1 to e_4 represent the aggregate demand curve AD_1. If aggregate expenditure changes, *at a given price level*, the shift in the AE curve also shifts aggregate demand, as indicated by AD_2, with a new equilibrium level of national income, e_5.

The excess supply that would result, when planned aggregate expenditure (at AE_1) is less than the real domestic output, would trigger the same adjustment process that was described earlier in the chapter. Workers would be laid off and output would fall until the economy was in equilibrium at real GDP of $20 billion.

A decrease in the price level would have the opposite effect: planned aggregate expenditure would shift upward from AE_2 to AE_3 as consumers found that they could purchase a greater quantity of output with their given financial assets. (A further drop in prices would shift the expenditure curve to AE_4.) As producers responded to the excess demand for goods and services, output would increase, and the equilibrium level of national income would rise.

Figure 6.11a shows four different planned aggregate expenditure curves, each associated with a different price level, and with four different equilibrium levels of national income. The higher the price level, the lower the AE curves and the lower the equilibrium level of national income; the four equilibrium combinations are identified as e_1 to e_4.

These same combinations of price level and national income at which the economy is in equilibrium (where planned aggregate expenditure equals domestic output) are plotted in Figure 6.11b. The curve obtained by plotting e_1 to e_4 is the economy's aggregate demand curve.

The aggregate demand curve represents, for each price level, the level of national income at which planned aggregate expenditure would equal actual domestic output. Note that the aggregate demand curve is *not* the summation of the market demand curves for individual items. Although these latter market demand curves are downward sloping, reflecting the greater quantity purchased at lower prices, they show the responses of consumers to change in prices for separate goods and services rather than the response of total spending to changes in the general price level. In the case of individual items, price changes result in quantity changes that are based mainly on substitutability or complementarity of goods and services; in the general case, the response to price variation is related to the purchasing power of given assets.

Shifts in Aggregate Demand

Shifts in the aggregate demand curve, such as the shift in Figure 6.11b from AD_1 to AD_2, occur because there are changes *other than* a change in the general level of prices. Any change in economic conditions that increases planned spending for consumption, investment, government expenditures, or net exports, and produces a shift in the AE curve, *at the given price level*, results in an increase (or outward shift) of the aggregate demand curve. That is, a change in prices shifted the aggregate expenditure curve from AE_1 to AE_2 in Figure 6.11a, and the equilibrium combination shifted from e_1 to e_2; this resulted in a *movement along* the aggregate demand curve, AD_1, from e_1 to e_2. But if the foreign exchange value of the Canadian dollar were to decline, so that

Canadian goods could be bought by foreigners at a lower price, or if a retail sales tax were removed and consumer spending increased, aggregate expenditure would increase from AE_1 to AE_2 *at the same price level*, and the new equilibrium would be shown as e_5 on AD_2 in Figure 6.11b. Conversely, a decrease in aggregate expenditure at the given price level results in a decrease, or inward shift, of the aggregate demand curve. Changes in economic conditions that produce a shift in aggregate demand are usually described by economists as "shocks" to the economic system. (Although the "shock" may occur gradually and without apparent trauma, the term does emphasize that the result is a shift of the entire AD curve rather than a movement along the curve.)

One should also note that the *distance* of the shift in the AD curve is related to the multiplier effect of a change in aggregate expenditure on national income. In Figure 6.11a, for example, the increased initial spending that produces the vertical shift from AE_1 to AE_2 increases national income by \$20 billion. This is the equivalent increase in national income indicated by the shift of AD_1 to AD_2, and e_1 to e_5, in Figure 6.11b.

Aggregate Supply

In the first stage in national income theory, the equilibrium level of national income occurred when planned aggregate expenditure was equal to the actual domestic output. Now the supply side of the economy, when the price level is no longer held constant, can be portrayed by aggregate supply.

Aggregate supply is the total output of final goods and services that firms would wish to provide at each level of output prices.

This definition of aggregate supply assumes that the level of *input* prices (for labour, energy, transportation, and so on) remains constant. Changes in input prices will be incorporated into the theory at a later stage. In the simple Keynesian model, the aggregate supply curve was assumed to resemble a reverse-L, as illustrated by the broken line in Figure 6.12a. As long as there were some unemployment, firms could increase real output at the prevailing price level because there would be no change in their output costs per unit. When the economy reached the full-employment level, however, there could be no further increase in real output and any increase in aggregate demand beyond that level would only lead to rising prices. Economic conditions of the 1970s and 1980s, however, showed that prices would begin to rise before full employment occurred; indeed, the rate of inflation would accelerate as the economy moved toward full employment. Consequently, the aggregate supply curve takes the shape shown in Figure 6.12a. This indicates that as the economy approaches full employment,

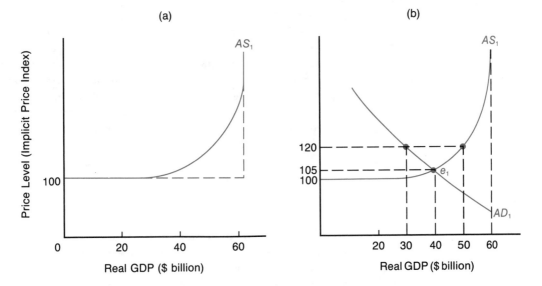

Figure 6.12　Aggregate Supply and Equilibrium with Aggregate Demand
The aggregate supply curve is approximately horizontal at low levels of real output and employment, but as the economy approaches full employment, greater output is offered only at higher prices because producers' costs per unit increase. (The simple Keynesian supply curve is shown by the broken line.)

The intersection of AS_1 and AD_1 indicates that when the price level is 105, the equilibrium level of national income is $40 billion. At the higher price level, there would be disequilibrium, because equilibrium could be achieved only at real output of $30 billion, but producers would want to offer $50 billion in output.

firms are able to increase their output — despite constant input prices — only at higher prices for their outputs because the production costs per unit are rising. These costs may increase for several reasons: additional workers that are hired to produce more output may be less skilled or experienced; machinery breaks down and employee absenteeism increases when firms operate beyond their normal capacity; less reliable sources and lower quality of inputs may be encountered as firms expand; and so on.

Equilibrium of AS and AD

The equilibrium level of national income, when the price level was constant, occurred when planned aggregate expenditure was equal to actual domestic output. Now, with the use of the aggregate demand

and aggregate supply curves, it is possible to determine the equilibrium combination of national income and the price level. This combination is shown in Figure 6.12b at the intersection, e_1, of aggregate demand (AD_1) and aggregate supply (AS_1). The meaning of this equilibrium can be better understood by considering the disequilibrium that would occur, for example, at a higher price level. In Figure 6.12b, at a price level of 120, there is excess aggregate supply of $20 billion. As firms adjust by reducing their output, the price level would fall, with purchasers then increasing the quantity demanded until equilibrium is reached.

Changes in Equilibrium

Changes in the combined equilibrium of the price level and national income occur whenever there are shifts in aggregate demand or aggregate supply. Changes in aggregate demand occur for reasons such as those mentioned previously—a drop in the foreign exchange value of the Canadian dollar or removal of a retail sales tax—as well as for other reasons. These include the factors that were described earlier to explain shifts in aggregate expenditure that would change the equilibrium level of national income. For consumers, these included changes in personal income taxes, in consumers' expectations about their future incomes, and in interest rates; for producers, they included changes in expectations about profitability (or yield rate) in general, or about future sales to export markets, and changes in corporate profit taxes.

Changes in aggregate supply also may occur for a variety of reasons. Improved productivity, with a greater output from a given quantity of inputs, reduces per unit costs and increases aggregate supply at any given price level. Other factors may increase output costs, even with input prices held constant; these would include costs imposed on employers such as increased premiums for unemployment insurance and health insurance, or costs imposed for compliance with government regulations concerning pollution or employee health and safety. Conversely, government subsidies to employers reduce output costs and increase aggregate supply.

Finally, one can consider the effect of changes in the prices of inputs such as labour, and materials, energy, and transportation. Input prices had previously been held constant to reduce possible confusion with the effects of changes in the general level of output prices. When input prices rise, there is likely to be an increase in output costs *at any given level of output*, and therefore an inward shift of the aggregate supply curve. (This differs from the upward slope of the aggregate supply curve depicting increasing costs per unit as output increases.)

The consequences of such shifts are illustrated in Figure 6.13. As aggregate demand increases from AD_1 to AD_2, given that aggregate supply is AS_1, the new equilibrium occurs at a higher price level and greater real output. But a further increase in aggregate demand, from AD_2 to AD_3, results mainly in a higher price level with little increase in real output. But with aggregate demand at AD_3, an increase in aggregate supply—even in the steeply sloped portion of the curve—from AS_1 to AS_2, results in some reduction of the price level but a large increase in real output.

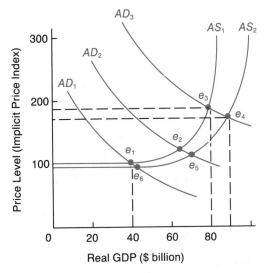

Figure 6.13   Changes in Equilibrium
Changes in the general equilibrium can occur because there are shifts in aggregate demand and/or in aggregate supply. As the *AD* curve shifts upward along AS_1, real output increases but the price level also rises more quickly. At e_2, there is both unemployment and inflation. An increase in aggregate supply to AS_2 would increase real output and reduce inflation and unemployment, for example, from e_3 to e_4.

Review of the Main Points

1. Classical economists argued that "supply creates its own demand", or that all output would be purchased. Flexible prices, wages, and interest rates would assure that there would always be full employment. However, Keynes observed during the Depression of the 1930s that an economy would become stuck at high levels of unemployment.

2. In the Keynesian model of national income determination, the components of aggregate expenditure are consumption, investment, government expenditures, and exports. Consumption is spending for domestic goods and services; saving represents the postponement of consumption. The fraction of total income used for consumption is the average propensity to consume; the fraction of additional income going to consumption is the marginal propensity to consume. Similar calculations are made for the average and marginal propensities to import and to save. $APC + APM + APS = 1$ and $MPC + MPM + MPS = 1$.

3. Investment is new plant and equipment, new residential construction, and real additions to inventories. As long as the marginal efficiency of investment, or the expected rate of return on each additional investment project, exceeds the interest rate on borrowed funds, there will be investment spending. In the simple case, investment is autonomous—or unaffected by changes in the level of national income. In a more realistic model, some investment is induced by increasing incomes.

4. Government spending in the national income model excludes transfer payments, since most or all of these increase aggregate expenditure through consumption spending out of individuals' incomes. Again, in the simple case, government spending may be assumed to be autonomous, but in a more complex model, government spending rises with national income. Export spending consists of foreign purchases and therefore is the component of aggregate expenditure least dependent on the level of national income. Imports are subtracted to reflect the total spending for domestically produced goods and services

5. Each major sector—consumers, investors, governments, and foreign buyers—determines planned expenditures independently and for each level of income. The economy is at its equilibrium level of national income when the total planned aggregate expenditure is equal to the actual domestic output. When the economy is not at equilibrium, inventories are above or below desired levels; producers adjust by decreasing or increasing employment. If any sector changes its planned expenditures, the economy will return to equilibrium at some other level of national income.

6. The multiplier effect of successive rounds of spending increases national income by more than the initial increase in spending. The size of the multiplier is determined by the size of the marginal propensity to consume. Two special cases of the multiplier—in the foreign trade sector and in the government's balanced budget—emphasize that an increase in exports will usually induce an increase in imports, and that an equal increase in government expenditures and tax revenues will increase national income by the same amount.

7. If individuals collectively try to increase saving at any given level of income, they will actually save less because the withdrawal of spending will lead to a lower level of national income: this is called the paradox of thrift.

8. The accelerator is the effect that a change in consumption has on the level of investment. Accelerated investment, when combined with the multiplier effect, can produce wide swings in the level of economic activity.

9. The deflationary gap is the additional spending required to raise

the level of planned aggregate expenditure sufficiently to lead the economy to the full-employment level of national income. An inflationary gap is the reduction in planned aggregate expenditure required to return the economy to the full-employment level of output.

10. Planned aggregate expenditure is the total spending desired at each level of national income, given a certain general level of output prices. Aggregate demand is the equilibrium level of national income that would occur at various price levels. Shifts in aggregate demand occur when aggregate expenditure changes for non-price reasons.

11. Aggregate supply slopes upward as the economy approaches full employment, and will shift with changes other than in the level of output prices.

12. The intersection of aggregate supply and aggregate demand determines the equilibrium level of national income and the general price level.

Key Concepts and Topics

laissez-faire
Say's law
Keynesian revolution
aggregate expenditure
consumption (domestic vs. total)
saving
investment
propensity to consume
propensity to save
propensity to import
average vs. marginal propensity
shift in aggregate expenditure
expected yield
marginal efficiency of investment
investment demand
government spending
exports
domestic output

equality line
equilibrium national income
unplanned inventories
planned injections
planned withdrawals
multiplier
balanced budget multiplier
foreign trade multiplier
paradox of thrift
accelerator (acceleration principle)
inflationary gap
deflationary gap
national income gap
aggregate demand
aggregate supply
general price level
output vs. input prices

Questions for Review and Discussion

1. What logical connection(s) is (are) there between the way the term "investment" is used in economics and the way this word is used in the world of financial affairs?

2. What is the difference between autonomous investment and induced investment? How does an autonomous increase in investment affect GDP?

3. Explain carefully the difference between a shift in the *MEI* curve and a movement along this curve, and outline the factors that cause each of these changes.

4. Explain why the domestic output curve is shown as a 45° line, when the scales on both axes are the same.

5. Why is the value of the multiplier calculated from the marginal propensity to consume rather than from the average propensity to consume?

6. "If the marginal propensity to consume were always equal to one, for all persons at all times, there would be no equilibrium level of national income." Do you agree? Explain.

7. Consider how the accelerator principle can be used to explain (and predict) the boom in school construction and the teacher shortage of the 1955–65 period compared with the closing of schools and the teacher surplus in the 1975–1985 period?

8. Which industries do you think would show the strongest influence of the acceleration principle? Explain carefully.

9. Why is the combination of price level and GDP at which the *AD* and *AS* curves intersect necessarily the only equilibrium position that can be sustained in the economy, all other things being equal?

Sources and Selected Readings

Dornbusch, R., S. Fisher, and G. Sparks. *Macroeconomics*, 3rd ed. Toronto: McGraw-Hill Ryerson, 1989.

Heilbroner, Robert L., and J.K. Galbraith. *Understanding Macroeconomics*, rev. ed. Englewood Cliffs, N.J.: Prentice-Hall, 1987.

Keynes, John Maynard. *The General Theory of Employment, Interest, and Money.* London: Macmillan, 1936.

Parkin, Michael, and Robin Bade. *Modern Macroeconomics*, 2nd ed. Scarborough, Ont.: Prentice-Hall, 1986.

Stewart, Michael. *Keynes and After*, rev. ed. Baltimore: Penguin Books, 1986.

Wilton, D.A., and D.M. Prescott. *Macroeconomics: Theory and Policy in Canada*, 2nd ed. Toronto: Addison-Wesley, 1987.

7 Money and Banking in Canada

What Is Money?

Since the next chapter will show that changes in the money supply can have substantial effects on the performance of the economy, it is important to know precisely what is meant by "money" and how it is possible to change the total quantity of money available to the economy.

In order to understand the nature of money, consider first something that interests most people, namely food. Two different answers might be given to the question, What is food? One answer would list the *functions* of food: it nourishes the body; it provides epicurean delight; it may even act as a pacifier for neurotics. A different type of answer would list the numerous *items that serve as food*, from raw fish to roast beef. Similarly, the question, What is money? is answered in terms of its functions and the items serving these functions.

What Does Money Do?

Medium of Exchange The most obvious use for money is as a *medium of exchange* in the innumerable transactions occurring every day in the Canadian economy. No longer does anyone purchase goods or services by offering goats, beads, or beaver skins. Occasionally a guitar may be swapped or traded for part ownership of a motorcycle, but this can be treated as a unique case; the person who gave up the guitar does not make a continuous practice of purchasing items by trading guitars. Instead, it is money that is normally used to buy goods and services and it is money that is readily accepted by the sellers of these commodities.

Money is therefore defined as something readily and widely accepted as a medium for the exchange of goods and services.

Unit of Account An equally common but less obvious function of money is as a *unit of account*; prices of all goods and services can be expressed in terms of money. The selling price of an automobile is stated as 12,295 dollars, not 7 cows or 165 days of manual labour. Anyone who has travelled in another country can appreciate how important it is that prices be expressed in terms of the medium of exchange (or currency) with which one is familiar. Canadian tourists have been heard to mutter in front of store windows around the world, "How much is that in our money?" Although they may be carrying foreign currency, the unit of account they are using to determine the relative prices of the goods is the Canadian dollar.

Store of Value   The third function of money is as a *store of value*. Since the value of the goods and services that can be purchased in the present can be expressed in terms of money, it follows that the total claim on future goods and services can also be expressed in terms of money. To say that one's assets are worth $10,000 is to say that one has a claim on goods and services valued or priced at a total of $10,000.

Money is an extremely convenient way to hold the value of postponed consumption of goods and services, since money can be stored more easily than any other commodity. One disadvantage, however, is that prices may rise, resulting in a lower future consumption in real terms. Some people who expect price increases may prefer to buy and store consumer goods, while others hold assets, such as real estate, which tend to rise in price as the prices of consumer goods rise.

Alternatively, if prices fall, persons who hold money rather than stocks of consumer goods will find that they can buy *more* goods in the future. But even if inflation seems inevitable, most persons will use money as some of their store of value because it is so convenient to have it available for short-term needs.

Standard of Debts   Since money serves so well as a store of value or as a measure of one's assets, it also serves well as a *standard of deferred payments*, or debts. One's debts can be recorded in terms of money, and can be repaid with money.

Characteristics of Money

The purposes that money must serve determine its major characteristics. There are many transactions to be made every day and in several locations: the bus stop, the cafeteria, the newsstand, the drycleaner, and so on. Money must be not only readily acceptable, it must also be *easy to carry*, but not so small that it is easily lost. A five-dollar coin the size of a Canadian nickel could be lost or misplaced easily. At the other extreme, the use of paper currency for denominations of less than one dollar would be a nuisance.

Money must also be *divisible*, so that very small transactions (such as the purchase of postage stamps and matches) can be accommodated. Thus most monetary units, whether dollars, pounds, francs, or liras, are divided into 100 parts, called cents, centimes, and so on. Money should also be *durable* enough to be exchanged in many transactions and to be carried or held by many persons in succession.

Evolution of Money

Money is one of the major inventions of mankind, an invention that made it possible to abandon the barter system and to develop the division and specialization of labour. Barter required what has been called a *coincidence of wants*. Someone who wanted a cow and was willing to offer fifty bushels of grain in exchange needed to find a person who not only wanted to trade a cow, but also was willing to take fifty bushels of grain (or less) in return. The major disadvantage of the barter system, however, was that it acted as a deterrent to the specialization of labour and trade. Under the barter system it was more convenient to be self-sufficient — to produce only the amount of each commodity that one's family required.

Early Problems   Items such as spices, salt, and finely made clothing or shoes could not be produced by each family, however, and early forms of money emerged to facilitate trade in these items. Gold, silver, and other rare metals were used because the demand for them for ornamental uses had established their high value. Furthermore, the physical amount required for most transactions was quite small.

The convenience of gold to facilitate trade was partly offset by other problems. Since every transaction required a different amount of gold, it was necessary to measure precisely the right number of ounces or grams in each case. This was not only a nuisance, it also provoked disputes about the reliability of the weigh-scales that were used. This problem was met by striking or making coins containing a specific amount of gold or other metal; this amount was then stamped on the face of the coin. Coins of various values were produced so that the proper combination of coins could be presented to meet almost any asking price.

Goldsmith Receipts   Money also had to be kept safe from theft. Persons who had considerable quantities of gold and gold coins began to deposit these with the local goldsmith or jeweller for safe-keeping. The goldsmith issued a receipt for the deposit, perhaps adding a promise that the required amount of gold would be available whenever the depositor required it. People soon realized that it was a nuisance to collect gold from the goldsmith each time a large purchase was made, and to take gold back to the shop following each major sale. Instead, the goldsmith's receipt could be exchanged for the item being purchased.

This process could continue as long as the recipients of the goldsmith's receipt were confident that there actually was gold "backing" the receipt or certificate. Only occasionally would someone demand gold from the goldsmith in exchange for the receipt, perhaps to make a purchase in another town, or because a prospective seller would not accept the receipt, or simply to confirm that the gold was available.

The goldsmith found that on any given day the depositors would ask for only a very small proportion of the gold. Some of the gold could be loaned to borrowers, provided that the goldsmith did not loan too much and that the repayments were arranged to assure that the goldsmith would always have enough to meet the depositors' demands.

The borrowers likely would not take loans in the form of gold, but rather as goldsmith's receipts, since they too were able to use the receipts to make purchases. Thus gold held by the goldsmith represented only a fraction of the claims on gold represented by the outstanding receipts. The smaller this fraction, the larger were the profits to be made on loans. But the risk of being unable to meet the demand for gold on any given day also became greater as the ratio of claims to actual gold holdings increased.

From Goldsmith to Banker

Gradually, the goldsmiths found it more profitable to spend their time as bankers than as craftsmen. As banks developed, the goldsmith's receipt was replaced by paper currency printed by the banks. This paper currency needed to be backed by gold or silver, at least to some reasonable fraction of the face value of the currency, if it was to be readily accepted. A "run" on a bank would occur when it was discovered that the bank could not meet demands to convert the bank currency into gold or silver. Even the suspicion that a bank was not holding sufficient gold could lead to its collapse, if enough depositors demanded their funds at one time. Many such "runs" occurred and many banks failed during the nineteenth and early twentieth centuries, until banks came under closer government regulation and supervision.[1]

Legal Tender

It is only relatively recently that the paper currency of the private banks has been replaced by the *legal tender* or *fiat money* issued by central banks under government direction. Most countries now have a

---

[1] Even with government regulation and supervision, banks can fail. The Canadian Commercial Bank and the Northland Bank both collapsed in 1986 because of a large volume of loans that could not be repaid. But most depositors were covered by insurance provided through the Canada Deposit Insurance Corporation, with funds augmented by the federal government.

central bank operating under varying degrees of government control. Canada's central bank, the Bank of Canada (described more fully later in this chapter), is the only institution in Canada that can issue *legal tender: the only currency that, by law, must be accepted for payments of debts.*

Legal tender includes both coins and paper currency. Although the metal contained in the coins has some value, it is much less than the face value of the coins. There is no gold, other metal, or any other commodity backing Canada's paper currency. What now matters more than whether paper currency is convertible into gold is whether the currency can be easily counterfeited, whether too much or too little money is put into circulation, and whether the government is pursuing other appropriate policies for price stability.

Cheques   The practice of depositing gold or gold coins with the goldsmith gave rise to another form of money, in addition to the goldsmith's receipt or gold certificate. Depositors might not wish to transfer *all* of their gold holdings to someone else; they could not therefore simply pass on the goldsmith's receipt for the full amount. Instead, the depositors could write a note requesting the goldsmith to give a stated amount of gold to the person(s) specified in the note. The recipient of the note might decide to "cash" the note, that is, actually withdraw the gold, or might simply have the goldsmith issue a receipt acknowledging the transfer of a claim to a specified amount of gold.

This process has continued almost unchanged in the modern use of bank deposits, with cheques written against these deposits or accounts to make payments as required. But it is the deposit account, and not the cheque, that is counted as money. The cheque simply provides a convenient method for transferring this money.

Similarly, it is important to recognize that credit cards are not money. They are simply a very durable and portable certificate of credit showing that a bank or other corporation is prepared to extend short-term credit to the cardholder, by agreeing to reimburse the merchant who accepts the individual's credit card.

Another innovation to assist consumers in making monetary exchanges is the *debit card*. In this case, the cardholder pays for a purchase by authorizing a bank or other financial institution to deduct from his or her account the appropriate amount and transfer this amount to the merchant concerned. The advantage of the debit card is that an individual does not need to use cheques to make monthly payments, the merchant does not need to submit credit-card vouchers to the financial institutions to receive monthly payments, and both merchants and banks can avoid the cost and risk in processing cash and cheques. Debit cards were introduced in small pilot programs in the late 1980s, and on a larger scale in Ottawa in 1990, but major retailers such as department and grocery chains have taken a "wait and see" approach.

Definitions of Money Supply

Money is a stock; that is, a certain quantity of it exists at a given point in time. It must be distinguished from income, which is a monetary measure of the output (or payment received) over a certain period of time.

The quantity of money available in the economy at any given time is often defined simply as the total value of coins and paper currency in circulation outside the banks and the total value of bank deposits.

Coins and paper currency held inside the banks cannot be included in a measure of the money supply since these are not immediately available for spending. They become available only when a deposit is withdrawn in the form of currency, or a cheque is cashed rather than deposited. The value of *coins and currency in circulation* at the end of 1990 was almost $20 billion.[2] About 90 per cent of this was in notes (or paper currency), and about 10 per cent was in coins. Yet, as Table 7.1 shows, coins and currency were only a small percentage of the total money supply.

M1   The total value of bank deposits includes many different types of deposits and hence requires more precise definitions of the money supply. The basic definition of money has been the narrowly defined money supply, M1. This includes *currency outside the banks* and *demand deposits at the chartered banks, excluding Government of Canada deposits.*[3] The latter are excluded from measures of the money supply because these deposits can be shifted from the chartered banks

---

[2] This quantity of coins and currency represents about $750 per person in Canada, an amount far greater than persons normally hold for transaction purposes. It would seem therefore that much of the currency "in circulation" is actually hoarded in cookie jars and elsewhere as an alternative to bank deposits. Much of the currency is also held by retail stores and similar firms that receive currency rather than cheques from their customers. Currency is also used extensively in the "underground economy" that was described in Chapter 5, since cash payments cannot be easily traced for income tax purposes. As that part of the economy grows, so does the use of paper currency.

[3] Demand deposits are payable on demand, as distinct from notice deposits, for which banks can legally require some days' notice before they are withdrawn. But this right is seldom if ever used. Term deposits are those committed for a specified period of time. A much lower interest rate is paid if the deposit is withdrawn before the specified due date.

Table 7.1

Money Supply in Canada, December 1990
(billions of dollars)

Items included	Amount	per cent of total M3
M1 = Currency outside banks (notes and coins) plus:	$ 19.8	6.3
Chartered banks demand deposits (Can.$) (excluding Government of Canada deposits of $3.2 billion)	20.9	
Total M1	$ 40.7	13.0
M2 = M1 plus:		
Personal savings deposits	198.9	
Non-personal notice deposits	24.5	
Total M2	$264.1	84.2
M3 = M2 plus:		
Non-personal fixed-term deposits	43.8	49.7
Foreign currency deposits of Canadian residents	5.9	
Total M3	$313.8	100.0
M2 + = M2 plus:		
Deposits at other financial institutions (Trust and mortgage loan companies, Credit unions and *caisses populaires*, Provincial banks (Alberta and Ontario))	136.3	
Total	$450.1	

Source: *Bank of Canada Review.*

to the Bank of Canada as part of a specific monetary policy and because the federal government deposits change in response to specific fiscal policies. Since these deposits are so closely related to the initial stages of economic policies, they also cannot be included in any measure used to monitor the effects of the policies. Federal government deposits are nonetheless available for spending, and amounted to about $3 billion at the end of 1990.

The demand deposits included in M1 consist of personal chequing accounts (but not chequable savings accounts) and the current or chequing accounts of businesses and of provincial and local governments and their agencies.

M2   The broadly defined money supply, termed M2, includes personal savings deposits plus non-personal notice deposits, in addition to the M1 items.

M3   Another category, M3, adds in all other deposits at the chartered banks (non-personal fixed-term, and foreign currency deposits of Canadian residents, but still excluding Government of Canada deposits).

M2 +   In recognition of the increasing importance of non-bank financial institutions, another category, M2 +, was created recently. This includes M2 items plus deposits at trust and mortgage loan companies, and credit unions and *caisses populaires*, and personal deposits at provincial governments' savings offices in Alberta and Ontario.

Near-Money   A related category, *near-money*, should be considered when the money supply is measured, because some types of assets can easily be converted into bank deposits, and thus represent a potential sharp increase in the money supply. Near-money includes the general public's holdings of federal government bills, bonds, and savings bonds, because these can be readily sold or redeemed and converted to chequable deposits. But they are not money because they cannot be used directly as a medium of exchange.

Canadian Banking System

Chartered Banks

The Canadian *banking system* consists of the chartered banks and a central bank, the Bank of Canada. These form an important part of the larger *financial system*, which includes institutions performing only some of the functions of chartered banks: trust companies, insurance companies, mortgage companies, savings banks, credit unions (and *caisses populaires* in Quebec), mutual and pension funds, consumer finance and other financial acceptance companies, and stock and bond brokers.

Until 1987, the four major components of the financial system — bankers, trust companies, investment dealers, and insurance companies — had separate functions and were chartered and regulated under separate legislation. But amendments were made to federal and provincial legislation in 1987 to permit each of these institutions to compete with the others in offering a full range of financial services. This meant that the banks could then act as investment dealers and advisors, while insurance companies could offer consumer and commercial loans.[4] In reality, however, the new services would be offered by subsidiary firms that would specialize in each function. Such firms could be acquired by take-overs since the new legislation permitted, for example, a bank to own 100 per cent of the shares in an investment dealership or insurance company. Supervision of these industries was unified by combining the previous Inspector General of Banks and the Supervisor of Insurance under the new Superintendent of Financial Institutions.

Each bank — but not each branch — continues to be chartered by Parliament under the Bank Act and is regulated by the provisions of this Act. At mid-year 1991 there were only ten domestic (or "Schedule 1") chartered banks in Canada. In order of their total assets these were: the Royal Bank, Canadian Imperial Bank of Commerce, Bank of Montreal, Bank of Nova Scotia, Toronto-Dominion Bank, National Bank, Laurentian Bank, Canadian Western Bank, B.C. Bancorp, and Continental Bank of Canada. There were fourteen domestic banks in 1981, but mergers and bank failures have reduced the total number. The first five banks listed — the "Big Five" — account for almost 95 per cent of the total assets of all Canadian chartered banks.

A revision of the Bank Act in 1980 altered the Canadian banking scene quite abruptly by granting full banking status to foreign (or "Schedule 2") banks. This opened the way for about 60 foreign banks to be licensed for operation in Canada, and assured a place for Canadian chartered banks to operate in other countries. Some of the largest foreign banks now include: the Hongkong Bank of Canada, Citibank (U.S.), Barclays Bank (England), Banque Nationale de Paris (France), the Bank of America (U.S.), and Morgan Bank (U.S.). While the new banks are expected to increase the competitiveness of the Canadian banking system, they are unlikely to dominate it. With the exception of American banks, foreign banks' Canadian assets are limited to 12 per cent of the total Canadian assets of all banks in Canada. Moreover, foreign banks operate primarily in making loans to medium and large corporations, particularly for financing exports.

Bank of Canada

The Bank of Canada Act of 1934 provided for the creation of a central bank, the Bank of Canada. The responsibilities of the Bank were summarized in the preamble to the Act in the following terms:

> to regulate credit and currency in the best interests of the economic life of the nation, to control and protect the external value of the national monetary unit (the dollar), and to mitigate by its influence fluctuations in

---

[4] But only the insurance companies were permitted to sell insurance.

the general level of production, trade, prices and employment, so far as may be possible within the scope of monetary action, and generally to promote the economic and financial welfare of the Dominion.

In other words, the Bank of Canada was to be responsible for regulating the supply of money in an effort to achieve full employment, price stability, economic growth, and a viable balance of payments.

Relationship to the Federal Government

The federal government appoints the Bank's directors who, in turn, appoint the Governor of the Bank for a term of 7 years. It must be emphasized, however, that the Bank of Canada is not a direct part of the government as is, for example, the Department of Finance. The Governor of the Bank is responsible to Parliament rather than to a particular cabinet minister. Nevertheless, the federal cabinet can veto the decisions of the Bank's executive council.

The Bank's monetary policy was therefore expected to be interdependent with the federal government's actions designed to meet economic goals. But the Bank of Canada was also intended to be *independent* of the direct control of the federal government, in order to exercise separate judgment on the policies most suitable for particular circumstances, and on the techniques for implementing these policies.

The principles governing the relationship of the Bank of Canada and the federal government were made more explicit in 1962 by the Governor of the Bank:

> I believe that it is essential that the responsibilities in relation to monetary policy should be clarified in the public mind and in the legislation. I do not suggest a precise formula but I have in mind two main principles to be established: (1) in the ordinary course of events, the Bank has the responsibility for monetary policy, and (2) if the Government disapproves of the monetary policy being carried out by the Bank, it has the right and responsibility to direct the Bank as to the policy which the Bank is to carry out.[5]

In practice, however, the Minister of Finance and the Governor of the Bank have tended to coordinate directly their economic policies in pursuit of their common goals.[6]

The regulation of the money supply to stabilize employment, prices, and the foreign exchange rate of the dollar is the main responsibility of

---

[5] *Submission by the Bank of Canada to the Royal Commission on Banking and Finance*, 31 May 1962, p. 23.

[6] One major exception to this practice was the growing conflict between the views of the Governor and the Minister of Finance in 1961, which ended with the resignation of the Governor.

the Bank of Canada. The Bank does, however, have a number of other important functions. These flow from its dual role as "the government's bank" and "the bankers' bank".

Government's Bank

Economic Advice   In its role as the federal government's bank, the Bank of Canada provides *economic advice* to the government, through meetings of Bank officials with people from the federal Department of Finance, and more formally through the Governor's annual report and occasional speeches.

Government's Deposits   The balance sheet of the Bank of Canada as presented in Table 7.2 illustrates some of the other ways in which the Bank serves the federal government. Some of the *government's deposits* are held at the Bank of Canada, although a comparison of Tables 7.2 and 7.3 shows that at the end of 1990, the government held only $11 million at the Bank of Canada, while it held $3.2 billion at the chartered banks. Although this ratio varies somewhat, the larger part of federal government funds are held at the chartered banks.

Bond Issues   The Bank of Canada manages the government's *bond issues*. These include the sale to the public of new federal government bonds, the retirement of maturing government bonds, and the conversion of existing bonds to new bonds. The Bank can also make *advances* or loans to the federal government, but this is not a significant function because the Bank can provide funds to the federal government in other forms.

Treasury Bill Auctions   Much more important is the Bank's role in handling the government's weekly sale of *treasury bills*. These are fed-

Table 7.2

Bank of Canada Assets and Liabilities, December 31, 1990
(billions of dollars)

Assets			Liabilities		
Government of Canada securities		20.0	Notes in circulation		23.0
Treasury bills	10.3		Held by chartered banks	5.0	
Other securities	9.8		Held by others	18.0	
			Deposits (in Canadian dollars)		2.1
Advances to chartered banks		0.5	Government of Canada	0.01	
and savings banks			Chartered banks	1.6	
			Foreign chartered banks		
Foreign currency		0.4	and others	0.5	
Other assets		4.4	Foreign currency liabilities		0.2
			Other liabilities		0.1
Total Assets		25.3	Total Liabilities		25.3

Source: *Bank of Canada Review.*

eral government securities issued each week to provide the government with some of its immediate cash needs. The bills are short-term: the principal amount is to be paid in 91, 182, or 365 days. Treasury bills differ from other bonds in that there is no prescribed interest rate. Instead, the treasury bills are sold at an auction at a price below their face value; the lower the price, the higher is the implicit yield rate. Box 7.1 presents an example of the calculation of the yield rate associated with a given price for a treasury bill.

The Bank of Canada and the Department of Finance determine prior to each Thursday auction the total amount to be borrowed and the reserve or minimum bid price that is considered appropriate for current monetary policy. The Bank of Canada will therefore accept the bids or offered prices starting with the highest prices (lowest yield rates) down to the price at which the total value of treasury bills sold would produce approximately the desired average yield rate. If the government's financial requirements exceed this total treasury bill value, the Bank of Canada will buy the remaining required bills (that is, loan the required amount to the government).

This mechanism enables the Bank of Canada to provide funds for the government, but only after funds have been sought from the private financial sector at competitive interest rates. It also enables the federal government to obtain the required funds without causing interest rates to be bid up, should the Bank decide that it is inappropriate for rates to rise in the existing circumstances. In a similar manner, the Bank of Canada may buy new federal government bonds if an insufficient number of these are sold in the private sector.

The Bankers' Bank   **Chartered Bank Deposits**   The Bank of Canada acts as a bankers' bank mainly by accepting deposits of the chartered banks and certain other financial institutions, foreign central banks, and other official foreign institutions. The *chartered bank deposits* are the portions of the chartered banks' cash reserves that these banks choose to hold at the Bank of Canada, rather than in the form of paper currency and coins in their own tills or vaults. The liability items in Table 7.2, notes held by the chartered banks and Canadian dollar deposits of chartered banks, show the proportion of each held in the central bank and at the chartered banks. The value for these two items equals the assets entry in Table 7.3, "Bank of Canada deposits and notes".

Advances and the Bank Rate   The Bank of Canada may also make *advances, or loans*, to the chartered banks, but only as "a lender of last resort". The Bank prefers not to make loans to the chartered banks and thus usually keeps the interest rate it charges on these advances, the *Bank Rate*, just high enough so that the chartered banks will look to other banks and financial institutions for the funds required. The Bank

---

Box 7.1   **Treasury Bill Yield Rates**

Consider, for example, a 91-day treasury bill with a face value of $100,000. At maturity—91 days after it is sold—the government will pay the bearer or holder of the bill $100,000. The interest earned on this loan to the government will be the difference between the purchase price and the $100,000 redemption value. The purchase price is determined at the auction conducted each Thursday noon by the Bank of Canada. Selected money market dealers (or bond brokers) submit their tenders or offers to purchase, at a specified price, a certain number of treasury bills of a given face value: for example, 10 bills at 91-day maturity with $100,000 face value for $97,000 each.

The actual interest rate or yield on these bills will be given by the following formula:

$$\text{Percentage Yield} = \frac{(100 - P)}{P} \times \frac{365}{T} \times 100$$

where P is the price paid per $100 of face value and T is the time to maturity in days. The term $(365/T)$ converts the yield rate to an annual basis. The yield on each treasury bill in the above example is $(100 - 97)/97 \times 365/91 \times 100 = 12.4$ per cent.

Rate has been set since March 1980 at one-quarter of a percentage point above the average 91-day treasury bill yield rate. Prior to 1980, the Bank of Canada set the Bank Rate by decree, and would change it in response to changing economic circumstances as part of the Bank's monetary policy. During the 1970s, the Bank Rate ranged between 5 and 10 per cent, but it reached a peak of 21.24 per cent in 1981. In practice, advances from the Bank of Canada are for a very short period—1 or 2 days—although they can be made for several months in unusual circumstances. This together with a Bank Rate at the appropriate level keeps Bank of Canada advances low, usually less than $50 million.[7]

The Bank Rate should be distinguished from the *prime rate*, which is the interest rate charged by the chartered banks on loans to their large, least risky customers. The prime rate is usually—but not always—about one percentage point above the Bank Rate.

Clearing House   The Bank of Canada also acts as the final *clearing house* for the chartered banks (and other financial institutions) by

---

[7] But these advances temporarily soared to about $4.5 billion during 1985 and 1986 when the Bank of Canada made loans to the Canadian Commercial Bank and the Northland Bank to try to prevent their collapse due to loans that could not be repaid. This was an unusual action by the Bank of Canada, and one for which it received much criticism.

transferring deposits from the account of one chartered bank at the Bank of Canada to the deposit account of another chartered bank. When cheques are cleared — at the Canadian Payments Association — by totalling the amounts drawn against one bank to be deposited in any of the others, the Bank of Canada is advised of the net credits or debits so that it can make these adjustments. The Canadian Payments Association includes banks, trust and mortgage companies, credit unions, and *caisses populaires*.

Banking as a Business

The Bank of Canada decides by how much the money supply should change at any given time, but the operations of the chartered banks are essential in determining whether this decision will be realized.

It is because banks operate as private, profit-seeking businesses that the monetary authorities can predict fairly accurately the effects of their initial decisions on the chartered banks. Banks have several sources of income. Although they pay interest on the savings accounts of their depositors, they also receive income from the services provided for depositors. A fee is charged for processing cheques on chequing accounts, for the use of safe deposit boxes, for cashing foreign cheques, and for exchanging foreign currencies. The major portion of bank income, however, is earned through the use of depositors' funds to purchase securities such as government bonds and to make loans for consumer purchases, business activities, and mortgages.

The consolidated balance sheet for all chartered banks is shown in Table 7.3 as a summary of the principal business activities of banks. About 75 per cent of the chartered banks' liabilities are in the form of deposit accounts. The banks hold some deposits of the federal and provincial governments and of other banks, but the largest part of the deposits are public savings and other notice or non-chequing deposits. Since these are the funds the banks will use to earn income, the banks compete actively to attract depositors.

Primary Reserves   About three-quarters of the banks' assets take the form of loans and mortgages. The amounts shown for these items would be even larger, since these are important income-earning assets, but for the fact that until 1992 the chartered banks had been required by the Bank Act to hold some assets in liquid or very short-term forms. The banks had to hold *primary* or *cash reserves*, as deposits at the Bank of Canada or currency notes at the banks, equal to 10 per cent of the demand or current deposits and 3 per cent of the savings and notice deposits. Since the dollar value of savings and notice deposits is always

Table 7.3

Canadian Chartered Banks Assets and Liabilities, December 31, 1990
(billions of dollars)

Assets		Liabilities		
Bank of Canada		Deposits (in Canadian dollars)		298.0
deposits and notes	6.5	Government of		
Canadian day-to-day		Canada	3.2	
loans**	—	Other demand	18.3	
Treasury bills	18.2	Personal chequing	5.5	
Government of Canada		Personal savings	202.6	
bonds	6.5	Other notice	68.3	
Call and short loans	1.0			
Net foreign currency assets	−7.3	Advances from Bank of		
Loans	181.1	Canada		0.5
Mortgages	110.1	Acceptances*		44.1
Other assets	86.1	Other liabilities		28.3
		Shareholders' equity		31.3
Total Assets	402.2	Total Liabilities		402.2

* Bankers' acceptances are drafts or cheques written by firms and guaranteed by banks. The draft is then sold to an investment broker to find a lender in the short-term money market. This is a way for small businesses to borrow at more favourable interest rates.
** Balances are under 50 million.
Source: *Bank of Canada Review.*

much larger than the value of demand deposits, the total cash reserves of chartered banks had been about 4 per cent of total deposits against which reserves were to be held. However, the 1992 revision of the Bank Act provided for a phasing out of the primary reserve requirement. This is expected to make the banks more competitive with trust companies, which have not been required to hold reserves.

Although there now are no official reserve requirements, the banks and other financial institutions hold some reserves as a precaution against unexpected fluctuations in deposit withdrawals. They also continue to hold deposits at the Bank of Canada to facilitate inter-bank settlement of net balances in the cheque-clearing process.

Secondary Reserves   The chartered banks were also required to hold *secondary reserves* of near-money in the form of day-to-day loans and treasury bills. (Day-to-day loans are very short-term loans made mainly to securities dealers.) Although most treasury bills have a 3-month maturity date, they can easily be bought or sold and therefore are highly liquid assets.

The secondary reserves requirement could be varied by the Bank of Canada, as a percentage of the chartered banks' total deposits, between 0 and 12 per cent. It was reduced from a high of 9 per cent in 1970–

71 to a low of 4 per cent in 1981, where it remained until statutory or legal requirements for primary and secondary reserves ended in 1992. Altering the secondary reserves requirement instead of the primary reserves enabled the Bank of Canada to alter the supply of funds available for longer-term loans, while still allowing the banks to earn some return on these reserves assets. Increasing the secondary reserves requirement also had the effect of forcing the chartered banks to increase their purchases of treasury bills at a time when the federal government needed to use this method to increase its funds.

Expansion and Contraction of Bank Deposits

The main purpose of this chapter is to show how it is possible to change the money supply. This occurs primarily through the actions of the chartered banks as the economy's principal source of loans.

One of the most fascinating aspects of the banking system is its ability to expand the total bank deposits on the basis of small initial changes in these deposits. This process can be illustrated by following a particular case through the banking system.

First Stage   Suppose that a college student receives a money order from England for $1,000 — an inheritance from the estate of her wealthy aunt. She takes the money order to the bank and asks to have it credited to her deposit account. This action increases the deposit liability of her bank by $1,000, but it also increases the bank's assets by $1,000 when the bank has cleared the money order with the English bank that originally issued the money order. To simplify calculations, assume that the bank wishes to hold cash reserves of 10 per cent against the deposits (but the actual ratio in Canada is much less than this). In the following example, reserves may be described as "required" or "desired." These are the cash reserves, held as currency or as deposits at the Bank of Canada, that banks believe are sufficient to meet deposit withdrawals and inter-bank settlements. "Excess" reserves are those in excess of the desired level.

The bank now has *excess reserves* of $900, since its cash reserves increased by $1,000 but it wishes to hold only $100 of that sum in reserves against the new deposit of $1,000. In order to increase its income, the bank will want to put the $900 into income-earning assets such as loans. These changes can be shown in an abbreviated form of the chartered banks' balance sheet. Instead of showing the several items appearing in Table 7.3, the balance sheet below simply indicates the changes that take place. Increases in the amounts of each item are shown by a plus sign and decreases by a minus sign.

Chartered Banks' Balance Sheet

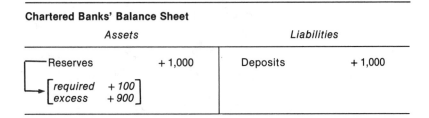

Assets		Liabilities	
Reserves	+ 1,000	Deposits	+ 1,000
required + 100			
excess + 900			

Second Stage Fortunately for the bank, another student appears to obtain a loan, and by convenient coincidence he would like $900. The bank makes the loan by crediting his chequing account with the $900; he can now write cheques to meet his outstanding account at the college for part of his tuition or residence fees. The bank holds 10 per cent or $90 reserves against this new chequing deposit. These further changes are shown as the second-stage changes in the banks' balance sheet.

Chartered Banks' Balance Sheet

Assets		Liabilities	
Reserves	+ 1,000	Deposits + 1,000 (*1st stage*)	
required + 100			
excess + 900			
Loans	+ 900	Deposits + 900 (*2nd stage*)	

Third Stage Since the borrowing student has immediate debts to meet, he writes cheques on his new account for $900 and gives these to the college fees office, which in turn deposits this amount in the college's chequing account at another bank. This transaction reduces the deposits at the first bank by $900, reduces the reserves held against this deposit by $90, but leaves the increased assets in the form of a $900 loan unchanged. Meanwhile the second bank has increased its deposit liabilities by $900 and the reserves held against this deposit by $90. But the new deposit liability also enables it to increase its loans by 90 per cent of $900, or $810. Note that the new $900 deposit at the second bank resulted in a transfer of $900 reserves from the first bank to the second bank. This transfer of reserves takes place between the accounts each chartered bank holds at the Bank of Canada.

Fourth Stage Again assume someone appears seeking a loan of $810, opens an account, and has this amount credited to his account. The banks' combined balance sheets would now show the following changes:

Chartered Banks' Balance Sheet		
Assets		Liabilities

Assets			Liabilities
First Bank			
┌─ Reserves		+ 1,000	Deposits + 1,000 (1st stage)
└─ required	+ 100		
excess	+ 900		
Loans		+ 900	Deposits + 900 (2nd stage)
Reserves		− 900	Deposits − 900
			(3rd stage)
Second Bank			
┌─ Reserves		+ 900	Deposits + 900
└─ required	+ 90		
excess	+ 810		
Loans		+ 810	Deposits + 810 (4th stage)

This process would continue as long as borrowers wrote cheques for the full amount of their new deposits, and recipients of these cheques deposited the receipts instead of cashing the cheques by requesting currency. Continuation of the process also depends on the banks' making loans for the full amount of their excess reserves.

Since the banks may not always be "fully loaned up" and since some of the cheques may be cashed, the process is unlikely to continue to the point where new loans and deposits are infinitely small. If the process continued through several stages, however, one can see that the sum of all the deposits resulting from the initial deposit of $1,000 would be substantial. By the end of the fourth stage shown in the balance sheet, net deposits have increased by $1,710 over the initial deposit. A further stage would show the cancellation of the $810 deposit credited to the second borrower but remaining for the recipient of these funds, then there would be a deposit of $729, and so on.

Final Result The final or total possible increase in deposits, including the initial deposit, can be calculated using the following formula:

The final change will depend on the required or desired reserve ratio: the larger the required reserve, the smaller the deposit expansion effect. The change therefore will be equal to $1/R$ multiplied by the value of the intial deposit, where R is the ratio of required reserves to the total deposits.

Thus, the final increase in this case will be $1,000 $\times$ 10, or $10,000. (If the desired cash reserve ratio had been 5 per cent or 1/20, the final change would have been $1,000 \times 20$, or $20,000$.) Deposits have increased up to the limit determined by the initial increase in reserves and the reserve requirement. This deposit increase had occurred through the expansion of loans made by the chartered banks.

Chartered Banks' Balance Sheet (*final changes*)

Assets		Liabilities
Reserves	+ 1,000	Deposits + 10,000
Loans	+ 9,000	

Since the actual cash reserve requirement in the Canadian banking system has averaged about 4 per cent, the potential expansion was about 25 times any initial change in deposits. The actual expansion, however, was limited by the secondary reserve requirement. That is, some of the banks' reserves in excess of the primary reserve requirement were to be held as secondary reserves—mainly treasury bills—rather than being available for loans. With the official reserve requirement removed, however, the banks will maintain a smaller reserve ratio, and consequently the expansion factor will be larger.

Although there is an apparent similarity between the national income multiplier (discussed in Chapter 6) and the expansion of bank deposits, particularly in the formulae for calculating the final results, these two processes should not be confused. They deal with quite different features of the economy. The term "multiplier" is reserved for the particular process of an expansion or contraction in national income, resulting from an initial change in spending. This term *cannot* be used for the expansion and contraction of the money supply. In fact, there is no similar, generally accepted term in the latter case; one simply refers to the deposit adjustment process. The process by which the money supply is contracted will be described in the next section on the operations of the Bank of Canada.

Techniques for Regulating the Money Supply

There is no longer any "backing" for money created by the banking system in Canada. Prior to World War II, the Bank of Canada was limited to creating money equal to four times the value of its holdings of gold, but this ceiling was removed in 1940 to allow the Bank to meet the increased monetary requirements of the wartime economy. The only factor now governing the expansion of the money supply is the confidence of the Canadian public (and other countries) that the Bank of

Canada is maintaining the proper monetary level for the best performance of the economy.

The most important activity of the Bank of Canada is regulating the
total amount of money that the banks can create through the process
just discussed. The Bank is able to do this through the techniques
described below, most of which involve the *unique power of the Bank
of Canada to create chartered bank deposits at the Bank of Canada.*

Open Market Operations

The Bank of Canada's buying and selling of securities such as federal
government bonds and treasury bills is termed the Bank's *open market
operations*. The market in which these securities are traded is the bond
market; it is "open" because there is essentially no restriction on who
can buy or sell bonds. The bond market is not as well defined as the
stock market—which has the Vancouver, Toronto, and Montreal Stock
Exchanges to bring buyers and sellers together. Nevertheless, bond
trading occurs daily on a large scale through a communications network linking bond brokers' offices.

The Bank of Canada, like the chartered banks and many other
financial institutions, holds government securities as part of its assets.
Of the federal government's outstanding marketable bonds and treasury bills, representing a debt of approximately $311 billion on
31 December 1990, the Bank of Canada held $20.4 billion and the
chartered banks held $19.5 billion. (The balance was held by other
corporations and individuals.)[8] Since the Bank of Canada's holdings
form such a substantial part of the outstanding government securities,
the Bank can exercise considerable influence on the prices of these
securities.

What happens when the Bank of Canada deals in government securities in the open market? The bonds that are traded carry a stated
maturity value and interest rate. A one-year bond may state, for example, that one year from the bond's date of issue the government will
redeem the bond for the face value of, say, $1,000 and will pay interest
of 12 per cent. If the Bank of Canada wishes to *sell* bonds, it can offer to
sell this $1,000 bond for $980.[9] The actual yield to the bearer will

---

[8] In addition to the $311 billion in marketable securities, the federal government had
a further debt of $35 billion in nonmarketable Canadian Savings Bonds, and $5.0
billion in securities held by federal government accounts and funds.

[9] The example used here is highly simplified. In fact, the Bank of Canada would offer
to sell bonds at a price just barely below the price at which the same kind of bonds
were being offered in the market by other sellers. It is this price comparison, rather
than the difference between the face value and the offered price, that is important to
prospective buyers.

therefore be the $120 interest payment plus the additional gain of $20 when the bond is redeemed. The yield is thus $140 on an asset of $980, or 14.3 per cent. If the Bank wishes to *buy* bonds, it would offer to pay a price above the face value—say, $1,020. Thus the Bank of Canada can alter the price at which it is willing to buy or sell bonds until other institutions dealing in the bond market, mainly chartered banks, are willing to buy or sell bonds to the total value desired by the Bank.

Deposit Expansion   The effect on the money supply of the Bank's open market operations can be traced in the following steps. If the Bank buys a bond for $1,000 from an insurance company, the company sends the bond to the Bank and in return receives a cheque for $1,000. The insurance company presents this cheque to its chartered bank to be credited to the deposit account of the company. The chartered bank thus increases its liability to the company by $1,000. When the chartered bank then presents the original cheque to the Bank of Canada, the Bank credits this to the deposit account of the chartered bank by creating assets for the chartered bank in the form of $1,000 bank reserves. The Bank of Canada has increased its liabilities by $1,000, in the form of chartered bank reserves, but it has also added the $1,000 bond to the Bank's assets. These changes are shown below in the balance sheets of the three institutions involved.

The process does not stop at this point. The initial increase in bank deposits leads to an expansion of deposits in the same manner as did the $1,000 inheritance discussed in the previous section on expansion of bank deposits. Assume a desired cash reserve ratio of 10 per cent; the chartered bank will wish to hold only $100 in reserves against the new deposit of $1,000. It is therefore anxious to loan the excess reserves

Insurance Company Balance Sheet

Assets		Liabilities
Securities	−$1,000	(no change)
Deposits	+$1,000	

Chartered Banks Balance Sheet

Assets		Liabilities	
Bank reserves	+$1,000	Deposits	+$1,000

Bank of Canada Balance Sheet

Assets		Liabilities	
Securities	+$1,000	Bank reserves	+$1,000

of $900 in order to obtain additional income in the form of interest on the loan. The process can be traced through to the point where the initial $1,000 deposit has led to an additional $9,000 in deposits, for an overall increase in the money supply of $10,000.

The Bank of Canada can be said to have *created* money to the extent that its cheque to the insurance company, which was written against no deposit account, became a $1,000 deposit in the banking system and thereby increased the excess reserves of the chartered banks. Of greater quantitative significance, however, is the subsequent *expansion* of the money supply that occurred through the banking system.

Deposit Contraction   If the Bank of Canada wishes to *contract* the money supply, it can do so by reversing the process that is initiated through its open market operations. Suppose the Bank of Canada *sells* a $1,000 bond to the insurance company. The company writes a cheque for $1,000 on its deposit account and sends this to the Bank of Canada (through a bond broker) in exchange for the bond. The Bank reduces its liability to the chartered bank in question by reducing the bank's deposit at the Bank of Canada by $1,000. The chartered bank in turn reduces its liability to the insurance company by deducting $1,000 from the company's account.

But again this is not the end of the process. The chartered bank's reserves have fallen by $1,000, only $100 of which was being held against the $1,000 deposit of the insurance company. The bank therefore has a reserves deficiency of $900. The bank will therefore reduce other loans, and hence deposits, until it is back to the desired level of cash reserves. Chartered banks do this either by calling in some of their demand loans or, more likely, by simply not re-lending funds received in repayment of loans. If the bank in question reduces its loans, and in the related deposits, by $9,000 — that is, in a 10-to-1 ratio with the reserves deficiency — the desired ratio will be restored. Thus, the initial sale of a $1,000 bond by the Bank of Canada leads to a $10,000 reduction in deposits and a $9,000 reduction in loans outstanding.

There is one important difference between the expansion and the contraction of the money supply. The extent of the expansion depends on whether banks are able to loan all of their excess reserves, and whether all payments from deposit accounts are redeposited. The full extent of the contraction *must* occur, however, unless the banking system has been holding substantial amounts of excess reserves.

Purchase and Resale Agreements

The Bank of Canada also uses "purchase and resale agreements" with financial institutions, whereby the institutions sell treasury bills or other short-term securities to the Bank, with an agreement to repurchase these at a specified price, usually within very few days. These agreements, with an implicit interest equal to the Bank Rate, increase bank reserves just as would a loan from the Bank. The converse arrangement, sale and repurchase agreements, is also used, and provides the Bank with another means to influence short-term interest rates.

Box 7.2   **Bank of Canada uses overnight market to influence rates, Crow says**

By James Rusk

Bank of Canada governor John Crow said yesterday that the bank has in recent years switched the focus of its money market operations to influence short-term interest rates from the treasury bill to the overnight market. . . .

"The tool we use most often to affect overnight rates is the day-to-day adjustment of the amount of cash reserves provided to the banking system." . . .

The overnight market to which Mr. Crow referred is a market in which investment dealers borrow cash from the banking system to carry their inventory of financial instruments such as treasury bills.

By taking cash out of, or putting it into, the overnight market, the central bank can influence short-term interest rates.

Mr. Crow said the bank decides early each evening on a cash position in the overnight market that takes into account the volume of reserves apparently being demanded by the banks and that tries to bring about the interest conditions the bank would like to see develop in the market. . . .

When, however, cash reserve management proves less precise than the bank would like, the bank has in recent years increasingly used market transactions, which are reversed a day later, to influence overnight rates.

The two types of market transactions the bank uses to take cash in and out of the system are purchase-resale agreements (PRA) and sales-repurchase agreements (SRA).

Under a PRA, the bank buys government securities from one of a designated group of investment dealers and agrees to sell it back the next day. The SRA operates the other way round—a government security is sold with an agreement to buy it back the next day. . . .

"Unlike traditional PRA, the bank sets the rate, amount and timing of these transactions. This, not surprisingly, gives us a higher profile in the overnight market.

"We have accepted this as a necessary reality if we are to signal our intentions efficiently."

Source: *The Globe and Mail,* 27 April 1989.

Transfer of Government of Canada Deposits

Since the Bank of Canada acts as a banker for the federal government, the Bank has available a third technique for changing the level of bank reserves, and hence deposits. This is the transfer of deposits belonging to the Government of Canada from the chartered banks to the Bank of Canada, and vice versa. If the Bank transfers federal government deposits from a chartered bank to the Bank of Canada (termed a "draw-down"), this has the same contracting effect as the sale of bonds in the open market. If the Bank switches $10,000 from the Government of Canada account at a chartered bank to the Government's account at the Bank of Canada, the Bank of Canada will also reduce the chartered bank's deposit at the Bank by $10,000. The chartered bank finds that it must make up cash reserves of $9,000. This leads to a contraction of deposits and loans at the chartered banks, as described previously.

Conversely, if the Bank of Canada switches $10,000 from the Government of Canada account at the Bank to the federal government's account at a chartered bank and increases the bank's cash reserves by $10,000 (termed a "redeposit"), there can be a further expansion of deposits and loans.

The transfer of government deposits is increasingly used as a day-to-day tool of monetary policy and provides a useful method for reinforcing the effect the Bank is trying to achieve through open market operations.

Changes in the Bank Rate

The Bank of Canada may also influence bank reserves and the money supply by significantly changing the Bank Rate. This is the interest rate the Bank charges for advances or loans it makes to the chartered banks and other financial institutions.

If the Bank of Canada, through the treasury bill auction, reduces the Bank Rate, financial institutions will also lower the rate they charge on loans to the chartered banks, and the chartered banks will lower the rate that they charge each other; otherwise, the chartered banks would borrow from the Bank of Canada at the new lower rate.

When a chartered bank borrows from the Bank of Canada, the Bank increases the chartered bank's cash reserves by the amount borrowed. The expansion of money then proceeds as in the previous cases of monetary expansion. But the effect will usually be short-lived, since these loans usually are made for only a few days. In practice, the Bank of Canada maintains the Bank Rate just high enough to encourage chartered banks to borrow elsewhere, especially from other chartered banks.

The Bank Rate is a useful technique, however, for the Bank of Canada to influence interest rates directly. The Bank Rate changes fairly frequently, as shown in Figure 7.1, both as a *signal* of the monetary policy the Bank is pursuing and in response to changing demands for funds in the private sector. A low Bank Rate indicates that banks will be able to obtain less expensive loans from the Bank of Canada if necessary, and that they should therefore lend to their customers more freely and at lower rates. A high Bank Rate would indicate that the Bank of Canada wants a reduction in the availability of loans and a higher interest rate. A change in the Bank Rate is used to bring about faster changes in the monetary situation than would be possible if the Bank relied only on its open market operations and transfers of federal government deposits.

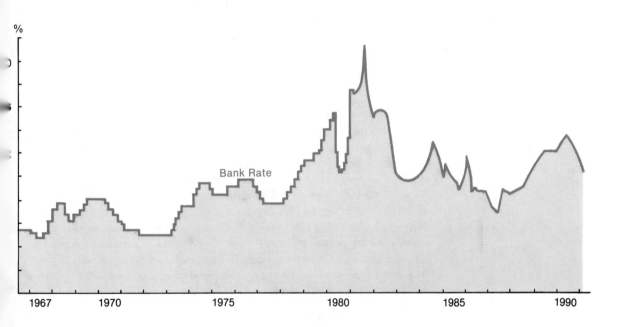

Figure 7.1 Bank Rate, Canada
The Bank of Canada changed the Bank Rate frequently in the 1970s, especially in 1973–1974 and 1978–1981, during periods of rapid inflation. Since 1980, the Bank Rate has moved with the 91-day treasury bill rate.

Source: *Bank of Canada Review.*

Changes in the Required Reserves Ratio

The first three techniques represent the methods commonly employed by the Bank of Canada in bringing about changes in the money supply. Another of the Bank's former powers, that of specifying the percentage of chartered bank deposits to be held as secondary reserves, was occasionally used to reinforce the effect the Bank was trying to achieve through its other methods.

When the Bank of Canada was established in 1934, there was no mention of secondary reserves in the Bank Act. The chartered banks were required to hold primary or cash reserves, equal to 5 per cent of their deposits. In 1954, this requirement was amended to allow the Bank of Canada to vary the cash reserve ratio from 8 to 12 per cent of deposits, in order to give the Bank another method of regulating the money supply. An increase in the cash reserve ratio would have the same kind of contractive effect as a sale of bonds in the open market or a transfer of government deposits to the Bank of Canada. If the chartered banks were "fully loaned up", that is, if they had no excess reserves, the need to increase their cash reserves would lead them to reduce their loans and hence their deposits.

Such a change in the cash reserve ratio, even if as small as a fraction of a percentage point, would require quite large and immediate changes in cash reserves on the part of all banks. Since this is such a powerful, blunt technique, a change in the cash reserve ratio has never been used by the Bank of Canada. The cash reserve requirement remained at 8 per cent from 1954 to 1967. Subsequent revisions of the Bank Act specified the requirements, until these ended in 1992.

A requirement of secondary reserves was introduced in 1967. The Bank of Canada was given the authority to vary this ratio between 0 and 12 per cent against all deposits. An increase in the required ratio compelled the banks to reduce their loans. But an increase in the secondary reserve requirement still allowed the banks to earn some income on their increased reserves of day-to-day loans and treasury bills. The secondary reserve requirement was reduced in stages from a high of 9 per cent in 1970 to 4 per cent in 1981, where it remained for the following decade.

Moral Suasion

No discussion of the Bank of Canada would be complete without a reference to "moral suasion". Because six chartered banks dominate the banking system in Canada, the Governor of the Bank of Canada should be able to call together these bank presidents and persuade them to follow the monetary policies desired by the Bank. For example, the Bank might wish to avoid overall increases in the money supply, while making more funds available for small businesses or residential mortgages.[10] A selective policy of this kind could not be achieved with other techniques such as open market operations, because their effects on the money supply are so widespread.

Selective controls, however, are difficult to implement, partly because the banks are in competition with the other near-bank financial institutions like the trust companies and savings banks. If the chartered banks did try to comply with the wishes of the Bank of Canada, the near-banks probably would provide the funds to potential borrowers who had been turned away from the chartered banks. The use of moral suasion depends primarily, however, on the attitude of the Governor toward the freedom of the chartered banks to operate within the conditions established by the Bank's other activities.

Another difficulty in implementing selective controls is the possibility that loans obtained for one purpose may be transferred to other uses. For example, if mortgage funds are to be made available but loans for consumer durables such as automobiles and household appliances are to be restricted, a family may take a larger mortgage on its new house and use some of the funds to purchase new appliances.

Review of the Main Points

1. Money is something that is readily and widely accepted as a medium for the exchange of goods and services. Money also serves as a unit of account, a store of value, and a standard of deferred payments or debts.

2. Precious metals, particularly gold, served as money for a long time; gold certificates and later bank deposits evolved from the practice of depositing gold for safekeeping. Coins and paper currency are legal tender — money the government decrees must be accepted for payment of debts or for exchange of goods and services.

3. An economy's money supply includes all coins and paper currency circulating outside the banks and the total value of chequable deposits at the chartered banks. Broader definitions of money include various components of time or notice deposits.

---

[10] One of the few clear examples of moral suasion was the Winnipeg Agreement of 1972, whereby the Governor obtained the agreement of the chartered banks to restrict the interest rate offered on large, short-term deposits so that these funds would be available to other borrowers. In July 1981 the Governor asked the chartered banks not to finance the Canadian purchases of firms in the United States, since this would increase the demand for American dollars and lower the value of the Canadian dollar.

4. The Bank of Canada acts as the federal government's bank by providing economic advice, holding some of the government's deposits, making loans to the government, and managing its issues of bonds and treasury bills. The Bank also acts as a final clearing house for the chartered banks and as a lender of last resort, making loans available at the Bank Rate.

5. The money supply can be expanded or contracted through the chartered banks, since the banking system can make loans equal to a large multiple of any initial change in deposits. The potential total expansion, equal to the reciprocal of the cash reserve ratio multiplied by the amount of the initial deposit, is realized only if the banks maintain no excess cash reserves and if all payments from deposit accounts are redeposited. The potential total contraction, calculated in the same way, occurs more quickly than expansion because banks move immediately to restore the intended or required reserve ratio.

6. The Bank of Canada regulates the money supply by creating or removing chartered bank reserves through open market transactions in government securities, by purchase and resale agreements and by transferring federal government deposits between the Bank and the chartered banks.

Key Concepts and Topics

money	balance sheets
functions of money	chartered bank assets, liabilities
characteristics of money	treasury bill
barter	"lender of last resort"
goldsmith receipts	cash reserves
legal tender	excess reserves
money supply	desired reserves
near-money	reserve ratio
banking system	Bank Rate
financial system	deposit expansion and contraction
chartered banks	open market operations
central bank	moral suasion
Bank of Canada	

Questions for Review and Discussion

1. It is sometimes said that Canada will soon be a "cashless" society. What does this mean? Describe some of the changes that would be required to achieve a completely cashless society. What advantages and disadvantages would there be? Could Canada also become a "moneyless" society?

2. What happens to the level of the money supply when someone withdraws $500 in currency from his or her bank account for a vacation trip? Does it ultimately matter whether the trip is within Canada or another country? Why?

3. Why can one say that the banking system creates money if a bank is permitted to lend only part of its deposits?

4. What determines the quantity of coins and paper currency in circulation?

5. Suppose that chartered banks held cash reserves equal to 100 per cent of their deposits. Would this mean that the Bank of Canada could no longer have an influence on the money supply?

6. Bank of Canada actions to increase the money supply have been described as "trying to push on a string." Is this a valid analogy?

7. Why does money have value if there is nothing "backing" the money supply?

8. What is the difference between money and bonds? Is there any difference between money and gold? Explain.

Sources and Selected Readings

Bank of Canada. *Report of the Governor of the Bank of Canada*. Ottawa: Bank of Canada, annual.

Bank of Canada Review. Ottawa: Bank of Canada, monthly.

Binhammer, H.H. *Money, Banking and the Canadian Financial System*, 5th ed. Toronto: Methuen, 1988.

Boreham, G.F., and R.G. Bodkin. *Money, Banking and Finance: The Canadian Context*, 4th ed. Toronto: Holt, Rinehart and Winston, 1992.

Government of Canada. *White Paper on the Revision of Canadian Banking Legislation*. Ottawa: Supply and Services Canada, 1976.

Martin, Peter. *Demystifying Monetary Policy: A Guide to Understanding What the Bank of Canada Does and How*. Vancouver: Fraser Institute, 1980.

——. *Inside the Bank of Canada's Weekly Financial Statements: A Technical Guide*. Vancouver: Fraser Institute, 1985.

Shearer, R.A. J.F. Chant, and D.E. Bond. *The Economics of the Canadian Financial System*, 2nd ed. Scarborough, Ont.: Prentice-Hall, 1984.

8 Money and National Income

In Chapter 6, it was seen that planned aggregate expenditure and domestic output of goods and services were the major factors determining the equilibrium level of national income. The next step is to see the role that changes in the quantity of money play in determining aggregate expenditure and the effect on the level of national income.

Money in Classical Economics

Quantity Theory of Money

The classical economists attached great importance to changes in the quantity of money in an economy. The classical *Quantity Theory of Money* in its crude or basic form stated simply that the general price level in the economy would vary directly and proportionately with the stock of money. This could be expressed as

$$P = kM$$

where k is the value of the constant relationship between the general price level, P, and the stock of money, M. If the quantity of money were doubled, the crude quantity theory would predict that prices would be doubled. This result was based on two of the classical assumptions outlined earlier: that individuals would spend all of their incomes, and that the economy was normally at the full employment level. Thus, if the quantity of money were increased, people would spend the increased quantity also. But since it was assumed that the economy was normally at full employment, the increased spending could only result in a bidding up of prices for the fixed levels of goods and services. Money in the crude classical model had the effect of increasing national income, but only by increasing the *monetary value* of the output, not by increasing the *real* output.

The *Sophisticated Quantity Theory*, or what is more commonly called the *quantity equation of exchange*, modified the crude theory to take into account the fact that it is not only the *quantity* of money available that affects the economy, but also the *velocity* of money, or how quickly money circulates in the economy. But two different measures of the velocity of money need to be clarified: the transaction velocity and the income velocity.

Velocity   The *transactions velocity of money* refers to the total value of all transactions or sales made during the period of a year compared with the average stock of money (usually defined as M1) available to finance these transactions. The formula for the transactions velocity is therefore:

$$V_T = \frac{PT}{M}$$

where V_T is the transactions velocity, P is the weighted average price of transactions, T is the total number of transactions, and M is the quantity of money. If one knew that the total value of transactions, PT, in one year was $300 billion and the stock of money was $30 billion, the velocity calculation would show that, on average, each dollar was exchanged ten times during the year. Indeed, the total value of all transactions in the economy is many times the value of final goods and services, such that the value of V_T would be large.

Income velocity is the proper concept, however, for examining transactions of final goods and services. The income velocity will be considerably smaller than the transactions velocity, since national income measures only the final goods and services and not the many transactions that occur as each good moves toward the final production stage, or the numerous transactions representing the change in ownership of property and financial assets. Income velocity is calculated by dividing the GDP for a given year by the stock of money.[1] The formula is the same as for the transactions velocity except that Q (output of final goods and services) is substituted for T, and P is the weighted average price of final goods and services. Hence:

$$V_Y = \frac{PQ}{M}$$

[1] The income velocity, based on the M2 definition of the money supply, has tended to fluctuate within a range of 2.5 to 3.5 over the past two decades in Canada. But the velocity of M1 money has increased from 9 to 17. See Figure 10.1.

The *quantity equation of exchange* is so called because it is an equation that relates the quantity of money to the value of goods and services exchanged. By definition, the total value of these commodities must be equal to the total spending. That is,

$$MV = PQ$$

because V_Y was defined as PQ divided by M. This equation is described as a *truism* or *identity* because it states what is necessarily true, rather than expressing a causal relationship.

The introduction of real goods and services into the equation, in the form of T or Q, opened the possibility that an economy at less than full employment would respond to an increase in M by increasing real output. The quantity equation of exchange also emphasized a point made by the later classical economists, namely, that the crude theory omitted the possibility of a change in the velocity of circulation of money. But they also assumed that the velocity was reasonably stable in the long run, and that changes in the quantity of money would lead directly to proportionate changes in the price level.

Finally, the equation also showed that even when the money supply remained constant, an increase in velocity could result in an increase in national income. Velocity tends to increase with higher interest rates because individuals and firms then hold smaller balances in current or chequing accounts.

Demand for Money

Although the quantity equation did try to show how money could affect the levels of real output and prices, it was not very effective in explaining how or why changes in the money supply would lead to such changes. Keynes argued that an analysis of the role of money needed to examine the *demand for money*, or why people would hold different amounts of money under different conditions. Money, in this context, refers to the M1 definition, namely, currency and demand deposits.

It is easy to understand why there is a demand for real goods and services, and why the quantity demanded should vary inversely with the price of a good. It may not be quite so obvious why people should want to hold money, apart from using it immediately to purchase commodities. The reasons or motives for holding money fall into three categories: transactions, precaution, and speculation.

Transactions The *transactions demand* for money arises because money is needed to make routine purchases. It would be possible — but foolish — to buy bonds or other financial assets with one's weekly or monthly pay as it was received, and then sell these each time money was needed to buy the groceries or pay the rent. In addition to the inconvenience, there are costs in buying and selling some financial assets. Thus, most people keep some cash in their wallets or purses and a reasonable balance in chequing accounts to meet regular expenses.

Precaution The *precautionary demand* for money is closely related to the transactions demand. One can estimate weekly or monthly requirements for regular expenditures on food, housing, clothing, and transportation, but other expenditures are less predictable. A sudden illness, the opportunity to join someone else on a trip, or a clearance sale of "real bargains" may suddenly require cash. One usually maintains a bank balance somewhat above the bare minimum for these and similar "rainy day" reasons.

Speculation The *speculative demand* for money is related to the small percentage of the population who hold some assets in bank accounts in order to take advantage of opportune times to buy other financial assets. When investors, for example, believe that common stock prices are about to fall for a short time, they may sell stocks and hold their funds as bank deposits until it seems time to buy stocks again.

The quantity of money demanded or held at any time, given one's level of income and preference for holding money, depends on its "price", which is the opportunity cost of holding money. This cost is represented by the interest that could have been earned on alternative forms of financial assets, such as savings deposits, bonds, or stocks.

Liquidity Preference The demand for money curve, D_M, as illustrated in Figure 8.1, resembles a typical downward-sloping demand curve: a larger quantity of money is demanded or held as the opportunity cost (the interest rate on alternative assets) falls.[2] Since the desire to hold money reflects the preference that people have for liquidity or liquid assets, as compared to holding purchasing power in other forms such as bonds, stocks, and real estate, *the demand for money is referred to as liquidity preference.* It is also described as a "preference" because it represents what individuals prefer or desire to hold at a given interest rate, by comparison with the actual quantity of money held. This distinction between desired and actual quantities is similar to the distinction made earlier between desired and actual levels of aggregate expenditure for real goods and services.

One can see individuals responding to changes in the opportunity cost of money in terms of the movement of deposits from chequing

[2] Throughout this chapter, "the rate of interest" should be thought of as an average of interest rates, since the interest rates on different types of assets tend to move together.

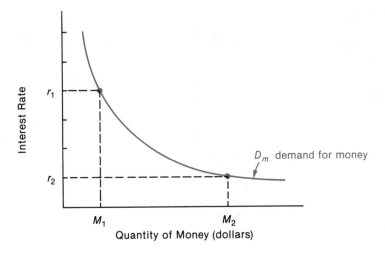

Figure 8.1   Liquidity Preference: Demand for Money
At any given level of income, the quantity of money that individuals and firms wish to hold as coins, currency, or bank deposits is greater, the lower the interest rate. As the interest rate falls from r_1 to r_2, the quantity demanded increases from M_1 to M_2 because the cost of holding money—the forgone return on other financial assets—is lower at lower interest rates.

accounts to (non-chequing) savings accounts, bonds, and stocks when interest rates rise sharply. When the interest rate is low, the opportunity cost of retaining these balances in a chequing account is much less. (Banks have responded by creating deposit accounts that blend chequing and savings functions.)

Nevertheless, some money must be held for transactions and for precautionary reasons, whatever the interest rate. This is reflected in Figure 8.1. M_1 is the amount of money being held for these reasons, even at a high interest rate. At this high rate virtually no money will be held for speculative reasons because there will be more rewarding opportunities in holding other assets. But as the interest rate falls, from r_1 to r_2, more money will be held for transactions and some will be held for speculative reasons. When the rate drops to r_2—which may be the counterpart of a 2 or 3 per cent interest rate on savings deposits—large amounts of money will be held for speculation.

Liquidity Trap   The liquidity preference curve is shown to flatten out at an interest rate of about r_2. This long "tail" on the right-hand end of the liquidity preference curve is described as the *liquidity trap*. At very low interest rates, investors will hold exceptionally large quantities of money instead of other assets. The cost of holding money at r_2 is not sufficient to offset the risk of holding assets in other forms. However, such low interest rates have not been experienced for so long that the liquidity trap is now considered to be of historical interest only.

Change in Demand for Money

The demand for money, like the demand for other commodities, shows the relationship between price (or interest rate) and quantity, with other factors held constant. The demand for money will change, as does the demand for other commodities, when there is a *change in income* or a *change in "tastes"*. At any given interest rate, the higher one's income, the larger the amount of money required for transactions, and the higher the cost one is willing to afford for the convenience of holding money for precautionary and speculative purposes.

The preference for liquidity—holding money rather than other assets—may change for various reasons. People vary significantly in their preferences for holding money rather than other assets, depending on their willingness to take some risk.

Determination of the Interest Rate

Since the supply of money is defined as the quantity held in currency and bank deposits, money can be "supplied" only to the extent that it is actually held. The quantity of money supplied is therefore the actual quantity of money held in the economy. The supply decision of monetary authorities is to determine what the level of this stock should be at any time. The important distinction, however, is between the quantity individuals *wish* to hold and how much they actually do hold. The supply curve for money is shown in Figure 8.2 as perfectly inelastic with respect to the interest rate—because the quantity of money supplied at a particular time is dependent on autonomous decisions of the monetary authorities, and not on the interest rate.

Money versus Bonds   In Figure 8.2a it can be seen that the quantity of money people prefer to hold (demand) and the quantity actually held (supply) will be equal only when the interest rate is r_1, given the demand curve, D_M, and the supply curve, S_M. Suppose that the interest rate is at r_2. In this case, the quantity of money "demanded"—that is, the quantity that the economy would prefer or desires to hold—is M_2. The quantity "supplied"—actually held—is M_1. The difference between the quantity people prefer to hold and the amount actually held, $M_2 M_1$, is the quantity that the economy would prefer to hold in the form of interest-bearing assets. The opportunity cost or forgone interest on $M_2 M_1$ is more than individuals collectively are willing to give up for the advantage of holding some of their purchasing power in the form of money rather than other assets such as bonds.

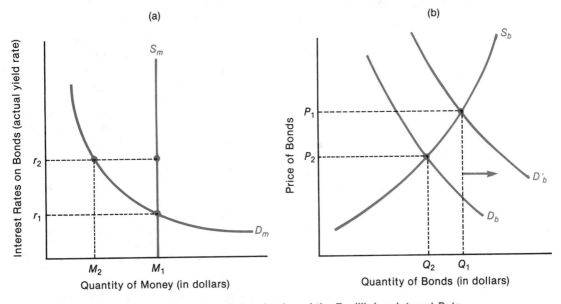

Figure 8.2 Determination of the Equilibrium Interest Rate
When the amount of money actually held, M_1, at a given interest rate, r_2, exceeds the amount that individuals and businesses wish to hold, M_2, they will begin to use the excess money to buy bonds (as representative of all other forms of financial and real assets). As the price of bonds is bid up toward P_1 through increasing demand toward D'_b, the implicit yield or interest rate declines until equilibrium is reached at r_1. The supply of money, M_1, is independent of the interest rate because the money supply is decided by the monetary authorities.

An attempt to reduce the actual stock of money from M_1 to M_2 by purchasing bonds will increase the demand for bonds,[3] as illustrated in Figure 8.2b. The increased demand for bonds then presses up the price of bonds to P_1.

As the price of bonds increases, the actual yield or interest rate on the bonds is falling, as described in detail in Box 8.1. This process would continue until the interest rate fell to r_1 (or the bond price rose to P_1), such that the quantity of money the economy preferred to hold was just equal to the quantity actually held, namely M_1.

The equilibrium rate of interest is the rate at which the actual supply of money—or the quantity actually held—is equal to the desired quantity as shown by the liquidity preference, or demand for money.

---

[3] This occurs in the bond market that was discussed in Chapter 7, with respect to the Bank of Canada's open market operations.

Box 8.1   **Bond Prices and the Interest Rate**

An increase in the price of a bond will decrease the actual yield or true interest rate on the bond. For example, suppose that a $100 bond had a stated interest rate of 10 per cent; that is, the face of the bond stated that the bondholder would be paid 10 per cent (or $10) per year as interest. But if the bond can be purchased for less than $100, say for $90, the $10 interest payment now represents 11.1 per cent of the price actually paid for the bond. Similarly, a bond price of $110, with the same annual interest of $10, would result in an actual yield or interest rate of 9.1 per cent.

One may ask why a person would sell a $100 bond for only $90, or would pay as much as $110 to buy a $100 bond. The answer is simply that individuals who hold bonds but need cash for a specific purchase of goods or services may find it financially better to sell the bond at a lower price rather than borrow at a high interest rate. One may also find it financially attractive to pay $110 for the bond if the resulting interest rate (9.1 per cent) is still better than the interest rate on other similar assets.

In the short run, the liquidity preference or demand curve tends to shift very little. The more important influence on the interest rate is a change in the supply of money. In the longer run, however, the demand for money tends to rise with increases in national income. Figure 8.3 shows how such changes in the supply of or demand for money lead to changes in the interest rate. The interaction of the supply of and demand for money is usually referred to as the *monetary sector*, in contrast with the *real sector*, where real goods and services are exchanged.

Money, Interest Rate, and Aggregate Expenditure

The monetary sector and the market for real goods and services are linked through the effect of the interest rate on the level of real investment, that is, on the demand for producer goods.

When interest rates are high, businesses will borrow less to undertake new investment projects because there will be fewer investment possibilities for which the expected rate of return exceeds the rate of interest. This effect is illustrated in Figure 8.4. In the initial equilibrium condition of the money market, the interest rate is r_1. At this interest rate, businesses find it profitable to continue investing up to a level of investment, I_1, since at this level of investment the marginal efficiency of investment, or rate of return, is just equal to the cost of borrowing money. If they invested more, the returns would fall below their interest costs, with a net loss as the result. When businesses plan a level of investment of I_1, planned aggregate expenditure will be AE_1, given the

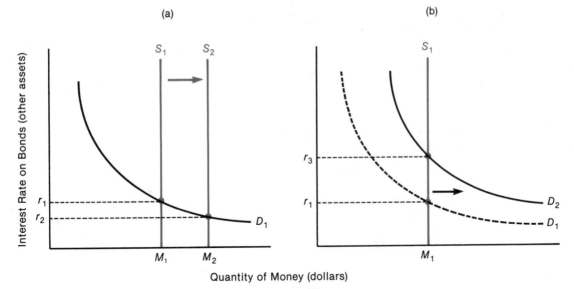

Figure 8.3   Changes in the Equilibrium Interest Rate
When the supply or stock of money is increased from M_1 to M_2, at a given interest rate r_1, there will be an increased demand for bonds to reduce the undesired level of money. This increases the bond price and reduces the bond yield or interest rate until there is a new equilibrium interest rate, r_2.

If there is an increase in liquidity preference to D_2, with the money supply still at M_1, people will sell bonds to increase their holdings of money. This lowers the bond price and increases the yield or interest rate until a new equilibrium rate is reached.

other components of aggregate expenditure, and the equilibrium level of national income will be GDP_1.

Now suppose the money supply is increased to M_2. Provided that the demand for money is unchanged, the interest rate falls to r_2. With this decline in the interest rate, investors will increase the level of their planned investments to I_2. The increase in planned investment increases the level of aggregate expenditure to AE_2. The increased investment spending *combined with the multiplier effect* increases the equilibrium level of national income to GDP_2, by an amount greater than the change in investment spending.

Conversely, if the amount of money available dropped below M_1 (the S_M curve shifts to the left), the interest rate would rise, planned investment would fall, aggregate expenditure would fall, and thus the equilibrium level of national income would fall.

This important effect of the interest rate on national income, through the effect on planned investment spending, is based on the assumption that investors' plans are sensitive to changes in the rate of interest, or that investment demand is not inelastic with respect to the interest rate.

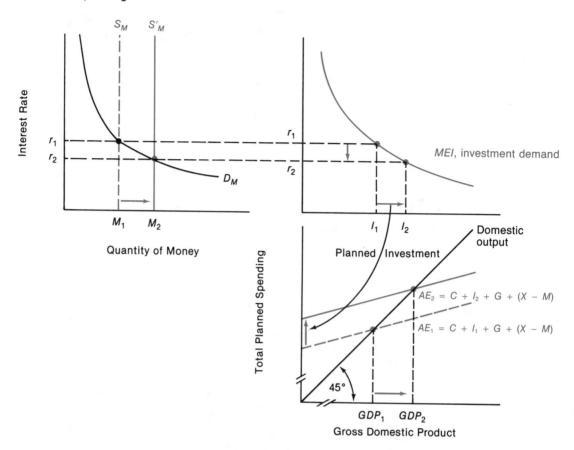

Figure 8.4   Interest Rates Link the Real and the Monetary Sectors
Suppose the monetary sector is in equilibrium with the money supply at M_1 and the interest rate at r_1, and the real sector is in equilibrium at GDP_1. An increase in the money supply to M_2 leads to a lower interest rate, r_2. This leads to an increase in planned investment to I_2, shifts planned aggregate spending upward to AE_2, and hence—through the multiplier effect— increases the equilibrium level of national income to GDP_2.

While it is true that, for large investment projects of, say, $10 million, an increase of one percentage point in the interest rate represents a sub-stantial cost increase—in this example it would be $100,000—several other factors must also be considered in a new project of this magni-tude. For example, the investment may be a new plant in an area where there is still some uncertainty about consumer response to the proposed product, or it may be the first plant ever to use a new technique. The risk of technical failures and the uncertainty of consumer response are frequently the major considerations. Furthermore, the usual financial sources for projects of this kind may have their funds "tied up" in loans for other projects. Some firms prefer to finance new projects from their retained earnings: whether or not they undertake a project could depend more on whether funds were available than on the current interest rate.

These factors have led some economists to emphasize the availability of money, rather than the interest rate, in explaining the effect money has on the level of national income. Although this is an important distinction it does not significantly alter the basic explanation, since both factors operate in the same direction. That is, an increase in the money supply has the effect of both increasing the availability of money and decreasing the interest rate; in either case, an increase in planned investment can be expected. However, firms with a large fund of retained earnings may use this fund to finance new projects even when interest rates are high. To this extent, the link between money supply and business investment is somewhat weakened. However, when it comes to investment in residential housing, empirical evidence indicates that the availability of money and the interest rate have a much stronger effect.

There is also an increasing effect of interest rates on consumption expenditures. At high interest rates, consumers are more likely to postpone purchases of major durable items such as automobiles, household appliances, and furniture. However, consumers' expectations of higher inflation rates may partly offset their reaction to high interest rates.

The model or explanation of the operation of the economy at the aggregate level is now complete—at least in its simple form! This is the model or the analytical framework that will be used later to examine the actions governments can take toward achieving the economic goals of full employment and price stability.

Review of the Main Points

1. Because the classical economists assumed full employment would prevail, they assumed that an increase in the money supply could only increase the level of prices.
2. Later, with the quantity equation of exchange, they recognized that an increase in the velocity of money could also increase prices, and that both increased money supply and velocity could increase real output if there was some unemployment.
3. Keynes linked the real sector with the monetary sector through the effect of interest rates on investment. Interest rates are determined by the supply and demand for money.
4. Money is demanded (or held) for transactions, precautionary reasons, and speculation. The higher the level of income, the more money will be held at any given interest rate. Thus the monetary sector can be in equilibrium at different interest rates.

Key Concepts and Topics

real sector	transactions demand
monetary sector	liquidity preference
stock of money	liquidity trap
quantity theory of money	supply of money
velocity of money	bond yield rate
income velocity of money	equilibrium interest rate
quantity equation of exchange	inverse relationship of
demand for money	bond prices and yields

Questions for Review and Discussion

1. Does an increase in the money supply always cause inflation? Explain.
2. Why is the quantity equation of exchange necessarily true?
3. Discuss the several circumstances or conditions under which an increase in the money supply might have little or no effect on the level of employment.
4. "The Bank of Canada should try to maintain a stable interest rate in order to avoid inflation or unemployment." Do you agree? Why?
5. What is the difference between money and income? Between money and wealth?
6. Use the *AD-AS* diagram to explain why complementary monetary and fiscal policies (such as increasing both the money supply and government spending) will have a stronger impact on GDP than either policy taken separately.

Sources and Selected Readings

Boreham, G.F., and R.G. Bodkin. *Money, Banking and Finance: The Canadian Context*, 4th ed. Toronto: Holt, Rinehart and Winston, 1992.

Dornbusch, R., S. Fisher, and G. Sparks. *Macroeconomics*, 3rd ed. Toronto: McGraw-Hill Ryerson, 1989.

Heilbroner, Robert L., and J.K. Galbraith. *Understanding Macroeconomics*, rev. ed. Englewood Cliffs, N.J.: Prentice-Hall, 1987.

Keynes, John Maynard. *The General Theory of Employment, Interest, and Money*. London: Macmillan, 1936.

Parkin, Michael, and Robin Bade. *Modern Macroeconomics*, 2nd ed. Scarborough, Ont.: Prentice-Hall, 1986.

Stewart, Michael. *Keynes and After*, rev. ed. Baltimore: Penguin Books, 1986.

Wilton, D.A., and D.M. Prescott. *Macroeconomics: Theory and Policy in Canada*, 2nd ed. Toronto: Addison-Wesley, 1987.

9 Fiscal Policy and the Public Debt

Major responsibility for reducing unemployment and inflation while encouraging a high rate of economic growth rests with the federal government, with the assistance of the Bank of Canada. Some provincial governments also try to design expenditure programs to counteract unemployment and inflation, but differences between the priorities of the various governments can result in conflicts between their policies for dealing with inflation and unemployment.

The federal government's responsibility for influencing total spending to maintain economic stability was widely accepted only about two or three decades ago. Keynes' analysis of the high unemployment levels experienced during the Depression led him to argue that governments must use their taxation and spending powers to offset swings in economic activity. This view was advocated in Canada in 1940 by the Royal Commission on Dominion-Provincial Relations, and stated as government policy in 1945 in a White Paper on employment and income, but it became common policy only in the 1960s.

Actions taken by the federal government and the Bank of Canada to reduce unemployment and inflation are collectively described as stabilization policies. These actions consist of *fiscal policy*, the government's expenditure and taxation programs, and *monetary policy*, the Bank of Canada's actions to regulate the money supply and influence interest rates. A third group of policies is concerned with international economic relations and includes *policies on tariffs, foreign exchange rates, and foreign investment*. International economic policies are determined to a certain extent in cooperation with other countries, and for the moment can be considered constraints within which domestic economic policies must be designed.

Inflation-Unemployment Trade-Off

The numerous combinations of actions available to the federal government and the Bank of Canada to influence aggregate demand and the money supply make it difficult to determine the most suitable stabilization policy for Canada at any particular time. Further complicating the situation is the need to choose between inflation and unemployment as the primary problem to be attacked.

In the simple Keynesian model, inflation would only occur after the economy had reached full employment. This condition was based on the assumption that if aggregate demand increased during periods of unemployment, there would be an increase in real output rather than higher prices. In actual experience, however, prices tend to rise even when there is substantial unemployment, and to rise more quickly as the economy approaches the full-employment level.

Phillips Curve

This varying combination of rates of unemployment and inflation can be shown by a curve relating the average unemployment rate and inflation rate for particular short-run periods. Such a curve has been called a *Phillips curve*, after one of the first economists to analyze the relationship of these and similar indicators of economic activity. Since it appeared that the government must trade off some inflation to reduce unemployment, and vice versa, the Phillips curve was also termed a *trade-off curve*.

Figure 9.1 presents a hypothetical Phillips curve to show the nature of the basic decision facing a government. Suppose the economy were experiencing a combination of inflation and unemployment represented by point *A*: inflation at the rate of 6 per cent annually and an average annual unemployment rate of 6 per cent. The government may choose to fight inflation, trying to reduce it from 6 to 4 per cent, but must then accept 9 per cent unemployment (point *D*). Alternatively, the government may try to reduce unemployment to 4.5 per cent, meanwhile allowing inflation to rise to 8 per cent (point *C*). Ideally, the government would like to move the economy toward point *B*, and certainly to keep it away from *E*, a combination of high unemployment and high inflation.

The curve shown in Figure 9.1 illustrates only the nature of the trade-off decision facing the government; it does not present actual data for the Canadian economy. Historical Phillips curves were useful in understanding how the economy performed in the past, but they did not provide an adequate basis for designing future stabilization policy. That is, the government could not determine how much inflation it should expect for each percentage point in the reduction of the unem-

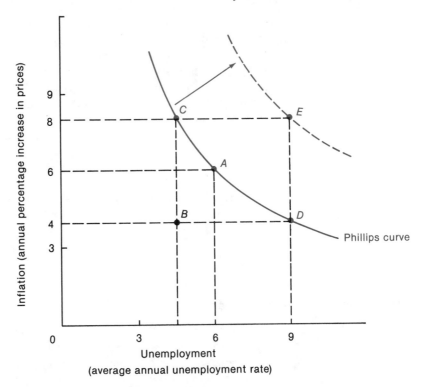

Figure 9.1   The Phillips Curve: Inflation and Unemployment Trade-Off
A Phillips or trade-off curve shows the various combinations of
unemployment and inflation rates that have occurred in an economy's
recent past. Usually, high unemployment rates have been associated with
low inflation rates, and vice versa. However, the historical Phillips curve
cannot be used to determine by how much inflation will increase for a given
decrease in the unemployment rate, for example in moving from *D* to *A*,
because the curve tends to shift with other economic changes.

ployment rate, because this relationship changed over time. Through
the 1960s and early 1970s, the trade-off curve for Canada was shifting
outward, and became less well defined.

This outward shift was said to be due partly to inflation expectations
or an "inflation psychology" in the population. If, for example, the
government is fighting unemployment and thus lets inflation proceed
at a higher rate than in the previous year, workers and lenders anticipate continuing inflation and demand higher wages and interest rates.
They thus create the inflation they expected. The prevailing unemployment rate is associated with a higher rate of inflation than in the
past; that is, the Phillips curve shifts outward.

Other reasons suggested for the changing relationship between inflation and unemployment include the possibility that the structure or nature of unemployment has changed. The greater number of "secondary" workers—persons who work part-time or who are in the labour force intermittently—may increase the measured unemployment rate at any given level of inflation, while there is a relatively low unemployment rate among "primary" workers, the full-time members of the labour force. The geographical immobility of workers may also affect the trade-off. If there is a strong demand for workers in one part of the country while unemployment is high in another region, the national relationship of inflation and unemployment is different from that when there is substantial unemployment in all regions. Other major events, such as the sharp rise in oil prices, will also increase the rate of inflation at any given unemployment level.

Natural Rate of Unemployment

During the 1970s, debate about the Phillips curve moved from a concern with the outward shift of the curve to whether such a relationship between inflation and unemployment still existed. As Figure 9.2 shows, there was an obvious trade-off relationship between unemployment and inflation for 1959 to 1967, with an outward shift of this curve for 1969 to 1971. But during 1971 to 1974 there was a sharp increase in inflation with little change in the high rate of unemployment. This led to the concept of a *"natural rate of unemployment"*, which meant that basic structural conditions of the labour market determined the rate of unemployment, and that fiscal and monetary policies could only influence inflation, with negligible effects on unemployment. The natural rate of unemployment therefore resembles the full-employment level of the economy that has been assumed in preceding chapters. The concurrent persistence of high rates of inflation and unemployment also became known as *"stagflation"*—the condition of an economy that was facing high inflation despite the fact that so many persons were unemployed.

Accelerating Inflation   The concept of a natural rate of unemployment can be explained by reference to Figure 9.3. This builds on the Phillips curve and its outward shifts due to expectations of increasing or *accelerating inflation*. Suppose that with an economy at point *A*, experiencing high unemployment and modest inflation, the government decides to pursue an expansionary program to reduce unemployment. As producers hire more

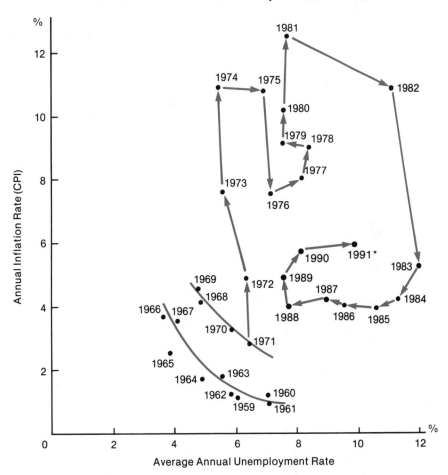

Figure 9.2 The Inflation-Unemployment Relationship in Canada
During the 1960s there appeared to be a Phillips curve type of relationship
between inflation and unemployment, with an outward shift of the curve for
1968 to 1971. Since 1972, there is more evidence of a "natural rate of
unemployment", with a breakdown in the trade-off relationship. The
"natural rate" appears to have shifted from about 6 per cent in the early
1970s to about 8 per cent for 1976–1981 and to about 11 or 12 per cent in
the early 1980s. From 1984 to 1990, it appeared that the economy was
returning to a natural rate of about 8 per cent.

* forecast

workers unemployment declines, but an increased demand for their
output raises prices and the economy moves along the Phillips curve to
point *B*.

Workers then become aware that their *real wages* have fallen. With
the rise in prices, the wages at which they agreed to work when the econ-

omy was at A will now buy fewer goods and services. If they demand, and receive, higher wages, they may set off an accelerating inflation that causes the government to shift its policy from employment creation to inflation control — that is, from demand expansion to demand contraction. This results in higher unemployment, with the economy moving back toward point C. Although the decreased demand is the main

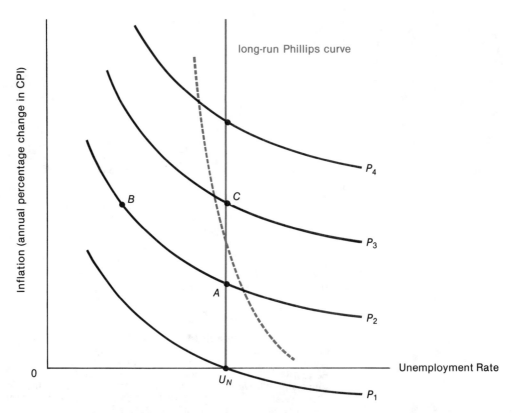

Figure 9.3   The Natural Rate of Unemployment
The short-run Phillips curves (labelled P_1, etc.) are said to show only the short-run trade-off between inflation and unemployment. In the longer run, the economy is expected to move to an inflation-unemployment combination that includes the natural rate of unemployment—but only if inflation can be correctly anticipated and taken into account in economic decisions. This would then generate the vertical long-run Phillips curve, as shown above, at the natural rate of unemployment. Some economists would argue, however, that the long-run relationship more closely resembles the broken line shown in the figure above.

cause of the higher unemployment, there may also be some workers who quit their jobs when they realize that their real wages are diminishing due to inflation. They believe that they would be further ahead to spend more time searching for a higher-wage job.

Some economists argue that the economy will move to point C, while others believe that it will move to the right of B but not necessarily all the way to C. The view that the economy will move to B assumes that the economy had adjusted to the level of unemployment represented by A, and that it will return to a similar level of unemployment when it adjusts to a higher level of inflation. This latter adjustment is reached when wages, prices, and profits all increase at the same rate.

The process would be repeated again if the government should try to increase demand to reduce unemployment, with the economy moving from C upward along the higher Phillips curve, P_3. Eventually, there would be a return to a new point directly above C. Thus, there would be a long-run relationship between inflation and unemployment traced out by the succession of points lying above U_N, the natural rate of unemployment—which is therefore defined as *the rate of unemployment that occurs when the economy (workers, producers, and consumers) has adjusted to or correctly expected the rate of inflation*. This is sometimes referred to as the *non-accelerating inflation rate of unemployment* (or NAIRU) to emphasize that there is nothing "natural" about this unemployment rate—that is, it is not intrinsic or permanently embodied in the economy.

Economists who disagree with the notion of a *vertical* long-run Phillips curve believe that the economy may not move all the way from B to C because workers may be concerned with more than their real wages. They may have a "money illusion" and thus be inclined to resist any cut in money wages (or nominal wages), or may respond positively to increases in money wages even if inflation is increasing at the same time. In this case, it is easier to maintain existing employment levels at higher inflation rates than with low inflation. In the latter case, employers could not afford to raise wages and workers would have to be laid off or would quit. To this extent, the long-run curve would not be as steep as the curve shown in Figure 9.3, but it would be steeper than the short-run Phillips curves.

The inflation-unemployment relationship since 1974 suggests that there may have been an outward shift of the "natural" rate for 1976 to 1981, followed by a further outward shift to 1982–1984. It must be emphasized, however, that there is still much debate about how to interpret this recent behaviour of the economy, especially the unusual pattern seen since 1985.

Rational Expectations   To explain how people form their expectations about future inflation, economists have introduced a theory of *rational expectations*. Supporters of this theory argue that people make their own economic forecasts — even if implicitly — on the basis of current policies and conditions. Although their forecasts or expectations may be wrong, they learn from their mistakes and incorporate this learning into future expectations. But the formation of rational expectations in this way depends on an understanding of the working of the economic system and the recurrence of similar circumstances to which the learning can be applied. The assumption that people are rational in their expectations of inflation is important to economists, who must incorporate popular expectations about inflation into their own forecasts. For example, the alternative short-run curves in Figure 9.3 would represent the behaviour of the economy under alternative expectations that the majority of people have about inflation.

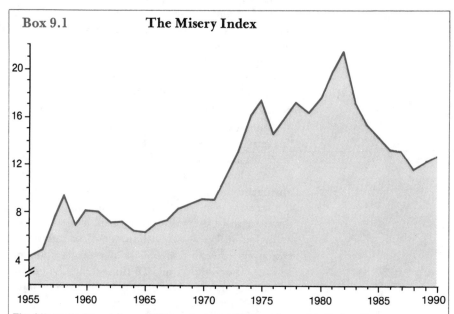

Box 9.1   **The Misery Index**

The Misery Index = Annual Unemployment Rate + Annual Inflation Rate

Another way to portray the severity of the combined rates of inflation and unemployment is the "economic misery" index shown in the graph above. The index has been above 10 for most of the 1970s and 1980s, and peaked at 21.8 in 1982. This index is not an official measure of economic activity, but it provides a simple comparison of differing economic conditions across the years.

Fiscal Policy

It is within this context of changing combinations of inflation and unemployment, with little repetition of historical experience, that fiscal policy must be designed and implemented. Although fiscal policy can be defined simply as the government's expenditure and taxation programs, discussion of a specific fiscal policy should consider the effects that particular taxation and spending measures are intended to achieve. Fiscal policy can be further defined as either *automatic* or *discretionary*.

Automatic fiscal policy consists of what are commonly called *automatic or built-in stabilizers*: government programs designed to vary the amount of tax revenues or government expenditures automatically as the levels of employment and prices change. *Discretionary fiscal policy* requires a specific decision by the government. That is, the government must use its discretion in determining the level and type of taxation and expenditures needed to combat current economic problems.

Automatic Stabilizers

Two types of automatic stabilizers are at work in the economy: private economic behaviour in response to changing incomes, and government programs. The private "built-in" stabilizers are the marginal propensities to save and to import. As individuals' incomes rise, the marginal propensity to save tends to rise also. The proportionately greater saving has a dampening effect on aggregate demand, thereby reducing the inflationary effect of rising incomes. Conversely, as incomes fall, the marginal propensity to save decreases and proportionately more income is directed to consumption or investment goods, with the effect of maintaining aggregate demand and employment at a higher level than would occur if the marginal propensity to save were constant for all levels of income. The marginal propensity to import tends to act in the same way, increasing with rising incomes and thus reducing their potential inflationary effect.

The automatic stabilizers built into government programs are always at work and respond relatively quickly to income changes. Depending on the level of economic activity, they are slowing down either the decline or the increase in disposable incomes. Although government action is needed to initiate the programs, and may be taken again to alter the payments or tax rates, no specific decision is needed as the economy moves through changing levels of inflation and unemployment.

Built-in stabilizers in the form of government programs include *transfer payments* for income and price maintenance schemes, and tax revenues from the progressive personal income tax structure. Transfer payment programs include unemployment insurance, welfare assistance, and agricultural price supports.

Unemployment Compensation

As the level of unemployment rises, accompanied by a fall in employment earnings, government expenditures for unemployment compensation are increased. Although these payments do not fully offset the decline in incomes, they keep consumer demand closer to its previous level than it would be without the payments. Similarly, when the economy is moving closer to full employment, unemployment compensation payments decline, so that aggregate demand does not push up prices quite so quickly.

Welfare Assistance Payments

Welfare assistance payments tend to act in the same way as unemployment compensation in stabilizing consumer demand. However, welfare schemes are generally provided for persons experiencing long-term unemployment or persons who are not in the labour force, and so do not perform quite so effectively as automatic stabilizers in short-run changes in aggregate demand.

Agricultural Price Supports

Agricultural price support schemes (described more fully in a later chapter) provide payments to producers whenever the price of the commodity concerned falls below the guaranteed price. Depending on the scheme in effect, the government either pays the difference between the price received in the market and the guaranteed price, or buys the quantity that is not sold at the guaranteed price. These payments have the effect of keeping agricultural producers' incomes closer to the previous level. As agricultural prices rise, the government payments to producers decline and vice versa.

Progressive Personal Income Tax Structure

The progressive tax structure on personal income acts as one of the strongest and most immediate stabilizers. When incomes rise, a larger percentage of the additional income is taken for taxes. Consumers' disposable incomes thus rise less quickly than their gross incomes. When personal incomes fall during a recession, a lower proportion of incomes is deducted for taxes, and disposable incomes fall more slowly than total incomes.

Fiscal Drag   The advantage of built-in stabilizers is that they operate automatically, but they also have a disadvantage: they reduce the effectiveness of discretionary policies to deal with inflation and unemployment. The progressive income tax structure, in particular, causes what has been termed *fiscal drag*: as government actions to reduce unemployment begin to take effect and national income rises, the higher marginal tax rates increase tax revenues and reduce aggregate demand. The opposite effect also occurs. As anti-inflation policies begin to work and national income falls, lower marginal tax rates leave consumers with a higher proportion of gross incomes available for spending. These effects are reinforced by the other automatic stabilizers. The government must therefore consider the action of automatic stabilizers when discretionary fiscal policy is being determined.

Discretionary Fiscal Policy

Discretionary fiscal policy can be defined as a *deliberate effort by the government to achieve not only stable prices and full employment but also economic growth, favourable income distribution, and equilibrium in the balance of payments, through the appropriate composition and size of its expenditures and tax revenues.*

Numerous alternatives on both sides of the budget are open to the government, each with different effects. Indeed, the government is constantly encountering pressure from various groups to favour them by reducing taxes or increasing government spending in each new budget.

Basic Effects of Fiscal Policy

Consider a situation in which the economy is experiencing high unemployment and only minor inflation. The government is formulating an *anti-unemployment* or *expansionary fiscal policy*. It has four basic choices:

- to increase government expenditures, leaving tax revenues unchanged;
- to decrease tax revenues, leaving government expenditures unchanged;
- to increase both government expenditures and tax revenues;
- to increase government expenditures and decrease tax revenues.

Assume further that government economists have determined that, to reduce unemployment to the desired level (presumably to create full employment), the required increase in national income is $6 billion and that the economy's marginal propensity to consume is $2/_3$. How large would the changes need to be in each of the four choices open to the government?

Increased Government Expenditures   Government expenditures for goods and services directly increase aggregate demand. Since any increase in government expenditures has a multiplied effect on national income, an increase of $2 billion in government expenditures will, with a multiplier of 3, increase national income by $6 billion. This is illustrated in Figure 9.4a. The result is an initial increase in government spending to G_2, with the multiplier effect resulting in a $6 billion increase in GDP.

Decreased Tax Revenues

A decrease in personal or corporate income taxes does not have the same effect as an equal increase in government expenditures. Although a decrease in taxes increases personal or corporate after-tax income, one-third of the increased income goes to savings, imports, and even some taxes. The multiplier effect will occur only on the additional spending for domestically produced goods and services; this is equal to two-thirds of the increase in disposable income. Tax revenues must therefore be reduced by more than an increase in government expenditures if this second approach is to have the same effect on national income as the first.

A $3 billion decrease in tax revenues produces an initial increase of $2 billion in domestic spending, and a final increase in national income of $6 billion. Thus the tax reduction needs to be 50 per cent greater than the increase in government expenditures to have the same effect on national income. (Note that when $MPC = \frac{1}{2}$, tax reductions must be double the expenditure increase; and when $MPC = \frac{3}{4}$, tax reductions must be $33\frac{1}{3}$ per cent larger than expenditure increases.) The effect of a tax reduction of $3 billion is illustrated in Figure 9.4b. Government expenditures and exports are unchanged but consumer spending and investment initially increase by a total of $2 billion, from C_1 to C_2 and I_1 to I_2.

Equal Increases in Taxes and Expenditures

The fact that tax reductions must be greater than increases in government expenditures to obtain the same increase in national income hints at the changes required if the government chooses to follow the third alternative: an equal increase in taxes and expenditures. If taxes are increased by $2 billion, domestic spending will decrease initially by two-thirds of this amount, or $1\frac{1}{3}$ billion, and the final decrease in national income will be $4 billion. An increase of $2 billion in government expenditures, however, leads to an increase in national income of $6 billion. The combined effect of a $2 billion increase in both government spending and taxes will therefore be a net increase in national income of $2 billion. Thus, to achieve the objective of a $6 billion increase in national income, both taxes and government expenditures must be raised by $6 billion.

This third alternative is a specific case of the *balanced budget multiplier*.[1] The particular result obtained here can be expressed in general terms:

[1] Recall from Chapter 6 that the balanced budget multiplier is based on the MPC for domestically produced goods and services. Leakages from spending are represented by MPS, MPM, and MPT.

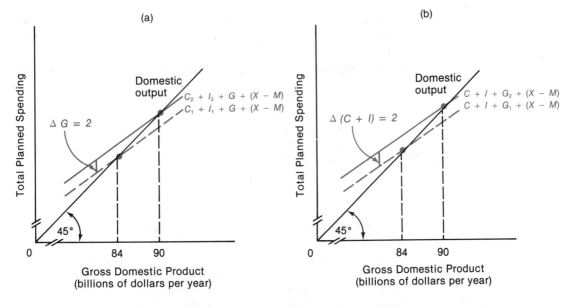

Figure 9.4   Changes in Government Expenditures or Income Taxes
A $2 billion increase in government expenditure will have a multiplied effect
on national income. When $MPC = 2/3$, the value of the multiplier is 3, and
GDP is increased by $6 billion.
A $3 billion decrease in personal and corporate income taxes increases
disposable income by $3 billion, but if the $MPS + MPM + MPT$ for
consumers and firms is $1/3$, C and I increase by only $2 billion. With a
multiplier of 3, this increase leads to an increase in GDP of $6 billion.

A balanced or equal change in taxes and government spending will
change national income by the same amount, given that the value of the
multiplier is uniform throughout the economy.

**Increased Expenditures
and Decreased
Revenues**

The government may also choose to combine two of the basic alternatives. To combat high unemployment, for example, it may combine tax
reductions with increased government expenditures. In this case, a $6
billion increase in national income can be achieved through decreasing
tax revenues by $1 billion and increasing government expenditures by
$1 1/3 billion. Alternatively, especially perhaps just prior to an election,
tax revenues might be decreased by $1 1/2 billion and government expen-
ditures increased by $1 billion, with the same effect on national income.

Limitations of Fiscal Policy

Although only the basic elements of fiscal policy have been outlined, it
should be clear that the government is faced with difficult decisions
each time it designs new fiscal policy. When unemployment is high,

should taxes be cut? government expenditures increased? some of each action taken? or a budget balance be maintained with much larger increases in both taxes and spending?

Some considerations in making these choices fall into three general categories:

- the timing of specific changes in taxation and spending;
- regional versus national effects;
- the problem of managing budgetary deficits that result when expenditures exceed revenues, and budgetary surpluses when revenues exceed expenditures. (This point will be dealt with in a separate section.)

Timing of Fiscal Policy   Several factors compound the problem of timing in implementing fiscal policies. It is so difficult to predict the future, even for a few months hence, that too much emphasis is often placed on present conditions in designing fiscal policy. This difficulty is illustrated hypothetically in Figure 9.5. For example, after a slow but steady growth in GDP through time periods t_1 to t_2, with unemployment probably at a higher than normal level, the economy begins to "heat up", GDP rises more quickly from t_2 to t_3, the unemployment rate drops slightly, and economic advisors warn that increased inflation is ahead. Should the government assume there will be a prolonged expansionary period, with the economy moving along path A? Or is the current burst likely to be as short-lived as it was during t_0 to t_1, moving the economy along path D? Or is the economy moving on to its long-term steady growth path shown as C?

Recognition   If the future path is actually A, this illustrates the first type of timing problem: there may be a *recognition lag* such that the economy is well into an inflationary period (or a recession) before corrective action is even considered. This lag is represented in Figure 9.5 as the period from t_2 to t_3.

Decision   Second, there is a *decision lag* — the time it takes government economists and advisors to agree that the economy is indeed on path A, that a contractionary fiscal policy is required, and that this should, for example, take the form of both reduced government expenditures and tax increases. The decision period may be prolonged because tax changes, in this case possibly an income surtax, are normally announced only when the finance minister presents the budget or the mini-budget.

Implementation   Even if this decision is announced by the government shortly after t_3, a further lag is experienced: this *implementation lag* means that changes, in income taxes particularly, are usually not effective until some time after the announcement.

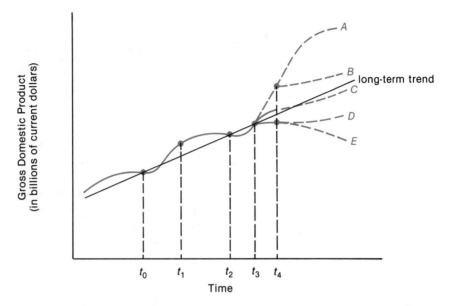

Figure 9.5 Predicting Future Economic Activity for Policy Decisions
At time period t_2, the economy may seem to be moving toward its long-term trend line (path C). There may therefore be a recognition lag between t_2 and t_3 before the actual path A is recognized. A further decision lag may delay action beyond t_2, with the implementation of a policy not occurring until t_4 or later. Contractionary policy implemented at t_4 may put the economy onto path B. But if the strength of the original expansion was wrongly judged, and the economy was moving onto path D, a contractionary policy will reinforce the recession, indicated by path E.

Expenditure changes can generally be effected more quickly than tax changes, but most major programs or projects cannot be terminated abruptly. A decision, for example, to cut back on defence expenditures would result in the signing of fewer new production contracts, rather than the breaking of existing contracts. Fewer personnel would be recruited, and military commitments abroad would gradually be reduced.

The same type of lags would occur if an expansionary policy was required: time to recognize the need, to determine a new policy, and to put it into action. New job creation programs, for example, require time to make the program known, for applications to be received, processed, and approved, for the first grants to be awarded, for the funds to be spent by the recipients, and for the multiplier to begin to take effect.

The combined decision lag and implementation lag is represented by the period from t_3 to t_4 in Figure 9.5. During this period, the rate of inflation has been high. Although the policy begins to have an effect at t_4, the economy moves along path B, representing a higher level of inflation than if it had been on path C without these lags.

There is an even more serious problem associated with these lags. Suppose that the economy were actually on path D, rather than on path A as determined by the government. A contractionary policy having its effect at t_4 would initiate a recession, represented by path E.

Regional versus National Effects   The second set of problems associated with fiscal policies concerns the location of their effects. If unemployment is high in some regions but not in others, a tax cut may reduce the high unemployment but add to inflationary pressures in the other regions. Such cases require government expenditure programs specifically designed to put purchasing power into the hands of low-income persons in the high unemployment regions. Conversely, if there is a widespread recession with unemployment at an unusually high level across the country, a tax cut is usually the preferable strategy. The implementation period can be short and the consequences immediate and widespread.

Budget Deficits

A major limitation on discretionary fiscal policy results from the diversity of views on the maximum budgetary deficit that government should incur. Three general views can be identified:

- the budget should be balanced each year;
- the budget should be balanced over the cyclical fluctuations in economic activity, or over a five- to ten-year period;
- balancing the budget is unimportant: use whatever combination of expenditures and taxes will bring about non-inflationary full employment.

Annually Balanced Budget   Prior to Keynesian analysis of national income determination, and especially during the Depression, it was generally accepted that a government should balance its budget each year; after all, that was what prudent individuals would do. When the economy was in a slump, it would be irresponsible for the government to push the country further into debt by allowing expenditures to exceed tax revenues. Advocates of this policy failed to recognize that when incomes declined during the Depression, tax revenues also fell. If a balanced budget was to be maintained, the government would need to increase tax rates in order to keep tax revenues constant, or decrease government expenditures, or do both. Each of these policies would reduce aggregate demand and produce further unemployment.

During an inflationary period, tax revenues would rise, and if expenditures remained constant, a surplus would result. Maintenance of a balanced budget would require the government to lower the tax rates, or increase government expenditures, or do some of each. These actions would increase aggregate demand and thus increase the rate of inflation. It is evident then, that an annually balanced budget would worsen whichever problem, unemployment or inflation, was present.

Budgets Balanced over the Cycle Some persons who recognized that an annually balanced budget could be an irresponsible fiscal policy argued that governments should pursue a counter-cyclical policy, but that the budget should be balanced over the cycle. As income rose, taxes should be increased faster than expenditures so that a budget surplus would be accumulated. But as this contractionary action slowed down the rate of inflation and unemployment began to increase, expenditures should be increased faster than tax revenues, wiping out the surplus and even producing a budgetary deficit. This approach seemed plausible when fairly regular cycles were experienced, but failed to answer the problem that arose when a recession continued for some time or when government expenditures were unusually large for some time, as occurred during World War II.

Deficit or Surplus as Required Recognition of the drawbacks to balancing the budget annually or cyclically led to acceptance of the government's budget as a tool for combatting inflation or unemployment, and realization that the resulting surplus or deficit was of only secondary importance. This position is sometimes referred to as *functional finance*: a budgetary deficit or surplus has a particular function and should be judged by how well this function is served, rather than by the size of the deficit or surplus. In fact, a recent version of this view suggests that what is relevant is not the actual deficit or surplus shown in the government's budget, but what the budgetary balance would be if the economy were at the full-employment level.

Full-Employment Balance Most economists now emphasize the full-employment deficit or surplus, or the *full-employment balance*.[2] It is recognized that a deficit budget introduced when unemployment is high may so effectively stimulate the economy that the increased incomes associated with full employment will produce a balanced budget, possibly a surplus, or at least a lower deficit. This concept can be illustrated as in Figure 9.6. Government expenditures, G, are assumed to rise slightly with increasing national income. Tax revenues, T, rise more rapidly due to the progressive tax rates and constant basic tax exemptions. The given tax and expenditure

---

[2] The Economic Council of Canada prefers to use the term "high employment" balance or budget, recognizing that the estimates are based on the best attainable unemployment rate.

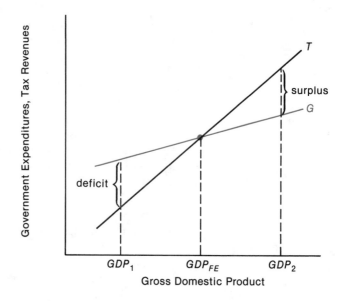

Figure 9.6   A Budgetary Deficit May Produce a Balanced Budget at Full Employment
Given the government's planned spending for various levels of national income, G, and the tax revenues realized as national income increases, T, a budget deficit (G − T) at GDP_1 may stimulate economic activity enough to produce a balanced budget (G = T) when the economy is at full-employment national income, GDP_{FE}. The given planned G and T would also produce the necessary surplus budget to restrain the inflation that could be expected at even higher levels of national income, such as GDP_2.

programs produce a deficit when the economy is at a less than full-employment level of national income, GDP_1, and a surplus when national income is beyond the full-employment level at GDP_2. The particular deficit incurred at GDP_1 produces a balanced budget at the full-employment level represented by GDP_{FE}. The government's role is to make sure that the tax structure and the level of government expenditures are such that a budgetary balance is achieved at the full-employment level.

Structural Deficit   The notion of a full-employment balance can be expressed or measured from another approach. This is what is often called the *structural deficit*, or the component of the deficit that would exist even if the economy were at full employment with no inflation. By focusing on this definition, one can see the portion of the deficit that results from under employment in the economy, with reduced tax revenue and greater government expenditures required for transfer payments. Over the longer term, it is the size of the structural deficit, rather than the total deficit, that is of concern, since this represents a continuing burden to the economy. The absolute level of the deficit should be adjusted for inflation, but by comparing the deficit with the Gross Domestic Product and assessing only this ratio, the effect of inflation is implicitly removed.

Managing the Deficit

The government may need to incur a deficit over an extended period to reduce a stubborn, high level of unemployment. Since a deficit represents expenditures in excess of tax revenues, where does the additional revenue come from to make these expenditures possible? One might think that the government should be able to draw on accumulations of past surpluses, but many governments have acquired such large debts in the past, primarily through war expenditures, that any previous surplus has already been used to reduce this debt. A deficit therefore requires that governments borrow.

Borrowing for Deficits There are two sources for such borrowing: the general public (including the chartered banks) and the Bank of Canada.

Borrowing from the Public If the government borrows from the public by issuing government bonds—such as the Canada Savings Bonds issued each fall—*private spending is reduced.* Individuals may reduce their consumption spending slightly to purchase government bonds. More likely, they hold their savings in the form of government bonds instead of other bonds or bank deposits that would have made their savings available for private investment spending. Borrowing from the public can increase aggregate demand only if government expenditures are directed to individuals whose marginal propensity to consume is higher than that of persons who would have received these funds through the private spending by consumers.

Crowding Out This reduction in private spending that results from increased government borrowing is often referred to as *"crowding out"*. There does seem to be some evidence supporting the argument that government borrowing crowds out, or reduces, private investment. In the United States, there has been a stable ratio of total outstanding debt to GNP throughout the postwar period, with changes in the relative size of the federal government's debt resulting in compensating changes in all other debt. In Canada, the debt-to-GDP ratio has been less stable because Canadian borrowers tend to look for foreign lenders whenever domestic interest rates rise relative to rates elsewhere. (But potential depreciation of the foreign exchange rate for the Canadian dollar also has to be taken into account, since both principal and interest would then cost more Canadian dollars than expected.)

Borrowing from the Bank of Canada Since borrowing from the public can diminish the stimulating effect of a deficit budget, the government is inclined to borrow at least a large portion of the required funds from the Bank of Canada. When the government sells bonds to the Bank, the bonds are added to the Bank's assets. The Bank's liabilities are increased in the form of Government of Canada deposits at the Bank. The government can then issue cheques directly against this account or transfer its deposit to the chartered banks. In either case, *the effect is to create new money.*

When a cheque drawn against the government's account at the Bank of Canada is deposited by a recipient at a bank, monetary expansion begins, following the process outlined previously. Thus, financing a budgetary deficit by borrowing from the Bank of Canada has a doubly stimulating effect. The deficit adds new government spending to aggregate expenditure, while the increased money supply encourages investment through lower interest rates and availability of loans. Note, however, that the effect on interest rates may be slight, since the increased national income due to new government spending will subsequently increase the demand for money.

If the stimulating effect of the government's deficit has only a modest impact on employment and real output, the result will be greater inflation. Consequently there is always a concern that financing government deficits through borrowing from the Bank of Canada may produce higher levels of inflation rather than reduced unemployment.

Disposing of Surpluses   Budget surpluses may be handled in either of two ways: the surplus revenues may be used to repay some of the government's debt, or they may be held in the government's bank accounts. A surplus budget, however, is intended to reduce inflation by reducing aggregate demand. If the surplus is used to reduce the debt, bond-holders will receive some of the surplus, probably use these funds for consumption and investment spending, and thus diminish the anti-inflationary effect of the surplus.

Alternatively, the government can retire some of the debt held by the Bank of Canada. The procedure is the reverse of that followed when the government borrows from the Bank of Canada. Cheques are drawn on the government's deposits at the chartered banks to pay the Bank of Canada for the government bonds it surrenders. The Bank of Canada "cashes" them by reducing the chartered banks' reserves at the Bank. Not only is aggregate expenditure reduced by the amount of the budget surplus; the money supply is being reduced, initially by the reduction of bank reserves, and later by the contractive process as the chartered banks seek to restore the minimum cash reserve requirement. Thus, using a surplus to retire publicly held debt may offset part of the deflationary effect of the budget, but retiring debt held by the Bank of Canada will augment the deflationary effect.

If the government holds the surplus as idle balances at the chartered banks, aggregate expenditure is reduced. The money supply is reduced to the extent that the deposits are transferred from individuals' and corporations' accounts to those of the government, since federal government deposits are excluded from the money supply.

Fiscal Policy in Canada

Economic policy-makers in Canada have a somewhat more difficult task than do their counterparts in the United States and many European countries, due to the division of powers between the federal and provincial governments. During the 1970s provincial and municipal government spending were each close to the level of federal spending, and their combined spending greatly exceeded federal spending. This is one important reason for the increasing number of first ministers' conferences in Canada, at which the prime minister meets with provincial premiers to seek cooperation on economic policies.

The 1940s   The federal-provincial jurisdictional conflicts have always presented problems for Canadian economic policies, but these were minimized in World War II when the Wartime Tax Agreements transferred the provinces' responsibility for income tax to the federal government. Although the immediate reason for this transfer was to raise revenues for war finance, it also centralized fiscal policy. A number of economists emerged from the closely controlled economy of World War II anxious to use the new Keynesian prescriptions for fiscal policy. These seemed ideally designed, particularly those concerning budgetary deficits, to deal with the anticipated recession following the war. Instead of a recession, however, there was rapid inflation in 1946 as consumers cashed their wartime savings bonds to buy cars and other items that had been rationed or unavailable during the war.

Since then fiscal policy has had to deal with several recessions, and fewer "booms". These periods have occurred approximately as follows:

Recession		Expansion
1948–1949	1967–1968	1949–1952
1953–1954	1970	1955–1956
1957–1958	1974–1975	1962–1966
1960–1961	1980	1968–1969
	1982	1971–1973
	1990–1991	1976–1979
		1984–1989

The 1950s and 1960s   Fiscal policy appears to have been roughly appropriate through most of the 1950s, with the federal government running a surplus budget in a period of high growth with inflation and unemployment at low levels. The recession of 1953-1954 was accompanied by a slight federal deficit. When it became apparent in mid-1957 that the economy was slowing down, the government moved toward a deficit budget, which it then continued through the high unemployment period of 1960 to 1962. This deficit was so small, however, relative to the levels of unemployment (which were at a post-Depression record high) that the government's fiscal policy could be described as neutral.

Through the growth period of 1962 to 1965, fiscal policy was mildly expansionary. A major tax cut was introduced in 1965, with personal income tax rates reduced by 10 per cent, in order to maintain the steady growth that had occurred since 1962. Emerging inflation, however, caught the government by surprise, since inflation had not exceeded 2 per cent since 1958. Consequently, taxes were raised in 1966 to offset the stimulus initiated by the 1965 budget. Fiscal policy was reversed again in late 1966 when it was recognized that growth was slowing, and a mildly expansionary program would be required. By 1969, the emerging inflationary pressures were clearly recognized and fiscal policy became strongly restrictive, in spite of increasing unemployment.

The 1970s   As the unemployment rate moved above 6 per cent in 1971 and 1972, fiscal policy moved from a large surplus position in 1969 to a deficit. The 1973 budget included a 5 per cent cut in personal income taxes, but increased inflation and real growth led to a federal surplus. (This surplus, and the budgetary deficits for succeeding years, are shown in Figure 9.7.) A more expansionary program in 1974 included an 8 per cent cut in personal income taxes, and tax reductions on building materials and construction equipment in order to stimulate the housing industry.

The antidote for increasing inflation in 1975 was *"indexation"* of the personal income tax structure. That is, the value of exemptions was to be increased each year in pace with the inflation rate. Although the 1974 budget had forecast a small surplus for 1975, this did not develop due to the almost negligible rate of real growth. In October 1975 the federal government introduced a formal wage and price control program, which is described in Chapter 11. The overall effect of the 1977 federal budgets in March and October appeared to be neutral, with both unemployment and inflation at about 7.5 per cent and rising.

The newly elected Conservative government presented a budget—on which the government was defeated in December 1979—that focused on energy prices. Crude oil prices were to rise to 85 per cent of world prices by 1984, and the gasoline tax would be more than tripled in order to reduce oil consumption.

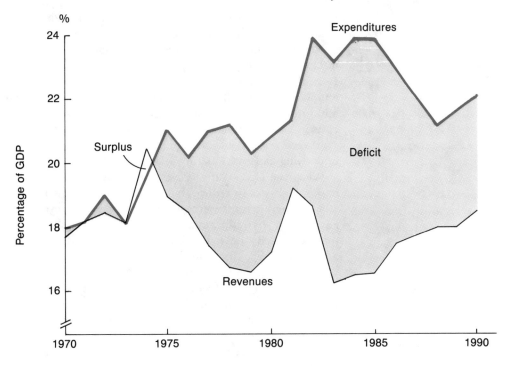

Figure 9.7   Federal Government's Deficit or Surplus (National Accounts Basis)
The federal government's revenues and expenditures are shown here as a percentage of GDP. Before 1975, there were short periods of budgetary deficit or surplus as the government responded to cyclical fluctuations in the economy. But in each year since 1975, there has been a deficit; this was especially large in 1982 and 1983 during a severe recession, but continued to grow during the recovery in 1984 and 1985.

Source: Department of Finance, *Quarterly Economic Review*, December 1990.

The 1980s   A Liberal government, elected in February 1980, brought in a "standpat" budget on the assumption that the current recession was ended, but that recovery would be slow and sporadic. The new National Energy Program, announced as part of the 1980 budget, was designed to replace Canada's consumption of foreign oil with Canadian oil, and to increase Canadian ownership of the gas and petroleum industry.

The budget of November 1981 faced unprecedented difficulties. The economy had reached record inflation rates of over 12 per cent, the unemployment rate was increasing beyond 8 per cent, and real economic growth had almost come to a halt. Economic stimulation would renew inflationary pressure, while contraction would worsen the impending recession. Consequently, the budget was designed to reduce the inflationary effect of a government deficit by increasing tax revenues from the higher income groups and large corporations.

When the June 1982 budget was announced, fear of impending inflation led the government to introduce its *six and five program*. Federal employees' pay raises would be limited to 6 per cent in 1982 and 5 per cent in following years until the program terminated. Grants and subsidies were provided for groups hit hardest by the high interest costs in 1981–82. A short-term budget in April 1983, at the peak of a short recovery, emphasized productivity improvements to overcome this underlying cause of inflation.

When the Conservative government was elected in 1984, one of its major goals was to reduce the government's deficit. In both 1985 and 1986, some attempts were made to increase tax revenues and reduce government expenditures, but these had only a slight impact on the total deficit. By 1987, the federal deficit seemed to have levelled off, and even to have diminished slightly.

Throughout the rest of the 1980s, however, the federal government budgets continued to focus on deficit reduction as a primary objective. Although the 1988 budget forecast a deficit of $29 billion, it remained above $30 billion. Increasing interest rates, designed to restrain inflation, increased the cost of financing the deficit and took a larger share of the federal expenditures. The 1989 budget increased personal and corporate income taxes, but the 1990 and 1991 budgets left these unchanged while imposing greater restrictions on government spending.

Public Debt

A distinction is seldom made between the terms *public debt*, *national debt*, and *federal debt*. Strictly speaking, the public debt includes the outstanding debt (or liabilities) of all governments — municipal and provincial, as well as federal. The federal debt obviously refers only to the debt of the federal government. Perhaps because the latter debt forms such a large part of the total public debt (see Figure 9.8), the two terms are often used interchangeably. Because "national debt" is used ambiguously to refer to either, this term should preferably not be used at all.

Some people have advocated an annually balanced budget because they fear that continuing deficits could lead the country to accumulate very large debts that never could be repaid. Whether the public debt *should* ever be completely paid off is a question to be considered shortly. Even supporters of budgetary deficits to control unemployment are concerned about the public debt, although less about the absolute size of the debt than about the effects of its existence and its management.

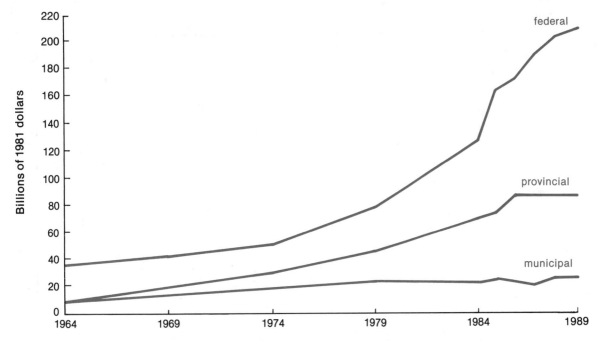

Figure 9.8   Public Debt*, in Constant (1981) Dollars,† by Level of Government, Canada
Through the 1960s and 1970s, the federal government's debt was just slightly greater than the combined debt of the provincial and municipal governments. But in the 1980s, the federal share of the public debt rose substantially. The federal debt increased, in real terms, by about 250 per cent in the decade 1979–88.

Source: Department of Finance, *Quarterly Economic Review, Annual Reference Tables*.

* Unmatured debt that includes marketable bonds, debentures, Canada Savings bonds, and treasury bills.
† Based on the GDP Implicit Price Index.

Size of the Public Debt

The public debt is the current total amount owed by all levels of government, principally municipal debentures, provincial bonds, and federal bonds and treasury bills. The largest component is the federal debt; it has amounted to more than the combined debt of the provincial and local governments throughout the 1970s and 1980s, and was relatively much greater in preceding decades. The federal debt increased rapidly during World War II, when the federal government borrowed heavily to finance defence expenditures. Although the debt has also grown considerably since 1945, the ability of the country to carry this debt grew even more quickly—at least until recent years. This is reflected in the

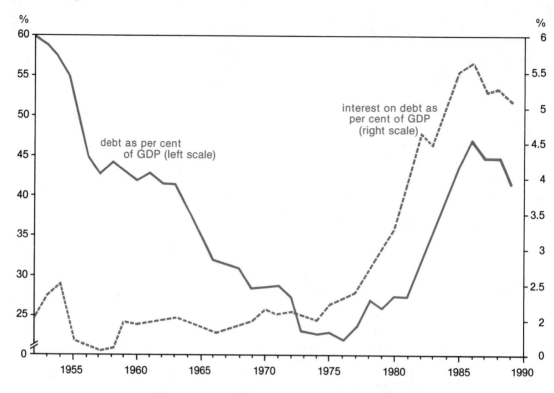

Figure 9.9   Federal Debt and Interest on the Debt Relative to Canada's GDP

The size of the unmatured federal debt, as a percentage of GDP, fell fairly steadily from 65 per cent in 1952 to a low of 22 per cent in 1976. But the accumulating budget deficits drove this ratio up again to almost 50 per cent by 1987. Interest payments on the federal debt amounted to about 2 per cent of GDP until the mid-1970s, when increasing interest rates and the larger debt pushed this ratio up over 5 per cent.

Source: Department of Finance, *Quarterly Economic Review, Annual Reference Tables*.

ratio of the federal government's debt to GDP, as is shown in Figure 9.9.

The federal debt was even greater than the level of GDP by the end of World War II, but during the 15 years from 1951 to 1976 the size of the federal debt fell from 65 per cent to 22 per cent of the GDP. The sudden and persistent increase in the federal deficit (as shown in Figure 9.7) that began in 1975 has reversed this long-run trend, such that by 1988 the size of the federal debt was equal to almost 50 per cent of the Canadian GDP. Expressed differently, the federal debt represented over $10,000 per person in Canada, and over $20,000 per member of the labour force.

Another comparison can be made, between interest payments required to carry the debt and the annual GDP. Figure 9.9 also shows that *the percentage of GDP required to meet the interest charges* on the federal debt has increased steadily due to higher interest rates as well as the increase in the debt. This second comparison represents the actual cost of the federal debt and is thus the comparison to be considered when budgetary deficits are evaluated.

Implications of the Public Debt

An evaluation of the costs and advantages of the public debt requires that some unique features of the debt be recognized.

Possible Burden on Future Generations

It is sometimes argued that the public debt places a burden on future generations by requiring them to pay interest and principal on a debt they did not incur. However, to the extent that government expenditures have been used productively, future generations will enjoy a higher level of goods and services than would have been possible otherwise. Current government expenditures for items such as education, health care, and transportation facilities are expected to produce substantial future economic benefits from which the costs of the debt can be met.

Wasteful government expenditures that did not produce such benefits would, however, represent a future burden. Furthermore, *failure* to increase the public debt can also become a burden if the current generation allows what is called "social overhead capital" to degenerate. If roads, schools, hospitals, airports, and other public facilities are not properly maintained, large future deficits with sharp increases in public debt will be required to bring these structures back to the original operating standard.

Income Redistribution

It is often said that "we all owe the public debt to ourselves". More correctly, the debt is owed by everyone in the country, but only to some persons. Repayment of outstanding debt can be made only by borrowing more money from ourselves or by raising our own taxes. This means that the total consumption of goods and services is not reduced, as it would be when a private debt is repaid, but there may be a transfer of income to the extent that the persons to whom the debt is repaid are different from those who provide the new borrowed funds or who pay the taxes.

Most bondholders are corporations or individuals in the higher-income groups, but some of the tax revenues raised to pay the interest charges or to repay part of the debt comes from the lower-income groups. The resulting income redistribution toward the higher-income groups can be considered a burden of the public debt, especially if one objective of the government's fiscal policy is to redistribute income toward the lower-income groups.

Externally Held Debt   Provincial and municipal governments do not have the advantage of being able to sell their bonds to the Bank of Canada to finance a budget deficit. Consequently, a significant portion of the provincial and municipal debt—and some of the federal debt—is held by residents of other countries. Foreign holdings represent about 30 per cent of provincial bonds, about 25 per cent of municipal bonds, and about 20 per cent of federal bonds and treasury bills. This externally held debt represents a burden to the extent that residents of Canada must forgo some consumption to pay the interest charges and eventually to repay the debt. In this sense, the public debt does resemble a private debt.

Limitations on Monetary Policy   Several times each year it is necessary to refinance part of the public debt as matured bonds are presented for payment. The government would like to arrange this refinancing—issuing new bonds to raise funds for repayment of mature bonds—during recessions, when interest rates tend to be low, in order to minimize future interest payments. But if the sale of government bonds is concentrated in such periods, this will increase the general level of interest rates, discourage private investment, and prolong the recession, just at the time when the Bank of Canada would be attempting to lower interest rates to stimulate the economy. Conversely, the government will be reluctant to see interest rates increased during inflationary periods if it must refinance part of the debt, while the Bank will be trying to raise interest rates to restrain aggregate demand.

Basis for Open Market Operations   The principal advantage of the public debt is the stimulating effect of the budget deficit financed by the debt. A second advantage is the existence of a large quantity of widely held government bonds, which are the basis for the Bank of Canada's open market operation. Recall that the Bank can effect subtle, daily changes in the money supply by buying and selling government bonds. In the absence of such a monetary tool, the Bank would be forced to rely on more disruptive devices, such as changing reserve requirements or the Bank Rate or both.

Tax Disincentives   If marginal tax rates are increased to raise tax revenues for interest payments or debt repayments, this may act as a disincentive, or discourage individuals from earning higher incomes and corporations from investing in new and riskier projects. However, even if higher marginal tax rates have such a disincentive effect, it would represent only a minor burden of the debt, since such a small part of tax revenues are used for payments of interest and principal on the public debt that the rate increase would be similarly small.

Inflationary Effects   The public debt represents the accumulation of budget deficits intended to have an expansionary effect. This effect may continue, however, even when the need for it has passed. Holdings of highly liquid assets like Canada Savings Bonds create what has been termed a *wealth effect*. Individuals feel wealthier than if their assets were in less liquid forms, like real estate, and consequently have a higher consumption level at any given income level. This can have an inflationary effect when the economy is close to full employment, and thus reinforce the inflationary effect that may result directly from a budget deficit.

Review of the Main Points

1. The federal government's fiscal and monetary policies are part of its overall stabilization policy to reduce inflation and unemployment. Because these generally occur together, the government must choose to reduce inflation while accepting higher levels of unemployment, or vice versa.

2. There is even some doubt whether a trade-off relationship still exists, because there is thought to be a "natural" rate of unemployment that determines the long-run equilibrium combination of inflation and unemployment.

3. Fiscal policy includes both automatic and discretionary elements. Automatic stabilizers include the higher marginal propensities to save and to import at higher income levels, government programs that automatically vary transfer payments as incomes change, and the progressive income tax structure that reduces the proportion of disposable income as gross incomes rise.

4. Discretionary fiscal policy includes the actions taken by the government to achieve not only stable prices and full employment but also economic growth, favourable income distribution, and balance of payments equilibrium, through the appropriate composition and size of its expenditures and tax revenues. Alternative fiscal policies are available, for example, to reduce unemployment. The three basic approaches are: an increase in government expenditures, a decrease in tax revenues, or an equal increase in both tax revenues and expenditures.

5. The size of the change required varies for each of these alternatives. Because the multiplier affects the full amount of government expenditures, these need to be increased the least. Since the multiplier acts only on the consumption component of increased disposable income, tax revenues must be decreased by more than the increase in government expenditures to have a given effect on national income. Finally, if the value of the multiplier is uniform throughout the economy, an equal change in tax revenues and gov-

ernment expenditures will change national income by the same amount.

6. A major problem in designing discretionary fiscal policy is to determine how long current increases in inflation or unemployment are likely to last if current fiscal policy is not revised. A strong deflationary policy, for example, could produce a recession if the strength of a current inflationary trend is overestimated.

7. Other problems include the time lags in recognizing an emerging problem, deciding on the proper action, and implementing this policy; there is also the problem of determining how this public action will indirectly affect private spending and how particular areas and individuals will be affected by a general policy.

8. An annually balanced government budget would reinforce any deflationary or inflationary trend in the economy. Balancing the budget over the cycle is generally impossible because the size and duration of recessions and expansionary periods are never equal. Instead, governments should have budget deficits or surpluses as required to guide the economy to non-inflationary full employment.

9. Deficits may be financed by borrowing from the general public or from the Bank of Canada. Borrowing from the public may have a "crowding out" effect because it transfers private consumption and investment to government spending. A net increase in spending results if private funds would have been dormant or used to purchase foreign securities, or if the multiplier is greater for government expenditures than for private spending. Borrowing from the Bank of Canada creates new money and thus has a much stronger expansionary effect. There is therefore a high risk of causing inflation.

10. Surpluses generally are used to reduce the outstanding public debt. Repayment of publicly held debt transfers aggregate demand from taxpayers to bondholders, but repayment of a debt held by the Bank of Canada reduces the money supply and then the level of aggregate demand.

11. Effective fiscal policy in Canada requires the cooperation of all three levels of government, since the federal level represents less than one-half of total public spending. Fiscal policy was centralized during World War II, when the provinces transferred their powers to tax incomes to the federal government; this centralizing trend continued during the postwar period.

12. Fiscal policy was roughly appropriate during the 1950s, but tended to lag behind the events in the 1960s that required stronger action. By the 1970s it became clear that high rates of inflation required stronger monetary policy to reinforce fiscal policy.

13. Indexation of the personal income tax structure in 1975 reduced the effect of fiscal drag. Subsequently, fiscal policy was designed primarily to restrain the growing budget deficit.
14. Public debt includes the outstanding debt of all levels of government, but the major part of it is the federal debt.
15. The public debt declined relative to the size of GDP until 1975, but has since increased. Furthermore, the interest charges on the public debt have also increased as a percentage of the GDP.
16. The public debt represents a burden on future generations who must repay the debt, only if the funds have not been used for real investment that will increase the productive capacity of the economy. There is, however, a redistribution of income to the extent that taxpayers at all income levels repay the bondholders in the upper income groups.
17. There may be limitations on the exercise of monetary policy to the extent that the government will be faced with higher interest charges when there is a restrictive monetary policy. Conversely, a large and widely held public debt provides the basis for open market operations.
18. There is some evidence that higher taxes to pay interest and principal on the debt act as work disincentives; as well, individuals who hold financial assets have higher consumption spending, which may foster inflation.

Key Concepts and Topics

stabilization policies	discretionary fiscal policy
fiscal policy	policy lags
monetary policy	recognition lag
Phillips curve or trade-off curve	budget deficit or surplus
natural rate of unemployment	functional finance
NAIRU	full-employment balance
"stagflation"	structural deficit
automatic stabilizers	public debt
fiscal drag	wealth effect

Questions for Review and Discussion

1. Under what conditions would the federal government's budget deficit have little or no expansionary effect on the economy?
2. If a Phillips curve represents an historical relationship between unemployment and inflation, which changes frequently, is the concept of a Phillips curve of any value in designing economic policy?

Why do some economists argue that the long-run Phillips curve is vertical?

3. "It is not the existence of a large public debt, but rather the changes in the debt that have an influence on the economy." Do you agree? Why?

4. Why is the problem of time lags so important in setting fiscal policies?

Sources and Selected Readings

Dornbusch, R., S. Fisher, and G. Sparks. *Macroeconomics*, 3rd ed. Toronto: McGraw-Hill Ryerson, 1989.

Economic Council of Canada. *Twenty-seventh Annual Review: Transitions for the 90s*. Ottawa: Supply and Services Canada, 1990.

Heilbroner, Robert L., and J.K. Galbraith. *Understanding Macroeconomics*, rev. ed. Englewood Cliffs, N.J.: Prentice-Hall, 1987.

Lamontagne, Maurice. *Business Cycles in Canada: The Postwar Experience and Policy Directions*. Ottawa: Canadian Institute for Economic Policy, 1984.

Riddell, Craig. *Dealing with Inflation and Unemployment in Canada*. Toronto: University of Toronto Press, 1985.

Rose, David. *The NAIRU in Canada: Concepts, Determinants and Estimates*. Ottawa: Bank of Canada, 1988.

Sargent, John. *Fiscal and Monetary Policy*. Toronto: University of Toronto Press, 1985.

Wilton, D.A., and D.M. Prescott. *Macroeconomics: Theory and Policy in Canada*, 2nd ed. Toronto: Addison-Wesley, 1987.

10 Monetary Policy and the Foreign Exchange Rate

Monetary Policy

Monetary policy is the deliberate effort by the government, acting through the monetary authorities (the Bank of Canada), to vary the money supply in order to move the economy toward full employment without inflation. In addition, monetary policy attempts to maintain a viable balance of payments and an appropriate foreign exchange rate.

The classical view of money's role emphasized its direct influence on the price level, but the neo-Keynesian view stresses the effect of the money supply on interest rates. Interest rates in turn are expected to have some effect on the level of investment, particularly in residential construction and inventories, and hence on employment and national income.

To trace the sequence of effects of monetary policy on national income (and thus on unemployment and inflation), assume that the Bank of Canada is pursuing an expansionary policy by buying bonds in the open market. The purchase of bonds increases chartered bank reserves, making more loans available, thus increasing deposits (the money supply) and reducing interest rates.

Bond purchases also directly cause changes in the interest rates. The Bank can usually acquire enough bonds to realize its policy objectives only if it offers a higher price for bonds than would otherwise prevail in the bond market. A higher bond price results in a lower yield or interest rate.[1] A lower interest rate is expected to encourage firms to increase their investment in plant and equipment, to increase their inventories of semifinished and finished goods, and to increase residential construction.

---

[1] Recall from Chapter 8 that the actual interest rate on a bond varies inversely with the price of a bond. This is because the actual rate (r) is determined by the equation $r = i/P_B$, where i is the nominal or face-value rate and P_B is the bond price.

Limitations of Monetary Policy

The use of fiscal policy was seen to have a number of limitations or qualifications. Monetary policy is similarly constrained as a means for reducing inflation and unemployment, particularly because of the conflict between domestic and external economic objectives.

Asymmetry of Monetary Policy

The major limitation is the asymmetry of monetary policy: the Bank of Canada can force a contraction in bank deposits, but it can only encourage an expansion (by increasing chartered banks' excess reserves). Monetary expansion is curtailed if the banks are not "fully loaned up", that is, if banks are not able to find borrowers for all of their excess reserves. Such a situation might occur when interest rates are quite high. In this case, stronger expansionary monetary policy would be required to force interest rates down far enough to attract a substantial number of borrowers. The banks might use some of their excess reserves to buy bonds from the general public—thus adding to bank deposits—but only reluctantly, since the yield on bonds is lower than on personal and business loans.

Timing of Effects

Monetary policy appears to have about the same overall time lag that is encountered with fiscal policy. The recognition or identification lag may be equally long, but the decision lag can be much shorter than for fiscal policy, since the Bank's senior officers alone usually decide day-to-day policy. (The Finance Minister and his advisors are consulted on longer-range monetary policy.) The initial stage of the implementation lag can also be somewhat shorter, because the Bank's techniques for changing the money supply act immediately to alter chartered banks' reserves; the subsequent expansion stage may take longer if the banks have difficulty in finding borrowers for their excess reserves. The contraction process, however, must proceed quickly, particularly when the banks have been holding no excess reserves.

Location of Effects

The location of the effects of monetary policy cannot be controlled as can some aspects of fiscal policy, particularly on its expenditure side. Effects of monetary policy are seen first in the larger financial centres of the country, but the branch banking system assures that these effects are quickly dispersed. An excess or deficit of bank reserves is reported only for each chartered bank; the head office of these banks can therefore manage its reserves within its branches as it chooses. In an expansionary situation, for example, all branches of a bank will be advertising for potential borrowers in order to loan out the total excess reserves held by that bank. This universality of effects can be an advantage when the entire country faces similar inflation or unemployment, but a disadvantage when conditions vary significantly among different regions.

Conflict with Debt Management

The discussion of the public debt raised the problems that debt management poses for monetary policy. The government would like to refinance its maturing bonds during recessionary periods when interest rates are low. But substantial sales of government bonds would increase interest rates and discourage investment expenditures. At the same time, the Bank should be buying bonds in the open market to lower interest rates in order to induce more investment spending. Thus the Bank faces a dilemma posed by its two roles as manager of the public debt and as agent of monetary policy.

Investment Inelasticity   Investment spending may in some cases be inelastic with respect to changes in the interest rate. If, for example, firms are sceptical that the government's expansionary policies will be effective in increasing aggregate demand, they will not increase investment spending even at much lower interest rates. This also illustrates, incidentally, another limitation on monetary policy: that business expectations contrary to the desired direction of government policy can severely weaken its effect.

Investment spending may also be interest-inelastic for high-yield, high-risk projects. Whether the project is undertaken will depend on the firm's assessment of many factors influencing the potential success of the venture, rather than on the interest rate.

Finally, larger firms may have sufficient funds among their highly liquid assets to undertake whatever investment projects they may be considering. The increased scarcity of loans would have little effect on their investment decisions; only a very high interest rate would cause them to question whether such funds should be held in higher yielding assets rather than in the firms' own investment projects. Smaller firms, however, are not so likely to have internal funds, and therefore are more affected by changes in monetary policy.

Effect of Near-Money   Asset holdings in the form of near-money or highly liquid assets can offset much of the potential effect of a contractionary monetary policy. Chartered banks can sell their government bonds to provide loan funds; firms and individuals can sell their more liquid assets to maintain their investment and consumption spending.

Velocity of Circulation   A problem similar to that posed by near-money is presented by changes in the velocity of money. Recall from the quantity equation of exchange, $MV = PQ$, that an increase in V will have the same effect on national income as an increase in M. Velocity tends to increase late in an expansionary period, when monetary policy usually is attempting to restrain increases in the money supply, because individuals want to hold less money as interest rates rise. Higher interest rates encourage savings and trust companies to be more active in attracting and loaning funds during an expansionary period, and higher interest rates also cause individuals to reduce their chequing account balances to the lowest possible amounts. This further increases the velocity of money, partly offsetting the effect of contractionary monetary policy.

The income velocities of M1 and M2 are shown in Figure 10.1. Until late 1982, the Bank of Canada focused on M1 as the stock of money it tried to control, but it is M1 that has had the greatest increase in velocity. For example, in 1979-82, when the Bank of Canada was attempting to restrain the growth of M1, the velocity increased sharply.

Liquidity Trap   At very low interest rates, the liquidity preference or demand for money curve is assumed to flatten out to form a *liquidity trap*. At such low interest rates, people are quite prepared to increase their bank deposits in exchange for bonds. At this point, the Bank's purchase of bonds has little effect on the rate of interest because only a small increase, if any, in bond prices is necessary to provide the Bank with whatever quantity of bonds it seeks. In these circumstances, the money supply can be increased, but interest rates cannot be pushed down further. But when interest rates have reached such a low level, the economy probably is experiencing such high unemployment that little investment or consumption spending can be induced simply by increasing the money supply to make loans available.

The concept of a liquidity trap was important to Keynes' analysis of Depression conditions, but it has less relevance in current economic conditions, with higher interest rates than have prevailed in previous decades.

Foreign Exchange Rates

International trade in goods and services and securities requires that payments be made in the currency of the country supplying these items. This in turn requires that a rate of exchange between foreign currencies be determined.

Perhaps the most serious limitation on domestic monetary policy is the Bank of Canada's responsibility "to control and protect the external value of the national monetary unit", that is, the foreign exchange rate of the Canadian dollar. The next section of this chapter shows how the foreign exchange rate is determined and how changes in the foreign exchange rate affect domestic monetary policy. The Balance of Payments accounts that are used to record international payments are discussed in Chapter 13.

Foreign Exchange Markets

Foreign exchange markets include all the buyers and sellers of particular currencies in every country. There is a separate market for each *pair* of currencies because a currency can be bought only with another currency. Hence, as illustrated by the market quotations in Box 10.1, there are many foreign exchange markets for the Canadian dollar: a Canadian dollar can be bought with Swiss francs, Italian liras, Greek drachmas, and so on.

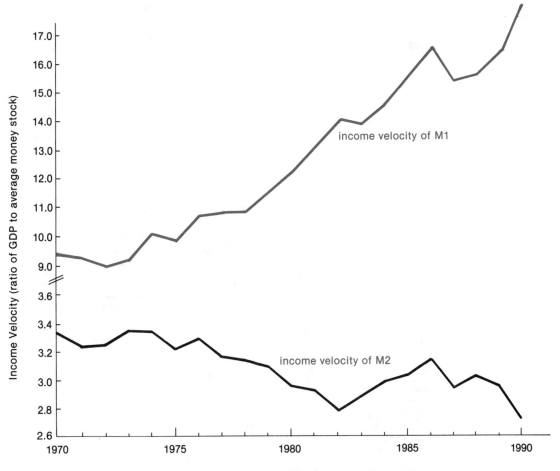

Figure 10.1   Income Velocities of M1 and M2
The continuing increase in the velocity of M1 and the recent increase in the
velocity of M2 have partly offset the effects of the Bank's attempts to
restrain the growth in money supply.

Source: *Bank of Canada Review.*

Exchange of currencies usually occurs in chartered or commercial
banks, which in turn deal with the central banks of each country or
with the major commercial banks of other countries. Foreign currencies
are also exchanged in firms that make foreign currency exchange their
principal business.

Exchange Rates   The foreign exchange rate or price of the Canadian
dollar can be expressed in terms of numerous other currencies,
although it is most often stated in terms of the American dollar. But
if Canadian dollars can be traded in many different places at the same
time, how can there be only one American price for the Canadian
dollar? Or one British price? Or one Spanish price?

Box 10.1

Foreign Exchange by Country

Supplied by: Canadian Imperial Bank of Commerce
Noon mid-rates

	Foreign in C$	C$ In foreign	% chng week		Foreign In C$	C$ In foreign	% chng week
Argentina (austral)	0.0002	5498.0025	–4.48	Italy (lira)	0.0010	961.60	+1.17
Austria (schilling)	0.1111	9.0000	+1.13	Jamaica (dollar)*	0.1512	6.6154	+0.36
Bahamas (dollar)*	1.1639	0.8591	+0.36	Malaysia (ringgit)	0.4316	2.3171	+1.26
Barbados (dollar)*	0.5787	1.7280	+0.36	Mexico (peso)	0.0004	2534.99	nil
Belgium (franc)	0.0379	26.3572	+1.11	Netherlands (guilder)	0.6934	1.4421	+1.11
Bermuda (dollar)*	1.1639	0.8591	+0.36	Netherlands Antilles (guilder)*·	0.6503	1.5379	+0.36
Brazil (cruzeiro)	0.0061	165.2562	nil	New Zealand (dollar)	0.6937	1.4415	+0.53
Bulgaria (lev)*	0.3919	2.5518	+0.36	Norway (krone)	0.1997	5.0067	+1.74
Chile (peso)	0.0110	91.2410	–0.30	Pakistan (rupee)	0.0529	18.9183	+0.36
China (renminbi)	0.2229	4.4865	+0.36	Peru (inti)*	0.0000	382040.47	+0.36
Columbia (peso)	0.0021	483.0018	–0.09	Philippines (peso)	0.0428	23.3687	+0.36
Costa Rica (colon)	0.0113	88.2770	+0.36	Poland (zloty)*	0.0001	8161.86	+0.36
Cuba (peso)*	1.4613	0.6843	+0.36	Portugal (escudo)	0.0088	113.41	+2.26
Czechoslovakia (koruna)*	0.0740	13.5057	+0.36	Singapore (dollar)	0.6746	1.4825	+1.44
Denmark (krone)	0.2030	4.9255	+1.11	South Africa (rand)	0.4570	2.1882	+0.95
Dominican Republic (peso)*	0.1069	9.3568	+0.36	South Korea (won)	0.0017	605.9195	+0.33
Egypt (pound)*	0.5820	1.7183	+0.36	Spain (peseta)	0.0124	80.37	+1.17
Finland (markka)	0.3231	3.0955	+1.48	Sri Lanka (rupee)	0.0290	34.5376	+0.14
Grand Cayman (dollar)*	1.4023	0.7131	+0.36	Sweden (krona)	0.2091	4.7833	+1.72
Greece (drachma)	0.0073	136.35	+0.87	Taiwan (dollar)*	0.0427	23.4460	+0.36
Grenada (dollar)*	0.4311	2.3197	+0.36	Thailand (baht)	0.0463	21.5904	+0.72
Guatemala (quetzal)	0.2238	4.4675	+0.36	Trinidad & Tobago (dollar)*	0.2739	3.6514	+0.36
Hong Kong (dollar)	0.1494	6.6944	+0.42	U.S.S.R (rouble)	2.0938	0.4776	+1.70
India (rupee)	0.0631	15.8514	+0.36	Venezuela (bolívar)	0.0227	44.0913	–0.79
Ireland (pound)	2.0811	0.4805	+1.81	Yugoslavia (dinar)	0.0889	11.25	+2.20
Israel (new shekel)	0.5782	1.7295	+1.76	* Indicates fixed rate			

Currency cross rates

Supplied by: Royal Bank of Canada

	C$	US$	DM	Yen	£	Fr.fr.	Sw.fr.	A$
Canadian dollar	·	1.16414	0.78026	0.00878	2.27532	0.22957	0.92107	0.90559
U.S. dollar	0.85900	·	0.67024	0.00754	1.95450	0.19720	0.79120	0.77790
Deutschemark	1.28163	1.49200	·	0.01126	2.91611	0.29422	1.18047	1.16063
Japanese yen	113.86	132.55	88.84	·	259.07	26.14	104.87	103.11
British pound	0.43950	0.51164	0.34292	0.00386	·	0.10090	0.40481	0.39800
French franc	4.35599	5.07100	3.39879	0.03826	9.91127	·	4.01218	3.94473
Swiss franc	1.08569	1.26390	0.84712	0.00954	2.47029	0.24924	·	0.98319
Australian dollar	1.10426	1.28551	0.86160	0.00970	2.51253	0.25350	1.01710	·

Source: *Financial Post*, 28 January 1991.

Foreign exchange rates express the price of one unit of a given currency in terms of a second currency. The published quotations of foreign exchange rates may therefore show "both sides" of the exchange, as is seen in this example: the price of one United States dollar was 1.16414 Canadian dollars, which is the equivalent of saying that the price of one Canadian dollar was .85900 United States dollars.

Arbitrage   There may, in fact, be slight differences in this price at any given time, but such differences are quickly reduced by arbitrage. Persons who watch for these differences and make a profit by buying and selling foreign currencies simultaneously are called arbitragers. If the Canadian dollar is selling for 60.9 Spanish pesetas in Toronto but for 61.2 pesetas in Madrid, an arbitrager in Toronto will call a broker in Madrid, buy one million pesetas, and sell them immediately in

Toronto. The one million pesetas will cost $16,340 in Madrid but they can be exchanged for $16,420 in Toronto, with a profit of $80. Since this may not cover the costs of telephone calls and broker's fees, the arbitrager will deal in larger quantities. As arbitragers rush to make their gains on these differences, their own actions move the prices for a particular currency toward a common level around the world.

Factors Influencing Exchange Rates

Although arbitrage does have a slight but important influence on the supply and demand for currencies, other factors determine the general level of prices for foreign currencies. The supply and demand for currencies derive from five types of international transactions:

- capital flows;
- trade in goods and services and transfer payments;
- speculation;
- government intervention to maintain pegged rates;
- arbitrage.

Capital Flows *Capital flows* arising, for example, when a Canadian firm borrows funds in New York, require that Canadian dollars be bought with the American dollars being loaned, so that the borrowing firm will have Canadian currency to spend in Canada. This transaction adds to the demand for Canadian dollars in the American foreign exchange market, or to the supply of American dollars in Canada. When the Canadian firm pays interest on the loan, its Canadian dollars must be converted to American dollars, with the opposite effects on the American or Canadian foreign exchange markets.

International Trade *Trade in goods and services* has the same type of effects. A Canadian firm importing automobiles from Japan must pay the producer in Japanese yen. The result is an increase in the demand for Japanese yen in Canada or in the supply of Canadian dollars in Japan. In the Balance of Payments accounts (see Table 13.7), receipts represent a demand for Canadian dollars and payments represent the supply of Canadian dollars.

Speculation *Speculation* in foreign currencies is essentially the same as speculation in other markets, from common shares to real estate to agricultural commodities; if speculators expect the price of the item to rise they will buy more, selling it later at (they hope) a higher price. Note that speculation differs from arbitrage: the speculator holds the item for resale later, while the arbitrager buys and sells simultaneously in two markets. If speculators expect the price of a currency to rise, they buy and hold the currency until the expected price is reached, or until it becomes unprofitable to wait longer. When speculators are especially active in buying or selling a particular currency, their own actions may bring about the results they anticipated.

Government Policy   *Government intervention*, through a central bank, to maintain pegged rates is described later in this chapter.

Determination of the Equilibrium Rate

The foreign exchange rate, or the price of one currency in terms of another, is determined by supply and demand forces, just as the equilibrium prices of goods and services are determined. Hypothetical supply and demand curves for Canadian dollars in terms of Swiss francs are shown in Figure 10.2. The demand curve indicates that when the price of the Canadian dollar increases in terms of Swiss francs (or when more Swiss francs must be paid for a Canadian dollar), fewer Canadian dollars would be demanded by persons wishing to buy them with Swiss francs. This reflects the fact that as the price of the Canadian dollar rises in terms of Swiss francs, Canadian goods become more expensive for Swiss importers. Although the price of a woollen blanket in Canada, for example, may remain at $20, an increase in the price of a Canadian dollar from 2 francs to 3 francs means that Swiss importers must pay 50 per cent more for a blanket. Thus, fewer Canadian goods would be bought and fewer Canadian dollars would be required. The demand curve for Canadian dollars therefore has the conventional downward slope to the right.

Why is the supply curve shown to slope upward to the right? An increase in the price of the Canadian dollar implies a decrease in the price of Swiss francs. Swiss watches, for example, would be less expensive in Canadian dollar terms and more of them would be purchased by Canadian importers. Although a greater quantity of watches would be purchased, it is not certain that a greater quantity of dollars would be offered for exchange with francs. This depends on the elasticity of demand for Swiss watches.[2] If this is *inelastic*, the total expenditure of Canadian dollars will be less, and fewer Canadian dollars will need to be exchanged for Swiss francs to purchase the greater number of watches. The supply curve will be downward sloping to the right. If there is *unitary* demand elasticity, the supply curve will be vertical because there is no change in the total expenditure of Canadian dollars or in the number of dollars to be exchanged for francs; and if the

---

[2] Recall from Chapter 3 that a price increase results in a greater total expenditure if demand is inelastic, but a lower total expenditure if demand is elastic.

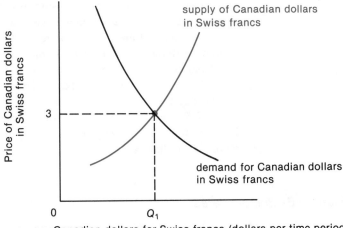

Figure 10.2   Unpegged Foreign Exchange Rates Are Determined by the Supply of and Demand for Currencies
When the foreign exchange rate of the Canadian dollar is free to fluctuate, the exchange rate between the Canadian dollar and, for example, the Swiss franc is determined by the supply of Canadian dollars exchanged for Swiss francs and the demand for Canadian dollars purchased with Swiss francs. At a price of 3 Swiss francs for one Canadian dollar, the quantity of Canadian dollars purchased in the given time period is Q_1. At a higher price there would be an excess supply of Canadian dollars, and at a lower price there would be an excess demand for Canadian dollars.

demand for watches is *elastic*, the quantity of Canadian dollars offered will rise. For the sake of simplicity, it is this last case that is assumed in the upward slope of the supply curve shown in Figure 10.2.

Note that the supply of dollars to the foreign exchange market is quite different from the supply or stock of money within Canada. Canadian dollars going into the foreign exchange market represent only a small percentage of the total money supply in Canada; and of course when dollars leave the country they are no longer a part of the money supply in Canada.

Money Supply and Foreign Exchange Rates

Foreign exchange rates can be determined either by government decree or by the unregulated market forces of supply and demand. In the first case, the rate is said to be *pegged* or *fixed*; in the second case, the rate is *floating* or *fluctuating*. When the foreign exchange rate is free to fluctuate, it is determined by the supply and demand for Canadian dollars related to international financial transactions and the flow of goods and services. When foreign consumers want to buy more Canadian exports, payment must ultimately be made in Canadian dollars. Foreign currencies offered in exchange for Canadian exports are sold for Canadian dollars in foreign exchange markets operated by the chartered banks. This increase in the demand for Canadian dollars raises the price of the Canadian dollar in terms of other currencies. In other words, the foreign exchange rate of the Canadian dollar rises. Similarly, if foreign countries buy fewer Canadian exports, or Canadians increase their import expenditures, the foreign exchange rate of the Canadian dollar falls.

Fixed (Pegged) Exchange Rates

From 1962 until 1970, the foreign exchange rate of the Canadian dollar was pegged by the Canadian government at the rate of $1.00 (Can.) = $.925 (U.S.). The Canadian dollar was therefore worth about 8 per cent less than the American dollar in terms of foreign purchases or payments. In fixing the foreign exchange rate at this level, the Canadian government agreed with other major industrial countries, through the International Monetary Fund (IMF), that it would take the appropriate action necessary to offset changes in supply or demand for Canadian dollars, in order to keep the rate within a narrow range on either side of the agreed rate.

When the foreign demand for Canadian dollars increased, the Bank of Canada used Canadian dollars from the government's account to buy foreign currencies. In this way, more Canadian dollars were made available and some foreign currencies were removed from the foreign exchange market, thus curtailing upward pressure on the Canadian foreign exchange rate.

The Canadian dollars used to purchase foreign currency either were originally drawn from the federal government's deposits at the chartered banks or were borrowed by the government from the Bank of Canada. The effect of the latter action was to increase the money supply, since the money created by the government's borrowing from the Bank of Canada was transferred to the chartered bank that sold the foreign exchange to the government. These actions to hold down the exchange rate of the Canadian dollar could therefore lead to an increase in the money supply that was not intended. It was possible, however, for the Bank of Canada to "sterilize" or offset this potential expansion of the money supply. By selling government bonds to the chartered banks, from whom the foreign currencies were purchased, the Bank of Canada was able to reduce the chartered banks' reserves, and thereby contract the money supply.

When the demand for Canadian dollars fell, putting downward pressure on the foreign exchange rate, the Bank of Canada would sell foreign currency in exchange for Canadian dollars. But this would reduce the foreign currency reserves held by the government in the Exchange

---

Box 10.2 **Reserves hit record as Ottawa cools hot dollar**

By Bruce Little

Canada's official monetary reserves reached yet another record last month as the Bank of Canada continued to lean against the upward pressure on the Canadian dollar by selling the currency into a relatively strong market. . . .

The country's reserves—a basket of foreign currencies used by Ottawa to finance its dealings in the foreign exchange market—rose $474.4-million to $6.5-billion on Feb. 28. It was the second consecutive record high for the reserves account. . . .

Ottawa has to borrow the Canadian dollars it wants to sell to foreign buyers and the strength of the dollar in recent weeks has forced the Government to seek new borrowing authority from Parliament and resort to special measures to finance its purchases of foreign exchange.

Two weeks ago, Finance Minister Michael Wilson tabled a borrowing bill asking for another $3.6-billion (Canadian) to finance the buying of reserves. Last week, he announced that he was using a provision in the Financial Administration Act to permit the Government to borrow an additional $600-million today in three- and six-month treasury bills. That money is expected to see the Government through until the new borrowing bill can be passed. . . .

Acting for the Government, the Bank of Canada sells Canadian dollars when the currency is rising too fast for its liking and buys dollars when the currency is falling too quickly. In both cases, such intervention moderates the push of the market in either direction.

In January, when the dollar rose 2.2 cents (U.S.) to finish the month at 74.64 cents, the Bank added almost $2-billion (U.S.) to its reserves of foreign exchange, which are always denominated in U.S. dollars. . . .

The bulk of the reserves are kept in U.S. dollars, which last month accounted for $4.467-billion of the total, up $272-million from Jan. 31. Other currencies, which normally account for less than $50-million worth of holdings, last month rose to $319.9-million, an increase of almost $240-million from the January level of $80.6-million. . . .

Source: *The Globe and Mail*, 5 March 1987

This newspaper article illustrates how the federal government intervenes in the foreign currency market when it wishes to influence the exchange rate. Note that this policy has a cost, namely, the interest charges on the borrowed funds.

Fund Account, possibly requiring the government to borrow the required amount of foreign currency.

The Bank's actions in changing the money supply as part of domestic economic policy could also have an impact on the Exchange Fund Account. Increasing the money supply would lower the interest rate. This in turn would cause short-term deposits to be moved to other countries in search of higher interest rates. This would result in a downward pressure on the Canadian foreign exchange rate. To offset this, the Bank of Canada would need to sell foreign currencies and buy Canadian dollars. Thus, when the Account's supply of foreign currencies is low, the Bank of Canada is constrained from increasing the money supply by as much as if only domestic conditions had been considered.

Floating Exchange Rates

From 1950 until 1962, and again since May of 1970, the foreign exchange rate of the Canadian dollar has been free to fluctuate with the supply and demand conditions in foreign exchange markets. The Bank of Canada therefore is not required to maintain an official exchange rate for the Canadian dollar, although it holds a view on the appropriate range for the exchange rate and frequently buys or sells Canadian dollars in the foreign exchange market to influence the rate. Box 10.2 presents an example of the Bank's intervention for this purpose. This arrangement is often described as a "managed float": the Bank intervenes frequently to keep the exchange rate within a narrow (but unannounced) range.

Fixed or Floating Exchange Rates?

Floating Rates   The unsettled international monetary situation in the early 1970s raised again the debate on the merits and disadvantages of fixed and floating exchange rates. Among the chief merits of a floating exchange rate is that the balance of payments can adjust automatically, except in the very unusual case of inelastic demand for both a country's exports and imports. When exchange rates are pegged, there can be only an informed guess about the rate that is most likely to achieve equilibrium even in the short run, and too frequent changes in the pegged rate will bring on the disadvantages of both systems. Furthermore, when currency prices (or exchange rates) are determined in the market rather than by arbitrary government decisions, there is no need to maintain foreign reserves simply to maintain a fixed rate. Acquiring foreign reserves can be difficult, expensive, and inflationary when a country has depleted its reserves and must borrow in international markets.

Domestic fiscal and monetary policies do not need to be tempered by considerations of the balance of payments situation. Moreover, inflationary pressures are reduced under a floating exchange rate system. If the exchange rate is fixed, the domestic price level rises with price increases in other countries. This occurs because higher foreign prices attract domestic production into exports, hence there is a fall in the supply of goods and services to the domestic market. Under floating rates,

---

Box 10.3

Dollar's rise aids areas tied to interest rates
By Bruce Little

The biggest winners from the latest rise in the value of the Canadian dollar may not even know what helped them.

Usually, the search for winners and losers from a move in the dollar focuses on Canadian exporters and importers. But the most dramatic effect of the dollar's 3.2 per cent rise in the past month has been a sharp reduction in interest rates.

. . . If the lower rates stick, the chunks of the Canadian economy most sensitive to interest rates should wind up with a brighter year than they were expecting only a few weeks ago. Among those are the construction industry and manufacturers of durable goods.

. . . During that period, the Bank of Canada — fearful of a repeat attack on the dollar — kept interest rates high in an effort to persuade potential speculators that it was serious about keeping the dollar above 72 cents (U.S.). The bank now has relaxed its grip. If the dollar stays in its current 74.6-cent range, the bank may be willing to cut rates further.

That could set the stage for a new round of home-building, which triggers higher purchases of household durables such as furniture and appliances.

. . . One economist figures that a one-percentage-point decline in interest rates, if it lasts, will add 0.5 per cent to the country's growth rate in each of the next two years. Industries turning out consumer goods will benefit first, but businesses should follow by increasing their own spending on new plants and equipment, especially if they see the growth in demand to justify new investment.

Source: *The Globe and Mail*, 31 January 1986

This newspaper report illustrates the potential conflict of domestic and external economic policy. In an effort to put upward pressure on the foreign exchange value of the Canadian dollar, the Bank of Canada had been restricting the growth of the money supply to push up interest rates and thereby increase the demand for Canadian dollars. But the higher interest rates reduced domestic spending on consumer and investment goods.

export sales cause the foreign exchange rate to rise; higher foreign prices are then less attractive to exporters.

Fixed Rates   Fixed exchange rates are usually defended on the grounds that they stabilize the prices of goods and services entering into international trade, and thus encourage such trade. This can be important in a recession when declining imports, under floating rates, would improve the trade balance, push up the foreign exchange rate, and thus reduce exports. Under pegged rates, the exchange rate would not rise and exports would be maintained.[3]

Floating exchange rates are said to encourage speculation, which in turn will reinforce any fluctuation in an exchange rate. A fixed exchange rage, however, can also encourage speculation. When a country has a serious deficit on its balance of payments, is running low on foreign reserves to maintain the agreed rate, and has too much unemployment to implement a restrictive stabilization policy, there is a high probability that it will devalue its currency. Speculation that this will occur involves large-scale selling of the country's currency on foreign exchange markets, creating extreme pressures on the lower limits of the agreed range for the currency's exchange rate. Such speculation is frequently the reason for the final decision to devalue.

Under a fixed foreign exchange rate, monetary policy designed to achieve domestic stability can cause difficulties for monetary authorities. If the money supply is increased and interest rates fall, short-term foreign capital tends to leave the country in pursuit of higher interest rates elsewhere. This puts a downward pressure on the foreign exchange rate, and consequently more foreign currency must be sold from the Exchange Fund Account in exchange for Canadian dollars to maintain the pegged rate within the agreed range. When holdings of foreign currencies are low, the Bank of Canada will be reluctant to pursue an expansionary policy that would further drain the Exchange Fund Account by lowering interest rates. Otherwise, it would be necessary to borrow foreign currencies, with the undesirable consequences of increasing foreign indebtedness and interest payments.

The Bank will also be reluctant to pursue a vigorous expansionary policy if there is a serious deficit on the current account in the balance of payments. Such a policy would tend to increase product prices, reduce exports, and increase imports, thereby worsening the current account deficit.

[3] A study by American economists found that floating exchange rates reduced trade between West Germany and the United States (two of the largest trading nations). West German exports would have been higher by 14 per cent and imports higher by 8 per cent, during 1977–1981. The impact on the United States was considerably less, partly because foreign trade is a smaller percentage of its Gross National Product.

There is no clear conclusion on the preferable exchange rate system — fixed or floating — although the experience with unpegged rates in the 1970s ironically led former proponents of both systems to be less certain of their positions. It has been argued that a formal fixed exchange rate system will not emerge in the foreseeable future because too much foreign currency is held privately, such that this could counteract official actions in the foreign exchange market, and because no single national currency dominates the world economy, as the American dollar once did.

Canada's Exchange Rate Policy

The rapid decline of the Canadian dollar's exchange rate (in terms of the U.S. dollar) from 1976 to 1979 increasingly raised the question, How far can the dollar fall?, amid speculation first of an 85-cent dollar and then an 80-cent dollar. The same question was asked again through the mid-1980s as the dollar fell to 75 cents and then to 70 cents. These fluctuations are shown in Figure 10.3.

Pre-1900 Such a rapid change, however, was not unique in the history of the Canadian dollar. The dollar was first adopted as the monetary unit of the Province of Canada (now Ontario and Quebec) in 1858 and then, in 1870, of the entire Dominion. Previously the "unit of account" had been pounds, shillings, and pence, while the "unit of exchange" was the dollar. The Canadian dollar was pegged in 1858 at par with the U.S. dollar and at $4.87 to the British pound. With the exception of a short-term drop in the U.S. dollar during the American Civil War, this relationship among the three currencies continued until 1914.

After World War I, the British pound fell sharply due to war debts; when Canadians rushed to pay off British debts at this improved exchange rate, the Canadian dollar fell also, reaching a low of US $.82 in 1920. By the mid-1920s the dollar had returned to par with the U.S. dollar; it was fixed at this level in 1926.

Canada floated the dollar again in 1931, when Britain unpegged the pound, and the dollar fell to US $.77. The Canadian dollar rose strongly in 1934 and floated close to par with the U.S. dollar until 1939.

The 1940s and 1950s With the beginning of World War II, Canada imposed foreign exchange controls and pegged the dollar at US $.909. This continued until 1946 when the Canadian dollar was returned to parity with the U.S. dollar. When Britain devalued the pound in 1949, Canada again dropped its exchange rate to US $.909 to maintain its trade competitive-

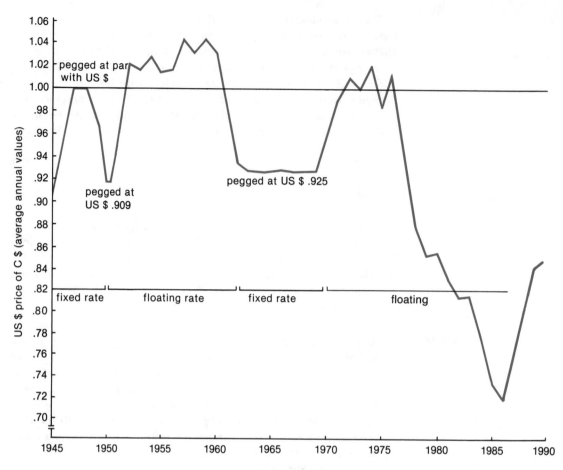

Figure 10.3   Canadian Dollar Exchange Rate in Terms of the American Dollar, 1945-1990
Canada's postwar exchange rate policy is unique in the world in that it has alternated fairly frequently between fixed and floating rates, together with short periods of closely managed "floating" rates. Note that the chart shows *average* values for each year, but that extreme highs and lows exceeded these values.

Source: Department of Finance, *Economic Review*.

*The chart shows the *average* annual value of the Canadian dollar for each year, but the dollar reached a daily peak of US $1.0575 in 1957; and, in 1986, it reached a low of US $.6924.

ness with Britain. The devalued dollar, however, attracted large inflows of American capital, with resulting strong pressure on the pegged rate. Rather than attempt to set yet another, higher pegged rate, the government floated the dollar in 1950. Throughout most of the 1950s, Canada had large inflows of American capital that held the dollar above US $1.00 from 1952 to 1960, with a peak of almost US $1.06 in 1959.

The 1960s   In 1960, the Minister of Finance began to challenge the restrictive monetary policy followed by the Bank of Canada, and in 1961 announced that the government would move to reduce interest rates while directly lowering the exchange rate by buying U.S. dollars.

The Canadian dollar fell so quickly that the government then attempted to support the dollar in early 1962 at about US $.95. This caused such a drain of foreign reserves that the government decided to return to a pegged exchange rate, at US $.925.

Speculation against the Canadian dollar continued after the rate was pegged. The government managed to dissuade the speculators with restrictive monetary and fiscal policies, foreign borrowing, and import surcharges. The dollar was generally strong from 1963 to 1966 due to large trade surpluses (including wheat sales to China and the U.S.S.R.) and the Canada-U.S. Auto Pact. Some weakening of the dollar resulted from Britain's devaluation of the pound to US $2.40 in 1967, when speculation ran against all major currencies.

The 1970s   In 1970, a strong inflow of long-term capital and a record trade surplus led to a large increase in foreign reserves. Since it was clear that the pegged rate was much too low, the government allowed the dollar to float.

The dollar rose sharply through 1970 and 1971 and moved above par with the U.S. dollar in December 1971. From 1970 through 1972 the government maintained a managed float by frequent intervention through the Bank of Canada in the foreign exchange markets, selling Canadian dollars to keep the dollar lower than it would have been otherwise. While this may have reduced unemployment in Canada by maintaining competitiveness for Canadian exports, the result was also to increase inflation.

The steady increase in the trade surplus that Canada had enjoyed since 1960 suddenly turned to a deficit in 1975 and the dollar dropped sharply to about US $.97. A return to a trade surplus in 1976 and a large inflow of capital in response to the wide spread between Canadian and U.S. interest rates caused the dollar to float back above par.

As the Bank of Canada eased off in 1977 from its earlier restrictive policy, the spread in short-term interest rates in the U.S. and Canada was narrowed. This reduced short-term capital inflows; at the same time there was a weakening of long-term capital flows resulting from uncertainty about Quebec's political and economic future. The dollar dropped fairly steadily as the government declined to intervene.

In 1978 the dollar fell to US $.84 as a result of rising inflation and a decline in exports and foreign borrowing. The government did intervene to buy Canadian dollars and also raised the Bank Rate in five short stages to raise interest rates such that they would attract short-term capital inflows.

The 1980s   The exchange rate fluctuated between $.81 and $.86 during 1979 to 1981 in response to occasional rapid rises in American interest rates.

Box 10.4   **The dollar and inflation**
                      Times staff

The strongest argument against a cheap dollar is that it will cause inflation to raise its ugly head even higher.

What casual everyday observers have trouble deciding is how much higher and what it really means for them.

For example, using Data Resources Canada's economic model, managing economist George Vasic has calculated that a 10% devaluation of the dollar, or a seven-cent decline, would add 3% to the consumer price index within two years. Inflation, roughly, would jump 1.5% each year.

Vasic also estimates that the 2% decline in the Canadian currency against the U.S. dollar over the past few months will have only "a negligible effect on the inflation rate".

On the overall inflation rate, Vasic is right.

However, on specific consumer goods, the depreciation of the Canadian dollar against other currencies has had a somewhat more substantial impact.

The decline against the Japanese yen, for example, "has affected our prices tremendously," says Ron Scoular, manager of Willowdale Nissan Ltd. car dealership in Toronto. "They have gone up about 7%."

Put another way, before the drop in the dollar, a not too fancy 1986 300 ZX sports car – no turbo, no leather interior – cost $24,000. It now costs $25,700. And, says Scoular, if the dollar continues to fall, the price will continue to climb.

Source: *Financial Times of Canada*, 13 January 1986.

Changes in the foreign exchange rate of the Canadian dollar affect various segments of the economy in different ways. A fall in the price of the Canadian dollar causes inflation because domestically produced goods become relatively less expensive, and consumers' demand shifts to those goods and away from foreign goods, thereby pushing up the prices of the domestic goods. But foreign goods will still be purchased, although in lesser quantity. The higher prices for these goods are included in the overall measure of inflation.

The government borrowed $1.6 billion in 1979 to replenish foreign reserves and obtained short-term credit for $600 million in 1980. The Bank Rate was raised to 21 per cent by August 1981, when the Canadian dollar reached its lowest value ($.8029) since 1931. Part of the decline was due to the outflow of investment funds following the government's National Energy Policy (1980), which specified that petroleum firms would have to be at least 50 per cent Canadian-owned.

The dollar fell further, however, in 1982 (to $.768) due to the cancellation of the Alsands project to extract heavy oil in northern Canada, the postponement of the Alaska Highway pipeline, lower inflation in the United States, and continuing recession in Canada. The dollar fell again in 1984 (to $.749), due to higher inflation in Canada than in the United States. The exchange rate floated apparently free from government intervention through 1985, during a period of modest prosperity and growth. Speculation then turned strongly against the Canadian dollar in 1986. Several different actions were used to reverse the speculation that had driven the dollar to its record low of $.6924. The Bank of Canada bought Canadian dollars in the foreign exchange markets, sold treasury bills and restricted growth in the money supply to push up interest rates, and added $2.4 billion to the Exchange Fund Account to show that it had strength to defend the Canadian dollar. In addition, strong moral suasion was used to try to reduce the chartered banks' financing and brokering in the speculative trading.

From its record low level in early 1986, the Canadian dollar appreciated steadily, reaching $.86 by the end of 1989. The government had borrowed several billion dollars in 1987 and 1988 to buy U.S. dollars in order to slow this growth. Consequently, Canada's official reserves of U.S. dollars rose from 1.7 billion in 1984 to 12.6 billion in 1988. The dollar fell briefly in early 1990, to $.836, but the high interest rates that were intended to constrain inflation, together with the Persian Gulf crisis, maintained the Canadian dollar around $.86 through the latter part of 1990. Even as interest rates declined in early 1991, and the U.S. dollar strengthened against other currencies, the Canadian dollar remained above $.86.

Canadian Experience with Monetary Policy

The preceding discussion of foreign exchange rate determination and Canada's diversity of experience with exchange rate policy can now be integrated with Canada's monetary policy—in an economy that is so sensitive to foreign economic conditions.

The Early Period   From the beginning of the Bank of Canada's operations in 1935 until 1939, the economy was recovering from the Depression. Since an expansionary policy was required throughout this period, there was little opportunity for learning to use the tools of monetary policy under various economic conditions.

The monetary situation during World War II also offered little opportunity to experiment with monetary policy. Large-scale government borrowing to finance war expenditures required a continuation of the expansionary policy to maintain low interest rates. This was accomplished through the Bank of Canada, which purchased large quantities of government bonds. This action both increased the money supply and directly maintained low interest rates by not allowing bond prices to fall. The Bank Rate was set at $2^{1}/_{2}$ per cent from 1935 until 1943; the chartered banks' prime rate stood at 5 per cent over the same period. At the end of 1943, the Bank Rate was dropped to $1^{1}/_{2}$ per cent, with the prime rate at $4^{1}/_{2}$ per cent.

Wartime monetary policy was continued into the immediate postwar years because a recession was expected to follow from the sharp reduction in the government's war expenditures. The strong inflationary pressure that emerged instead, as individuals spent their savings on the limited output of consumer goods, was not recognized for a few years. The Bank took little action except to suggest, in 1948, that chartered banks restrain their granting of loans. There was a mild recession in 1949, but serious inflationary conditions returned in 1950.

Monetary policy was largely ignored in the period immediately after World War II. The Bank of Canada's first significant use of monetary policy took the form of *increasing the Bank Rate* from $1^{1}/_{2}$ to 2 per cent in late 1950.

The 1950s   In early 1951, moral suasion was used to gain the chartered banks' agreement to restrict less essential loans and to accept an overall *ceiling on deposit expansion*. Setting a ceiling rather than attempting to restrain monetary expansion by using open-market operations indicated the Bank's initial reluctance to develop day-to-day use of monetary policy.

The ceiling was removed in 1952, but loans continued to be restricted. The recession that emerged in late 1953 brought no monetary action until late 1954, when the money supply was increased by *reducing the cash reserve ratio* from 10 to 8 per cent. The return of inflation in 1955 evoked a stronger monetary policy consisting of open-market operations, an increase in the Bank Rate, and moral suasion. The latter included an agreement by the chartered banks to restrain loans and to maintain an additional 7 per cent reserve in highly liquid assets. This became an *informal secondary reserve requirement*, but in 1967 such reserves were made mandatory by the revision of the Bank Act. Direct control of the Bank Rate was abandoned from late 1956 until mid-1962, during which time the Bank Rate was set each week at $1/4$ per cent above the yield rate on three-month treasury bills.

A restrictive monetary policy was maintained throughout the late 1950s until early 1961, despite the serious recession that developed in 1958 through 1961, when unemployment rose to over 7 per cent.

This perverse monetary policy reduced the effectiveness of the government's expansionary fiscal policy, resulting in a sharp dispute between the Governor of the Bank and the Minister of Finance and the eventual resignation of the Governor.

The 1960s   The new Governor immediately introduced an expansionary monetary policy based on *open-market bond purchases*. Except for monetary restraint in 1962 when the Canadian foreign exchange rate was pegged at $.925 in terms of the American dollar, the expansionary policy continued to 1965, using open-market purchases and reductions in the Bank Rate. Some restraint was exercised in 1965 as sustained economic growth threatened to bring faster price increases, but expansionary conditions generally prevailed until 1967.

Early in 1968, the Bank introduced severe monetary restraint to increase rates and attract foreign deposits to support the dollar. But the restrictive monetary policy was not as effective in restraining inflation as had been thought, and unemployment became a more serious problem. Monetary restraint was again exercised by open market bond sales, and a number of *increases in the Bank Rate and the secondary reserve requirements*. This restrictive policy was maintained until mid-1970.

The 1970s   An expansionary policy in 1971 and 1972 brought large increases in M1 and M2. From 1970 until late 1972 the Bank Rate was reduced frequently, from a high of 8 per cent to $4\frac{3}{4}$ per cent. The secondary reserve requirement was maintained at its high of 9 per cent until the end of 1971, but then was reduced twice within a month to 8 per cent to allow the banks to divert funds from treasury bills into loans and hence encourage expansion of consumer and investment spending.

The rapid increase in the money supply that occurred through 1971–72 was tempered during 1973, in a belated effort to restrain inflation. The Bank Rate was raised from $4\frac{3}{4}$ to $7\frac{1}{4}$ per cent; in early 1974, the Bank Rate was raised again, to $9\frac{1}{4}$ per cent.

The secondary reserve requirement had been held at 8 per cent from 1972 to the end of 1974, when it was reduced to 7 per cent. This was the first step in a further reduction to 6 per cent in January 1975, and to $5\frac{1}{2}$

per cent in March 1975. Since the federal government had met its revenue requirements through record sales of Canada Savings Bonds in the fall of 1974, it did not need to rely on the chartered banks to take up its offerings of treasury bills, and hence the Bank of Canada could reduce their secondary reserve requirements.

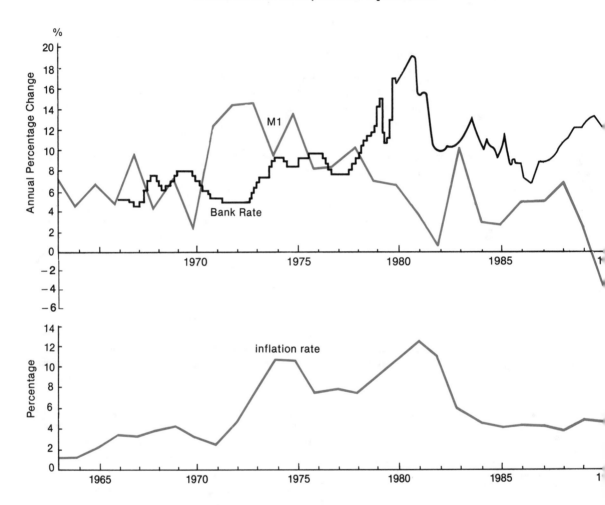

Figure 10.4   Changes in the Money Supply and the Bank Rate
Canadian monetary policy since 1962 has made frequent use of changes in the Bank Rate to accompany changes in the money supply, especially for the narrow definition (M1) of the money supply. M1 increased rapidly in 1971 in response to low inflation, but grew much more slowly during the high inflation of 1974–82. With inflation apparently under control in 1984 and 1985, the money supply was allowed to grow more quickly in 1986, but then was sharply reduced to control inflation in 1988–90.

Source: *Bank of Canada Review.*

A number of economists have argued that the monetary policy of 1972 to 1975 had a much stronger impact on economic events than is commonly realized. The essence of their views is that a rapid increase in the money supply in 1972–73—especially in M1, as shown in Figure 10.4—was a major cause of record inflation in 1974–75, and similarly that the more restrictive policy of late 1975 and early 1976 was more significant in restraining inflation than was the Anti-Inflation Board and fiscal policy.

In 1975 the Bank of Canada moved explicitly to what has been termed "monetarism" in its monetary policy; that is, it set explicit targets for the growth rate of the money supply. These targets reflected the underlying monetarist view that the long-run money supply growth should be equal to the real growth rate of the economy.

The Bank's emphasis in conducting its monetary policy was on changes in M1, whereas some economists would have preferred to focus on M2 because this represented a larger absolute base and appeared to explain economic conditions better than the changes in M1. The *target range* announced in November 1975 was an annual growth rate in M1 of 10 to 15 per cent. The apparent intent was that the mid-point of this range, $12\frac{1}{2}$ per cent, would be equal to an 8 per cent inflation target plus $4\frac{1}{2}$ per cent real growth. The monetary target range was dropped in stages during the next five years—until it was at a range of 4 to 8 per cent in early 1981. Rather than set a new target, the Bank abandoned this strict form of monetarism in November 1982.

Meanwhile the Bank of Canada continued to influence interest rates, primarily with an eye to the spread between the short-term rates in the United States and Canada and the effect of this on the dollar's exchange rate.

The Bank Rate was raised sharply from $8\frac{1}{4}$ to 9 per cent in 1975, just before the anti-inflation program was announced, and then to $9\frac{1}{2}$ per cent in March 1976. From November 1976 to May 1977, the Bank Rate was dropped in four steps from 9 to $7\frac{1}{2}$ per cent, partly to narrow the international difference in interest rates. The Bank Rate reductions were also a response to the fact that increases in M1 in 1976 were below the lower range of the monetary targets.

By early 1978, however, the Bank was again moving to higher interest rates in an attempt to restrain the rapid decline in the dollar's exchange rate. The Bank Rate was raised in five steps through 1978 from $7\frac{1}{2}$ per cent to $10\frac{3}{4}$ per cent, and in four further steps through 1979 to 14 per cent.

By early 1978, however, the Bank was again moving to higher interest rates in an attempt to restrain the rapid decline in the dollar's exchange rate. The Bank Rate was raised through 1978 from $7\frac{1}{2}$ per cent to $10\frac{3}{4}$ per cent, and through 1979 to 14 per cent.

The 1980s In March 1980 the Bank of Canada put the Bank Rate on a floating basis, with the Rate set at $\frac{1}{4}$ percentage point above the average yield on 91-day treasury bills. This latter rate is influenced by the Bank's bidding at the weekly auction of treasury bills. From April to August 1980 the Rate fell from almost 18 per cent to 10.45 per cent, and then climbed to a record high of 21.24 per cent in August 1981.

The record-high interest rates in 1980–81 were due largely to monetary conditions in the United States. The U.S. Federal Reserve Board was attempting to restrict the money supply severely in order to reduce inflation; this resulted in high and fluctuating interest rates and downward pressure on the Canadian dollar exchange rate. This had an inflationary effect in Canada due to higher prices for foreign oil and other imported goods. By late 1982, inflation had subsided, and dropped to less than 5 per cent by 1984. Although the tight money policy had brought inflation under control, this policy had also induced a severe recession.

Money supply growth was again tightened in 1986, to raise interest rates and boost the value of the Canadian dollar from its low of $.70; throughout 1987 to 1990, interest rates were held at a high level in order to keep inflation below 5 per cent. Indeed, the explicit objective of the Bank of Canada during this period was "zero inflation". By 1991, however, the Bank was persuaded to adopt more attainable inflation targets, namely 3 per cent inflation by the end of 1992, and 2 per cent by the end of 1995.

Review of the Main Points

1. Monetary policy is the deliberate use of variations in the money supply to move the economy toward non-inflationary full employment. When the foreign exchange rate is pegged or managed, effects of monetary policy on the balance of payments and on the exchange rate must also be taken into account.
2. Monetary policy effected through open market operations influences aggregate expenditure by changing bank reserves available for loans and thus the interest rate on loans, and by directly changing interest rates through changing bond prices.
3. The limitations on monetary policy include: the asymmetry of its effects (contraction of the money supply must occur, but expansion depends on the ability of banks to increase their loans); the liquidity trap, or the inability of the Bank to reduce interest rates further

once they have reached a low level; the interest-inelasticity of investment under certain conditions; the possibility of near-money, or highly liquid assets, being converted to money and thus offsetting a restrictive monetary policy; changes in the velocity of circulation, which tend to vary inversely with the money supply; the difficulty of keeping interest rates low during a recession while the sale of government bonds exerts an upward pressure on interest rates; the time lag in implementing an appropriate policy; and the universality of effects when they may be inappropriate to specific regional needs.

4. Foreign exchange markets operating in each country are closely linked by arbitrage, the simultaneous buying and selling of two currencies in two countries.

5. Foreign exchange rates, whether floating or pegged, reflect the supply and demand for foreign currencies and, indirectly, the supply and demand for exports and imports. Speculation in currency also affects foreign exchange rates.

6. The foreign exchange rate of the Canadian dollar—the rate at which it is traded for foreign currencies—may be pegged or fixed by the government, or it may be free to fluctuate according to the supply and demand for Canadian dollars. When the rate is pegged, the Bank of Canada is responsible for holding the rate within the agreed range by selling or buying foreign currencies through the Exchange Fund Account.

7. When there is a low stock of foreign currencies in the Exchange Fund Account, the Bank of Canada is restrained from increasing the money supply. An increase would lower the interest rates, some deposits would leave the country, and there would be a downward pressure on the exchange rate, requiring the Bank to buy Canadian dollars with its diminishing stock of foreign currencies.

8. When the exchange rate is unpegged, the Bank is required to modify the supply or demand for Canadian dollars if there is a danger of a continuing deficit in the balance of payments. This will also restrain the Bank from increasing the money supply when the exchange rate is unduly low, or from decreasing the money supply when the rate is unduly high.

9. Fluctuating exchange rates allow the balance of payments to adjust automatically, but entail more variation in prices of internally traded goods. Fixed exchange rates can stabilize such prices but fixed rates require an arbitrary decision on the appropriate rate and a foreign exchange account to maintain the agreed rate. Fixed exchange rates also curtail the use of monetary and fixed policy in pursuing domestic objectives, and attract speculation when a country is having difficulty maintaining a fixed rate.

10. Canada's exchange rate policy has alternated between fixed and floating rates. Until 1914 the dollar was pegged at par with the U.S.

dollar. The rate was also pegged at US $.925 from 1962 until 1970; it has floated since then, rising first to over $1.05, then falling to the $.70 level, and recovering to about $.86 by 1990-91.

11. A restrictive monetary policy was generally maintained throughout the 1950s, without regard to changing economic conditions. A more active, expansionary policy following 1960 included regular open-market operations, but the pegging of the exchange rate from 1962 to 1970 limited its effectiveness on domestic conditions. An anti-inflation policy was pursued from 1968 to 1970. An expansionary policy followed from 1970 to 1972; from 1973 to 1978 monetary policy was mildly contractionary, except for temporary easing in 1977, and has been increasingly restrictive since 1978. Monetary policy since 1960 has included greater use of changes in the Bank Rate, including weekly adjustment since 1980 by setting the Bank Rate at 0.25 per cent above the treasury bill rate. In 1975, the Bank adopted monetary targets as a basic component of its policy, but in 1982 dropped their use.

Key Concepts and Topics

asymmetry of monetary policy
investment inelasticity
income velocity
arbitrage
foreign exchange rates
foreign exchange markets

fixed or pegged exchange rates
floating or fluctuating exchange
 rates
Exchange Fund Account
foreign exchange reserves

Questions for Review and Discussion

1. Chapter 8 showed that there are several steps or links in the process by which a change in the money supply has its effect on employment, prices, and output. Is this the reason there is said to be a long lag in the effect of monetary policy?

2. Why is monetary policy likely to be more effective in curtailing inflation than in reducing unemployment?

3. What is the opportunity cost associated with accumulating foreign exchange reserves in the government's Foreign Exchange Account?

4. Who supplies the Canadian dollars in the foreign exchange markets?

5. Distinguish between an increase in the money supply in Canada and an increase in the supply of Canadian dollars on the foreign exchange markets.

Sources and Selected Readings

Boreham, G.F., and R.G. Bodkin. *Money, Banking and Finance: The Canadian Context*, 4th ed. Toronto: Holt, Rinehart and Winston, 1992.

Courchene, T.J. *No Place to Stand? Abandoning Monetary Targets: An Evaluation*. Toronto: C.D. Howe Institute, 1983.

_____. *The Strategy of Gradualism: An Analysis of Bank of Canada Policy from Mid-1975 to Mid-1977*. Montreal: C.D. Howe Institute, 1977.

Dobson, Wendy. *The Exchange Rate as a Policy Instrument*. Toronto: C.D. Howe Institute, 1980.

Tew, Brian. *The Evolution of the International Monetary System, 1945–1988*, 4th ed. New York: New York University Press, 1988.

Williamson, John. *The Failure of World Monetary Reform, 1971–74*. London: Nelson and Sons, 1977.

Wilton, David, and David M. Prescott. *Macroeconomics: Theory and Policy in Canada*, 2nd ed. Toronto: Addison-Wesley, 1987.

Appendix: Reforming the International Monetary System

Fixed Exchange Rates and the Role of Gold

Gold Standard   The origin of fixed exchange rates lies in the *gold standard* that governed the financing for foreign trade until the Depression of the 1930s. Countries that were "on the gold standard" agreed to buy and sell gold at a fixed price expressed in terms of their own currencies. Since the prices of currencies were fixed in terms of a common commodity, gold, they were also fixed in terms of each other. This was brought about by the arbitrage process, although some small variation in exchange rates could remain, due to the cost of shipping gold.

The rate of exchange among currencies remained fixed despite changing supply and demand for imports and exports because gold formed part of the money supply of the countries concerned. When a country's international payments exceeded its receipts, the deficit resulted in a net outflow of gold. Since this reduced the country's money supply, prices of its goods and services would fall—or so it was assumed under the crude quantity theory of money. The inflow of gold to other countries would raise their prices; exports to those countries would increase and imports from them would decrease, until there was a balance in foreign trade. The gold flow would then cease. To the extent that prices were flexible and responded quickly to changes in the money supply, a country would not incur a deficit or surplus on its balance of payments for very long. Note that, under the gold standard, domestic prices change to maintain an equilibrium in the balance of payments; under floating exchange rates, domestic prices are constant and exchange rates change to maintain an equilibrium in the balance of payments.

Gold-Exchange Standard

A *gold-exchange standard* evolved early in this century as smaller countries began to hold the currencies of larger countries such as the United States and Great Britain in place of gold, and as the gold standard countries made more of their international payments in foreign currencies instead of gold. The prices of currencies continued to be expressed in terms of gold, but a world shortage of gold diminished its actual use in foreign trade.

Toward the end of World War II, most of the major nations met to establish the *International Monetary Fund* (IMF), in an effort to stabilize foreign exchange rates and to help countries that would have balance of payments difficulties in the postwar period. In joining the IMF, countries agree to fix their exchange rates in terms of gold or the American dollar.

Under a fixed exchange rate system, a government agrees to maintain the price of its currency within a very narrow range around the *par value* or pegged rate.

It does this by buying or selling foreign currencies from its Exchange Fund Account, or a similar account, to offset the effects of supply and demand for its currency arising from other international transactions.

Gold in International Payments

During the late 1930s and World War II, much of the world's stock of gold was accumulated in the United States. This was partly due to the movement of gold out of Europe as the Nazis rose to power in Germany, and partly to the United States' commitment to buy gold from world producers at a *fixed price of $35 per ounce*. This price, established in 1934, was inadequate to stimulate substantial gold production in the face of rising mining and smelting costs. However, as long as the United States was running large balance of payments deficits, gold and American dollars were being made available to other countries to finance their international payments.

In the early 1960s, however, the American gold stock was sharply reduced. A shortage of *world liquidity*—gold and key currencies such as the American dollar—was foreseen since world trade was expanding much more rapidly than the output of gold and the movement of key currencies into international finance. Moreover, industrial and other private demand for gold was increasing. The international monetary system clearly was dependent on continuing balance of payments deficits in the United States to increase holdings of gold and foreign exchange in other countries. *A common proposal was to increase the price of gold*: this would both stimulate increased gold production and increase the value of the existing gold stock. But it would also entail a devaluation of the American dollar, a consequence the American government was not prepared to accept.

By early 1968, there was mounting speculation that the price of gold would be raised. Speculators bought gold at an increasing pace. This upward pressure on the price of gold was offset by the American Federal Reserve, which sold gold to foreign central banks. Some of these in turn sold the gold to speculators, thus continuing the upward pressure on gold, draining the American gold reserves, and pushing the American dollar closer to devaluation.

Two-Tier System   In March of 1968, the ten major trading nations agreed to suspend payments of gold to private purchasers and thus separated the official gold market from the private gold market. Gold would continue to be exchanged at $35 per ounce in the "official tier", but would be free to find its own price in the "free market tier". The existing gold reserves in the central banks would be used for international payments, when gold was required, at the official price.

In 1971 the United States announced that it would raise the price of gold to $38 per ounce, but that the U.S. dollar would no longer be convertible into gold. Meanwhile, the free market price of gold jumped to $70 per ounce, and then to a peak of $127 in 1973 when the U.S. raised the official price to $42.22.

The End of Gold   The separation of the official and private gold markets became less distinct in November 1973, when it was agreed that central banks would be able to sell gold in the free market. The "two-tier" system was completely abandoned in 1975, when the IMF members agreed to abolish the official price of gold and to end the requirement that gold be used in transactions with the IMF. One-sixth of the Fund's gold would be sold at market prices and the resulting profits used to provide financial assistance to developing countries experiencing chronic balance of payments problems. Another sixth of the Fund's gold would be resold to member countries at the previous official price.

By these actions, official holdings of gold were made more valuable: central banks could use gold to settle transactions at the market price ($140 per ounce when the IMF decision was made) rather than at the previous official price. Even though the market price of gold fell sharply with the announcement that the IMF would be willing to sell some of its gold, the value of the total official holdings of gold increased by more than 200 per cent. Consequently, countries with large holdings would be able to finance balance of payments deficits longer than they could at the previous official price, with the further result of continuing inflationary pressures in world trade.

SDRs: Special Drawing Rights

The 1968 agreement on a two-tier system for gold prices temporarily solved the problem of speculation against an increase in the price of gold, but it did not solve the problem of an inadequate stock of gold for international payments. This was partly resolved when members of the International Monetary Fund agreed in 1967 and again in 1969 to create *Special Drawing Rights* or SDRs; these have been termed "paper gold", since they serve the same function as gold in international payments.

SDRs are an international fiduciary currency: they are created and accepted by agreement of IMF members. The annual stock of SDRs is determined by an 85 per cent vote of IMF members and is distributed in proportion to the quota of reserves that members are required to hold at the IMF. SDRs came into effect in 1970 with the decision to create $9.5 billion of SDRs for the 1970–1972 period; a second allocation of $12 billion occurred in 1979–81.

SDRs will not become the major medium for international payments—at least not for some time. Nevertheless, the international agreement to create a world currency represents a major step toward replacing the unpredictable output of gold by the regulated creation of a currency that can match the world's needs for international payments.

Although SDRs are viewed as currency, they are treated as a loan to the extent that countries using SDRs to make payments to other countries are encouraged to redeem (or buy back) these SDRs; countries using SDRs are to pay interest to the recipients of their SDRs.

An SDR was originally valued at US $1.00, but in 1974 the IMF decided to let the value of the SDR fluctuate with the rate of exchange between 15 major world currencies and the American dollar. In 1981, this was reduced to the five largest exporting countries. Each currency used in computing this average would be weighted in proportion to its country's share of world trade.

Floating the American Dollar

The third major change in the international monetary system occurred in 1971, when the United States announced that it would increase the price of gold to $38 per ounce, but that the American dollar would not be convertible into gold. This effectively unpegged or *floated the foreign exchange rate of the American dollar* and, with it, the foreign exchange rates of all other countries. During the four months from President Nixon's August announcement until the December meeting of IMF members, the value of currencies in terms of each other was determined by the same interaction of supply and demand that was described earlier for floating exchange rates.

When the IMF members met in December 1971, they established a new structure of pegged foreign exchange rates (termed the Smithsonian Agreement), but with wider margins within which the rate was to be maintained, namely, plus or minus $2^1/_4$ per cent instead of the original 1 per cent. (A few countries did not establish new pegged rates due to continuing uncertainty about what the rate should be. Canada's foreign exchange rate had been unpegged since May 1970.) This was the first major realignment of foreign exchange rates to occur since the original structure was set in 1944, although some countries had individually changed their foreign exchange rates during this long period.

The new agreement did not remain intact for long. In June of 1972, Britain announced that it was floating the pound; the Swiss franc was floated in January 1973. Then, following several months of trying to maintain the American dollar at the agreed exchange rate, the United States devalued its dollar by 10 per cent in February 1973. The counterpart of this action was an increase in the price of gold from $38 to $42.22 per ounce. At the same time, Japan and Italy decided to allow their currencies to float.

Joint Float Shortly thereafter, however, continued downward pressure on the American dollar led the EEC countries (except Britain, Ireland, and Italy) to agree on a "joint float": the exchange rates of the EEC members' currencies would be fixed in relation to each other but would float with respect to all other currencies. This final attempt at pegging exchange rates was substantially weakened as the composition of countries in the float agreement changed frequently from 1974 to 1978.

In January 1976, the IMF officially acknowledged the worldwide floating exchange rate that had evolved through the 1971 and 1974 period.

European Monetary System In another effort to maintain fixed European exchange rates, the European Monetary System (EMS) was created in early 1979. It was also planned that this would lead to a monetary union based on the European Currency Unit (ECU), which resembled the SDRs issued by the International Monetary Fund. Each country (West Germany, The Netherlands, Belgium, Luxembourg, Ireland, Denmark, France, and

Italy) agreed to maintain its exchange rates within $2\frac{1}{4}$ per cent of the official exchange rate. The EMS has been able to coordinate changes in the money supply in each country, but the European Community is still several years from a common currency and monetary policy.

Managed Float or Sliding Pegs?

Some countries were reluctant to shift to an international monetary system based on floating exchange rates completely free of any government intervention. There was general agreement, however, that the previous rigid structure of fixed exchange rates made it increasingly difficult to effect the large rate revisions necessary to overcome long-run disequilibria in balances of payments. The emerging compromise on floating exchange rates was based on assurances — particularly from the United States — that governments would intervene in foreign exchange markets to prevent erratic currency movements. There remained some doubt, however, that a "managed float" could survive.

An exchange rate system based on "sliding pegs" is therefore often proposed as a means for retaining the stability of pegged rates, while providing for the gradual and continuing correction of imbalances through flexible rates. The sliding peg system would also widen the range within which exchange rates would be allowed to fluctuate.

Under a sliding peg system, a par value or official rate would be established. A country would be permitted, however, to change the par value according to an agreed formula by, say, 1 or $1\frac{1}{2}$ per cent a year. Such changes could continue on a monthly or annual basis until the balance of payments disequilibrium was corrected. Moreover, the range of permitted fluctuations around the par level would be widened to a proposed 10 per cent above and below the parity rate. Thus, exchange rates could move over a relatively broad range in reaction to short-term influences, but would be changed gradually in response to longer-term conditions. Such a system could be expected to avoid the international monetary crises experienced in the recent past due to speculation that a currency would be devalued.

But such a system must be recognized as the compromise that it is. Increasingly it is seen that the only possibility for a truly fixed exchange rate system lies in having an international currency — that is, a system in which there are *no exchange rates* because there is only a single currency. This is the system that Keynes had in mind in advocating a world currency he called "bancor". But failing the arrival of this unlikely situation, the second-best arrangement is for greater international cooperation in the formulation of macroeconomic policy in each country.

Review of the Main Points

1. Numerous proposals have been made for reforming the international monetary system. Recent changes include: the implementation in 1968 of a two-tier system to separate the official and the market price of gold, and the abolition in 1975 of an official price for gold; the introduction in 1970 of Special Drawing Rights to finance a small part of international trade; and in 1971 the floating and depreciation of the American dollar, with subsequent changes in the relative exchange rates of several other national currencies.

2. A frequently proposed compromise between fixed and floating exchange rates is an exchange rate system based on "sliding pegs", whereby a country's foreign exchange rate could be changed frequently and could fluctuate within a wider range.

Key Concepts and Topics

gold standard
gold-exchange standard
two-tier system

special drawing rights (SDRs)
managed float
sliding pegged rates

Questions for Review and Discussion

1. Discuss the advantages and disadvantages of using the following as the means for international payments: (a) gold, (b) major foreign currencies, and (c) SDRs.

2. In what respects is a "managed float" like a pegged exchange rate, and in what respects is it like a floating exchange rate?

11 Monetary, Fiscal, or Other Policies?

Monetary or Fiscal Policy?

Monetary and fiscal policies represent two distinct sets of actions the government can take in its efforts to reduce inflation and unemployment by influencing aggregate demand. Each policy has limitations and advantages. Which should be emphasized, and when? Economists have debated this question extensively. The argument is perhaps even more vigorous in the United States, where the Federal Reserve System has much more independence in designing a monetary policy than does the Bank of Canada.

Keynesians   Supporters of fiscal policy—sometimes termed "Keynesians"—maintain that, although both fiscal and monetary policy should be used, the former is more effective in bringing about economic stability because it can be designed to act more directly on particular problems. Monetary policy, they argue, has its main effect, through changes in interest rates, on the level of residential construction and consumer durables; this can be slow and unpredictable. Monetary policy should therefore be used only to reinforce fiscal policy, and specifically to offset the effects of higher interest rates generated by deficit financing in an expansionary fiscal policy. It is also sometimes claimed that monetary policy based on high interest rates adds to inflation, since interest costs are part of the sellers' total costs. Evidence for Canada shows, however, that interest costs were about 1.5 to 2.0 per cent of total sales revenues until 1979. This ratio rose to about 6 per cent in 1980 but dropped back to 5 per cent in 1981, despite even higher rates in 1981. Increasing interest rates do appear to create adjustment problems, but probably do not raise retail prices significantly over the longer run.

Monetarists   The advocates of monetary policy—the "monetarists"—argue that fiscal policy acts too slowly, and indeed has worsened economic problems when, for example, an expansionary policy has its major effect after the recession is past and inflation has become a serious threat. Fiscal policy therefore should be restricted to the minimum government expenditures required to provide necessary public services, with sufficient tax revenues to finance these. Moreover, money is said to have a stronger, more direct impact on aggregate demand than simply its influence on interest rates.

The key to this argument is the stability in the demand for money. There is said to be a normal relationship between the quantity of money that individuals and firms wish to hold and the level of national income. This implies that the velocity of money tends to return to a normal rate following any fluctuations in velocity. If the money supply increases beyond the quantity individuals want to hold at a particular level of national income, this excess money will be spent, increasing national income to the point where the normal relationship between the demand for money and national income is reestablished. Similarly, a reduction in the money supply will lead to a reduction in spending until national income has fallen to the level appropriate to the quantity of money held. This can be recognized as a restatement of the quantity equation of exchange: $MV = PQ$. If V is assumed to be constant, an increase in M will increase P or Q or both; that is, the level of national income will rise.

In this context, fiscal policy can be viewed as a special case of monetary policy. When a deficit budget is financed by borrowing from the public, the expansionary effects are not nearly so strong as when the government borrows from the Bank of Canada. In the latter case, money is created and deposit expansion occurs. The monetary advocates point out that it is actually the increase in the money supply that increases aggregate spending, rather than the deficit budget per se.

Rules versus Policy   Professor Milton Friedman has argued[1] that analyses of money's impact on national income lead not only to the conclusion that monetary policy is more effective than fiscal policy for economic stability, but that a monetary *rule* should replace discretionary monetary policy: *that the money supply should be increased each year at the same annual rate projected for real growth in Gross National Product*. This follows from his view that not only is monetary policy important, but that changes in the money supply have too strong an effect on the economy to leave decisions about these changes to monetary authorities. In fact, he suggests that monetary policy has had a destabilizing effect because

---

[1] Milton Friedman, *Dollars and Deficits*. Englewood Cliffs, N.J.: Prentice-Hall, 1968.

changes have been too large or too small in given situations, and have been made too late to have their intended effect. If the economy is basically stable, as Friedman claims, applying his rule would allow economic growth to proceed steadily.

The Bank of Canada's monetary targets described earlier are a pragmatic form of the "Friedman rule", particularly in their emphasis on gradualism and an arbitrary determination of the timing for shifting targets. Also, as noted previously, the Bank has continued to use Bank Rate changes to directly influence interest rates and the foreign exchange rate. The Bank has been criticized for its gradualism on the grounds that faster, stronger monetary action would have been more effective, and thus would have reduced the period for which high interest rates were required.

Normative Aspects of the Debate

Economists have recently given more attention to the use of monetary policy, but most are not prepared to abandon discretionary policies, fiscal or monetary, in favour of rules, because the economy is not basically stable: each period requires judgment and knowledge about economic conditions and policies to design an appropriate policy for the following period. Thus, more emphasis has been placed on selecting appropriate combinations of fiscal actions, proper financing of deficits, timing of policies, and especially coordinating monetary and fiscal policies.

The debate as outlined above is concerned with positive economic analysis. Despite extensive research on the efficacy of monetary and fiscal policies, much disagreement remains on basic relationships in the economy (such as between income and the demand for money) and on the data and techniques used in analyzing policy impact on economic activity. In time, such disagreements may be resolved through further theoretical and empirical research.

An overriding aspect of the debate, however, concerns normative judgments about the role of government in the economy.

Some advocates of more emphasis on monetary policy would like to see the Bank of Canada become more independent of the federal government, so that it is free of what such advocates regard as short-run, political considerations. However, even given the close relationship between the Bank and the federal government, they argue that more reliance on monetary policy would slow down the expansion of the government sector in the economy. (Total government spending, including transfer payments, now accounts for over 45 per cent of the Gross Domestic Product.) Fiscal policy, in practice, is seen as gradually increasing the government share of GDP, because politically it is difficult to eliminate or to reduce spending on specific programs after they have been in effect for a few years. Thus, contractionary fiscal policy can be implemented only by increasing taxes: the alternative action, of reducing expenditures, is said to be virtually unavailable to the government. It is, for example, easy to establish a new hospital or college, but almost impossible politically to close one.

To a certain extent, this second level of debate could be resolved by examining government budgets to discover whether significant expenditure reductions had occurred when restrictive fiscal policies were required, but the disagreement is largely a matter of political ideology. Nevertheless, economists have an obligation to show how economic policies affect the political organization of the country, as well as how they affect specific economic objectives. From this perspective, normative disagreements can be a stimulating, enlightening contribution to policy-making, provided that they are based on sound evidence and reasoning.

Labour Supply Policies

In the early 1960s, when there was increasing support for the structural-change explanation of unemployment, there were frequent proposals for what were then called manpower policies designed to reduce such unemployment through retraining, and hence to shift the Phillips curve to lower levels of inflation and unemployment.[2] At the same time there was considerable support for these policies in order to encourage economic growth, and to reduce shortages of skilled labour that contributed to cost-push inflation. These were longer-range objectives, however, and any success in meeting these through the original programs would not be available immediately.

The government's manpower programs were sometimes used primarily as stabilization programs, but not in a way that would necessarily improve the trade-off relationship. In the case of retraining programs, for example, putting unemployed persons into classrooms would temporarily reduce the unemployment rate and their maintenance allowances would stimulate aggregate demand, but if they returned to the labour

---

[2] The term "manpower policies" was generally used to describe the group of policies acting on the supply side of the labour market. The term "employment policies" was reserved for those affecting the demand side. But with increased emphasis on gender-neutral language, this distinction has been blurred. The most recent emphasis is on "job strategies".

force without adequate training in appropriate occupational skills the process would be repeated during the next recession. However, if these policies are properly designed—and applied—to meet the objective of economic growth by improving labour productivity, they can at the same time contribute to economic stabilization. In this sense, the programs of the 1960s were an earlier example of a supply-side policy. The major components of Canada's labour supply policy include programs for retraining, counselling and job placement, and labour mobility.

Retraining   Although some provinces have their own retraining programs, the major program in Canada is conducted under the federal government's National Training Act (1982). Training is provided to persons who are expected to benefit through increased earnings, who are above the school-leaving age, and who have been out of school for at least one year. The training generally consists of classroom instruction in educational institutions established by provincial governments. There is increasing evidence, however, that on-the-job training is more effective in improving workers' skills and future employment opportunities, and hence the federal government has tended to shift the program in this direction. The Industrial Training program and the Critical Skills Training program provide for direct agreements with employers to provide training.

Counselling and Job Placement   Canada Employment Centres are located in more than 300 municipalities across Canada to collect and provide information on job vacancies, to counsel workers on employment prospects and training opportunities, and to refer workers to specific training programs.

Labour Mobility   A federal Manpower Mobility program (now called the Canada Mobility program) was introduced in 1965 to assist workers in finding employment in other geographical areas. Grants are available for workers who need to travel to other areas to take training programs not available in their home areas, to assist workers in exploring job possibilities in nearby areas, and to cover moving and travel expenses for workers and their families who have secured employment elsewhere. Eligibility for such grants is restricted to persons who are unemployed or underemployed and who cannot find suitable work in their home areas.

Other programs, both federal and provincial, are concerned with improving the operation of the labour market. One important policy is legislation forbidding discrimination in employment practices, particularly regarding race, religion, national origin, and—in some provinces—sex and age.

Prices and Incomes Policies

The dilemma of simultaneous inflation and unemployment is a serious enough problem for government policy-makers, but *two additional factors* led them to look more widely for other stabilization policies — particularly in the late 1970s and early 1980s. First, the Phillips curve was shifting outward: that is, higher inflation was associated with any given unemployment rate; and second, monetary and fiscal policies were not working as well as desired, requiring massive and often disruptive changes to obtain significant reductions in inflation or unemployment. Attention turned to prices and incomes policy as an additional tool for dealing with these problems, particularly for restraining inflation while attempting to reduce unemployment with longer-term programs.

A prices and incomes policy has three components: a set of general targets or objectives concerning incomes that are expected to lead to economic stability, such as a statement that the average level of wages should rise by not more than 8 per cent or that inflation should fall to 4 per cent over three years; a set of principles for translating the general targets into specific wage and price decisions in each sector, industry, and firm; and a method for either inducing voluntary acceptance of these objectives and principles, or for enforcing them if a voluntary program is not successful.

A basic criticism of wage and price controls is that they do not allow *relative* prices and wages to change. It is often these relative changes that are necessary if there are to be structural changes in labour markets and product markets. Workers tend to move among occupations, industries, and regions in response to wage differentials, and especially to differences in the rate of change in wages. A wage freeze or limit on wage increases will suppress these differentials and impair the required adjustments.

Wage and price controls were intended to deal with increasing inflation levels resulting from *expectations* of further inflation. By such controls it was thought that governments could change expectations. Inflation due mainly to other causes, however, cannot be reduced significantly by such an incomes policy. Other policies that are designed to overcome constraints on the supply side of markets would be necessary to reduce inflationary pressures.

Canadian Experience

Voluntary Restraint   Faced with accelerated inflation in 1966, the Canadian government suggested that wage increases should be *voluntarily restrained* to not more than 6 per cent annually. Workers responded by pressing more vigorously for wage increases, to keep ahead of both the rising cost of living and possible government attempts to introduce a more formal wage policy.

Prices and Incomes Commission In 1969, the federal government appointed a Prices and Incomes Commission to examine the major causes of the rapid inflation and to suggest means for dealing with it. The Commission attempted to obtain *voluntary support* for restraint of wage and price increases but the labour unions refused to cooperate. The Commission's final report took note of experience with wage and price controls elsewhere and suggested that something similar might be necessary in Canada, at least for a temporary period. Any temporary controls, however, may be expected to have only temporary effects, with the result that such controls would need to be reintroduced from time to time. This seems to have been the experience in the United States, and particularly in Britain, as described in the section below.

Anti-Inflation Board Temporary wage and price controls, as proposed by the Conservative party in the July 1974 election, were rejected by the Canadian electorate. In October 1975, the Liberal government introduced a restraint program that limited most wage, salary, and professional fee increases to 10 per cent annually—inflation had exceeded 11 per cent—and allowed prices to rise only by the amount of increased production costs. An Anti-Inflation Board was appointed to monitor and control wage and price increases, to seek public support for the program, and to coordinate the federal program with the provincial legislation that was required to give legal power to some parts of the program. At the same time, the Bank of Canada was following the restrictive monetary policy described earlier.

Soon after the program began, the Prime Minister stirred national controversy by suggesting that "the market system was not working". This was a direct reference to the problems described in Chapter 4. That is, where markets have become monopolistic, cost-push inflation becomes stronger, and governments must encourage greater competition. An incomes policy is useful, however, only if it provides a period within which other legislation can be introduced to improve the market system over the long run.

The major aim of the 1975 controls program was *to change widely-held expectations* about continuing high inflation. Hence the three-year duration of the program was an important part of the strategy because temporary controls used in other countries had been viewed simply as temporary interruptions in the inflation spiral. Inflation was to be reduced to no more than 8 per cent in 1976, 6 per cent in 1977, and 4 per cent in 1978. The desired impact on expectations was lessened, however, when the AIB approved some wage increases exceeding the maximum rate in recognition of "catching up", and when the Minister of Finance began to comment on possibilities of early termination of the program.

Many economists would agree with the Economic Council's assessment that "It is probably impossible to make a clear-cut judgment on the overall benefits and costs of the federal government's anti-inflation program. . . ."[3] One study concludes however, that the major effect of the program was to reduce wage increases in major collective agreements in the private sector by 1.7 percentage points annually and in the public sector by 4.3 percentage points. A similar result was that when the controls were removed during the latter part of 1978, there was not the rapid increase in wage rate settlements that had been predicted earlier. Although wage increases were restrained, it appears that the program had little effect on inflation. Price increases did drop to 5.9 per cent in the last quarter of 1976 but by 1978 inflation was back to 9 per cent annually.

CSIP   Toward the end of the controls program, responsibility for monitoring price changes passed to the Economic Council of Canada in the form of a newly created Centre for the Study of Inflation and Productivity (CSIP). The Centre's role was to *research and offer advice* on inflationary trends. When it became clear by March 1979 that inflation was not declining and wage increases were again approaching 10 per cent, the government created a National Commission on inflation. Although this Commission would not only monitor changes in prices, profits, and wages but would also investigate specific increases, it lacked the power to order reduction in prices and wages. This Commission ended with the election of the Conservative government.

"Six-and-Five"   In 1982 the federal government introduced wage controls for federal employees and encouraged the private sector to follow a similar scheme voluntarily. Federal wage increases were limited to 6 per cent for 1982–83 and 5 per cent in the following years. With the drop in inflation to less than 5 per cent by the end of 1983, the government phased out the mandatory "Six-and-Five" program during 1984–85 but retained a guideline of 4 per cent for price increases on goods and services sold by the federal government, its Crown corporations, and federally regulated industries.

American Experience

Guideposts   The American experience with an incomes and prices policy began in 1962. The U.S. President's Council of Economic Advisors advocated wage and price "guideposts". These recommended average wage increases in each industry equal to the annual increase in productivity (or output per labour unit). Prices were to be reduced if an

---

[3] Economic Council of Canada, *Fourteenth Annual Review: Into the 1980s*. Ottawa: Supply and Services Canada, 1977, p. 19.

industry's productivity increase was greater than the national average, and vice versa. The guideposts had no legal status, but they did have the strong support of Presidents Kennedy and Johnson. Generally it is agreed that this approach had some restraining effect on prices and wages, largely because the presidents were prepared to cite specific cases as being contrary to the public interest.

Nixonomics   As inflation became a more serious problem in the late 1960s, presidential influence was much less effective, partly because this inflation stemmed from the government's Vietnam War expenditures. President Nixon finally turned, in 1971, to direct controls forbidding any increases in wages and prices for 90 days. Following this period, a Cost of Living Council was created to direct two agencies, a Pay Board that would review and judge proposed wage increases, and a Price Commission to do the same for prices. Controls of this type might have been instituted in any case, but they seemed to be particularly necessary in 1971 because Nixon was also proposing several tax reductions in order to reduce unemployment. The wage and price freeze was intended to curtail inflation so that increased disposable income would generate more real output and employment. This was followed in January 1973 by a voluntary system of price restraints, then in mid-1973 by a short return to a price freeze, and then by wage and price review boards again.

Carter   In 1978, President Carter introduced a voluntary anti-inflation program. This included a Council on Wage and Price Stability that would identify firms not complying with price standards. Following the Carter era, no further use was made of price and wage controls, because the Reagan and Bush administrations favoured less governmental intervention in markets.

British Experience

Freezes and Pauses   The British experience with incomes policies has been long and rather unsuccessful. The postwar Labour government introduced a "wage freeze" and "dividend restraint" policy in 1948, but wages nevertheless increased by an average of 6 per cent during the following year. Although wages for a particular occupation and grade classification remained fixed, employees were simply promoted to higher classifications. That is, employers competed for labour by offering higher job classifications instead of higher wages. During the early 1950s, the Conservative government relied on exhortations to management and unions to restrain wage increases. In 1961, a "pay pause" was introduced to give the government's new National Economic Development Council time to discover means for increasing productivity that would justify subsequent wage increases.

Guiding Light   In 1962, about the same time the Americans were being urged to follow wage and price "guideposts", the British government issued a White Paper proposing a "guiding light": that wage increases should average 2.5 per cent annually. A National Incomes Commission that was to assist the government in implementing this policy received little support from the unions, with the result that the guiding light was ignored in many industries.

The election of a Labour government in 1964 led to an agreement by government, employers, and unions, to plan jointly for increasing productivity and income restraints. Two further White Papers in 1965 set a norm of 3 to 3.5 per cent as the average annual increase in money incomes, but earnings rose by three times this amount during the following year. The result was a tougher policy: from October 1966 until August 1967 an "incomes freeze" was in effect. This was more successful than the earlier recommendations and exhortations.

Nonetheless, Britain found it necessary to devalue the pound in November 1967 to maintain competitive prices in international markets, and then to allow the foreign exchange rate of the pound to float in June of 1972. In early 1973, a 90-day wage and price freeze — this time a "standstill" — was introduced. For the rest of 1973, wage increases could not exceed 6.5 per cent. Nevertheless, Britain experienced rampant inflation and in July 1975 introduced new guidelines that imposed a range of wage increases in the following year — from 7 per cent, for low-wage earners, to no increases for those with above-average earnings. When Britain followed this with a 10 per cent "pay guideline", average earnings rose by 14 per cent. Undaunted, the government then introduced a voluntary wage limit of 5 per cent.

In the late 1970s and 1980s, however, the Thatcher government used monetary policy to control inflation, and deliberately avoided intervention in the market mechanism.

Alternative Proposals

TIPs   A frequently proposed alternative to direct wage and price controls is a *tax-based income policy* (TIP). This policy would specify a maximum permissible wage increase for each industry, region, and occupation. Firms that granted wage increases greater than the maximum would pay a surcharge (or additional tax) on their income taxes. In order to keep some wage increases below the maximum, there might also be a tax credit for employees in firms that paid less than the permitted wage increases. Proponents argue that this scheme could be effective by having it apply only to the very largest firms, since these employ a large part of the labour force and tend to set the patterns for wage increases. The same limits would apply to the public sector (governments, schools, and hospitals), which also represents a large part of the labour force.

Supply-Side Policies   A recent important factor in higher inflation rates has been the decline in productivity. This evoked proposals for *"supply-side" policies*, especially in the United States during the early years (1980–84) of the Reagan administration. Whereas fiscal, monetary, and incomes policies attempt to regulate aggregate demand, the supply-side policies would try to reduce inflation by increasing output through influences on aggregate supply conditions. The labour supply policies described previously are examples of programs intended to improve the operation of the labour market.

Supply-side policies include reduction in corporate income taxes in order to encourage investment in more and better productive capacity, and deregulation of much of the private sector's economic activity. This would be expected to increase efficiency through competition and to reduce the bureaucratic costs associated with government regulations. Policies such as these, however, are more likely to be effective only over the longer run and in cases of strong "demand-pull" inflation. Where the inflation is due mainly to "cost-push", an increase in productive capacity will have less effect on inflation.

Review of the Main Points

1. Controversy exists among economists on the appropriate roles for fiscal and monetary policy. Fiscal policy is preferred by some because it can be designed to deal directly with specific problems, while others argue that fiscal policy can act so slowly that an expansionary policy may spur the economy at the wrong time.

2. Still others argue that even discretionary monetary policy is too destabilizing and propose that the money supply be increased at the same rate as the potential growth rate of GDP.

3. Labour supply programs (long known as manpower programs) have been introduced, partly in an effort to shift the Phillips curve downward by reducing cost-push inflation and structural unemployment. Retraining, job counselling and placement, and mobility programs are designed to increase the supply of specific labour skills in areas where there appear to be an excess demand for these skills.

4. A prices and incomes policy has often been proposed as an additional stabilization policy. The United States and Britain have both resorted to direct control of wage and price increases, with limited success.

5. Canada introduced a mandatory restraint program in late 1975; this was gradually removed during 1978. A wage restraint program for

federal employees and some provincial employees was in effect from 1982 to 1985.
6. Other recent proposals include a tax-based incomes policy (TIP) and supply-side policies to increase output in response to increasing demand.

Key Concepts and Topics

Keynesians	labour supply policy
monetary (Friedman) rule	prices and incomes policy
monetarism	supply-side policies

Questions for Review and Discussion

1. Distinguish between discretionary monetary policy and monetary targets. Does it mean that monetarism has failed if the targets are changed periodically?
2. "If economists could obtain more accurate, up-to-date data on the aggregate economic activity of the economy, fiscal and monetary policy could eliminate inflation and unemployment." Do you agree? Explain carefully.
3. How are incomes policies expected to have an effect on high rates of inflation? Why have incomes policies generally not been very successful in controlling inflation?

Sources and Selected Readings

Carr, Jack, et al. *Tax-Based Income Policies: A Cure for Inflation?* Vancouver: Fraser Institute, 1983.

Courchene, Thomas J. *No Place to Stand? Abandoning Monetary Targets: An Evaluation.* Toronto: C.D. Howe Institute, 1983.

Howitt, Peter. *Monetary Policy in Transition: A Study of Bank of Canada Policy, 1982–1985.* Toronto: C.D. Howe Institute, 1986.

Lamontagne, Maurice. *Business Cycles in Canada: The Postwar Experience and Policy Directions.* Ottawa: Canadian Institute for Economic Policy, 1984.

Maslove, A., and G. Swimmer. *Wage Controls in Canada, 1975–78.* Montreal: Institute for Research on Public Policy, 1980.

Riddell, Craig. *Dealing with Inflation and Unemployment in Canada.* Toronto: University of Toronto Press, 1985.

Sargent, John. *Fiscal and Monetary Policy.* Toronto: University of Toronto Press, 1985.

Wilton, David, and David M. Prescott. *Macroeconomics: Theory and Policy in Canada,* 2nd ed. Toronto: Addison-Wesley, 1987.

12 Economic Growth and Productivity

Economic Growth as a Basic Goal

The causes of economic growth, and policies to encourage growth, are fundamental concerns in economics. They appeared early in the first chapter, in the discussion of production-possibility boundaries and the reasons for an outward movement of these boundaries or frontiers. An economy could reach its potential output by using all of its available resources and applying the most efficient technology available. To achieve a still higher level of output—beyond the current potential—would require that either of those conditions was changed. That is, an economy could grow only if it acquired more resources, or if it could improve technology such that existing resources could be used more effectively. If, however, there were underutilization of resources—due to unemployment or inefficient technology—an improvement in these circumstances could also increase output; this would be a case of moving the economy toward or onto its production frontier.

This chapter builds on those elementary but important principles from Chapter 1 to examine the rationale for the goal of economic growth, the causes for Canada's experience with fluctuations in its growth rates, and policies for fostering higher and sustained economic growth.

The previous chapters dealing with the theory of income determination and stabilization policies explained how national income and output could be increased, given the existing level of productive resources and the current state of technology. However, since these conditions limit the potential economic growth, they also limit the extent to which stabilization policy can increase output. Long-run growth depends on increasing the quantity of productive factors, and improving the available technology.

Measures of Growth and Productivity

When economic growth was discussed in Chapter 5, it was seen that there are two basic approaches to measuring economic growth. The first approach focuses directly on economic growth, or on the actual output of goods and services, while the other approach measures growth indirectly by reference to productivity, that is, to an increase in an economy's effectiveness in using productive resources.

Economic growth is defined as the *increase in real output per capita*, measured on an annual basis. Real output is the total Gross Domestic Product in constant prices. That is, the nominal GDP is adjusted for inflation by using the implicit GDP price index. Growth in the economy's total output is also adjusted for increases in the population, to arrive at the real GDP per person. The effect of this adjustment for population growth can be seen clearly in Figure 12.1. Even though the net growth in the population may be no more than 1 to 2 per cent annually, its cumulative effect is substantial.

A distinction is also made between two different but closely related measures of productivity. First, there is *total-factor productivity* — the value of output divided by the total value of all productive factors, and *labour productivity* — the total value of output divided by the number of labour units. The latter may be the total number of persons employed or the number of labour-hours.

Economic growth in terms of actual output therefore depends on the productivity of the economy's inputs multiplied by the quantity of those inputs. It is in this sense that productivity is viewed as an indirect measure of growth.

An Imperfect Measure   The real GDP per capita is an imperfect measure of the average standard of living or well-being in an economy for several reasons. This measure of growth includes the additional goods and services available, but does not take into account other important changes that may have occurred at the same time. Since these changes include both positive and negative impacts on well-being, the measured growth rate both understates and overstates the true change in individuals' well-being.

First, increased output has been achieved over the long run while the average *length of the work week* has been reduced, so that most individuals can now enjoy both more goods and services, and more leisure time. Second, there has been an improvement in the *quality of most goods and services* that cannot be included in the quantitative measure of commodities produced. Third, there have been changes in the environment due to *pollution and congestion* that reduce the enjoyment associated with any given level of goods and services. These latter problems are discussed more fully in the section on the costs associated with economic growth.

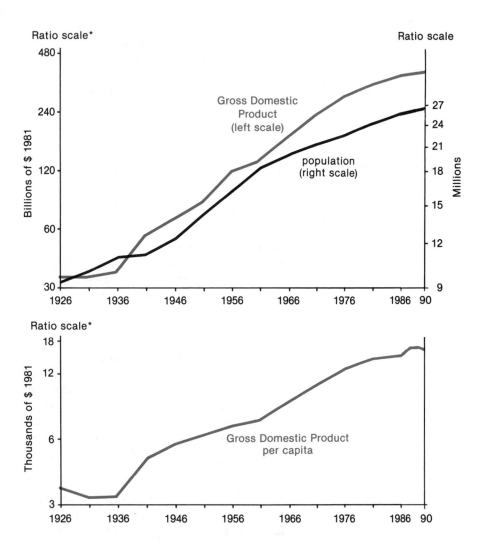

* Equal vertical distances represent equal percentage increases, or rates of growth

Figure 12.1 Total and per Capita Real GDP, Canada, 1926–1990
The total real GDP (in 1981 prices) increased more than ten times during
the six decades, 1930 to 1990. Since the total population increased by 170
per cent, the real GDP per capita (or per person) increased by only 320 per
cent.

Source: Statistics Canada, *Historical Statistics of Canada*, 2nd ed.; and
Bank of Canada Review.

Rationale for Economic Growth

Economic growth is included among the basic economic goals because increasing the goods and services enjoyed by individual consumers is a major step toward improving their well-being. But well-being also depends on several other conditions, such as the quality of the physical and social environment of daily life. These simple, preliminary considerations lead to a more comprehensive assessment of the goal of economic growth, in terms of its expected benefits and its potential hazards.

Standard of Living   The strongest reason for economic growth is to improve the standard of living, at least in terms of a greater quantity of goods and services. Although there may be some controversy about the desirability of certain consumer goods in the luxury class (such as electric meat-carvers and battery-powered golfball polishers) there is general agreement that more adequate housing, better health care, greater availability of legal services, and a greater diversity of training opportunities are all important economic objectives. An improvement in the "standard of living" frequently is interpreted too narrowly, as including only more and better private consumer goods such as luxury automobiles and fashionable clothing, but it also includes many other basic personal and social needs.

By increasing the output of goods and services, economic growth also makes it possible to control inflation. Since a basic cause of cost-push inflation is a faster increase in wages than in labour productivity, an economy that can maintain a steady increase in productivity can also maintain a steady increase in wages. Similarly, because demand-pull inflation is the result of "too few goods", a high rate of economic growth makes it possible to avoid this type of inflation as well.

Quality of Life   Economic growth is also expected to improve the "quality of life", as well as the quantitative standard of living, in several ways. For example, labour-saving machinery and safer equipment may evolve from technological changes that were primarily intended to increase labour productivity and profitability. An increase in the size of an economy's output is also usually accompanied by a greater *diversity* of products, and of the jobs involved in the production of those products. Consequently, consumers have more choice, and should find that goods and services more nearly match their specific preferences, when an economy is expanding. In the same way, workers should find a wider range of jobs available, and can therefore better match their jobs to their skills and preferences.

Income Distribution Economic growth is also a means for making some progress toward another basic economic goal—an equitable distribution of income. When there is a high rate of economic growth, with most people enjoying rapidly rising incomes, they are more willing to support government programs to redistribute that additional income more equitably. This is a different notion, however, from the "trickle-down" argument that greater total output will benefit everyone, on the assumption that those who receive the income in the first instance will spend this income on goods and services provided by the rest of the population. In fact, the additional income may be subject to a high marginal propensity to save, or the spending may be concentrated within a small section of the economy.

Building Social Capital Infrastructures Just as economic growth makes it possible to redistribute some of the rising income, it also makes it possible to create a larger and better "social capital infrastructure". This is the term used to describe collectively the public institutions such as schools, colleges, and hospitals, and it sometimes includes public facilities such as highways, ports, and broadcasting systems. These are structures that are important to the economic and cultural prosperity of a country, and that are usually financed from tax revenues. With high rates of economic growth, and rising personal and corporate incomes, governments are able to increase tax revenues to finance more extensive construction of this kind. The most notable example of this phenomenon was the rapid expansion of schools and colleges in the 1960s. Although these were "required" by the demographic boom, they were financially possible only because of the economic boom.

The Costs of Growth

People increasingly realize that the methods used to achieve economic growth have serious consequences for their total well-being. The processes and products of growth—such as smelters and pulp mills, automobiles and pop-cans—may also have a negative impact on the environment, and the enjoyment of a higher level of consumption. Although this effect is generally recognized, there are other less obvious disadvantages of economic growth.

Postponed Consumption and Leisure The basic economic decisions facing any economy were seen in Chapter 1 to include a decision about the rate of economic growth. In addition to the production-possibilities boundary facing an economy, there were also alternative consumption possibilities. That is, it could choose to consume fewer goods and services currently, and allocate more resources to producing investment goods, which in turn would be expected to yield a greater output of consumer goods and services in the future. In other words, an economy needed to have a higher current rate of *saving* if it were to have a higher future rate of *consumption*. The extent to which an economy would be prepared to do this would depend on its *rate of time preference* — or the quantity of current consumer goods that it would trade off against a given, greater quantity of consumer goods at a specific time in the future.[1]

This represents a further paradox in the "paradox of thrift" that was explained in Chapter 6. It was seen that an increase in intended saving in an economy would lead to a decrease in national income and in actual saving, due to the reduction of spending that occurred as individual consumers each tried to increase saving by cutting back on consumption. That was an important conclusion concerning the short-run, cyclical behaviour of an economy that was operating inside its production frontier. When one turns to the long run, however, where the objective is to increase output by pushing the production frontier outward, it becomes obvious that more physical capital (producer goods) can be obtained only by saving, that is by postponing the enjoyment of consumer goods. In this case, increased saving is necessary to finance the increased investment, or addition to the stock of physical capital.

Environmental Quality   A common concern is that economic growth has many adverse impacts on the social and natural environment. As mentioned above, increasing industrialization and urbanization can result in more air and soil pollution, more noise, and more congestion — in residential neighbourhoods, roadways, and retail areas. This is the result of not only a greater concentration of people required for the labour force to operate the economy, but also the increased use of transportation systems to move these workers, the material inputs, and the outputs. All of these processes also produce more waste materials that must be removed to disposal sites.

Some of these costs can be internalized by requiring the producers concerned to provide for waste disposal and to curtail air pollution, but the larger costs of noise and congestion of urbanization seem to be a part of the unavoidable social costs of growth.

These concerns are the counterpart of the argument that economic growth *improves* the quality of life, as discussed above. While higher real incomes make it possible to afford more medical research and medical treatment, the adverse effects of pollution and psychological stress have increased the illness and death rates related to these conditions.

---

[1] For example, if a student is indifferent between being paid $100 today or $110 one year from today (assuming there is no inflation and no risk of default on the agreement), the student's rate of time preference is 10 per cent.

Personal Costs   In addition to the environmental issues arising from economic growth, there are personal problems associated with the industrialization process and changes in labour demands. Some people find that their skills have become obsolescent, or that the industry in which they were working is moving to another region of the country in pursuit of cheaper materials and labour, or a larger market. Workers who remain employed in an area or industry may be required to go through a retraining program to retain their jobs.

Finally, the higher standard of living associated with economic growth may impose a hidden cost—the attempt to "keep up with the Joneses". As a greater variety of goods and services become available, there is a human tendency increasingly to include these in the category of necessities, such that a family feels deprived if it does not have all of the electronic home entertainment available, take a winter holiday for skiing or sunning, or join in whatever is the current consumer fad.

Economic Growth in Canada: Experience and Policies

Canada's Economic Growth Record

Over the past century, and even over the past few decades, Canada has had a very high rate of economic growth. During the period from 1930 to 1990, total real GDP rose from $35 billion to $461 billion, when adjusted to 1981 price levels. At the same time, population rose from 9.5 million to 26.6 million. Consequently, the real GDP per person rose from $3,680 to $17,330, also in 1981 prices. This represents a growth of 470 per cent in 60 years, or a compound growth rate of about 2.5 per cent annually. The annual growth rate, however, has varied widely, from 16 to −14 per cent. But it is important to have a high and *sustained* rate of economic growth in order to achieve a major improvement in real GDP per capita over a given period.

The results of a sustained growth rate can be seen in an arithmetic example of the compounding effect of growth rates that differ only slightly on an annual basis, but lead to substantially different totals over a short period of time. For example, at an annual growth rate of 3 per cent, an economy's real income would double in 24 years; but at a 4 per cent growth rate, the income would double in only 18 years.[2] At 5 per cent, if this growth rate could be sustained annually, the real income of a worker would increase to 5 times its original level within 33 years, or in less than the typical working lifetime.

[2] This comparison is derived from the *Rule of 72*, which is a quick method for calculating the "doubling time" based on a given growth rate. By dividing the annual growth rate (or interest rate) into the number 72, one can calculate the number of years required for a doubling of the amount in question.

Balancing the Benefits and Costs of Growth

For most of Canada's history, it has been assumed that economic growth was not only a desirable goal, but also an essential factor in its political development as an independent nation. Confederation in 1867 and the creation of the Canadian Pacific Railway in the 1880s were based on the expected economic benefits of expanding and diversified markets. Later, the industrialization of the 1920s showed that greater output and higher incomes were also accompanied by more variety in consumer goods. The growth experience of the 1930s and 1940s, as illustrated in Figure 12.2, was quite erratic, ranging from negative rates of 8 to 14 per cent during the Depression in the early 1930s, to exceptionally high rates of 12 and 16 per cent during World War II. The emphasis on peacetime economic growth in the 1950s was accompanied by an enthusiasm for the foreign investment that was resulting in more employment and newer technology, as well as greater output.

High growth rates during most of the 1950s and steady growth in the 1960s led to a shift in emphasis concerning the basic economic goals. Redistribution of income was accorded higher priority when it was recognized that significant segments of the population were not benefiting directly from the higher levels of economic growth. This shift in goals was especially noticeable in the United States, where the Democratic administrations of Presidents Kennedy and Johnson emphasized the economic war on poverty. Similar economic and political circumstances prevailing in Canada led to a similar shift in goals. At the same time, there was increasing doubt about the social value of increases in the material standard of living that were not accompanied by at least comparable increases in the quality of that standard, but were indeed accompanied by increasing pollution, noise, congestion, crime, and a variety of other social problems.

Slower growth in the later 1970s and the 1980s, including the recessions of 1975, 1982, and 1990, led to a renewed emphasis on economic growth as a primary economic goal. This time, however, the objective was not so much to secure a high level of consumer goods and services, as it was to improve productivity as a means to avoid the high levels of inflation encountered from 1975 to 1982.

Determinants of Growth and Increased Productivity

Attempts to analyze the sources or causes of economic growth have begun by recognizing that there are three basic factors in growth: additions to physical capital (and land), additions to labour, and technical progress. But technical progress cannot be as easily defined or measured as can physical capital and labour. Consequently, the sources of growth traditionally were estimated by calculating the growth rates for capital

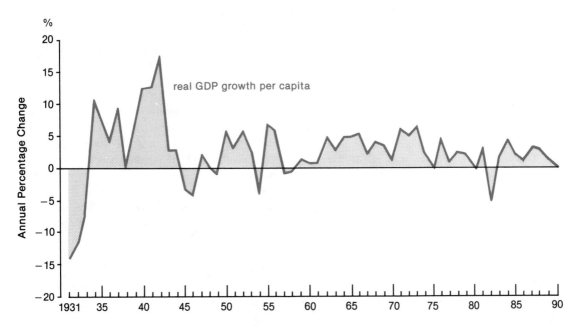

Figure 12.2   Annual Rates of Economic Growth in Canada, 1931–90
The annual rates of economic growth, measured as the real Gross Domestic Product per capita, fluctuated widely during the Depression of the 1930s and the Second World War in the early 1940s. The 1950s were years of generally high but unstable growth rates, preceding a period of sustained growth in the 1960s. Since 1974, growth rates have been lower and less stable.

Source: Economic Council of Canada, *Strengthening Growth: Options and Constraints*. Ottawa: Supply and Services Canada, 1985, Chart 3-1; and *Bank of Canada Review* for 1983–90.

and labour, subtracting these from the economic growth rate, and treating the residual as a measure of technical progress.[3] For example, if an economy's average annual growth rate were 5 per cent, with an annual labour force growth rate of 1.5 per cent and an annual increase in physical capital of 2 per cent, the residual of 1.5 per cent would be attributed to technical progress, or technological improvements.

While this approach offered rough estimates of the sources of growth, it became increasingly inadequate, with changes occurring in the *quality* of physical capital and of the labour force. Additions to the stock of physical capital represented both a greater quantity and a higher quality, in terms of newer technology. Similarly, additions to the labour force not only increased the quantity of labour, but also raised its qual-

---

[3] Technical progress and technological improvement are terms that are commonly used interchangeably.

ity because of the more advanced education and training received by new members of the labour force. Consequently, more recent analysis of economic growth has attempted to estimate those changes in quality, and to disaggregate the various components of the capital stock and the labour force.

Economists had tried to explain why some economies had higher growth rates than others, both by developing theories of economic growth and by empirical analysis of economic data. But it was not until the 1960s that the combination of better statistical data and more sophisticated analytical techniques made it possible to determine the component factors in economic growth. A study of Canada's economic growth for the period 1950-67, at an average annual rate of 5.2 per cent, found that this could be attributed to a 1.6 per cent increase in the quantity of labour (in terms of labour hours) plus a 3.6 per cent improvement in labour productivity. The increase in labour hours was the net result of a 1.8 per cent rise in number of persons and a 0.2 per cent decline in number of hours worked. Factors accounting for the 3.6 per cent average annual improvement in labour productivity included a 1.1 per cent increase in capital, improved resource allocation (0.6 per cent), greater economies of scale (0.7 per cent), improved quality of the labour force (0.3 per cent), plus other unidentified factors that added a further 0.9 per cent.[4]

Improved resource allocation was due partly to reductions in the tariffs on imported goods, such that resources were redirected to production where Canada was using resources more efficiently, and to a shift of resources out of the less efficient parts of the agricultural industry and into the more efficient areas of production. The greater economies of scale were the result of growth in consumer demand, based both on a larger domestic population with a higher per capita income and on an expanded export market. The residual component of "unidentified factors" would include changes in technology that could not be included elsewhere.

A subsequent study, for the 1973-78 period, analyzed the 3.3 per cent average annual growth rate for those years.[5] The contribution attributed to increased labour hours had risen slightly (1.8 per cent) as the net result of increasing numbers of workers, but with each working fewer hours. Labour productivity had declined to 1.5 per cent, despite a higher rate of capital accumulation. The declining productivity in this case was attributed to fewer opportunities for resource allocation,

[4] Dorothy Walters, *Canadian Growth Revisited, 1950-67*. Ottawa: Economic Council of Canada, 1970.
[5] See J.W. Kendrick, "International Comparisons of Recent Productivity Trends", in Wm. Fellner (ed.) *Essays in Contemporary Economic Problems*. Washington, D.C.: American Enterprise Institute, 1981.

diminishing gains through economies of scale, and lower utilization of productive capacity.

Another study of Canada's economic growth covers the period 1962 to 1986, when Canada's growth became less stable and fell below growth rates in some other countries. The study divided the period into three parts, 1962-73, 1974-79, and 1980-86. The most relevant results are presented in Table 12.1. This shows a decline in the growth rate of gross output from 5.4 per cent to 4.2 per cent to 2.7 per cent. Although the basic inputs, labour (or employment) and capital, continued to grow at about the same rates in the 1960s and 1970s, there were sharp declines in growth of total factor productivity. During the 1980s, both productivity and employment grew more slowly.

Canada has recently faced two separate questions about its growth and productivity rates: first, why does Canada's growth rate differ from other countries' growth rates? and second, why has Canada's productivity been declining over the past several years? These questions are addressed in detail in the following two sections.

Canada's Growth Rates in International Perspective

During the past decade, Canada's annual rate of economic growth per capita has been lower than in earlier periods, but it still compares favourably with that of other countries such as the United States, the United Kingdom, and Germany. (See Figure 12.3.) The differentials in growth rates among various countries have been attributed to a number of factors, but international economic comparisons of any kind

Table 12.1

Components of Economic Growth in Canada, 1962–86

	Average Annual Percentage Change		
	1962–73	*1974–79*	*1980–86*
Gross output	5.4	4.2	2.7
Employment	2.8	2.8	1.4
Capital accumulation	0.6	0.4	0.8
Total factor productivity	2.0	1.0	0.5

Source: Economic Council of Canada, staff study on Canadian productivity (unpublished).

must always be interpreted carefully. Consequently, only certain factors can be identified with any reliability; each of those is discussed below.

Saving and Investment   As emphasized previously, if there is to be economic growth, there must be an increase in saving. This reduces current consumption and makes resources available for producer goods, in the form of more physical and human capital. Although Canada has had a higher saving rate than the United States since the early 1970s, it has also had a lower rate than Japan and West Germany. It is not surprising, therefore, that the stock of physical capital in Japan and West Germany has grown at the rate of about 5 per cent annually for the past decade, while in the United States and Canada, it grew at 2 to 3 per cent annually.

Not only does this greater expansion of the capital stock increase the quantity of productive resources, it also incorporates the most modern

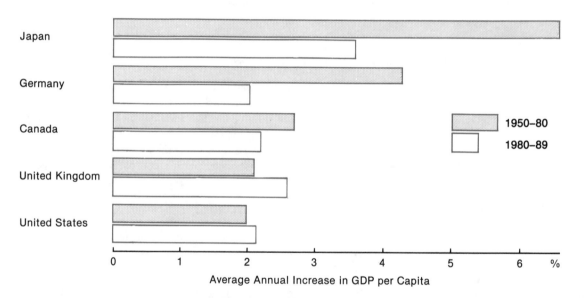

Figure 12.3   Canada's Growth Rate in International Perspective, 1950–89
Canada's average annual increase in GDP per capita during 1950–80 was 2.7 per cent, but this was exceeded by Japan and Germany. During the 1980–89 period, including the severe recession of 1982, three of the countries had lower growth rates, but the United Kingdom and the United States had higher growth rates than in the earlier period.

Source: U.S. Department of Commerce, *Statistical Abstract of the United States*, 1982–83; and Organization for Economic Co-operation and Development, *Main Economic Indicators*.

technology. Since the capital stock has grown faster than the labour force, there is an increase in the capital/labour ratio. These three factors—greater productive capacity, more modern technology, and higher capital/labour ratio—combine to provide a major advantage in achieving a higher rate of economic growth.

Enterprising Spirit and Culture

Economists writing about economic growth in the 1920s to 1950s were not reluctant to emphasize the importance of the entrepreneur—the individual who would combine existing resources, new technology, and an unexplored market, to bring about innovations that led to economic growth. But with the emergence of large corporations in the 1960s and 1970s, the emphasis on entrepreneurship gave way to the more abstract and de-personalized notion of physical capital and technology. More recently, there has been a recognition that a major factor in Japan's economic success was its entrepreneurial culture, and this has revived the same emphasis in Canada. In fact, several innovations of international importance had emerged in Canada—such as the Bombardier line of vehicles, from snowmobiles to rapid transit cars—but these have only recently been cited as examples of the innovations that can stimulate employment and trade.

Such enterprising spirit must be evident among ordinary workers, as well as in senior management, if there is to be sustained economic growth. Consequently, there has been much attention given to the concept of "quality circles", or groups of workers who are collectively responsible for the complete, high-quality production of a specific product. No longer is a worker concerned only with a small step in the assembly of a product, but rather he or she shares the responsibility for the complete product. This production system has been shown to increase both the quantity and quality of output for given inputs, but it has been only slowly introduced in North America.

Length of Production Runs

One of the long-standing factors reducing Canada's growth rate and its relative productivity has been the fact that it has shorter production runs than other countries that are its major competitors. Shorter runs—that is, a lower quantity produced using the same basic productive resources—mean that the fixed costs of physical plant are spread over a smaller quantity of output. Consequently, the production cost per unit is higher than in countries that can operate with longer production runs. The smaller production runs in Canada are the result of several factors, but a major one is the tariff on certain imported goods that protects Canadian producers from foreign competition.

The Productivity Puzzle

Compared with a rate of growth in labour productivity of 3.6 per cent annually during the 1950–67 period, a drop to less than 1.0 per cent in the 1970s presented a serious challenge to economic analysis and policy. Total factor productivity has performed even less satisfactorily, as shown in Figure 12.4. This all-inclusive measure of the economy's effectiveness in using productive resources declined from an average of about 2.5 per cent during the 1960s and early 1970s, to a negative level of −1 to −2 per cent during the early 1980s. These lower levels of productivity have been attributed to several factors.

Declining Capital/ Labour Ratio   When the labour force increases at a faster rate than the rate of investment (or the addition to the stock of physical capital), the capital/labour ratio declines. With less capital per worker, labour productivity

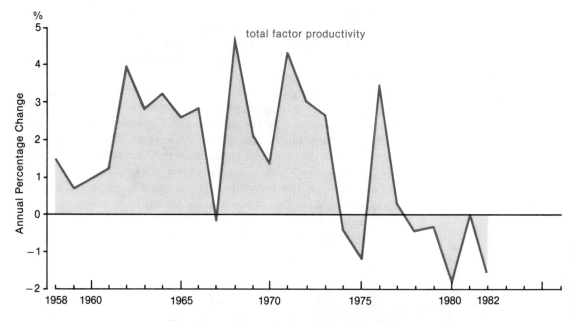

Figure 12.4   Change in Total Factor Productivity, Canada, 1958–82
Prior to 1973, the annual increase in total factor productivity was the major determinant of total economic growth. For the period 1958–73, total factor productivity increased at an average of 2.6 per cent per year. But during the period 1973–82, this long-run average was exceeded only in 1976, and in most years, productivity declined.

Source: Economic Council of Canada, *Strengthening Growth: Options and Constraints*, Cat. No. EC21-1/1985E. Ottawa: Supply and Services Canada, 1985. Chart 3-3. Reproduced with permission of the Minister of Supply and Services Canada.

also declines, all else being equal. The Canadian labour force grew rapidly during the 1960s and 1970s, first, due to the population boom following World War II; and second, due to a sharp increase in the labour force participation rate for females during the 1970s. Although the expansion of the labour force contributed to a much greater total output, the productivity of each labour unit was reduced since additions to capital occurred at a lower rate. The economy has therefore, while attempting to meet the goal of full employment, reduced labour productivity.

Growth of the Service Sector

The composition of Canada's labour force has changed substantially during the past four decades, with a much smaller proportion now employed in the primary industries (agriculture, mining, forestry) and in secondary industries (manufacturing and construction), but with a much larger proportion now employed in the service sector. This includes transportation, telecommunications, government services, health, education, and personal services, such as dry-cleaning and hair-dressing.

Productivity in several of the service industries has grown slowly, if at all, over a long period of time. This is because many services are labour-intensive, that is, there is very little physical capital per worker. Consequently, there is less opportunity to improve the worker's output through providing better equipment. In the case of professional occupations such as teaching, law, and accounting, the service is produced almost exclusively by the professional's labour. (The extreme case is in the performing arts—live theatre or symphonies—where productivity has not changed in three centuries because a cast or orchestra of the same size is required to produce any given work today as was required originally.) As the labour force shifts from industries with high productivity, to low-productivity service industries, there is a decline in the productivity rate for the whole economy.

Rising Energy Prices

An unexpected factor has emerged in the attempts to explain declining productivity, namely, higher prices for energy, including petroleum, natural gas, and electricity. It is argued that techniques using less energy were adopted in response to the higher oil prices especially, and that these less efficient techniques reduced productivity. In addition, the higher prices led to practices and expenditures that had not occurred before, such as increasing the amount of insulation in new buildings and redesigning automobiles to be more energy-efficient, but also more expensive to produce. It is very difficult to estimate the percentage of the productivity decline that can be attributed to rising energy prices, because their effects are so diffused in the economy—including not only the specific changes in producer and consumer goods just mentioned, but also changes in arrangements for transporting goods and in sources of supply.

Inadequate Research and Development

A frequent comparison is made between the levels of expenditure for research and development (or R and D) in Canada and in other countries. These expenditures are necessary to produce the innovations in materials used, processing equipment, and methods for distributing the finished products. The original research may be done in universities and government laboratories, but ultimately it must be adapted and developed in the private sector. This requires shared expenditures and a coordination of development efforts.

Expenditures by private industry for R and D have been less than 1.0 per cent of Canada's Gross Domestic Product during the past two decades. Not only does this seem a small fraction to invest in the development potential of the economy, but it is also lower than in most other industrialized countries. Reasons for this low level of R and D expenditures are not clear, but there is general agreement that Canada's close link with manufacturing in the United States in the past has retarded Canada's R and D activity. Figure 12.5 shows that, whatever the reasons, spending for research and development in Canadian industry is only about one-half the proportionate amounts that are spent for R and D by some of Canada's major trading partners. Spending for R and D by both private and public sectors totalled only 1.4 per cent of the GDP in Canada in the late 1980s, but was double that level in the United States and Japan.

Diminished Opportunities for Resource Reallocation

Another result of the shift in the industrial structure was the diminished opportunity for resource reallocation. During the 1950s, the agricultural sector experienced two major economic changes: there was a movement of labour out of agriculture and into other industries; at the same time, more and better equipment improved the capital/labour ratio in agriculture. Consequently, this industry experienced a sharp rise in its labour productivity. But those changes had a diminished impact in the 1970s because the major improvements had already been realized, and agriculture had become a much smaller sector of the economy. Similar, although not quite as substantial, changes occurred in the manufacturing and construction industries.

Policies for Improving Growth and Productivity

Since there is a diversity of factors influencing economic growth and productivity, there is also a diversity of policies that could be or have been implemented in pursuit of these goals.

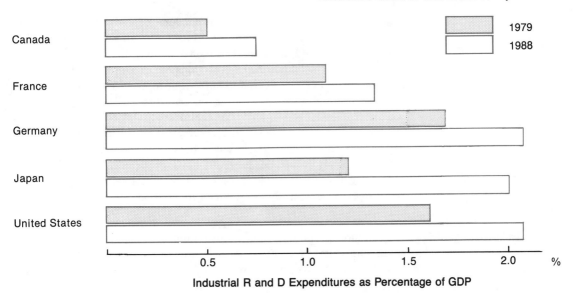

Figure 12.5 **Industrial Expenditures on Research and Development**
Industry in Canada spends a smaller percentage of its Gross Domestic
Product on research and development than is the case in several other
countries. This is thought to be one of the reasons for lower economic
growth in Canada than in Germany and Japan.

Source: Statistics Canada, *Industrial Research and Development Statistics.*

Supply-Side Policies   Within the past decade, however, popular attention has been drawn to
what are termed "supply-side" policies—following from the Reagan
Administration's initial emphasis on supply-side economics in the
United States. This approach to economic policy was based on the view
that Keynesian-style macroeconomic management of aggregate demand
could not solve the dilemma of simultaneous high levels of inflation and
unemployment. Instead, it was agreed that policies were needed to
encourage a more efficient allocation of resources and a higher rate of
technological improvement. These changes would occur more quickly,
it was further argued, if governments would reduce corporate taxes and
remove many of the regulations that restricted the economic activity of
the private sector.

Other policies have also been proposed for some time. These are
policies to encourage more investment, and to develop an industrial
strategy that would focus on the development of a small group of
selected industries.

Increased Investment   Throughout this chapter, there has been repeated attention to the level
and quality of investment, and the capital/labour ratio. An obvious

policy, therefore, would be one that encouraged a higher rate of investment. The federal government introduced a major tax revision in 1985 that was intended to meet this goal, namely the exemption from income tax of $500,000 in capital gains over an individual's lifetime. This exemption was expected to encourage more investment in the economy's productive capacity, but it was criticized for the unlimited scope of its applicability. It led, for example, to higher housing prices because speculators purchased residential properties, intending to resell them at a substantial tax-free profit. (If this activity provided a regular stream of income, however, the profit would be treated by the tax department as taxable income rather than a capital gain). Consequently, the exemption was reduced to $100,000.

Industrial Strategy   A common proposal is that there should be an *industrial strategy* for Canada. Certain industries would be identified for special treatment in the form of grants for research and development, tax incentives, tariff protection, and other types of government assistance. At the same time, industries with declining productivity and declining demand for their products would be assisted in closing their plants and transferring resources to other industries. But this proposal has not been implemented as a complete package because it is difficult for governments to identify correctly the industries that should be supported. (It is also difficult to convince the public that these choices are the correct ones.) It is at least as difficult politically to identify industries where production should cease.

Review of the Main Points

1. An economy can increase its potential output — that is, push out its production-possibilities frontier — only by acquiring more resources or by improving its technology so that existing resources can be used more effectively.
2. There are two basic approaches to measuring economic growth: one approach — the real GDP per capita — measures growth directly; the second approach — productivity — measures growth indirectly by measuring how effectively an economy's resources have been used. The productivity approach includes both total factor productivity and labour productivity; the former compares total output with the total input of all productive factors, while the latter compares total output with the total labour input.
3. Measures of growth have certain limitations; they do not take into account changes in the amount of leisure time available, or in the quality of goods and services produced, or in the environment.
4. There are several reasons for an economy's choosing to increase its

economic growth rate: this would increase the standard of living, improve the quality of life, enhance the possibility for income redistribution, and provide the means for enlarging the social infrastructure, or the public institutions and facilities such as hospitals and highways.

5. Several costs are associated with economic growth. These include: the postponed consumption and leisure that would be available with existing resources and technology, but which must be allocated to increasing the stock of physical and human capital; the adverse impact of growth on the social and natural environment; and personal costs or problems such as the increasing obsolescence of labour skills and a shift in the demand for labour to other industries or regions.

6. Canada has had an average annual growth rate of about 2.5 per cent over the past six decades, but this rate has varied widely. The political emphasis on economic growth has also varied. In the years following Confederation in 1867, economic growth was seen to be essential for both the economic and political development of a new nation and especially to maintain its independence from the United States. There was also a strong emphasis on economic growth in the 1920s and 1950s, to enjoy the benefits of rapid industrialization and a greater diversity of consumer goods. During the 1960s and 1970s, however, an increasing priority was accorded to income redistribution. But when it was seen, in the late 1970s, that economic growth could not be taken for granted, attention again turned to that basic goal.

7. Early attempts to identify the relative importance of various factors contributing to economic growth focused on changes in the stock of physical capital and labour, with any residual component being attributed to technical progress, or technological change. Later analysis made it possible to distinguish changes in the quality and quantity of capital and labour. These studies showed that Canada's economic growth during the postwar period was due primarily to an improvement in the quality of labour, greater factor productivity, and an increased stock of physical capital.

8. In international comparisons of economic growth rates, Canada has not performed as well as countries such as Japan and West Germany. Some of the factors explaining these international differences are Canada's lower rate of saving, less emphasis on entrepreneurship and managerial training, and shorter production runs.

9. Declining productivity in Canada during the past decades has caused much concern and study of the problem. Although it is still not clear what all of the factors are that account for this decline, they are thought to include the declining capital/labour ratio, a shift of resources to the less productive service sector, factor substi-

tution due to rising energy prices, inadequate research and development, and diminished opportunities for resource reallocation.

10. Policies that the federal and provincial governments might implement to increase productivity would include greater incentives for investment, and an industrial strategy to identify and support industries that are likely to have high productivity levels.

Key Concepts and Topics

economic growth	social capital infrastructure
potential output	rate of time preference
technological change and technological progress	capital/labour ratio
	entrepreneurship
total-factor productivity	length of production run
labour productivity	service sector
real vs. nominal GDP	supply-side policies
standard of living	industrial strategy
quality of life	

Questions for Review and Discussion

1. Why is measurement of productivity considered to be only an indirect measure of economic growth? How are these two measures related?

2. Discuss the limitations on real GDP per capita as a measure of individual well-being in Canada.

3. Distinguish between the productivity of labour and the productivity of capital, and then show how these are closely related.

4. What factors offer the greatest potential for increases in productivity in Canada during the next decade? Why? What policies, if any, might the federal and provincial governments implement to encourage this growth?

5. Why might an increase in energy prices cause declining productivity?

6. "Industrial strategy" is a popular term, but what exactly is meant by strategy in this context, what industries would be involved, and how is this policy expected to improve economic growth?

Sources and Selected Readings

Baldwin, J.R., and P.K. Gorecki. *The Role of Scale in Canada-U.S. Productivity-Differences.* Toronto: University of Toronto Press, 1985

Economic Council of Canada. *Strengthening Growth: Options and Constraints.* Ottawa: Supply and Services Canada, 1985.

_____. *The Bottom Line: Technology, Trade, and Income Growth.* Ottawa: Supply and Services Canada, 1983.

Maital, S., and N.M. Meltz, eds. *Lagging Productivity Growth: Causes and Remedies.* Cambridge, Mass.: Ballinger, 1980.

McFetridge, D.G. *Technological Change in Canadian Industry.* Toronto: University of Toronto Press, 1985.

Sargent, John. *Economic Growth: Prospects and Determinants.* Toronto: University of Toronto Press, 1985.

Schott, Kerry. *Industrial Innovation in the United Kingdom, Canada, and the United States.* Toronto: C.D. Howe Institute, 1981.

Schumacher, E.F. *Small Is Beautiful: Economics as if People Mattered.* New York: Harper and Row, 1973.

Statistics Canada. *Aggregate Productivity Measures.* Ottawa: Supply and Services Canada, 1983.

Stuber, Gerald. *The Slowdown in Productivity Growth in the 1975–83 Period: A Survey of Possible Explanations.* Ottawa: Bank of Canada, 1986.

Usher, Dan, and Basil Blackwell. *The Measurement of Economic Growth.* London: Oxford University Press, 1980.

Zohar, Uri. *Canadian Manufacturing: A Study in Productivity and Technological Change.* Ottawa: Canadian Institute for Economic Policy, 1982.

13 International Trade and the Balance of Payments

Why do countries trade with other countries? Why not attempt to become a self-sufficient economy? One might suggest that one way to increase a country's employment and income is to increase exports. But this policy necessitates buying the exports of other countries if they are to have the funds to buy one's own exports. This brings us back to the question, Why do some countries import goods and services rather than produce domestically all that the country needs?

This chapter discusses the theory of international trade, developing a general answer to that question, and then examines Canada's policies and experience with international trade.

Canada's Pattern of Foreign Trade

Canada's pattern of foreign trade is examined by asking the following questions: How large is Canada's foreign trade relative to its GDP? Who are the major trading partners? What is exported and to whom? What is imported and from whom?

Merchandise Trade
Most of the world's international trade has consisted of merchandise, or goods. But trade in services—such as shipping and tourism—has increased significantly in recent decades.[1] This section deals exclusively with merchandise trade, but the importance of trade in services will be seen later in the chapter when the Balance of Payments is discussed.

In 1989 Canada ranked seventh in the world in the total value of its merchandise exports. More significantly, Canada's merchandise exports equalled 21 per cent—more than one-fifth—of its total production of goods and services; Canada also had the second largest

---

[1] Services formerly included interest and dividend payments but these are now treated separately in an investment income account.

exports per capita. Although the United States is the world's largest exporter, Table 13.1 shows that it exports only 7 per cent of its GNP.[2] But West Germany stands out on all three measures: absolute value of exports, percentage of GDP, and exports per capita. Another notable observation is that the seven major exporting countries account for one-half of the world's trade in tangible goods.

Trading Partners   Canada's major trading partners are shown in Table 13.2. Note that in most cases the main purchasers of exports are also the main suppliers of imports. In 1989, Canada had a negative balance of trade with most of these trading partners, but a large positive trade balance with the United States. Although only one-quarter of American exports (about 2 per cent of the American GNP) came to Canada in 1989, Canada's trade with the United States far exceeds that with any other country, accounting for 73 per cent of Canada's exports, or about 15 per cent of Canada's GDP.

For this reason, Canada is very much concerned about the domestic economic policies of the United States. When unemployment is high in the United States, Canada's export sales may fall; when inflation is a problem in the United States, Canada may "import" some of this inflation through purchases of American goods.

Exports   The major commodities exported by Canada are displayed in Table 13.3. Motor vehicles and parts head the list of exports, a result of the Canada-United States Automotive Agreement (signed in 1965) by which tariffs were removed from motor vehicles and parts imported by automobile manufacturers, to increase specialization in automobile production and expand Canada's sale of these to the United States. Most of the other items in this list reflect the importance of *products from primary industries*: newsprint, wood pulp, and lumber from forestry; wheat from agriculture; crude petroleum, natural gas, and coal from mining. The value of the least-processed products on this short list alone—wood pulp, wheat, lumber, crude petroleum, natural gas, and coal—accounts for about 17 per cent of Canada's exports.

Imports   A large part of Canada's imports are fully manufactured or finished products. The imports of motor vehicles and parts also reflect the effects of the Automotive Agreement. The net trade effect of this agreement can be seen in Table 13.4 by subtracting the value of vehicles and parts imported from those exported.

The apparent paradox of both exporting and importing crude petroleum is explained by the concentration of petroleum production in

---

[2] The United States continues to use GNP as its primary measure of national income.

Table 13.1

Major Exporting Countries, 1989

Country	Value of Exports (US$ billions)	Percentage of World Exports	Percentage of Own GNP/GDP	Exports per Capita (US$)
United States	364	12	7	1,462
West Germany	341	11	29	5,500
Japan	274	9	10	2,228
France	179	6	19	3,189
United Kingdom	153	5	18	2,677
Italy	141	5	16	2,449
Canada	117	4	21	4,455
Total, 7 countries	1,569	51		
Total, world[1]	3,100	100		

Source: Organization for Economic Co-operation and Development, *Main Economic Indicators.*

[1] Preliminary estimate.

Table 13.2

Canada's Major Trading Partners, 1989

Country	Merchandise Exports		Merchandise Imports		Trade Balance ($ billions)
	Value ($ billions)	Percentage of Total	Value ($ billions)	Percentage of Total	
United States	97.9	73.3	87.9	65.2	10.0
Japan	8.7	6.5	9.5	7.0	−0.8
United Kingdom	3.4	2.5	4.6	3.4	−1.2
West Germany	1.8	1.3	3.7	2.7	−1.9
China	1.1	0.8	1.2	0.9	−0.1
South Korea	1.6	1.2	2.4	1.8	−0.8
U.S.S.R.	0.7	0.5	0.1	0.1	+0.6
Belgium-Luxembourg	1.2	0.9	0.5	0.4	+0.7
Netherlands	1.5	1.1	0.8	0.6	+0.7
France	1.3	1.0	2.0	1.5	−0.7
Italy	1.1	0.8	2.0	1.5	−0.9
Taiwan	0.9	0.7	2.4	1.8	−1.5
Hong Kong	1.0	0.7	1.2	0.9	−0.2
Rest of World	12.3	9.2	16.0	12.3	−4.3
Total (excludes re-exports)	133.5	100.0	134.9	100.0	−1.4

Source: Statistics Canada, *Exports: Merchandise Trade* and *Imports: Merchandise Trade.*

Table 13.3

Canada's Major Merchandise Exports, 1989

Item	Value ($ billions)	Percentage of Total
Motor Vehicles and parts	34.8	25.1
Lumber	5.6	4.0
Newsprint	5.9	4.2
Wood pulp	6.8	4.9
Crude petroleum	4.5	3.2
Wheat	2.6	1.9
Natural Gas	3.0	2.2
Coal	1.6	1.2
Total Merchandise Exports (including re-exports)	138.9	100.0

Source: Statistics Canada, *Exports: Merchandise Trade.*

Table 13.4

Canada's Major Merchandise Imports, 1989

Item	Value ($ billions)	Percentage of Total
Motor vehicles and parts	32.0	23.8
Office machines	6.3	4.7
Communications equipment	7.6	5.7
Crude petroleum	3.7	2.8
Aircraft and parts	3.4	2.5
Iron and steel	3.2	2.4
Farm machinery and parts	1.9	1.3
Total Merchandise Imports	134.3	100.0

Source: Statistics Canada, *Imports: Merchandise Trade.*

Western Canada, its consumption in Eastern Canada, and the high cost of transporting or moving petroleum between these two areas. Thus Quebec imports petroleum from Venezuela by means of ocean tankers to Maine and pipeline from Maine to Quebec, while Alberta exports petroleum to the United States.

These patterns of foreign trade vary somewhat from year to year as new sources of raw materials are discovered and developed, as new agreements are made with other countries, as wheat harvests change with weather conditions in Canada and abroad, as technology and consumer demands change, and as international monetary arrangements are revised. Nevertheless, some of the main features have dominated Canada's foreign trade pattern throughout its history: the export of raw or semi-finished materials and the import of manufactured goods; the prominence of trade with the United States; and the large export component in Canada's total production of goods and services.

Rationale for Trade

Comparative Advantage

The explanation of the benefits to be realized through trade is stated in terms of *the principle of comparative advantage*. The argument that individuals and regions can be better off through specialization of labour and exchange is widely applied in economics; economists frequently refer to the "comparative advantage" of certain individuals or regions. But the principle of comparative advantage also needs to be emphasized with respect to different countries, because there are so many barriers or limitations to the exchange of goods and services between countries.

Specialization of Labour

The rationale for foreign trade is the same as the rationale for trade between regions within a country, or for the specialization of labour. In the latter case, individuals specialize in providing the type of labour service that will earn them the highest monetary return, and then sell their goods or labour services so that they can purchase other goods and services. A dentist, for example, may also be skilled as a do-it-yourself carpenter. He may be even more skilled in carpentry than are the carpenters available locally. Nevertheless the dentist will probably hire a carpenter to put an exercise room in his basement rather than do the job himself. When the dentist calculates the income he can earn during the three days it would take him to build the room (after subtracting income tax from such earnings), he finds that he can earn more as a dentist than he must pay the carpenter. Thus, by hiring a carpenter he can have his exercise room and extra income as well. The carpenter gains through having a higher income than he would have had otherwise.

Specialization and Exchange

Similarly, some areas of Canada are especially suited to the production of apples: the Annapolis Valley of Nova Scotia, the Niagara Peninsula of Ontario, and the Okanagan Valley of British Columbia. Each of these areas could also support beef production, but if this were done the value of the potential beef output would be less than the value of apple production on these lands. Other areas can produce beef cattle, perhaps not so efficiently as the areas mentioned above, but more efficiently than they can produce apples. Specialization in the commodity produced more efficiently, with subsequent exchange of goods between the areas, leaves each area better off than if each produced both beef and apples.

The gains realized through specialization in each of the above cases — the dentist and the carpenter, the apple and beef producers — were possible only because there was an exchange of services or goods.

International trade is an extension of this local and regional specialization and exchange that further increases the economic gains from specialization.

Principle of Comparative Advantage in Foreign Trade

Assumptions   The principle of comparative advantage in specialization and free exchange between countries can be illustrated by a simple example. Suppose that there are only two countries to be considered: Canada and England. Assume further that each country produces and consumes only two goods, cheese and beef. Each country has only land and labour resources; labour is fully employed but there is no limit on available land. All labour is of uniform quality within each country, but the quality of labour and land differs between the countries. Productive resource requirements can be expressed simply in terms of labour units, such as one day of labour.

The production conditions in each country are such that, as shown in Table 13.5, Canada can produce both cheese and beef more efficiently than can England. The production of 100 kilograms of beef requires 3 units of labour in Canada and 6 units in England; the production of 100 kilograms of cheese requires 2 labour units in Canada and 3 in England.

Absolute Advantage   Canada has an *absolute advantage* in the production of both beef and cheese because fewer labour units are required to produce a given quantity of each good in Canada than in England. One might suggest that Canada should produce both beef and cheese for its own consumption, ignoring any possibility of trade with England, since Canada can produce both goods more efficiently. The principle of comparative advantage, however, will show that it is not absolute advantage or absolute efficiency that matters, but rather comparative advantage or comparative efficiency.

Comparative Advantage   Table 13.5 shows that Canada is twice as efficient as England in producing beef: 3 labour units compared with 6. But Canada is only $1\frac{1}{2}$ times more efficient in producing cheese: 2 labour units compared with 3. Canada is *relatively* more efficient in producing beef than cheese: Canada's *comparative* advantage is in beef production and England's *comparative* advantage is in cheese production.

Table 13.5

Relative Efficiency and Costs before Trade

| | Resource Requirements in Labour Units | | Opportunity Costs | |
	Beef (100 kg)	Cheese (100 kg)	Beef (1 kg)	Cheese (1 kg)
Canada	3	2	1 1/2 kg cheese	2/3 kg beef
England	6	3	2 kg cheese	1/2 kg beef

The principle of comparative advantage states that the commodities (goods and services) that a country should produce and trade with other countries are the commodities that it produces relatively more efficiently than do other countries.

Two-Country Model   Now the example must be pursued to see how both Canada and England can gain by specialization and trade. The information in Table 13.5 indicates the cost of each product in each country in terms of productive resources. But the cost of each good can also be expressed in terms of its opportunity cost, or how much of the other good must be given up to increase the output of the first good. At this point, the comparison is not between countries; rather, it is a comparison of the opportunity cost of the two goods *within* each country.

For every 100 kilograms of beef produced in Canada, 150 kilograms of cheese must be given up or forgone because the 3 labour units required to produce beef are not available for cheese production. This is another illustration of the *opportunity cost* concept introduced in Chapter 1. The cost of 100 kilograms of beef is the opportunity that is forgone to enjoy 150 kilograms of cheese. Thus one can say that 1 kilogram of beef "costs" 1 1/2 kilograms of cheese. Similarly, the price of 1 kilogram of beef in England is 2 kilograms of cheese. The price of 1 kilogram of cheese in Canada is 2/3 kilogram of beef and the price of 1 kilogram of cheese in England is 1/2 kilogram of beef. This is another way of determining comparative advantage: beef is relatively cheaper in Canada (one kilogram costs 1 1/2 kilograms of cheese, compared with 2 kilograms in England) and cheese is relatively cheaper in England (1 kilogram costs 1/2 kilogram of beef, compared with 2/3 kilogram in Canada).

It is because these cost ratios are different in each country that trade can be an advantage to both. The principle of comparative advantage therefore states that the countries should specialize in the commodities for which their opportunity costs are lowest.

Equal Ratios   If the ratio of opportunity costs were the same in each country, this would mean that neither country was *relatively* more efficient in the production of one good than the other and that therefore neither country had a comparative advantage in the production of either good. If in Table 13.5, for example, England's production cost of cheese had been 4 labour units, Canada would have been *equally more efficient* in producing both goods and England would have been *equally less efficient*. In this case there would be no benefit to either country in specialization and trade. Canada would, of course, have a higher consumption level than England because its resources were more productive, but it could not become even better off through trade. Canada and England each could only attempt to produce the particular combination of beef and cheese that gave the greatest satisfaction to the consumers in each country.

The possibility that the production cost ratios will be exactly the same for each country is quite unlikely. The many conditions affecting the production of any good vary so much among countries that a country can be expected to have a comparative advantage in some goods, and therefore have a reason for foreign trade.

Constant Costs   If the production cost of cheese in England had been 4 labour units *at a given level of production*, for example when labour resources were equally divided between beef and cheese production, the cost of cheese might have dropped to 3 labour units at a higher level of cheese production. This would indicate that there were *economies of scale* (cost per unit decreased with increases in output) in England's cheese production. If this were the case, then specialization would be an advantage. However, in this simple example illustrated by Table 13.5, it is assumed that the production costs per unit are constant for all levels of production; economies of scale are temporarily ruled out. This important assumption underlies the preceding discussion of equal ratios of opportunity costs.

Gains from Trade   The increased output made possible when countries produce according to their comparative advantages can be seen by extending this simple example of two countries and two commodities. Assume that Canada's labour resources are 1,200 labour units per week and England's are 1,800 labour units per week. How these labour resources are actually divided between the production of beef and cheese in each country depends on relative supply and demand conditions for each product. Assume the labour distribution is as follows: Canada allocates 450 labour units for beef and 750 for cheese; England allocates 1,200 for beef and 600 for cheese.

Since in Canada 3 labour units are required to produce 100 kilograms of beef, 450 labour units will yield 150 units of beef, each unit weighing

100 kilograms. The production level for each of the other cases is shown in Table 13.6. Total world production is 350 units of beef and 575 units of cheese. But if Canada produces only beef and England produces only cheese, world output increases to 400 units of beef and 600 units of cheese.

The sharing of increased production between the two countries will depend on the *terms of trade* that are established, or the quantity of one good that will be traded for a given quantity of another good.

Terms of Trade   The precise terms of trade, or the prices for each good when trade takes place, depend on the supply and demand conditions in each country. But the *limits* of these terms of trade or exchange prices can be determined from the relative production costs assumed earlier.

Prior to specialization, 1 unit of beef cost or was exchanged within Canada for 1½ units of cheese. Consumers in Canada will therefore not be willing to pay more for 1½ units of cheese imported from England than the 1 unit of beef they paid or gave up previously for Canadian cheese. Similarly, prior to specialization in England, 1 unit of beef was exchanged for 2 of cheese. If trade is to take place, the consumers in England will not pay more than this price for imported beef. The terms of trade must lie between the ratios 1:1½ and 1:2. If the ratio is 1:1¾ both countries will be willing to trade because Canada will receive 1¾ units of cheese, instead of 1½ units, for each unit of beef it gives up, while England needs to give up only 1¾ units of cheese, instead of 2 units, for each unit of beef.

Table 13.6

Gains in Real Output through Specialization and Trade

	Beef		Cheese		Total Labour Used (units)
	Produc-tion (100 kg)	Labour Used (units)	Produc-tion (100 kg)	Labour Used (units)	
Before Specialization					
Canada	150	450	375	750	1,200
England	200	1,200	200	600	1,800
World	350		575		
After Specialization					
Canada	400	1,200	0	0	1,200
England	0	0	600	1,800	1,800
World	400		600		

In Figure 13.1 the full range of consumption possibilities is shown for Canada and England before trade and after trade, on the assumption that the terms of trade remain at 1 beef for 1¾ cheese. This emphasizes again that both countries—despite Canada's absolute advantage in both commodities—can gain by specializing in the commodity in which they have a comparative advantage.

International specialization and trade has one major benefit: prices of goods and services are reduced. Stated alternatively, real wages are increased. Since labour and other resources are directed to their most productive use, a given number of labour units will yield a greater output and thus a higher real wage.

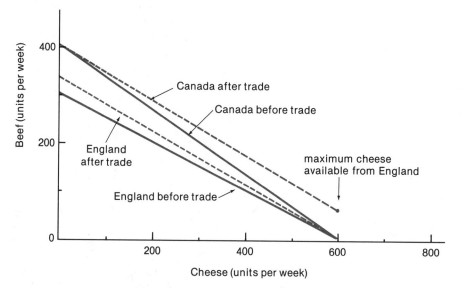

Figure 13.1   Consumption Possibilities before and after Trade
With the given technology and resources, Canada can produce 400 units of beef per week or 600 units of cheese or any other combination of beef and cheese shown by its before-trade consumption-possibilities curve. By producing only beef—in which it has a comparative advantage—Canada can shift its consumption-possibilities curve outward and thus enjoy a greater combination of beef and cheese. The same is true for England, even though it is less efficient in producing both commodities. Note the parallel after-trade curves that reflect the assumed international terms of trade of 1 beef for 1³/₄ cheese. The maximum cheese available to Canada is 600 units because this is the maximum England can produce with its labour resources and the required labour per unit of cheese produced.

Conditions Fostering International Trade

There are numerous conditions that contribute to the development of international trade, through enhancing the comparative advantage each country has in the production of particular commodities. Nevertheless, the following general factors encompass most of the reasons that enable a country to produce some goods at relatively lower costs.

Physical or Geographical Differences

Unique combinations of climatic and geographical features account for a large proportion of the cases of specialization in agricultural products. Wheat could be grown in almost every temperate-zone country of the world, but the special combination of terrain, precipitation, and temperature gives only a few countries such as Canada, the United States, Australia, and Argentina a strong comparative advantage in wheat production, and indeed an absolute advantage.

The combination of a large water supply and a sharp drop in land elevation at Niagara Falls gave Ontario a comparative advantage in producing low-cost hydro-electric power for a long time. Development of other sources of energy, however, has diminished much of this cost advantage. The combination of natural resources close to ocean ports has also been a spur to foreign trade. British Columbia's forest industries depend on shipping from Vancouver and other ports; Venezuelan oil can be shipped to many countries due to its proximity to the sea. In these cases, the transportation costs per unit are much lower than they would be for countries with similar natural resources located farther from water transportation.

Differences in Technology and Labour Resources

Some countries, such as Japan, Great Britain, and Germany, do not have major cases of comparative advantage based on geographical conditions, but they have become major exporters through technological innovations and development of skilled labour. Other countries have enhanced their natural advantages by adding massive amounts of physical capital to the productive process. The United States, for example, has been able to maintain a comparative advantage in producing some agricultural commodities, despite increasing land and labour costs, by mechanizing and automating much of its agricultural industry.

Economies of Scale

The realization of economies of scale is a case of developing a comparative advantage that did not exist at lower output levels. One reason that Britain joined the European Common Market was to maintain a large enough European market for some of its products so that it could continue to enjoy economies of scale. Similarly, the Canada-U.S. Automotive Agreement was designed to encourage such economies in Canadian automobile production by increasing the length of production run—the number of automobiles of a specific model that are produced on a given assembly line without change-overs.

Restrictions on International Trade

Although the general validity of the principle of comparative advantage has been widely recognized, and many economists have long advocated free or unimpeded international trade, several types of barriers remain. Restrictions are found on both sides of international trade; some such restrictions directly or indirectly discourage exports, while others impede imports. Most of the attention in this section is directed to imports because restrictions on these are generally quite specific. But there are some issues on the export side that must at least be raised because they have increasing importance in Canadian economic policies.

Barriers to Exports

Transportation Costs   A general factor limiting international trade should also be noted. This is the *cost of transporting goods* between countries. Some countries may have a comparative advantage in certain products when only the domestic production costs are considered, but the cost of moving the goods to foreign markets may wipe out this advantage. Tropical countries clearly have an absolute advantage in the production of cut flowers, but these are so perishable that expensive air transportation is necessary to deliver them to snow-bound Canadian consumers. The result is domestic greenhouse production of such flowers in Canada with little foreign competition. However, the importance of transportation costs varies with the mode of transportation required and the size of the item relative to its selling price.

Conservation Policies   What is often described as "an abundance of natural resources" has been a major source of Canada's exports throughout its history. But doubts are being raised about whether Canada should export natural resources such as water and petroleum. The economic problem, however, is not whether to export but how to determine the proper price. By exporting large quantities of water at a price that currently seems reasonable, even attractive, Canada may find in future years that the price of domestic water is much higher than it would have been otherwise.

Given some uncertainty about the size and location of industry and population in the future, projecting the future domestic demand for water is difficult. The problem is one of weighing increased current income and consumption against the possibility of lower real income and consumption in the future if the cost of bringing water to Canada's domestic users should increase. This question becomes more complex when income distribution is taken into account: only some people would benefit directly from the sale of water, but all consumers would pay the higher future prices. For the same reason, there is increasing opposition to export sales of crude petroleum and other non-reproducible resources such as copper and iron ore. Again, it is a question of whether the price should be higher or an export tax levied.

Export Duties   *Export duties*, or taxes on exports, are more common in less-developed countries that rely on income from export sales. When such incomes are unusually high they are taxed to provide income for the periods when receipts from exports are low, and to redistribute the benefits of export sales.

A form of export tax was introduced in Canada in 1977 in the form of an export charge on crude oil and oil products exported from Canada. The rate was set equal to the difference between the price for Canadian consumers and the international price. A 15 per cent export tax was also applied in 1987 to forest products shipped to the United States. But these oil and forest taxes were designed to offset the implicit subsidies to producers that were contrary to international trade agreements.

Diversification   Indirect restraints on exports operate through policies for *diversification*, rather than specialization, of industrial production, and through various factors *reducing the geographical, occupational, and industrial mobility of labour*. Diversification of industrial production may be advocated for several reasons; one is to reduce dependence on income from exports if there tend to be fluctuations in export sales of commodities such as wheat. When export sales drop, governments are pressed to provide income supplements to the producers. Another reason for diversification is to maintain a basic self-sufficiency in essential commodities to avoid dependence on other countries in case of war, adverse economic policies, or simply changes in the terms of trade.

Labour Immobility   Specialization usually requires the mobility of labour within a country. In most cases this would be carried out at a high economic and social cost to the individuals concerned. Plants in some parts of the country would have to be closed, families would need to move to other centres to find work, and workers would need to be trained for new jobs. Although the monetary costs of such adjustments would be more than offset if the area for specialization were properly identified, some persons would place a high value on remaining in a familiar community and region. The result is pressure for industry to be subsidized in various ways so that geographical relocation is not necessitated by economic pressures.

These considerations do not invalidate the principle of comparative advantage. Rather, they emphasize the broader range of costs and the distribution of potential benefits and costs that need to be taken into account when potential areas of specialization are examined.

Restrictions on Imports

Although there are several kinds of restrictions on imports, these can be divided into two basic categories: *tariffs* and *quotas*.

Tariffs   *Tariffs* or *import duties* are taxes on imports. An *ad valorem* tariff states the tax as a percentage of the price of a good; a *specific* tariff specifies the amount to be paid on each unit regardless of its price. Another minor type of import tax is a *licence fee*, which may be required to import specific goods. The cost of the licence usually is fixed, whatever the quantity imported, and thus the effective tax rate is reduced with an increasing quantity of imports.

Quotas   *Quotas* are limitations on the quantity of a good that can be imported. Such quotas may be expressed in terms of the quantity that can be imported each month or each year, or from particular countries. Quotas may also be combined with an import licence, so that the importer is paying a fee to import a specific amount. The most stringent form of quota is an *embargo*, or *sanction*, such as an embargo or prohibition against the importation of cattle when there is an outbreak of a cattle disease in another country. Sanctions are usually imposed for political reasons; this is the case with the sanctions that were imposed by some countries against imports from South Africa to protest against its discrimination policies.

Comparative Effects   Economic effects of tariffs and quotas can be explained using supply and demand analysis. Figure 13.2a shows the supply and demand for imported children's toys in Canada prior to any restriction on such imports. The equilibrium price is $10 per unit, and quantity is 90 per year. If a specific tariff of $2 per unit is imposed, importers are willing to supply 90 units of the toys only if the price is high enough to cover previous costs plus the new tax. The result shown in Figure 13.2b is an upward shift of the supply curve to S_1, by the amount of the tariff. A new equilibrium price is established at $11, with the quantity demanded reduced from 90 to 80. Note that, as in the case of a sales tax, the less elastic the demand for a product, the greater will be the increase in the price as a result of a tariff.

The same effect would follow, as indicated by Figure 13.2c, if a quota on imported toys were set at a quantity of 80. This represents a

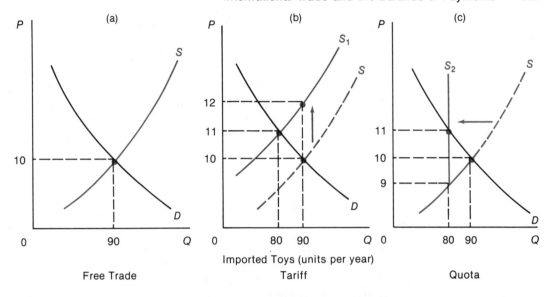

Figure 13.2   Tariffs and Quotas Reduce the Quantity of Imports and Increase Prices
When there are no restrictions on international trade, 90 units of toys are imported each year and the price is $10 per unit. Imposing a tariff shifts the supply curve upward, to S_1, by the amount of the tariff, $2. The price increases by less than the tariff amount to $11, and the quantity imported falls to 80. A quota that restricts the quantity imported to 80 effectively shifts the supply curve to S_2 and increases the price to $11.

shift of the supply curve from S to S_2, with S_2 being perfectly inelastic at a quantity of 80. The new price is again $11. Since the price and quantity effect of tariffs and quotas can be the same from the perspective of the consumer, governments usually favour the tariff form of restriction, since it produces tax revenues as well as the quantitative limitation on imported goods.

Tariffs or Quotas?   Quotas tend to be used for commodities, mainly from the agricultural sector, whose prices fluctuate substantially, such that it is difficult to set an effective protective tariff rate. Quotas are also used if there is such an inelastic demand for the foreign product that a tariff would not reduce imports enough to encourage expanded capacity in the domestic industry for that product. The inelasticity of demand suggests that consumers do not regard the domestic product as a close substitute for the foreign product, for example, in fashionable clothing, shoes, and fancy foods.

Quotas can also be used to limit import consumption so that domestic products may gain a larger share of the market as consumers begin to treat them as substitutes for the foreign products. For example, the Canadian dairy industry has proposed a quota on imported specialty cheeses such as brie and camembert so that Canadian producers can diversify from the traditional cheddar cheeses.

Canada imposed a quota on automobiles imported from Japan in 1980. (This was formally termed a "voluntary export restraint" on the part of Japan.) This action dealt more directly with the competition faced by the Canadian producers than would an increased tariff, which would have to apply to imported automobiles from all other countries. The latter option could have provoked protests and possible retaliation from several other countries. That 1980 quota also provided an incentive for the Japanese manufacturers to establish assembly plants in Canada.

Reasons for Tariffs and Other Trade Restrictions

If tariffs raise the prices of imported goods and reduce the quantity that consumers can enjoy, why do governments continue to impose tariffs? There are many reasons; some are based on political objectives while others are related to economic objectives. Only in some cases, however, do tariffs contribute effectively to achieving these objectives.

Political Independence   Any country wants to be as independent as possible in determining its foreign relations. Unless it is willing to be closely allied with some other countries in mutual defence agreements, it must develop its own defence industries and encourage other industries that can be converted to defence production in wartime.

Countries also want to be independent of foreign decisions about the domestic services they will have. Most countries, for example, have established national airlines so that they can determine how their cities and regions will be served, rather than depend on foreign airlines, even if they might be less expensive, to provide this service. By limiting the access of foreign airlines, countries are in effect imposing a quota on foreign air service.

Countries also tend to protect their agricultural producers by high tariffs, when food products could be obtained more cheaply abroad, because it would be so disruptive socially and politically to re-establish the numerous small farmers in other occupations and because countries fear the uncertain consequences of losing part of their agricultural industry and becoming dependent on other countries for their basic needs.

The net cost of pursuing political goals by restricting imports and encouraging higher-cost domestic production is not easily determined. Such political objectives could be accomplished more precisely, with a full appreciation of the cost of doing so, if selected domestic industries or commodities were *subsidized* directly. Foreign suppliers would then be discouraged by the lower domestic prices made possible by the subsidy. Governments and their electors could then determine whether the cost of their objectives—as shown by the amount of the subsidy—was too great or whether even more should be spent to pursue these objectives more effectively. Although people might complain about paying more taxes for such subsidies, they would need to weigh this against the higher prices they pay for domestically produced commodities when foreign goods and services are excluded through the use of tariffs.

Maintenance of Full Employment and Protection of Industry

The most common economic reason given for tariffs is that they protect established industries and their employees. If tariffs on certain commodities were reduced or removed, prices of the imported commodities would fall and domestic firms would be forced either to close, putting employees out of work, or to become more efficient in the use of resources. This, of course, is exactly the process implied in the principle of comparative advantage. It is also the main reason why free trade is not more widely practised, in spite of its economic advantages. Although consumers pay a higher price for some domestic goods because foreign competition is excluded by tariffs, governments find it politically more desirable to maintain tariffs than to admit cheaper imports and face the complaints of domestic industries.

Alternatively, tariffs could be removed if there were a tax placed on consumers who enjoy cheaper goods, to subsidize the establishment of more competitive firms and retrain or relocate the workers for the new firms. Governments are seldom willing to consider this alternative, however, because consumers seem more willing to pay higher prices than to be taxed to assist the readjustment of production. Similarly, firms and employees appear to be more concerned about short-run relocation costs than about the longer-run benefits from the more productive use of resources.

A related argument states that tariffs "help keep money in the country". When consumers buy domestic goods instead of imports, employment and incomes are maintained. But this is only another form of the argument considered above. Specialization based on comparative advantage would raise real incomes and increase real purchasing power, such that employment would increase with the removal of tariffs.

Increased Government Revenues

If the demand for the imported goods is *elastic* with respect to price, a tariff decreases the quantity demanded proportionately more than the price increase. (Recall the explanation of price elasticity in Chapter 3.) Government revenue from a tariff on such a good may not be very substantial, but at least it is greater than zero. However, an attempt to increase this tax revenue by raising the tariff further will reduce the total tariff revenue because of the reduced quantity sold.

Tariffs are more effective in producing government revenue in cases where the demand is *inelastic*. But inelastic demand implies that there are no close substitutes, and particularly that domestic commodities are not directly in competition with that particular import. Thus, a tariff that raises substantial government revenue usually provides little protection for domestic industry. Furthermore, tariffs yielded only an estimated $4 billion for 1990, while the cost of tariffs in the same year in terms of inefficient production has been estimated as well over $15 billion. At existing federal rates, this additional output would yield an additional estimated $5 billion in tax revenues.

Improved Balance of Payments

When a country is experiencing a continuing deficit in its balance of trade, there may be much support for raising tariffs to curtail imports. This action will reduce the physical volume of imports. If the demand for imports is *inelastic*, total expenditures on imports will increase due to the price increase, but payments abroad will decrease since the import duty goes to the home government. This temporarily improves the balance of payments situation.

If demand for imports is *elastic*, total expenditures on imports as well as payments abroad will fall, again temporarily improving the balance of payments. The decrease in foreign payments, however, provides other countries with less foreign currency. The result may be a reduction in exports to those countries and, therefore, possibly a return to an adverse balance of payments condition.

Retaliation

Even if any of the preceding reasons were valid arguments for imposing tariffs, there would be the danger that other countries would retaliate by imposing tariffs on their imports. This would reduce exports sales and at least partly offset any advantage resulting from the tariff. It should be emphasized that the least acceptable argument for tariffs is simple retaliation in reaction to tariffs being imposed elsewhere. When one country takes the initiative in raising tariffs, this presents one barrier to the economic gains of free trade, but retaliation by the second country further diminishes the possibility of gains through specialization and trade.

Protection of Certain Infant Industries

The one economic argument for tariffs that does not conflict with the principle of comparative advantage is that a tariff should be imposed to protect an industry or firm that appears to be developing a comparative advantage. If a tariff is not imposed, it may be difficult for the industry to get past the initial stage of high costs associated with low levels of production. However, the danger in governments' acceptance of this argument is that, once the low-cost production level has been reached, it will be politically difficult to remove the tariff.

The argument can also be appealing to governments anxious to justify support for a certain industry. In such circumstances, protective tariffs may be imposed without satisfactory evidence that the industry is likely to develop a comparative advantage. Even in this case, the objective might be achieved more effectively by subsidizing the developing industry, rather than by imposing a protective tariff. The subsidy can be identified clearly as a cost of obtaining future gains from trade; judgments can therefore be made about the amount of present consumption that should be given up for potential increased future consumption from more productive use of resources. The subsidy also provides a reason for the government to scrutinize the operations of a new industry more closely, whereas the tariff offers the industry little incentive to reduce costs — unless there is an explicit timetable for the gradual reduction of the tariff. However, the subsidy could also be reduced gradually to provide the same incentive.

Conclusion   There is only one response to the reasons given for tariffs: raising the price of imports maintains domestic industries at a less efficient level of production than would occur under free trade and encourages tariff retaliation from other countries, thus compounding the loss of real income and output that would be realized by specializing in areas of comparative advantage. The non-economic arguments for tariffs that are related to other political or social objectives cannot be sustained either, since subsidies provide a more efficient means for pursuing these objectives.

Opening the Way for Trade

Both the international and domestic conditions facing an economy change substantially from time to time and, with these changes, attitudes toward free trade or protective tariffs also vary. The result has been a variety of arrangements for obtaining some of the advantages of foreign trade while retaining some features of a protected economy. These have ranged from special trade agreements on particular commodities to the economic integration of geographical areas.

GATT: General Agreement on Tariffs and Trade

International agreements on reducing tariff barriers may be either *multilateral agreements* or *bilateral agreements*, that is, among several countries or between only two countries. The most important multilateral agreement is the *General Agreement on Tariffs and Trade*, or GATT. Immediately after World War II, a number of countries tried to establish an international trade organization to act as an agency of the United Nations and as a counterpart to similar United Nations organizations concerned with labour, agriculture, and education. Opposition to the proposed international trade organization led to the substitution of the somewhat weaker arrangement, GATT.

The General Agreement on Tariffs and Trade, now signed by over 80 countries, sets out regulations governing the conduct of international trade, including the frequently cited "most-favoured nation" clause. This states that a country may not discriminate among trading partners by imposing a higher tariff against the imports of one country than against another. (Some of the discriminating tariff schedules that existed at the signing of GATT, such as the Imperial Preference tariffs levied by British Commonwealth countries on each other's imports, were allowed to continue through a transitional period.)

The other major effect of GATT arrangements has been a succession of multilateral trade negotiations designed to reduce tariff schedules by stages. An important round of negotiations (the Kennedy Round) lasted from 1964 to 1967, and resulted in an agreement that the average tariff level in most of the major exporting countries would drop to 7 or 8 per cent within five years.

The subsequent, Tokyo Round of negotiations began in late 1973, but GATT meetings continued until mid-1979. The results of these negotiations went into effect gradually from 1980 to 1987, reducing tariffs on industrial goods by about one-third. For example, the average tariff in Canada prior to the Tokyo Round was 12.7 per cent; this dropped to about 9 per cent by 1987. For the United States, the reduction was from 7 to about 5 per cent.

The most recent round of GATT talks began in Uruguay in 1986. These negotiations were adjourned without reaching agreement because they were concerned with difficult problems relating to agricultural subsidies and protectionism.

Non-tariff barriers have received particular attention in these recent negotiations because they were used more frequently in the 1970s, partly in response to the Kennedy Round tariff reductions and partly to the 1975 and 1982 recessions. Such barriers include: export subsidies, tax concessions, and other government aid to exporters; customs procedures that delay shipments, and product standards that are more stringent for imports than for domestic goods; some anti-dumping regulations; legislation and campaigns to give preference to domestically produced goods; and quotas on quantity or total value of specific imports.

Commodity Agreements   A number of *multilateral trade agreements* have been concerned with only a single commodity: wheat, tin, cotton, and others. These agreements sought primarily to establish a price range within which the commodity would be traded internationally, in an effort to stabilize prices. Such stability would encourage continued specialization by the exporting countries in the particular commodity and thus continue the gains to be realized from that trade.

Bilateral Agreements   *Bilateral agreements* are, strictly speaking, in contravention of the GATT "most-favoured nation" clause, but have won acceptance where other countries are not seriously harmed, or where the protests of injured nations have been successfully ignored.

The Canada-U.S. Automotive Agreement of 1965 is a prominent example of a bilateral agreement, requiring that each country remove tariffs against imports of motor vehicles and parts from the other country. However, the Agreement is discriminatory only on the American side: the United States has removed tariffs from Canadian automotive products but not from those of other countries, whereas Canada's side of the agreement permits Canada to remove tariffs on automotive products from other countries. (The Canada-U.S. Free Trade Agreement is discussed below.)

The textile industry is another case where Canada has attempted to reduce tariff protection while offering adjustment assistance. Canada's 1970 textile policy was designed to move the industry toward more competitive products; and in 1976 the emphasis shifted explicitly from textiles to clothing. The federal government provides grants to establish new employment and to help displaced workers in communities where textile and clothing industries cannot compete effectively with imported goods; and to assist in modernizing the technology of textile and clothing firms that are potentially competitive with foreign producers.

Integration of Trade Policies

Agreements of the type just discussed are concerned either with partial reduction of tariffs on all commodities, or complete removal of the tariff against specific commodities. The next step toward free trade is the integration of trade policies, but this can take different forms.

Free Trade Areas or   *A free trade area* or *free trade association* is a group of countries that
Associations   have agreed to reduce the tariffs imposed against imports from each of the other countries, usually with the objective of complete removal of these tariffs. However, each country can maintain its own trade policy with respect to other countries outside the free trade area.

A major example of this kind was the *European Free Trade Association* (EFTA) maintained through the 1960s by seven European countries: Austria, Denmark, Great Britain, Norway, Portugal, Sweden, and Switzerland. This group was formed in an effort to replace the trade they feared would be lost when other European countries (France, Germany, Italy, Belgium, the Netherlands, and Luxembourg) established the European Economic Community (EEC). EFTA currently includes Sweden, Norway, Finland, Iceland, Switzerland, and Austria.

A free trade area was established in 1989 when Canada and the United States signed the Free Trade Agreement removing any remaining tariffs and other barriers to trade between these two countries.

Customs Unions and Common Markets

A *customs union* goes one step further than the free trade area in integrating members' trade policies. In addition to removing the tariffs against imports from each other, the member countries agree to a common tariff schedule that each will charge against imports from outside the group. A *common market* takes integration another important step by permitting the free flow of productive resources, namely labour and capital, among the member countries. At the final stage of development of the common market, common fiscal and monetary policies are required, as well as a common trade policy. By this point, the countries will also have provided for substantial political integration as well.

The *European Community* (EC) is commonly called the Common Market, but it has not yet reached the final stages of the pure common market described above. Nevertheless, the EC has since its formation in 1957 succeeded in establishing free trade in the products of each country and in permitting the free flow of labour and capital among its members. The EC has also had a fixed exchange rate system for several years. When Britain, Denmark, and Ireland joined the EC in 1973, the remaining EFTA countries signed free trade agreements for non-agricultural products with the EC.

Canada's Tariff Policies

Protective tariffs have had a substantial, long-term effect on the character of the Canadian economy. Long periods of high tariffs on manufactured goods have stimulated a larger manufacturing sector than would have emerged otherwise and, with it, a higher proportion of foreign capital. Tariffs have also led to more inefficiency in manufacturing than would have occurred otherwise and, consequently, lower real incomes, higher relative prices, and fewer exports of manufactured products.

National Policy   Until 1879, tariffs served mainly as a major source of government revenues. Sir John A. Macdonald's National Policy shifted the emphasis to protection: tariff rates were raised to 25 to 30 per cent, from a previous average of about 10 per cent, to encourage the diversification and expansion of Canadian manufacturing. Tariff rates continued upward for another decade to reach an average of over 30 per cent of the value of dutiable imports.[3] British preference tariffs were introduced in 1899. These provided for lower duties on British goods than on goods imported from other countries, but Britain did not extend the same preference to Canadian goods.

Reciprocity   In 1911, the Laurier government negotiated a trade reciprocity agreement with the United States. Each country would remove all tariffs on imports of lumber, fish, agricultural produce, and mineral ores from the other country, and lower tariffs would be applied on some manufactured goods. But the government was defeated in the 1911 election, partly on its Reciprocity policy, and the trade agreement was never implemented.

Imperial Preference   Tariff rates fell gradually from the introduction of British preference until 1930. Tariffs were then raised quickly to the former high levels, partly in an effort to protect domestic employment during the Depression and partly as retaliation against sharp increases in American tariffs. In 1932, the Ottawa Agreements established Imperial Preference tariffs among British Commonwealth countries, thus extending the preferential tariffs Canada and Britain had established earlier. A trade agreement with the United States in 1935 reduced the tariffs that had been pushed so high five years before.

GATT   The General Agreement on Tariffs and Trade (GATT), initiated in 1948, has been the major element in Canada's postwar tariff policy. Through periodic meetings of GATT members, a series of multilateral tariff reductions have been achieved. This continuing effect of GATT agreements is evident in Figure 13.3, which portrays a century of Canada's tariff policies. Since GATT was established there have been eight major tariff-negotiating conferences: in 1947, 1949, 1951, 1956, 1960-61, 1964-67, 1973-79, and 1986-90.

The 1973-79 negotiations were influenced mainly by the U.S. proposal to reduce all tariffs by 55 to 60 per cent and by the European Community's emphasis on "tariff harmonization", or the reduction of high tariffs to the most common tariff level, which would entail cuts of 25 to 50 per cent. Canada agreed to reduce its tariffs by an average of

---

[3] Since some imports were (and still are) admitted duty-free, the average tariff on *total* imports was 22 per cent.

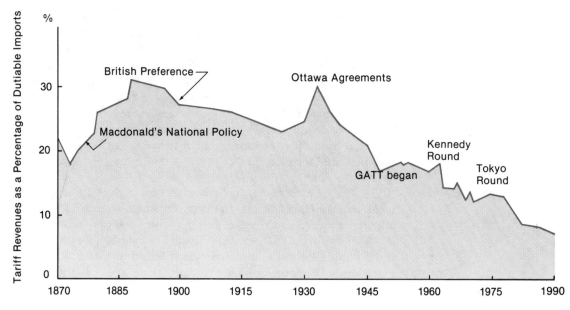

Figure 13.3   Canada's Tariff Policy
Canada's tariff policy began as a means to raise tax revenues, but in 1879
the National Policy shifted emphasis to protection of the manufacturing
sector. Preferential tariffs on British imports reduced the average tariff until
the Depression of the 1930s, when tariffs rose sharply to protect
employment and in retaliation against increased American tariffs. The
British preferential tariff was extended to all Commonwealth countries in
1932. GATT led to lower tariffs, especially in the 1960s, but slower real
growth in the 1970s hindered progress toward further reductions. The 1979
agreements made minor tariff reductions and tried to reduce non-tariff
barriers.

Source: J.H. Young, *Canadian Commercial Policy* (Royal Commission on
Canada's Economic Prospects, 1957); Statistics Canada, *Canadian
Economic Observer*.

36 per cent over the years 1980 to 1988, to bring Canada's average
tariff rate to about 9 per cent. At the same time, the average tariff in
the United States was about 5 per cent; and in Japan and the European
Community it was less than 7 per cent.

The 1986–90 talks focused on the removal of subsidies to agricultural
producers; these subsidies were said to reduce the potential for specialization in agricultural trade.

In 1973, Canada and a number of other industrialized countries
introduced a general preferential tariff for the developing countries, to
provide for reductions in the tariffs on imports from these areas.

As noted previously, another important component in Canada's postwar tariff policy has been the Canada-United States Automotive Agree-

ment, which was signed in 1965. This removed the 15 per cent tariff Canada had levied previously on American automobiles and parts. In addition to the trade in automobiles, about 35 per cent of the trade in other goods between Canada and the United States was also duty free.

Free Trade Agreement

The Economic Council of Canada proposed in 1979 that Canada should pursue a free trade policy, preferably with all nations but particularly with the United States, the European Community, and Japan. Even if bilateral free trade could not be obtained, Canada should undertake unilateral abolition of its tariffs. The Council recognized, however, that despite the substantial economic advantages, Canada would need to examine the social and political implications of free trade.

The major reason for the Council's recommendation was that Canada's rate of increase in productivity, under tariff protection, was one of the lowest among the industrialized countries. The Council estimated that in the late 1970s the cost of tariff protection in terms of lower productivity was at least 5 per cent of the GDP. A more recent study confirmed that Canadian real income could rise by 8 to 10 per cent with a free trade (no tariff) policy in the manufacturing sector, and that labour productivity could increase by 20 to 25 per cent.[4]

In 1985 the federal government was strongly urged by the Macdonald Commission on the Economic Union and Development Prospects for Canada to pursue a free trade treaty with the United States. The Commission proposed that trade in services (not currently covered by GATT rules) and non-tariff barriers should also be covered by a free trade treaty. The benefits of free trade were forecast to include an increase in per capita real income of 3 to 8 per cent, due to increased investment and employment, and lower prices for imports. These long-term benefits would require some reallocation of labour and physical resources among industries, for which the government would need to provide adjustment assistance.

Although the commission argued that Canada should pursue free trade multilaterally through GATT negotiations, it also argued that a bilateral treaty with the United States was even more urgent, because such a large percentage of Canada's international trade was with that country.

Within a year the federal government began negotiations with the United States. A tentative Free Trade Agreement was achieved in 1987,

---

[4] Economic Council of Canada, *Looking Outward: A New Trade Strategy for Canada*, Ottawa: Information Canada, 1975. Also see R. G. Harris and D. Cox, *Trade, Industrial Policy, and Canadian Manufacturing*, Toronto: Queen's Printer, 1984.

and was ratified in 1988. The two countries established a free trade area that would eliminate tariffs and other trade barriers, made it easier to invest in each other's economy, and established the framework for resolving trade disputes. All tariffs are to be removed by 1998, with some already eliminated as early as 1989. In addition, firms providing services in sectors such as architecture, finance, transportation, and telecommunications are able to operate more freely in both countries. Finally, the Agreement established a trade dispute panel that can resolve disputes regarding attempts by one country to interfere with trade from the other country.

In 1990, the United States and Mexico began discussions on a bilateral Free Trade Agreement; Canada was later invited to join these deliberations. Although Canada's trade with Mexico is very small, Canada has participated in the talks in order to preserve the benefits of the Canada-U.S. Free Trade Agreement.

Balance of International Payments

The fourth major economic goal recognized by the Economic Council of Canada was the maintenance of "a viable balance of payments". This refers to the Balance of International Payments, another important set of accounts used to measure Canada's international economic performance.

The Balance of International Payments is a record of all economic transactions between residents of Canada and the residents of all foreign countries during one year.

The goal of a viable balance of payments has been defined by the Economic Council as being not merely the maintenance of an inflow of payments from other countries equal to the outflow of payments from Canada to all other countries, but also as a strengthening of Canada's international economic position. This would be reflected particularly in the reduction of "the current account deficit" relative to Canada's Gross Domestic Product, and in a reduction of "net capital inflow" relative to domestic investment. The terms used in expressing this goal are drawn from the following description of the Balance of International Payments.

Balance of Payments Accounts

The separate factors influencing the overall balance of payments can be seen by examining the detailed structure of the international accounts.

There are two major sections in the Balance of International Payments: the *Current Account* and the *Capital Account*. A supplementary account, *Changes in Official International Reserves*, will be seen later to provide the balancing amount between the two major accounts.

Each account is divided into a number of sections related to the specific form or nature of the transaction. Entries in each account are categorized as either *receipts* or *payments*. Items that increase the flow of payments into Canada are receipts; items that increase the flow of payments out of Canada are payments.

Current Account

The current account is divided into sub-accounts for merchandise (or goods), services, investment income, and transfers. The *balance on merchandise account*, or the *balance on trade account*, shows the net position for the year with respect to trade in goods. Countries have traditionally attempted to develop a "favourable balance of trade" by exporting more than they imported in order to accumulate gold or foreign currencies. A glance at the current account in Table 13.7, however, shows that Canada's positive balance on the merchandise account was more than offset in 1990 by the negative balances in the *services account* and the *investment income account*. In the past three decades there has usually been a negative current account balance, as is shown by Figure 13.4.

The major service items include travel, freight, and shipping. When Canadians travel abroad or use foreign transportation services, they are "importing" services provided by other countries. The *investment income account* (which was part of the services account prior to 1986) includes interest and dividend payments, especially the large outflows of such payments for the use of foreign-owned capital. Inheritances and migrants' funds are not payments for foreign goods or services; rather, they represent international *transfer payments* through bequests or funds accompanying immigrants or emigrants.

These components of the current account can thus be used to monitor the effects of policies to stimulate exports, reduce imports, encourage foreign tourists to visit Canada, and so on. The balance on current account reflects the net effect of these policies and is one key indicator of progress toward a viable balance of payments.

Capital Account

The capital account is divided to show the flows of *long-term capital* and *short-term capital*. An inflow of foreign capital has the same effect on currency movements as does an outflow of export goods: there is an inflow of payments to Canada. Inflows of foreign capital are therefore treated as receipts in the balance of payments. This should not be confused with the fact that borrowings (or receipts) of foreign capital add to Canada's foreign indebtedness; the inflow of currency is accompanied

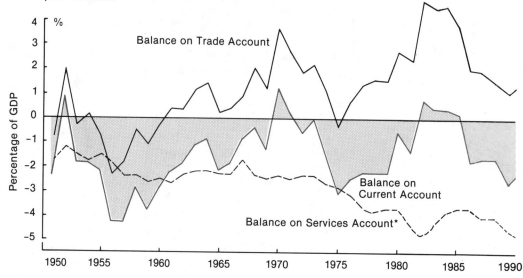

* Services in this figure include Investment Income.

Figure 13.4   Balance of Payments Accounts as a Percentage of GDP, Canada
Items in the Balance of Payments are shown here as percentages of the GDP, mainly to reduce the effect of inflation. The (usually negative) current account balance tends to reflect movements in the trade account because the services account deficit has smaller annual fluctuations. (Note that Net Transfers are not shown here.)

Source: Statistics Canada, *Canadian Balance of International Payments.*

by an outflow of certificates (stocks and bonds) indicating foreign ownership and Canada's foreign indebtedness.

Movements of long-term capital can take the form of direct investment in Canada by foreigners (a receipt) or Canadian residents' direct investment in other countries (a payment). Such investment would include the purchase of an existing Canadian firm, for example, or the construction of a new branch plant to be operated by the foreign owners. International purchases of stocks and bonds include both new and existing issues of these securities.

Short-term capital movements include changes in bank deposits and short-term bills that foreigners hold in Canada or that Canadian residents and governments hold abroad.

Changes in Official International Reserves   The third main section of the balance of payments shows the changes in official or government holdings of foreign exchange reserves and gold

Table 13.7

Canadian Balance of International Payments, 1990
(billions of Canadian dollars)

Accounts		Current Receipts		Current Payments	Balance[1]
Current Account					
Merchandise (exports or imports)		146		135	+11
Services		22		30	−8
Travel	7		12		
Freight and shipping	5		5		
Other services	10		13		
Investment Income		9		33	−24
Transfers		11		5	+5
Total		188		204	−16
Capital Account					
Long-term capital					+15
Direct investment				+4	
Stocks and Bonds				+11	
Short-term capital[2]					+2
Total net capital movements					+17
Changes in Official International Reserves					
Net change in official international reserves[3]					+1

Source: Statistics Canada, *Quarterly Estimates of the Balance of International Payments (Preliminary).*

Note: Items may not add to totals due to rounding.

[1] A minus sign, except for changes in official reserves, indicates net outflow of funds from Canada.
[2] Includes net errors and omissions.
[3] Includes Special Drawing Rights.

in the Exchange Fund Account. These changes reflect the net deficits or surpluses on the other two accounts.

A net inflow of foreign currencies is the result of a net inflow of foreign payments to Canada in the current or capital accounts. The foreign currencies have initially been acquired by the chartered banks and other currency dealers in exchange for the Canadian dollars required to complete the original transactions. These foreign currencies are then acquired by the Exchange Fund Account as part of the official monetary actions in stabilizing the foreign exchange rate.

Consequently, a net increase (or positive sign) on official reserves is the balancing item, or offset, for a positive balance in the current and/or capital accounts. *It is in this sense that the Balance of Payments must necessarily be in balance*. However, reference to a deficit or surplus in the balance of payments means only the net balance of the current and capital accounts. Nevertheless, a deficit in those accounts will be accompanied by a decrease in official reserves; similarly, a surplus would result in an increase in official reserves.[5]

Balance of Payments Equilibrium

The balance on current account is often cited as a measure of health of the balance of payments since a chronic deficit or current account represents a growing debt to other countries. But a surplus on capital account can offset part or all of this deficit.

Basic Balance   The concept of a *basic balance* has been developed to show the net effect of movements in both the current and capital accounts, in order to calculate the net result in holdings of foreign currencies. *A basic balance exists when the current account balance is equal to the long-term capital balance.* Movements of gold and foreign currencies and the short-term capital balance are removed from this equation, since a balance that depended on either of them would be precarious, particularly under a fixed foreign exchange rate. Countries could not sustain an outflow of foreign exchange and gold over a long period, since stocks of each of these are limited. Nor can short-term capital movements be depended upon, since the movement of these funds changes quickly with changes in short-run conditions.

The balance of payments is therefore said to have a "basic balance" only when these latter movements are not required as the balancing items; that is, when the current account balance is equal to the long-term capital balance. *When the balance of payments does not have this basic balance, there is either a surplus or deficit in the balance of payments and thus it is in disequilibrium.*

Disequilibrium   A country attempts to overcome a balance of payments disequilibrium, particularly a continuing deficit, because this requires a continuing payment of gold and foreign exchange to other countries, and rising indebtedness to them, neither of which can be sustained indefinitely. A continuing surplus entails a continuing accumulation of foreign exchange and debts of other countries. Although this may seem desir-

---

[5] The item that brings the balance of payments into balance statistically is the "other short-term capital", because it also includes a "statistical discrepancy" component. This is a residual item that is calculated after all other entries in the international accounts have been estimated. But this statistical adjustment must be distinguished from the true balancing item, the federal government's holdings of foreign currencies.

able, a continuing surplus can be a source of inflation; because the net inflow of foreign currency could increase the money supply, the chartered banks sell this currency to the central bank in exchange for the domestic monetary unit.

A continuing surplus on current account also represents a giving up of current consumption (in the export of goods and services to other countries) in exchange for a claim on goods and services in some indefinite future. Like a large personal savings account, a surplus yields satisfaction only when it is being spent. A country will wish to correct a balance of payments disequilibrium—whether a deficit or a surplus—but the way it does so will depend on whether it has a floating or pegged exchange rate.

Floating Exchange Rates and the Balance of Payments

When a foreign exchange rate is free of government control, it fluctuates with changes in the supply and demand for the currency. To see how this affects the balance of payments, consider the case of Canadian demand for Swiss watches. If there is an increase in the price of Canadian-made watches, there will likely be an increase in Canada's demand for Swiss watches. The supply of Canadian dollars to be exchanged for Swiss francs increases: there will be more Canadian dollars offered in exchange for Swiss francs at any price level (that is, at any exchange rate). Figure 13.5a shows this outward shift of the supply curve with the resulting decrease in price of the Canadian dollar, as more are offered in exchange for Swiss francs.

When the price of a currency falls, it is said to *depreciate*; if it rises, it is said to *appreciate*. Figure 13.5b shows that depreciation of a currency can occur not only with an increase in its supply, but also with a decrease in demand for the currency. The downward shift of the demand curve reflects a decrease in the Swiss demand for Canadian dollars, perhaps because Canadian blankets have become relatively more expensive than English blankets, or because Swiss investors are buying fewer shares on a Canadian stock exchange.

What will be the effect on Canada's balance of payments of a depreciation in the Canadian dollar's exchange rate? (Although the analysis is presented for Canadian-Swiss trade only, the conclusion can be generalized to include trade with all other countries.) Assume that both the long-term capital account and the current account are in balance before depreciation occurs. The net effect will depend on the price elasticity of demand by the Swiss for Canadian imports and the demand by Canadians for Swiss imports.

If both demands are elastic, a depreciated Canadian dollar lowers the price of Canadian goods in terms of Swiss francs, resulting in a greater quantity of goods exported and an increased inflow of Canadian dollars. Meanwhile the original depreciation of the dollar increases the Canadian-dollar price of Swiss goods, resulting in a lower quantity of Swiss goods imported and a reduced outflow of Canadian dollars. This temporarily produces a surplus on Canada's current account. But the increased quantity of Canadian dollars demanded by the Swiss, and the decreased quantity of Swiss francs demanded by Canadians, results in an *appreciation of the Canadian dollar*. The balance of trade shifts in the other direction and Canada's surplus on current account disappears. Thus when both demands are elastic, the balance of payments will tend toward long-run equilibrium.

When both demands are inelastic, depreciation of the Canadian dollar leads Canada to buy fewer Swiss goods but to pay more Canadian dollars in total for them. The Swiss buy more Canadian goods and pay more dollars in total because the Swiss pay the same dollar price per unit, even though the price of Canadian goods has fallen in terms of Swiss francs. Hence, there *may* be a net deficit on current account for Canada. In this case the *Canadian dollar would depreciate* further still and if the elasticity of the Swiss demand plus the elasticity of the Canadian demand, for each other's goods, is less than one, the balance of payments will tend toward a long-run disequilibrium.

This disequilibrium can persist only if there is a continuing surplus on the long-term capital account. If the Swiss (or all other countries generally) are willing to continue buying Canadian stocks and bonds, the deficit on current account may be offset. But in some countries, and notably in Canada, concern has been expressed about the level of foreign indebtedness or foreign investment. It may be deemed an unacceptable price to pay for a continuing current account deficit.

A country faced with a balance of payments disequilibrium due to inelastic demand for its exports and imports would find a solution difficult. Apart from direct controls, which are discussed later, the main attack on the disequilibrium must come through domestic policies designed to lower the price of domestic goods in order to reduce imports. This would include anti-inflation policies as well as longer-run programs for improving labour productivity. In most cases, however, this problem would not arise. The demand for another country's goods tends to be elastic because there are a number of close substitutes, either produced domestically or available from a number of other countries.

Fixed Exchange Rates and the Balance of Payments

Because the foreign exchange rate is not allowed to fluctuate significantly under a fixed exchange rate policy, there are no effects on the balance of payments equilibrium of the kind described in the preceding section. This does not mean, however, that a fixed exchange rate has no implications for the balance of payments. Indeed, a serious problem

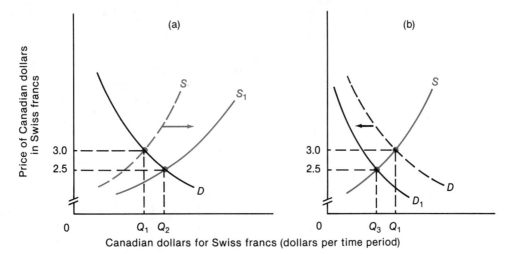

Figure 13.5   Shifts in Supply or Demand for Currencies Cause Foreign Exchange Rates to Change
An increase in the supply of Canadian dollars that can be exchanged for Swiss francs shifts the supply curve outward to S_1, hence lowering the exchange rate of the Canadian dollar in terms of Swiss francs and increasing the quantity of Canadian dollars demanded. Alternatively, a decrease in the demand for Canadian dollars, to D_1, also lowers the exchange rate but reduces the quantity of Canadian dollars demanded.

arises if there is a persistent or chronic deficit, because a country must continue paying out foreign currencies to meet this deficit.

A chronic balance of payments deficit is usually an indication of an *overvalued currency*: that is, the exchange rate has been set too high. At the fixed exchange rate of an overvalued currency, the price of a country's own goods will be expensive compared with the same goods in other countries. The result is a strong incentive to import and a difficulty in promoting exports.

An *undervalued currency* leads to chronic surpluses on the balance of payments. Although this may be considered a less serious situation, an undervalued currency requires a country to pay more for its imports and to earn less from its exports.

Correcting Balance of Payments Deficits

A country experiencing a chronic deficit due to an overvalued currency can take a number of different actions to reduce its deficit. It can:

- pursue contractionary monetary and fiscal policies;
- impose tariffs;
- subsidize exports;
- devalue its currency;

- impose exchange controls;
- allow the exchange rate to float.

Contractionary monetary and fiscal policies should have the effect of restraining inflation, thus improving the competitive position of exports and discouraging imports. Such policies also curtail imports by slowing the growth of incomes. At the same time, high interest rates implied in the restrictive monetary policy should encourage a large inflow of short-term capital. Such actions may impose a high cost in terms of unemployment, but a government must weigh this against the problem of a chronic deficit.

Imposing tariffs will reduce imports by making them expensive, but at best will have no stimulating effect on exports. It is more likely that imposing or increasing tariffs will cause other countries to retaliate. There likely will be no improvement in the balance of payments and any previous advantages of foreign trade will be lost.

Export subsidies probably will encourage increased receipts from exports and reduce the balance of payments deficit. But subsidies designed explicitly to increase exports are illegal under international (GATT) trading rules. There may also be retaliation by other countries. In any case, taxes must be raised to pay the subsidies; this represents a gift to other countries who enjoy the cheaper exports at the expense of the taxpayers.

Devaluation is a reduction in the pegged value of the foreign exchange rate. This represents an abrupt change in the rate compared with the gradual depreciation that might occur with a floating exchange rate. The effect of the devaluation will be the same as in the case of depreciation: the quantity or volume of imports will decline, and the value of exports will rise. The net effect on the balance of payments, however, depends on the price elasticities of demand for imports and exports.

Exchange controls are used by some countries that have experienced chronic deficits for some time. Persons receiving foreign currency, whether through export sales, gifts, or other sources, are required to present it to the government in exchange for the domestic currency at a specified rate. Persons who require foreign currencies to pay for imports, travel abroad, and so on, must apply to the goverment; currency can thereby be rationed for purposes receiving government approval. Such controls act as direct restraints on imports.

Allowing the exchange rate to float is usually the final alternative that a country would consider. Britain, for example, devalued the pound twice in the postwar period, from US $4.03 to US $2.80 in 1949 and to US $2.40 in 1967, before it allowed the pound to float in June 1972.

By mid-1973, most of the major currencies were also floating. Some of the other remedies described above were still relevant, however, as countries tried to manage the range within which they thought their currencies should float. Hence, monetary policy was usually designed with both domestic and international considerations in mind.

Review of the Main Points

1. Canada's annual exports of goods are equal to about one-fifth to one-quarter of its GDP; the country ranks seventh in the world in total value of exports. Trade with the United States accounts for about 70 per cent of Canada's exports and imports. Apart from trade in motor vehicles and petroleum, Canada's major exports come from primary industries, while imports are mainly manufactured goods.

2. The principle of comparative advantage states that a country should produce and trade those commodities in which it has a comparative advantage, namely, commodities it can produce relatively more efficiently than can any other country. Even if a country has an absolute advantage in all commodities, that is, if it is more efficient in the production of all commodities than other countries, it will be still better off by producing commodities in which it has a comparative advantage.

3. The terms of trade between countries or within a country is the ratio of the quantity of one good that will be exchanged for a given quantity of another good. No trade will occur between countries unless this ratio is within the limits established by the terms of trade within each country.

4. International trade, when based on the principle of comparative advantage, reduces commodity prices or, alternatively, increases real wages.

5. Import restrictions include tariffs and quotas. The reasons generally advanced for tariffs are: to maintain political independence; to protect domestic industries and employees; to raise government revenues; to reduce a balance of payments deficit; to retaliate against tariffs imposed by other countries; and to foster new industries that are expected to develop a comparative advantage. Tariffs reduce the gains from trade and implicitly impose a tax on consumers, by requiring them to pay a higher price for commodities, or a tax on workers, by reducing real wages.

6. International trade has been encouraged by international agreements, such as GATT, which have led to reduced tariffs, and by integration of trade policies through free trade associations, customs unions, and common markets.

7. The goal of a viable balance of payments is concerned with maintaining an acceptable balance between the inflow and outflow of international payments for goods and services, and of long-term capital.

8. The Balance of International Payments includes the Current Account of payments for goods and services and international transfer payments, the Capital Account of international long- and short-term capital flows, and the account showing Changes in Official International Reserves.

9. A country's balance of payments is in disequilibrium when there is a deficit or surplus in the combined balances of the current account and the long-term capital account. The effect on the balance of payments of fluctuating exchange rates depends on the elasticity of demand for exports of the two countries involved. If both demands are elastic, there will be a tendency to long-run equilibrium; if inelastic with a combined value of less than one, there will be long-run disequilibrium. A chronic deficit on current account can be sustained by a surplus on the capital account, but this implies an increasing level of foreign indebtedness.

10. Under fixed exchange rates, a balance of payments disequilibrium is not corrected automatically. A continuing deficit (or surplus) reflects an overvalued (or undervalued) currency. A country can try to correct a deficit by establishing restrictive monetary and fiscal policies, imposing tariffs, subsidizing exports, devaluing the currency, imposing exchange controls, or allowing the exchange rate to float.

Key Concepts and Topics

Canada-United States
   Automotive Agreement
absolute advantage
comparative advantage
terms of trade
export duties
ad valorem tariff
specific tariff
quota
embargo
sanction
retaliation
"infant industry" argument
GATT
"most-favoured nation" clause
non-tariff barriers
free trade area
customs union
common market

foreign exchange rate
pegged exchange rate
floating exchange rate
balance of payments disequilibrium
   (surplus or deficit)
appreciation
depreciation
devaluation
revaluation
overvalued currency
undervalued currency
exchange controls
Balance of International Payments
   (or balance of payments)
balance of trade
current account
capital account
basic balance

Questions for Review and Discussion

1. Why is comparative advantage, rather than absolute advantage, the relevant concept for explaining international trade?
2. "International trade is indirect production." Explain.
3. "A tariff cannot be effective in providing government revenues if it provides effective protection for domestic producers." Do you agree? Explain.
4. Discuss the relative advantages and disadvantages of import tariffs and quotas as a method for protecting domestic industries in the short run.
5. Why do policy-makers seem to be more concerned with the balance of trade or the balance on current account than with the balance on capital account?
6. A deficit in the balance of trade indicates that a country is enjoying a higher standard of living than if there were no deficit. Why then do governments try to reduce trade deficits?
7. What are the possible effects of a decline in the Canadian dollar exchange rate on (a) the balance of payments, (b) the level of employment, and (c) the rate of inflation? Explain how these effects would occur.
8. Should Canada have a fixed or floating foreign exchange rate? Give a detailed explanation for your position.

Sources and Selected Readings

Dales, John H. *The Protective Tariff in Canada's Development*. Toronto: University of Toronto Press, 1966.

Eastman, H.C., and S. Stykolt. *The Tariff and Competition in Canada*. Toronto: Macmillan, 1967.

Harris, Richard G. *Trade, Industrial Policy and International Competition*. Toronto: University of Toronto Press, 1985.

Hill, Roderick, et al. *Canada-United States Free Trade*. Toronto: University of Toronto Press, 1985.

Lazar, Fred. *The New Protectionism: Non-Tariff Barriers and their Effects on Canada*. Ottawa: Canadian Institute for Economic Policy, 1981.

Lindert, P.H. *International Economics*, 8th ed. Homewood, Ill.: Irwin, 1986.

Lipsey, R.G., and M.G. Smith. *Taking the Initiative: Canada's Trade Options*. Toronto: C.D. Howe Institute, 1985.

Markusen, J.R., and J.R. Melvin. *The Theory of International Trade and Its Canadian Applications*. Toronto: Butterworths, 1984.

Purvis, Douglas. *The Canadian Balance of Payments: Perspectives and Policy Issues*. Montreal: Institute for Research on Public Policy, 1983.

Smith, M.G., and F. Stone, eds. *Assessing the Canada-U.S. Free Trade Agreement*. Halifax: Institute for Research on Public Policy, 1988.

Stone, Frank. *Canada, the GATT and the International Trade System*. Montreal: Institute for Research on Public Policy, 1984.

Whalley, John, et al. *Canadian Trade Policies and the World Economy*. Toronto: University of Toronto Press, 1985.

14 Economics of the Public Sector

Government policies determine the framework for all economic activity in Canada. It might therefore seem unnecessary to devote a separate chapter to the economics of governments, or the public sector, when public policies are examined in most of the other chapters. This chapter, however, emphasizes governments' direct involvement in allocating resources and distributing final products, through their expenditures and taxation programs. It is here that the "mixed" aspect of a mixed economy is most pronounced. The second part of the chapter examines the principles and structure of the taxation system used to collect the revenues for financing these expenditures.

Government Expenditures

Growth in Government Expenditure

Total expenditures by all levels of government in Canada have increased dramatically in the past several decades. The federal government's expenditure in 1867 was about $14 million, by 1926 it was $306 million, and by 1990 it was about $120 billion. Such growth is due to a number of factors. Inflation is the most obvious one. The price level has risen by over 800 per cent since 1926, which means that the real increase in government expenditures is much less than a comparison expressed in current dollars would indicate. Second, the population of Canada has increased by over 150 per cent since 1926. One would therefore expect an increase in government expenditures that at least matched the population growth. Third, Canada was involved in two major wars during this century, and in other defence commitments, which resulted in continuing expenditures for veterans' pensions and other benefits, and for interest payments on the debt incurred during the war periods.

If these were the only factors influencing government expenditures, the increase would be much less than the above comparison indicates. Governments would still be spending approximately the same low share of the Gross Domestic Product that they controlled several decades ago. Figure 14.1 indicates, however, that the combined governments— federal, provincial, and municipal—continued to claim an increasing share of the Gross Domestic Product until government spending almost reached 50 per cent of GDP. Since 1985, this share has declined slightly.

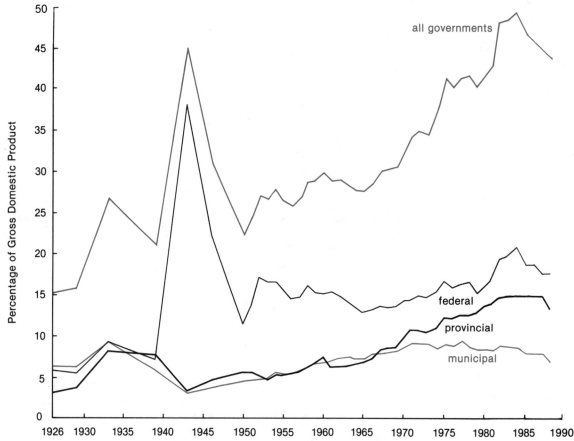

Figure 14.1 Governments' Spending, Including Personal Transfer Payments, as a Percentage of Canada's GDP
Federal government spending increased sharply, to over 35 per cent of GDP, during World War II, but provincial and municipal governments reduced their spending at that time. The federal share of GDP rose slightly in the 1953–54 and 1960–61 recessions but rose sharply in the early 1980s. The municipal and provincial governments' shares of GDP increased fairly steadily in the postwar period, with provincial governments showing the sharpest increase since the mid-1960s. Intergovernmental payments are excluded. The total for all Governments includes hospitals.

Source: Canadian Tax Foundation, *The National Finances.*

Government expenditures represented about 45 per cent of the GDP during World War II but fell sharply to 22 per cent by 1950. The government share rose slowly during the 1950s and early 1960s, reaching temporary peaks as government expenditures were increased to deal with the recessions of 1953-54 and 1960-62. Since 1965, however, the government share has risen substantially; it reached a peak at 47 per cent in 1983 and then receded slightly to 44 per cent.

The relative sizes of federal, provincial, and municipal expenditures have also changed during the same period. Prior to the 1930s, municipal expenditures were about double those of the provincial governments. From 1945 to 1970, the total expenditures of these two levels of government were roughly equal, but since then provincial expenditures have risen more quickly than those of the municipalities.

Expenditures by Government Function

The primary reason for the absolute growth in government expenditures in Canada — in addition to the effects of inflation, population growth, and war — has been an increasing emphasis on governments' role in providing education, health, and welfare assistance. Figure 14.2 shows the percentage of the total government expenditures allocated to each major function, for 1959 and 1988.

A comparison of the percentages of total government spending allocated to specific functions in 1959 and 1988 shows that the traditional functions of government — defence and protection — have received a lower or constant share of the total spending. The major increases in the share of government spending have been in health and social welfare. This reflects increases in the relative costs of providing such services, increases in the proportion of transfer payments, and a shift of expenditures for some of these services, especially in the health field, from the private to the public sector.

Public expenditures for health services rose sharply with the introduction of the Medical Care Act (now the Canada Health Act), under which the federal and provincial governments shared the cost of health programs arranged by the provinces. Welfare assistance expenditures include old age pensions and family allowances, which are paid to all eligible persons regardless of income level, in addition to income-support payments under the Unemployment Insurance programs and the Canada Assistance Plan.

Education expenditures, as a percentage of total government spending, rose quickly for three reasons: the proportion of the population in the school-age group increased in the 1950s and 1960s; the percentage of the school-age group remaining in the educational system beyond the compulsory age has continued to rise, as have the real educational costs

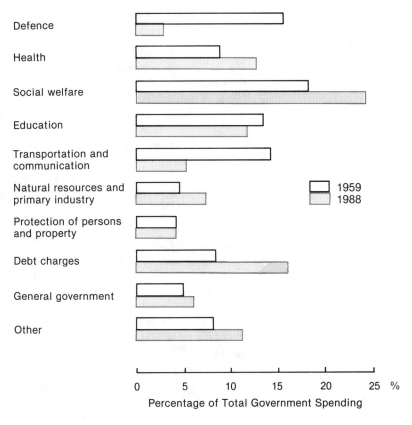

Figure 14.2   Major Government Expenditures as a Percentage of Total Government Spending
About 46 per cent of the combined spending by all levels of government in 1988 went to education, health, and social welfare. The share of governments' budgets directed to the latter two categories increased substantially from 1959 to 1988, while the share going to defence and transportation and communication declined. Debt charges became a much larger share of government spending in the 1980s, because of increasing interest rates and a larger government debt.

Source: Statistics Canada, *Consolidated Government Finance.*

per student. However, the declining birth rate of the past two decades may lead to a levelling off or decline in the share of government spending going to education.

Economic Functions of Government

The expenditure patterns show how the relative importance of spending by different levels of government, and of their specific expenditure programs, has changed substantially in the past several decades. The economic roles of government (as outlined in Chapter 4) are:

- to stabilize the level of economic activity over a long-term upward trend in GDP;
- to assure that income is distributed in a manner that is considered equitable or fair; and
- to encourage more efficient use of productive resources and to provide commodities that would not be produced in sufficient quantity, if at all, in the absence of government action.

Governments also have political and social functions such as curtailing crime; setting and enforcing safety standards; and regulating social practices concerning marriages, divorce, and property ownership. Some of these functions have economic consequences, but this section discusses only the direct economic responsibilities of government listed above, and particularly the allocation function.

The *stabilization* role of government involves government expenditures and taxation to influence the level of aggregate expenditure, and thus the level of employment, output, and income. This role is exercised through the discretionary and automatic fiscal policies that governments pursue in an attempt to stabilize prices and employment.

To agree on what constitutes an acceptable combination of inflation and unemployment — or what constitutes a stable economy — is difficult enough, but it is even more difficult to agree on what represents an equitable *distribution* of income. Governments must therefore constantly seek and guide a national consensus on this question, and then determine what means can be used to achieve the appropriate redistribution of income. The pattern of income distribution, and especially the incidence of poverty, is discussed in Chapter 26.

Stabilization of the economy and redistribution of income involve governments primarily in decisions about the transfer of purchasing power both over time (in the case of deficit and surplus budgets) and among individuals.

The *resource allocation* role of government is more directly concerned with determining how resources should be used. The many factors influencing these latter decisions will be considered next.

Preparing the Public Budget

Even if it can be assumed, at least for the moment, that the redistribution and stabilization functions of the government budget have been taken into account, the allocation function raises a number of problems. Not only do governments need to decide which of the several methods should be used for providing or encouraging public services, they must also decide how much of each good or service should be available. How much *should* be allocated to each of the many government activities?

The traditional answer to this question has been that the elected representatives of the people vote on each issue and thereby determine how much will be allocated to each activity. The debate on governments' spending estimates is an important feature of the parliamentary process and, especially where there are strong opposition parties, gives rise to close scrutiny of a government's proposed expenditure program.

Theory of Public Choice

Do the elected members always know what their constituents want, and do they always vote according to these wants? Some economists have developed a public choice theory to explain how the political process is used to determine the output of public goods and services.[1] Models based on this theory suggest that individual members and political parties arrange their voting to maximize the probability of their being re-elected, and especially re-elected as the government. Governments will therefore provide the minimum services required to gain the votes of each interest group, and try to realize the maximum number of votes with a minimum of tax revenues. The voting process can partly take account of externalities, but since each voter has only one vote, the size or importance of external effects cannot be reflected in voting. Someone who will be severely harmed by a new expressway or airport has no more effect on the political decision than someone who will realize almost negligible benefits. Consequently, political pressure groups or lobbies are formed to offset this inadequacy in the voting system.

Benefit-Cost Analysis

A technique sometimes used by governments to evolve rational expenditure programs is program budgeting. Its full name is the *Planning-Programming-Budgeting System*, or PPBS. The essential feature of this approach is that government expenditures are allocated to programs or functions of governments, rather than to government departments. However, departments have been retained for administrative purposes. Under PPBS, a government decides how much to allocate to its total health program, and then assigns the administration of various parts of the program to different departments. Developing the total expenditure program through PPBS has three steps: a government outlines its objectives and priorities in the form of a *plan*; this plan is then translated into the *programs* required to meet the various objectives; and the total *budget* is the sum of expenditures allocated to each program.

How could a government determine how much to spend on each program? The approach usually used in PPBS is *benefit-cost analysis*. Although benefit-cost analysis is regarded by some people as a complicated approach to government spending decisions, the basic concept is

[1] See, for example, Albert Breton, *The Economic Theory of Representative Government*; Anthony Downs, *An Economic Theory of Democracy*; Douglas G. Hartle, *A Theory of the Expenditure Budgetary Process*; and Dennis C. Mueller, *Public Choice*.

familiar to everyone. It is simply a comparison of the benefits of a project with its cost — a comparison that everyone makes, although perhaps sometimes unconsciously, when deciding how to spend his or her time or money.

Box 14.1 An Example of Benefit-Cost Analysis

With the increasing use of this technique, there has been increasing criticism of the interpretation of its results. Benefit-cost analysis, and the difficulties associated with its application, can best be understood through an example. Consider the case of a government that must decide whether a community college should be added to the postsecondary educational system. Since governments are responsible for encouraging the most productive use of an economy's resources, this project should be evaluated from the point of view of the whole economy; *all* benefits and *all* costs must be included in the analysis.

The costs include the direct costs of constructing, or renting, the college buildings, as calculated on an annual basis; the salaries of instructors and other staff; the books, supplies, and transportation costs of students; and other miscellaneous expenses. Indirect costs include the earnings that students forgo because they are not in the labour force; and the cost of municipal services supplied to the colleges, such as snow and garbage removal, and police and fire protection. There may also be some non-monetary costs, such as the noise of students' motorcycles in the neighbourhood.

The direct benefits include the additional output of the graduates, beyond what they would have produced had they not attended the college. The indirect benefits vary from local prestige related to the presence of a college, to the community involvement of its staff, to the availability of more meeting and conference spaces if these facilities are open to the community.

A conceptual outline of the costs and benefits can be prepared without much difficulty, but problems arise when one attempts to put dollar values on each item in the list. How should the buildings be depreciated in estimating the annual cost of their use? Are high school graduates' wages a satisfactory measure of the forgone earnings of college students? Does it cost the municipality anything more to include the college within its fire protection program? How can the neighbourhood's costs, such as motorcycle noise, be measured?

Even more difficult questions arise in evaluating the benefits. Are the earnings of other college graduates a suitable measure of the potential output of the college graduates in question? How will these estimated earnings change over the years with changing conditions in the supply and demand for such graduates? What is the possibility that the graduates will emigrate, or that they will not be in the labour force, or that they will not live to retirement — whatever that age might be? How should one estimate the value to the community of locating a college there?

These are the kind of questions that the critics of benefit-cost analysis have raised, and indeed the questions that analysts must answer. However, the difficulty is not insurmountable; assumptions can be made to deal with each question. By using alternative sets of assumptions, one can determine whether varying the value assigned to any one cost or benefit component has a significant effect on the final calculations.

The actual calculations of the costs and benefits include an estimate of the total cost of producing one "average" college graduate and the total benefits associated with the graduate for his or her lifetime.* If the benefits exceed the costs, the college represents a reasonable use of productive resources. Whether the project will actually be undertaken depends on whether the net benefit is greater in this project or in some other public projects under consideration. That is, priorities will be established on the basis of the benefit-cost calculations and other political considerations.

It remains for the government to decide what share of the costs should be borne by the individual student and what share should be met by public funds. Again leaving aside other considerations of income redistribution (or equality of opportunity) and stabilization of employment, the public contribution should be just large enough to attract enough students so that the increasing cost of instructors' salaries and the declining average benefits associated with an increasing number of graduates will reduce the net benefits to zero; at this point the total benefits are just equal to the total costs.

In practice, governments do not determine their policies quite so precisely. This type of calculation, however, affords some guidance on whether public policies are even moving in the appropriate direction. A project, for example, that cannot be justified on the basis of benefit-cost analysis requires the politicians to justify or reject it by looking more closely at the nonmonetary and indirect effects.

* The benefits and costs must be *discounted* to a common base year before the net benefit, or *net present value*, is calculated.

Benefit-cost analysis was used initially in public allocation decisions to evaluate proposed water resource developments. Since there were many potential benefits of a proposed dam, some way had to be found to include all of them—flood control, irrigation, electric power production, and recreational use—within a single measure that was to be compared with the costs of land acquisition and dam construction. More recently, benefit-cost analysis has been used to evaluate expenditure proposals in education—such as the proposal illustrated in Box 14.1— vocational training, health, transportation, parks, research and development, housing, and crime prevention. In fact, the list could include almost all government programs.

Which Level of Government?

The history of the public sector in Canada includes many disputes about which level of government should be responsible for which public service. Generally the issues have focused on an interpretation of the responsibilities allocated to the federal and provincial governments by the British North America Act of 1867 (now known as the Constitution Act, 1867), or on the fiscal resources available to different governments to meet their responsibilities. These questions are considered more closely in connection with the intergovernmental tax agreements and revenue transfers, discussed later in this chapter.

Economies of Scale   The *economic* rationale for determining the appropriate level of government to be responsible for different public services is essentially the same as the justification for the public provision of services other than pure public goods, namely, the existence of *economies of scale* and *externalities*. The existence of economies of scale, for example, led some provinces to amalgamate local school boards into county or district units. Specialized programs could be provided by small, local boards only at very high per-student costs, but county boards can provide a wider variety of programs at lower average costs — or so it was assumed. There is some concern, however, that these economies of amalgamation may be partly offset by higher costs for administering the larger units.

Spillover Benefits   Education also provides an example of how external benefits, or *spillover* benefits, lead to a change in the level of government responsible for a given function. Although the increasing share of education costs assumed by some provincial governments is explained in part by problems associated with using property taxes to finance education, this shift in responsibility is also based on the argument that graduates of the local schools are more likely to leave the local community than was the case in earlier years. Local residents are less willing to bear the education costs of children who will not be productive members of the local labour force.

In contrast, residents of larger metropolitan areas often object to paying for the welfare services of persons moving into the area from other centres. The provincial governments, and in some cases the federal government, are pressed to assume larger shares of the cost of what have traditionally been municipal functions, as the population becomes more mobile.

Decentralization   The external effects argument is, however, not inconsistent with *decentralization* of the provision of public services. Local residents, and their elected municipal representatives, may be in a better position to determine, for example, whether the benefits of a neighbourhood park justify the cost of providing it. Governments may not make the proper decisions about public services if they are too far removed from persons who will enjoy the benefits or who will bear the nonmonetary costs of some types of projects. For this reason a number of provinces, and particularly the higher-income provinces, are arguing that they can determine the value or priority of some public services better than the federal government. At the municipal level, local rate-payers' associations are beginning to discuss the establishment of ward councils, as municipal councils enlarge their geographical areas and become further removed from specific neighbourhood problems.

Taxation

Principles of Taxation: Who and What Should Be Taxed?

There is much truth in the old adage about the inevitability of death and taxes. Almost anything can be — and has been — taxed. Taxes have been levied on every type of luxury, on necessities such as salt, and on the incomes of the poor as well as the wealth of the rich. Economic analysis can indicate how governments should allocate their expenditures to achieve specific objectives, but it is more difficult to say how governments should collect revenues to finance these expenditures. There is not, for example, an analytical technique like benefit-cost analysis that can be applied to the taxation side of government budgets. Instead, a set of principles or standards must be used to judge the merits of a proposed tax.

Although normative judgments underlie taxation decisions, objective analysis is important in assessing the effects of different types of taxes. In discussing these principles, it is again assumed that the government's stabilization function has been taken into account. But the question of redistribution must be given at least as much attention as the allocation function in examining a proposed tax, as will be evident from the following principles of taxation.

The principles or standards for assessing the effects of taxation have evolved through a long history of financing public expenditures. Although there is widespread agreement on the principles, the relative emphasis to be placed on each one will vary among different groups in the population and at different times. There can also be considerable disagreement about the extent to which any particular tax is in accord with the accepted principles.

The three basic principles of taxation are: *equity*, *neutrality*, and *efficiency*.

Tax Equity

The equity principle states simply that the tax system should be fair. But what constitutes a fair, just, or equitable tax system? Three conditions have been proposed as a test of equity. Each of these yields a different answer as to whether a particular tax can be said to be "fair". As a result, the major disagreement about taxes centres on which of these tests is most appropriate. The three alternatives for judging tax equity are the *benefits received*, the *ability to pay*, and the *equal treatment of equals*.

Benefits Received   The principle of benefits received states that *individuals (and corporations) should pay taxes equal to the benefits they receive from government programs*. As governments increasingly move into areas of quasi-public goods, and especially those areas that have come under public control for reasons of efficiency, there is growing support for the principle of benefits received.

This is often expressed in the proposal that public services be financed by "user charges", or that the user of the service be charged directly. Thus subway riders would be charged the full cost of providing subway transportation. But this proposal can err in focusing only on those who benefit directly from a service. The beneficiaries of a city's subway system include not only the subway riders, but also the inner-city residents who are freed from automobile noise and congestion, the merchants who no longer need to provide customer parking, and so on. Obviously, it would be difficult to assess a benefits tax against this wider group.

It is at least as difficult to determine who benefits, and especially to what extent, from most other public services. Does everyone benefit equally from national defence or police protection? If some persons benefit more than others, how are the relative amounts to be measured? This is not to suggest that the benefits principle is inappropriate, but rather that its application is not as easy as some advocates would argue.

There are, however, cases in which the benefit principle has been applied using some rough approximations. For example, the gasoline tax was initially "earmarked", or reserved, for use in highway construction and maintenance, on the assumption that the amount of gasoline purchased would be in direct proportion to the benefits derived from highway use. But "earmarked" taxes have become less popular because the revenues from such taxes were sometimes insufficient to meet the demand for the services they were to provide, or alternatively, because governments wanted to use those revenues for other programs.

Ability to Pay   The principle of ability to pay, sometimes termed the principle of equal sacrifice, states that *individuals should be taxed according to their ability to pay*. The underlying reasoning is that individuals should make an equal sacrifice in paying taxes, in terms of the private goods and services they forgo in order to enjoy the public services. Since a tax of $100 represents a larger sacrifice for the poor than for the rich, the rich are expected to pay more in order to make a comparable sacrifice. What constitutes an equal sacrifice, however, is also an almost impossible question to answer. The debate on how the ability-to-pay principle should be applied has therefore produced a third equity principle, which is in fact a refinement of these two preceding principles.

Equal Treatment of Equals
The third equity principle states that *equals should be treated equally: persons with equal ability to pay, or enjoying equal benefits, should pay equal taxes*. Since this suggests looking at persons who, by some standard, are considered to be at the same level, this condition is termed *horizontal equity*. It follows from this principle that "unequals should be treated unequally", and that such a condition can be termed *vertical equity*. While it is difficult to be certain that apparent "equals" are indeed equal in every important respect, it is an even greater problem to determine how unequally the unequals should be taxed.

The application of the ability-to-pay principle, together with the conditions of vertical and horizontal equity, raises the same type of questions about what constitutes ability as were raised in determining who benefits and by how much. In this case, there are two basic questions: how should ability to pay be defined, and how much should be paid by persons at any specific level of ability?

Ability Measures   Several measures of ability to pay have been used or proposed. Annual incomes are an obvious indication of individuals' ability to pay, but difficulties arise in determining what constitutes income. In addition to employment earnings, incomes are received in the form of interest, rent, dividends, profits on unincorporated businesses, sale of assets, gifts, inheritances, as well as in the form of tangible goods and services. Some incomes are easier to identify than others and the recipients of these are less likely to be able to evade taxes. Partly in an attempt to get around the evasion and measurement problems, other measures of ability to pay have included real estate or property holdings, wealth or assets in other forms, and purchases of consumer goods, especially luxuries.

Progressive and Regressive Taxes   The second question is one of determining what represents an equitable sacrifice for each ability level: how much tax should be paid by each group? The tax burden, when compared with an individual's income, can be described as *regressive, proportional, or progressive*. At first glance, it might appear that a proportional tax, with everyone paying the *same percentage* of his or her income, would be most equitable. It is generally agreed, however, that the same percentage — and especially the same dollar amount — would represent a greater sacrifice for low-income groups. A tax of 10 per cent of an income of $5,000 would require a greater sacrifice, it is argued, than 10 per cent of a $50,000 income. Progressive taxes, with the higher-income persons paying a *higher percentage* of their income in taxes than the low-income persons, have therefore become more acceptable. The opposite case, a regressive tax, is one that claims a *lower percentage* from the higher-income persons. Note that the emphasis is on the *percentage* of income that is paid in taxes. High-income persons may pay a higher absolute amount in the case of a regressive tax, even though the percentage is lower than for low-income persons.

Other Taxation Principles

Neutrality Prior to the discussion of the equity principles, two other desirable features of a tax system were also mentioned. These were neutrality and efficiency. The *neutrality principle states that taxes should have a neutral effect on private decisions and on the operation of private markets*, unless a tax is explicitly intended to alter private sector activities in some way. A tax on pollution or on liquor is an example of a tax intended to be non-neutral in its effects. Alternatively, there are many taxes that are not primarily intended to alter private decisions but that do have that effect. It is unlikely that any tax is perfectly neutral. Rather, taxes must be compared on the basis of their relative neutrality—or the comparative strength of their effects on private decisions.

Efficiency *The principle of efficiency includes several features in the administration of a tax system.* This system should be viewed by the taxpayers as *reasonable and fair*, so that tax evasion does not become widespread. It should be *simple to administer* so that the costs of collecting the tax do not represent a high percentage of the tax revenue. It should be *enforceable*; when evasion of a tax is fairly common, it is no longer regarded as fair and tax revenues decline as a result. Finally, the tax should provide a *predictable* revenue for the government so that it is not necessary to change the tax rates or the tax base too frequently.

The above taxation principles do not, unfortunately, point to what can be regarded as the ideal tax. Instead, the existing tax system in Canada reflects a compromise; the continuing analysis and debate on the tax system represent attempts to discover what is, at any particular time, the most widely accepted compromise.

Taxation in Canada

Direct vs. Indirect Taxes

The British North America Act (now known as the Constitution Act, 1867) specifies the types of items that can be taxed by each level of government. Under this Act, the federal government has the right to collect revenues by "any mode or system of taxation", but the provincial governments are restricted to direct taxation within their own jurisdiction. Since municipalities are governed by provincial legislation, they are also confined to direct taxation.

Direct taxes are those levied on the persons intended to pay the tax: these include income taxes, estate taxes or succession duties, and real estate taxes. *Indirect taxes* are those levied on goods and services, and therefore indirectly on persons who are not identified until they purchase the commodities taxed; these include excise or sales taxes and tariff duties on imports. By explicit agreements with the federal government, however, provinces have been permitted to levy sales taxes.

Federal Taxes

Personal Income Tax   The federal government's major source of revenue is the tax on personal incomes. Table 14.1 shows that 45 per cent of federal tax revenue was raised by this means in 1988. This percentage has increased sharply in the postwar period and may continue to do so as personal incomes rise. This follows from the progressive rate structure for personal income taxes, shown in Table 14.2, whereby a higher percentage of one's income is paid in taxes with increasing income levels.

The personal income tax meets most of the criteria of a good tax: it is simple to collect, provides a predictable level of revenue, and is difficult to evade. Although it bears no direct relationship to benefits received, it is based on one of the best measures of ability to pay.

A major criticism of the personal income tax is that it is hard to determine how unequally the unequals should be treated. That is, how progressive should the progressive rate structure be? The rate levied on the highest bracket of a person's income, the *marginal tax rate*, is the one a person considers when deciding whether to take a higher-paying job, or to earn additional income through overtime work or "moonlighting". Because a high marginal rate, of say 50 per cent, may discourage a person from earning additional income, a highly progressive rate structure—where the marginal tax rates increase sharply—is said to restrain economic activity. How serious this effect actually is, however, is still strongly debated among economists. Nonetheless, the 1972 tax reform legislation removed the progressivity of the personal income tax structure at the higher income levels by setting 47 per cent as the marginal rate of federal tax on taxable income over $60,000. The 1981 budget reduced this still further by setting 34 per cent as the top marginal rate for the federal tax; and in 1987, the top rate was reduced to 29 per cent. (Provincial income tax rates then bring this marginal rate to between 44 and 48 per cent.)

Table 14.1

Tax Revenue Sources by Government Level, Canada, 1988

	Percentage of Total Tax Collected		
Tax Source	*Federal*	*Provincial/Municipal*	*Total*
Incomes			
Corporations	11	6	9
Individuals	45	31	39
Interest, dividends going abroad	1	—	1
Health and insurance levies	16	11	14
General and other sales	16	22	17
Gasoline, fuel oil sales	3	5	4
Customs and excise duties and excise taxes	8	3	6
Real and personal property	—	21	10
Other	2	—	2
Total tax revenue ($ billions)	104	91	196
Total revenue	108	124	334
Tax as % of Total	96	73	59

Source: Canadian Tax Foundation, *The National Finances.*

Table 14.2

Personal Income Taxes and Tax Rates, 1989,
for Taxpayer with Two Dependent Children under Age 16

Assessed Income[1]	*Marginal Tax Rate*[2] *%*	*Taxes Paid*	*After-Tax Income*
$ 20,000	26.2	737	19,263
25,000	26.2	2,125	22,875
30,000	26.2	4,057	25,943
50,000	40.0	13,079	36,921
100,000	44.7	35,202	64,798
200,000	44.7	79,427	120,573

[1] Deductions from assessed income include personal exemptions for a taxpayer (who supported 2 dependent children), unemployment insurance and Canada Pension Plan contributions.

[2] Federal tax rate plus (nominal) provincial tax at 50 per cent of federal tax.

Another important feature of the 1972 tax reform was the addition of capital gains to personal and corporate incomes for tax purposes. A capital gain (or loss) is the difference between the purchase and selling prices of assets such as real estate, common shares, and works of art. This capital gains tax was effectively removed for virtually all Canadians in the 1985 budget; a taxpayer was exempt from such tax for capital gains of up to $500,000 realized during his or her lifetime. But the 1987 reform proposals limited the capital gain exemption to $100,000 in most cases.

A reform introduced in 1973 provided for adjustment of tax deductions, exemptions, and "tax brackets"—the taxable income levels at which higher marginal rates were applicable—according to changes in the Consumer Price Index. Without such "tax indexing", especially in years of high inflation rates, taxpayers would be paying a higher percentage of their incomes in taxes, even though their increased incomes might represent no increase in their real standard of living. But with lower levels of inflation and increasing federal deficits, there was diminishing support for this measure. Adjustments are now restricted to 3 percentage points below the actual inflation rate.

Corporation Income Tax

The corporation income tax also provides a large part—about 11 per cent—of the federal government's tax revenues. This tax is levied on the net income of corporations, after eligible business expenses have been deducted from the firm's gross receipts.

The corporate income tax has been criticized because it is said to represent double taxation of income—the earnings of firms are taxed as corporate income and again as personal income in the form of taxes on shareholders' dividends. This problem is met in part by providing a tax credit for a part of the dividend income of individuals: that is, this amount can be deducted from the total tax that would otherwise be paid if dividends are included in income. Another criticism of the corporate income tax is that it is *shifted forward*, or passed on, to individuals through higher prices of goods and services.

Excise and Sales Taxes and Customs Duties

Excise taxes are taxes levied on specific goods, while sales taxes are levied on broad categories of goods. (Most services are not included.) The federal government, for many years, had levied a *general sales tax* at the manufacturer's or wholesaler's level, with the exception of some goods such as most foodstuffs, and equipment used in certain industries. There were proposals to replace the general sales tax with a *value-added tax* (or VAT), such as is used in the United Kingdom and several European countries, levied on the difference between the buying and selling prices of all goods and services at every stage of production or distribution, from supplies of raw materials to the final consumer. Small businesses objected to this tax because so much effort would be required in collecting and reporting the tax. The 1987 tax reform proposals presented three options for further examination: a national sales tax that would replace both the federal and provincial sales taxes; a federal goods and services tax; or a federal value-added tax.

In 1991, a goods and services tax (GST) was introduced (at a rate of 7 per cent of the retail price, although the initial plan was for a 9 per cent rate) and caused considerable adverse reaction, partly because taxpayers did not associate this new tax with the removal of the manufacturers' sales tax and the reduction in personal income tax rates.

There are also *special excise taxes* levied, in addition to the general sales tax, on items such as tobacco products, wines, cosmetics, and jewellery. Excise taxes are levied on what may be regarded as luxury items, or what one provincial treasurer called "avoidable tastes". Such taxes produce high levels of revenue relative to the price of the goods because the demand for these tends to be price-inelastic. That is, an increase in the price results in a less-than-proportionate decrease in the quantity of the goods purchased.

Taxes in the form of *tariffs* or *customs duties* are levied on many goods imported into Canada. Such taxes are intended both to produce revenues for the federal government and to protect domestic producers from the competition of lower foreign prices. To the extent that the tariff succeeds in reducing the purchase of imports, however, it reduces government revenues from such duties. Sales and excise taxes and customs duties account for about 27 per cent of federal tax revenues.

Provincial Taxes

Personal and Corporate Income Taxes

Each province levies a personal income tax, in addition to that levied by the federal government. In 1990 these were equal to 46 to 61 per cent of the basic federal tax. (The Quebec personal income tax is levied directly on taxable income reported to the province.) The federal government collects this tax for the provinces, with the exception of Quebec, and "abates" or refunds the appropriate amounts to the provinces. Similarly, the corporation income tax imposed by each province is collected and refunded by the federal government, with the exception of Ontario and Quebec, where the corporation tax is collected directly.

Sales and Excise Taxes

All provinces except Alberta and the Yukon and Northwest Territories impose a general sales tax, of from 5 to 12 per cent. Sales taxes are an increasingly important source of revenue for these provinces, both because total sales revenues are increasing and because sales tax rates have been increased as provinces require more tax revenues. Some of the provinces have designated the sales tax according to the purpose for which the revenue is raised, an example being the "social security tax"; nevertheless these are sales taxes since they are levied on the sale of goods and expressed as a percentage of the retail price.

Provinces also levy excise taxes on specific goods, often the same goods that bear a federal excise tax, such as tobacco products and alcoholic beverages. Other commodities such as gasoline or motor fuel are taxed by what is essentially a sales tax, but this tax was originally justified as a user charge on vehicles using the highways constructed by the provinces. Taxes are also levied on the transfer of land and securities as these are bought and sold.

Estate and Gift Taxes The federal estate and gift taxes were eliminated under the 1972 tax reform. In 1985, Quebec became the last province to eliminate estate and gift taxes.

Property Taxes Some provinces also levy a property or real estate tax, usually because a province has assumed responsibility for most or all of the costs of local services such as education, and thus uses the property tax that would have been levied by the municipalities to finance these costs.

Municipal Taxes

Property or Real Estate Taxes A property tax may be levied on *personal property* such as jewellery and antiques or on *real property* including land and buildings. Personal property taxes are now so rare that the terms "property tax", "real property tax", and "real estate tax" are used interchangeably. Almost all of the municipalities' tax revenues are raised through the real estate tax. Historically, this was considered to be related to benefits received when municipal expenditures were mainly for police and fire protection, roads, and garbage disposal. Reliance on this tax has been criticized recently, however, because property owners have borne the rapid increases in education costs without necessarily having a proportionate increase in the means to pay this tax.

Business Taxes Municipalities may also levy a business tax directly on the tenant or the operator of a business, based on the value of the property or the inventory or the annual rental value.

Other Revenue Sources

Each level of government has other sources of revenue in addition to the taxes outlined above. The federal government receives income from some of its crown corporations, and realizes interest on its loans, deposits, and special funds. Other non-tax revenue includes licences and fees charged on a variety of activities controlled by the federal government.

Provincial governments derive substantial revenue from motor vehicle registrations and operators' licences, profits on the sales of alcoholic beverages and other provincial enterprises, and several other fees and licences, as well as fines and penalties.

Municipal governments realize some additional revenue through charges for water service and by licence fees on the operation of businesses such as retail stores, barber shops, and taxis, and from traffic and parking fines.

Fiscal Federalism and Intergovernmental Transfers

In addition to tax revenues, provincial and municipal governments derive substantial revenue from grants made by the higher level of government. Such grants may be either *conditional*, paid for definite purposes and under specific conditions, or *unconditional*, leaving the recipient government free to spend the funds in any way.

Federal Grants

Unconditional Grants   Historical circumstances account for the unconditional grants paid by the federal government to the provinces. The British North America Act (Constitution Act) required the provinces to withdraw the sales and excise taxes that had provided such a large part of their revenues. In compensation, the federal government provided *statutory subsidies*, based on provincial populations, with additional allowances for costs of government administration, debt charges, and special grants. These amount to only $34 million.

The BNA Act permitted the provinces to levy personal and corporation income taxes, but when the federal government required a sharp increase in its revenues to finance expenditures for World War II, it entered into Wartime Tax Agreements with the provinces, whereby they withdrew from the income tax field. In return, the federal government made a cash grant to the provinces equal to the previous year's revenue from these taxes. The wartime agreements were replaced in 1947 with agreements that are renewed every five years, currently termed the Federal-Provincial Fiscal Arrangements and Federal Post-Secondary Education and Health Contributions Act.

Under this Act, the federal government makes three types of payments to the provinces: abatements, equalization grants, and stabilization grants. Throughout the postwar period, the federal government has gradually transferred or abated to the provinces a larger share of the revenue collected from personal and corporate income taxes. The payments made to the provinces are referred to as *tax abatements*.[2] Some provinces receive lower tax abatements per capita than other provinces because, for example, one percentage point of the federal personal income tax produces lower revenues per capita where the taxable income base is lower.

The federal government therefore makes an *equalization payment* to the lower-income provinces, so that an abatement of one percentage point in the personal or corporate income tax is of equal value per capita to each province. *Stabilization payments* are made when necessary, to maintain a province's tax revenue at not less than 100 per cent of the previous year's revenues, on the basis of the previous year's tax rates.

Conditional Grants   Conditional grants, or grants-in-aid, are made as the federal government's portion of cost-sharing programs. There are now fewer such programs, both because it was difficult for the federal government to control the expenditures under these agreements, and because some provinces chose to "opt-out" of the programs, receiving instead increased tax abatements. Recent examples of shared-cost programs were the Hospital Insurance Plan and Medicare (which are now combined under the Canada Health Act), as well as the Canada Assistance Plan. Under the latter plan, for example, the federal government paid 50 per cent of the provincial expenditures for a variety of welfare assistance programs. A special form of *adjustment payment* was also made to the provinces under an arrangement whereby the federal government paid 50 per cent of postsecondary education costs. If the tax abatements specified for this purpose were less than 50 per cent of the costs, an adjustment payment was made for the difference.

The federal grants for "established programs" were replaced in 1977 by revenue transfers equal to 9 percentage points of the federal personal income tax, in addition to income tax "points" granted by the federal government in 1967 to finance postsecondary education. These tax revenues are also subject to equalization payments. A further payment is calculated using the base year (1975-76) expenditure per capita for these programs, multiplied by a province's population.

---

[2] Formerly the abatements were calculated as a percentage of the federal tax. This system has been replaced by a downward adjustment of federal tax rates so that provinces can each determine the revenue to be raised directly by an increase in the provincial tax rate.

Federal Grants to Municipalities   Federal grants are also made to municipalities to compensate them for the federal properties (such as airports and post offices), which are exempt from real property taxes.

Provincial Grants

Provincial governments make both unconditional and conditional grants to municipalities; these account for about one-half of municipal governments' total revenues from taxes and other sources. Unconditional grants, including payments in lieu of property taxes on provincial government properties, are designed to reduce the municipal tax burden on residential and farm properties. About three-quarters of the conditional grants represent contributions to primary and secondary education; other shared-cost programs include roads and highways, unemployment assistance and winter works projects, police services, recreation, and housing.

Review of the Main Points

1. Total government expenditures in Canada increased in the postwar period from one-quarter to almost one-half of the Gross Domestic Product. These expenditures increased sharply due to inflation, population growth, wars, and increasing emphasis on public provision of education and health services.

2. Benefit-cost analysis is the principal technique in the Planning-Programming-Budgeting System (PPBS) that most governments have introduced for determining their expenditure programs; benefit-cost analysis consists of comparing all benefits with all costs of a project and selecting the projects with the highest net benefits.

3. The appropriate level of government to provide particular services depends on economies of scale and externalities associated with each program. The greater the economies of scale, and external benefits for other areas, the stronger is the case for passing responsibility to a higher level of government. However, lower levels of government may be better able to determine the local benefits of a program.

4. The three basic principles of taxation are: equity, neutrality, and efficiency. Three alternatives for judging tax equity are the benefits received, the ability to pay, and the equal treatment of equals. The first alternative states that taxes should be equal to the benefits received; however, some direct benefits—and most indirect benefits—are hard to measure, and such taxes usually are difficult to collect. Ability to pay is defined as requiring an equal sacrifice from all individuals, but this too is difficult to determine. Equal treatment of equals applies to each of the other two alternatives; the major difficulty is deciding how unequally the unequals should be treated.

5. A progressive tax is one that collects a higher percentage of income, the larger the income; a proportional tax collects the same percentage; and a regressive tax collects a lower percentage from larger incomes.

6. The neutrality principle states that taxes should have a neutral effect on private decisions and on the operation of private markets, unless a tax is explicitly intended to alter these. The efficiency principle requires that a tax be reasonable and fair, simple to administer, enforceable, and predictable as a source of revenue.

7. The federal government relies on personal and corporation income taxes, excise and sales taxes, and customs duties for its tax revenue; about three-quarters of federal revenue comes from income taxes and levies for health and insurance. Provincial governments raise one-half of their tax revenue through income taxes, about one-quarter through sales taxes, and the balance through taxes on gasoline and other sources. Municipal governments raise most of their tax revenues through real property taxes. Each level of government also has non-tax revenues from crown corporations and other public agencies, interest on financial assets, and various licences, fees, and fines.

8. Unconditional grants are made by the federal government to provincial governments, mainly as equalization payments to compensate lower-income provinces, which would otherwise have to impose higher taxes on their populations to provide public services comparable to those in higher-income provinces. Conditional grants represent the federal contributions to shared-cost programs, but many of these grants are being replaced in a shift from federal to provincial income tax revenues.

Key Concepts and Topics

public sector	proportional tax
transfer payments	progressive tax
government functions	direct taxes
benefit-cost analysis	indirect taxes
PPBS	marginal tax rate
principles of taxation	capital gain
equity	tax brackets
neutrality	excise tax
efficiency	tax credits
benefits-received principle	tax abatements
ability-to-pay principle	equalization payments
equal treatment of equals	
regressive tax	

Questions for Review and Discussion

1. Why has the total government share of GDP increased so much over the past decade? What should this percentage be? Why?

2. Should governments provide any services they do not now provide? Are there any services currently provided by governments that should be provided instead by the private sector? Specify and explain why in terms of the principles outlined in this chapter.

3. Do you favour the ability-to-pay or the benefits-received principle of taxation? Why? Which principle is the easier one to apply? Which of the taxes collected by any level of government do you favour and which do you oppose most strongly? Why?

4. Do you think a tax on gasoline is progressive, proportional, or regressive? Why?

5. To which government programs might benefit-cost analysis be applied most easily? For which programs would it be difficult to do benefit-cost analysis? What are the key characteristics that determine how easy or difficult it is to apply benefit-cost analysis to different programs?

6. An automobile mechanic was overheard saying, "The government should stay right out of the whole business of designing automobiles. People know best what they want." Do you agree? Explain.

Sources and Selected Readings

Auld, Douglas G., and F.C. Miller. *Principles of Public Finance: A Canadian Text*, 2nd ed. Toronto: Methuen, 1982.

Bird, Richard M., and Enid Slack. *Urban Public Finance in Canada*. Toronto: Butterworths, 1983.

Boadway, Robin W., and Harry M. Kitchen. *Canadian Tax Policy*. Toronto: Canadian Tax Foundation, 1981.

Breton, Albert. *The Economic Theory of Representative Government*. Chicago: Aldine, 1974.

Canada, Treasury Board. *Benefit-Cost Analysis Guide*. Ottawa: Supply and Services Canada, 1976.

Canadian Tax Foundation. *The National Finances*. Published annually by the Foundation.

_____. *Provincial and Municipal Finances*. Published biennially by the Foundation.

Economic Council of Canada. *Financing Confederation—Today and Tomorrow*. Ottawa: Supply and Services Canada, 1982.

Hartle, Douglas G. *A Theory of the Expenditure Budgetary Process*. Toronto: University of Toronto Press, 1976.

McCready, Douglas J. *The Canadian Public Sector*. Toronto: Butterworths, 1984.

Maslove, A.M., G.B. Doern, and M.J. Prince. *Public Budgeting in Canada.* Ottawa: Carleton University Press, 1988.

Mueller, Dennis. *Public Choice.* Cambridge: Cambridge University Press, 1979.

Perry, J. Harvey. *Taxation in Canada*, 4th ed. Toronto: Canadian Tax Foundation, 1984.

Strick, J.C. *Canadian Public Finance*, 3rd ed. Toronto: Holt, Rinehart and Winston, 1985.

PART THREE

Consumers
and Producers

15 Consumer Demand

Consumer demand was discussed earlier (Chapter 3) to show how prices are determined in individual markets. That analysis of supply and demand provided an explanation for the behaviour of prices, and the response to prices in terms of quantities demanded, but it did not offer an explanation of the overall economic behaviour of consumers. The law of demand, for example, states that consumers will buy more of a good when its price falls, but this provides no answers on how consumers will spend their incomes in making choices between the thousands of goods and services available.

Why does a consumer buy some goods and not others? Why does he or she buy a great deal of one product but only a little of another? If one's income increases by 10 per cent, will 10 per cent more be spent on each good previously purchased, or will some of the increase be allocated to new goods? How will one's collective purchases change if the prices of some goods rise while the rest remain constant? Answers to these questions require a *theory of consumer behaviour*. Such a theory, which might also be called "On getting more for one's money", assumes that the consumer's goal is to maximize the total satisfaction obtainable with his or her income, given a set of prices and preferences.

Marginal Utility and Consumer Decisions

Utility and Satisfaction

Toward the end of the last century, economists gave increasing attention to the satisfaction that consumers derived from their purchases. This satisfaction or usefulness was termed *utility*. The utility of a particular commodity would vary among consumers, depending on each consumer's set of preferences or tastes. Moreover, the utility derived from each particular unit of a commodity would depend on how much of that commodity an individual had previously consumed or used during a given time period.

Marginal Utility

At the same time, economists recognized that a consumer did not decide how to spend the whole of his or her income at any given moment. Rather, the consumer was constantly faced with specific decisions such as whether to buy another shirt or another roast of beef. These items were described as being at the *margin* of the consumption of such goods. Although "marginal" is the term usually used in economics for this concept, other terms such as "additional" or "incremental" also appear occasionally.

The concepts of utility and marginal units are combined in the term *marginal utility*, which is the additional satisfaction gained from an additional unit of the commodity. While granting that utility cannot be measured objectively, economists assume that individuals can and do make subjective comparisons of marginal utility, both between marginal units of various commodities and between various quantities of the same commodity.

Marginal utility can be illustrated by the example presented in Table 15.1 and Figure 15.1. Someone who has not had a milkshake for a long time probably derives a great deal of enjoyment or utility from a milkshake, especially on a hot day. In fact, he may decide to have a second. But the second milkshake probably is less satisfying than the first. A third milkshake may also be enjoyed, but with even less satisfaction than the second. And a fourth milkshake is only barely satisfying. Partway through the fifth milkshake he is beginning to feel sorry that he ordered it. Irrationally, he goes on to order a sixth and soon regrets it! In this case, the *total utility* or enjoyment of the milkshakes increased during the consumption of the first four, but the fifth shake contributed nothing and the sixth shake reduced his overall enjoyment. The *marginal utility*, however, declined for each additional milkshake following the first one; this decline continued until there was even some *disutility* associated with the last one.

Table 15.1

Individual's Utility Schedule for Milkshakes

Milkshakes per Day	Total Utility	Marginal Utility
0	0	
1	12	12
2	19	7
3	23	4
4	25	2
5	25	0
6	24	−1

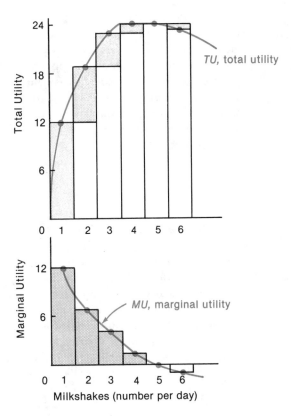

Figure 15.1 Diminishing Marginal Utility
Marginal utility is the change in total utility associated with each additional
unit consumed. The total utility curve, *TU*, shows the cumulative total utility
at each level of consumption. Shaded areas represent the additional
utility or satisfaction associated with each subsequent milkshake. Marginal
utilities plotted in the lower graph illustrate the law of diminishing
marginal utility: each additional unit provides less utility. When marginal
utility becomes negative, total utility begins to decline; this would be
evidence of an irrational decision.

Diminishing Marginal Utility

The declining satisfaction obtained from each additional unit of a commodity is described as *diminishing marginal utility*.

The declining satisfaction obtained from each additional unit of a
commodity was observed so widely that economists chose to regard it as
one of the basic premises of economics. More recently, economists have
questioned whether something that cannot be measured — utility —

should be the basis of an economic theory. Nevertheless, they are sat-·
isfied that consumers behave *as if* diminishing marginal utility is universally valid. As the marginal utility or satisfaction derived from each
additional unit diminishes, it is apparent that consumers will buy additional units only at a lower price. Diminishing marginal utility thus
provides a logical basis for the law of demand and the downward sloping demand curve: if consumers will buy *additional* units only at a
lower price, they will buy a larger total quantity only at a lower *average*
price per unit.

Rational Consumer Decisions

Diminishing marginal utility provides the key to an explanation for
consumers' purchases of particular combinations of commodities, given
their income levels. At the same time, this explanation provides an
approach for determining a consumer's optimal combination of purchases. The theory of consumer decision-making assumes that the consumers' objective is to derive the greatest possible utility or satisfaction
from their individual monetary incomes or, in other words, that consumers wish to maximize their total utility. This will lead to an equilibrium condition for consumers, just as an equilibrium condition has
been found previously for commodity markets and for national income.

Consumer Equilibrium   The combinations of a consumer's purchases are in equilibrium when a
consumer has obtained the maximum total utility with his or her given
income, with relative prices and preferences held constant.

This equilibrium condition for consumer decision-making becomes
more apparent if one focuses on a consumer's *marginal expenditure*,
rather than on her total expenditure. Although a consumer may agree
that her marginal dollar should be spent where it will realize the highest marginal utility, she may wonder what to do when a certain good
will afford more utility, but also costs more than another potential purchase. In this case *she must choose the good that yields the highest
marginal utility per dollar.* If a $50 sweater will give exactly twice as
much satisfaction as a $20 shirt, the shirt should be purchased since it
provides more utility per dollar than does the sweater.

This suggests how one could maximize utility in allocating one's
income:

The total income should be allocated among various commodities
until the marginal utility per dollar spent on one commodity is equal to
the marginal utility per dollar spent on each and every other commodity.

This condition can be expressed in general terms as follows:

$$\frac{MU_a}{P_a} = \frac{MU_b}{P_b} = \frac{MU_c}{P_c} = \ldots = \frac{MU_n}{P_n}$$

where MU_a is the marginal utility of good a, and P_a is the price of good a, and so on to the last or nth good.

Nonmonetary Decisions   The condition for optimal allocation of incomes has a wider application to the use of all resources. Most people who are concerned about making good use of their time follow this rule, perhaps without realizing how "economical" they are. In the time remaining before leaving for a trip, writing an examination, or moving to a new job, they will spend their time on those activities that are most important, or whose results will be most effective in achieving their objectives. Consider a student, for example, who wishes to obtain a high average mark on his examinations. He may be able to improve the mark in his best subject by five points if the entire remaining week is spent on that subject. But his average mark, or the total mark for all examinations, may be improved even more by allocating study time so that the anticipated improvement (or marginal gain) per hour of study is the same for each subject.

Changing Equilibrium Conditions

No one is likely to be able to estimate the marginal utility derived from each unit of a commodity so accurately that he or she can achieve precisely the optimum allocation of expenditures. Moreover, even if one could achieve the equilibrium condition, forces would be acting in such a way that a new combination of expenditures very likely would be indicated. Changes in tastes leading to changes in marginal utilities of different goods, changes in the relative prices of commodities, and the availability of new commodities would all require reallocations of expenditures. Commodities would therefore be purchased in different quantities until their marginal utilities are again proportional to their prices.

Consumer Surplus

An old proverb states that "He who knows the price of everything knows the value of nothing". Although this exaggerates the case, it nevertheless makes the basic point that troubled early economists: the value, or usefulness, of a commodity often seems to be quite different from the price of the item. Water is valued highly because it is so important to life, yet water is either free or available at a low price. Conversely, some luxury items such as diamonds and silks command high prices.

The concept of marginal utility provides some insight into this puzzle, namely, that the value of a good may seem unrelated to its price. Consider the case of someone who is very fond of corned-beef sandwiches. Figure 15.2 shows this person's demand curve for her particular gastronomical delight. At the prevailing price of corned-beef sandwiches, $2.50, she purchases four per week. The *economic* or *market value* of these four sandwiches is $10.00. But the demand curve indicates that she would have been willing to pay about $6.00 for the first sandwich, almost $5.00 for the second, about $3.50 for the third, as well as $2.50 for the fourth. The total value to the individual of the four sandwiches (about $17.00) is much greater than the market value calculated by multiplying the price by the number of sandwiches purchased ($10.00). This total value to the individual is a reflection of her total utility, although the actual total utility cannot be calculated in dollar terms. What is clear, however, is that the sandwich-lover would be willing to pay more in total for her four sandwiches than she has been required to pay. The differences between these two amounts (about $7.00 in this example) is termed the *consumer surplus*.

Suppliers would, of course, like to be able to collect this consumer surplus, as well as the total revenue they realize from their market sales. One technique for realizing at least a large part of this surplus is to sell goods by *auction*. At an antique auction, for example, there may be four Early Canadian crocks to be sold. Instead of offering the four crocks at one time, the auctioneer will usually sell them individually. The person who offers the highest price for the first one will get it. That buyer may also be willing to pay more than anyone else for the second. And for the third. If he buys the four crocks separately, he will have paid a higher total price than if he had bought the four at once.

He might, however, have been willing to pay still more for the crocks. He has only been required to offer a higher price than anyone else, and to that extent is paying only a fraction above the marginal utility of the next closest bidder.

Substitution and Income Effects

The law of demand expressed an almost universal observation that when the price of a commodity falls there is an increase in the quantity purchased. This occurs for two reasons. First, a lower price for butter, for example, has the effect of increasing the *relative* price of margarine.

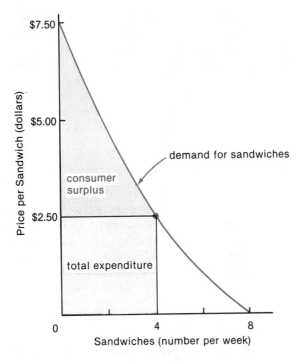

Figure 15.2 Consumer Surplus
The consumer's demand curve indicates that she would be willing to pay more than $2.50 for 1, 2, or 3 sandwiches, but since the market's equilibrium price is $2.50, she can buy each of her 4 sandwiches for that price. The difference between what she would be willing to pay in total for the 4 sandwiches if purchased separately, and what she does pay, is called consumer surplus.

To the extent that butter and margarine are substitutes, there will be more butter and less margarine consumed as a result of the *substitution effect*.

The substitution effect is the effect of a change in the relative prices of two goods, leading to a substitution of some of the good that has become relatively cheaper, for some of the good that has become relatively more expensive.

Substitution effects of changes in relative prices can be seen frequently in cases of close substitutes. For example, the conversion to natural gas for residential heating was due primarily to the abrupt change in the relative prices of natural gas and fuel oil when petroleum prices rose suddenly in the 1970s. Similarly, some wine consumers switched to Canadian wines when some provincial liquor commissions increased the price of foreign wines relative to domestic wines, in an effort to promote that domestic industry.

Second, a fall in the price for any commodity also has the effect of increasing a consumer's *real* income. That is, one can purchase a greater quantity at the lower price, just as if the price had been unchanged while one's income rose. This part of the change in the quantity demanded is termed the *income effect*.

The income effect is the effect of a price change on the total purchasing power of a given monetary income.

The increased real income due to a lower price for one commodity may also be used, of course, to purchase greater quantities of other goods whose prices are unchanged. If there were a drop in the price of automobile gasoline, for example, consumers would likely purchase more gasoline, but they would also be able to afford slightly greater quantities of some other commodities.

Consumer Expenditure Patterns

When aggregate expenditure was examined in Chapter 6, it was seen that the total expenditure for consumer goods and services tended to take a declining share of personal income as incomes rose. This was expressed as a declining marginal propensity to consume. But that referred only to aggregate consumption expenditure. Now it is time to consider the separate components of consumer expenditures to see how these change at increasing levels of consumers' incomes.

Engel's Law   Comparisons of consumer income and expenditures for food, housing, and clothing were examined by a nineteenth-century statistician, Ernst Engel. By using data for expenditures on broad categories of consumer goods at different income levels, Engel observed that the percentage of consumer incomes spent on food usually declined as incomes increased. This commonly observed relationship became known as *Engel's Law*.

Other related observations were that as consumers' incomes increased, the percentage spent on housing remained almost constant; the percentage spent on clothing remained the same or increased slightly; and the percentage spent on most other items increased. With minor exceptions, these relationships have been observed in different countries and over long periods of time.

Surveys of families and individuals provide information that can be used to plot similar curves for broad categories of consumer items.

Table 15.2 shows, for example, how consumer expenditures in Canada in 1986 varied by income level for food, shelter and household operation, transportation, clothing, and recreation. Consumption expenditure patterns for selected levels of income, as shown in Table 15.2, are generally in accord with Engel's Law. As income increases, there is a decline in the percentage spent for food (from 22 to 12 per cent) and shelter (from 29 to 13 per cent).

Note also that total expenditures for all consumption items, as a percentage of total income, decline as income rises. Savings and personal income taxes make up the difference. As real incomes rise over a period of time, and a larger percentage of families move into the higher income classes, the share of national income going to consumption expenditures tends to fall. From 1960 to 1990, for example, consumer expenditure as a percentage of GDP fell from 65 per cent to 58 per cent.

Table 15.2

Consumption Expenditure Patterns of Families and Unattached Individuals, by Income Quintiles, Canada, 1986

		Family Income Quintile Group				
	All Classes	*Lowest Quintile*	*Second Quintile*	*Third Quintile*	*Fourth Quintile*	*Highest Quintile*
			(percentage of total consumption expenditure)			
Food	19	24	20	19	19	17
Shelter	22	31	24	22	21	19
Household operation	5	6	6	5	5	6
Furniture, equipment	5	3	5	5	5	6
Clothing	8	6	7	8	8	11
Health, personal care	5	5	6	5	5	5
Tobacco, alcoholic beverages	4	5	5	5	4	5
Travel, transportation	18	11	17	18	19	20
Recreation	7	4	6	6	7	8
Reading, education	1	2	1	1	1	2
Miscellaneous	4	2	4	3	4	4
Total[1]	100	100	100	100	100	100
Consumption Expenditures as percentage of net income before taxes	74	93	84	77	73	66

Source: Statistics Canada, *Family Expenditure in Canada.*

[1] Components may not add to totals due to rounding.

Review of the Main Points

1. The theory of consumer behaviour attempts to explain why consumers allocate their expenditures as they do, and how consumers will change their purchases as relative prices change.

2. Utility is the satisfaction, enjoyment, or usefulness that individuals derive from a commodity. Marginal utility is the utility derived from the marginal or additional unit purchased. Total utility is the utility derived from the total quantity of the good consumed in a given period.

3. A basic premise in economics is that as more of a particular good is consumed, the marginal utility of each additional unit will diminish.

4. Consumers can maximize the total utility derived from a given level of income by arranging their purchases so that the marginal utility per dollar spent on one commodity is equal to the marginal utility per dollar spent on every other commodity. This is the equilibrium combination of purchases, given the consumer's tastes and the relative prices of consumer goods. The equilibrium combination will change whenever there is a change in tastes, relative prices, or an introduction of new commodities—unless the influences of these changes exactly offset each other.

5. Consumer surplus is the difference between the total revenue that suppliers receive for the total quantity exchanged in the market for a good, and what consumers would be willing to pay as an expression of the total utility they derive from the good.

6. The combined income and substitution effects of a change in the price of a commodity provide an explanation for the downward slope of a consumer's demand curve. That is, a price decrease results both in an increase in a consumer's real income and in a change in the relative price of two goods, leading to the substitution of some of the cheaper good for some of the more expensive good.

7. Data from surveys of family expenditures tend to confirm Engel's Law, that as income increases, a lower percentage is spent for food. It is also usually observed that a constant or declining percentage is spent for housing, and a slightly increasing percentage is spent for clothing.

Key Concepts and Topics

utility	price vs. value
marginal utility	consumer surplus
total utility	substitution effect
law of diminishing marginal utility	income effect
utility maximization rule	Engel's Law

Questions for Review and Discussion

1. "Consumer sovereignty is a fiction. Producers develop new products and then use advertising to persuade consumers that they should buy these products." Do you agree? Why?

2. Why does the optimum allocation of a consumer's income require the same ratio of marginal utility to price for all commodities purchased? What basic objective is assumed in stating this rule?

3. Since diminishing marginal utility seems to be encountered by all consumers, a government program that taxes the rich and gives the proceeds to the poor can be rationalized by this fact alone. Do you agree? Why?

4. Name three or four commodities for which you enjoy a substantial consumer surplus. Explain carefully why consumer surplus exists.

5. Suppose someone who has an average income says, "I really do need a new suit but I can't afford it". How would you explain this statement in terms of the theory of consumer behaviour?

6. "If a consumer's income elasticity of demand for some goods is greater than unity, there must be some goods for which the income elasticity is less than unity." Explain why you do or do not agree.

7. Assume that your tastes and relative prices remain unchanged but that you suddenly become five times better off financially than you are now. What would you expect to buy more of, less of, and in the same amount? What would you conclude about the income-elasticities of the commodities in each of these three categories? Is there any commodity for which the income-elasticity is zero?

Sources and Selected Readings

Baumol, Wm. J. *Economic Theory and Operations Analysis*, 4th ed. Englewood Cliffs, N.J.: Prentice-Hall, 1977.

Duesenberry, J. S. *Income, Saving and the Theory of Consumer Behavior*. Cambridge: Harvard University Press, 1949.

Ferber, Robert. "Consumer Economics: A Survey". *Journal of Economic Literature* (December 1973).

Green, H.A.J. *Consumer Theory*, 2nd ed. Harmondsworth, Middlesex: Penguin, 1976.

Mansfield, Edwin. *Microeconomics: Theory and Applications*, 6th ed. New York: Norton, 1988.

Scitovsky, Tibor. *The Joyless Economy*. New York: Oxford University Press, 1976.

Stonier, Alfred W., and Douglas C. Hague. *A Textbook of Economic Theory*, 5th ed. London: Longmans, Green, 1980.

Watson, Donald S. *Price Theory and Its Uses*, 5th ed. Boston: Houghton Mifflin, 1981.

Appendix: Indifference Analysis of Consumer Decisions

The consumer's equilibrium condition, that the ratio of marginal utility to price be equal for all commodities, is useful for a general or qualitative explanation of consumer behaviour, but it does not provide an operational method for quantitative analysis of consumer behaviour. Economists have therefore modified this approach so that it is not necessary to measure utility directly. The more modern method for examining consumer behaviour is *indifference curve analysis.*[1]

Indifference Schedule

Even though someone cannot say by how much more or less she would enjoy a slice of pizza compared with a piece of barbecued chicken, she should be able to say how much pizza would give her approximately the same satisfaction as one piece of chicken. If the answer is three slices, then she is said to be *indifferent* between having one piece of chicken and three slices of pizza. Furthermore, she will be indifferent between various combinations of pizza and chicken. By listing these combinations in an *indifference schedule* and then plotting this schedule on a graph, one can obtain the individual's indifference curve for these two goods. This is the initial step in obtaining an objective picture of the consumer's tastes or preferences.

Table 15.3 presents one person's indifference schedule for combinations of pizza and barbecued chicken. The information provided indicates that she is equally satisfied with, or is indifferent between, four different combinations of pizza and barbecued chicken. Any one of these combinations might be consumed each week: 25 slices of pizza and 5 pieces of chicken provide the same satisfaction or utility as 10 slices of

Table 15.3

Combinations Yielding Equal Total Satisfaction

Combination	Pizza (pieces per week)	Chicken (pieces per week)
A	25	5
B	20	6.5
C	15	10
D	10	15

[1] A still more recent approach examines the consumer's "revealed preference". This is presented in more advanced textbooks included in the Sources and Selected Readings of this chapter.

pizza and 15 pieces of chicken. Different persons could have quite different combinations of pizza and chicken, depending on their relative tastes for these two foods.

Indifference Curve

The four combinations shown in Table 15.3 are plotted as points A to D in Figure 15.3. A smooth curve is drawn through these points to show the other combinations that would be equally acceptable. This becomes indifference curve, I_1. Note that the individual is indifferent between each *combination* of goods; it is *not* a matter of being indifferent, for example at point A, between 25 pizza slices and 5 pieces of chicken.

The process can be repeated to develop other indifference curves for the same individual and the same goods. By beginning with a less desirable combination of, say, 15 pieces of pizza and 5 of chicken (point E), and obtaining other equally satisfactory combinations, a lower indifference curve, I_0, is obtained. Alternatively, asking for other combinations that would yield the same satisfaction as 15 pieces each of pizza and chicken (point F) provides the higher indifference curve, I_2. That is, the combination represented by F—and all other equally satisfactory

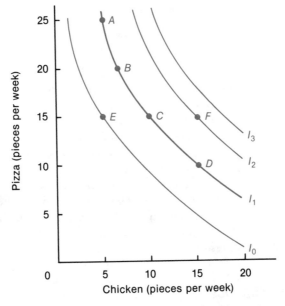

Figure 15.3 An Individual's Map of Indifference Curves
Each indifference curve represents a specific level of satisfaction that can be derived by consuming various combinations of pizza and chicken. Examples of equally satisfying combinations are shown as points A, B, C, and D, on indifference curve I_1. Total satisfaction increases as one shifts to combinations represented by points on higher indifference curves, such as F on I_2, which are farther from the origin.

combinations—would yield a higher level of satisfaction or utility (I_2) than the combinations represented by I_1.

Each indifference curve presents a distinct level of utility or satisfaction provided by various combinations of the two goods.

Indifference Map

Since there can be many different levels of utility or satisfaction derived by consuming various amounts of one good while the quantity of the second is unchanged, there can similarly be many indifference curves relating to these two goods. For example, points E and F in Figure 15.3 were derived by holding the quantity of pizza constant at 15 pieces and varying the quantity of chicken combined with the pizza, to yield lower and higher levels of satisfaction than are represented by combination C.

Then alternative combinations are determined that yield the same satisfaction provided by combination E, and similarly for combination F, to derive the two additional indifference curves I_0 and I_2. One can imagine the other indifference curves that would result as the quantity of chicken combined with the fixed quantity of pizza varied from 1 to 20 pieces, and the alternative, equal-satisfaction combinations were determined. The end result would be a whole *family of indifference curves* or an *indifference map*.

The indifference map presents a complete picture of an individual's preference for various combinations of two goods.

It is also a map of the total utility she enjoys with different combinations of the goods. The indifference curve I represents a higher level of total utility than does I_1, although one cannot measure the difference between these two utility levels.

Indifference curves can never intersect. If I_2 intersected I_1 at B, this would imply that the consumer was indifferent between combinations B and F. But since she is also indifferent between B and C, this would also imply that she was indifferent between C and F. Such a result would be foolish, because combination F provides her with more chicken than does combination C, while the quantity of pizza remains the same. Since she cannot be indifferent between F and C, curves I_1 and I_2 cannot intersect.

Marginal Rate of Substitution

Note that the indifference curves in Figure 15.3 have a particular shape: they bow inward, or are *convex to the origin*. This reflects the fact that as one moves downward along the indifference curve, or as more chicken is combined with less pizza, more chicken is required to compensate for the loss of each additional unit of pizza if total utility is to remain unchanged. Figure 15.4 shows that as one moves from *A* to *B* on indifference curve I_1, $1\frac{1}{2}$ pieces of chicken can be substituted for 5 of pizza. But in moving from *C* to *D*, 5 pieces of chicken must be substituted for 5 of pizza. As the individual consumes more chicken, each additional piece of chicken provides less satisfaction, and thus more must be added to compensate for the reduction in pizza.

Diminishing Marginal Rate of Substitution

The diminishing marginal utility discussed earlier reappears in indifference curve analysis as the *diminishing marginal rate of substitution*.

The marginal rate of substitution is the quantity of one good that an individual will give up in exchange for one unit of another good, without changing the total satisfaction obtained from the two or more goods consumed.

In Figure 15.4 the marginal rate of substitution between points *A* and *B* is 5 pieces of pizza for $1\frac{1}{2}$ of chicken, or $3\frac{1}{3}$ to 1. But when more chicken and less pizza is included in the combination, the marginal rate of substitution is 1 to 1, that is, 1 piece of chicken for 1 of pizza.

The assumption of diminishing marginal rate of substitution therefore means simply that as more of a good is consumed, the marginal rate at which it can be substituted for another good will diminish.

Consumer Decisions with Given Incomes

Budget Line

If a consumer is indifferent among a large number of alternative combinations of pizza and chicken, how does she decide which specific combination of purchases to make? The answer lies in relating her income and the relative prices of these goods to her indifference map.

To present a simple example, suppose that a consumer allocates $60 each week for lunches or snacks; that these consist of only pizza or chicken; that pizza is $1.20 per slice while chicken is $2.00 per piece. This information provides a *budget line* or *consumption-possibilities curve*. If she spends all of the $60 on chicken, she can buy 30 pieces; alternatively, the $60 would buy 50 slices of pizza. These alternatives are illustrated in Figure 15.5. The budget line, *PC*, shows the various combinations of pizza and chicken that can be purchased with $60—from 50 pizza slices and no chicken, to 30 chicken pieces and no pizza.

The budget line is a straight line because *the slope of the line is the ratio of the prices of the two goods*. Since the prices do not change with different quantities purchased by any one person, the ratio of prices, or slope of the line, is constant for all combinations of the two goods.

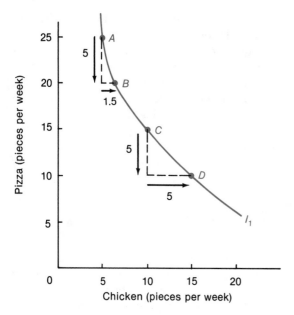

Figure 15.4 Diminishing Rate of Substitution
A movement downward along indifference curve I_1 implies that equal satisfaction combinations include more chicken and less pizza. More chicken must be added in moving from C to D, than in moving from A to B, to compensate for the loss of a given quantity (5 pieces) of pizza, because each additional piece of chicken provides less satisfaction. That is, as more of a good is consumed, the marginal rate at which it can be substituted for one unit of another good will diminish.

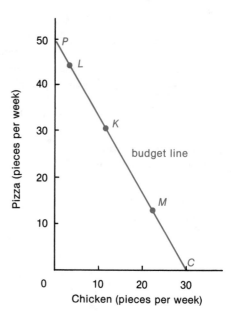

Figure 15.5 Consumer's Budget Line
The budget line PC shows the various combinations of pizza and chicken that can be purchased with a given money income per week ($60) and at given prices ($1.20 per slice of pizza and $2.00 per piece of chicken). L, K, and M represent only three of the numerous possible combinations. Higher incomes would shift the budget line outward since more of each good could be purchased, provided prices remained constant.

Consumer Equilibrium By plotting the budget line on the indifference map, it is possible to determine the combination of pizza and chicken that will yield the highest total utility, given the level of income and prices of each good. This combination can be described in terms of Figure 15.6 as point K: 30 pieces of pizza and 12 pieces of chicken. Since the budget line is just touching the indifference curve I_2, or is tangent to I_2, this is the highest level of utility that can be obtained with an expenditure of $60. Other combinations, such as those represented by L and M, would just exhaust the $60 budget, and the consumer is indifferent between them, but

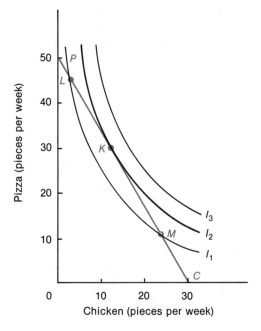

Figure 15.6 Consumer Equilibrium
The consumer will reach her maximum satisfaction level, given her budget
line *PC*, by consuming combination *K*: 30 pieces of pizza and 12 pieces of
chicken. Although her income would also buy combinations *L* and *M*, these
are on a lower indifference curve, I_1, and thus provide less satisfaction. The
greatest satisfaction she can afford is represented by the highest
indifference curve she can reach; this occurs at *K*, where *PC* is tangent to I_2.
Unless the consumer's tastes or income change, or there is a change in prices
of these goods, the consumer will continue to purchase combination *K*.

these would provide a lower level of satisfaction because they are on a
lower indifference curve. Point *K* thus becomes the consumer's equilibrium position, given the information assumed at the beginning of this
example. The combined purchase of 30 pieces of pizza and 12 pieces of
chicken per week is the most rational expenditure she can make.

The consumer's equilibrium condition is defined as the purchase of
two goods such that their marginal rate of substitution is equal to the
ratio of their prices.

This condition is derived from the fact that at the point where the
budget line is tangent to the indifference curve, the *slopes of the two
lines are equal*. Since the slope of the budget line is the ratio of prices
and the slope of the indifference curve is the marginal rate of substitution or the substitution ratio of the two goods, these two ratios must be
equal at point *K*, the consumer's equilibrium position.

Notice the similarity of this equilibrium condition with the rule for consumer expenditures under marginal utility analysis. This latter rule required expenditures on two goods such that

$$\frac{MU_1}{P_1} = \frac{MU_2}{P_2} \text{ or } \frac{MU_1}{MU_2} = \frac{P_1}{P_2}$$

That is, the ratio of marginal utility is equal to the ratio of prices for two goods. In indifference curve analysis, the rule is

$$\frac{P_1}{P_2} = MRS_{(2 \text{ for } 1)}$$

where MRS is the marginal rate of substitution between good 1 and good 2. Thus, MU_1/MU_2 has been replaced by $MRS_{(2 \text{ for } 1)}$. This provides an objective measure of utility, but in terms of quantities of goods that substitute for one another. To obtain such a measure, it is necessary only that a consumer be able to say which combinations of goods provide equal satisfaction, and not how much more satisfaction she derives from one good than from another.

Consumer's Demand Curve

Indifference curve analysis makes it possible to derive the consumer's demand curve from her indifference map. For each of the two goods involved, the quantity that would be demanded at each price can be found by varying the price of the good and determining the quantity of that good that would be included in the various equilibrium combinations of purchases. This is illustrated in Figure 15.7. When the price of chicken is $2.00, the consumer will buy 12 pieces. If the price drops to $1.50, with the price of pizza unchanged, the budget line becomes PC_2, since an expenditure of $60 would buy 40 pieces of chicken. The new equilibrium is on a higher indifference curve, at point N, and 24 pieces of chicken would be purchased. Similarly, if the price of chicken increases to $3.00, the budget line shifts to PC_3, the new equilibrium point is R and only 6 pieces of chicken are purchased.

The combinations of chicken prices and quantities demanded are plotted on the lower diagram of Figure 15.7. These provide three points on the consumer's demand curve for chicken. By assuming alternative prices for chicken, other equilibrium points could be found and plotted. These points could then be joined to derive the complete demand curve, given a specific level of the consumer's income, constant prices of other products, and no changes in the consumer's tastes.

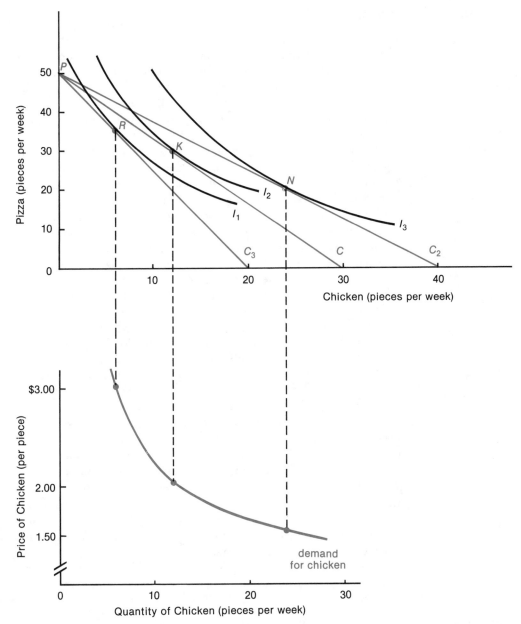

Figure 15.7   Deriving the Demand Curve
A decrease in the price of chicken enables the consumer to buy more
chicken with a given income: the budget line shifts to PC_2, and the highest-
satisfaction combination is N. Similarly, an increase in the price of chicken
shifts the budget line to PC_3 and combination R is purchased. The quantity
of chicken that would be purchased at each of the prices represented by
the three budget lines is shown by combinations R, K, and N.

Income and Substitution Effects

Diminishing marginal utility provided one explanation for the downward slope of the consumer's demand curve. This explanation was not entirely satisfactory, however, because marginal utility could not be measured, and one needed to rely on intuitive or subjective judgments about the validity of this explanation. Indifference curve analysis affords a more precise and objective explanation in terms of the *income effect* and the *substitution effect*.

The income and substitution effects can be explained by reference to Figure 15.8. A fall in the price of chicken shifts the budget line from PC_1 to PC_2. In moving to the new equilibrium combination, the consumption of pizza decreases and the consumption of chicken increases. The income effect is measured by drawing another line, P_3C_3, parallel to the original budget line and tangent to the same indifference curve reached by the new budget line, PC_2. Budget line P_3C_3 shows the extent to which the consumer is better off, or enjoys a higher level of real income, as a result of the decreased price of chicken. That is, the consumer can buy more pizza, as well as more chicken, when the price of chicken falls. This analysis shows that the income effect of the price change has increased consumption of chicken from 12 to 18 pieces.

The substitution effect has increased consumption further still, from 18 to 30 pieces. The income effect is measured by moving from one indifference curve to the other; the substitution effect is measured by moving along the new indifference curve. It is these two effects taken together that explain the downward slope of the consumer's demand curve: as the price of a good falls she buys more, both because the relatively lower price leads her to substitute this good for other goods and because the lower price makes it possible for her to buy more goods including the good in question, with her given monetary income. [2]

Indifference curves are used in the previous section to analyze a consumer's response to price changes, but indifference curve analysis can also be used to determine how consumers will respond to income changes. In Figure 15.8, for example, the budget line P_3C_3 shows the real income effect of a price change. However, P_3C_3 also shows how consumption would change if prices remained constant and the consumer's income increased. The income increase is shown by a shift of the budget line from PC_1 to P_3C_3. Similarly, if several budget lines, representing

---

[2] Interested students should refer to more advanced economic texts for a fuller discussion of these effects. Note especially that the substitution effect is always positive (an increase in price reduces the quantity, since indifference curves have a negative slope) but the income effect may be negative. When the negative income effect exceeds a positive substitution effect the overall price effect is negative, representing an exception to the law of demand.

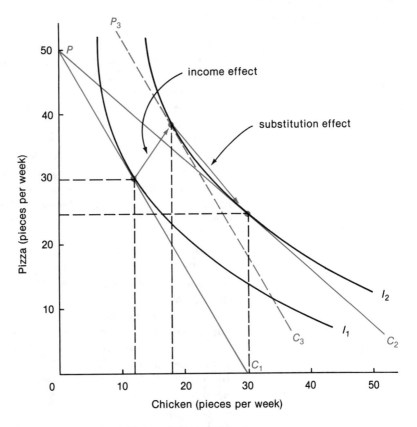

Figure 15.8 A Price Change Has Two Effects
When the price of chicken falls, the budget line shifts from PC_1 to PC_2.
Chicken consumption increases from 12 pieces to 30 pieces. Part of the
increase is an income effect: since a price decrease enables one to
purchase more real goods with a given money income, there is an increase
in real income. This is represented by a parallel shift of PC_1 to P_3C_3, and an
increase in chicken consumption to 18 pieces. The further increase in
chicken consumption from 18 to 30 pieces is a substitution effect: the
decreased chicken price relative to the pizza price leads one to substitute
chicken for pizza.

different income levels, were drawn parallel to P_3C_3, a line connecting
the points of tangency of the budget lines and the various indifference
curves would show the quantities of chicken and of pizza that would be
consumed at various income levels.

From this information one could plot a curve, termed an *income-
consumption curve*, which shows the quantity of each good that will be
purchased at various levels of income.

Review of the Main Points

1. Indifference schedules are lists of combinations of goods such that each combination provides the same satisfaction to the consumer. Indifference schedules can be plotted on a graph as indifference curves. An individual's indifference map is a set of indifference curves, with each curve representing a specific level of satisfaction or utility. Since each indifference curve represents a different level of utility, indifference curves cannot intersect.

2. The shape of indifference curves — downward sloping and convex to the origin — is due to the diminishing marginal rate of substitution. That is, as the quantity consumed increases, more of a good must be substituted for a given reduction in the consumption of another good.

3. A budget line shows the combination of two goods that can be purchased, given their prices, with a given total expenditure. The slope of this line is the ratio of the prices of the two goods. Since the ratio is constant for all combinations of the two goods, the budget line is a straight line.

4. The consumer equilibrium condition, or the condition for maximizing total utility with a given income, is reached by purchasing the combination of goods represented by the point of tangency of the budget line and an indifference curve. The slopes of these two curves are equal at the tangency point, indicating that the ratio of prices is equal to the marginal rate of substitution of the two goods, or that $P_1/P_2 = MRS_{(2 \text{ for } 1)}$.

5. As the price of a good changes relative to the price of another good, the position of the budget line changes and thus the equilibrium combination of goods also changes. By plotting the quantities of a good that will be purchased as its price changes, the consumer's demand curve can be derived from an indifference map.

6. An income-consumption curve, showing the quantities of a good that will be purchased at different income levels, can be derived by shifting the budget line outward across a consumer's set of indifference curves.

Key Concepts and Topics

indifference schedule	diminishing marginal rate
indifference curve	of substitution
indifference map	budget line
marginal rate of substitution	consumer equilibrium

Questions for Review and Discussion

1. Draw the indifference curves for the commodities in the following cases and explain your answer:

   (a) two commodities—skis and ski bindings—purchased separately; and

   (b) white eggs and brown eggs.

2. Explain in non-mathematical terms how the diminishing marginal rate of substitution is logically related to diminishing marginal utility.

16 Production Costs

In the introduction to the market system in Chapter 3, a supply curve was simply assumed. The quantity supplied varied directly with the market price, while the entire supply curve depended on prices of inputs and the technology used. This chapter now examines more precisely how production costs vary under different conditions, how these costs determine individual producers' supply decisions, and thus how market supply is determined. It will also provide the underlying rationale for the upward-sloping supply curve that was assumed earlier.

What Are Costs?

Opportunity Cost

The basic cost concept, *opportunity cost*, has previously been defined as the satisfaction or output forgone by choosing one alternative instead of the next best alternative. The opportunity cost of a productive factor is the output forgone by using that factor for the given purpose rather than in its best alternative use. The cost of labour hired by a firm, for example, will be the wage the firm must pay to attract that labour away from its best alternative employment. In the same way, all of a firm's costs for other productive resources can be viewed as opportunity costs.

Explicit and Implicit Costs
A firm's costs are both *explicit* and *implicit*. Explicit costs are a firm's direct expenditures for labour services, materials, electricity, transportation, rental of space, and so on. Implicit costs are related to the use of productive factors owned by the firm. Most firms recognize, for example, that if part of the plant stands idle, a cost is involved even if the firm makes no mortgage payments or maintenance expenditures for the idle space. This is the opportunity cost, represented by what could be earned through the productive use of the space. Since implicit costs can only be estimated or imputed, they are also referred to as imputed costs.

Using the opportunity cost concept to estimate implicit costs often leads to the erroneous impression that only implicit costs are opportunity costs. However, *all costs are opportunity costs*. The firm could use the productive resources purchased with direct expenditures, as well as the factors it owns, to produce other commodities.

Normal Profits Are Costs One of the opportunity costs of producing a particular commodity is the profit forgone by not producing some other commodity.

Implicit costs therefore include a normal profit. This is the minimum profit required to retain the firm in the production of the specified commodity and is determined by the profit that could be earned in the next most profitable industry.

Any profit made in excess of the normal profit is termed an *economic profit* or *pure profit* because it exceeds the profit that would just keep the firm in that industry. (Normal profits are also termed zero profits because they include no pure profit; conversely, pure profits are also termed excess, supernormal, or extranormal profits because they are in excess of normal profits.)

Although a businessperson may be inclined to calculate a firm's profit by subtracting explicit costs from total revenues, pure profit is calculated in economics by subtracting both explicit and implicit costs, including normal profits, from the total receipts.

Short Run and Long Run Production costs are also classified according to the period within which the firm can vary the quantity of specific factors. Some factors such as casual labour can be changed on a daily basis. Other factors such as skilled labour and some materials may be varied according to a contractual period of perhaps three months to two years, while changes in machinery or plant size may require an even longer time.

The *short run* is the period within which it is possible to change the quantity produced by altering the quantity of *some* factors, such as labour and raw materials, but within which it is not possible to alter the quantities of all factors.

During the short run, for example, the firm may employ more labour to utilize idle machinery or to work an additional shift.

The *long run* is the period long enough to enable a firm to change the quantity produced by changing the quantity of *all* resources used to produce the good, including any changes in the type of resources used.

Variable and Fixed Factors Factors that can be used in varying quantity during the short run are *variable factors*; those that can be changed only in the long run are *fixed factors*.

The short run and long run do not refer to specific time periods of weeks or months; they can be defined only by reference to the production of particular commodities and prevailing practices concerning, for example, contractual employment of managerial personnel and the length of collective agreements with labour unions. Thus the short and long runs are more appropriately viewed as *planning periods* than as calendar time periods.

Short-Run Production and Costs

Production costs per unit of output usually vary with the length of the planning period, because different combinations of productive resources can be used in the different planning periods. The resources required and the cost per unit produced in the short run can be examined using a simple *production function*. This shows how a firm's total output changes as additional units of a factor are added to the firm's existing productive factors. Such a function is illustrated by the *production schedule*, shown in Table 16.1, and plotted as a *total product curve* in Figure 16.1. (Throughout this discussion of production costs, it is assumed that the firm produces only one product. The case of multiproduct firms is examined in more advanced textbooks.)

Suppose that a firm is producing a standard ceramic coffee mug for sale in craft and gift shops. Assume for the sake of simplicity that the only productive resources required are physical capital in the form of potter's wheels, and skilled labour, or potters. (The raw material, clay,

Table 16.1

Production Schedules for a Pottery Firm

Variable Factor[1] (units of labour) Q_L	Total Product (per day) TP	Average Product (per day) AP	Marginal Product (per day) MP
0	0	0	
			20
1	20	20	
			56
2	76	38	
			107
3	183	61	
			121
4	304	76	
			106
5	410	82	
			76
6	486	81	
			32
7	518	74	
			2
8	520	65	
			−7
9	513	57	

[1] Fixed factor consists of five potter's wheels.

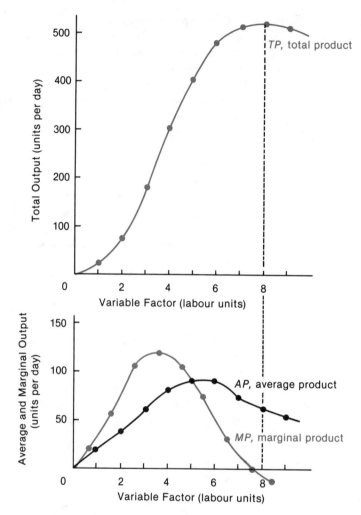

Figure 16.1   The Law of Diminishing Returns
When the quantity of one productive factor is fixed, the addition of
increasing quantities of a variable factor eventually leads to a decline in the
total product. In this example, adding a ninth unit of labour to the pottery
firm's five wheels results in lower total product. The shape of the total
product curve, *TP*, is determined by the marginal product, *MP*, associated
with each additional unit of labour. When *MP* becomes negative, *TP* begins
to decline. Average product, *AP*, is the total product divided by the quantity
of labour. Marginal product is equal to average product where average
product is at a maximum.

is assumed to be a free good in a huge mound outside the pottery shop.)
Assume also that the firm has five potter's wheels—the fixed factor—
and is determining how its output would vary with different amounts of
labour—the variable factor.

The quantity produced by the combined factors of production is described in terms of the total, average, and marginal product. How the quantity of output varies with changes in the quantity of labour is shown as production schedules in Table 16.1. *Total product, TP,* is the total quantity produced per time period (one day) by the total productive factors of the firm. *Average product, AP,* is the quantity produced per unit of a variable productive factor, or by each unit of labour service in this particular example. *Marginal product, MP,* is the change in the total product associated with each additional or marginal unit of a productive factor, in this case with an additional unit of labour. Thus:

$$AP = \frac{TP}{Q_L} \text{ and } MP = \frac{\Delta TP}{\Delta Q_L}$$

where Q_L is the quantity of labour used per period of time.

The production schedules of Table 16.1 are plotted as curves in Figure 16.1. The shape of the marginal product curve determines the shape of the total and average product curves. The marginal product reaches a maximum with the addition of the fourth labour unit. The total product increases at a slower rate from this point until the total product is at a maximum, and then declines due to the negative marginal product of additional labour. The average product reaches a maximum where the average and marginal products are equal. This occurs because when the marginal exceeds the average, the average increases, and vice versa. To see why this is so, consider an arithmetic example: if the *average* value of the first three units is 7, and the fourth or *marginal* unit has a value of 3, the average of the four units declines to 6.

Law of Diminishing Returns

Average output may differ with any given change in the quantity of a productive factor for a variety of reasons. Generally, this is due to the fixed relationship between labour and machinery, and the possibility for division of labour. For example, the machinery/labour relationship in the pottery firm is that one person operates one wheel. If fewer than five persons are employed, at least one wheel is idle. If more than five persons are employed, the additional workers can add to total output only by performing other specialized tasks such as preparing and rough-shaping the clay, fitting handles to the mugs, glazing, packing, and handling orders. But the number of persons required for these additional tasks is also related to the fixed capital, the total number of potter's wheels. When all wheels are in use, the data provided in Table 16.1 indicate that the ninth person cannot be fully occupied and distracts the other workers; as a consequence, the firm's total output is reduced.

The marginal product is not necessarily the actual quantity produced by a particular additional person, but reflects the effect of adding one worker to the total productive process—the effect usually being to make further specialization of labour possible.

The effect of combining increasing amounts of the variable factor with a given fixed factor is so consistent that it can be described as an economic law:

The law of diminishing returns states that the economies realized by division of labour eventually diminish as increasing quantities of a variable factor (labour) are added to a fixed quantity of another factor. The continued addition of the variable factor eventually leads to a decrease in the total product.

Because the proportions of the two factors vary as more of one is added, the law is also termed the *law of variable proportions*.

Total, Average, and Marginal Costs

The production costs of the firm can be determined from its production schedule and the prices it pays for productive resources. In this simple example, it is assumed that the firm's purchases of productive resources (potter's wheels and labour) are too small to influence their prices, so that the price per unit of any factor of production is constant, regardless of the amount the firm buys.

Fixed and Variable Costs   The total cost of producing any given quantity of output can be broken down into the costs associated with fixed factors—fixed costs—and the costs associated with variable factors—the variable costs.

Fixed costs are those costs that do not vary with changes in quantity of output.

Fixed costs are also termed *overhead costs*; they must be incurred even if the firm produces no output. They would include payments for insurance, licences, property taxes, interest on loans and bonds, and imputed costs of plant and equipment. In the pottery firm example, the estimated or imputed cost of the potter's wheels is treated as a fixed cost.

Variable costs are costs that vary directly (but not necessarily in proportion) with changes in the quantity of output.

Variable costs usually include items such as wages, materials, fuel, and transportation. The variable costs of the pottery firm are its wage payments. The fixed, variable, and total costs are shown in Table 16.2, and are plotted as curves in Figure 16.2. The total fixed cost is set at $50, the imputed cost of the five wheels, for all levels of output.

Table 16.2
Production Costs for a Pottery Firm

| Variable Factor (units of labour) Q_L | Total Product (mugs per day) TP | Total Cost | | | Average Cost | | | Marginal Cost[1] (per unit) MC |
		Fixed TFC	Variable TVC	Total TC	Fixed AFC	Variable AVC	Total ATC	
1	20	$50	$100	$150	$2.50	$5.00	$7.50	$ 1.79
2	76	50	200	250	.66	2.64	3.30	.94
3	183	50	300	350	.27	1.64	1.91	.83
4	304	50	400	450	.16	1.32	1.48	.94
5	410	50	500	550	.12	1.22	1.34	1.32
6	486	50	600	650	.10	1.23	1.33	3.11
7	518	50	700	750	.10	1.35	1.45	50.00
8	520	50	800	850	.10	1.54	1.64	

Note: $TC = TFC + TVC$
$AFC = TFC \div TP$
$AVC = TVC \div TP$
$ATC = AFC + AVC$
or $TC \div TP$

[1] $MC = \Delta TC \div \Delta TP$

ΔTP can also be shown as one unit of output, but in this example ΔTP varies because it is related directly to the variable input, labour.

The total variable cost curve in Figure 16.2 rises slowly at first because the marginal product of additional labour is rising. When the point of diminishing marginal productivity is reached with the fourth labour unit, the total variable cost begins to rise more quickly because additional units of labour produce fewer additional units of output. Note that the total fixed cost is added to the total variable cost at each level of output to determine the total cost.

Average Costs *Average total cost, ATC, or the total cost per unit, is the total production cost for a given quantity of output divided by that quantity or number of units produced.* The average fixed cost and average variable cost are defined and calculated similarly. These cost schedules are also shown in Table 16.2, and are plotted as cost curves in Figure 16.3. The average fixed cost curve falls continuously as output increases because the fixed cost is being divided by an increasingly larger quantity. This is the effect commonly described as "spreading overhead costs".

The average variable cost curve, *AVC*, is U-shaped; it declines initially, reaches a minimum cost, and rises again. The output level at which the *AVC* curve is at its minimum is the same point at which the average product curve reaches its maximum in Figure 16.1. When the average product per unit of labour is at a maximum, the cost of labour in each unit of output, the *AVC*, is at a minimum. Similarly, when the average product is rising, the *AVC* is falling and vice versa. Thus the law of diminishing productivity implies that the average cost,

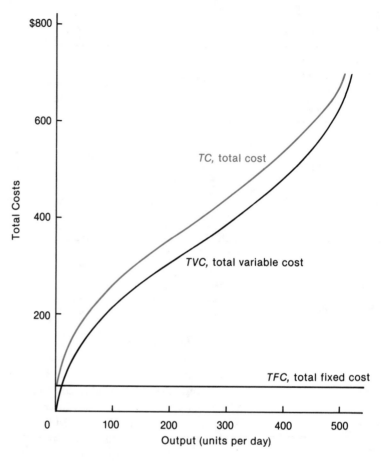

Figure 16.2   Total Cost Curves
The total cost curve, *TC*, is obtained by adding the total variable cost, *TVC*,
and total fixed cost, *TFC*, at each level of output. Fixed cost does not vary
with output. Variable cost usually increases at a decreasing rate, and then
at an increasing rate, as output increases, because of the diminishing
marginal productivity of variable factors such as labour.

or cost per unit, will eventually rise. The actual point at which this
occurs, as noted before, depends on the particular conditions for producing each commodity. If the firm is a relatively large employer of
labour, the average cost will rise sooner since the firm will be bidding up
the price of labour services as it employs increasing numbers of workers,
unless the large number of employees also make substantial specialization of labour possible.

The average total cost curve, ATC, is again determined by adding
the average variable and average fixed costs at each level of output, or
by dividing the total cost by the quantity produced. At the lowest out-

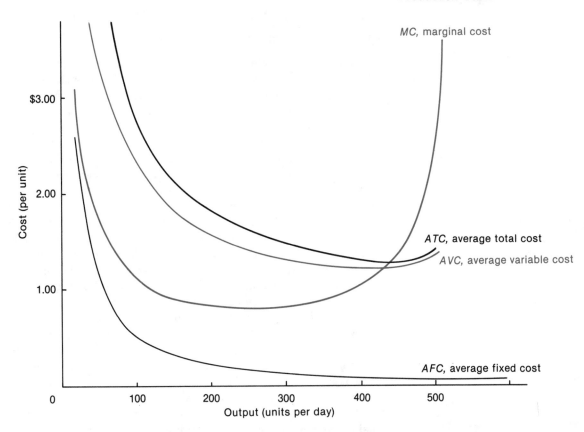

Figure 16.3 Average and Marginal Cost Curves
The average fixed cost, *AFC*, average variable cost, *AVC*, and average total
cost, *ATC*, are calculated by dividing the total cost by the quantity
produced. The marginal cost, *MC*, is the change in total cost associated
with each additional unit produced. *AFC* declines with increasing output,
but *AVC* and *ATC* fall and then rise as *MC* rises more sharply. *MC* always
intersects the *AVC* and *ATC* curves at their lowest points.

put levels, the shape of the *ATC* curve is influenced mainly by the
AFC curve, but as *AFC* diminishes, the *ATC* curve is more strongly
influenced by and approaches the *AVC* curve.

The output level at which the *ATC* curve is at a minimum is defined
as the firm's *capacity or optimum rate of output*. Although the firm can
produce more than this quantity, operating above capacity increases
average costs; operating with excess capacity, or at a lower output level,
also results in higher average costs.

Marginal Cost   Apart from the basic concept of opportunity cost, the most important
cost concept in economic analysis is marginal cost.

Marginal cost is the change in total cost associated with the production of each additional unit.

Marginal cost can also be calculated from changes in the total variable cost, since fixed cost does not vary with the quantity produced. It is possible to have a change in the fixed cost within the short-run period, such as an increase in property taxes or in the price of a business licence, but this increase must be paid even if there is no change in output.

The marginal cost curve, as shown in Figure 16.3, is U-shaped for the same reasons that the average variable cost curve takes this shape. Marginal cost is at its minimum at the output level where the marginal product curve begins to fall, the point of diminishing marginal productivity. Note that as the marginal cost curve rises, it intersects the average variable cost curve from below and at the minimum level of the *AVC*. The output level at which this equality of marginal cost and average variable cost occurs is that associated with the same level of variable factor inputs at which marginal product and average product are equal.

Marginal cost schedules and curves are important because they show the increase in total cost for each additional unit of output. The average cost schedules do not provide this information: although average costs vary with level of output, the change in average cost is not the cost of producing one more or one less unit. The significance of marginal cost in a firm's decision about the quantity to produce is explained in the next chapter.

The marginal cost and average variable cost curves shown in Figure 16.3 have a pronounced U-shape. In many actual cases, however, marginal cost remains constant over a wide output range because diminishing returns are not experienced until higher output levels are reached. But this constancy cannot continue indefinitely. Eventually, the law of diminishing returns has its effects, and marginal cost begins to rise. It will be seen later that this rising portion of the marginal cost curve is critical to a firm's output decisions; it is this section of the curve, therefore, that is commonly used in analyzing such decisions.

Long-Run Production and Costs

The long run was defined as the time required to change or vary all factors of production, particularly plant and equipment. In the long run, a firm can change its plant size or the amount and type of machinery it uses, as well as the amount and proportions of such factors as labour, raw materials, and so on. Moreover, the *number of firms* in the industry producing a specific commodity may also change; some firms may leave and others enter the industry.

Since all factors are variable in the long run, the distinction between fixed and variable costs is not relevant in the long run; the only relevant concept is total costs. The alternatives open to a firm in the long run are examined in terms of average total costs and various plant sizes.

Suppose the pottery firm from the example above were trying to determine the plant size at which it could produce 500 mugs at the lowest possible average cost.

In Figure 16.4, each ATC curve represents a different plant size. A plant size of 5 potter's wheels, represented by the ATC_1 curve, would result in an average total cost of $1.40. The 500 mugs could be produced in the smaller plant represented by ATC_0 or in the larger plant represented by ATC_2, but at a higher average cost in each case, namely, $2.00 for ATC_0 and $3.15 for ATC_2. Note that it is not a question of finding the *output* at which the average cost is minimized in a plant of given size, but rather, finding the *plant size* at which a given output can be produced at the lowest average cost.

The firm could similarly determine the plant size that would result in the lowest average cost for producing 1,000 mugs. Figure 16.4 indicates that a plant size with either ATC_2 or ATC_3 would lead to approximately the same average cost for 1,000 mugs (about $1.40), but the larger plant would enable the firm to expand production at lower average costs per

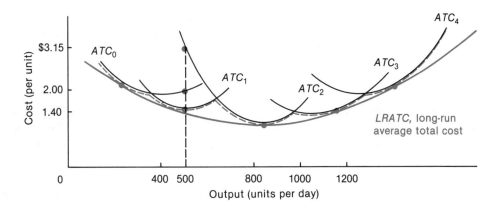

Figure 16.4 Long-Run Average Total Cost Curve
When all possible short-run average total cost curves are plotted on a graph (only five are illustrated here), the minimum ATC for producing any given level of output can be determined. Joining the lowest ATC for each level of output provides the long-run average total cost curve, *LRATC*. Note that only at the minimum point of the *LRATC* (at about 850 units) does the *LRATC* curve coincide with the minimum point of any short-run ATC curve; in this case, it is ATC_2. The broken curve shows the *LRATC* if only five plant sizes are possible; the smooth curve shows the *LRATC* when there are an unlimited number of plant sizes.

unit than would the smaller plant. This would be true until output reached about 1,300 mugs, when the firm would want to increase to the plant size implied in the ATC_4 curve.

If the ATC curves of all possible plant sizes were plotted in Figure 16.4, it would be possible to determine the plant size with the lowest average total cost for producing each level of output.

The curve showing the lowest possible average total cost for any given output level is the long-run average total cost curve, *LRATC*.

The *LRATC* curve is also described as the *envelope curve*: if one drew all the possible short-run ATC curves that correspond to different plant sizes and then drew the envelope that would enclose them, the result would be the *LRATC* curve.

Returns to Scale

The shape of the long-run average total cost curve is determined by variations in the returns to scale. *Returns to scale result from varying the quantities of all factors*. They are *not* due to the law of diminishing returns; that law described the effect on output of continuing to add more of one productive factor while the quantity of all other factors was held constant.

There are three different cases of returns to scale: *increasing returns, constant returns*, and *decreasing returns*. The decreasing portion of a long-run average total cost curve, such as the *LRATC* curve in Figure 16.4, reflects increasing returns. The flatter portion reflects almost constant returns, and the increasing portion represents decreasing returns.

Increasing Returns   Firms or industries experiencing increasing returns are sometimes called decreasing-cost firms or industries, and are said to be realizing *economies of scale*. This is the case when doubling *all* inputs results in more than a doubling of the output.

Increasing returns occur for various reasons: technical, managerial, marketing, and financial. *Technical economies* can be realized in several ways: large batches or mass production make increased specialization of labour possible; some machinery may be quite expensive and therefore lead to low unit costs only with large-scale production; a large firm may be able to enlarge the number of commodities it produces and thus make use of by-products from the production of its major item. A common technical economy in the chemical and petroleum industries, for example, is realized by increasing the diameter of pipelines. The volume carried per hour can thus be increased without an increase in labour.

Managerial economies can be realized by large plants that use special managers for each type of activity, who can afford to purchase more information and advice on their part of the plant's operations. Some managerial personnel may be underutilized in a small plant because they are capable of dealing with more responsibility than they have, in terms of production, sales, or employees.

Marketing economies are possible because some sales activities, such as market research, advertising, and establishment of distribution outlets, usually require large expenditures to be effective.

Financial economies are related, for example, to a large firm's ability to borrow funds at lower interest rates, or even to issue public shares to raise investment funds, and to finance a broader research and development program, which in turn leads to further economies.

Constant Returns   Constant returns or constant costs mean that output and the use of productive factors are increasing at the same rate. This is the case of a firm that has become large enough to take advantage of the economies of scale just described, but that has not expanded to the point where diseconomies begin to take effect. Since constant returns are often realized over a wide range of output, many of Canada's larger firms are in a constant-returns situation.

Decreasing Returns   Decreasing returns to scale, or increasing average total costs, would occur for reasons opposite to those explaining increasing returns. For example, management of very large firms may become less effective in controlling and coordinating the firm's diverse activities, as the firm expands. Beyond a certain size, there may be no further economies to be realized through specialization of the managerial function. Also, one important assumption made thus far — that the quantity of labour and materials purchased by the firm is such a small part of the market quantity that their prices are unaffected — usually does not hold for very large firms. If the automobile producers, for example, substantially expanded their scale of production, their purchases of more steel and certain skilled workers would increase the prices of these factors, and thus raise their average total costs, unless there is a perfectly elastic supply of these factors in the long run.

While any one of these situations may be found in large firms, it is doubtful that the net effect of many factors would be to increase the average total costs with large-scale production. That is, the production level at which decreasing returns begin for one factor may also be the level at which increasing returns begin for other reasons. There has been much debate, but relatively little evidence, on whether the long-run average total cost curve normally rises at high levels of output.

Review of the Main Points

1. All costs are opportunity costs: these include explicit or direct costs and implicit or indirect costs. Normal profit, the minimum profit required to retain a firm in a particular industry, is also a cost of production.

2. The short run is the period within which the quantity produced can be varied even though some factors, such as plant size, remain constant. The long run is the period within which all factors of production can be changed. Variable factors are factors that can be varied in the short run; fixed factors are those that can be varied only in the long run.

3. Total product is the total quantity produced in a given time period; average product is the quantity produced by one unit of a variable factor; marginal product is the change in total product associated with an additional unit of the variable factor. The quantity of the variable factor employed when the total product reaches a maximum is the point of diminishing total productivity.

4. The law of diminishing returns states that as increasing quantities of a variable factor are combined with a fixed factor, the total product will eventually decline.

5. Fixed costs are those that must be incurred regardless of the level of output; variable costs vary directly with changes in the level of output. Total costs include both fixed and variable costs.

6. The average fixed cost decreases as long as output is increasing; the average variable cost usually declines initially, then increases at the output level where average product begins to decline. The average total cost curve is also U-shaped; a firm's capacity is defined as the output level at which average total cost is at a minimum. Marginal cost, the change in total cost associated with producing an additional unit, begins to increase at the output level where marginal product reaches a maximum. When AVC and ATC are at a minimum, they are also equal to the marginal cost. The long-run average total cost curve shows the lowest average total cost at which each quantity can be produced.

7. Returns to scale may be increasing, constant, or decreasing. These refer to variations in the average total cost for a given quantity of output that are associated with different quantities or fixed factors. Increasing returns arise for technical, managerial, marketing, and financial reasons, including, for example, fuller utilization of managerial skills at higher output levels.

Key Concepts and Topics

opportunity cost
explicit cost
implicit cost
imputed cost
normal profit
economic or pure profit
short run
long run
production function
production schedule
total product
average product

marginal product
diminishing productivity
law of diminishing returns
law of variable proportions
fixed costs
variable costs
total cost
average cost (variable, total)
marginal cost
long-run average total cost
returns to scale

Questions for Review and Discussion

1. Why are normal profits, but not pure or economic profits, considered to be a cost of production?
2. Explain the relationship between marginal cost per unit of output and the law of diminishing marginal productivity.
3. Explain why the *MC* curve always intersects the *ATC* and *AVC* curves at the lowest points on these curves. Why does the *ATC* curve usually fall at low levels of output and then rise as output is increased further?
4. "The existence of economies of large scale contradicts the law of diminishing returns." Do you agree? Why? Which concept is relevant in the short run? Which is relevant in the long run? Explain.

Sources and Selected Readings

Eckert, R.D., and R.H. Leftwich. *The Price System and Resource Allocation,* 10th ed. Hinsdale, Ill.: Dryden Press, 1988.

Mansfield, Edwin. *Microeconomics: Theory and Applications,* 6th ed. New York: Norton, 1988.

Stigler, G. *The Theory of Price,* 4th ed. New York: Macmillan, 1987.

17 Supply Decisions in Competitive Markets

Market Structure

The objective of this chapter is to explain the response of a firm and an industry to a change in their costs or revenues. The quantity of output that a firm will supply to a market depends on both its production costs and its revenues, which in turn depend on the structure of the market.

Market structure is defined in terms of the nature and number of buyers and sellers in the market and the characteristics of the product. Each supplier or seller is treated as a single firm; all firms supplying a particular product are collectively described as the industry for that product.

Although many types of market structure have been identified, four basic types are sufficient to illustrate the principles governing a firm's output decisions under alternative market conditions. Two market structure models represent the extreme limits of possible conditions: *perfect competition* and *pure monopoly*. Two other models represent the actual conditions faced by a large number of firms: *monopolistic competition* and *oligopoly*. Only perfect competition is discussed in this section; the other three models are considered in the next chapter.

Perfect Competition

The distinguishing feature of perfect competition is that *individual firms cannot influence the price of the product in any way*. Regardless of the quantity supplied, a firm faces the price prevailing in the market at any given time. Firms in perfect competition are therefore described as *price-takers*.

A second basic feature of perfect competition is that *there are no barriers or obstacles preventing new firms from entering the industry, or preventing existing firms from leaving it*. Any firm that wishes to produce and sell a product in a perfectly competitive market is free to do so.

A number of conditions give rise to these two essential characteristics of perfect competition:

1. There are *many sellers* of the product, such that no individual seller produces a significant share of the quantity available to the market. The actions of any one firm, for example, in offering the product at a different price, can be ignored by other firms because that firm represents such a tiny share of the market.

2. All firms produce exactly the *same product*. Because "product" is defined broadly enough to include associated services such as free delivery, advice, and maintenance service, buyers have no reason to purchase the product from one firm rather than another. The products of all firms are therefore said to be homogeneous.

3. All buyers and sellers have *full information* about the market, in terms of the product, prices, and suppliers. For example, if one firm offered the product at a lower price than its competitors, all potential buyers would be aware of this.

4. Productive *resources are perfectly mobile*; any firm or potential firm can acquire whatever resources it requires for producing the commodity in question.

Such conditions rarely exist in any market. Perfect competition is therefore almost unknown in actual practice. Nevertheless, an analysis of firms' behaviour under perfect competition is a useful approach to studying the diversity of existing market conditions. As successive features contrary to the conditions of perfect competition are introduced into market structure models, the separate effects of such conditions can be identified. It will also be shown later that perfect competition generally leads to the most efficient use of resources, and therefore provides a standard for evaluating the efficiency of resource use under other market conditions.

Agriculture and Fishing There are, however, some markets that are more closely approximated by the perfect competition model than by other models. The markets for farm products have traditionally provided examples of perfect competition. The classic case portrays, for example, the egg industry, which has many producers and numerous buyers, standard products (determined by egg-grading standards), resources readily moved into or out of egg production, and buyers aware of many, if not all, producers and their prices. Any single egg producer supplies such a small share of the market quantity that it cannot affect the market price. Firms can easily enter or leave the industry because resources such as grain, labour, land, and buildings can be readily transferred between egg production and other agricultural uses.

In many countries, including Canada, *producer cooperatives* or *marketing boards* have been established for several agricultural commodities. These have often been formed in response to the declining number and increasing size of the buyers, such as large supermarkets or food processors. The result is a market with only one seller, the cooperative or board, and a few buyers. A substantial element of perfect competition remains in such a market, however, in that individual producers receive the same price for their products and each producer can supply any quantity at that price, unless there are quotas assigned to each producer. The creation of the Canadian Egg Marketing Agency thus ended most of the conditions necessary for perfect competition in the egg industry: production is regulated by quotas and most eggs are marketed through a provincial board.

The fishing industry has also provided examples of perfect competition, but here also cooperatives have been formed to market the fish from local areas. Both fishing and agricultural production have also been modified by contractual arrangements whereby a large buyer agrees to buy all, or a specified quantity, of the product from individual suppliers, and at predetermined prices. Furthermore, the supplier may sell its product only to the buyer holding the contract.

Examples that closely resemble perfect competition can also be found in local markets, for example, for handicraft products such as leather goods, pottery, woodcarvings, and hooked rugs, where any of these is a specialized handicraft of the area. Tourists travelling in resort or vacation areas frequently encounter a series of roadside stands, with each producer offering essentially the same product at very similar prices.

Output and Price under Perfect Competition

The effect of *time* on production conditions has previously been described in examining short-run and long-run production costs. In the short run, the quantity produced can be changed only by altering the use of variable resources, but in the long run, the quantity produced can vary more widely because all resources are variable. *The elasticity of supply therefore varies with the time period*: the longer the period considered, the more elastic is the supply, because producers have more opportunities to change the productive process as well as the quantity of factors employed.

Market Period In addition to the short run and the long run, there is the *market period* or *momentary period*. This is *the period within which the quantity to be supplied has already been produced.*

The market period is appropriate only to perishable products that, once produced, must be supplied to the market because they cannot be held for future sale. Since the quantity of such products is fixed, supply is perfectly inelastic.

Consider an example such as lettuce. The quantity of lettuce offered in a particular market area on any given day is represented in Figure 17.1 by the vertical or perfectly inelastic supply curve, S, at quantity Q_M. The market price, P_1, is determined by the intersection of the supply and demand curves. If the quantity of lettuce supplied each day remains at Q_M, the price of lettuce will vary only with shifts in the demand curve.

Short-Run Output under Perfect Competition

Firm's Objectives   In the market or momentary period, a firm has no choice about the quantity to be supplied; this has already been determined. In the short run, however, a firm must decide what quantity will be produced. This will depend on the firm's objectives or reasons for being in business.

The long-standing assumption has been that firms want to realize the highest possible profit; firms are described as "profit maximizers".

Some controversy has arisen, however, on the validity of the profit-maximization assumption. Critics have argued that firms, especially the larger ones, may have objectives other than profit maximization. Two alternative hypotheses about the firms' objectives are actually variations of the profit-maximization assumption.

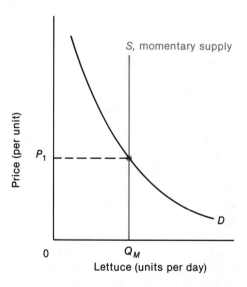

Figure 17.1   Momentary or Market Period
In the momentary or market period the quantity supplied, Q_M, has been determined previously, and thus the supply curve, S, is perfectly inelastic. The equilibrium price can vary only with changes in demand.

One hypothesis is that firms are concerned only with *long-run profit maximization*, and will take whatever short-run decisions are necessary to achieve this goal. Maximizing the short-run sales revenue, for example, is said to be a short-run means toward this long-run end. Increasing sales will enable the firm to expand in the longer run, and thus to realize economies of scale and higher profits.

An alternative assumption is that *firms hold sales maximization as their major objective, even in the long run.* Firms want to achieve the highest possible sales revenue, even if this means sacrificing some profits. The basis for this argument is that the objectives of large firms (especially the giant corporations) are determined by managers rather than shareholders. Such firms will make sufficient profits to satisfy shareholders, but will be primarily concerned with the salary and prestige of the higher levels of management. A large firm generally pays higher managerial salaries and confers more prestige and political power than a smaller firm, even though its profit rate *may* be lower.

Hypotheses about objectives of firms are difficult to test and validate. Because each hypothesis advanced here has contained at least some element of profit maximization, and because of other factors given above, the profit maximization assumption remains a basic element in the economic analysis of firms' behaviour.

Short-Run Profit Maximization

A perfectly competitive firm was described as a price-taker, since it could not affect the product price regardless of the quantity it supplied. This was because its output would represent only a very small share of the market quantity. A perfectly competitive firm therefore faces a *perfectly elastic demand curve* for its product. As shown in Figure 17.3, there can be wide variation in the quantity purchased from the firm even though there is no change in the price.

Given the firm's cost conditions and the perfectly elastic demand for its product at the prevailing market price, the firm has two decisions to make: What quantity should it produce? and Should it produce at all?

Two approaches or rules can be used for answering these questions. The firm can compare its total revenues with its total costs, or it can compare marginal revenues and marginal costs. Both approaches will be seen to provide the same answers. These are illustrated by returning to the example of the pottery firm producing ceramic coffee mugs that was introduced in the previous chapter.

Total Revenue Minus Total Cost Rule

The total revenue received from the sale of the firm's mugs is calculated by multiplying the quantity sold by the price per mug. This is expressed as $TR = Q \times P$. The firm's total revenue is shown in Table 17.1, along with the total cost data from Table 16.2. The product price is assumed to be \$2 per unit. The profit (or loss) for each level of production is calculated by subtracting the total costs from the total revenue. A loss is incurred at low levels of production because the fixed costs must be paid regardless of quantity produced, and because the marginal product of the first few workers is low. (See Table 16.1 again.) A profit can be made as output approaches 183 mugs, but the maximum profit can be obtained by producing 486 mugs.

The total revenue and total cost data are plotted in Figure 17.2. Note that the total revenue curve is a straight line; this is because the perfectly elastic demand curve faced by a purely competitive firm means that the firm receives the same price for each unit it sells. The total cost curve increases throughout its length, but rises more quickly at high levels of output due to the diminishing marginal productivity of additional units of labour.

The profit or loss is the vertical distance between the total revenue and total cost curves, measured at each quantity level. The level of output at which the total cost curve lies farthest below the total revenue curve is therefore the quantity at which maximum profits are realized. In Figure 17.2, this is again found to be at 486 mugs.

Suppose the price had been $1.25 per mug instead of $2.00. The total revenue received by the pottery firm when the price is $1.25 is shown as TR' in Figure 17.2. The new total revenue curve is again a straight line because the price received for each mug is constant for all levels of output, but the curve has shifted downward as a result of the lower price. This new total revenue curve lies below the total cost curve for all output levels, indicating that the firm cannot make a profit. It can, however, *minimize its loss* when the price is $1.25, by producing 410 mugs. At this point, the loss is $38.

Table 17.1

Total Revenues and Costs for a Pottery Firm

Variable Factor (units of labour) Q_L	Total Product (mugs per day) TP	Total Revenue (p = $2.00) TR	Total Costs TFC	TVC	TC	Profit (+) or Loss(−) TR − TC
0	0	$ 0	$50	$ 0	$ 50	$− 50
1	20	40	50	100	150	−110
2	76	152	50	200	250	− 98
3	183	366	50	300	350	+ 16
4	304	608	50	400	450	+ 158
5	410	820	50	500	550	+ 270
6	486	972	50	600	650	+ 322
7	518	1,036	50	700	750	+ 286
8	520	1,040	50	800	850	+ 190

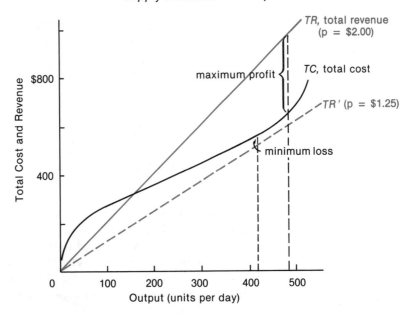

Figure 17.2   Pure Profit = *TR* − *TC*
Pure or economic profit (or loss) at each level of output is represented by
the vertical distance between the total revenue curve, *TR*, and the total cost
curve, *TC*. When the price per unit is $2.00, profit is maximized at 486 units.
When the price falls to $1.25, *TR'* Is below *TC* at all output levels: no profit
is possible and the loss is minimized at 410 units. The *TR* curves are
straight lines because the price received by the firm does not vary with
output in the case of perfect competition.

**Marginal Revenue
Equals Marginal Cost
Rule**

The second approach to calculating the firm's profit-maximizing quantity of output is to compare the marginal revenue and marginal cost.

Marginal revenue, *MR*, is the change in total revenue due to the sale
of an additional unit of output.

That is,

$$MR = \frac{\Delta TR}{\Delta Q}$$

Since the price or revenue received by the firm remains the same for
each additional unit sold, marginal revenue is equal to the price. Given
that $TR = P \times Q$, average revenue is also equal to the price since

$$AR = \frac{TR}{Q} = P$$

Thus, for the purely competitive firm, $P = AR = MR$. Furthermore, since the demand curve is a horizontal straight line at the market

price, the marginal revenue and average revenue curves are the demand curve for the firm. These curves are shown for the pottery firm in Figure 17.3.

An alternative rule for determining the profit-maximizing quantity is:

> The firm should produce the quantity at which marginal revenue is equal to marginal cost, or at which $MR = MC$.

Since marginal revenue equals price in the case of a purely competitive firm, this can also be stated as *the quantity at which price equals marginal cost* or $P = MC$. This rule follows from the fact that a profit is realized on each unit of output that can be produced at a cost less than the revenue received for that unit. Each unit of output that returns a profit adds to the total profit of the firm. Thus the firm should increase the quantity produced to the point where the cost of an additional unit is just equal to the additional revenue. At this point there is no further increase in total profits; the *maximum profit* point has been reached. This is illustrated in Figure 17.4, again using the case of the pottery firm. The cost data are drawn from Table 16.2, but the MC curve is smoothed to permit estimation of specific values from the diagram.

First, note that the marginal cost curve is plotted with the MC values at the midpoints of the TP (or total product) values, since marginal

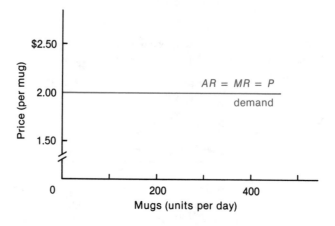

Figure 17.3   Perfectly Competitive Firm's Demand Curve
The demand curve facing a perfectly competitive firm is perfectly elastic, or a horizontal line at the prevailing market price ($2.00 per unit). The price received by the firm at each level of output is the average revenue, *AR*. Since this is constant for a perfectly competitive firm, the average revenue is also the marginal revenue, *MR*.

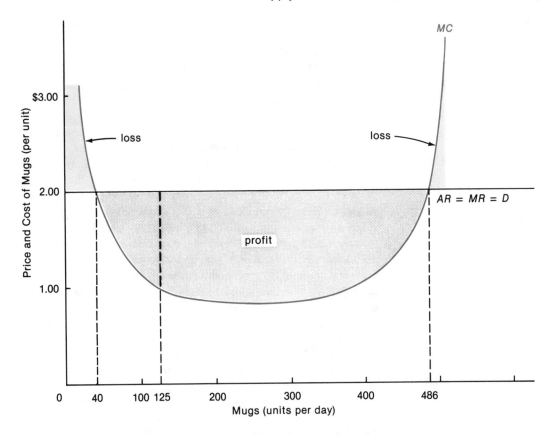

Figure 17.4   Maximum Profit Is Realized When *MC* Equals *MR*
Profit is realized on any unit of output for which the marginal revenue
exceeds the marginal cost. Thus output should be increased to the point at
which *MC* equals *MR*, or 486 units. Beyond this level, *MC* exceeds *MR* and
the loss reduces the total profit realized on previous units. Although *MC*
also equals *MR* at 40 units, this is not a profit-maximizing output because
MC intersects *MR* from above and thus represents the level at which the
firm only begins to realize a profit on each additional unit.

values are the *changes* in the total values. The marginal cost curve intersects the marginal revenue curve at two points, indicating that *MC*
equals *MR* at quantities of 40 units and 486 units. The first point, where
the *MC* curve intersects the *MR* curve *from above, or where the MC
curve is falling*, is *not* relevant to the profit-maximization rule. On all
quantities of less than 40 units the firm realizes a loss. Since marginal
cost refers only to variable costs, this is a loss *in addition to the fixed
costs*. Only at quantities greater than 40 units does the firm begin to
make a profit, and only in terms of the variable costs. But profit is *not*

realized on each of the units; it is realized on only those units in excess of 40 units. The losses on previous units, plus the fixed costs, need to be set against this profit.

The total profit on 125 units, for example, is found by calculating the total loss on the first 40 units (including the fixed costs) and subtracting this from the total gain on the next 85 units. The shaded area above the *MR* curve in Figure 17.4 represents a loss; the shaded area below the *MR* curve represents a profit. Comparison of these areas, keeping in mind that the *MC* curve extends much farther up the vertical axis than is shown in Figure 17.4, suggests that a small profit is realized on 125 units. But this is still based only on variable costs. The relationship between this profit and the fixed costs will be explored in the following pages.

On each additional unit between 40 units and 486 units, the firm realizes a profit; the total profit therefore continues to increase up to an output of 486 units. Above this quantity level, marginal cost exceeds marginal revenue, so that each unit produced in excess of 486 reduces total profit. The profit-maximizing level of output is therefore 486 units. This concurs with the result obtained by subtracting total cost from total revenue, as shown in Table 17.1. The quantity of 486 units was associated with the employment of six workers. Adding a seventh worker would bring output to 518 units, at a marginal cost per unit of $3.11; at this point the firm begins to incur losses that would reduce its profit.

It is therefore at the quantity level where MC = MR, when marginal costs are increasing, that the firm reaches its profit-maximizing output. At this point the firm is in equilibrium; given the market price and its production costs, the firm will not alter this profit-maximizing level of output.

The relationship between the $TR - TC$ and $MR = MC$ rules for profit maximization now becomes apparent. A review of Figure 17.2 will show that at the output where profit is maximized, the slope of TR is equal to the slope of TC. Recall that the slope of $TR = \Delta TR/\Delta Q = MR$ and that the slope of $TC = \Delta TC/\Delta Q = MC$. Hence the output at which $MC = MR$ is also the point at which the slopes of TC and TR are equal and profit is maximized.

Shutdown Price: Two Approaches

First Approach To this point, the discussion has emphasized the profit-maximizing level of output, but this should also be seen as the *loss-minimizing* level of output.

Should the firm produce at all if it cannot make a profit? At a price per mug of $1.25, the answer is yes. In fact, as long as the market price per mug is greater than $1.22, the firm should produce. Although the firm loses $38.50 by producing 410 mugs when the price is $1.25, it would lose the full amount of its fixed costs, $50, if it did not produce at all. By producing 410 mugs, it receives a total revenue of $512.50. This provides $500 to meet its total variable costs, with an additional $12.50 to meet part of its fixed costs.

When the price drops below $1.23, however, the firm should shut down. At $1.22, total revenue for the 410 mugs is $500.20, just about enough to cover total variable costs but with nothing left over to meet fixed costs. At a lower price, the total revenue will be less than total variable costs; there is clearly nothing to be gained by continuing production.

The firm's shutdown price, therefore, is defined as *the price at which total revenue is equal to or less than total variable costs at all except zero output*. Since the total revenue is the price multiplied by the quantity sold, the average revenue (total revenue divided by the quantity) is equal to the price. Thus, another definition of the shutdown price is the *price that is equal to or less than average variable cost at all possible levels of output*. This can also be expressed as the price equal to or less than the minimum average variable cost.

The shutdown condition can be stated simply as:

$$TR \leq TVC \text{ or } P \leq \text{minimum } AVC$$

Second Approach   The profit-maximizing rule, produce the quantity at which MC equals MR, can also be used to determine whether or not the firm should shut down. For the sake of brevity, the pottery firm is momentarily set aside to consider the two general cases illustrated in Figure 17.5.

In Figure 17.5a, the firm realizes its minimum loss at quantity Q_1, where MC equals MR. Total revenue is price, P_1, times quantity, Q_1. Total cost is average total cost, P_2, times quantity, Q_1. Total cost exceeds total revenue at Q_1 by the amount of loss shown as a shaded area, namely, $(P_2 - P_1)$ times Q_1. However, at Q_1 the average variable cost, AVC, is less than the price or marginal revenue. The firm therefore receives more than the cost of variable factors used to produce Q_1, and has some revenue to offset part of its fixed costs. The firm pictured in Figure 17.5a should continue to operate, producing quantity Q_1.

In Figure 17.5b, the firm minimizes its losses at Q_2, where $MC = MR$. But at Q_2 the average variable cost is greater than the price. The firm therefore does not receive a high enough price to cover the variable cost of producing Q_2. The firm illustrated by Figure 17.5b should shut down because its average variable cost exceeds the price received. Only if the AVC curve falls, or the price rises, is it rational for this firm to remain in operation.

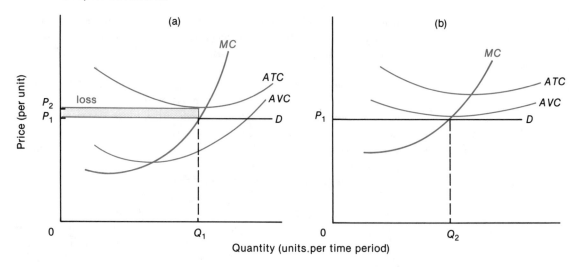

Figure 17.5   Alternative Short-Run Loss Conditions
The firm represented by Figure 17.5a minimizes its loss by producing Q_1. At this point its average revenue, P_1, exceeds its average variable cost, AVC, so it is earning some revenue to meet its fixed costs. It will therefore continue to produce Q_1 in the short run. The firm in Figure 17.5b, although it would minimize its loss at Q_2, will not produce at all. There is no output level at which its average revenue, P_1, would exceed its average variable cost, AVC, and hence it will shut down in the short run.

In each of these approaches, the firm would continue to operate if it could at least cover its variable costs and earn at least some small part of its fixed costs; that is, it would operate if $TR > TVC$ or $P >$ minimum AVC.

Competitive Firm's Short-Run Supply Curve

The perfectly competitive firm has been shown in the preceding section to adjust its output, given the market price and its cost conditions, in order to maximize profits. Perfectly competitive firms can therefore be described as "quantity-adjusters" as well as "price-takers". If a firm's cost conditions remain unchanged, the firm simply adjusts the quantity it supplies as the market price changes. But the supply of a commodity was defined in Chapter 3 as the quantity that would be supplied at each price. Thus, in adjusting quantity to different market prices, the firm is actually determining its supply curve.

Since the quantity that will be provided at each market price is determined by the marginal cost curve, the firm's supply curve is its marginal cost curve above the shutdown point (or the minimum average variable cost).

The fact that the supply curve is determined by the marginal cost curve is illustrated in Figure 17.6, which again shows the pottery firm example. It was determined previously that the firm would shut down if the price were $1.22 or less, that is, at these prices the quantity supplied would be zero. The firm's marginal cost curve is shown as a broken line at prices below $1.22 in Figure 17.6 to emphasize that this lower part of the marginal cost curve is not part of the supply curve. Instead, a solid horizontal line is drawn at $1.22 to indicate that zero quantity would be supplied at this and any lower price.

The supply curve above the $1.22 price is derived by drawing a series of demand or marginal revenue curves—horizontal lines—at alternative prices. The quantities at which the MR curves intersect the MC curve are the quantities that would be supplied at each of the alternative prices. Thus, 448 units would be supplied at a price of $1.32, 486 at

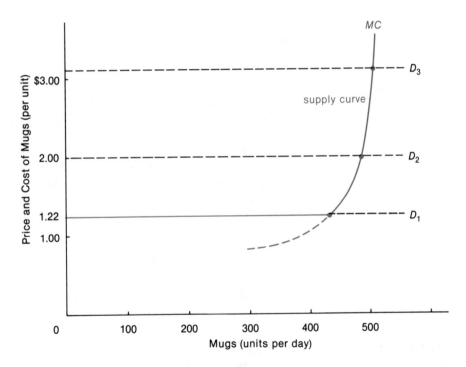

Figure 17.6 Marginal Cost Curve Is Competitive Firm's Supply Curve
Since maximum-profit output is realized when MC equals MR, any point on the firm's MC curve represents a potential output level. But since P equals MR for a purely competitive firm, any point on the MC curve also indicates the quantity that would be supplied at the related price level. Hence, the purely competitive firm's MC curve, above the price at which the firm would shut down ($1.22), is also the firm's supply curve.

$2.00, and 502 at $3.11. The supply curve is found by joining these points. Since all of these points are on the marginal cost curve, the supply curve is the marginal cost curve — *but only above the price at which the firm would shut down.*

Short-Run Equilibrium of Competitive Industries

An industry is defined as the total of all of the firms producing a particular commodity. An industry's supply curve is therefore the summation of the supply curves for all individual firms in the industry.

These are summed or aggregated in the same way that consumers' demand curves were added to find the market demand curve in Chapter 3: the total of quantities supplied by each firm at a particular price is the total quantity supplied by the industry at that price.

Suppose that there are 20 pottery firms supplying identical ceramic mugs. If one firm supplies 448 mugs at a price of $1.32, each of the other firms is expected to supply about the same number. This is the outcome of other specified conditions of a perfectly competitive industry, such as the mobility of resources and full knowledge of production and marketing in the industry.

The total quantity supplied to the market at $1.32 would be about 8,960 mugs. Similarly, assume that the 20 firms supply a total of 9,720 at $2.00 and 10,004 at $3.11. These points are plotted in Figure 17.7 to show the industry's supply curve.

Although a single firm in pure competition faces a perfectly elastic demand curve, the industry as a whole faces the downward-sloping demand curve for the market. That occurs because the individual firm is such a small part of the industry that it can sell virtually any quantity at the prevailing market price. But for the market as a whole, a greater quantity can be sold only at a lower price — due to the diminishing marginal utility that was discussed in Chapter 15. Such a market demand for ceramic mugs is also shown in Figure 17.7. The equilibrium price and quantity is $2.00 and 9,720 mugs per day; this market equilibrium price is thus the given price, shown in Figures 17.3 and 17.4, to which individual firms adjust their output in the short run.

Long-Run Equilibrium: Industry and Firm

Firms and industries can be in short-run equilibrium — equating marginal cost and marginal revenue — without being in long-run equilibrium.

Adjustments to achieve long-run equilibrium are likely to involve changes in both the number of firms in the industry and the average size of firms.

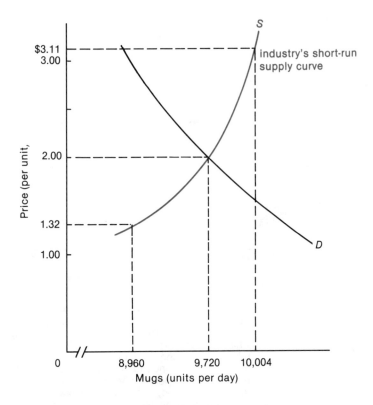

Figure 17.7   Industry's Supply, Demand, and Equilibrium Price
Supply curves for individual firms are added horizontally to obtain the
industry's supply curve, S. Intersection of the supply curve with the market
demand curve, D, determines the equilibrium price, $2.00 per unit, which is
the price faced by individual firms.

Changes in the number of firms will depend on whether any existing
firms are making pure profits or realizing losses in the short run. Firms
will continue to enter or leave the industry until the total revenue of
each firm is sufficient to cover its total costs, including a normal profit,
but no firm is realizing a pure profit. This will occur when each firm is
at the *output level where its average total cost is at a minimum.*

To see how this adjustment occurs, suppose that existing firms in the
particular industry are making economic or pure profits. A typical firm
in this industry is illustrated in Figure 17.8. The firm is in short-run
equilibrium producing Q_1 units per week, the quantity at which
$MC = MR_1 = P_1$. Pure profit is the area between price and average
total cost, ATC, for Q_1 units. The industry is also in equilibrium, at P_1
and ΣQ_1, which is the sum of the quantity produced by each firm in the
industry. The total demand for the industry's product is shown by
the demand curve, D, and is assumed to remain unchanged throughout

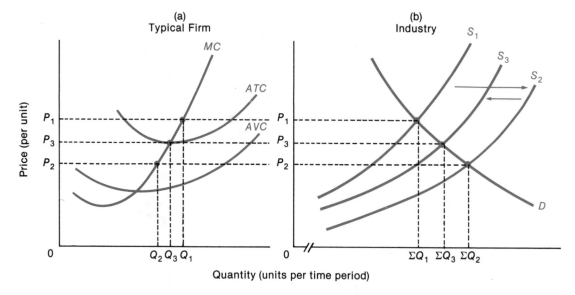

(a) Typical Firm

(b) Industry

Quantity (units per time period)

Figure 17.8 Entry of Firms Reduces Existing Firms' Profits
The industry is initially in short-run, but not long-run, equilibrium, at price P_1, and a typical firm in this industry is realizing its maximum profit at Q_1, where the profit is $P_1 - ATC$. New firms enter the industry in response to this profit, shifting the industry's supply curve outward to S_2 and reducing the equilibrium price to P_2, with a total quantity of ΣQ_2. The firms are then realizing a loss per unit equal to the difference between P_2 and ATC at Q_2. In the next period, some firms will leave the industry, the industry's supply curve will shift leftward to S_3, and the equilibrium price will increase to P_3. The remaining firms will have adjusted their output to Q_3, at which they will realize only a normal profit.

this example. The industry's supply curve is S_1, representing the sum of the supply curves for all firms in the industry.

When it is known that pure profits are being made in this industry, new firms will be established to produce the same commodity. The increase in the number of firms results in a greater quantity being supplied. Assume that the number of new firms is such that there is an outward shift of the short-run supply curve to S_2. If demand remains constant (no shift in the demand curve), the outward shift in the supply curve leads to a lower equilibrium price, P_2. (The new and the old firms had, however, based their output decisions on the assumption that the price would remain at P_1, and hence produced Q_1. That led to the excess supply that pushed the price down to P_2.) The fall in price to P_2 causes the firms to adjust their output to Q_2, but they still incur a loss, the difference between P_2 and the average total cost at Q_2. Firms will continue producing in this second short-run period because the price, P_2, more than covers their average variable cost at Q_2. Some firms will leave the industry, however, because they are not covering their fixed costs; they are not making the normal profit required to keep them in the industry.

The departure of firms reduces the total quantity supplied in the next short-run period, shifts the industry supply curve back toward S_3, and leads to a higher equilibrium price. If the new price happens to be P_3, the remaining firms will make a sufficient profit to keep them in the industry, but there will be no pure profit to attract new firms. The firms will have reached the output level, Q_3, where their average total cost is at a minimum. But since at this output quantity, marginal cost equals marginal revenue, and this is equal to price, the minimum average total cost is also equal to the price.

This is one of the conditions for long-run equilibrium of a perfectly competitive industry, namely that the market price is equal to the firm's minimum average total cost. The second equilibrium condition is that firms adjust their size so that they are producing the quantity at which the long-run average total cost is at a minimum.

This means that, in terms of Figure 17.9 (note the similarity with Figure 16.4), firms will adjust their fixed factors until their average total cost curve is represented by ATC_1. If, for example, firms are producing Q_1 at an average total cost of P_1 (and price equals MC_1), the industry will be in equilibrium but only to the extent that firms are neither leaving nor entering.

The long-run average total cost curve, $LRATC$, of Figure 17.9 indicates that there are returns to scale to be realized if firms adjust their fixed factors to increase their plant size. In pure competition, this opportunity is available to all firms since there are no restrictions on the use of resources. The same process that leads firms to produce where price equals minimum average total cost will lead them to expand their output to Q_2, with a resulting market price of P_2. *This fulfills the second condition for long-run equilibrium of a perfectly competitive industry: that firms produce the quantity at which price equals the minimum long-run average total cost.*

Changes in Long-Run Costs

It has been implicitly assumed that the entry or exit of firms did not change production costs by raising or lowering the prices of productive factors. This would be the case of a *constant-cost industry, one in which changes in the number of firms does not affect the prices of productive factors.* The long-run supply curve of such an industry will be perfectly elastic—a horizontal straight line at P_1—shown in Figure 17.10 as S_{LR}. An increase in demand, or a shift of the demand curve from D to D_1,

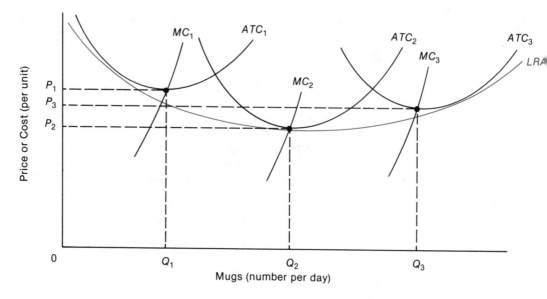

Figure 17.9 Long-Run Equilibrium in Perfectly Competitive Industry
In the long run, the number of firms in a purely competitive industry is adjusted, such that each firm is producing the output, Q_2, at which the market price, P_2, is equal to the average total cost. Each firm adjusts to the plant size, represented by ATC_2, at which it can produce Q_2 at the minimum long-run average total cost, P_2.

will initially raise the market price to P_2, leading to pure profit, and attract new firms. As explained previously, this will shift the short-run supply curve outward and reduce the market price to P_1, where no pure profit can be made. Hence the perfectly elastic long-run supply curve. But this curve will shift downward if production costs fall. For example, with demand D given and a supply increase to S_1, the new price would be P_3, with long-run supply now being perfectly elastic at that price.

However, if prices of productive factors are increased due to the entry of new firms, production costs are also increased. Cost curves will therefore be shifted upward. The short-run supply curve will not be shifted outward quite as far as in the constant-cost case, and a higher equilibrium price and a lower quantity will be established. *This is the case of an increasing-cost industry, in which the entry of new firms raises the prices of productive factors, causing the industry's long-run supply curve to slope upward to the right.*

As shown in Figure 17.11, a third possibility may exist: *the decreasing-cost industry, in which entry of new firms reduces the prices of productive factors.* Such a case is unlikely because an increased demand for productive factors would normally lead to higher production costs.

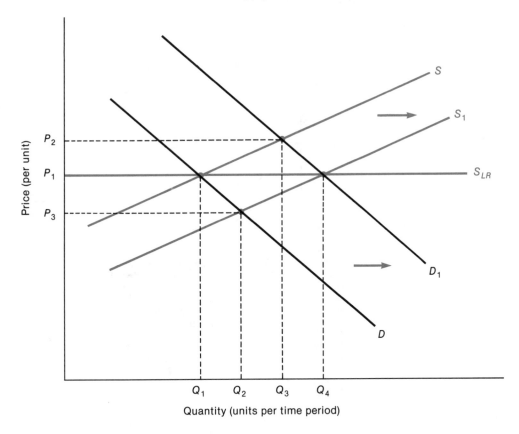

Figure 17.10   Long-Run Industry Supply Curve
The long-run supply curve for an industry is determined by the short-run
responses to changes in demand. If demand increases to D_1 this would
temporarily increase price to P_2, where existing firms would realize a profit.
This situation attracts new firms, causing an increase in supply to S_1 until
the price returns to P_1, where firms realize no pure profit. The total quantity
is increased to Q_4 by the additional firms. If, however, there were no change
in demand from D, but supply increased to S_1 due to lower input prices, the
price would drop to P_3 and the new long-run supply would be horizontal at
this price.

However, it may happen, for example, that an increase in the number
of firms employing welders in a certain area would stimulate the training of welders, resulting in so many with this skill that the price of weld-
ing services would fall. The general explanation for decreasing-cost
industries is the existence of external economies. Additional firms in an
area, for example, may attract services such as improved transportation
that will reduce the costs of all firms.

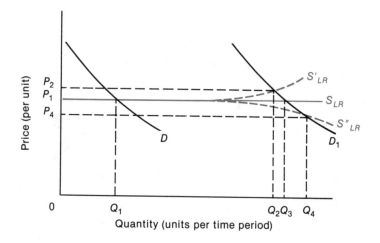

Figure 17.11 Alternative Long-Run Industry Supply Curves
The long-run supply curve of a purely competitive industry may be either upward-sloping (S'_{LR}), perfectly horizontal (S_{LR}), or downward-sloping (S''_{LR}). The shape of the long-run supply curve depends on the effect that new firms have on the costs of productive factors. If these rise with increased output, the supply curve is upward-sloping, and a long-run increase in demand, to D_1, results in a higher product price, P_2. A downward-sloping supply curve is usually due to external economies. In the latter case, a long-run increase in demand can result in a lower product price, P_4.

Review of the Main Points

1. "Perfect competition" describes a commodity market in which individual firms face a perfectly elastic demand curve and thus adjust their output quantities to a given price, and a market in which any firm is free to enter or leave. Conditions for this situation are: there are many sellers, none of which produces a significant share of the quantity supplied to the market; all firms produce the same product; all buyers and sellers have full information about product prices and production costs; productive resources are available without restriction to any firm.

2. Equilibrium quantity and price for a commodity market will vary for different planning periods. The momentary or market period is the period within which the quantity to be supplied has already been produced. In the short run and the long run, however, firms can adjust output in accordance with their objective. This is generally assumed to be profit maximization, although other objectives have been hypothesized.

3. The profit-maximizing output can be found by determining the output level at which the difference between total revenue and total cost

is greatest. A firm may produce even though total revenue is less than total cost, but it should shut down if total revenue does not exceed total variable costs.

4. The maximum profit is also realized at the output level where marginal revenue equals marginal cost. For a purely competitive firm, marginal revenue is constant and is equal to average revenue or price. Thus the profit-maximizing output is that at which marginal cost equals price, when marginal cost is rising.

5. A firm's short-run supply curve is the portion of its marginal cost curve above the price at which it would shut down.

6. All firms producing a specific commodity constitute the industry for that commodity. Hence, the industry's supply curve is the summation of the supply curves of all firms in the industry. The intersection of the industry's short-run supply curve, which is also the market supply curve, with the market demand curve determines the equilibrium output and price.

7. If existing firms are making economic profits or incurring losses, the number of firms will be altered in the long run, such that each firm is producing the quantity at which its average total cost is equal to the market price. The size of each firm will be adjusted until all firms are producing at the long-run minimum average total cost.

8. The shape of the industry's long-run supply curve depends on the effect new firms have on production costs. An increasing-cost industry has an upward-sloping long-run supply curve; a constant cost industry, a perfectly elastic supply curve; and a decreasing-cost industry, a downward-sloping supply curve.

Key Concepts and Topics

market structure	short-run supply curve
perfect competition	firm
price-takers	industry
freedom of entry	industry supply curve
momentary (or market) period	short-run equilibrium
profit maximization	long-run equilibrium
total revenue	long-run supply curve
marginal revenue	constant-cost industry
average revenue	decreasing-cost industry
shutdown price	increasing-cost industry

Questions for Review and Discussion

1. "Since a perfectly competitive firm faces a perfectly elastic demand curve, each firm could produce an infinite quantity without affecting the market price." Do you agree? Explain.

2. Why does $P = MR$ for a perfectly competitive firm?
3. Are there any circumstances under which the MC curve would intersect the AVC curve at other than the minimum point of the AVC curve?
4. List the conditions that must be present for perfect competition to exist. Explain why the absence of any one of these conditions would result in less than perfect competition.
5. Explain carefully why the profit-maximizing (or loss-minimizing) output occurs where $MC = MR$.
6. An individual beef farmer does not advertise his product but the Canadian Cattlemen's Association may decide to advertise to encourage beef consumption. Is each acting rationally? Why? Use a supply and demand diagram to show the possible effects of advertising for the beef industry and for the individual farmer.

Sources and Selected Readings

Eckert, R.D., and R.H. Leftwich. *The Price System and Resource Allocation,* 10th ed. Hinsdale, Ill.: Dryden Press, 1988.

Mansfield, Edwin. *Microeconomics: Theory and Applications,* 6th ed. New York: Norton, 1988.

Stigler, G. *The Theory of Price,* 4th ed. New York: Macmillan, 1987.

18 Monopoly and Imperfect Competition

Perfect competition is the form of market structure with which all other market conditions can be compared. Other market structures are therefore generally described collectively as *imperfect competition*. While there are several different cases of imperfect competition, the important ones include pure monopoly, monopolistic competition, and oligopoly. Each of these is examined in this chapter, and is compared with perfect competition in the following chapter.

Pure Monopoly

A pure monopoly exists if only one firm produces a commodity for which there are no close substitutes.

A pure monopolist faces no competition from other producers since there are *no close substitutes* for its product. But such a condition is rare because there are substitutes for almost all commodities. The products of firms commonly regarded as monopolies have some substitutes: a telegram substitutes for a telephone call; natural gas and fuel oil can substitute for electricity used in heating; aircraft and buses provide transportation alternatives to trains.

The definition and identification of monopoly depends on *the closeness or similarity of such substitutes, and thus on the extent of the firm's power to affect the price of the product by controlling the quantity supplied to the market*. A monopolist therefore is described as a *price-maker*.

Barriers to Entry

Other firms are prevented from producing the same commodity by various barriers. Some monopolistic conditions are created by *government actions*, including the granting of patents, creation of public utilities, sale of franchises, and the placing of quotas or embargoes on specific imports.

Government Policies   *Patents* granted to inventors give them exclusive right to produce their products for a period of 17 years. Alternatively, patent holders may sell their rights to other firms or license firms to produce the patented products. A patent may also create a monopoly in the production process of a product, as well as in the product itself; it may also allow a firm to extend a monopoly position if the firm requires licencees to purchase other products from it as well.

Public utilities are often created when only one producer could realize the economies of large scale associated with large fixed costs. This is the case of a natural monopoly, described in Chapter 20. There may also be situations in which competition may reduce the quality of service or increase its price. Urban bus transportation, for example, is generally provided by a single firm—a public utility—due both to economies of large scale and the inconvenience to passengers of a variety of bus tokens and incompatible timetables if a number of firms provided this service. In public utilities, governments retain the right to regulate the prices and types of services offered.

Franchises are granted, often with some payment made to a government, for the exclusive right to provide a service. In some cities, for example, a taxi company has the exclusive right to transport people from the airport to the city, although other taxis may take them to the airport. Fares might be lower if several firms could transport people from the airport, but in granting the franchise the government is able to insist that sufficient taxis be available at all times to meet travellers' needs.

Quotas limit the quantity produced or sold, and *embargoes* forbid the importation of specific imports, to the advantage of a domestic producer. For a monopoly position to be maintained against potential domestic producers, however, other types of barriers must exist.

Control of Inputs   In addition to such government actions, a second general type of barrier is a monopolist's *ownership or control of unique resources* used in producing the particular commodity. Such control is particularly evident in cases of rare deposits of mineral ores. For example, the International Nickel Company (INCO) controls most of the world's nickel deposits, and the Aluminum Company of America, prior to World War II, controlled virtually all sources of the bauxite ore used in producing aluminum.

Costs of Entry   A third general type of barrier can arise with *large-scale production relative to the size of the market, especially when the firm has been established for some time*. The costs of entry are thus extremely high and discourage potential firms from entering the industry. When the quantity that could be sold, even at a very low price, is relatively small and there are significant economies of scale, it may not be possible for more than one firm to make a profit. Potential competitors may recognize that if they or other firms enter the industry, all firms will incur losses. An existing monopolist will, of course, try to encourage this impression. Furthermore, a large, well-established firm will have a well-known product and dependable sources of financing, which place a new entrant at a distinct disadvantage.

Short-Run Price and Output in Pure Monopoly

In the monopoly case, *the firm is the industry*, because the monopoly is the only seller of the commodity.

The demand curve faced by the monopolist is the market demand curve for the product in question.

Since the demand curve indicates what quantity will be purchased at each price, the price set by the monopolist will be the price associated with the quantity it has produced and wishes to sell.

As in the case of perfectly competitive firms, a monopolist's objective is assumed to be profit maximization. A monopolist is thus concerned with determining the quantity of output required to meet this objective. The basic decision rules for maximizing the monopolist's profit are the same as those for the purely competitive firm: produce the quantity at which total revenue exceeds total cost by the greatest amount, or at which marginal cost is equal to marginal revenue.

For a perfectly competitive firm, the profit-maximization rule could be expressed in terms of marginal cost equalling price, because the demand curve facing the firm was perfectly elastic. It is highly unlikely, however, that a monopolist would face a perfectly elastic demand curve, because it faces the total demand curve for the market. This difference in the demand curves facing the two types of firm is one of the two major features distinguishing perfect competition from pure monopoly; the other feature is the difference in ease of entry to the industry.

A monopolist's price and output decision can be illustrated by the following example. Suppose someone holding a commercial pilot's licence decides to provide an air service in a small, remote community. The service offered is measured as kilometres of air travel. To avoid the complication of unfilled seats, it is assumed that the plane carries only one passenger and that only chartered service is offered. Fixed costs are high relative to the small market to be served, and the pilot has an outstanding reputation for long, accident-free experience with local flying conditions. It is improbable therefore that there will be competition from other firms.

Monopolist's Revenue

A market research firm engaged by the monopolist has found that the demand for local air service is as shown in Table 18.1. This market demand schedule indicates the number of kilometres of air travel that will be purchased each week at each of several prices, and thus the number of travel-kilometres the monopolist can expect to sell at each price.

The total revenue that can be realized at each quantity is calculated by multiplying the price by the quantity that would be sold at that price. From the total revenue schedule the marginal revenue schedule can be calculated, since *marginal revenue is the change in total revenue associated with each additional unit sold*. The demand schedule is also the average revenue schedule, because average revenue is the total revenue, at each price, divided by the quantity.

These schedules are plotted in Figure 18.1 as the demand or average revenue curve, marginal revenue curve and, below them, the total revenue curve. These show important differences from the revenue curves of the perfectly competitive firm. The monopolist's average revenue curve slopes downward because it faces the total demand curve of the market for its product, and that demand curve has been assumed to be downward sloping. Its marginal revenue curve is not identical with its average revenue curve because the monopolist can increase the quantity it sells only by reducing the price. The lower price relates not just to

Table 18.1

Revenues and Costs for a Monopoly Airline Service

Price (per kilometre)	Quality Demanded (kilo- metres per week)	Total Revenue	Average Revenue	Marginal Revenue	Total Cost	Average Total Cost	Marginal Cost	Profit (+) or Loss (−)
$1.00	0	0			1,000*			− 1,000
.91	1,000	910	.91	.91	1,250	1.25	.25	− 340
.81	2,000	1,620	.81	.71	1,490	.75	.24	+ 130
.72	3,000	2,160	.72	.54	1,740	.58	.25	+ 420
.63	4,000	2,520	.63	.36	2,000	.50	.26	+ 520
.54	5,000	2,700	.54	.18	2,300	.46	.30	+ 400
.45	6,000	2,700	.45	.00	2,640	.44	.34	+ 60
.36	7,000	2,520	.36	− .18	3,030	.43	.39	− 510
.27	8,000	2,160	.27	− .36	3,490	.44	.46	− 1,330
.18	9,000	1,620	.18	− .54	4,020	.45	.53	− 2,400
.10	10,000	1,000	.10	− .62	4,670	.47	.65	− 3,670
.00	11,000	0	.00	− 1.00	5,410	.49	.74	− 5,410

*There is a fixed cost of $1,000 per week for the leasing of the aircraft.

the additional unit sold, but also to all other units sold. For example, the pilot can sell 4,000 kilometres at $.63 per kilometre, but to sell 5,000 kilometres the price must be lowered to $.54 per kilometre. Thus the average revenue per kilometre drops only from $.63 to $.54, but the marginal revenue per kilometre for the additional 1,000 kilometres is only $.18 because the firm has had to accept a lower price for the first 4,000 kilometres in order to sell the additional 1,000 kilometres. *At any level of output the marginal revenue will be less than the average revenue, if the average revenue or price is declining.*

Although the average revenue is always positive, *marginal revenue becomes zero* when the quantity produced increases from 5,000 to 6,000 kilometres, and becomes negative for higher levels of output. This effect is due to the price elasticity of demand for the air service. At low quantities, a decrease in price leads to a proportionately greater increase in quantity demanded. The result is an increase in total revenue: in this range, the demand is elastic. As the price is decreased from $.54 to $.45, however, there is no change in total revenue, indicating unitary elasticity. At higher quantities, total revenue declines as price is decreased: demand is inelastic. Figure 18.1 shows that *marginal revenue becomes negative just beyond the quantity where total revenue reaches a maximum and at the point of unitary elasticity on the demand or average revenue curve.*

One rule for profit maximization is to produce the quantity at which marginal cost equals marginal revenue. The monopolist therefore will not produce beyond the quantity at which marginal revenue becomes negative, since marginal cost cannot be negative. When demand is inelastic, producing larger quantities always reduces total revenue. Production of larger quantities will be possible only at the same or higher total costs. Therefore the monopolist never sells in the price range where demand is inelastic. This leads to the further conclusion that *a monopolist will be concerned only with the range of output associated with the elastic portion of the demand curve.*

Price and Output Where $MC = MR$

The precise shapes of the monopolist's cost curves depend on the degree of competition in the markets for productive factors, and on the technology employed. In the example used here, the cost curves are assumed to be of the same general shape shown in the last chapter. Specific cost data are presented in Table 18.1 and plotted as cost curves in Figure 18.2. The fixed cost of $1,000 per week is the leasing charge for the aircraft. Variable costs are primarily for fuel and maintenance. These costs are assumed to increase faster than output at higher quantity levels; therefore the marginal cost curve will turn upward. The average

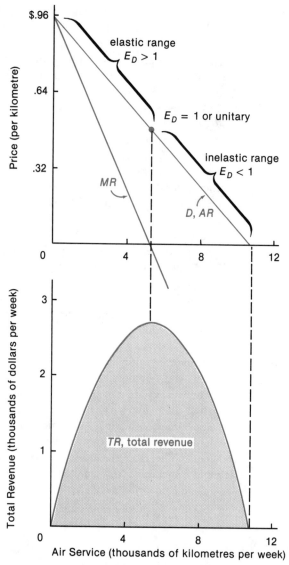

Figure 18.1   Monopolist's Revenue Curves
The demand curve faced by a monopolist is the market demand curve, since
the monopolist is the only firm producing the product. The demand curve is
also the average revenue curve, *AR*, because the demand curve indicates
the price one can charge to sell any given level of output. The marginal
revenue curve, *MR*, lies below the *AR* curve because additional output can
be sold only if a lower price is charged on all units. At high prices, demand
is elastic, total revenue (*TR*) increases with increasing sales, and *MR* is
positive. When demand is of unitary elasticity, *MR* is zero and *TR* reaches a
maximum. At lower prices, demand is inelastic, *MR* is negative, and *TR*
declines.

variable cost curve is not shown because this is required only to determine the firm's short-run shutdown point. Note the other similarities with the cost curves examined in the last chapter: marginal cost is equal to average cost at the output where average cost is at its minimum level. At lower outputs, marginal cost is less than average cost, and at higher outputs, marginal cost is greater than average cost. Average total cost falls sharply at low output levels, as the fixed costs are averaged over increasing quantities, and then rises as variable costs form a more significant portion of total costs.

Figure 18.2 shows that the monopolist's marginal revenue exceeds the marginal cost on each additional unit up to a quantity of 4,000 kilometres. At higher levels of output, the additional cost of each kilometre of air service is greater than the additional revenue: total profit therefore declines beyond that point. The maximum profit is realized by providing 4,000 kilometres of air service per week. The demand curve indicates that this quantity can be sold at a price of $.63 per kilometre. The

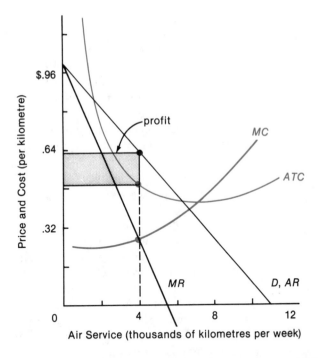

Figure 18.2 Monopolist's Maximum Profit, Output, and Price
The monopolist maximizes profit at the output where *MC* equals *MR*, namely 4,000 kilometres per week. The demand curve indicates this quantity can be sold at a price of $.63 per kilometre. Pure profit is the difference between *AR* and *ATC* for 4,000 units.

profit on 4,000 kilometres is shown in Figure 18.2 as the shaded area between the average revenue and average total cost curves, for an output of 4,000 kilometres.

Table 18.1 confirms the profit-maximizing quantity indicated by Figure 18.2. The marginal revenue in going from 3,000 to 4,000 kilometres is $.36 per kilometre, but marginal cost is only $.26 per kilometre. If output is increased to 5,000 kilometres, marginal revenue drops to $.18 while marginal cost rises to $.30. The monopolist should therefore restrict output to 4,000 kilometres per week. Note that at this quantity, demand is still elastic; the general conclusion that a monopolist will not produce where demand is inelastic is confirmed in this example. The total revenue minus total cost rule for determining maximum profits provides the same result: the final column of Table 18.1 indicates that the maximum profit, of $520 per month, is realized at a quantity of 4,000 kilometres per month.

Two important observations should be drawn from this analysis of the monopolist's revenue and cost conditions.

First, a monopolist does not necessarily make a profit.

Suppose, in the example used here, that the price of aircraft fuel rises sharply. Marginal costs increase for each output quantity: the marginal cost curve thus shifts upward to MC_1, as shown in Figure 18.3. The average total cost curve also shifts upward. The new marginal cost curve determines a new profit-maximization output at a lower quantity, and therefore a higher price. At this new quantity, average total cost exceeds average revenue: the "maximum-profit" level is actually the output at which the monopolist's loss is minimized. This loss is shown as the shaded area in Figure 18.3. *The monopolist will continue to operate in the short run, however, provided that the average variable cost is less than average revenue at this quantity; otherwise, the monopolist should shut down.*

The monopolist can also realize a lower profit or incur a loss even when marginal costs do not increase. If the fixed cost is increased, perhaps by a new tax on air service operators, the average total cost curve will again shift upward. However, because there is no change in the marginal cost, the profit-maximizing (or loss-minimizing) quantity is unchanged. There is no reason therefore for the monopolist to raise the price. The monopolist simply absorbs the cost of the new tax by reducing its profit or increasing its loss. Moreover, this tax cannot force the monopolist to shut down if it was rational for it to operate prior to the tax, because average variable costs are also unchanged.

The second observation is that there is no supply curve for a monopolist.

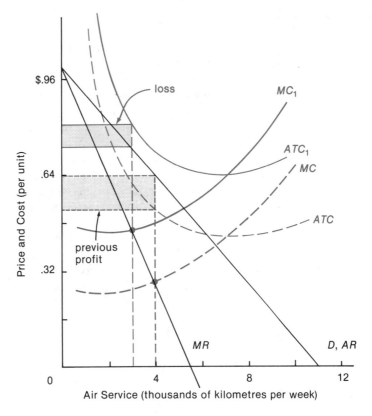

Figure 18.3 Monopolists May Incur Losses
The monopolist's profit illustrated in Figure 18.2 can become a loss if
production costs increase but there is no increase in demand. Increased
prices for productive factors, such as labour, shift the MC curve to MC_1 and
the ATC curve to ATC_1. The new short-run output is the level at which MC_1
equals MR. At this level (about 3,000 kilometres), the selling price indicated
by the demand curve is less than ATC_1 and a loss is incurred.

A supply curve indicates the quantities that will be offered *in response
to* various market prices. A supply curve can therefore be determined
for a perfectly competitive firm because it adjusts its output quantity to
the given market price. Although a monopolist has a marginal cost
curve, it does not have a supply curve because its output depends on
both the demand and the cost for its product. That is, the monopolist
determines profit-maximizing output and then sets the price at which
this quantity can be sold.

Long-Run Price and Output in Pure Monopoly

The rule that a firm will obtain maximum profit if it produces the quantity at which marginal cost equals marginal revenue is also applicable for long-run decisions. In this case, however, it is the *long-run marginal cost* that must be considered. As shown in Figure 18.4, this is the marginal cost that is associated with the profit-maximizing level of output, for each of the various short-run positions.

The lowest short-run average total cost for producing Q_1 is associated with the short-run plant size represented by ATC_1. The short-run marginal cost for Q_1 is also C_1; thus the long-run marginal cost for Q_1 is also C_1. Similarly, the long-run marginal cost is obtained from the other short-run cost conditions, shown as ATC_2 and ATC_3, to produce the long-run marginal cost curve, *LRMC*.

The *LRMC* and *LRATC* curves of Figure 18.4 are reproduced in Figure 18.5, together with the average revenue and marginal revenue curves. Assuming that no forces are acting to shift these revenue curves over time, they are the same revenue curves faced by the monopolist in

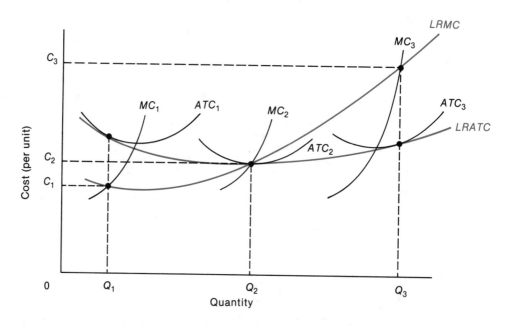

Figure 18.4   Monopolist's Long-Run Cost Curves
The monopolist's long-run average total cost curve, *LRATC*, is obtained by determining the lowest *ATC* for producing each possible level of output. The lowest *ATC* for Q_1, for example, is possible only in a plant size represented by ATC_1. The marginal cost curve, MC_1, associated with ATC_1 is the marginal cost of Q_1. Similarly, the marginal cost is found for each output level; these are plotted to obtain the long-run marginal cost, *LRMC*.

the short-run case. The long-run profit-maximizing quantity, where *LRMC* equals *MR*, is Q_{LR}; the price is P_{LR}. If the monopolist was previously in the short-run position represented by ATC_1 in Figure 18.4, the long-run price will be lower, but the profit will be greater. This can be determined from the fact that total revenue increases as price falls when demand is elastic, and *LRATC* is less than ATC_1 except where *LRATC* equals ATC_1 at Q_1.

Note that this calculation of the monopolist's long-run equilibrium output and price has assumed that it is able to maintain its monopoly position, that there is no change in demand, and that there is no change in the prices of productive factors. Variation from any of these assumptions would lead to different results.

Price Discrimination

Some monopolists are able to increase their profits by practising price discrimination. This can occur where a firm can charge different prices to different buyers of the same commodity produced under the same cost conditions. Price discrimination is quite common, even in markets that are not supplied by pure monopolists. For example, children are charged lower prices for public transportation, theatres and

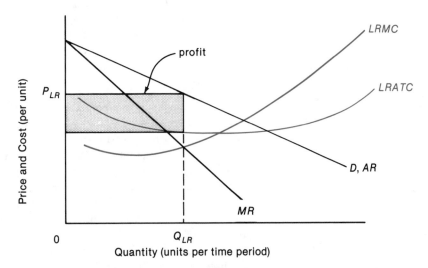

Figure 18.5   Monopolist's Long-Run Equilibrium Output and Price
The monopolist's long-run profit-maximizing output level is the quantity at which *MR* equals *LRMC*, namely Q_{LR}. The demand curve indicates that this quantity can be sold at price P_{LR}. The monopolist's profit is the difference between *AR* and *LRATC* at output Q_{LR}, multiplied by Q_{LR}.

concerts, and haircuts, although the cost of such services is seldom different for children and adults. Lawyers sometimes charge their wealthier clients higher fees—for the same service provided at the same cost—than they charge the less wealthy. These examples of price discrimination, although not cases of absolute monopoly, are examined here because they are possible only when the producer has some control over the price of the product.

Conditions for Price Discrimination

Price discrimination by price-makers is potentially possible because different buyers are willing to pay different prices for a single unit of a commodity; that is, because individuals have different demand curves for the commodity. But price discrimination can actually occur only if different groups of individuals with different demand curves can be identified and segregated into the sub-markets of the total market for the commodity. (In the examples cited above there are sub-markets consisting of children and of adults.) Not only must the groups having different demand curves be treated separately; it is also essential that the commodity cannot be transferred or resold between individuals in these different groups. Otherwise, the group charged the lowest price would resell the commodity to the other groups, until everyone would buy at the lowest price and no discrimination would exist.

Price discrimination is possible when a supplier can control both the quantity and distribution of the product, when it can distinguish between buyers with different demand curves, and when transfer of the product between buyers is impossible, preventable, or more costly than the difference between the prices charged different buyers.

The circumstances meeting these conditions include the following: (a) the product is a service, such as a concert, haircut, or surgical operation, and thus cannot be transferred to anyone else; or (b) one group of buyers is not aware that another group of buyers is paying a different price: an example of this is secret rebates or discounts; or (c) there is a barrier to the transfer of goods from one group of buyers to another: such barriers would include high transportation costs, tariffs, quotas or embargoes on imports, or explicit restrictions imposed by the seller as a condition of a lower price.

A special case of price discrimination exists when a single buyer may be charged different prices for additional quantities. Electricity and natural gas, for example, are commonly sold according to a rate structure, whereby initial quantities have a high price and successive quantities are provided at lower prices. Electricity or natural gas could be transferred to another buyer only by an extension of the power or gas lines, an arrangement forbidden by the suppliers. The differentiated rate structure allows the producer to obtain more of the total revenue represented by the area under an individual's demand curve. The more complex the set of rates, the larger the revenue realized. In other words, *if a different price could be charged for each unit consumed*, the producer would obtain all the revenue represented by the demand curve, up to the quantity level at which the price no longer exceeded the marginal cost of producing the commodity.

Effects of Price Discrimination

In the case of perfect or complete price discrimination between different buyers in a market, the monopolist will charge a different price for each level of output, in accordance with the declining demand curve. The monopolist that can segregate its market into several groups will increase its output to the point where its marginal cost is equal to the price at that quantity level. The demand curve will therefore become its marginal revenue curve, since the price charged for an additional unit will be the marginal revenue for that unit. (Note that in cases of price discrimination the seller does not reduce the price of all units in order to sell an additional unit.) *Thus, equating marginal revenue and marginal cost is, for the perfect price-discriminating monopolist, also equating price and marginal cost.* The consequence of this, as shown in Figure 18.6, is a higher profit and larger output than occurs in the case of a non-discriminating or single price monopolist.

A single-price monopolist, producing where MC equals MR, would be seen in Figure 18.6 to produce Q_1 at an average total cost of P_2 and to sell at price P_3. Its profit is $(P_3 - P_2) \times Q_1$. A monopolist that can carry price discrimination to its limit by charging a different price for each unit will produce quantity Q_2, where MC equals AR. Its total revenue is the area under the demand curve up to quantity Q_2, namely P_4BQ_2; total cost is the average total cost at quantity Q_2 (shown as C) multiplied by Q_2, or area P_1CQ_2. Its profit is the difference between these areas, namely triangle P_4P_1A less triangle ACB. From Figure 18.6, it can be clearly seen that the discriminating monopolist has a substantially higher profit and a greater output than a non-discriminating monopolist.

Monopolistic Competition

Monopolistic competition is the case of an industry where there are many small firms selling similar but not identical products.

Each small firm supplies only a small share of the total market quantity and hence is not concerned about the reaction of other firms to its

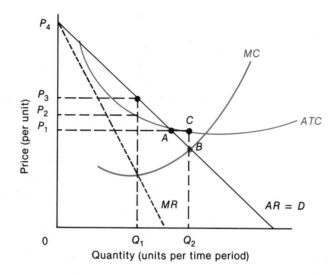

Figure 18.6   Price Discrimination from a Monopolist's Perspective
Price discrimination involves selling the same product at different prices to different buyers. The monopolist who sells at only one price maximizes profit at output Q_1, which can be sold at price P_3. The profit is $P_3 - P_2$ on quantity Q_1. Under perfect or complete price discrimination, when each unit is sold at the maximum price a consumer is willing to pay, the demand curve (D) becomes the monopolist's marginal revenue curve. Maximum profit is then realized at output Q_2, the level at which MC intersects the demand curve. Total revenue is the area under the demand curve up to Q_2, and total cost is $Q_2 \times P_1$. Profit for the price-discriminating monopolist is the difference between these two areas, namely, P_4P_1A less ACB.

price and output decisions. However, because the product of each firm is slightly different from that of other firms, the products in question are not perfect substitutes for each other. Thus, a monopolistically competitive firm's demand curve is not perfectly elastic, with the result that it can adjust its price to accord with the output where it will maximize its profit. Since there are a large number of firms in the industry, it follows that barriers to entering the industry are negligible.

The competitive aspects of this model are thus the existence of many sellers, each with a small market share, and the ease of entry to the industry. The monopolistic aspect is the differentiation of products resulting in a demand curve that is not perfectly elastic, such that individual firms have some effect on market price.

The monopolistic competition model is a reasonably good explanation for a large number of industries, including those producing clothing, shoes, and furniture, as well as numerous retail service industries such as drugstores, shoe repair shops, laundries, dry cleaners, and restaurants. Product differentiation in such industries takes many forms:

clothing and shoes differ in style, workmanship, and material; small retail establishments vary mainly in their selling conditions such as location, service, and credit policy.

Short-Run Price and Output in Monopolistic Competition

The profit-maximizing rule that applies to monopolists also applies to the firm in monopolistic competition: produce the quantity at which marginal cost equals marginal revenue and set the price for this quantity as indicated by the demand curve facing the firm.

The monopolistically competitive firm faces a highly elastic demand curve because its product is a close but not perfect substitute for the products of its competitors. If the monopolistically competitive firm raises its price slightly it will lose a substantial number of sales, but not all sales, because some buyers will pay slightly more for the closer location of a drugstore or the reliability of a product that has given satisfactory results in the past. Similarly, a price reduction will attract many, but not all, customers from other producers.

The cost conditions of firms in monopolistic competition are assumed to be generally the same as those described for firms in other market conditions, except that costs likely include expenditures for advertising and other sales promotion that were unnecessary for the perfectly competitive firm. (However, a monopolist may advertise to raise its demand curve or improve public relations to prevent government controls.) The profit-maximizing output level, Q_1, and price, P_1, shown in Figure 18.7a are the short-run equilibrium conditions for the monopolistically competitive firm.

Selling Costs Maximum profit in the short run can vary, depending on the firm's decisions about selling costs. These costs are the expenditures for sales promotion. Assume that a firm can shift its demand curve outward and make it less elastic by increasing advertising, paying higher commissions, spending more for a more attractive package, and so on. These costs are assumed to vary with the quantity produced, with resulting upward shifts in the marginal cost and average total cost curves as shown in Figure 18.7b. The new marginal cost and marginal revenue curves intersect at output Q_2, with the new, larger profit shown as the shaded area. The product price also increases, from P_1 to P_2.

Many monopolistically competitive firms thus face the further problem of estimating the extent to which their demand curves can be altered in the short run by increasing such selling costs. An advertising program, for example, may not always have the substantial effect on the demand curve illustrated in Figure 18.7b. If the demand curve had remained as it was in Figure 18.7a, despite the additional sales promo-

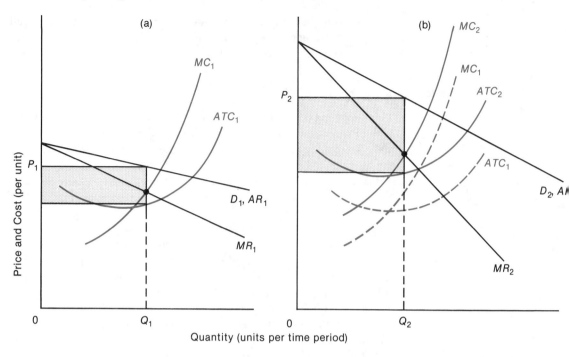

Figure 18.7   Advertising Sometimes Increases Profits
A monopolistically competitive firm that does not advertise maximizes its profit, as in Figure 18.7a, at output Q_1 and price P_1. By advertising, the firm shifts its demand curve to AR_2 (Figure 18.7b), and its marginal revenue curve to MR_2. Advertising costs shift marginal costs to MC_2 and average total cost to ATC_2. The new profit-maximizing output is reduced to Q_2, which is sold at a higher price, P_2. Profit is increased in this case, but a profit reduction could occur when large advertising costs have little effect on the demand curve.

tion, the new marginal cost curve would have intersected the original marginal revenue curve at a lower output level than Q_1, the average total cost of that level of output would be higher, the profit would be reduced, but the product price would be higher than P_1.

Long-Run Price and Output in Monopolistic Competition

In the long run, a monopolistically competitive firm can change its plant size, as can firms in other types of industries, to take account of whatever economies of scale are possible. This opportunity will be curtailed, however, by the entry of new firms. The absence of barriers to new firms enables them to enter the industry, when they are attracted by short-run profits of existing firms. As new firms attract existing customers in the market, *the demand for products of existing firms will be*

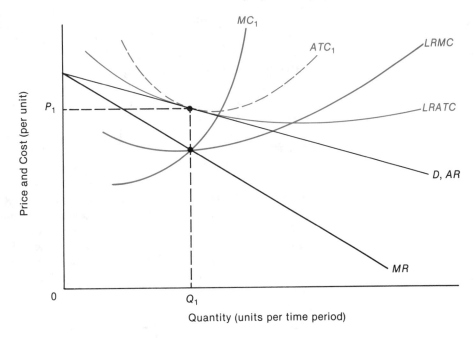

Figure 18.8   Long-Run Output and Price of a Monopolistically Competitive Firm
A monopolistically competitive firm, like firms under other market structures, maximizes profit at the output where *LRMC* equals *MR*, namely Q_1. The free entry of new firms reduces pure profit to zero through an adjustment process that decreases the firm's demand and increases its costs, until ATC_1 is tangent to the demand curve at Q_1. However, the firm is not producing at either its short-run optimum capacity (the minimum level of ATC_1) nor at its long-run optimum scale (the minimum level of *LRATC*).

reduced. This process will continue until so many firms have entered the industry that a firm's demand curve has shifted downward or to the left to the point where, at the quantity equating long-run marginal cost and marginal revenue, pure profit has been reduced to zero. This is shown in Figure 18.8. The long-run profit-maximizing output is produced at a plant size (represented by ATC_1) too small to realize the economies of scale implied by the downward slope of the *LRATC* beyond the quantity Q_1.

Oligopoly

An oligopoly is an industry with so few firms that the actions of one firm directly affect the decisions of other firms in the industry.

There may actually be more than a few firms; that is, there may be a number of small firms in addition to the few large firms dominating the industry. The important fact in an oligopoly is that each large firm produces a large share of the total output of the product concerned. Although the actions of the small firms are occasionally of some consequence, it is the actions of the large firms that are significant in oligopolistic behaviour.

Because there are only a few major producers, each has some control over the price of its product. This distinguishes oligopoly from perfect competition. But oligopolists do not have the independence in setting prices that characterizes a monopolist; the price and output decisions of one firm affect the decisions of all the other firms. The second distinguishing feature of an oligopoly, in addition to the small number of firms, is thus the *interdependence* of the actions of firms.

The equilibrium price and output of oligopolistic firms and industries cannot be determined quite as readily as those for perfect competition and monopoly, because oligopolistic firms' decisions reflect not only cost and revenue conditions but also how they *expect* other firms in the industry will react. This unpredictable behaviour has led economists to suggest that oligopolistic price and output are *indeterminate: a given set of cost and revenue conditions does not always lead to the same price and output decision because other variable factors—primarily competitors' responses—also influence the decision.*

Price and output are, of course, decided somehow. Several hypotheses have been proposed to describe firms' behaviour in oligopolies. A recent approach has involved applying the *theory of games*, or strategies for successive responses to the actions of rivals.

Conditions for Oligopoly

Conditions fostering the existence of oligopolies are primarily *economies of scale*, *cost advantages*, and *mergers*.

Economies of Scale   *Economies of scale* make it possible for only one firm to operate profitably in the case of a monopoly; similarly, economies of large scale may prevent more than a few firms from realizing a profit in an oligopoly. Oligopolies often emerge from more competitive conditions in which several firms are operating at a small-scale output level in the short run. Longer-run expansion to realize economies of scale results in fewer firms, each providing a large share of the market quantity, with other firms leaving the industry.

This process tends to follow *technological changes* that make economies of large scale possible. The firms that first adapt their production and marketing techniques to the new technology are the ones to remain in the industry; the laggards cannot match the lower prices or improved quality of the other firms and are forced to cease operation. Most of the current oligopolies, such as the automobile, steel, and petroleum industries, once included several other firms, which gradually dropped out or were bought by the remaining firms.

Cost Advantages   *Cost advantages* enjoyed by existing firms are major barriers to new firms that might wish to enter an oligopoly. A new firm would need to become a large-scale producer immediately in order to realize the low average total cost at which existing firms are operating. But this would require extremely large expenditures for plant, equipment, senior management, advertising, and distribution. Such a venture might be regarded as a high risk by potential creditors or shareholders. In the few cases where new firms do enter an oligopoly, financing is often provided by large firms that operate in a related oligopoly and that can realize further economies of scale by sharing management and distribution with the new firm.

Even if a new firm could arrange financing of a large-scale plant, the existing firms would have other advantages that would give them a lower long-run average total cost curve than the new firm would have. Existing firms may control necessary patents or raw materials, may have a specialized knowledge of production and marketing in their industry that can be learned only by experience, or may have a well-established group of customers or "brand loyalty" that the potential new firm must penetrate.

Mergers   *Mergers* are often the outcome of the two other conditions fostering oligopolies, and thus reinforce the oligopolistic nature of an industry. The few firms in an oligopoly, although large, often differ significantly in their output. Two of the smaller firms may merge in order to gain the economies of scale and market power held by the largest firm; they thereby become less susceptible to the effects of its actions. Also, each firm in the oligopolistic industry may have particular advantages, such as outstanding management or established customers, and may find that it can improve its cost and profit positions by merging and sharing these advantages with another firm.

Short-Run Price and Output in Oligopoly

Different models or explanations of oligopolists' behaviour are based on the nature of their products: these are described as being *differentiated* or *undifferentiated*. The products of the various firms in an oligopoly may differ slightly in design or composition, or buyers may simply *believe* that the products are different. The oil companies, for example, put much effort into persuading buyers that their automobile gasolines are significantly different. Other differentiated-product oligopolies include the automobile, tobacco, and soap industries. In other oligopolistic industries, such as those producing primary aluminum, cement, and basic steel, the product is undifferentiated, or essentially the same for all firms.

Oligopolists' Revenues

The interdependence of oligopolists' actions makes it difficult to specify precisely their demand or average revenue curves, since the elasticity of demand for the product of a particular firm depends on how other firms react to the firm's price changes. Consider the case of a paint industry dominated by about five major producers. If one firm, currently selling 10,000 litres per week of its standard white paint at $6.00 per litre, should lower its price to $5.00 per litre, its rivals could react in a number of ways. If they do not change their prices, the firm will increase its sales both because the total market sales will increase and because the firm will gain sales from its competitors. If the other firms also lower their prices, total market sales will increase but each firm will gain a share of this increase roughly proportionate to its previous market share. The firm initiating the price change will thus increase its sales less than it would if rivals firms' prices were unchanged. The demand elasticity is therefore lower in the second case than the first.

The other firms may decide that the price-cutting firm is in financial difficulty and can be squeezed out of the industry if they reduce their prices still further. Despite this competition, the price-cutting firm may still increase its sales slightly if it has a sufficiently different product or if there is strong brand loyalty among its buyers; otherwise its sales may remain unchanged, but will likely decrease. Thus, in estimating its demand curve, the firm must be able to predict both how buyers and other firms will react to its own price changes, and how buyers will react to price differentials between its product and those of other firms.

It is assumed in the following discussion that an oligopolist will face a normal, downward-sloping demand curve. Although the precise shape or elasticity of the curve may not be known, this assumption can still provide important comparisons between alternative oligopolistic situations. In the case of differentiated products the market demand curve is also imprecise, since slightly different products are being treated as if they were the same. The problem is one of determining how different products may be and still be considered within a single market. Again, a downward-sloping demand curve can be assumed for the industry; its precise position, however, remains in question.

Price and Output in Differentiated-Product Oligopoly

Kinked Demand
A model of the behaviour of oligopolistic firms whose products are differentiated has been developed to explain why prices tend to remain unchanged despite changing cost conditions. This is the *kinked demand model*. It assumes that if a firm lowers its price other firms will do the same, but if a firm raises its price the others will not follow; it also assumes that firms recognize that none will benefit by price-cutting since each would move away from its profit-maximizing output level.

The kinked demand curve facing a firm in this situation is shown as the solid D,AR curve in Figure 18.9. It actually combines segments of two demand curves. Suppose the firm's current price and quantity are P_1 and Q_1. If the firm expects that its rivals will match any price change, its demand curve will be the steeper, less elastic one. If all firms raise their prices, this firm will lose some sales, but so will the other firms; if all firms lower their prices, this firm will gain few sales. Alter-

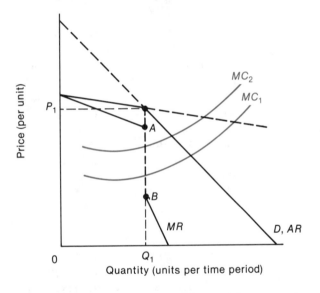

Figure 18.9   Oligopolist's Kinked Demand Curve
An oligopolistic firm is selling Q_1 units per period at P_1 per unit. It believes that if it raises its price, the quantity sold will decrease proportionately more (demand is elastic) because rivals will not raise their prices. A price reduction, however, would be matched by rivals. Hence there is a "kink" in the demand curve (D, AR) that produces a discontinuity in the MR curve between A and B. An increase in production costs, shifting marginal costs up to MC_2, has no effect on price and output because MC_2 equals MR at the same output, Q_1, at which MC_1 equals MR.

natively, if the firm expects its rivals to ignore its price changes, its demand curve will be the flatter, more elastic one because a price increase will sharply reduce sales and a price decrease will lead to many more sales.

The firm facing the kinked demand curve, however, expects that its price increase will be ignored by rivals because they can then gain a larger share of the market, while its price decrease will be followed by other firms attempting to preserve their market shares. But all the firms recognize that there is nothing to be gained if they all reduce their prices. Thus the price remains fixed at P_1.

One might expect, however, that an increase in costs would cause a firm to raise its price as part of its adjustment to a new profit-maximizing price and output combination. *Within a certain range of cost changes, no such price change occurs.* Figure 18.9 illustrates why this is rational behaviour for the firm. While the demand curve has a kink at quantity Q_1, the marginal revenue curve derived from the segments of the two demand curves has a discontinuity, or vertical section, AB, at this output level. If the firm's marginal cost curve is MC_1, marginal cost is equal to marginal revenue at output Q_1 and the firm is at its maximum-profit position. Suppose an increase in the price of a variable factor such as labour shifts the marginal cost curve upward to MC_2. *The output level at which marginal revenue is equal to the new marginal cost is still Q_1. The price thus remains at P_1 despite the cost increase.*

Note that the kinked demand explanation does not account for the initial price, nor can this explanation be expected to apply to all cases of differentiated products. The range within which marginal revenue is constant, and thus the range within which marginal cost changes have no effect on price, depends on the relative elasticities of the two segments of the kinked demand curve.

This model would lead one to expect that:

- prices will remain unchanged in oligopolies even when costs change;
- only substantial shifts in costs will cause prices to change;
- firms will advertise to differentiate their products and thus make the upper segment of the kinked demand curve less elastic, thereby reducing the degree of the kink. This will enhance their opportunity for freedom of action in setting prices.

In the real world, these results are observed: prices of products offered by oligopolistic firms change infrequently, and then in pronounced jumps, and oligopolists generally spend a larger percentage of the selling price of the product for advertising than do firms in other industries.

Price and Output in Undifferentiated-Product Oligopoly

Since oligopolistic firms cannot be certain how their rivals will react, they cannot be certain what their profit-maximizing price and output should be. This is especially true for firms producing essentially the same product as their rivals, because buyers' responses to any price difference will be greater than when products are differentiated.

Firms that are uncertain about their rivals' reactions thus have a strong incentive to work together to maximize their joint profits as a means of maximizing their individual profits.

At the same time, as a firm increases its certainty about rivals' reactions by cooperating with them, it will have an incentive to use this knowledge to operate independently, and thus to improve its profit position still further.

Collusion

The joint decision-making of firms, particularly concerning the setting or changing of prices, is termed collusion. It rarely occurs in any market other than those characterized by oligopoly, because it is not necessary in monopoly, and too difficult in monopolistic competition. Collusion can take several specific forms, which can be categorized as *overt or explicit collusion* and *tacit or implicit collusion.*

Cartels The most formal type of overt collusion is the cartel, which is an arrangement whereby firms agree to establish a central authority that determines the price and output for the industry, tells firms how much each should produce, and regulates marketing by individual firms. The cartel can thus behave as a pure monopolist. Profit-maximizing output is determined by aggregating the firms' marginal costs to derive the industry's marginal cost curve and find the quantity at which marginal costs and marginal revenues are equal.

The cartel then allocates output quotas among the firms, such that each firm is operating at the same marginal cost. The profit of each firm is the difference between the industry price and its own average total cost at the output allocated to it. Individual firms thus have an incentive to reduce their marginal costs relative to those of other firms, because this increases both their quota and their profit on each unit. While this arrangement would maximize joint profits, cartels are unlikely to obtain the agreement of all firms.

Cartels were common in Europe during the 1920s and 1930s but are now forbidden in most countries by anti-trust, anti-combine, or unfair trade practice legislation. However, international groups such as OPEC (Organization of Petroleum Exporting Countries) closely resemble cartels and continue to exist because they are subject to no other authority. Less formal but explicit collusion in the form of price schedules that reflect the joint-profit-maximization price can also be agreed upon without the formal machinery of a cartel organization. This too is illegal in most countries. In Canada, collusive agreements are forbidden by the Competition Act.

Tacit Collusion

Tacit or implicit collusion is also generally illegal, but this type is more difficult to identify and prove in the courts. A common form of implicit collusion is *price leadership*. One firm, often the largest in the industry, becomes the acknowledged price setter. Whenever it raises its price, other firms do likewise. This pattern serves to reduce uncertainty because the largest firm, knowing that its costs are likely to be lower than other firms', can expect that other firms will welcome a price increase. Similarly, the smaller firms know that each of the other firms has more to gain by a price increase than by holding price constant, once the industry leader has raised its price. They may also fear retaliation if they refuse to cooperate.

Disintegration of Collusion

In addition to legislation, other factors can prevent or break down collusive activity. These include the *number and size of firms in the industry, the degree of product similarity or differentiation, the rate of technological change, and the temptation to take independent action.* The more firms there are and the more dissimilar they are in size, the weaker will be their sense of interdependence and hence their willingness to act in concert. Agreement is also less easily reached and enforced when seven or eight firms, rather than three or four, are involved. In an industry where there are a few large firms and a number of small ones, the smaller firms may decide they have something to gain by setting prices below those of the large firms and attempting to increase their scale of operation.

The more differentiated are the products of collusive firms, the more likely are their revenue and cost conditions to be different. But even firms producing the same product may have different cost curves, and thus different profit levels at the agreed price. In either case, some firms may decide they can improve their profits by leaving the agreements. Where products are differentiated by quality, firms may not be able to agree on a price differential commensurate with the quality difference. Firms may also believe that they can achieve a greater profit through product differentiation than by cooperation.

In oligopolies where technological change is slow or seems to have been halted, cost conditions are more stable and the possibilities for product differentiation are minimized. Hence there is less incentive for firms to act independently. Conversely, in periods of rapid technological change, each firm may think that by aggressive, individual action it can dominate the others and reduce the importance of their reactions to its own decision.

Finally, there is always the temptation to betray an informal price agreement by offering secret price reductions to a few customers in order to take sales from other firms. Alternatively, a firm may simply declare open price war in the hope of getting and holding customers of the other firms. These secret or open violations of a price agreement are probably the single most significant factor in disrupting collusive activity in an industry. Each firm becomes wary of future agreements with the offender, and often with the other firms as well.

Long-Run Price and Output in Oligopoly

Long-run profit-maximizing price and output decisions are even more difficult for oligopolists than are short-run decisions. In the short run, a firm at least knows its rivals' production capabilities, and hence the range of their possible reactions. In the long run, the possibility of change in plant size and technology increases the firm's uncertainty about its competitors' reactions. Otherwise, the same principles would apply that were described for the long-run decisions of monopolistic and competitive firms, namely that each oligopolistic firm should produce the quantity at which its long-run marginal cost is equal to its long-run marginal revenue. Estimation of long-run costs raises the possibility of economies or diseconomies of scale, and estimation of long-run revenues raises the possibility that other firms will enter the industry. Possible barriers to the entry of other firms are the same as those discussed in explaining the existence of oligopolies: the large investment needed to enter the industry and the cost and other advantages enjoyed by the established firms.

Non-Price Competition   Since joint-profit maximization through collusion is illegal and otherwise difficult, and individual profit-maximizing output is subject to uncertainty, oligopolistic firms are likely to engage in *non-price competition*. This includes the use of advertising and emphasis on product style and quality in order to shift the firm's demand curve to the right, and to make the demand less elastic by increasing product differentiation.

Price decreases, especially the substantial reductions evident in some price wars, often reduce short-run profits and do not result in *permanent gains* in absolute sales or share of the market, since rivals can and usually do follow with similar price decreases. Non-price competition,

Box 18.1

Top Canadian advertisers

The 15 largest buyers of space and time in 1990:

Company	$millions
1 Thomson Group	75.8
2 General Motors	68.3
3 Gov't of Canada	67.3
4 Procter & Gamble	67.2
5 Sears Canada	63.9
6 Molson Breweries	52.7
7 Paramount Commun.	44.7
8 Unilever	43.8
9 Cineplex Odeon	42.9
10 John Labatt	40.9
11 Kraft Foods	39.0
12 George Weston	37.9
13 Eatons	37.6
14 Ontario Gov't	35.9
15 McDonald's	32.5

Figures compiled by Media Measurement Services, Inc., Markham.

Source: *The Globe and Mail*, 2 April 1991.

The largest advertising budgets are usually associated with oligopolistic firms. The above data on Canada's major advertisers indicate that the soap, beer, and automobile producers—with only slightly differentiated products—are among the major advertisers.

The federal and provincial governments need to provide their public with information about programs and regulations, and to advertise tourist attractions; but some critics argue that the governing party also advertises to differentiate itself from the opposition parties and thereby retain political support.

however, may enable a firm to make slower but permanent gains. Advertising and design changes, of course, increase a firm's costs; hence, non-price competition may be seen as a kind of cost competition—an attempt to increase marginal revenue as much as possible for a given increase in marginal cost.

Massive advertising has also been shown to form a barrier to the entry of other firms. A potential new firm would not only need to match the large advertising budgets of existing firms; it might need to spend even more to alter the attitudes and habits of buyers in an established market.

Another advantage of non-price competition is that *competitors' reactions* to non-price actions can usually be predicted with more certainty than otherwise. An advertising campaign tends to provoke a similar campaign, style changes are countered with similar style changes, and promotional games and contests soon compete with other such attractions. Moreover, the cost of an advertising campaign is known in advance; the cost of a price war in terms of increased costs and decreased profits is much less certain. Through non-price competition, a firm hopes that it can do better than its rivals in altering its product or image, and therefore achieve a permanent gain, even if its rivals attempt to do the same.

Review of the Main Points

1. Pure monopoly is a market in which only one firm produces a commodity for which there are no close substitutes. Monopoly exists because other firms are prevented from entering the industry by barriers such as patents, public utilities, restricted access to raw materials, and economies of scale.

2. A monopolist can set the price of its product according to the quantity it decides to produce. Its demand curve is also the market demand curve; since there are no close substitutes this curve is less elastic than the demand curve facing a firm in any other market structure. There is no supply curve for a monopolist because it does not adjust the quantity produced to a given market price.

3. A monopolist maximizes profit (or minimizes loss) by producing the quantity at which marginal cost equals marginal revenue. A monopolist does not necessarily make a profit. Marginal revenue, the change in total revenue for each unit of output, declines with increasing output: the marginal revenue curve is downward-sloping and lies below the average revenue curve.

4. Price discrimination is charging different prices to different buyers of the same commodity produced under the same cost conditions. This is possible when the commodity cannot be transferred or resold because it is a service, or when buyers are not aware that others are paying a different price, or when there is a barrier to the transfer of the commodity. A special case of price discrimination is charging a single buyer lower prices for additional quantities. The perfect price discriminator, who could charge a different price for each unit sold, would produce the quantity at which marginal cost was equal to price and would have a higher output and profit than if it charged only one price.

5. Monopolistic competition describes a market or industry in which there are many small firms selling similar but not identical products; the market share of any firm is too small for it to be concerned about reactions of other firms. Products are different enough that the demand curve facing each firm is not perfectly elastic. There is

also easy entry to the industry. The firm's profit-maximizing output
level occurs where marginal cost equals marginal revenue, but by
changing its selling costs the firm may be able to alter its demand
curve and hence its maximum-profit output level.

6. In the long run, new firms will enter a monopolistically competitive
industry where pure profits have been realized; the result will be to
shift the demand curves facing existing firms to the left, until
all firms make only normal profits. The downward slope of the
demand curve, however, means that this break-even point will
occur at a lower quantity, higher price, and higher average cost
than occurred in pure competition.

7. An oligopoly is an industry or market with so few firms that the
actions of one firm affect the decisions of other firms in the industry. Oligopolies develop where there are economies of scale, cost
advantages for particular firms, and a tendency for firms to merge.

8. Behaviour of oligopolists may depend on whether other firms
in their industry produce the same or slightly different products. In
the latter case, oligopolists are sometimes assumed to face a kinked
demand curve: an increase in price will not be matched by other
firms but a decrease will be. A firm's price can therefore remain the
same even if there is a change in the marginal cost.

9. Firms in undifferentiated-product oligopolies tend to practise collusion, agreeing to set a common price for their products in order to
maximize the total profit for the industry. Collusion is illegal in
most countries, but governments can control overt or explicit collusion such as a cartel more easily than tacit or implicit collusion such
as price leadership. Collusion is less stable where there are more
firms and firms of varying sizes, where products are less similar, and
where technological change occurs more quickly.

10. Oligopolists engage in non-price competition such as advertising
and other forms of sales promotion to avoid the less predictable
effects of price wars.

Key Concepts and Topics

imperfect competition

monopoly power

pure monopoly

price discrimination

oligopoly

perfect price discrimination

monopolistic competition

selling costs

barriers to entry

interdependence of oligopolists

patent

differentiated products

natural monopoly

kinked demand curve

franchise

collusion (overt vs. tacit)

long-run marginal cost

price leadership

monopolist's long-run equilibrium

non-price competition

Questions for Review and Discussion

1. Why are there numerous retail automobile dealers but only a few automobile producers?

2. List several monopolistically competitive firms whose products you buy. What are the specific features of the products that led you to describe the firms as monopolistically competitive?

3. It has been claimed that advertising reduces product prices and also that it increases product prices. Could each claim be correct? Under what conditions?

4. "The greater the degree of interdependence among firms in an oligopoly, the greater will be the pressure for collusion among them." Do you agree? Why?

5. Would an increase in the size of the market (the number of potential buyers) for a particular commodity increase or reduce the degree of competition? Explain.

6. "Price discrimination increases monopolists' profits and therefore cannot be justified from the consumers' point of view." Explain why you agree or disagree.

Sources and Selected Readings

Clarkson, Kenneth, and Roger Miller. *Industrial Organization*. New York: McGraw-Hill, 1982.

Friedman, James W. *Oligopoly Theory*. New York: Cambridge University Press, 1987.

Hirshleifer, Jack. *Price Theory and Applications*, 4th ed. Englewood Cliffs, N.J.: Prentice-Hall, 1988.

Eckert, R.D., and R.H. Leftwich. *The Price System and Resource Allocation*, 10th ed. Hinsdale, Ill.: Dryden Press, 1988.

Stigler, George. "The Literature of Economics: The Case of the Kinked Demand Curve". *Economic Inquiry* 16 (1978): 185–204.

19 Evaluation of Market Structures

Four types of market structure have been described in the preceding chapters: perfect competition, pure monopoly, oligopoly (of two types), and monopolistic competition. As a first step toward understanding the significance of alternative market structures, the *conduct* or *behaviour* of firms and industries under each alternative was examined in terms of output, prices, responses to competitors' decisions, collusive activity, product differentiation, and non-price competition. Table 19.1 presents a summary of the major features distinguishing different basic market structures.

Performance of Firms

An evaluation of alternative market structures cannot be based only on the conduct of firms. Collusive activity, for example, cannot be judged desirable or otherwise without evaluating its consequences. A further step is therefore required, namely, an evaluation of the performance of firms in terms of their contribution to general economic objectives. It is here that the elaboration of market structure models becomes most useful.

No single theory of the firm can include all characteristics of each firm in an economy when there is such a diversity. Comparing the characteristics and behaviour of any given firm with those in the market structure models, however, often makes it possible to place the firm in a particular category and thus predict how it will perform.

Criteria for evaluating the performance of firms include:

- the efficient use of productive resources;
- innovation in products and techniques to stimulate and adapt to technological change; and
- contribution to product variety, providing a broad range of choice to correspond with the range of effective consumer demand for goods and services.

Table 19.1

Distinguishing Features of Market Structures

Features	Perfect Competition	Monopolistic Competition	Imperfect Competition		Pure Monopoly
			Oligopoly		
			Different Products	Standard Product	
Number of Sellers	many	several	few	few	one
Product Differentiation	none	much (also differing service, location)	little to some	little or none	one product, no close substitutes
Typical Demand Facing Firm	perfectly elastic	quite elastic	moderately elastic, perhaps kinked	same as market, if collusion exists	slightly elastic, as for market
Control over Price	none	little	some	some	much
Competitor Reaction	none	little	much	much	none
Barriers to Entry	none	slight or none	some	some	complete
Examples	some products in agriculture and fishing	some retail stores, clothing, furniture	automobiles, gasoline, cigarettes	aluminum, steel, cement	rare (some public utilities)

Efficiency

Relative efficiency in the use of productive resources within alternative market structures can be judged, given some strict assumptions, by comparing firms' long-run equilibrium positions. These equilibrium positions are valid, however, only as statements of the *tendencies* of firms, because long-run equilibrium is seldom reached: forces inevitably emerge to change the firm's long-run cost or revenue conditions.

Figures 19.1 to 19.3 compare the short- and long-run equilibrium positions of firms in perfect competition, monopolistic competition, and pure monopoly. Oligopoly is omitted to avoid complicating the comparison further, and because the two general cases of oligopoly can be roughly approximated by either pure monopoly or monopolistic competition. To clarify the effects of different revenue conditions, the same cost curves are assumed for each type of firm.

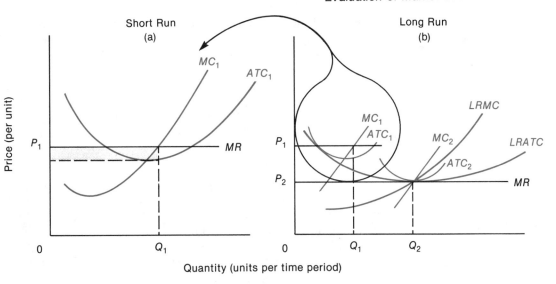

Figure 19.1   Firm in Perfect Competition
A perfectly competitive firm can realize a pure profit in the short run but not
in the long run, at which point it reaches its optimum scale (ATC_2) and
capacity, Q_2. Its price, P_2, equals *LRMC*.

Perfect Competition   The perfectly competitive firm may make a pure profit in the short run;
it is doing so in Figure 19.1a. Because the firm faces a perfectly elastic
demand curve, its marginal revenue is the average revenue for each
level of output. Its profit-maximizing output, Q_1, at which marginal
cost equals marginal revenue, therefore is priced at marginal cost, P_1.
However, it is not necessarily producing at the minimum short-run average total cost. The latter would occur only if the demand curve happened to be tangent to the short-run average total cost curve, ATC_1.

In the long run (Figure 19.1b), the firm produces the quantity, Q_2, at
which its long-run marginal cost equals its marginal revenue. Again, its
perfectly elastic demand curve is also its marginal revenue curve, and
long-run output is priced at marginal cost. Because other firms have
been attracted into the industry by short-run profits, the demand curve
facing an original firm is lower than it was in the short run. The downward shift of the firms' demand curves and their expansion of plant size
continue until no pure profit can be made, that is, until long-run average total cost is equal to average revenue or price. Thus, in the long
run, the purely competitive firm's output is produced at the minimum cost; output is as large and price as low as possible under perfect
competition.

Monopolistic   The monopolistically competitive firm may make a short-run pure
Competition   profit; it is doing so in Figure 19.2a. Because the firm faces a downward-
sloping demand curve, its short-run profit-maximizing output, Q_3, is
priced above marginal cost. The difference between marginal cost and
price is not large, however, because the typical demand curve facing
this firm is quite elastic; the marginal revenue curve thus lies not far
below the demand curve. Short-run output would be produced at the
minimum average total cost only if the marginal revenue curve happened to intersect the ATC_1 curve at its minimum point.

In the long run (Figure 19.2b), the firm increases its plant size to produce the quantity, Q_4, where its long-run marginal cost equals its marginal revenue. The entry of other firms attracted by short-run pure
profits shifts downward the long-run demand and marginal revenue
curve, until no pure profit can be made. However, the downward slope
of the demand curve causes this point to be reached to the left of the
minimum point of the long-run average total cost curve. *Given the same
cost conditions for perfectly competitive and monopolistically competitive firms, the long-run output of the latter firms will always be less, and
the price will be more, than for the former. Furthermore, long-run output, Q_4, will be priced above marginal cost and produced at more than
the minimum of the long-run average total cost.*

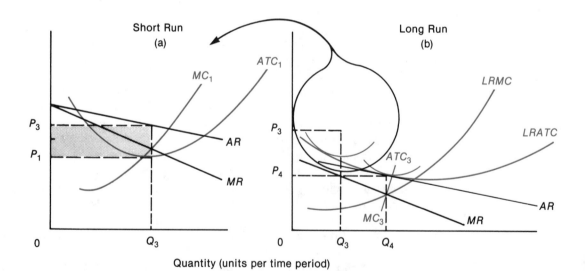

Figure 19.2   Firm in Monopolistic Competition
A monopolistically competitive firm makes no pure profit in the long run,
does not produce at its lowest possible *LRATC*, and its price, P_4, exceeds
its *LRMC*.

Pure Monopoly The pure monopoly firm may make a pure profit in the short run; it is doing so in Figure 19.3. The demand curve it faces is generally less elastic than that for the monopolistically competitive firm; hence, its marginal revenue curve lies farther below its average revenue curve at any given quantity, and there is a greater difference between the marginal cost and price of its profit-maximizing output, Q_5. (Again, short-run output would be produced at the minimum average total cost only if the marginal revenue curve happened to intersect the ATC_1 curve at its minimum point.)

Since new firms cannot enter the industry, the demand curve will not shift in the long run (Figure 19.3b), other things being equal. The firm may, however, need to increase its plant size to produce the output, Q_6, at which its long-run marginal cost equals marginal revenue. If output is increased, pure profit will also increase, otherwise the monopolist would not alter its output. Although the price decreases, there is a greater difference between marginal cost and price. As in the short run, output will be produced at the minimum average total cost only if the marginal revenue happens to intersect the *LRATC* curve at its minimum point. This is illustrated in Figure 19.4. If the marginal revenue curve is MR_1, marginal revenue equals long-run marginal cost at Q_1.

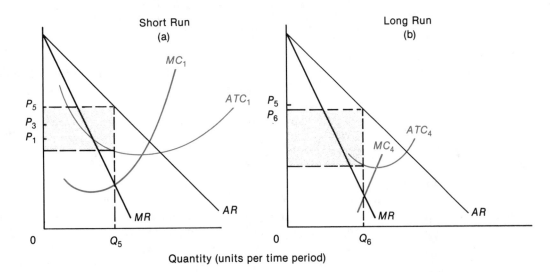

Figure 19.3 A Monopoly
A monopoly firm can realize a long-run profit and usually produces with excess capacity and at a scale (ATC_4) that does not realize further potential economies of scale. Its long-run price, P_6, is much higher than its MC at Q_6.

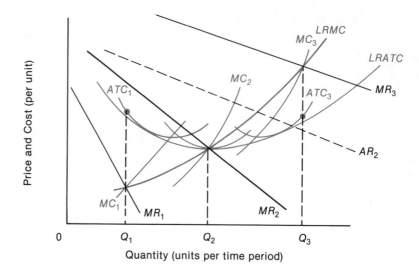

Figure 19.4   A Monopoly May Produce below, at, or above Its Optimum Scale
Depending on the relationship between a monopoly's marginal revenue and marginal cost curves, a monopoly may produce in the long run below, at, or above its optimum scale. When marginal revenue is MR_1, the firm produces Q_1 at less than optimum capacity and scale. At MR_3, it produces Q_3 at more than optimum capacity and with decreasing returns to scale. If the demand curve happens to be AR_2, the firm produces Q_2, at which $LRMC$ equals MR_2, at the optimum capacity and scale that would also be the long-run equilibrium position of a purely competitive firm. However, the monopolist realizes a profit since AR_2 is above $LRATC$ at output Q_2.

The lowest short-run marginal cost for Q_1 is realized with a plant size represented by ATC_1. If marginal revenue is MR_3, output is Q_3, and is produced at an average total cost shown by ATC_3. Only in rare cases, if marginal revenue is MR_2, is the output Q_2 produced at the lowest long-run average total cost. However, the price is greater than the average cost, and a pure profit is also realized in the long run.

Oligopoly   In the short run, the oligopolist *may* make a pure profit and will price its output above marginal cost; only by coincidence will it be operating at its minimum average total cost. In the long run, if there is freedom to enter the oligopolistic industry, the equilibrium condition resembles that of monopolistic competition, to the extent that the demand curve facing a firm is shifted downward until it is tangent to the long-run average total cost curve and no pure profit is realized. Because the oligopolist's demand curve typically has a greater slope, output is produced at a cost further above the minimum average total cost than in the case of monopolistic competition.

If, however, there are substantial barriers to entering the industry, there will not be enough new firms to shift the firm's demand curve downward to the point of tangency with long-run average total cost. The situation then resembles that of pure monopoly, in which long-run pure profit is possible and output might only by chance be produced at minimum average total cost. In either long-run case, however, oligopolist firms price their output above minimum average cost.

Comparative Efficiency

The efficiency of firms under alternative market structures may be compared on two grounds: optimum scale of plant and rate of output, and equality of price with marginal cost.

Optimum Scale and Output   The *optimum rate of output* is defined as *the quantity at which the short-run average total cost is at a minimum*. The *optimum scale of plant* is the one at which *all economies of scale are realized but diseconomies of large scale have not been incurred*. It is represented by the short-run average total cost curve whose minimum point coincides with the minimum point of the long-run average total cost curve. (See, for example, ATC_2 in Figure 19.1b.) Thus the optimum rate of output using the optimum scale of plant is the quantity at which long-run average total cost is at a minimum. (Note: Optimum output should not be confused with the profit-maximizing level of output.)

A brief review of the firms' performance shows that the long-run tendency is for perfect competition to lead to both the optimum scale of plant and the optimum rate of output for that scale.

Production under perfect competition is therefore at the lowest possible average total cost.

Under monopolist competition, firms do not quite reach the optimum scale, and they produce at less than the optimum rate of output for that plant size. *This is the general criticism of monopolistic competition: that there is necessarily an underutilization of resources because firms operate with excess productive capacity.* Similarly, in an oligopoly to which there is free entry, and in which firms face a less elastic demand curve than in monopolistic competition, firms tend to have a still smaller than optimum plant size and to produce at still less than the optimum rate of output. *The result is that there may be even more excess capacity in a free-entry oligopoly than in monopolistic competition.*

Whether firms in pure monopoly and restricted-entry oligopoly will produce at the optimum scale and rate of output is uncertain — but quite unlikely. As explained above, this would occur simply by chance. The probability therefore is that they will produce in plants either smaller or larger than the optimum; *there will thus likely be some inefficient use of resources in pure monopoly and restricted-entry oligopoly.*

Price and Marginal Cost   *Only in perfect competition is the price of the output equal to its marginal cost,* because only in this case are the firms facing a perfectly elastic demand curve. (A monopoly that can practise perfect price discrimination prices only the *final* unit of output at marginal cost.)

This second case of efficiency relates to maximizing consumer satisfaction or consumer surplus, given the resources available. Consumers are willing to pay more than the price charged for every unit preceding the last unit sold. The lower the price and the greater the quantity, the greater will be consumer surplus associated with any commodity. Now turn to Figure 19.5. Under monopoly, output will be Q_1, priced at P_1. Consumer surplus is represented by the area P_0P_1A. If the industry illustrated in Figure 19.5 is in perfect competition, however, the marginal cost curve is the industry's supply curve. Output will be Q_2 and priced at P_2. Consumer surplus is P_0P_2B, and clearly much greater than if the industry is a monopoly.

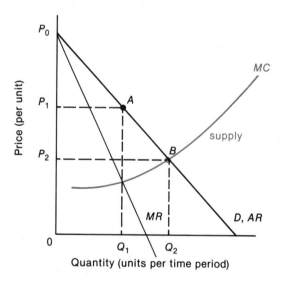

Figure 19.5   Marginal Cost Pricing Maximizes Consumer Surplus
A monopoly facing the cost and revenue conditions shown here will produce Q_1 and sell its output at price P_1. Consumer surplus is represented by area P_0P_1A. A purely competitive industry with the same cost and revenue conditions will supply Q_2, which will be sold at price P_2. Consumer surplus will be increased to P_0P_2B. One advantage of competition for consumers is the increased consumer surplus represented by P_1P_2BA.

Furthermore, output under perfect competition is increased to the point where the marginal cost of producing the last unit is just equal to the marginal utility derived from this last unit, as evidenced by the price consumers are willing to pay. Resources are being used as efficiently as possible to provide consumer satisfaction or utility. When this condition is realized in all markets, the maximum possible consumer satisfaction is reached.

Pure Profit   Note that whether pure profit is possible is not an issue in evaluating the performance of firms. In the long run, monopolistically competitive firms, for example, do not realize a pure profit, but they do price output above marginal cost and operate with less than the optimum plant scale. The persistence of profits in the long run is of interest, however, as evidence that there is restricted entry to the industry and thus that an oligopolistic or monopolistic situation exists.

How Valid Are the Assumptions?   Two of the assumptions made in comparing the efficiency of resource use under alternative market structures have important implications for this evaluation. One assumption is that *the market is large enough to accommodate many firms*, each of which can attain the optimum plant size in the long run. However, the long-run cost conditions may be such that the optimum output is, for example, 100 units per day produced at a marginal cost and price of $2.00. Market demand may be such that, at this price, only 300 units can be sold per day: only three firms can exist in what would then become an oligopolistic industry. The first three firms to enlarge their plants to this optimum size would survive, and the others would leave the industry.

Changes in technology, often requiring larger fixed costs for more complex equipment, have tended to increase the optimum plant size. In some industries, these changes have occurred faster than the expansion of demand for the industries' products and thus have reduced the number of firms in the industry. If the number of firms were to be increased artificially, by government regulation or court order, the result likely would be lower output and higher prices.

A second major assumption underlying the comparative efficiency of alternative market structures is that these structures have *no differential effect on cost conditions*. However, there may be monetary economies or diseconomies to be realized by having fewer firms produce any given level of output. This is not a case of economies of scale within a firm. Rather, it is, for example, the consequence of having one firm instead of ten firms buying raw materials, or one firm instead of one hundred firms hiring semiskilled labour. One large firm can usually influence prices of its inputs more than can a single small firm.

Innovation and Costs

A second general criterion for evaluating the performance of firms is their record for innovation: the use of new raw materials, new sources of existing raw materials, new techniques or processes, and the development of new products, or improved quality in existing products. The latter two types of innovation are discussed in the next section; the first three are considered here because each of them can potentially reduce production costs for existing products.

From the firm's point of view, the *incentive to innovate* is the possibility of larger profits through cost reductions. A special case of this condition, of course, is the incentive to maintain existing profits, or even to survive as new firms enter the industry or market demand falls. All types of firms can realize a profit in the short run and thus all have an incentive to innovate within this period. But the range of potential short-run innovations is limited to changes in the variable inputs: alternative sources of labour or raw materials might be found or a new raw material might be used, provided that these can be substituted within the constraints of the fixed plant and equipment.

In the long run, only the monopolist and restricted-entry oligopolist have an incentive to innovate. Their long-run profits are protected by barriers to entering the industry. Firms under other market structures are unlikely to make long-run innovations because the resulting increased profits would attract even more firms. These newcomers would imitate the cost-reducing innovations of the original firms and wipe out profits for any of them. One important exception occurs when the innovation can be kept secret for some time or, as is commonly the case, if it requires some time to introduce. A perfectly or monopolistically competitive firm might decide that the profit to be made in this interim was sufficient to undertake the innovation.

Since there are usually substantial economies of scale in research and development programs, innovation is also more likely to occur in oligopolies in which the few firms are large enough to undertake their own research and development programs and to introduce a large-scale technique, such as automated assembly, that represents a cost saving only at high levels of output.

One public policy consequence of the lack of incentive for perfectly competitive firms to innovate is that governments sponsor, for example, agricultural research and extension programs in an effort to have agricultural commodities produced at lower cost. This policy is sometimes extended to oligopolistic industries, since lower costs, despite increased pure profits, will lead to lower prices and greater output. Similarly, public policy may be directed to the encouragement of oligopolies that have innovation potential, on the grounds that output will be expanded and will be sold at lower prices, even though there may be a greater difference between price and marginal cost.

Product Variety

Product variety is also a criterion for evaluating the performance of firms, because there is such a great diversity in consumer tastes. A wide choice in products, of varying quality and style, can be produced only at higher cost than if a similar number of identical units were produced. For example, if the only cars made in Canada were standard Fords, Chevrolets, and Dodges, the same number of cars could be supplied each year at lower per-unit costs than when the choice is so much greater. But consumers apparently place a high value on variety in automobile models, colours, and options.

Product variety is likely to be greatest in oligopolies. These firms have a large enough plant size to produce great quantities of a standard unit, such as a basic automobile chassis or washing machine frame, and then add enough superficial features or options to offer several "different" products. Product differentiation also occurs under monopolistic competition, but it more often involves variation that has less effect on costs. The threat that other firms will enter the industry and thus reduce profits means that the monopolistic competitor has little scope for introducing a range of styles or colours if these lead to higher per-unit costs. Perfect competition, by definition, is restricted to one standard product. No variation will emerge under perfect competition unless the market *for each different product* is large enough to support many firms at the optimum plant size; this is obviously quite improbable.

Firms in oligopolies and monopolistic competition will tend to offer different products in an effort to attract sales from their competitors, but the differentiation cannot be so great that it alienates potential customers. North American automobile producers, for example, could have introduced compact cars many years ago, but waited instead until the small-car market was well established and they were forced to compete with imported cars. One of the domestic producers could have introduced compact cars earlier, to offer variety, but this would have involved the risk of losing sales of larger cars to other domestic producers.

Models of Firms' Behaviour: A Critique

The alternative models for behaviour and performance of firms are usually referred to collectively as the *theory of the firm*. This theory is clearly useful for predicting the responses of different types of firms to changing revenue and cost conditions, and for designing public policies to create the industrial organization most favourable to the public interest. The theory of the firm has been subjected to much criticism (and has also been vigorously defended) for many years. Among the continuing objections, the most important are the following: firms do not necessarily have profit maximization as their primary objective; even if they do attempt to maximize profits, they may not produce at the level where marginal cost equals marginal revenue; and even if they do try to do this, firms may not have enough information about costs and revenues at various outputs to use the theory of the firm.

Profit Maximization   Firms' objectives were considered previously in Chapter 17. Although the assumption that profit maximization is the primary objective has had widespread and long support, an alternative hypothesis, that firms seek to maximize sales revenue in order to maximize management's prestige and political power, is also popular. Support for this alternative objective has been cogently presented in J. Kenneth Galbraith's book, *Economics and the Public Purpose*. Galbraith argues that separation of ownership and control of the giant corporations has enabled management — Galbraith calls it the "technostructure" — to set its own objectives. These are primarily related to the security of management's position. This need for security in turn requires managers to retain control, earning sufficient and steady profits to satisfy shareholders and isolating the firm from market disturbances by controlling suppliers of raw products and financing expansion with internal funds. Increasing sales and numbers of products provide both direct job satisfaction and prestige.

All of these conditions, however, can be incorporated within the traditional theory of the firm. Earning sufficient profit, if not maximum profit, requires an analysis of costs and revenues at different output levels. New products cannot be introduced without regard for their effect on the firm's existing profit position; and at some point, sales maximization encounters diseconomies of large scale. However, Galbraith has effectively portrayed in detail the behaviour of oligopolistic firms striving to protect their position from the entry of new firms, and thus the process by which oligopolies have risen to a dominant position in the modern mixed economies.

Markup Pricing   An attack on the hypothesis of pricing according to the demand curve has provided the alternative hypothesis that firms practise *markup pricing: setting a price that is a specified percentage above the producer's average cost per unit*. This argument suggests that firms calculate the average cost per unit for producing their output and add 5, 10, 20, or 50 per cent to this cost to determine the price. Since the average cost frequently does not include all fixed costs, particularly imputed costs of plant and equipment and a normal profit, the markup is expected to cover these as well as to provide a pure profit. A firm's standard markup percentage often sets a base price that can be modified if the firm thinks demand conditions are changing.

If demand and cost conditions are fairly static, the firm can discover the relevant section of its demand curve: a too-high price will result in unsold units and a too-low price will leave the firm unable to fill all orders. A price that just clears its output identifies one point on its demand curve. Since the difference between its total cost and total revenue at this price is the firm's total profit for that level of output, the firm, by altering its output level in either direction, can determine the direction it must move to increase its profit, until it has identified a maximum profit output. Earlier it was shown that the output at which total revenue exceeded total cost by the greatest amount is also the output at which marginal cost equals marginal revenue. *Thus, by a trial-and-error process, the firm arrives at the point predicted by the theory of the firm.* It is not important to the theory that the firm determines its output by explicitly equating marginal cost and marginal revenue, but simply that it act as if it did this. Given this, the theory remains a valid tool for explaining and predicting firms' behaviour.

Cost and Revenue Information   Another criticism of the theory of the firm is that it assumes that firms have full information about their cost curves and the demand curve they face. One answer is given above: firms may discover the relevant portion of the demand curve by offering various quantities at different prices. The firm may also estimate a larger segment of its demand curve by observing the experience of other firms with similar products, or it may simply ask consumers, as part of its market research program, how much they would buy at various prices.

Some cost curves are more difficult to estimate than are the demand curves. Fixed costs can be determined with reasonable accuracy, except in firms that produce several products using the same plant and senior management. Variable costs present a greater problem due to the difficulty of estimating the marginal productivity associated with successive units of productive factors such as labour. Firms thus tend to assume that marginal productivity and prices of productive factors do not vary with output, at least over the relevant quantity range, and thus implicitly assume constant marginal costs. As suggested previously, actual experience shows this to be a reasonable or workable assumption in many cases.

Review of the Main Points

1. The performance of firms under alternative market structures can be evaluated in terms of their efficiency, innovation, and product variety.
2. Perfectly competitive firms are more efficient than other firms in their use of resources because, in the long run, they produce at the lowest possible average total cost. This occurs in monopoly and restricted-entry oligopoly only if the firms' marginal revenue curves intersect their *LRATC* curves at the lowest point.

3. Only in perfect competition do firms price their output at marginal cost. These advantages of perfect competition assume that the market is large enough to accommodate many firms, and that firms' cost conditions are the same, regardless of the market structure.

4. Although all firms, regardless of market structure, may make a pure profit in the short run, and therefore have an incentive to innovate, long-run innovations will occur only under monopoly and restricted-entry oligopoly.

5. Product variety is likely to be greatest in oligopolies.

6. An examination of some basic criticisms of the theory of the firm indicates that these criticisms do not invalidate the predictions yielded by the theory, even though firms may not follow the same reasoning, in determining their level of output, that economists use in explaining why that is the level that firms will tend to choose.

Key Concepts and Topics

efficiency	innovation
optimum rate of output	product variety
optimum scale	markup pricing
marginal cost pricing	theory of the firm

Questions for Review and Discussion

1. If innovations, produced under conditions of imperfect competition, improve the efficiency in the use of resources, why should perfect competition continue to be an economic ideal?

2. Distinguish between innovation and product variety as desirable features of market structures. Which would you rate more highly, and why?

3. There are no cases of the perfectly competitive ideal in the real world, but are there any cases of monopolistic competition? Describe these carefully in terms of their product differentiation and freedom of entry.

4. Distinguish between optimum rate of output, optimum scale of plant, and profit-maximizing output. Are there any cases when the three concepts are coincident, that is, when a given level of output would be representative of each condition?

5. "The degree of excess capacity in a firm depends on the price elasticity of demand for its product." Do you agree? Why?

6. Explain carefully why $P = MC$ is a necessary condition for the most efficient use of resources.

Sources and Selected Readings

Clarkson, Kenneth, and Roger Miller. *Industrial Organization.* New York: McGraw-Hill, 1982.

Friedman, James W. *Oligopoly Theory.* New York: Cambridge University Press, 1987.

Hirshleifer, Jack. *Price Theory and Applications,* 4th ed. Englewood Cliffs, N.J.: Prentice-Hall, 1988.

Eckert, R.D., and R.H. Leftwich. *The Price System and Resource Allocation,* 10th ed. Hinsdale, Ill.: Dryden Press, 1988.

20 Industrial Organization and Public Policy

Industrial Organization in Canada

The performance of firms under different types of market structures, as presented in preceding chapters, provides the primary basis for examining government regulation of business. Public policy in this area emphasizes the nature of industrial organization, or the conditions influencing the supply side of product markets. Thus the term "market structure" gives way to the term "industrial organization" in the following discussion. Before turning to specific legislation and government programs, however, it is useful to have an understanding of the number, size, and types of firms in the Canadian economy.

Industrial Concentration

One measure for defining monopoly power in an industry is the *concentration ratio*. This shows the number of sellers in an industry relative to the market size. It is usually defined either as the percentage of total market sales for the four largest firms in the industry, or as the number of firms producing 80 per cent of the industry's output. Variations of these measures are also used: number of employees or value of assets may be substituted for sales.

Evidence on changes in industrial concentration in Canadian manufacturing, using the value of shipments as the concentration measure, is seen in Table 20.1. Industrial concentration increased in Canadian manufacturing during the postwar period. Most of this increase occurred in the early 1950s, with concentration remaining generally stable since the 1970s.[1] Canadian manufacturing is more highly concentrated than American manufacturing, mainly because Canadian

[1] *Report of the Royal Commission on Corporate Concentration*. Ottawa: Supply and Services Canada, 1978, Chapter 2.

markets are much smaller while firms generally are not much smaller than American firms. Moreover, national data understate the degree of concentration in local markets. While the focus here is on manufacturing because detailed data are available, it should be noted that manufacturing accounts for roughly 20 per cent of the GDP and total employment; in other sectors there may be greater or less industrial concentration.

Size of Firms

Another dimension of industrial organization is the size of firms, which can be measured in terms of sales, employees, or assets. Size is assumed to be important in determining whether firms are likely to be realizing economies of scale, and indirectly suggests areas where industrial concentration may be high. Some evidence on the relative size of manufacturing establishments in Canada can be seen in Table 20.2. Note that establishments producing goods valued at less than $500,000 annually in 1986 represented 42 per cent of the total number of manufacturing establishments, but produced only 1.3 per cent of the total value of output. At the other end of the size scale, establishments that individually produced at least $10 million in goods annually accounted for only 11 per cent of all establishments, but produced over 80 per cent of the total value of output.

Table 20.1

Concentration in the Largest[1] Manufacturing Industries, Canada, 1982 and 1965

	1982		1965	
Industry	No. of Enterprises	Concentration Ratio[2]	No. of Enterprises	Concentration Ratio[2]
		(%)		(%)
Motor vehicle manufacturers	14	95	20	93
Iron and steel mills	37	82	32	79
Petroleum refining	16	61	12	84
Motor vehicle parts manufacturers	286	50	149	54
Slaughtering and meat processors	426	40	365	48
Dairy products	236	40	1,165	25
Paper and pulp mills	57	40	56	37
Sawmills and planing mills	1,081	18	2,464	17

Source: Statistics Canada, *Industrial Organization and Concentration in the Manufacturing, Mining and Logging Industries.*

[1] Size is based on total value of shipments in 1982.
[2] Concentration ratio defined here as the percentage of industry's total value-of-shipments accounted for by the four largest firms or enterprises in the industry.

Some of these large firms are included in the list in Table 20.3. Such a list is interesting because it shows that size tends to be associated with the automobile and petroleum industries. But it has limited significance for economic analysis since sales data are not strictly comparable and since other firms are omitted for lack of data.

Table 20.2

Size of Manufacturing Establishments, Canada, 1986

Production ($ thousands)	Percentage of the total number of establishments	Percentage of the total value of production
0-100	12	0.1
100-200	12	0.3
200-500	18	0.9
500-1,000	14	1.5
1,000-5,000	26	9.3
5,000-10,000	7	7.8
10,000-25,000	6	13.8
25,000-50,000	3	13.1
50,000 and over	2	53.3
Total per cent	100	100.0
number	38,380	253.4 billion

Source: Statistics Canada, *Manufacturing Industries of Canada.*

Table 20.3

Ten of the Largest Firms in Canada, Measured by Sales, 1989

Company	Sales ($ billions)
General Motors of Canada	19.7
Bell Canada Enterprises (BCE Inc.)	16.7
Ford Motor Co. of Canada	15.3
Canadian Pacific Ltd.	11.0
George Weston Ltd.	10.5
Alcan Aluminum Ltd.	10.5
Imperial Oil Ltd.	10.0
Noranda Inc.	9.3
Chrysler Canada Ltd.	8.2
Brascan Ltd.	6.8

Source: *The Financial Post 500.*

Type of Firm

The legal form or organization of the individual firm is another aspect of industrial organization. This has been of less importance to economic analysis than industrial concentration or size of firms, largely because one type of organization—the corporation—accounts for a very large proportion of the economy's output. Nonetheless, it is useful to examine the different types of firms to understand why corporations have attained this dominant position, and why the behaviour of some larger corporations has spurred the suggestion that not all firms hold profit maximization as their primary objective.

There are four basic forms of business organization: single proprietorships, partnerships, corporations, and cooperatives. Corporations can be further classified as holding companies, public or crown corporations, corporations holding either provincial or national charters, and multinational corporations.

The relative importance of these forms of business in manufacturing is illustrated by Table 20.4. In 1986, about 90 per cent of the establishments in manufacturing were corporations, but they accounted for 98 per cent of the total sales; fewer than one-tenth were proprietorships, but they produced less than one per cent of the total sales. Proprietorships are more significant in retailing than in most other industries, both in percentage of establishments and of sales, but again corporations dominate with the large majority of the sales. In fact, corporations account for the largest share of sales in every broad industry group except agriculture. In 1986, about 90 per cent of Canada's farms were single proprietorships.

Single Proprietorships

A single proprietorship is a business or firm wholly owned by one person. The owner almost always manages or operates the business, although there may be a number of employees. Proprietorships can be established easily—by simply going to the city hall to complete a business registration form. Certain types of business also require an annual business licence. Single proprietorships predominate among retail and service establishments such as confectioneries, cigar stores, and restaurants, and in professional groups such as doctors, dentists, engineers, and consultants of various kinds. Farmers are also mainly single proprietors.

Proprietorships are usually restricted to businesses with low financial requirements, because the individual owners must rely on their own assets and whatever they can borrow personally. Moreover, they are often unwilling to undertake large financial ventures because they are

Table 20.4

Type of Organization in Canadian Manufacturing

	Manufacturing			
	Percentage of Establishments		Percentage of Sales	
	1971	1986	1971	1986
Proprietorships	22	8	1	*
Partnerships	6	2	*	*
Corporations	71	90	97	98
Cooperatives	2	*	2	1
Totals	31,908	38,380	$50.3 billion	$253.4 billion

Source: Statistics Canada, *Manufacturing Industries of Canada.*

* less than 1 per cent.

subject to *unlimited liability*. This means that creditors can claim personal assets such as a home, automobile, and furniture, as well as business assets, should the proprietor be unable to meet financial obligations. One result of unlimited liability has been a greater use of the bankruptcy law, whereby an individual can declare bankruptcy or inability to meet all claims. The individual can then accumulate personal and business assets again that cannot be claimed by previous creditors.

The major disadvantage of the proprietorship is the difficulty it imposes on obtaining financing to expand a successful business. Profits of proprietorships are taxed as individual income; the owner may find that he or she is paying as much as 50 per cent of net profit in taxes and thus cannot depend on savings for business expansion. Borrowing requires collateral, which may involve pledging some personal assets and perhaps buying additional life insurance. Interest rates paid by small businesses for borrowed funds are usually higher than the rates paid by larger corporations.

Proprietorships come to an end with the owner's death or the sale of the proprietorship's assets to another person or firm.

Partnerships

A partnership is a firm formed by two or more persons who agree to own and operate a single business. The partnership agreement usually specifies what each partner contributes to the firm in terms of funds, management, physical assets, or even prestige; how each will share in the profits or losses; and what each will receive should the business be dissolved.

Forming a partnership is one way for a single proprietor to obtain financing for a business expansion. It may also provide a means for joining with another single proprietor in a related business, or acquiring some special managerial or technical talent.

Partnerships are subject to the same unlimited liability described for single proprietorships. Each partner should therefore have an equal share in the firm's decisions, although each partner can act independently in the name of the firm, committing other partners to this action, unless restrictions on individual action have been agreed to previously. Partnerships may also include "limited partners" who contribute funds but who do not participate in managing the firm, and who are liable only to the extent of their financial contributions.

A partnership is dissolved by the death or withdrawal of one of the partners. Although it can be re-established by the agreement of the remaining partners, other partners may use the occasion to leave the partnership, perhaps because they must find the funds to purchase part of the share held by the deceased or withdrawing partner. This uncertainty in the partnership's lifespan can be a serious disadvantage to a successful, growing firm, which needs permanence for financing and for holding skilled employees.

Corporations

A corporation is distinguished from a proprietorship or a partnership by two main features: it has *limited liability* and is a *separate legal entity*.

Limited Liability *Limited liability means that persons who own part of a company are financially liable only for the particular share of the firm's assets they own.* Creditors of an incorporated firm cannot make claims beyond this on the personal and other business assets of individual owners, should a firm be unable to meet its obligations. This feature has made it possible for corporations to raise substantial sums by offering small shares to a large number of individuals.

The limited liability feature applies not only to the firms that are listed for trading on the public stock exchanges, but also to the firms owned privately by a few persons. These are the private companies whose shares are not offered to the general public. Many family businesses have been limited private corporations in the past, but are gradually "going public" as the need arises for more financing to maintain or expand the business.

Separate Legal Entity   Corporations are created by the granting of a provincial or federal charter that gives them the right to engage in specific business activities, as separate legal entities. This means that corporations have *the same legal rights and responsibilities as an adult human being under civil law regarding property and contracts*. The chief executive officers of a corporation can, however, be prosecuted personally for offences under the criminal law, even though the actions were taken in the name of the firm.

A corporation can be a more permanent form of business than a partnership or a proprietorship: its lifespan is terminated only if it seriously deviates from its stated (albeit broadly worded) purposes or if its directors so decide. This feature is important in raising funds since owners know that, provided the corporation is soundly managed, they will be able to sell their shares at some future time. Furthermore, specialized or skilled personnel can be more easily attracted because there are reasonable prospects of permanent employment.

Corporation Financing

Corporations obtain financing by issuing shares, selling bonds, or using retained earnings.

Stocks or Shares   A stock certificate is evidence of a share in the ownership of a corporation; the terms "stock" and "share" are thus often used interchangeably. Stocks are further classified as common stocks or preferred stocks.

Common stocks are the basic stocks issued by all corporations. A stockholder receives one vote in the general affairs of the corporation for each common stock held; any individual or group holding 51 per cent of the common stock would therefore be able to control the corporation. In cases where the stock is held by a very large number of persons, control of the corporation can sometimes be gained by holding only 10 to 20 per cent of the stock.

There is no guarantee that a stockholder will obtain the original price of the stock when it is sold or receive any return on this asset, but any profits the corporation may realize and decide to distribute are paid out as dividends in proportion to the number of stocks held.

Preferred stocks also represent ownership in the corporation, but the holder of preferred stock surrenders voting rights in exchange for "preferences". These include a stated annual rate of return on the face value of the share, the guarantee that this dividend will be paid before dividends are paid on common stocks, and a prior claim against the corporation's assets should it be dissolved. Although the preferred stock carries a stated rate of return, this payment does not need to be made if there is insufficient profit. Preferred stock therefore sometimes has additional features: a *cumulative preferred stock*, for example, provides for the cumulation of stated dividends until profits are large enough to meet these accumulated obligations.

Corporate Bonds   Corporate bonds differ substantially from stocks, in that the amount of the bond must be repaid on or before the stated maturity date, and interest payments generally must be made annually unless alternative provisions are made. The bond holder is thus a creditor rather than a part-owner of the corporation and, as such, has a prior claim on the corporation's assets in the event of dissolution.

Internal Financing   The increasing size of corporations, which is usually accompanied by a greater total profit, has made it possible for more corporations to meet their financing needs internally. When expansion or alterations are planned, the directors may decide not to pay dividends and to retain the net profits or earnings for reinvestment in the corporation. *Retained earnings* provide a major financial source for many corporations; although dividends are less than they would be otherwise, retained earnings increase the value of the common stock. Another internal source is the *depreciation allowance* that is set aside each year to provide for the replacement of plant and equipment. Finally, both retained earnings and depreciation allowances may be used to acquire assets such as government bonds or stocks of other companies; the annual income from these supplements the other two sources.

Ownership and Control of Corporations

The separation of ownership and control of corporations has become a popular theme in the criticism of corporations. Reference was made in the previous chapter to Galbraith's description of the managerial "technostructure" that gains control of large corporations to pursue its own objectives. This situation arises when shares are widely held; individual investors each hold perhaps only a few hundred shares of possibly three or four million common shares issued. These small shareholders are seldom familiar with the detailed affairs of the corporation and choose not to spend the time or money to travel to the annual meetings. The managers, many of whom are likely also directors, can therefore easily persuade such shareholders to vote by proxy and assign their votes to the controlling group.

When management holds control in this way, they may become less concerned with profits as such because they can vote themselves larger salaries, bonuses, and other benefits. For other shareholders to regain control can be extremely difficult in such circumstances; dramatic "proxy battles" have been fought between incumbent managers and directors and other groups wanting to gain control. An interesting recent development, however, has been the use of annual shareholders' meetings to press policy changes on management. Persons holding perhaps only one or two shares have, through the skillful use of news media, been able to call attention to what they deem the corporation's neglect of specific social and political responsibilities.

Holding Companies

The possibility of maintaining control of a corporation by holding only a small percentage of the stock has stimulated the rise of *holding companies* and *conglomerates*. These are corporations that produce no goods or services but instead are established explicitly for the purpose of holding stock in other companies. A pyramidal structure of corporations can be built up by holding perhaps 40 per cent of the stock in a company that holds controlling interest in two or three other companies, each of which holds controlling interest in a number of other companies. Thus, by investing $5 million in the company at the top of the pyramid, it is possible to control companies whose assets total $100 million or more. Two of the largest holding companies in Canada are Argus Corporation and Power Corporation.

Public Corporations

Crown corporations, or public corporations, enable governments to be directly involved in the provision of goods and services, without this activity being subject to day-to-day politics. A few of these corporations are not far removed from government, since they are *responsible for administrative or supervisory functions comparable to government departments* and draw all of their operating revenue from government budgets. Examples of such corporations at the federal level include the National Research Council, the Atomic Energy Control Board, and the Unemployment Insurance Commission.

Other crown corporations are *responsible for the production or trading of goods and services* and are expected to earn substantial revenues from these activities. Any deficit, however, is provided from government budgets. Examples of these are the Northern Canada Power Commission and Atomic Energy of Canada.

A third group of crown corporations are those that are responsible to Parliament or a provincial legislature but that are *expected to cover all costs from operating revenues*. These include, for example, the provincial hydro-electric power commissions and the Canadian National Railways.

Cooperatives

A cooperative is a unique form of corporation, retaining several of the partnership's features, established by a society of individuals to buy or sell commodities cooperatively, according to a set of principles governing the organization. The cooperative movement originated with a retail store in Rochdale, England, in 1844. The principles governing cooperatives are therefore still commonly referred to as the "Rochdale principles". A similar cooperative store was first established in Canada in 1861. Later, the Antigonish Movement helped Maritimes fishermen start their own cooperatives for selling fish. In the Prairie provinces, grain cooperatives have been an important feature of the social and political, as well as economic, life of the communities.

There are two basic types of cooperatives: *producer cooperatives*, which sell their members' products, and *consumer cooperatives*, which buy goods from wholesalers for retailing to their members or provide financial services such as insurance and loans.

The principles governing most cooperatives include the following:

- each member has one vote, regardless of the number of shares he or she holds in the cooperative, so that control of the society remains democratic;
- each member receives a fixed rate of return on his or her capital contribution to the society, because the society is not intended as a means for increasing one's investment income;
- net earnings or profits are returned to the members in proportion to the purchases made or produce delivered by each member, so that members will be encouraged to use the society.

The major advantage of the cooperative is that it can obtain for individuals the benefits of large-scale selling or buying. The growth of some cooperatives has been restricted because, unable to issue shares or bonds as other corporations do, they have found it difficult to raise capital. Competition with giant retail chains is increasingly difficult. A further issue is that management must be able to deal with the democracy of control by the membership.

Nonetheless, cooperatives have a significant role in some sectors of the economy. Approximately one-third of all agricultural products marketed in Canada are sold through producer cooperatives, mainly the grain cooperatives on the Prairies. The credit unions, and *caisses populaires* in Quebec, account for over 10 per cent of all consumer credit.

Public Policy on Industrial Organization

"Effective Competition"

Among other objectives, public policy on industrial organization is concerned with attaining and supporting an industrial structure that will increase competition and thus foster increased efficiency in resource use and greater total consumer satisfaction. The conditions necessary for an optimal industrial structure, however, are widely considered to be unattainable, if only because the path of technological development appears to be leading the economy further from the basic features of pure competition. Some economists have therefore proposed a modified guide for public policy on industrial organization. This is intended to create what is termed "workable competition" or "effective competition".[2]

Desirable conditions for "workable competition" include a market structure with at least several buyers and a few sellers, but preferably more; a mixture of large and small firms; no collusion or coercion among sellers; as much market information as can possibly be made available to buyers and sellers; and no barriers to entry and exit. These conditions suggest a blend of oligopoly and monopolistic competition, with a leaning toward the latter.

Some existing conditions also contribute to greater competition. These include: the universal competition of producers for the *limited incomes* of consumers, such that producers of a wide variety of household appliances and furniture are effectively in competition with each other (that is, inter-industry competition as well as competition within the industry); the high degree of *substitutability* that exists for many products (aluminum can be substituted for steel or wood in many cases); the rapid pace of invention and *innovation*, which makes it difficult to maintain monopoly power; and finally, *public policy* for strengthening competition, which makes firms cautious about assuming control of markets.

Public policy on industrial organization has emerged slowly, uncertain of how to define competition and wavering under strong, persistent arguments that some industries should have only a few sellers. Different policies have been designed to meet different types of problems: there are policies on monopoly and oligopoly, on the support of existing competition in agriculture, on the protection of consumers by setting standards for products and conduct, and on Canadian ownership and control of industry.

---

[2] J.M. Clark, "Toward a Concept of Workable Competition," *American Economic Review*, Vol. XXX, June 1940, pp. 241-56; also see J.M. Clark, *Competition as a Dynamic Process*. Washington, D.C.: The Brookings Institution, 1961.

Public Policy on Monopoly and Oligopoly

Public policy on monopoly and oligopoly has taken two major forms: *legislation* to prevent reduction of competition, and *public ownership* or *regulatory agencies* to control or set prices for "natural monopolies". These are industries in which the existence of more than one or two firms would waste resources and increase prices.

Maintaining Competition through Legislation

Legislation that was intended to prevent the most adverse consequences of monopoly or oligopoly was consolidated in the Combines Investigation Act. This Act—whose purpose was to prevent firms from taking actions that would "unduly lessen competition"—was first passed in 1889 and was modified by new acts or amendments on several subsequent occasions. It was replaced in 1986 by the Competition Act. The purpose of this Act is to maintain and encourage competition in Canada in order to promote the efficiency and adaptability of the Canadian economy:

- in order to expand opportunities for Canadian participation in world markets while at the same time recognizing the role of foreign competition in Canada;
- in order to ensure that small and medium-sized enterprises have an equitable opportunity to participate in the Canadian economy;
- in order to provide consumers with competitive prices and product choices.

Three general types of activity are forbidden by the Competition Act: agreements between suppliers that would unduly restrict competition; certain mergers and the abuse of monopoly power; and a number of restrictive trade practices.

Agreements   The Act forbids suppliers to make agreements that unduly restrict entry into an industry, to fix prices, or to limit production or distribution of goods. Nevertheless, firms are still permitted to make agreements on the exchange of statistics and credit information, definitions of product standards, cooperation in research and development, and restriction of advertising, provided that these do not restrict competition.

This section of the Act also exempts agreements relating to the export of Canadian-produced goods, in recognition that such agreements may make economies of scale possible and hence improve Canadian competition in world markets.

Mergers and Monopolies

The Act also prohibits mergers that would have the effect of "substantially" lessening competition. A merger is the acquisition of any control over or interest in the whole or part of a competitor's business, or the control of markets or sources of supply. The preceding Act had also forbidden the formation of a monopoly, but the new Act replaces this by forbidding the "abuse of dominant position". This means that a firm that dominates the market for any product cannot attempt to block the entry of new firms, eliminate existing competitors, or restrict price competition, where the result would be a substantial lessening of competition.

Restrictive Trade Practices

A number of restrictive trade practices are made illegal by the Act. These include price discrimination, loss-leaders ("predatory price cutting"), misleading price advertising, and resale price maintenance. A supplier may not sell at different prices to different buyers who are buying similar quality and quantity; may not sell at lower prices in some localities than in others, or at unreasonably low prices anywhere in order to eliminate a competitor; may not refuse to deal with a potential buyer; and may not misrepresent the price of goods in its advertising, especially regarding the "regular" and "bargain" price of the good. Finally, a supplier may not practise resale price maintenance, that is, may not set a specific price at which wholesalers or retailers are to sell the good.

Effectiveness of Competition Legislation

The Competition Act is administered by the Bureau of Competition Policy, in the federal Department of Consumer and Corporate Affairs. The Director of Investigation and Research is responsible for investigating complaints, which may be brought by any six citizens. If the Director finds reasonable evidence of a violation of the Act, it is reported to the Competition Tribunal, which has replaced the Restrictive Trade Practices Commission. When the Tribunal—composed of judges and lay managers—has heard the evidence, it can determine appropriate solutions to the problem, rather than impose fines or imprisonment. That is, it can order the accused to cease whatever action was at issue, or to sell assets, or make other financial changes. But if the Tribunal's order is not followed, there can be penalties under criminal law. Moreover, the Tribunal can forbid a merger before it occurs, in the case of large companies that would dominate an industry following the proposed merger.

Canada's previous competition (or anti-combines) legislation was largely ineffective because the Act failed to define what was meant by *unduly* lessening competition. Moreover, the nature of the violations made it difficult to establish proof: agreements are generally verbal, and stating that a situation *appeared* to be the outcome of collusion was seldom acceptable evidence. The courts also refused to consider evidence based on the *economic performance* of firms. One result of this was that only five merger cases were taken to court. One defendant pleaded guilty, but the other four were acquitted either directly, or on appeal.[3] Only one monopoly offence was prosecuted successfully.

In addition to the necessity of showing that there was a lessening of competition, it had to be proved that there was a "public detriment" such as higher prices and/or profits. Since one could not prove with certainty the future economic effects of a merger, this part of the Act became virtually inoperative. Consequently, the new Act set less rigorous or restrictive criteria for proving that there was a lessening of competition that was detrimental to the public interest.

Because the Combines Investigation Act was based on criminal law, the courts were concerned with proving that a criminal act had occurred beyond a reasonable doubt.[4] This legal attitude to dealing with what is generally considered an economic problem (apart, perhaps, from such offences as price-fixing and misleading advertising) led to the shift in emphasis in the new Competition Act, from the criminal law to the civil law.

This approach was advocated by economists and others for at least the past two decades. For example, it was argued more than twenty years ago that:

> . . . there would seem to be a valid argument for a less legalistic and a more economic-commission approach to deal with some questions such as mergers. For example, one might want greater justification (unit-cost reductions) for a merger in circumstances of high concentration. In some cases, lower costs from a merger might outweigh the anticompetitive potential. The net effect of commission decisions could well be less merger activity in some industries and more in others.[5]

---

[3] See *Report of the Royal Commission on Corporate Concentration*, pp. 157-58; and C. Green, "Canadian Competition Policy", *Canadian Public Policy*, VII (3), pp. 418-32.

[4] The Act had been treated as a matter of criminal law because other bases for such federal legislation had been declared *ultra vires*, or unconstitutional, in light of section 92 of the Constitution Act (formerly the British North America Act), which gave provinces jurisdiction over civil and property rights within a province. But the Competition Act is based on the federal jurisdiction over trade and commerce.

[5] Max D. Stewart, "Industrial Organization", in L.H. Officer and L.B. Smith, eds. *Canadian Economic Problems and Policies*, Toronto: McGraw-Hill, 1970.

In fact, a primary concern of the Competition Tribunal is to weigh the gains in efficiency that might follow from a merger against the lessening of competition. Amendments to the former Act, as well as changes in the Competition Act, also came in response to proposals that service industries, including professional services, and the banking sector should be included under this legislation.

The impact of the Competition Act may have been diminished by certain court rulings in 1990: that the price-fixing section violates the Charter of Rights and Freedoms because it does not require that intent to restrict competition be proved; and that the Competition Tribunal lacks authority to determine and punish guilt. These rulings may yet be reversed by appeal courts, but they have at least raised doubts about the potential impact of the Act.

Public Control of Natural Monopolies

In a few industries, a firm's optimum size is so large relative to the market size that only one or two firms can operate efficiently. Such industries are termed *natural monopolies*. Common examples include those providing electricity, natural gas, telephone communication, and railroad and local bus transportation. These industries are similar, not only in that economies of scale can often be realized even at quantities larger than the market would buy at low prices, but also in that they are *public utilities*: they provide energy, transportation, or communication used by much of the population.

If several such firms were in competition in each industry, consumers might find the services offered both more expensive and less satisfactory—especially if railway transportation entailed coordinating different timetables; or if reaching a telephone subscriber of a different firm required making the connection through a central agency; or if competitive ferries at a popular crossing had a record of frequent collisions.

Although the one or two firms in such industries may have the potential to make more efficient use of resources by producing at the lower average costs of large scale, their profit-maximizing quantity may be at a point where average costs are still quite high. In any case, their services will be priced well above marginal cost; this difference will be greater the fewer close substitutes there are for the service provided.

Principles of Price Regulation

Public policy for natural monopolies therefore involves some means of regulating their prices, and sometimes their output. Two means have been used: *regulatory agencies*, which regulate prices for specific industries, and *public ownership of the industry*. In either case, the analytical principles for specifying a price are the same.

Figure 20.1 shows the hypothetical revenue and cost conditions for a natural monopoly. The long-run average total cost curve, *LRATC*, is decreasing throughout, reflecting continuing economies of scale. If public policy required breaking up natural monopolies into several small firms operating under monopolistic competition, each might be producing approximately quantity Q_1 for sale at price P_1 in long-run equilibrium. Governments may realize that a lower price is attainable, and therefore reject this approach. But if a government decides instead to regulate the price, what should that price be?

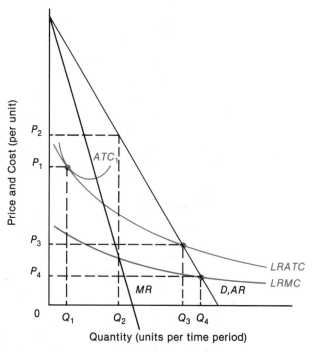

Figure 20.1 Alternative Prices under Natural Monopoly
A natural monopoly is an industry with extremely large economies of scale: the *LRATC* is decreasing throughout the relevant output range. If several firms were operating in this industry (under monopolistic competition), the output of each, Q_1, would be sold at a high price, P_1, even though no profit is realized. A monopoly firm would produce Q_2, to be sold at a still higher price, P_2. If a regulatory agency were to set the price equal to marginal cost, Q_4 would be the quantity that could be sold at P_4, but the firm would have a loss equal to the difference between *LRATC* and *AR* at Q_4. Hence the agency is likely to set the price at P_3; at the related output level, Q_3, the firm realizes only a normal profit, since *AR* equals *LRATC*.

The profit-maximizing quantity, and thus the quantity that would be produced in the absence of public regulation, is Q_2: the quantity at which $MR = LRMC$. This quantity would be sold at price P_2, which in this particular case is an even higher price than would occur with a large number of inefficient firms.

A public agency might decide that the monopoly should produce where price is equal to marginal cost, since this is the criterion for the optimum allocation of resources. At such a quantity, Q_4, the monopoly would incur a loss because its average revenue is less than its average total cost.

Since marginal-cost pricing would usually cause the monopoly firm to go out of business, public policy requires instead that a price be set that will give the firm a "fair return". Although this is a difficult concept to define operationally, the fact that the average total cost includes the cost of a normal profit suggests that pricing at average total cost will provide the firm with just enough profit to keep it in business. This would entail producing quantity Q_3, to be sold at price P_3.

Regulatory Agencies

One approach to implementing public price regulation of natural monopolies is to appoint a *regulatory agency*. Boards or commissions are established by governments for each industry or utility concerned.

These may be appointed by federal, provincial, or municipal governments in accordance with the scope of the market served by a particular utility. Any of these agencies, however, faces the same general problems in regulating prices: What is a fair return? How should the firm's assets be valued in determining a base for calculations of a fair return? Are the firm's statements of costs reasonable? Additional problems are also faced by regulatory agencies: Is there a place for more firms in the industry? What are the relative merits of allowing a utility to discontinue part of its service, rather than raising the price for all service, to maintain a fair rate of return?

What Is a Fair Return?   Setting prices that will enable a firm to realize a fair rate of return on its physical and financial assets has been the traditional principle of public price regulation, but a "fair rate" remains undefined. Economic principles suggest that this should be the opportunity cost of the assets, or the rate that could be earned in another industry, allowing for the higher risk usually found in industries other than public utilities. Regulatory agencies pay some attention to this principle, to the extent that they consider the average rate of return for the whole economy. "Fair rates" have normally been defined as about 6 to 9 per cent. In recent years, however, these rates have been in the range of 11 to 14 per cent. When prices reflecting this rate are set, there is, of course, no guarantee that the rate will be realized. Demand and cost conditions may change following the agency's decision. Any actual variation from this rate is therefore taken into account when prices are set in the subsequent period.

What Is a Fair Assets Value?

The set rate of return is related to the value of the firm's assets to determine what the total revenue should be, and thus what the price should be. Estimating a fair value for these assets raises a controversial issue: should assets be valued at *original cost* or *replacement cost*? The original cost approach gives a more accurate statement of actual costs of land, buildings, and equipment, but does not include enhanced value due to inflation. Depreciation must be deducted, but this can be calculated several different ways. Replacement costs, however, require arbitrary estimates that may provoke much dispute in price-setting deliberations. The higher the value of assets, the higher the total dollar return will be for any given rate. Regulated monopolies also lack incentive to restrain their spending for plant and equipment; regulatory agencies must therefore also assure that all such expenditures are necessary.

Are Costs Reasonable?

This approach to price-setting is essentially a matter of adding a fair profit to the firm's costs. A regulatory agency is thus watching for exaggerated cost statements and unnecessary expenditures. Cases of inefficiency or waste are not easily identified and proved; regulated monopolies therefore also lack incentives to control their operating costs.

Other Problems

In examining the cost data of regulated monopolies, boards or commissions will also question whether another firm could enter the industry without seriously reducing the economies of scale realized by existing firms. The possibility of such expansion arises when demand for the service is increasing quickly. For example, boards are required to decide whether a particular air route should be served by one, two, or more airlines, and whether new firms should be added to the television broadcasting industry.

Second, regulated monopolies such as the railways sometimes request permission to discontinue services in an area that is unprofitable, as an alternative to setting higher prices for all services. The regulatory agency faces the difficult task of weighing the social benefits of maintaining the service against the additional cost to be borne by all users of the service.

Regulatory Agencies in Canada

Regulatory agencies are used principally at the federal level; municipalities and provinces have tended to adopt the public ownership approach to natural monopolies. The three major federal agencies are the National Transportation Agency, the Canadian Radio-Television and Telecommunications Commission, and the National Energy Board.

National Transportation Agency

The National Transportation Agency was organized in 1989 to replace the Canadian Transport Commission; this had been established in 1967 to consolidate several agencies that regulated different types of transportation. The Transportation Agency regulates railway service (but no longer the rates) and tolls on international bridges and tunnels; licenses commercial air services and formulates transport regulations but no longer sets fares; licenses and sets rates for commercial shipping on inland waterways, with the important exception of the bulk carriers that constitute much of the Great Lakes shipping; regulates interprovincial commercial trucking and all international motor vehicle transportation; and licenses interprovincial and international pipelines and sets pipeline rates. The Agency is required by previous legislation to maintain special rates on railway freight transportation for the Maritime provinces, under the Maritime Freight Rates Act. The special rates for grain shipping in the West under the Crow's Nest Pass Agreement were discontinued in 1983 and replaced with new subsidies to the railways.

Canadian Radio-Television and Telecommunications Commission

All broadcasting in Canada comes under the regulation of the Canadian Radio-Television and Telecommunications Commission (CRTC). This agency regulates the number of firms or stations that can broadcast in each area, their programming, and the proportion of advertising time. It also regulates the cable-television industry by establishing rates and the areas to be served by each firm, and granting licences to operate pay-television facilities. The Commission regulates the rates or tolls charged for telephone and telecommunication services by, for example, Bell Canada and CNCP Telecommunications, and determines whether other firms will be allowed to enter that industry.

National Energy Board

Responsibility for oil and gas pipelines is shared by the National Energy Board and the National Transportation Agency. They regulate the construction and operation of such pipelines and set the rates or tolls. The National Energy Board also regulates the export and import of natural gas and oil and the export of electricity.

Public Ownership of Natural Monopolies

In some cases, public ownership of natural monopolies has been favoured not only because of the problems associated with regulatory agencies, but also because outright public ownership seemed preferable to the operating subsidies and public capital financing that appeared necessary for some regulated agencies. For example, the federal government amalgamated several railways to form Canadian National Railways, and created Air Canada, which was originally a division of the CNR. Similarly, some provinces have owned hydro-electric power systems since they were established.

Public ownership has two basic advantages. First, since the commission responsible for operating the utility has a direct knowledge of its production costs, it should be able to control them more effectively than can regulatory agencies. This also makes it possible to pursue a "break-even" policy, rather than a "fair return" policy. Second, the commission can take more direct account of the social benefits of its services. This may mean, for example in the case of urban public transit, that the utility should be permitted a deficit, to be subsidized from tax revenues. Such a utility thus becomes another municipal service like parks, sewers, and fire protection. A publicly owned utility should be able to take positive action to serve the public interest, whereas a regulatory agency can only prevent a utility from acting contrary to the public interest.

Most urban public transit systems, and water and electricity utilities, are municipally owned. Provincial electricity utilities (which sell power to the municipal systems) are also under public ownership, as are the provincial telephone systems in the Prairie provinces.

Public Support for Restricted Competition

Governments are pressed by consumers and small businesses to legislate against monopolistic practices and decreasing competition. But there is also pressure from other groups to support restricted competition. Such support may take the form of public licensing and chartering to restrict entry, the issuing of patents for the production of specific items, and even governments' own monopolizing of an industry.

Public Monopolies for Non-Economic Reasons Governments have extended public ownership to some cases that can not be justified by economies of scale. One common example is the liquor control boards established by the different provinces to be responsible for liquor retailing. The result is a standard price for liquors and wines, by contrast with the situation in several American states of intense price competition and a wider product variety. Provincial governments apparently maintain ownership of liquor retail stores because they are highly profitable.

Licensing Provincial and municipal governments license a number of *occupations* ranging from medicine, dentistry, law, and engineering, through plumbing, electrical and plastering trades, to undertaking and barbering. Legislation protecting these occupations usually allows the municipality to restrict the number licensed for the construction trades, or allows the occupation's governing association itself to raise admission standards or requirements enough to maintain the desired numbers. Some professional associations were also allowed to set their own suggested fee schedules, but recent changes in the competition legislation prevent strict imposition of fees. Licensing of this kind is usually said to be in the public interest, to the extent that the public is protected from unsatisfactory service or workmanship. However, prices are higher than if there were unrestricted entry and there is a possibility that the service is worse, especially when an excess demand for such services means the public must accept unsatisfactory work or go without.

Box 20.1   **Report urges Metro to issue more licences for taxicabs**

By Sean Fine

Metro Toronto has overprotected its taxi industry from competition, heating up the market for taxi licences, lowering driver income and reducing service to the public, a report by a consultant says.

Coopers and Lybrand Consulting Group, in a study done for the Metro Licencing Commission, recommended that an extra 203 taxi licences be issued to make up for the backlog and that the system of calculating how many are issued be improved.

The increase of 203 licences would expand Metro's fleet of 2,943 taxis by 6.9 per cent.

The report cited several reasons why demand for service has grown faster than the supply of new taxi-owner licences, including tighter drunk-driving laws, greater traffic congestion downtown, higher automobile costs and an underestimation of cab use by tourists and visitors.

Licences, issued by the commission at a cost of $5,000 to owners, are selling on the street at an average of $83,000, which compares with the $45,000 cost in 1982, the study said.

The scarcity of taxi licences, high demand and low interest rates helped push the cost up, the report said.

The higher price has hurt drivers, who usually pay the owner or an intermediary a certain amount for each shift worked.

Of the $60 paid by a driver for each nine- or 10-hour shift, $15 is "a direct result of licence plates having a scarcity value," the study said, adding that the owners are the only ones to gain from the licence shortage.

The scarcity of licences has meant a serious shortage of cabs available through dispatch services, the report said, adding that the problem is compounded by difficulty in getting enough drivers.

Source: *The Globe and Mail*, 5 March 1987.

Taxi licences are issued in almost every municipality in Canada by a public committee that must decide how many such licences are adequate to serve the public needs. But as the above article indicates, an inadequate quota of licences can impose additional costs on the public.

Taxis are also licensed by most municipalities. Some cases present the appearance of a natural monopoly because only one or two firms are operating in a city. That this is unnecessary is shown in other cases where several taxi firms are operating, whether in small towns or large cities. The effect of taxi licensing is to create a substantial financial asset for the existing operators: taxi "plates" are said to be worth several thousand dollars in major metropolitan markets. (See Box 20.1.) Again, licensing is defended as being "in the public interest", although the public interest would probably be better served simply by setting minimum standards for taxi operations rather than by fixing the number to be licensed.

Box 20.2   **Why Regulation?**

Government may decide for many reasons to intervene in the market and regulate industries. For example, certain industries have economic characteristics that qualify them as "natural monopolies": a single supplier will have lower unit costs than would a group of competing suppliers, either because of economies of scale or because of high fixed costs of capital installations.

In other instances the market for one reason or another may not allocate to the industry the amount of resources desired by society. The size of the project or its risk of technological failure may be too high to attract private investment (e.g., in energy development). The free market may lead to unacceptable price fluctuations (e.g., in agricultural products). Some industries are thought to be so important to the country that their adequate and proper functioning must be ensured by government; communications and transport are examples of this.

These traditional economic reasons sometimes merge with social or political goals such as subsidizing service to particular groups (urban transit), regional development (rail and air transport), regional planning (electric power), preservation of the family farm (marketing boards), use and upgrading of natural resources (energy boards), and the maintenance of cultural and political integrity (communications). Often the non-economic reasons may well be more important than the economic ones.

Regulation and regulated industries cannot be analyzed from a purely economic standpoint because many of the regulators' decisions are not based on economics, and are not particularly intended to achieve efficiency either in the use of existing resources or in the allocation of resources to an industry. Usually regulation involves social and political questions at least as much as economic ones. Regulation often is put in place, therefore, when the free market system fails to achieve the allocation of resources desired by the public. The lack of a single or dominant criterion by which to evaluate many regulated industries leads to serious problems of accountability and control.

Source: Privy Council of Canada, *Report of the Royal Commission on Corporate Concentration*, pp. 396–97. Reproduced with the permission of the Minister of Supply and Services Canada, 1991.

Patents   Patents constitute legal support for restricted entry without public regulation of the consequences. A patent grants its holder the exclusive right to produce a specific item without direct competition for 17 years. The purpose of the patent law is to encourage the invention of new products and processes. Although this purpose obviously has been served, other undesirable consequences have followed. Firms have been able to extend their protected period by patenting "improvements" on the original item. Some large firms have patented what appears to be every possible aspect of their particular technology. Several years ago, for example, the International Business Machine Corporation (IBM) acquired patents on all aspects of tabulating machinery, hired most of the known inventors in the field, and harassed competitors by charging them with patent infringements. Finally, IBM was forced by threat of legal proceedings to make some of its patents available on a royalty basis.

Box 20.3   Why Regulation Reform?

The introduction of regulations . . . may also lead to outcomes that are not socially preferable. Direct regulations can raise costs and prices, causing too little of the service or commodity to be produced. And failure to adjust to changed circumstances has meant that some direct economic regulations no longer suit the industries and activities to which they apply . . . . Rather than declining or disappearing in the face of changed conditions, many direct regulations have persisted . . . .

Finally it is our impression that the increasing complexity of the regulatory maze and the sheer physical constraints on legislators' time are overloading governments and control agencies well beyond their limits. As a result, many highly regulated markets may be suffering from administrative constraints and may no longer be operating efficiently.

Source: Economic Council of Canada, *Reforming Regulation*, p. 10. Reproduced with the permission of the Chairman of the Economic Council of Canada, 1991.

To Regulate, or Not?   The complex set of reasons for government regulation of business is illustrated briefly in the quotation in Box 20.2. These few paragraphs also emphasize the non-economic arguments that enter into the regulatory process.

The second quotation, in Box 20.3, highlights a recent movement of reform economic regulation. There is an increasing concern that regulations may become outdated or excessively costly to administer. The Economic Council of Canada, following a study of certain regulated industries, found that regulation frequently did not serve the purpose intended, or was unevenly applied due to wide discretionary powers of officials and overlapping responsibilities, or simply reduced efficiency

Box 20.4   **Storm warnings on deregulation**

When it comes to the federal regulation of economic activities, most econo-mists agree: the less, the better. The record of Washington's campaign to deregulate a host of vital industries proves the point. Since the deregula-tion wave began in 1978, individual and business customers have reaped enormous benefits in the form of lower prices in air travel, trucking, and long-distance telephone use. Operating efficiencies made possible by deregulation have virtually saved a once-moribund railway industry.

But the experts on deregulation are not ready to proclaim the great experiment a total success. The critical result was supposed to be a flower-ing of competition. Free entry into and survival of new ventures in the deregulated industries was considered essential to ensure continued price and productivity benefits. However, an initial burst of competition didn't last. Instead, the trend has been strongly toward concentration in the three transportation industries, and AT&T's dominance in long lines has barely been dented.

There's no conspiracy here. These industries seem to gravitate toward natural monopoly as the majors capitalize on the economies of flow pro-vided by their network structure to maintain or increase market shares. But natural or not, the trend raises the spectre of the re-emergence of car-tels that would eventually undo the gains achieved under deregulation. The Reagan administration has firmly adhered to free-market principles on the regulatory front but has failed to match that commitment in anti-trust enforcement. If this neglect permits anticompetitive abuses to spread, it will fuel demands for extensive reregulation. Deregulation must be made to work, and that requires far greater vigilance in the antitrust arena.

Source: *Financial Post*, 12 January 1987. Reprinted from 22 December 1986 issue of *Business Week* by special permission. Copyright © 1987 by McGraw-Hill Inc.

through excessive costs of compliance.[6] But the increased efficiency and lower prices that were expected to follow from the deregulation policies have occurred more slowly and less frequently than the policy sup-porters had claimed. One major reason for this is that, as illustrated in Box 20.4, there may be greater industrial concentration when govern-ments remove their regulatory restraints.

Review of the Main Points

1. Canadian manufacturing industries tend to be more highly concen-trated than American manufacturing. This leads to an uneven size

---

[6] Economic Council of Canada, *Reforming Regulation*.

distribution of firms: about 80 per cent of the total production in manufacturing comes from about 11 per cent of the establishments.

2. There are four basic forms of business organization: single proprietorships, partnerships, corporations, and cooperatives. Proprietorships and partnerships have unlimited liability: creditors may claim the personal assets of the firms' owners should they be unable to meet financial obligations. Corporations have limited liability because they are treated as a separate legal entity.

3. Corporations are financed by issuing stocks or bonds, or by drawing on retained earnings or depreciation allowances. Control of a corporation nominally requires ownership of 51 per cent of the common shares, but in large public corporations control can be gained with a lower percentage of shares. This has led to holding companies or conglomerates that control large accumulations of assets through a pyramidal structure of holdings.

4. Two special types of corporation are the public or crown corporations established by governments and the cooperatives established by societies of individuals to buy or sell commodities cooperatively.

5. Public policy concerning monopolies and oligopolies takes the form of competition legislation, and public ownership or regulatory agencies to control natural monopolies (industries in which the existence of more than one or two firms would waste resources and increase prices). The Competition Act forbids certain agreements between suppliers that would restrict competition, certain mergers and the abuse of monopoly power, and a number of restrictive trade practices. The forerunner to this Act was not very effective, but major amendments are expected to overcome some of the previous weaknesses.

6. Natural monopolies are common in the transportation, communications, natural gas, and electricity industries because firms have large fixed costs relative to the total output of the market. Such industries are either controlled by regulatory agencies appointed by governments, or are brought under direct control by public ownership. Regulatory agencies are usually required to determine a "fair return" on the firm's assets. The major regulatory agencies in Canada are the National Transportation Agency, the Canadian Radio-Television and Telecommunications Commission, and the National Energy Board.

7. Public support for restricted competition takes the form of licensing only some persons or firms in some professions, trades, or businesses, and issuing patents, which restrict the production of a specific item to one firm. Recent studies indicate a need for continuous review and reform of regulations.

Key Concepts and Topics

industrial organization	holding company
industrial concentration	crown corporation
concentration ratio	cooperative
single proprietorship	Competition Act
partnership	restrictive trade practices
corporation	merger
unlimited liability	natural monopoly
limited liability	regulatory agency
common stock	"fair return"
preferred stock	National Transportation Agency
corporate bond	Canadian Radio-Television and
depreciation allowance	Telecommunications Commission
ownership vs. control	National Energy Board

Questions for Review and Discussion

1. Would you prefer to hold financial assets in the form of corporate bonds, as common shares, or as preferred shares? Explain. Would your answer be different in a recession than at the peak of an economic expansion?

2. Why are corporations relatively more common in manufacturing than in retail services? Than in agriculture?

3. Discuss the uses and limitations of "concentration ratios" as a measure of industrial concentration.

4. Some economists have proposed that there should be more, rather than fewer, mergers in some industries in Canada. Why might they argue this way? Would you?

5. "All natural monopolies should be purchased by the government and be operated by a public commission." Do you agree? Why?

6. Do you think the patent system should be continued? Why or why not?

7. It is frequently suggested that urban public transportation should be provided at a lower price between 10 a.m. and 3 p.m. than during rush-hours. How should the lower price be determined? Do you agree with this proposal? Why?

Sources and Selected Readings

Armstrong, Donald. *Competition versus Monopoly: Combines Policy in Perspective*. Vancouver: Fraser Institute, 1982.

Caves, Richard. *American Industry: Structure, Conduct, Performance*, 6th ed. Englewood Cliffs, N.J.: Prentice-Hall, 1987.

Economic Council of Canada. *Reforming Regulation.* Ottawa: Supply and Services Canada, 1981.

Green, Christopher. *Canadian Industrial Organization and Policy,* 3rd ed. Toronto: McGraw-Hill Ryerson, 1989.

Jones, J.C.H. "Mergers and Competition: The Brewing Case". *Canadian Journal of Economics and Political Science* (November 1967): 551–68.

Khemani, R.S., D.M. Shapiro, and W.T. Stanbury. *Mergers, Corporate Concentration and Power in Canada.* Halifax: Institute for Research in Public Policy, 1988.

Prichard, J. Robert, W.T. Stanbury, and Thomas A. Wilson. *Canadian Competition Policy.* Toronto: Butterworths, 1979.

Royal Commission on Corporate Concentration. *Report* (and various research studies published separately). Ottawa: Supply and Services Canada, 1978.

Rugman, Alan M., and John McIlveen. *Megafirms: Strategies for Canada's Multinationals.* Toronto: Methuen, 1985

Tupper, A., and G.B. Doern, eds. *Public Corporations and Public Policy in Canada.* Toronto: Institute for Research on Public Policy, 1981.

21 Economics of the Natural Resource Industries

The natural resource industries include the renewable resources of forestry, and fishing and trapping, and the non-renewable resources of mining and petroleum. Agriculture is also included here because its basic input, land, is a non-renewable resource, and because it — like the other natural resource industries — provides an economic basis for the other industrial sectors. Indeed, the natural resource industries are also referred to as the primary industries, because they form the first tier of economic activity. The issue of foreign ownership of Canadian industry is also discussed in this chapter because some of the major concerns about ownership are with the mining and petroleum industry, and with foreign control over the depletion of Canada's natural resources.

Significance of the Natural Resource Industries

National Economic Significance

The natural resource industries are important to the Canadian economy for several reasons. Specifically, they:

- contribute directly to the total Gross Domestic Product, and offer employment to a significant part of the labour force, especially in certain regions of the country;
- provide a source of raw materials for further processing in the manufacturing industries and for use in the construction industries, and generate a demand for the services of a large part of the distribution, sales, and financial divisions of the service sector;
- provide a majority of the commodities that Canada exports to other countries.

Output from the natural resource industries has declined as a percentage of the total GDP, but only as a result of more rapid growth in the output of the secondary and service sectors, which depend on the primary sector. From Figure 21.1, it can be seen that output from the resource sector dropped from 24 per cent of total GDP in 1926 to 8 per cent in 1971, rose to 9 per cent in 1981, and then declined to about 7 per cent. Almost all of this decline can be attributed to agriculture, where output fell from 18 per cent to 2 per cent of GDP. Over the same period, however, output in mining and petroleum has increased its contribution to the total GDP.

Similar patterns have occurred with respect to the percentage of the total labour force that is employed in each of these industries. About one-third of the labour force was employed in natural resources in 1926, but this dropped to 7 per cent by 1990. Again, the major decline was in agriculture, but there was very little change over the period in the share of the labour force employed in mining and petroleum.

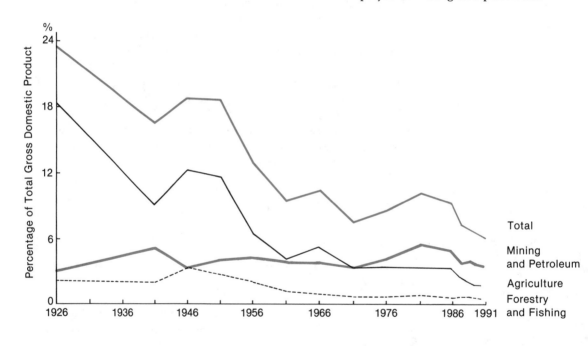

Figure 21.1   Percentage of Total Gross Domestic Product Contributed by Natural Resource Industries
The share of Canada's Gross Domestic Product contributed by the natural resource industries has declined since 1926 from almost 25 per cent to about 10 per cent. Their economic significance is greater than this suggests, however, because their output is essential for the manufacturing, construction, and service industries.

Source: Royal Commission on the Economic Union and Development Prospects for Canada, *Report*, Vol. 2, Table 11-1; and Statistics Canada, *Gross Domestic Product by Industry*.

With respect to exports, however, the natural resource industries have had a much more substantial contribution to make. Immediately following World War II, this sector accounted for 80 per cent of the total value of Canada's merchandise exports. By 1951, this share had risen to 87 per cent. But Figure 21.2 shows the sharp decline that occurred during the 1960s, as the exports of both agriculture and forestry formed a much smaller share of total exports. This was a consequence of the Auto Pact, which added automobiles and parts as a leading factor in Canada's exports and imports. Nonetheless, more than one-half of Canada's exports still come from the products of the resource sector, but mining and petroleum have replaced agriculture and forestry as the major components in this trade.

Statistics on the value of goods produced in each industry measure only the value added in that industry. For example, the value of beef

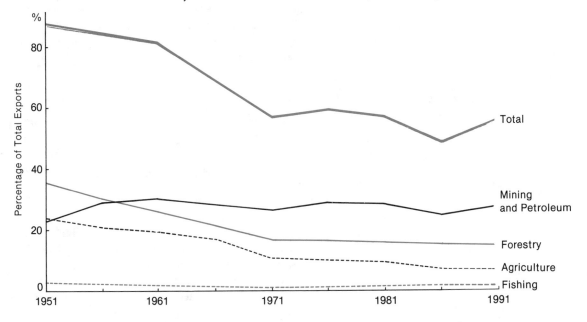

Figure 21.2   Percentage of Exports Contributed by Natural Resource Industries, Including Related Products
The natural resource industries provide the majority of Canada's exports. Although this sector's share of outputs has declined in the postwar period, the decline was attributable mainly to the Auto Pact with the United States, signed in 1965, which provided for free trade in motor vehicles and parts. Some of this effect can be seen in the decline in the natural resources share between 1961 and 1966, but the major effect occurred between 1966 and 1971. The data include related products, such as pulp and paper, in the forest industries.

Source: Royal Commission on the Economic Union and Development Prospects for Canada, *Report*, Vol. 2, Table 11-3; and Statistics Canada, *Summary of Canadian International Trade*.

produced in the agricultural industry reflects the value added up to the point where the cattle are sold to the buyers for the meat-processors, but does not include the final value of beef sold in Canadian supermarkets. In this sense, the GDP data understate the full economic importance of the natural resource sector. If there were a sudden reduction of output in the primary industries, the result would be much higher prices and reduced availability of raw materials as inputs to the processing stages in the manufacturing industries, and fewer goods to distribute in the transportation, wholesale, and retail industries. It is in this sense that the natural resource industries form the base on which the economy is built.

The natural resource sector has had a significant, but indirect, effect on the performance of the economy through that sector's considerable gains in productivity. Employment in the agricultural industry, for example, declined sharply in the 1950s because improved technology led to substantial increases in productivity. This not only reduced the relative price of agricultural goods; it also released part of the labour force for employment in other industries.

Regional Significance

The relative economic importance of the natural resource sector varies across the regions or provinces of Canada. While these industries account for only 3 per cent of the GDP in Ontario, they contribute 15 per cent in Alberta and 20 per cent in Saskatchewan. In a similar way, the share of provincial government revenues derived from these industries varies from a negligible amount in Ontario, to 20 per cent in Saskatchewan, to 40 per cent in Alberta. The following sections highlight this regional diversity in the economic impacts of the various natural resources; these differences illustrate the reason for political tensions among the regions, and with the federal government, in the development of public policies on the resource industries. The effect of this regional concentration is accentuated by the constitutional issue; namely, that the natural resources are owned by the provinces, but the federal government is responsible for interprovincial and international trade. Both levels of government therefore attempt to devise policies that fit within, and enhance, their interests.

Agriculture

Major Conditions Facing the Agricultural Industry

Although the agricultural industry accounts for only about 2 per cent of the total GDP and 4 per cent of the labour force, it produces most of the inputs for Canada's food processors, and buys its inputs from a wide range of manufacturing and service industries.

The major feature of the agricultural industry, however, is the *large number of producers*. In 1986, there were about 290,000 farms in Canada, as defined in the census as having at least one acre and annual cash sales of $1,200 or more. These of course include farmers producing diverse products—milk, beef, horticultural products, poultry and eggs, hogs, and so on. The number of producers nevertheless far exceeds, for example, the number of firms in the retail trade, which is also characterized by many small establishments.

Second, the *price elasticity of demand for farm products in Canadian markets is quite low*, although many individual producers face the almost perfectly elastic demand curve typical of pure competition.[1] The low market elasticity results in a substantial price reduction, with a decreased total revenue, if output is increased when there is no change in demand.

The third major feature is that *supply curves for agricultural products have shifted outward* rather quickly, with postwar improvements in agricultural productivity. Because agriculture is such a competitive industry, farmers who do not adopt new techniques, varieties, breeds, or machinery are not able to break even and are forced out of the industry. Those who remain receive lower prices and lower total revenues, as illustrated in Figure 21.3.

The rapid increase in supply has not been matched by a similar increase in demand. The latter is influenced mainly by population and per capita real incomes, but Canada's population has grown by only about 2 per cent annually, and much of the increase in per capita incomes allocated to food has been for more food preparation and processing, rather than more agricultural products. In high-income countries the income elasticity of demand for food tends to be quite low.[2] The result, as shown in Figure 21.3, is that agricultural prices have fallen *relative* to prices for most other commodities during the postwar period. Occasionally, as in 1951 and 1973-74, farm prices may rise quite rapidly, but the gains in real net farm income in these years are more than offset by the long-run decline.

Short-run supply conditions also complicate the problem: *weather and disease can substantially alter output from year to year*. When output is unusually low, prices and total revenue will rise, but frequently this additional income is used to purchase machinery or make repairs

---

[1] For example, price elasticities for farm products in Canada have been estimated as follows: .95 for beef; .56 for chicken; .24 for vegetables; and .12 for eggs. From Z. A. Hassan and S. R. Johnson, "The Demand for Major Foods in Canada," *Canadian Farm Economics*, Vol. 12, No. 2.

[2] Income elasticities have been estimated as follows: .51 for beef; .15 for chicken; and .09 for vegetables. (*Ibid.*)

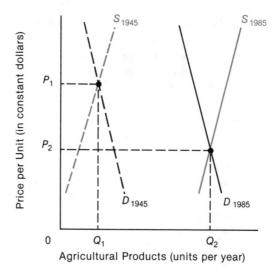

Figure 21.3   Decline in Relative Prices of Agricultural Products
The prices of agricultural products have declined relative to prices of other commodities in the past four decades, because improved agricultural productivity has increased supply proportionately more than the increase in demand, and because the demand for agricultural products in general is inelastic.

that were postponed from previous years. Few farmers are able to save substantial amounts as protection against the bad years.

About 20 to 25 per cent of Canada's agricultural products are exported, but they must compete with highly subsidized farm produce in many countries; some foreign governments not only subsidize all agricultural production, they add a further subsidy for exported agricultural products.

Consequences of Conditions in the Agricultural Industry

There are two major consequences of the conditions described for the agricultural industry: farm incomes are both low and unstable.

The low net farm incomes follow mainly from the large number of producers, which follows in turn from the lag in adjusting to improved productivity in agriculture. Since each producer faces a perfectly elastic demand curve (except where output is limited by quotas, as for fluid milk, eggs, and tobacco), the incentive is to produce as much as possible with the fixed assets of land and buildings. With each farmer doing this, the market quantity is usually in the inelastic portion of the market demand curve. This is shown as quantity Q_2 in Figure 21.4. The industry supply curve is also its marginal cost curve. Hence, if the industry were a monopoly or an oligopoly, the profit-maximizing output would be determined as Q_1 (where MC equals MR) and the price would be P_1. Although marginal cost pricing is desirable for consumers, it results in lower prices and incomes for the more competitive industries such as agriculture.

A further problem arises because producers have tended to plan future production in response to previous prices. The result is instability of farm incomes. Economists have termed this phenomenon the "hog cycle" because it has been prominent in hog production, or the "cobweb theorem" because its diagrammatic explanation resembles a cobweb — as Figure 21.5 may suggest.

Suppose the equilibrium price for hogs has been P_1 with quantity Q_1 produced. A short-run increase in supply (perhaps due to improved feed) results in a new supply curve, S_1. In the following production period, there is a greater quantity, Q_2, produced in response to the previous price. The price of hogs then falls to P_2. Producers therefore decide to reduce output to Q_3, but this increases the price to P_3. The response to this is quantity Q_4, and on it goes until the market is in equilibrium again, but at a lower price and larger quantity than before.

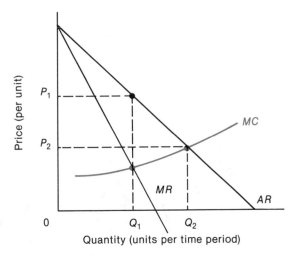

Figure 21.4 Competition in Agriculture Leads to Lower Farm Incomes
If a monopoly faced the revenue and cost curves shown here, it would produce Q_1, to be sold at price P_1. Competition in the production of most agricultural products results in the production of Q_2, to be sold at P_2. Although competition increases consumer surplus, it lowers net farm incomes below what they would be in less competitive conditions, unless producers cooperate as monopolistic selling agencies.

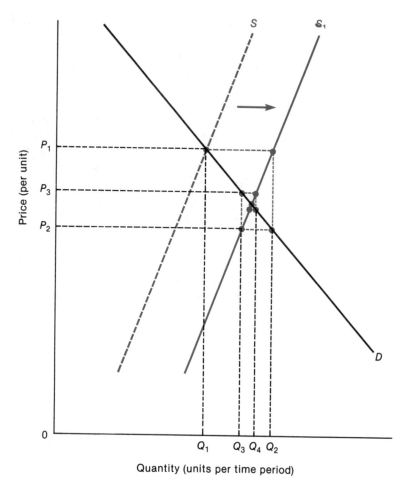

Figure 21.5   The Cobweb Theorem of Income Instability
Farm incomes tend to be unstable to the extent that producers determine
the quantity to be supplied in the next period on the basis of current prices.
Suppose a market is in equilibrium at P_1. A shift in supply, to S_1, leads
producers to offer Q_2 with the expectation of price P_1. But Q_2 is sold at the
lower price P_2, in order to avoid excess supply. Producers therefore plan to
offer only Q_3 in response to price P_2. This lower quantity raises the price to
P_3. Given D and S_1, this cyclical pattern would lead to a new equilibrium
price; but another shift in either demand or supply would start the cyclical
process again.

Meanwhile, of course, either supply or demand, or both, may have
shifted, setting off a new cycle of quantity responses to price changes.
Since the demand for hogs is assumed to be price-inelastic, the price
increases result in higher incomes; the price decreases produce lower
incomes. The outcome is unstable farm incomes.

Public Assistance for Agriculture

Public policies supporting agriculture are directed toward several dimensions of the "farm problem" in Canada. Such policies are intended as much to raise the low average incomes of farmers as they are to encourage competition in the agricultural industry and protect it from the consequences of dealing with other less competitive industries. These two goals were described by a federal task force on agriculture as "the basic conflict in agricultural policy, a cheap food policy together with a small farm maintenance policy."

Several types of government programs provide public assistance for agriculture. These can be classified as programs to maintain higher, more stable incomes through price supports; to decrease or subsidize production costs; to improve prices through more effective marketing; and to assist in the reallocation of resources within agriculture, or from agriculture to other uses.

Price Support Programs

Often confused with subsidy programs, price support programs consist of a government gurarantee that the producer will receive a specific minimum price per unit for his product. If the market price is higher than the guaranteed price, no government payment is made. A subsidy, however, is a payment of a specific amount per unit produced; payment is therefore made regardless of the market price.

The federal government's price support program is conducted under the Agricultural Stabilization Act. This provides for a Board to set support prices for three produce categories: cattle, hogs, and sheep; industrial milk and cream (i.e. for butter, skim milk powder, and cheese)[3]; corn, soybeans, and wheat, oats, and barley grown outside the Prairie provinces. The support price must be at least 90 per cent of the previous 5-year weighted average price for each product, plus the difference between current direct costs of production and the average cash costs in the preceding five years. Thus the support price is based on both the producer's selling price and the production cost. The Board may recommend to the federal Cabinet that support prices be established for a number of other agricultural products, and it may also authorize subsidy payments. Two types of price support may be used: an *offer to purchase* produce not sold in the market when the price is set at the guaranteed minimum, and a *deficiency payment* or a payment of the difference between the free-market price and the guaranteed price.

---

[3] Price support programs for butter and cheese (and dry skim milk) have been administered by the Canadian Dairy Commission since 1967. Egg production and prices have been the responsibility of the Canadian Egg Marketing Agency since 1972.

Offer-to-Purchase Method

Under the offer-to-purchase method, the government agrees to buy any unsold produce at the support price. The effect of this scheme is illustrated by Figure 21.6. Suppose the equilibrium price of butter, for example, is P_1 and the quantity sold is Q_1. A guaranteed price is now set at P_2. Producers therefore decide to increase output to Q_3, but consumers will buy only Q_2 units at the higher price. The government buys the unsold butter, the difference between Q_2 and Q_3, at the price of P_2 per pound.

What can the government do with the butter it has purchased? It cannot sell the butter in Canada, because consumers have bought all they will take at the floor price. It may be able to sell some butter in foreign countries, provided that this does not violate anti-dumping agreements: that is, international agreements that a product will not be sold abroad at less than the price received at home. Destroying produce always provokes public criticism, and donating produce to low-income countries requires further transportation and administration expenditures.

Produce such as butter can be stored for a few months. If the demand curve should shift rightward and/or the supply curve shift leftward until

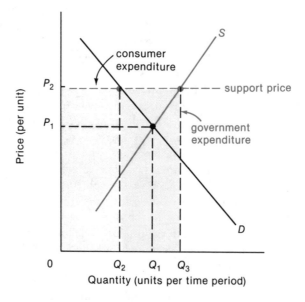

Figure 21.6   Offer-To-Purchase Method
Under the offer-to-purchase method for supporting agricultural prices, the government announces a floor price, P_2. Producers supply Q_3 at the floor price, but consumers buy only Q_2. The government purchases the balance, $Q_3 - Q_2$. If the equilibrium price and output prior to the floor price were P_1 and Q_1, farmers now receive a greater revenue, but consumers pay a higher price and have a lower quantity and less consumer surplus.

the equilibrium price was above the guaranteed price, the government could then add its stored butter to the current quantity supplied until the price fell back to the guaranteed price. However, the probability that this situation will arise within the safe storage period of butter is slight. Moreover, such a support program involves transportation and storage costs in addition to the cost of purchasing the product. Finally, consumers must pay a higher price for a lower quantity of the product. Offer-to-purchase programs therefore are not commonly used; specifically, this price support method has been used only for butter, cheddar cheese, and skim milk powder under the Canadian Dairy Commission's price support program.

Deficiency Payment Method

Under the deficiency payment method for supporting prices, no minimum market price is set. Instead, the government guarantees to pay producers the difference between the national average market price for the product and the support price. Each producer therefore receives the same deficiency payment per unit, regardless of the particular market price received for his own produce. The effect of this scheme is shown in Figure 21.7. Assume the same supply and demand curves, equilibrium price and quantity, and guaranteed price that were used in Figure 21.6. Producers decide to supply quantity Q_3 at the guaranteed price of P_2. In this second case, the new market price will be P_3, the price at which consumers will buy all of quantity Q_1. The government payment per unit is the difference between P_2 and P_3; this amount is paid for Q_3 units.

The advantages of the deficiency payment method are that there is no problem of surplus disposal, no additional costs for transportation and storage (although each method has administrative costs), and there is an increased quantity for consumers at a lower price. However, if the demand for the product is inelastic, government payments are higher under a deficiency payment program than under an offer-to-purchase program. Under both programs, using the example illustrated by Figures 21.6 and 21.7, producers receive a total revenue of P_2 times Q_3.

The portion of this revenue received from consumers is larger under offer-to-purchase due to the inelasticity of demand: total revenue (from consumers) is greater at a higher price. The portion remaining for the government to pay is therefore smaller under the offer-to-purchase method. However, despite the higher goverment payments required by a deficiency payment program when demand is inelastic, this program is frequently preferred because of its other advantages. Moreover, if demand is elastic, the government payments to producers are lower under the deficiency payment method. Finally, payments can be limited to a specific quantity for each producer, thereby reducing the quantity that will be offered at the support price, and giving proportionately

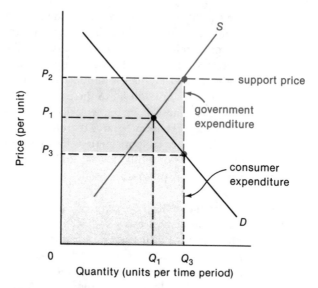

Figure 21.7   Deficiency Payment Method
Under the deficiency payment method for supporting agricultural prices, the government guarantees producers a price of P_2 per unit. Producers supply Q_3 units, which are sold in an otherwise free market at P_3. The government pays producers the difference between P_2 and P_3 for Q_3 units. Consumers pay a lower price than the previous equilibrium price, P_1, and enjoy a larger quantity, Q_3, and a larger consumer surplus. Producers' total revenue is P_2 for Q_3 units.

more assistance to the smaller producers. The deficiency payment method is thus the one more commonly used by the Agricultural Stabilization Board.

Production and Transportation Programs

Several agricultural assistance programs are directed to reducing or subsidizing production costs. *Agricultural research* is conducted by the federal and provincial departments of agriculture, with information made available through their publications, demonstration farms, and provincial extension or advisory services. Loans are made available to farmers in larger amounts and/or at lower rates than could be obtained normally, under the federal government's Farm Credit Act, Farm Improvement and Marketing Cooperatives Loans Act, and the Farm Syndicates Credit Act. Some provincial governments also have farm credit legislation. *Tax exemptions* or *rebates* are applicable to some farm items: farmers are eligible for a rebate of the gasoline tax for gasoline used on the farm. No duty is charged on imported farm machinery and most farm supplies.

Subsidies are paid for selected products or specific costs. A direct subsidy is paid for milk and cream used in manufacturing butter, cheese, and skim milk powder. Subsidies are also paid for the transportation of prairie-grown grains to other provinces, under the Livestock Feed Assistance Act. Before 1984, prairie-grown grains benefitted from the Crow's Nest Pass Agreement, which limited railway freight rates for exported prairie grains to the rates prevailing in 1898. This was revised in late 1983 such that rates are not controlled, but subsidies to the railways should keep rates down. The federal government also subsidizes premiums charged under provincial programs for crop insurance.

Marketing Programs

Federal and provincial governments set and administer *grading standards* so that a producer can realize a higher price for high-quality products and so that buyers can have confidence in the uniform quality and size of products.

Marketing boards have been established for almost every agricultural commodity. The Canadian Wheat Board administers a price support program for prairie-grown wheat, oats, and barley by making a guaranteed initial payment to producers. All grain entering into interprovincial or international trade is delivered to and sold by the Wheat Board. Deliveries are based on quotas set by the Board to ration the limited elevator space. All revenues from wheat sales, less operating costs, are distributed to producers such that each producer receives the same price for the same quality delivered to the same terminal.

The federal Farm Products Marketing Agencies Act provides for the creation of national marketing agencies for all farm products except those covered by the Canadian Wheat Board and the Canadian Dairy Commission. Under this Act, an egg marketing agency was established to assign quotas to the egg producers' council in each province, based on provincial shares of total egg production prior to the agency, between 1967 and 1971. The provincial councils, in turn, assigned quotas to each egg producer.

Provincial marketing boards are established by a vote of the producers of the particular commodity concerned. These boards do not administer price support programs; rather, most boards negotiate with the major buyers, such as food processors, for a minimum price for the commodity. Transportation charges and price differentials for quality differences may also be negotiated. Some boards have even established processing facilities to compete directly with the major processors. A few provincial boards have also established production or marketing quotas to restrict the total quantity supplied to the market.

The Ontario Tobacco Growers Marketing Board, for example, establishes production "rights", or the right to plant tobacco on a specified number of acres. The effect of this restriction is illustrated by Figure 21.8. Suppose that in the absence of such restrictions, the equilibrium price is P_1 and quantity sold is Q_1. The effect of the restrictive tobacco "rights" is to shift the supply curve leftward and make it perfectly inelastic above its intersection with the former supply curve at quantity Q_2. The price obtained for quantity Q_2 is P_2. Because the demand for tobacco is inelastic (due to the inelastic demand for tobacco products), the total revenue is greater for Q_2 than for Q_1. Since tobacco is a more profitable crop when such restrictions are applied, the "rights" increase land values for the owner of an established tobacco farm and cause considerable criticism of this system.

An alternative method of restricting supply is to specify quotas or quantities that each producer is permitted to supply, or for the marketing board itself to withhold part of the total quantity produced. This has the further advantage of controlling the quantity supplied more precisely; when quantity is specified in terms of acres planted, farmers cultivate these acres more intensely to obtain the highest possible yield.

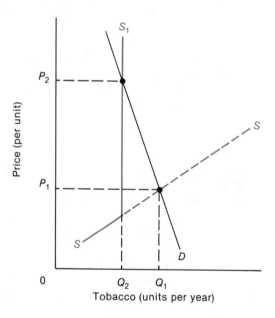

Figure 21.8   Crop Restriction Can Increase Total Revenue
When demand, D, is inelastic, a price increase also increases total revenue. By restricting the quantity of tobacco supplied to Q_2, tobacco producers can increase the price from its free market level of P_1 to P_2, and thus increase the total revenue.

The Economic Council of Canada examined the economic effects of agricultural marketing boards and concluded that these boards had improved the bargaining power and incomes of producers. However, the Council criticized the "supply management" actions of boards "with exclusive powers to determine prices and to set production quotas for individual producers, particularly when these powers essentially establish a cartel and are buttressed by import controls."[4] The commodities concerned included eggs, chickens, turkeys, tobacco, and milk. The problems identified by the Council were that the quota system could provide a capital gain to the producer who sold the quota (or right to produce) to another producer; the largest share of additional income resulting from supply management goes to the largest producers; provincial quotas impede the efficiency of a national market; and the higher costs of domestic production encourage the adoption of tariffs on related processed products.

Effectiveness of Agricultural Assistance Programs

Some of the less expensive programs appear to have been of greatest long-run benefit to Canadian agriculture: research in developing and breeding higher-yielding plants, livestock, and poultry; development of fertilizers, insecticides, and herbicides, and improved production techniques; expansion of information and advisory services, particularly in specialized subjects; and the establishment of marketing boards. Price supports have had some effect in raising farm prices and especially in reducing the instability of farm incomes. There has been rather disappointing progress, however, in dealing with the problem of agricultural surpluses such as wheat, and in coping with the long-run causes of rural poverty.

The report of a federal task force on agriculture recognized these problems in 1970, recommending that farm surpluses be controlled by restricting production and transferring some agricultural lands to other uses; that more emphasis be placed on management training for farmers, supplemented by better market information and forecasts; and that younger farmers on farms that cannot provide an adequate income by farming alone be provided with retraining and other employment opportunities.

While some progress was made in the 1970s in implementing these recommendations, the problem became more urgent in the early 1980s. The need for farmers to invest in new and more equipment, in order to remain competitive, together with high interest rates, led to serious

---

[4] Economic Council of Canada, *Reforming Regulation*. Ottawa: Supply and Services Canada, 1981, p. 65.

financial problems for many Canadian farmers. Additional public support was given through the federal government's Farm Credit Corporation and a few provincial programs, but the need for further additions to capital stock remains. Any financial relief has been gained only temporarily as a result of the lower interest rates prevailing in the later 1980s.

Forestry

The basic forest industry in Canada directly contributes only a tiny portion of the total GDP; but it provides the base for the forest products section, which accounts for 15 per cent of the manufacturing sector, and employs about six times as many persons as the forest industry. Furthermore, the forestry industry is concentrated in British Columbia, Ontario, and Quebec, so that the importance of forestry to these provinces is greater than the national totals would suggest. Forestry in British Columbia provides the raw material for one-half of the province's manufactured output.

Regeneration and Harvesting of Forests

The forests on which the forestry industry depends are generally considered to be renewable resources, especially in Canada, since they can regenerate themselves naturally—although at a slow rate. When this *rate of regeneration* is brought into consideration, it becomes apparent that the "renewability" of the forests is a matter of the size of the existing stock, and the rate at which the forests are harvested, compared with the rate at which they are replenished.

The basic decision in forestry management is the *rotation decision*, or the optimal rate of utilization of the existing stock. If utilization occurs too quickly, the stock will be depleted faster than it can naturally replace itself. When that happens, costs must be incurred to assist the regeneration artificially—by planting trees, thinning woodlots, spraying with insecticides to speed up the growth rate. But these programs must then be analyzed using benefit-cost analysis (as described in Chapter 14) to determine whether it is worthwhile to use these artificial interventions in the natural regeneration process.

Another factor to be considered in the harvesting decision is the fact that—so long as the trees continue to grow—the longer the harvest is postponed, the larger is the volume of timber to be harvested. This aspect of the decision brings in the *rate of time preference* (as described in Chapter 12) and estimates of the future prices of forest products. In addition, forests also play a major role in the physical environment through their effects on the climate (and specifically, on the water and oxygen cycles) and the preservation of soil. Increasingly, forests are recognized for their economic and aesthetic value in the tourism and recreation industries.

Public Policy for the Forest Industry

Stumpage Charges   Private firms that harvest trees on crown lands (publicly-owned lands) are required in all provinces to pay "stumpage charges", or fees, based on the volume of timber harvested. The setting of these fees becomes an important aspect of forestry policy, because a very high fee may erode any potential profit for the logging company, with the result that government revenues are sharply reduced and too few trees are harvested. Alternatively, a fee that is set too low would cause excessive, wasteful harvesting of trees, and leave the logging firm with a part of the profit that ought to have gone to the government for the use of a public resource.

Multiple-Use Policies   The conflicting proposals for forest management, arising from different interest groups, have led to a variety of policies that attempt to reconcile the different uses of the forests—logging, environmental stability, recreation, and wildlife habitat. Some lands have been set aside as wilderness areas, where logging is permanently prohibited. But in other areas, different sections are allocated to logging and recreation, with the intent that these uses will not overlap each other. The costs of access to such areas, however, both for logging and for recreation, and the demand for each use, will determine whether the quantity and location of the allocations have been appropriate.

Fishing

Canada is the world's largest exporter of fish. About 80 per cent of the total catch, valued at $2 billion in 1988, is exported—to the United States, the European Community, and Japan. The fishing industry consists of three separate fisheries: the Atlantic coast, the Pacific coast, and inland waters (such as the Great Lakes). The Atlantic fishery is largest, accounting for about three-quarters of the total value of the fishing industry, and includes cod, scallops, and lobster. The Pacific fishery amounts to one-fifth of the total, and is based on herring and salmon. The inland fishery contributes about five per cent of the industry's output.

This regional concentration suggests why fishing is so important in Canada, even though it represents a minute share of the total GDP. About one-fifth of the Newfoundland labour force is employed in fishing, and more than one-quarter of the population of the Atlantic provinces lives in the fishing villages. The fishing industry therefore forms the cultural as well as the economic base of these areas.

Maximum Sustainable Yield

The central focus of fisheries policy has been the management of the annual catch and the reproduction of the fish population, represented by the concept of the *maximum sustainable yield*. This is related to a "biomass", or biological growth model, as illustrated in Figure 21.9. The growth of the fish population is a function of the size of the population at any time. As the population increases in size, it can expand, but at a decreasing rate. Thus, a larger population would have a larger annual increase that could be harvested without depleting the base population. But this positive or direct relationship between annual increase and the base population can continue only to a certain population size. Beyond that point, the supportive environment, and particularly the food resources, begin to restrain the growth, until the population becomes so large that it can only support itself, and cannot add to its size.

The maximum sustainable yield is the largest amount that can be harvested (or fished) without reducing the base population. This occurs in Figure 21.9 at the peak of the yield curve, at point *B*. The diagram also shows that, with the exception of the maximum point, any given yield can be obtained at two different population sizes, such as at *A* and *C*, that is, on both the rising and falling portions of the yield curve. It can also be seen that by forgoing a portion of the yield in one year, in the rising portion of the yield curve, the base population and the future yields can be increased.

The maximum sustainable yield measure has been criticized for a number of reasons. First, the future fish populations are not as predictable as a simple model would suggest, with the possible result that the catch in a given year could be too large to allow the fishery to be sustained. Second, the maximum yield determined by this approach may not be the economically most efficient catch. If the fish population were allowed to grow, so that a larger catch could be obtained at a lower cost, the quota would need to be adjusted accordingly each year. Third, there is a biological consideration relating to the interdependence of species; namely, that the optimum population size for each species must take into account the effect on the species of any change in the size of another species.

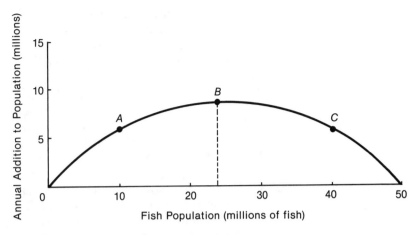

Figure 21.9   Potential Annual Fishery Yield
The curve illustrates the annual increase in a hypothetical fish population.
For example, with a relatively small population of 10 million, the annual
increase would be about 6 million. But a larger population, at 25 million,
would produce an annual increase of 10 million fish. This is called the
maximum sustainable yield because it is the maximum number that could
be caught each year (if the base population is 10 million) without reducing
the population. A larger population, of 40 million, produces a smaller annual
increase because the population is too large relative to its habitat and does
not have the food and protection required for the maximum increase.

Fisheries Policies

**Competition from
Foreign Fishing**

Foreign fishing boats have fished the Atlantic waters since before the
discovery of North America. With the development of modern fishing
trawlers that incorporated packing and freezing facilities, foreign fleets
were able to travel farther to the Atlantic fisheries and to take larger
catches. Canada has attempted to restrict this competition by declaring
a 200-mile limit, or zone. That is, Canada—and other nations that
joined in the agreement—would have the exclusive right to fish within
200 miles of its own coast. This would be a dramatic increase from the
3-mile limit that has prevailed for decades by international convention.
This arrangement has not yet received international agreement, but
Canada and several other countries have attempted to use diplomatic
and economic pressure to enforce the declaration.

Excess Capacity

A further policy problem concerns the larger number of persons
employed in the inshore (or near-shore) fisheries where the fish populations are being depleted; the fishermen are not well equipped, and there
is little alternative employment in the off-season, or for those who want
to leave the fishing industry. By contrast, the offshore (or distant)

fisheries are dominated by expensive, modern trawlers that are owned by, or are in contract with, the fish processing companies.

In both cases, there is excess productive capacity in the form of too many trawlers and too much capital invested in the on-board equipment, as well as in the on-shore processing plants. Much of this occurred when the 200-mile limit was introduced in 1977 and Canadian fishermen expected they would both increase their catch, and their exports, as a result of excluding foreign trawlers. But the slight increase in demand that actually occurred did not warrant the rapid expansion of the fishing and processing facilities.

Stinting Rights   In order to control the catch by Canadian fishermen, and to increase the incomes of those who remain in the industry, it has been proposed that quotas be assigned, in the form of "stinting rights". These are licences that specify a maximum catch, or quota, of a given species that the licence-holder can take each year. The size of these quotas would be determined by dividing the optimum total yield by the number of persons to whom the stinting rights would be issued. These quotas could be restricted to either the inshore or offshore fisheries (with a common proposal that quotas for inshore gradually be reduced), and could be transferable, through purchase-and-sale in an open market.

The problems of the Pacific fishery are less severe. Incomes are higher than on the Atlantic coast, and alternative employment is more readily available. But depletion of the fish population is a continuing policy issue, and there have been proposals similar to those advocated for the Atlantic fishery: namely, stinting rights and a reduction in the number of trawlers.

Unemployment Insurance   In addition to over-fishing and excess capacity in the Atlantic inshore fishery, much of the fishing is done in a short season. Consequently, incomes are supplemented with Unemployment Insurance (UI); and indeed, the active fishing season is influenced by the eligibility rules for UI compensation. Recent reports have suggested that the UI program be replaced by an income stabilization plan that would be based on criteria designed to encourage more efficient fishing practices, as well as to provide an income supplement.

Foreign Markets   A further policy problem is that 80 per cent of the fish output is exported; only 20 per cent is consumed in Canada. This means that the economic future of Canada's fishing industry is largely dependent on conditions in the world market, and in the major buyer of Canadian fish, the United States. Canadian exporters face the competition of other fish producers, and the protectionist lobbying of the American fishing industry.

Mining

There are certain similar features shared by the Canadian mining and fishing industries. In each case, Canada is the world's largest exporter, and exports 80 per cent of its total national output. Despite this, in each case, Canada has little impact on the world market because other countries are also significant producers of the same commodities.

Output of minerals has been declining in some cases, and growing only slowly in others, partly because of increasing international competition, but also because there has been a substitution of plastics, ceramics, and glass for traditional minerals such as copper, steel, and lead. It is commonly suggested, therefore, that the mining industry will need to develop new uses for its products in order to maintain its economic vitality.

A major feature of the mining industry is the oligopolistic pricing of output:

> Market structure in the minerals sector is dominated by a few multinational corporations that often set prices among themselves in an oligopolistic style, and pre-empt the market through vertical integration and long-term contracts. For instance, the world prices for aluminum, asbestos, sulphur, uranium, and potash are set by multi-national corporations, as are the American, Canadian and South American prices for copper and zinc, and the European price for zinc.[5]

Policies in the Mining Industry

Taxation   There has been continuing debate about the appropriate type and level of taxation on the mining industry. Two basic types of tax have been used: a tax on profits; and a tax, or "royalty", on the quantity or value produced. A royalty tax is easy to administer, provides a stable source of revenue for governments, may have a modest conservation effect, and is independent of changes in production costs. But a royalty tax can also distort mineral production by making it less profitable to extract the lower quality deposits, and hence may encourage companies to "take only the best and leave the rest". A profit tax, however, avoids this inefficiency.

The Macdonald Commission recommended that

> the federal government and the provinces collaborate in the establishment of a tax system that is more closely related to profits, while retaining a minimum gross royalty. After collection of a low-level gross royalty, taxes should be levied on profits rather than on output.[6]

[5] Royal Commission on the Economic Union and Development Prospects for Canada, *Report*, Vol. 2, p. 467.
[6] *Ibid.*, p. 478.

Oil and Natural Gas

The production of oil and natural gas provides about one-half of Canada's energy needs; two-thirds of this is oil and one-third is natural gas. (The other half of Canada's energy is provided by electricity from hydro, nuclear, or coal generators.) As in the case of other natural resource industries, the oil and gas industry is concentrated in a few provinces: the output of oil and gas contributes about one-quarter of Alberta's GDP, and 5 to 10 per cent of the GDP in Saskatchewan.

Canada's Petroleum Policies

National Oil Policy   The first stage in a petroleum policy in Canada was the National Oil Policy of 1961. A basic feature of this policy was the "Ottawa Valley Line", which followed the Ottawa River boundary between Ontario and Quebec. The areas west of this line were supplied by oil from western Canada, while provinces to the east could import foreign oil. This resulted in an agreement with the United States whereby oil from western Canada could be sold to the American mid-west, and no restrictions would be placed on the importation of American-controlled Venezuelan oil into eastern Canada. This arrangement provided for stable oil prices, production, and distribution through the 1960s, as illustrated in Figure 21.10.

The Response to OPEC   Early in the 1970s, however, increased use of oil and impending shortages began to push up oil prices. The Arab-Israeli war of 1973 showed that the Arab oil-producing countries held considerable economic power in the international oil market. Consequently, the Organization of Petroleum Exporting Countries (OPEC), consisting mainly of Arab countries, announced an abrupt increase in the price of oil. The result in Canada was that oil produced in western Canada was suddenly more valuable in world markets, while the price of imported oil in eastern Canada also increased sharply. At the same time, there was a sudden concern about the remaining oil reserves (in the ground) in Canada.

The federal government reacted by freezing the price of Canadian oil for home consumption, but allowing the price of exported oil to rise to the international level. The difference between the domestic and the world price would be taxed as an export tax by the federal government and would be used to subsidize the higher cost of imported oil in eastern Canada. These arrangements assured that there would be no oil shortages or rapid price increases, and consequently, Canada survived the earlier stages of the OPEC price increases with less inflationary impact than occurred in the United States and elsewhere.

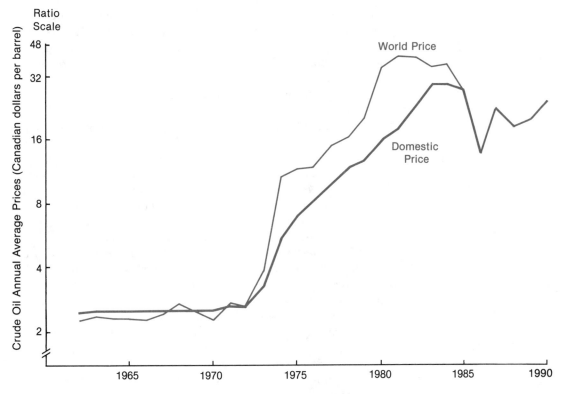

Figure 21.10   Comparison of World Oil Prices and Prices of Domestic Oil in Canada
The world price of oil was $2.50 to $3.00 per barrel through the 1960s. At the same time, the price of domestic oil was fixed at $2.65. But these levels and relationships began to change in 1973 when OPEC increased the world price to $3.95; this was quickly raised to the $12–$16 range for 1974–78; and to $43 in 1981. Meanwhile, the price of Canadian oil was held much below world prices; in 1980, it was only 42 per cent of the world price. But as the latter fell in the 1980s, the Canadian price rose to meet it until, in 1985, control of the Canadian price was discontinued. Oil prices remained in the range of $20 through the later 1980s, and rose briefly to about $45 in late 1990 due to the Iraqi invasion of Kuwait.

Source: Canada Department of Finance, *Economic Review*.

This arrangement resulted, however, in less concern about alternative energy sources and energy conservation, and less oil exploration and development, than was occurring in other countries. During the rest of the 1970s, the price of oil for domestic consumption was gradually adjusted upward, until it had reached more than 80 per cent of the world price. But the world oil price doubled between 1978 and 1980; as a result the Canadian price was only 45 per cent of the world level.

The situation presented a policy dilemma. The federal government preferred to restrain the price increase, both to avoid rapid inflation in the prices of the many goods and services that were dependent on petroleum inputs, and to allow the manufacturing sector to increase its competitiveness in world trade. But to lower oil prices would also encourage inefficient use of this nonrenewable resource.

National Energy Program

The result was the National Energy Program (NEP) of 1980. It was designed to reduce the uncertainty of oil supply by reducing petroleum imports, to increase the Canadian ownership of the petroleum industry, and to establish petroleum prices and a distribution of the revenues that are generally regarded as "fair". The government proposed to decelerate the consumption of oil by offering subsidies for conversion to more plentiful energy sources such as natural gas, and by increasing the prices and taxes for petroleum. The NEP was successful in shifting some demand from oil to natural gas, while oil prices were allowed to rise gradually. Subsequently, the world oil price fell sharply, and exploration and production slowed down. The Canadian oil price was approaching the world oil price so quickly that in 1985, the Canadian price was allowed to move to, and with, the world oil price.

The Macdonald Commission recommended that this policy, whereby domestic crude oil is sold within Canada at world prices, should be continued and that the government should intervene only to smooth out any abrupt changes in oil prices. The Commission stated clearly the opportunity cost to Canada that is imposed if the domestic price is set below the world price.

> The world price is the real opportunity cost for Canadian supplies, even if it is only the "artificial" creation of OPEC's market power. The difference between the world price and the domestic Canadian price is the value that is forgone every time a barrel of oil is consumed domestically rather than sold abroad. Likewise, it is the cost of replacing the same oil if we are forced to turn to the international market. To assign any price to oil other than the world price is to distort both supply incentives and demand incentives as well.[7]

Taxation of Oil

A continuing issue will be the appropriate balance of taxation by the federal and provincial governments. Since the provinces own the natural resources, they can impose a royalty tax; but the federal government, with its responsibility for interprovincial and international trade, can impose import and export taxes, as well as the general profits tax. Periodic federal-provincial negotiations will be necessary to

[7] Royal Commission on the Economic Union and Development Prospects for Canada, *Report*, Vol. 2, pp. 496-97.

assure that the combined taxes are not stimulating inflation or curtailing production, but still provide sufficient revenue to compensate the public for the permanent depletion of these resources.

Future Availability of Oil

A major public concern throughout the past two decades has been the future availability of domestic oil, and the extent to which Canada might become dependent on foreign oil. Although the lower prices for oil helped to reduce inflation during the 1980s, they also reduced the incentive to seek alternative energy sources and more energy-efficient production processes. Low oil prices also reduce the incentive for exploration and production.

Since it has been argued that Canadian oil prices should be free to follow the world prices, it will be necessary to develop policies other than price regulation, to have the desired impact on future oil reserves. This requires a combination of policies that both encourage exploration, development, and more efficient production in the petroleum industry, and encourage the continuing conversion to energy-efficient processes and products and to other energy sources. One component of such a set of policies was implemented in 1987 as the Canadian Exploration and Development Incentive Program (CEDIP). This provides for government payment of cash incentives of one-third of private expenditures for exploration and development expansion in the oil and gas industry.

Pricing of Natural Gas

Since natural gas cannot economically be transported long distances from its source, there is not a world market for natural gas, such as there is for oil. Consequently, the price is established within the Canada-United States market. Moreover, Canada's exports of natural gas to the United States account for less than 5 per cent of that country's total gas consumption, which means that Canada has virtually no market power to influence the price there. And in each country, the reserves of natural gas have *increased* throughout the postwar period, so that supply conditions have not had the same extreme impact on prices as in the oil market.

Until 1985, the domestic price for natural gas had been government-regulated, and determined by a somewhat complex arrangement. The price of natural gas at Toronto was set at 65 per cent of the domestic price of crude oil, but the price paid to Alberta producers was set separately by federal-provincial agreement. The difference between these two prices was offset by federal taxes or subsidies. The minimum export price for natural gas was to be the same as the Toronto price; but this generally was higher than the American domestic price and therefore restricted Canada's exports of natural gas. Since 1985, there has been less regulation of the gas prices, especially to open the opportunity for setting the export price in line with the American domestic gas market.

Foreign Ownership and Control of Canadian Industry

One of the most popular current issues in the Canadian economy concerns foreign ownership and control of Canadian industry. Ownership and control, however, are not synonymous. Ownership of 51 per cent of a corporation's common stock is nominally required to control the firm's affairs, but when shares are held by many people, a smaller percentage may be sufficient. Each of these issues requires separate consideration. For simplicity, however, this section will use only the term "foreign ownership", unless specific reference to control is necessary.

Table 21.1 summarizes some of the available information on foreign ownership in Canadian industry. Regrettably, no aggregative data are available on actual foreign control. Instead, estimates have been devel-

Table 21.1

Ownership and Control of Capital Employed in Selected Industries, Canada, 1985

	Total Capital Employed ($ billions)	Canada		United States		Other Foreign	
		Own	Control	Own	Control	Own	Control
		(percentage of total capital)					
Manufacturing	102	54	51	36	37	10	12
Petroleum, natural gas	80	59	65	29	27	12	8
Mining, smelting	22	61	68	21	17	18	15
Railways	11	65	100	22	0	13	0
Other utilities	115	70	97	18	3	12	0
Above industries plus merchandising, construction	411	67	76	23	18	10	6

Source: Statistics Canada, *Canada's International Investment Position.*

oped by including firms in which at least 51 per cent of the common stock is owned by non-residents, plus those in which less than 51 per cent is owned by non-residents but for which it is known or believed that control lies abroad.

Comparisons with similar data for previous years show that there has been a slight decline in the percentage of foreign ownership. Foreign control increased steadily in the postwar period until 1972, but there has been a gradual increase in Canadian control since then.[8] The major increase in Canadian control occurred in mining and petroleum between 1976 and 1985. Foreign ownership had occurred because foreign investors, particularly in the United States, were looking more widely for profitable uses of their financial assets and were increasingly buying larger blocks of stock in a few foreign firms, instead of bonds and small shareholdings in several firms. Another factor was the growth of *multinational corporations*, or firms that have plants in a number of countries. These are generally firms concerned with product areas where technology is changing rapidly, and where there are thus increasing opportunities for realizing economies of very large scale. Because some countries have retained high tariffs on the products concerned, these large firms are encouraged to establish plants in each country, rather than supply world markets from a home base.

The Major Issues

The question of foreign ownership might be included in a chapter on international trade and finance, since foreign direct investment obviously has important effects on a country's balance of international payments and its foreign exchange rate. The current issues, however, extend much beyond the matter of international economics, and indeed beyond economic considerations. This is evident in some of the proposals for dealing with foreign-owned firms. The suggestion that such firms be brought under public ownership, for example, has more to do with a general political ideology than with the specific consequences of foreign control. Public ownership may be appropriate, however, if the firm in question is a case of natural monopoly.

There appear to be five basic economic issues in the debate on foreign ownership. These concern the relationship of foreign ownership, Canadian economic growth, and the balance of payments; the effect of foreign-owned firms' international trade on Canada's balance of payments; foreign governments' influence on Canadian industry and governments; the behaviour of foreign-owned firms concerning research, development, and employment; and the accelerated depletion of Canada's natural resources.

[8] Statistics Canada, *Canada's International Investment Position.*

Economic Growth versus Balance of Payments Problems

Foreign ownership has generally been defended on the grounds that it would contribute to a substantial increase in the rate of economic growth. However, this argument usually fails to distinguish between an increase in foreign ownership due to the reinvestment of earnings of foreign-owned firms and that due to the importation of capital. The latter case also must distinguish between foreign *direct investment* (ownership of most or all of a firm's physical assets) and *portfolio investment* (holdings of bonds and small blocks of common stocks). Much of the foreign borrowing is done by provincial governments and has no direct bearing on the foreign ownership question; similarly, foreign holdings of small blocks of common shares in Canadian firms is not the nub of the issue. Moreover, much of the increase in the percentage of foreign-owned firms in Canada reflects reinvestment of earnings realized in Canada and borrowing from Canadian financial institutions.

The argument favouring foreign ownership for economic growth reasons thus shifts from the simple importation of capital to the special features of foreign capital. Two claims are made for this. Foreign-owned firms are: (1) willing and able to undertake riskier ventures than are Canadian-owned firms because they are part of the large, diverse operation of a foreign parent firm that can afford greater risk; and (2) able to draw on the advanced production, marketing, and financing experience of the parent company. Estimates of the effect of foreign-owned firms on Canadian economic growth vary with the data and assumptions used, but foreign-owned capital in Canada likely contributes less than 5 per cent of the current GDP.

Earlier criticism was directed against foreign investment rather than foreign ownership, since the former necessarily would require that interest payments, and likely some dividend payments, be made abroad for many years hence. If the exchange rate were pegged, this would impose an additional burden on foreign exchange reserves; if the foreign exchange rate were floating, it would increase the price of imports. Foreign ownership, however, has no immediate effect on the balance of payments if earnings are retained in Canada. Nevertheless, these retained earnings increase the base from which future earnings are paid abroad. Earnings transmitted abroad are likely to vary with business conditions; these payments would thus be highest when export earnings were highest.

International Trade of Foreign-Owned Firms

Because they tend to import more and export less than the rest of Canadian industry, foreign-owned firms are said to contribute to a current account deficit and to contractionary pressures on national income. This argument follows from the belief that Canadian subsidiaries are required to import much of their raw material or semifinished products from foreign parent firms. This, however, is inconsistent with the argument that Canadian subsidiaries are established to get around tariffs preventing foreign firms from exporting directly to Canada. Foreign-owned firms do, in fact, import more than similar Canadian firms, but the explanations for this vary; for example, it may be because parent firms export finished products through their subsidiaries rather than deal with independent importers.

That Canadian subsidiaries can be expected to export less than other firms follows from the assumption that Canadian subsidiaries are restricted to Canadian markets, leaving other markets to the parent firm or subsidiaries in other countries. The evidence does not support this as a general assumption: where foreign-owned firms can be compared with like Canadian firms, the export performance of the two types is similar, "whether one considers all such firms, larger ones only, or only those in manufacturing."[9] This general conclusion is consistent, however, with the existence of specific cases of marketing restrictions, and special advantages such as access to the parent firm's marketing system, since the evidence suggests that these features have offsetting effects. Moreover, the export performance of foreign-owned firms can be improved by diminishing the restrictions and encouraging the special advantages.

Foreign Influence   Current opposition to foreign ownership would appear to be based primarily on the view that Canadian subsidiaries and other foreign-owned firms are or can be a channel of influence on Canadian governments, and that policies of foreign governments are extended to the behaviour of foreign-owned firms in Canada. The latter condition does exist; for example, American-owned firms in Canada are subject to American anti-trust legislation. Since American anti-trust legislation has been more effective than Canada's anti-combines law, foreign control of this type might be welcomed by most Canadian consumers.

Foreign influence through Canadian subsidiaries pressuring the federal government on instruction from their parent firm has not been documented or studied, but there is no reason why the federal government should be particularly susceptible to this kind of pressure. Moreover, such subsidiaries have no bargaining power other than threatening to leave the country, and are more likely to seek government favour rather than express criticism. There have been a few cases of foreign governments pressing the federal government on behalf of foreign-owned firms, but this is a case of normal pleading, which can be resisted or not as the federal government chooses.

[9] A.E. Safarian. "Issues Raised By Foreign Direct Investment in Canada", in L.H. Officer and L.B. Smith (eds.), *Issues in Canadian Economics*. Toronto: McGraw-Hill Ryerson, 1974, p. 82.

Research and Employment in Foreign-Owned Firms

The suggestion that there can be foreign political influence through Canadian subsidiaries should be distinguished from the argument that these plants are controlled by the parent firm, frequently contrary to the Canadian public interest. Two specific concerns are the alleged lack of research and development undertaken in the subsidiary and the employment of foreign personnel in senior management; the effect of these is to curtail Canada's research and development capacity and to reduce job opportunities for highly trained personnel.

Evidence shows that much of the research and development work related to Canadian subsidiaries is done in the parent firm. At the same time, the subsidiaries do at least as much research and development work in Canada as similar Canadian firms do. The important question then is why Canadian firms conduct relatively little research and development activity. The association of Canadian subsidiaries with the research and development divisions of the parent firm is one of the major advantages credited to foreign ownership, since new technology can be transmitted more quickly through this close international linkage.

Foreign-owned firms do have a higher proportion of foreign personnel in senior management, but this can be beneficial in the transmission of management skills to Canadian firms. The loss of employment opportunities for Canadians would be serious only when unemployment in the managerial category is high. The presence of non-resident directors on the boards of foreign-owned firms in Canada also causes some concern, but it is not clear why they should be expected to act differently from Canadian directors, provided that one assumes the general objective of profit maximization in each case.

Depletion of Canada's Natural Resources

One of the most controversial issues is whether foreign-owned firms should dominate any industry, and particularly the mining industry. The basic question here, however, is whether Canada has an appropriate policy for mining development, including taxation policy, rather than whether foreign firms should be excluded from this field. Nevertheless, an important related problem is that foreign-owned firms extract and export raw materials, such as lumber, pulp, and mineral ores, for processing elsewhere, instead of providing the potential employment associated with processing these materials in Canada.

Public Policy on Foreign Ownership and Control

Public policy has evolved more slowly on the question of foreign ownership than on almost any other economic matter. The question became a political issue following the report of the Royal Commission on Canada's Economic Prospects in 1957. Commission chairman Walter

Gordon aroused some public support for his criticism of foreign ownership, and particularly for his proposed Canada Development Corporation. Gordon later persuaded the government to establish a Task Force on Foreign Ownership, which reported in 1968. This led to the Foreign Investment Review Act (FIRA), which provided for a government agency to screen proposed foreign take-overs of Canadian-owned firms, as well as new foreign investment in Canada. The basic test for allowing foreign ownership was that it should "bring significant benefit to Canada", particularly in terms of employment, investment, and improved productivity. FIRA was replaced in 1985 by the Investment Canada Act. This requires federal cabinet approval for the take-over of a Canadian firm by a foreign-controlled firm, but the federal cabinet has been more lenient in its decisions than was FIRA.

The slow evolution of public policy on foreign ownership follows not only from governments' attempts to find a compromise between the restrictive proposals of the nationalists and the international orientation of traditional liberals. There appear to be quite different effects of foreign ownership on different groups of people and in different regions of the country. There is also the difficulty of determining the effects of foreign ownership in particular industries and under a diversity of circumstances. It is the problem of reconciling these various differences that helps explain the difficulty of determining a policy to encourage those effects that are most in the public interest.

Review of the Main Points

1. The natural resource industries, broadly defined, include agriculture, forestry, fishing, mining, and petroleum. These are also described as the primary industries because they provide the inputs for the secondary and tertiary (or service) industries.

2. The natural resource industries have contributed a smaller share of Gross Domestic Product as other industries developed, but they continue to provide a large share of merchandise exports. The decline in employment in these industries was due primarily to increased labour productivity. Each of the natural resource industries tends to be concentrated in one or two provinces; thus, its contribution to the national economy may be small, while it plays a significant role in the province's economy.

3. The agricultural industry has an unusually large number of firms, faces a low price elasticity of demand for its products, has experienced rapid increases in supply, and is subject to sharp changes in product prices due to weather and disease. Consequently, farm incomes tend to be low and unstable. Public assistance takes the form of programs to support and stabilize prices, to decrease or

subsidize production costs, and to improve prices through more effective marketing.

4. Two types of price supports are used: an offer to purchase produce not sold in the market when the price is set at the guaranteed minimum, and a deficiency payment or a payment of the difference between the free-market price and the guaranteed price. The advantage of the latter method is that the government does not need to accumulate stocks of the supported product, although the total deficiency payments are larger than the offer-to-purchase payments would be for a given product, if the demand for that product is inelastic.

5. Other assistance programs include agricultural research and extension services provided by the federal and provincial governments, tax exemptions or rebates on farm supplies, subsidies for production or transportation of some products, and the establishment of marketing boards. Some boards set quotas, which, when the demand is inelastic, have the effect of raising the total revenue for the product; but these boards have been criticized for raising consumer prices. Finally, the federal government has been actively encouraging the formation of larger, more efficient farms, and the shifting of land and labour into other industries.

6. The forests have been considered to be naturally renewable, but their rate of regeneration depends on the rotation decision, or the rate of harvesting compared with the natural replacement rate. Replanting programs and programs to speed forest growth also influence the availability of forest resources. Logging decisions should also consider the future value of a greater harvest if current logging is carried on at a reduced rate.

7. Public policy issues in the forest industry include the setting of stumpage charges or fees (a provincial royalty tax) at appropriate levels, and the development of arrangements for multiple use of forest lands. Benefit-cost calculations in these public policies need to include the several environmental benefits associated with these lands.

8. The fishing industry consists of three fishing areas: the Atlantic coast, the Pacific coast, and the inland waters. The Atlantic fishery accounts for about three-quarters of the total value.

9. The concept of a maximum sustainable yield, which relates the optimum catch to the annual increase in the fish population, given the level of that population, has been the central focus of fisheries policy. But this concept has certain limitations: the fish population cannot be measured or predicted accurately; the biological optimum yield likely differs from the economic optimum; fish species

are interdependent ecologically, and therefore species need to be considered together when a maximum yield is determined.

10. Increased foreign fishing in the Atlantic offshore fishery led Canada to declare a 200-mile limit within which it would have exclusive right to fish. Although some other countries participated in this declaration, there has not been international agreement.

11. Fishery policies must take account of the excess capacity and depleted stocks in the inshore fishery, with little alternative employment opportunity. There have been proposals for stinting rights, or quotas. A major problem, over which Canada has almost no control, is that 80 per cent of the catch is exported and these exports face increasing world competition and protectionist pressure in other countries.

12. The mining industry has been growing more slowly, in terms of output, because it faces competition from foreign producers, as well as the substitution of other materials for copper, lead, and steel.

13. Pricing of mineral products is not a public matter, but is determined by a few multinational firms that set prices oligopolistically. The major policy issue is to levy the appropriate type and level of taxes on the mining industry so that the public gains some benefit from these resources, exploration is encouraged, and the minerals are extracted efficiently.

14. Public policy for the petroleum industry was consolidated and expanded by the National Energy Program of 1980 and its subsequent amendments. This program is intended to decelerate energy consumption, reduce dependence on foreign sources, increase Canadian ownership and control, and provide equitable energy prices and revenue distribution.

15. The future availability of domestic oil, and dependency on foreign oil, are continuing policy concerns. Low oil prices restrain inflation, but they also reduce the incentive to develop alternative energy sources and more efficient production processes, and the incentive to explore for and develop new oil reserves.

16. Foreign ownership and control of firms in Canada has become a major problem for public policy on industrial organization. There appear to be five basic issues: the relationship of economic growth and the balance of payments to foreign ownership; the international trade pattern of foreign-owned firms; the influence of foreign governments on Canadian industry and government; the research, development, and employment practices of foreign-owned firms; and the accelerated depletion of Canada's natural resources. Public policy on foreign ownership includes the federal government's plan to review proposed foreign take-overs of Cana-

dian firms and rules concerning the extent of foreign ownership in some industries, but policy has evolved slowly because foreign ownership has different effects on different groups of people and in different regions.

Key Concepts and Topics

natural resource industries
price supports
offer to purchase
deficiency payments
hog cycle or cobweb theorem
marketing boards
production rights or quotas
rotation decision
rate of time preference
stumpage charges

maximum sustainable yield
200-mile limit
stinting rights
National Oil Policy
National Energy Program
domestic vs. world oil price
foreign ownership vs. foreign
   control
multinational corporations

Questions for Review and Discussion

1. Conservation of natural resources is a popular public issue, yet there is seldom consideration of how much conservation there should be. Discuss approaches that might be taken in determining the rate of depletion or use of these resources. Consider also the arguments against an extremist who proposes that, since these resources will be more valuable in the future, none should be taken now.
2. Why are the prices received by farmers less stable than the prices paid by farmers?
3. "The farm problem becomes worse the more government attempts to intervene. The only solution is to let the free market take its course." Explain carefully why you agree or disagree.
4. The cobweb theorem is often used to explain fluctuations in the prices of agricultural commodites. What examples can you think of in other industries where the cobweb theorem may be applicable?
5. List the advantages and disadvantages, for producers and consumers, of controlled or regulated prices for domestically produced oil; and of high versus low prices for oil.
6. The OPEC cartel set both the level of oil prices, and output quotas, at various times during the past two decades. Can it do both of these successfully? Why? Which approach would you recommend, and why?
7. The control of a major part of the Canadian petroleum industry lies in the United States. Do you think the public concern about foreign control would be lessened if this same degree of foreign control were distributed about evenly over four or five countries instead? Why?

Sources and Selected Readings

Anderson, F.J. *Natural Resources in Canada: Economic Theory and Policy.* Toronto: Methuen, 1985.

Brinkman, G.L. *Farm Incomes in Canada.* Ottawa: Supply and Services Canada, 1981.

Carmichael, E.A., and C.A. Herrera, eds. *Canada's Energy Policy, 1985 and Beyond.* Montreal: C.D. Howe Institute, 1984.

Danielsen, A.L. *The Evolution of OPEC.* New York: Harcourt, Brace, Jovanovich, 1982.

Economic Council of Canada. *Connections: An Energy Strategy for the Future.* Ottawa: Supply and Services Canada, 1985.

Fisher, Anthony C. *Resource and Environmental Economics.* New York: Cambridge University Press, 1981.

Forbes, J.D., R.D. Hughes, and T.K. Warley. *Economic Intervention in Canadian Agriculture.* Ottawa: Economic Council of Canada, 1982.

Globerman, Steven. *U.S. Ownership of Firms in Canada.* Montreal: C.D. Howe Institute, 1979.

Hartwick, J.M., and N.D. Olewiler. *Economics of Natural Resource Use.* New York: Harper and Row, 1986.

Pomfret, R. *The Economic Development of Canada.* Toronto: Methuen, 1981.

Rees, Judith. *Natural Resources: Allocation, Economics and Policy,* 2nd ed. New York: Routledge, 1990.

Royal Commission on the Economic Union and Development Prospects for Canada. *Report,* Vol. 2, Part IV. Toronto: University of Toronto Press, 1985.

Rugman, Alan M., and John McIlveen. *Megafirms: Strategies for Canada's Multinationals.* Toronto: Methuen, 1985.

Safarian, A.E. *Foreign Ownership of Canadian Industry.* Toronto: McGraw-Hill, 1986.

PART FOUR

Distribution of Incomes

22 Demand for Factor Services

Prices of productive factors have a direct effect on the costs of producing final products, and thus on their prices. But factor prices also allocate or ration factors among industries and firms producing different commodities, and determine the particular combination of resources used to produce each commodity.

Of even wider significance is the influence that factor prices have on the total income of the population and the distribution of this income among various groups and individuals. This *functional or factor distribution* of income is determined largely by factor prices, because it is individuals who have ultimate ownership or control of the productive factors and who receive the income from the use of them. Each individual's income thus depends on the quantity of each kind of factor services he or she supplies and the prices of these services.

In previous chapters that were concerned with the prices and output of finished products, the prices of productive factors were taken as given. This chapter turns to a general explanation of the demand for productive factors and then considers the determination of factor prices in the form of rent, interest, and profit. An examination of wage determination in labour markets is reserved for the following chapter.

Factors and Factor Services

Two terms are used in this chapter that are similar, but actually have different meanings: *factors* and *factor services*. A distinction must be made, for example, between one worker and one hour of a worker's labour.

A productive factor is something that can make a contribution to the process of producing a good or service. A factor is thus a *stock*, a stock of potential contributions to production that the factor can provide over a period of time.

Factor services are the actual contributions of the factor and are described as a *flow* of the services over a specified period. The prices of factor services are therefore expressed in terms of time periods: the price of labour service, for example, is its hourly wage or annual salary.

The services of many different factors are used in the production of most commodities, but for convenience these different factors are generally classified as *land*, *labour*, and *capital*. This traditional classification, however, no longer represents clear distinctions among different factors. At a time when there were few improvements to land through draining, clearing, or levelling, and few improvements to labour through education and training, these two types of "natural" factors could be differentiated from *capital*, which was defined simply as a *man-made means of production*. However, the use of resources to make improvements to land and to the skills of labour, as well as to create new plant and equipment, has blurred this earlier distinction.

A fourth factor should be added to the list, namely, *management* or *entrepreneurship*. This addition emphasizes the particular contribution made by individuals who take the initiative, and the risk, in employing and organizing the other factors in the productive process.

Demand for Factor Services: Marginal Productivity Theory

There is a basic similarity between the demand for finished products and the demand for factor services. Consumer demand was explained primarily in terms of the utility or satisfaction obtained from additional units of a given commodity. Similarly, producer demand can be explained in terms of the output or revenue obtained from additional units of factor services. This explanation, termed the *marginal productivity theory*, can be illustrated by the example of the pottery firm used in Chapter 16 to illustrate the cost conditions facing a firm.

The pottery firm was assumed to use only two productive factors in producing its ceramic coffee mugs—capital and labour. Capital was the fixed factor consisting of five potter's wheels; labour was the variable factor. The firm was assumed to be in a perfectly competitive industry: it could sell any quantity of its mugs at a constant price of $2 per mug. Since there are many other pottery firms in the industry, this particular firm has no influence on the price of labour services because it employs only a small fraction of the potters in the industry.

Marginal Revenue Product Some of the production information included in Table 16.1 is presented again in Table 22.1. As an increasing number of worker-days are added to the firm's five potter's wheels, the *total product* increases up to the eighth unit of labour, but the *marginal product* decreases after the fourth labour unit.

Table 22.1

Marginal Revenue Product of a Perfectly Competitive Firm

Variable Factor (Units of Labour) Q_L	Total Product TP	Marginal Physical Product MPP	Product Selling Price P	Marginal Revenue Product MRP
0	0			
		20	$2	$ 40
1	20		2	
		56		112
2	76		2	
		107		214
3	183		2	
		121		242
4	304		2	
		106		212
5	410		2	
		76		152
6	486		2	
		32		64
7	518		2	
		2		4
8	520		2	
		−7		−14
9	513		2	

The terminology changes in an important way in Table 22.1: what was previously termed "marginal product" is now termed *marginal physical product*, to emphasize that it is the additional number of units of output that are being measured. Thus, the additional physical product is distinguished from the additional revenue associated with additional units of the variable factor. By multiplying the selling price of the product by the marginal physical product, one can calculate the *marginal revenue product*.

The marginal revenue product is the change in total revenue associated with each additional unit of the variable factor or input.

Note that $MPP = \Delta TP/\Delta Q_L$ and $MRP = \Delta TR/\Delta Q_L$. (Notice that marginal revenue product differs from marginal revenue, which is the change in total revenue associated with each additional unit of output.)

The cost conditions facing the firm are also differentiated in this fashion. Previously, the additional cost per unit of output has been termed the marginal cost. An additional term, *marginal resource cost* (*MRC*), is now introduced to describe the additional cost per unit of productive resources, or inputs, that are purchased or employed by the firm. In the definition of this new term, $MRC = \Delta TC/\Delta Q_L$, the quantity ($Q$) refers to input rather than to output.

MRP = MRC Rule   A firm's demand for the services of the factor depends on the marginal revenue product and the price of a factor's services. The rule for determining the profit-maximizing output—produce the quantity at which marginal revenue equals marginal cost—can be modified to establish a profit-maximization rule for determining the quantity of factor services to be employed. The purely competitive firm will maximize its profits if it continues to purchase additional units of the factor service up to the point where the factor price—the marginal resource cost (*MRC*)—is equal to its marginal revenue product.

In the pottery firm example, the price per day of potters' services is assumed to be $100. At a price of $100 per labour unit, Table 22.1 shows that the pottery firm will maximize its profit by employing six potters, because the cost per labour unit of $100 is less than the marginal revenue product, $152, of the sixth potter. If the firm increased its staff to seven potters, the additional cost would be $100, but the marginal revenue product would be only $64, with a loss of $36 incurred by hiring the seventh potter. Note that this result is the same as that found by following the profit-maximization rule for determining the level of output.

Firm's Demand Curve   By assuming a schedule of alternative prices per unit of potters' services, the firm's demand curve for this factor can be plotted, as in Figure 22.1. As the price (or wage) of potters' services declines, more labour units are used because the firm can add to its profit as long as the marginal revenue product of the last unit of the factor's service exceeds the price of that unit.

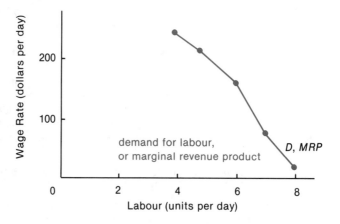

Figure 22.1   Competitive Firm's Demand for Factor Services
Although a competitive firm faces a perfectly elastic demand for its product, its demand for factor services is downward-sloping, due to the diminishing marginal productivity of variable factors. The firm will purchase the quantity of labour services at which the marginal revenue product, *MRP*, equals the wage rate. Hence the declining portion of the firm's *MRP* curve is also its demand curve for labour services.

The marginal revenue product curve is therefore a firm's demand curve for the services of a particular factor.

Only a portion of the demand curve has been plotted in Figure 22.1, namely, the portion corresponding with diminishing marginal productivity. As long as marginal productivity is increasing, the firm will add to its profit (or reduce its loss) by adding more of the variable factor; this portion of the curve is therefore irrelevant to the firm's decision. It is only when marginal productivity is diminishing that the firm must decide how many units of the variable factor it should employ.

Derived Demand   The demand for factor services is said to be a *derived demand*, because such services are useful or desirable only to the extent that they contribute to the production of final products desired by consumers. Furthermore, other things being equal, a shift in the demand for a final product will cause a shift in the demand for the factor services used in producing that product.

One might expect that the market demand curve for a factor's services would be derived by adding horizontally the individual demand curves of all firms, in the same way that a market demand curve is obtained for final products. This cannot be done for factor services, however, because the *industry* normally faces a downward-sloping demand for its product; that is, the product price declines with increasing output, whereas the product price received by a *single firm* in a competitive industry remains constant. Consequently, if each firm attempts to expand its output when the price of a factor's services declines, the price of its product falls. The effect of an industry's declining product demand curve is that its labour demand curve is less elastic than the sum of the demand curves of the individual firms.

Elasticity of Demand for Factor Services

The price elasticity of demand for factor services is defined and calculated in the same way as the price elasticity of demand for final products: the percentage change in the quantity demanded is divided by the percentage change in the price of the factor service.

Some of the reasons for differing degrees of elasticity are similar to those given for the different elasticities of consumer products. First, if there are *close substitutes* for a factor, the demand for that factor's service is likely to be highly elastic. If, for example, a technician is a close substitute for an engineer in a particular process, the demand for an engineer's service is likely to be quite elastic. A small increase in engineers' salaries relative to technicians' salaries will result in a proportionately greater decline in the number of engineers employed (and an increase in technicians employed).

Second, the elasticity of demand for a factor's service will reflect the *elasticity of demand for the final product* to which it contributes. If the demand for ceramic coffee mugs is quite elastic, a small increase in the price of mugs will result in a substantial decline in the quantity of mugs sold; hence there will be a sharp decline in the number of potters hired to produce the mugs.

Third, the *relative significance of the factor* in the total production costs of the firm will also influence the elasticity of its demand for the factor. If labour costs represent only a small portion of the total costs, a 10 per cent increase in wages, for example, may have little effect on the quantity of labour employed; but if labour is the firm's major production cost, the same percentage increase in wages may sharply reduce the number of labourers employed.

A fourth factor influencing the demand elasticity of factor services is the *rate at which marginal productivity is declining*. When the marginal productivity of a factor declines quickly, the demand for that factor is likely to be highly inelastic: even substantial decreases in the factor price result in small increases in the quantity used, because the additional units add so little to the total revenue.

Shifts in Demand

The demand curve for a factor's services may shift for any of three general reasons. One of these was suggested above in reference to derived demand. The demand curve for a factor's services is influenced by the *demand for the related final product*. When the demand for the latter increases, the demand for any factors used in its production is also likely to shift outward.

Another major reason for a shift in demand is a *change in the productivity* of each unit of a factor. This has been especially important in increasing the demand for particular kinds of skilled labour. With improved machinery and plant organization, the productivity of each labourer can be increased, with a resulting increase in marginal revenue product. Labour productivity can also be increased by combining more of the fixed factors—capital and land—with each unit of labour. One worker controlling several automated lathes is more productive than the same worker associated with only one lathe. Labour productivity is also increased by providing additional training for workers. Each of these factors can increase the marginal revenue product of a worker and hence lead a firm to employ more workers at any given wage level.

Finally, as was suggested above in the case of engineers and technicians, a *change in the relative prices of other factors* can shift the demand curve for a factor. A decrease in the relative wage of technicians will shift inward the demand curve for engineers, to the extent that these are close substitutes. Note, however, that shifts in the demand for factor services do not usually occur within a firm's short-run planning period, unless it is possible to vary the quantity of factors such as labour.

Imperfect Competition in the Product Market

The pottery firm's demand for factor services was based on the assumption of perfect competition in the product market. This implied a perfectly elastic demand curve for the firm's product, and hence a constant selling price of $2 per mug. In an *imperfectly competitive market*, the firm would face a downward-sloping demand curve: there would be a lower price per unit for each higher level of output. Moreover, the price applies to the total quantity sold. The result, as seen previously in the discussion of imperfect competition in Chapter 18, is that marginal revenue is less than the average revenue and declines more quickly than the average revenue.

Marginal Revenue Product

This outcome is found again when the marginal revenue product is calculated for the imperfectly competitive firm. Table 22.2 shows the same production information presented in Table 22.1, but assumes a downward-sloping demand curve: the product's selling price declines with increasing output. Total revenue is obtained by multiplying the price by the total product.

Table 22.2

Marginal Revenue Product of an Imperfectly Competitive Firm

Variable Factor (Units of Labour) Q_L	Total Product TP	Marginal Physical Product MPP	Product Selling Price P	Total Revenue TR	Marginal Revenue Product MRP
0	0		$4.00	$ 0	
		20			$ 70.00
1	20		3.50	70.00	
		56			158.00
2	76		3.00	228.00	
		107			229.50
3	183		2.50	457.50	
		121			150.50
4	304		2.00	608.00	
		106			48.00
5	410		1.60	656.00	
		76			24.40
6	486		1.40	680.40	
		32			−58.80
7	518		1.20	621.60	
		2			−101.60
8	520		1.00	520.00	
		−7			
9	513				

The marginal revenue product in the imperfect competition case must be calculated as the change in total revenue with each additional unit of the variable factor, and *not* as a result of multiplying price and marginal physical product.

The marginal revenue product schedule is plotted in Figure 22.2 as the firm's demand curve for the factor service. If the price of the factor service remains at $100 per unit, as assumed previously, the firm's profit-maximizing level of input will be four labour units, since the marginal revenue product of the fourth unit is $150.50, but for the fifth unit it falls to only $48. This result is in line with the general conclusion reached earlier, namely, that an imperfectly competitive firm will have a lower level of output than a perfectly competitive firm in the short run, and will underutilize its productive resources, which in this case are the potter's wheels.

MC = MR versus MRC = MRP

Although there is a similarity between the calculation of marginal revenue and marginal revenue product, marginal revenue is associated with each additional unit of *output*, while marginal revenue product is associated with each additional unit of the factor service or *input*.

Similarly, the profit-maximization rule discussed in Chapter 17, of equating marginal revenue with marginal cost, is used to determine the firm's level of *output*. In order to distinguish this rule from that for determining the profit-maximizing level of *input*, the marginal cost of productive resources was termed the marginal resource cost, *MRC*. The profit-maximizing level of input of factor services is thus defined as the level at which the marginal revenue product equals the marginal resource cost. Both rules, however, lead to the same conclusion, since a particular level of output is associated with a specific level of the variable input.

Demand for More Than One Factor Service

Firms have thus far been assumed to use only one variable factor, but most productive processes require several variable factors, if only in terms of different types of labour service. How can the firm determine the *profit-maximizing combination of productive resources*? The same rule applies for each input in the combination as was used when only one factor was involved.

The firm should employ each factor up to the point where its marginal revenue product is equal to its marginal resource cost.

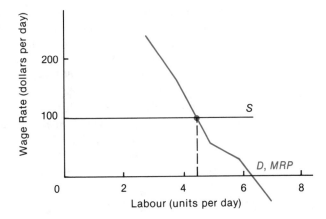

Figure 22.2 Imperfectly Competitive Firm's Demand for Labour
An imperfectly competitive firm's demand for labour services (or other productive factors) is less elastic than that of a perfectly competitive firm because it faces a less elastic demand for its product, as well as the diminishing marginal productivity of productive factors. If the labour market is perfectly competitive, the firm faces a perfectly elastic labour supply curve, *S*, at a wage rate of $100 per day; the firm will employ four units per day.

Thus, the ratio of *MRP* to *MRC* for each factor will be equal to 1, and the profit-maximizing rule can be expressed as:

$$\frac{MRP_1}{MRC_1} = \frac{MRP_2}{MRC_2} = \frac{MRP_3}{MRC_3} = 1$$

where the subscripts 1, 2, 3, etc., refer to different factor services. Unless the firm has some influence on the price of factor services such that their prices change with different quantities purchased by the firm, this rule can also be expressed as:

$$\frac{MRP_1}{P_1} = \frac{MRP_2}{P_2} = \frac{MRP_3}{P_3} = 1$$

where *P* is the price per unit of each factor service.

Profit Maximizing and Cost Minimizing

The profit-maximizing rule is used to determine the most desirable combination of factor services at each of various alternative *product* prices. As the product price increases, the marginal revenue product of each unit of factor service also increases; hence the firm must decide how much more of each factor should be used.

A different rule is required when the relative prices of *factor services* change. In this case, the firm will be seeking the *lowest-cost combination of factor services*. As the relative prices of factor services change, the firm should determine which factor will provide the largest marginal physical product for any given additional expenditure on productive resources. If an additional $100 for semiskilled labour will yield a higher marginal physical product than $100 for skilled labour, the firm will choose the former alternative. This approach yields the conclusion that:

> The cost of producing a given level of output is lowest or minimized when the marginal physical product of each factor is the same for any given level of expenditure on each factor.

The minimum-cost rule for determining the most desirable combination of resources to produce any given level of output can be expressed as:

$$\frac{MPP_1}{MRC_1} = \frac{MPP_2}{MRC_2} = \frac{MPP_3}{MRC_3}$$

Or, if the firm's purchases of factor services influence the prices of these, the rule is expressed as:

$$\frac{MPP_1}{P_1} = \frac{MPP_2}{P_2} = \frac{MPP_3}{P_3}$$

Review of the Main Points

1. The distribution of income among productive factors depends on the prices of factor services and the quantity of these services supplied. Factors are stocks of potential contributions to production; factor services are the flows of actual contributions of a factor during a specified period. Factors are generally categorized as land, labour, and capital, with the occasional addition of entrepreneurship.

2. The marginal productivity theory is an explanation of the demand for factor services. The marginal revenue product of one unit of factor service is the change in a firm's total revenue associated with the use of an additional unit of the factor's service. A firm will employ additional units only if the price per unit does not exceed its marginal revenue product. The marginal revenue product curve is therefore a firm's demand curve for the services of a particular factor.

3. The demand for a factor's service will have a greater price elasticity (a) the closer the substitutability of other factors, (b) the more elastic

the demand for the related product, (c) the larger the cost of the factor in the total production cost, and (d) the more gradual the decline in the factor's marginal productivity.

4. The profit-maximizing quantity of a factor's service to be employed is the quantity at which the marginal resource cost equals the marginal revenue product. The lowest-cost combination of factor services is determined by employing the quantity of each factor's services such that the ratio of the marginal physical product to the marginal resource cost is the same for each factor.

Key Concepts and Topics

factors of production	marginal resource cost
factor services	derived demand
entrepreneurship	profit-maximizing factor
marginal productivity theory	combination
marginal physical product	cost-minimizing factor
marginal revenue product	combination

Questions for Review and Discussion

1. Distinguish carefully between a factor and factor services, using the concepts of stocks and flows. Why is factor service the relevant concept for an analysis of demand?
2. Why is entrepreneurship considered to be different from labour service, and what is its contribution to production?
3. Distinguish between the terms "marginal revenue" and "marginal revenue product". Why does marginal revenue product decline more quickly for an imperfectly competitive firm than for a firm in perfect competition, in the product market?
4. Why is the marginal productivity theory of demand for factor services a major part of the explanation for income distribution? What limitations do you see in using the marginal productivity theory as the only explanation for the distribution of incomes?

Sources and Selected Readings

Barlowe, Raleigh. *Land Resource Economics*, 4th ed. Englewood Cliffs, N.J.: Prentice-Hall, 1985.

Eckert, R.D., and R.H. Leftwich. *The Price System and Resource Allocation*, 10th ed. Hinsdale, Ill.: Dryden Press, 1988.

23 Labour Markets and Wages

Wages and salaries constitute the largest share of the total income received by all factors of production in Canada. Consequently, labour costs account for the largest share of total production costs for all goods and services. Consequently, the conditions determining the price of labour services in the Canadian economy warrant careful attention. This chapter considers the determination of wages under different labour market conditions; the following chapter examines the effects of labour unions and the collective bargaining process on wages and employment.

Wages and Wage Rates

Payment for labour services takes a variety of forms, and statistical reports of such payments use different terms and definitions, with the result that some clarification of the term "wages" is essential to the following discussion.

Wages

Wages, as used in a general analysis of labour markets, include all forms of payment for labour services: not only hourly wages or annual salaries but also commissions, tips, royalties, and bonuses. In addition to these direct payments, indirect compensation in the form of medical insurance premiums and benefits, supplementary unemployment benefits, and pensions are also included. Such indirect costs or "fringe benefits" amount to about 10 per cent of the direct labour costs in Canada.[1] This all-inclusive concept of wages is broader than that implied in the terms, *earnings* or *employment income*, which refer only to the direct payments to labour.

[1] See Statistics Canada, *Labour Costs in Canada—All Industries*.

For some purposes, such as an analysis of consumer expenditure patterns, the relevant measure is *take-home pay*, or what remains after deductions such as those for income taxes, social security and unemployment contributions, and union dues. Other studies focus on *gross earnings*, or total direct payments prior to payroll deductions.

Real Wages   A distinction must also be made between money wages and real wages. *Money wages* are the actual wages paid. An increase in one's money wage of 3 per cent will, however, represent no increase in purchasing power if prices also increase by 3 per cent. Comparisons of money wages paid in different years should thus take account of price changes over the same period; this is done by dividing the current money wage by the Consumer Price Index for the given year. Many studies of wages therefore concentrate on this estimate of *real wages*, as a measure of the real income that workers enjoy in terms of the quantity of goods and services that can be purchased in return for their labour services.

Wage Rate   Wages are also expressed in terms of the length of time over which the payment is made: $5.50 per hour, $250 per week, $900 per month, or $11,800 per year. Such expressions actually indicate the wage rate, the amount paid per unit of time. An exception to this is payment based on the number of units of output produced by a worker, usually referred to as a *piece rate*. In the following discussion, however, labour service is viewed in terms of time periods and thus the wage rate is the appropriate measure of payment. Furthermore, just as the broad structure of interest rates can be represented simply as "the interest rate", the broad structure of wage rates paid to different types of labour and in different areas will be represented, for convenience, as "the wage rate".

Labour Service

Another simplification involves a reference to "labour service" as if all labour services were of the same quality in terms of skills. This is a convenient means for dealing with a wide range of physical and mental skills and other personal differences that partly account for the range of wage rates. Labour services have become increasingly differentiated in recent years by opportunities for vocational training at all levels of the educational system. The effect of this differentiation is considered further in the section on occupational wage differences.

Labour Markets

A general definition of labour markets would parallel the definition of commodity or product markets: namely, the interaction of buyers and sellers of particular labour services, such that there is a market for each identifiable type of labour service. In an economy that covers as large an area as Canada, there are even more labour markets than distinct types of labour services, because individuals are unaware of conditions in distant regions. There are almost as many markets, for example, for unskilled labour as there are municipalities, because buyers or sellers of such labour generally find that it does not pay to devote time and expense to searching more widely for lower-wage labour, or higher-wage jobs, at the same skill level, or to incur the related moving costs.

Markets for some other types of labour service, however, especially those associated with higher levels of education, are closely interrelated. On the demand side, an employer may decide that a particular job can be filled equally well by graduates of a number of different technology programs, and thus will seek potential employees in the various markets for different types of technologists. On the supply side, a recent graduate in chemical technology may seek employment in the markets for salespersons, research assistants, production supervisors, and so on. Labour markets are therefore more or less distinct or separated according to the difference in job functions and the mobility of persons offering labour services.

Supply of Labour

Short-Run Supply

When the behaviour of firms in product markets was examined, a clear distinction was made between their decisions in the *short run* and in the *long run*. These terms are also used in describing the supply side of labour markets, but with less precise meanings. For the present purpose, the short run may be defined as the period within which the total population and its level of schooling and training does not vary significantly. That is, the total quantity and quality of potential workers are fixed. In the long run, these factors may change and hence alter the supply of labour.

The supply of labour is a schedule or curve showing the quantity of labour services that will be offered during a specific period at each of alternative wage rates.

Two major factors determine the short-run supply of labour: the percentage of the population seeking employment or in employment at a given time—the *labour force participation rate*[2]—and the *number of*

---

[2] The labour force participation rate is defined as the percentage of the population aged 15 years or over who are in the labour force. The labour force consists of persons who are employed plus those who are unemployed, as determined by the monthly labour force survey.

hours per day or week that these persons are willing to work. The labour force participation rate and the length of the work week are treated separately for empirical studies in labour economics, but for the present purpose they can be treated as one. The decision about whether to enter the labour force can be considered a special case of the decision regarding the number of hours to offer: namely, to offer zero hours or to offer some hours. This decision is examined with the help of indifference curve analysis in the Appendix to this chapter.

Labour Supply in the Long Run

An economy's total supply of labour services in the long run is determined primarily by changes in the population due to *international migration* and *birth and death rates.*

Migration Where there are no barriers to migration, labour may be expected to respond to changes in the relative real wages of different countries. If the wage rate in Canada, for example, should increase more quickly than in the United States, one would expect there to be an increasing flow of American immigrants to Canada. A reverse movement of the relative wage rates would result in an increased number of emigrants from Canada to the United States, all other things being equal. The assumption of constancy in other factors influencing migration is clearly not appropriate, in light of actual experience with immigration policies and political and social changes in particular countries. Nonetheless, changes in relative wage rates will partly offset or augment the other influences on migration, except where there are complete barriers to migration due to political decrees.

Natural Increase The natural factors of births and deaths, while not directly related to the wage rate, influence the quantity of labour services available in the long run. An increasing birth rate combined with a declining death rate, which was Canada's experience in the 1950s, will increase the total population and thus the potential labour services. The elasticity of the long-run labour supply curve, however, depends on whether the rate of increase in the natural population together with net immigration is proportionately more or less than the rate of increase in real wages.

Wage Determination under Perfect Competition

When product markets were described in terms of alternative structures, emphasis was placed on the number of suppliers in different markets; there were assumed to be many buyers in all product markets. In describing the degree of competition in different labour markets, however, both the demand and supply sides must be considered, since the numbers involved on either side can range widely. Until the expansion of the National Hockey League, for example, there were only two buyers in Canada for the labour services of professional hockey players — the Toronto Maple Leafs and the Montreal Canadiens.[3] A perfectly competitive labour market therefore requires that there be not only many sellers of a service, but also many buyers. The other conditions are also similar to those necessary for a perfectly competitive product market: workers and employers have full knowledge of market conditions such as job opportunities and wage rates; workers are perfectly mobile; and each worker and employer acts individually in making employment decisions.

Demand for Labour

The demand for labour by an individual firm was examined in the preceding chapter. Two demand curves were derived, one for a firm in a perfectly competitive product market and one for a firm in an imperfectly competitive product market. Each of these firms, however, may be buyers in a perfectly competitive *labour* market. For example, the oligopolistic automobile firms enter what are almost perfectly competitive labour markets when employing typists, security guards, or cafeteria workers.

The labour demand curve of the perfectly competitive firm was seen to be more elastic than that of the imperfectly competitive firm, because the former firm faced a perfectly elastic demand, and thus received a constant price for its products. The downward slope of its labour demand curve reflected only the diminishing marginal product of additional units of labour service, whereas the labour demand curve of the imperfectly competitive firm reflected a decreasing product price, as well as diminishing labour productivity.

Elasticity   The market demand for labour is less elastic than the summation of the individual firm's demand curves. Moreover, since these usually reflect the demand of firms operating in different product markets, it is not possible to make a general statement about the degree of elasticity in the market demand curve.

Demand Shifts   The demand for particular kinds of labour services will increase with an *increase in the demand for a commodity* requiring those labour services for its production. The increased commodity demand represents an outward shift of a firm's marginal revenue product curve — its labour demand curve — because a higher price can be obtained for each unit sold.

---

[3] Some of the provincial hockey leagues could also be included as buyers if one used a broader definition of "professional" than is implied here.

The demand for labour will also increase if there is an *increase in the marginal physical product of labour*. Because the marginal physical product of labour declines as additional labour is added to a given quantity of other inputs such as capital, an increase in the latter will extend to the point at which diminishing marginal productivity of labour begins, and hence will shift outward labour's *MPP* curve.

A second reason for an increase in marginal physical product is an improvement in the *quality* of labour services, usually resulting from further education or training that makes a given unit of labour more productive.

Single Firm in a Perfectly Competitive Labour Market

The labour supply curve facing a firm in a perfectly competitive labour market is horizontal or perfectly elastic, as shown in Figure 23.1a, because there are so many buyers of the given type of labour service that a single firm has no control over the wage it pays. If the firm offers a wage below the prevailing rate, W_1, it will not be able to find any workers because they can obtain the prevailing rate at other firms. Nor will the firm offer a higher rate, because it can obtain as many or as few workers as it wants at the prevailing rate.

The firm is thus concerned only with determining the profit-maximizing quantity of labour to be hired at the given wage rate. This quantity will be realized when the marginal revenue product of labour is

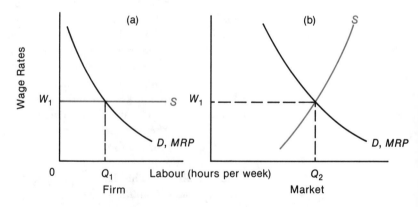

Figure 23.1   Perfectly Competitive Labour Market
Firms that buy labour services in a perfectly competitive labour market face a perfectly elastic labour supply curve, such that any quantity can be purchased at the market equilibrium wage rate, W_1. Given the firm's demand curve, *D*, it buys Q_1 hours of labour per week. The equilibrium wage rate, W_1, is determined by the intersection of the market demand and supply curves; the equilibrium quantity at this wage rate is Q_2.

equal to its marginal resource cost. Since the supply curve is perfectly elastic, the marginal resource cost is the same as the average resource cost: the given wage rate. Thus the profit-maximizing quantity is the level at which the marginal revenue product curve, the demand curve, intersects the labour supply curve. For the firm illustrated in Figure 23.1a, this is Q_1 hours per week. In practice, this quantity will be converted into the number of employees to be hired, by dividing Q_1 by the firm's standard work week.

Equilibrium in a Perfectly Competitive Labour Market

The supply curve for any given labour market is determined by summing individuals' supply curves; these in turn are the outcome of the labour/leisure choices made by individuals willing to supply their labour services to the particular market. As noted previously, the demand curve is approximated by, but is less elastic than, the aggregate of the firms' demand or marginal revenue product curves. The market equilibrium quantity and wage rate, as shown in Figure 23.1b, is determined at the intersection of the supply and demand curves.

If the wage offered is higher than W_1, the quantity of labour supplied will exceed Q_2 but employers will want less than Q_1. The result will be an excess supply of labour, or unemployment. Some labour will be transferred to other labour markets or will move out of the labour force, while other unemployed workers will be willing to work at a lower wage. Employers thus hire workers only at a lower wage until the rate falls to W_1, where there is neither an excess supply nor an excess demand. The opposite process would occur if the wage rate were less than W_1, since employers could actually pay a rate higher than W_1 for any labour less than Q_2, without incurring a loss on the marginal unit employed. Thus, employers would gradually offer a higher wage rate to attract more workers, until W_1 was reached.

Wage Determination under Imperfect Competition

Imperfect competition in labour markets may arise because there are either relatively few buyers or relatively few sellers, or both. The latter two possibilities are considered in the next chapter, where the economic effects of trade unions are examined. The existence of only one buyer in a given labour market is termed *monopsony*, and the single employer is said to have monopsonistic power.

Monopsony, like monopoly, is rare. The closest example of monopsony is the company that employs almost everyone in a town's labour force in mining or logging areas — hence the term "company town". To the extent that workers are prepared to move to other areas, however, they can participate in a labour market that is larger than the company town. But the cost of moving may be substantial, and employees in remote areas are often unaware of other employment opportunities.

Labour markets may be imperfect for reasons other than the limited number of buyers and sellers. The cost of moving to other areas and the lack of information about other employment opportunities, as just mentioned, are examples of two major limitations on the perfect operation of a labour market: *immobility of labour* and *incomplete knowledge* of labour market conditions.

The effect of these imperfections is to reduce the geographical movement of workers among labour markets in response to changing relative wage rates in these different areas. The supply curve will be farther to the right in a low-wage market, and farther to the left in a high-wage market, such that the wage difference will be greater when there is immobility and lack of information than if these conditions did not exist.

The federal government and some provincial governments have therefore introduced programs to make more information available concerning wage rates and job vacancies in various occupations and areas, to assist workers in moving to other areas, and to retrain workers for occupations where demand is increasing most quickly. Employment counselling programs also provide information to workers who may be unaware that they could seek employment in other occupations with their existing basic skills.

Labour Supply Curve

The labour demand curve for a monopsonistic firm is the same marginal revenue product curve that was explained previously. It is on the labour supply side that the monopsonist's condition differs from that of a firm in a perfectly competitive labour market. Since the labour supply curve facing the monopsonist is the market supply curve, it will be upward-sloping. In order to attract increasing numbers of workers away from other labour markets, or into the labour force, successively higher wage rates must be offered. Moreover, the marginal resource cost of an additional worker will exceed the higher wage rate required to attract an additional worker, because persons currently employed by the firm will also have to be paid the same higher wage to retain their services. Thus, for any quantity of labour services hired, the marginal resource cost exceeds the wage rate.

In a firm with five employees, for example, the marginal cost of hiring a sixth employee includes the full wage paid to this employee plus the amount required to raise the wages of the other five employees to the new wage rate. This is illustrated in Figure 23.2, where the *MRC* curve is above the supply, or average resource cost curve, *ARC*, and rises more steeply. This situation is similar to one seen in Chapter 18 for a firm in an imperfectly competitive product market. In that case, the *MR* curve was below the *AR* curve and fell more steeply, because an additional unit could be sold only at a lower price, but all units were then sold at this lower price.

$MRC = MRP$

The profit-maximizing quantity of labour for the firm illustrated in Figure 23.2 is the quantity at which the marginal resource cost equals the marginal revenue product, namely Q_1. The wage rate to attract Q_1 units of labour is W_1, since the supply curve indicates that workers will be willing to supply Q_1 hours per week at a wage of W_1. Note that if there had been many buyers in this labour market (that is, if it had been purely competitive), the equilibrium wage and quantity would both have been greater, at W_2 and Q_2, because the equilibrium levels would

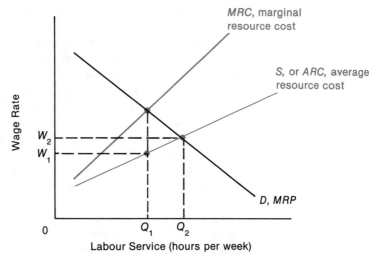

Figure 23.2 Wage Determination in Imperfect Labour Markets
When there are only a few buyers of labour, the buyers face an upward-sloping labour supply curve. A single, or monopsonistic, buyer faces the market supply curve, *S*. The supply curve is the firm's average resource cost curve, *ARC*, because it indicates the wage rate that must be paid to attract a given quantity of labour. The marginal resource cost, *MRC*, shows the increase in total cost associated with additional units of labour and rises more steeply than the *ARC* curve. The firm's profit-maximizing quantity of labour, Q_1, is the quantity at which $MRP = MRC$; this quantity can be hired at wage W_1. In a perfectly competitive market, the equilibrium wage would be W_2, with Q_2 units of labour hired.

have been determined by the intersection of the supply and demand curves. One can also see that the monopsonistic firm does not have a demand curve for labour inputs, just as the monopolistic firm does not have a supply curve for its output. In each case, the firm examines its costs and revenues to determine the profit-maximizing combination.

Figures 23.1 and 23.2 illustrate the cases of perfect competition and monopsony, respectively, in the labour market. The effects of labour unions, acting as monopoly sellers of labour services, are examined in the following chapter.

Structure of Wages in Canada

Wage Differences

The wage rates determined in the many labour markets in Canada constitute the *structure* of wages. The analysis, just presented, of wage determination in competitive and monopsonistic markets has suggested a few reasons for the existence of different wages in different labour markets. These reasons are not sufficient, however, to explain, for example, why some persons are paid $5.00 per hour while others receive $150 per hour.

Such wage differences are assumed to take account of the net advantages of some jobs compared with others. Jobs differ, it is suggested, in five basic ways: pleasantness or disagreeableness of the work, cost of training required, regularity or uncertainty of employment, degree of responsibility, and probability of advancement. On the basis of such criteria, some jobs woud be preferable to others; differences in wages represent the amounts necessary to attract persons into the less desirable jobs. These wage differences that compensate workers for the relative disadvantages of their jobs are usually termed *equalizing differences*.

However, it is commonly observed that higher-wage jobs are often associated with some of the best working conditions. This suggests that a substantial component of wage differences represents a *non-equalizing difference* — that part of the wage difference is compensation for something other than the characteristics of particular occupations. Numerous labour market imperfections account for many of these differences: imperfections such as monopsonistic employers, labour unions and professional associations, labour immobility, and inadequate information about labour markets.

Differences in labour quality, due to different levels of education or training, also explain a substantial part of wage differentials. The economic rent associated with individuals whose rare skills are much in demand forms a large part of the difference between, for example, the wage paid to a hockey club's outstanding player and that paid to its assistant accountant. (Economic rent is defined at the beginning of Chapter 25.)

Occupational Differences

Occupational income data such as those presented in Table 23.1 may provide very few surprises. More detailed occupational data, however, contain important evidence that is not apparent from average incomes reported for broad occupational groups. Occupations vary greatly in their range of wages, with wider ranges being found in the lowest- and highest-income occupations, where there is more irregularity of employment or variation in skills and personal factors, than in the salaried occupations at the middle-income levels.

Education is a major factor in occupational wage differentials. Table 23.2 shows that the higher the average income for an occupation, the higher usually is the percentage of persons in that occupation who have above-average schooling. Formal education not only develops certain occupational skills, it also provides the basis for further training. Several studies have shown that the higher the level of one's formal education,

Table 23.1

Earnings by Occupation, Canada, 1987

Occupational Category	Average Earnings of Full-Year Workers[1]		Relative Earnings[2]	
	Males	Females	Males	Females
Managerial	$41,814	$24,933	147	146
Professional	36,666	23,113	129	136
Processing, Machining	27,376	15,363	96	90
Product Fabrication	26,211	14,289	92	84
Sales	26,228	13,534	92	79
Transportation	25,012	14,625	88	86
Construction	25,374	**	89	**
Clerical	23,310	16,292	82	96
Service	19,290	10,075	68	59
Farming	20,473	14,076	72	83
All occupations, average	28,369	17,036	100	100

Source: Statistics Canada, *Income Distributions by Size in Canada.*

[1] Workers who reported having worked 50-52 weeks.
[2] Earnings as a percentage of the average for all occupations.

** Sample too small for reliable estimate.

the more likely one is to participate in on-the-job training programs or other forms of continuing education that lead to still higher incomes.

Part of the occupational wage differentials are also explained by the fact that certain occupations have a very high proportion of *female workers*. There are several implications of such a situation. For example, the annual incomes in such occupations tend to be lower, due to what Ostry and Zaidi term "discontinuous work experience", or intermittent participation in the labour force. It is suggested that this "might have prevented female workers from taking up jobs in higher positions or positions of responsibility and thus affecting their earnings adversely".[4] Even within narrowly defined occupations, however, male/female wage differentials remain. It has been found that:

> . . . adjusting for differences in productivity-related factors tends to raise the ratio of female to male earnings, but a wage gap of 5 to 10 percent still seems to prevail within the same establishment. This can be thought of as narrowly defined wage discrimination involving comparisons within the same establishment and occupation . . . . There appears to be a consensus in the literature that occupational segregation is a more important channel of discrimination than is narrowly defined wage discrimination, suggesting that occupational segregation would account for more than the .05 to .10 of the .40 gap that can be attributed to narrowly defined wage discrimination. But how much larger is difficult to determine.[5]

For some predominantly female occupations such as clerical work, there are many experienced or qualified persons not currently in the labour force. A slight increase in the wage rate in such occupations may attract a proportionately larger number of persons into the occupation. That is, the labour supply curve is highly elastic, resulting in only a small wage increase even though demand may increase substantially. In other occupations, the short-run supply curve is much less elastic; a similar increase in demand results in a much larger wage increase.

Finally, some occupations, such as medicine, dentistry, and law, have a high proportion of *self-employed persons*. Their reported incomes include some return to capital (a dentist's net income, for example, includes a return to the investment in office equipment and tools), which should be deducted to determine the true payment for labour ser-

---

[4] Sylvia Ostry and Mahmood A. Zaidi, *Labour Economics in Canada*, 3rd ed., Toronto: Macmillan, 1979, p. 541. This source presents a comprehensive examination of occupational, industrial, and geographical wage differentials.

[5] Morley Gunderson, "Discrimination, Equal Pay, and Equal Opportunities in the Labour Market", in W. Craig Riddell, ed., *Work and Pay: The Canadian Labour Market*, Toronto: University of Toronto Press, 1985, p. 230.

Table 23.2

Selected Occupations, Income and Schooling, Males, Canada, 1985

Occupation	Average Employment Income	Percentage with at least Grade 12 Schooling
Physicians and surgeons	$90,600	100
Lawyers and notaries	60,900	100
Architects and engineers	39,400	99
Accountants	39,300	94
Police officers	37,300	85
Tool and diemakers	31,300	81
Bus drivers	27,853	44
Carpenters	23,300	53

Source: Statistics Canada, *1986 Census of Canada.*

vices. Also, self-employed persons have more freedom in deciding how many hours to work; this total tends to be higher than the average number of hours per week for employees.

Review of the Main Points

1. "Wages" include all forms of payment for labour services, including direct payments and indirect compensation in the form of various benefits and facilities. Distinctions must be made, however, between gross earnings and take-home pay, and between money wages and real wages. Although reference is frequently made to "the" wage rate and "the" labour market, there are actually many labour markets and therefore many wage rates. Labour markets are interrelated, however, because workers and employers may be in several labour markets at the same time.

2. The short-run labour supply period may be defined as the period within which the total population and its level of schooling and training does not vary significantly. Two major factors therefore determine the short-run labour supply: the labour force participation rate and the number of hours offered per day or per week.

3. The economy's long-run labour supply is influenced primarily by population changes due to international migration and birth and death rates.

4. A firm's demand for labour is determined by the marginal revenue product of workers, and is more elastic the higher the degree of competition in the product market supplied by the firm in question. A firm in a purely competitive labour market faces a perfectly elastic

labour supply curve and hence has no influence on the wage it pays; it is thus concerned only with determining the quantity of labour to be hired at the given wage rate. This is the rate at which the quantity of labour supplied to the market is equal to the quantity demanded.

5. The opposite of a purely competitive labour market is a monopsonistic labour market, in which there is only one buyer of labour services. The labour supply curve faced by this firm is the upward-sloping market supply curve. The marginal cost of hiring an additional worker exceeds the prevailing wage rate because more must be paid to attract an additional worker. Furthermore, the existing workers must be paid the same wage as the additional worker in order to retain their services. The profit-maximizing quantity of labour for the firm is the quantity at which the marginal resource cost is equal to the marginal revenue product.

6. The structure of wages in Canada reflects many differences in jobs, from working conditions to the cost of training for a particular occupation. Other factors such as monopsonistic employers, labour unions and professional associations, labour immobility, and inadequate information also have a differential influence on wage rates.

Key Concepts and Topics

wages	labour supply (short- and
earnings	long-run)
gross earnings	labour force participation rate
take-home pay	demand for labour
money wages	monopsony
real wages	equalizing differences
piece rate	

Questions for Review and Discussion

1. If there was perfect competition in all labour and product markets, would there still be wage differences among occupations? Explain.

2. What is meant by "derived" demand for labour? And how does this affect the price elasticity of demand for labour?

3. Distinguish between monopolists and monopsonists. Is it possible to be a monopolist but not a monopsonist, and vice versa? Describe examples of each case.

4. What is meant by the labour force participation rate? List as many reasons as you can for the increasing labour force participation rate for women aged 30 to 50.

5. Distinguish between a change in the demand for labour and a change in the quantity of labour demanded. What would cause each of these changes?

6. Describe or list some labour markets in your area in which short-run supply is fairly elastic, and others where supply is inelastic. Why do these differences exist?

7. Discuss all the reasons you can think of for higher incomes to be associated with higher levels of education. What examples can you suggest where a higher education may *not* increase one's income very much, if at all? Explain why these cases occur.

Sources and Selected Readings

Ehrenberg, R. G., and R. S. Smith. *Modern Labor Economics: Theory and Public Policy,* 4th ed. Glenview, Ill.: Scott, Foresman, 1991.

Fleisher, Belton M., and T. J. Kniesner. *Labor Economics: Theory and Evidence,* 3rd ed. Englewood Cliffs. N.J.: Prentice-Hall, 1984.

Gunderson, Morley, and Craig Riddell. *Labour Market Economics: Theory, Evidence and Policy in Canada,* 2nd ed. Toronto: McGraw-Hill Ryerson, 1988.

Hamermesh, Daniel S., and Albert Rees. *The Economics of Work and Pay,* 4th ed. New York: Harper & Row, 1988.

Killingsworth, Mark R. *Labor Supply.* New York: Cambridge University Press, 1983.

Ostry, Sylvia, and Mahmood A. Zaidi. *Labour Economics in Canada,* 3rd ed. Toronto: Macmillan, 1979.

Riddell, Craig, et al. *Work and Pay: The Canadian Labour Market.* Toronto: University of Toronto Press, 1985.

Appendix: The Labour/Leisure Choice Model

The Choice: Labour versus Leisure

Decisions about the number of hours per week (or weeks per year) to offer as labour services are decisions about allocating one's time between labour and leisure. In this simple explanation of labour supply, labour is defined as any income-earning activity; leisure is all other activity. This approach assumes that labour services are offered to the market only to earn income that in turn can be used to purchase goods and services; it is further assumed that leisure is also a good, yielding satisfaction or enjoyment. Although this view may seem to ignore the satisfaction that people find in their work, and the dissatisfaction associated with some forms of leisure, such as mowing the lawn, these circumstances are at least partly reflected in labour/leisure decisions.

One might also object that individuals are not free to determine how many hours they will work each week, because the minimum is set by individual firms and the maximum in many cases is set by legislation. Individuals do, however, have some freedom in choosing whether to work at part-time or full-time jobs, whether to work for a few months or for a full year, whether to take a second job as "moonlighters", and so on.

The labour/leisure choice and the derivation of an individual's labour supply curve can be illustrated using the *indifference curve analysis* that was introduced in Chapter 15 to explain an individual's demand curve. Figure 23.3 presents an individual's indifference curves for different levels of satisfaction derived from various combinations of leisure and other goods (and services) purchased with labour income. Each indifference curve shows that, in moving upward along the curve, more goods must be purchased to compensate for fewer leisure hours if the same level of satisfaction is to be maintained. A higher-level indifference curve indicates that a greater total satisfaction is realized by combining more goods with a given quantity of leisure, or more leisure with a given quantity of goods.

At a wage rate of $6 per hour, one can enjoy 16 hours of leisure (not counting the minimum of 8 hours necessary for sleeping and eating) but no goods and services, or $96 worth of goods and services but no leisure (assuming a 16-hour work day), or any intermediate combination of leisure and other goods. These alternative combinations are indicated by the budget line WW_1. The greatest satisfaction possible at this wage rate is at A, the tangency point of WW_1 and I_1, with 8 hours of leisure being "consumed" and 8 hours of labour offered to acquire $48 worth of goods and services.

A higher wage rate, $12 per hour, will move this person to a higher level of satisfaction, shown by point B. Only 5 hours of leisure are consumed because the income from each hour of labour will now buy more goods and services. The move from A to B consists of an *income effect* (A to C) and a *substitution effect* (C to B). The income effect results from the increased wage rate: for any given number of labour hours, the individual receives a higher income due to the higher wage per hour. The substitution effect results from the increased price of leisure: for any given number of leisure hours, the individual "pays" a higher price because more goods and services are forfeited in forgoing an hour of labour at $12 per hour than at $6 per hour. In moving from C to B, more goods are substituted for fewer hours of leisure. The *substitution effect outweighs the income effect* because, on balance, the individual offers more labour time at the higher wage rate.

When the wage rate rises to $18 per hour, the net result is different. Figure 23.3 shows that the most satisfactory combination, represented by D, is 8 hours of leisure and 8 hours of labour. Again there is both an income and a substitution effect of the wage increase (imagine a budget line drawn parallel to WW_2 and tangent to I_3 at E), but this time the *income effect outweighs the substitution effect*. For a given number of labour hours, this person can buy so many more goods that he or she decides to enjoy more leisure hours than at a wage of $12 per hour.

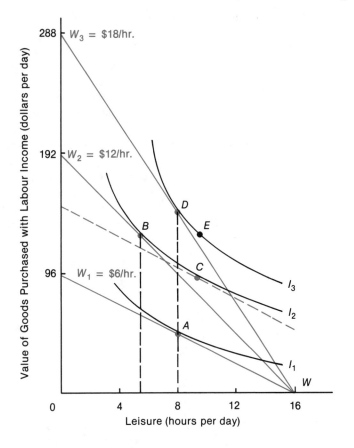

Figure 23.3 The Labour/Leisure Choice
Combinations of leisure and labour income yielding the same level of
satisfaction are shown by the indifference curve, I_1. At a wage rate of $6
per hour, one can enjoy either 16 hours of leisure per day, or goods
purchased with 16 hours of labour income, or various combinations of
goods and leisure, as indicated by the budget line, WW_1. (The budget line
assumes 16 hours per day are available for the allocation decision.)
Satisfaction is maximized by combination A, 8 hours each of leisure and
labour. At a wage of $12 per hour, the optimum combination is B, 5 hours of
leisure and 11 hours of labour. The income effect of the wage increase
would lead one to "buy" more leisure, about 9 hours as indicated by C, but
the substitution or price effect of the wage increase outweighs the income
effect. Since leisure is now more expensive, one substitutes more goods for
leisure, and chooses to offer 11 hours of labour.

The quantity of labour offered at each wage rate is plotted in Figure
23.4. In this particular case, the number of hours worked increases as
the wage rate increases through the lower range of wage rates, but at
higher wage rates the number of hours declines with further increases in

the wage rates. In this example the substitution effect outweighs the income effect at low wage rates; at higher rates the income effect outweighs the substitution effect. *Which effect outweighs the other depends on the particular shape of the indifference curves and the slope of the budget line.*

The shape of labour supply curves has been the subject of much controversy among economists. Since actual experiments with different wage rates to determine individuals' offerings of labour services at any given time are not possible, one can only speculate on the general shape of labour supply curves. Nevertheless, the income and substitution effects are present in wage changes, and provide useful explanations for the number of hours offered by individuals at different wage rates. There is, for example, some evidence of a backward-bending labour supply curve in the historical data on wages and average length of

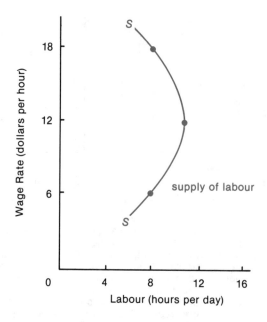

Figure 23.4   Individual's Labour Supply Curve
An individual's labour supply curve can be derived from Figure 23.3. The number of labour hours offered at alternative wage rates is shown by points *A*, *B*, and *D*. These are plotted here to produce the supply curve, *S*. At a wage below $12 per hour, the price or substitution effect outweighs the income effect, but the reverse is true at wage rates above $12 per hour.

the work week. Although these data must be interpreted carefully, the decline in the average work week from over 60 hours to less than 40 hours during the past century, while real wages have increased substantially, suggests that the income effect has been dominant.

When the supply curves for individuals are aggregated to obtain a supply curve for a market or the economy, the full influence of the income effect is not evident because individuals enter the labour market at different wage rates. That is, the backward-bending portion of one individual's supply curve may be offset by the upward-sloping portion of the supply curve of another individual who enters the labour market at a higher wage rate. It is therefore generally assumed that the economy's short-run labour supply curve is upward-sloping over the relevant range of wage rates, but is highly inelastic.

Review of the Main Points

1. Indifference-curve analysis can be used to examine workers' decisions about allocating their time between labour and leisure, when leisure is defined as any non–income-earning activity. An individual's short-run supply curve depends on his or her marginal rates of substitution of labour income for leisure over the range of possible working hours, and the relative size of the income and substitution effects across different wage rates. Although an individual's labour supply curve is thought to be backward-bending, the short-run labour supply curve for the economy is assumed to be upward-sloping, but highly inelastic, over the relevant range of wage rates.

Key Concepts and Topics

labour vs. leisure
income vs. substitution effect
backward-bending supply curve

Question for Review and Discussion

1. What impediments are there in the real world to the precise expression of a person's relative preference for labour income and leisure? Would most people you know in the labour force like to increase or decrease the number of hours they work per week, at the prevailing wage rates? Why?

24 Labour Unions and Collective Bargaining

Size and Structure of Unions in Canada

Approximately one-third of all non-agricultural employees in Canada belong to labour unions. A complete picture of labour organizations should also include members of professional associations, such as doctors, lawyers, and engineers. Many of these associations resemble labour unions in some organizational aspects and economic effects. These two types of labour organization have traditionally been treated differently in government policies and legislation; consequently there is less information available on the scope and impact of professional associations than on labour unions.

Union Growth

Union membership in Canada has increased substantially, although not steadily, as a percentage of all workers—from less than 20 per cent prior to the Second World War to a peak of 40 per cent in the 1980s. Public attitudes tended to favour unionism during the two World Wars and the Depression, but employer opposition halted its growth in the 1920s. In the postwar period, unions have expanded steadily but not as quickly as in the 1930s and 1940s, because the most easily organized workers had already been brought into unions, and because employment growth was greatest in the service sector where union organizing was more difficult. Thus, as Figure 24.1 indicates, the percentage of non-agricultural workers belonging to unions declined slightly in the 1960s but increased again in the 1970s and early 1980s.

Craft and Industrial Unions

Economic analysis of the effects of labour unions requires that a distinction be made between craft unions and industrial unions. *Craft unions* were the first type of labour organization to emerge, and included crafts such as shoemaking, carpentry, and printing. These unions consist of members from particular occupations, regardless of the industry in which they are employed. They are thus identified as carpenters' unions, plasterers' unions, electrical workers' unions, and so on. *Industrial unions* developed during the 1930s, particularly with the rapid growth of the automobile and steel industries. These unions draw their members from specific industries or groups of industries, and thus include workers in many occupations with a wide variety of skills.

Local, National, and International Unions

The organizational structure of labour unions includes local, national, and international unions, as well as federations of unions.

Local Unions   A union member's direct association is with a local union, which usually consists of the members in one plant, firm, or local area. Locals range in size from less than 10 to over 30,000 members, and may be chapters of a national or international union, or chartered directly by a federation, or independent of other associations.

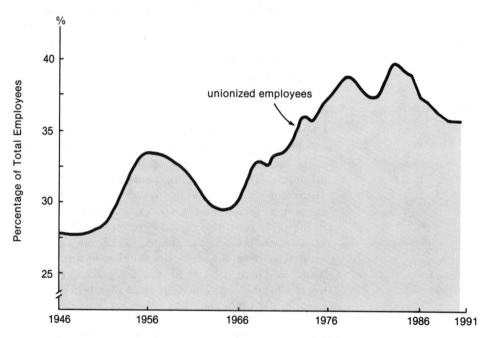

Figure 24.1   Union Membership in Canada, 1946 to 1990
Union membership in Canada as a percentage of all employees rose from about 28 per cent in 1946 to about 40 per cent in the early 1980s. This growth was fairly steady except for a slight decline in the early 1960s.

Source: Canada Department of Labour, *Labour Organizations in Canada.*

National and International Unions

National unions, such as the Canadian Union of Public Employees (CUPE), may have many local chapters, but these are located only in Canada. An international union often has many locals and a large membership in Canada, but the union headquarters and most of the membership are in the United States. International unions include some of the largest unions in Canada, such as the United Steel Workers of America. The International Union of United Automobile, Aerospace and Agriculture Implement Workers of America (UAW) was also in this group until the Canadian branch of the UAW separated from the American organization in 1985, to form the new Canadian Automobile Workers (CAW).

Federations and Congresses

Most unions are in turn affiliated with a federation or congress of unions, which acts as a national voice for labour unions but has little direct control over individual unions. The Canadian Labour Congress (CLC) includes provincial federations of labour, Canadian branches of international unions, and most national unions. The CLC also has close ties with its American counterpart, the American Federation of Labour and Congress of Industrial Organizations (AFL-CIO). The Confederation of National Trade Unions (CNTU), based mainly in Quebec, comprises about 5 per cent of all union members. Two newer union federations are the Confederation of Canadian Unions (CCU) and the

Table 24.1

Union Membership by Type of Union and Affiliation, January 1, 1990

Type of Affiliation	No. of Unions	Membership Number (thousands)	Percentage
International Unions	61	1,284	32
AFL-CIO/CLC	39	877	22
AFL-CIO/CFL	10	203	5
Others	12	204	5
National Unions	234	2,563	64
CLC	48	1,468	36
CNTU	8	212	5
Unaffiliated	136	720	18
Others	44	163	4
Directly Chartered Local Unions	341	48	1
Independent Local Organizations	380	136	3
Total	1,016	4,031	100

Source: Canada Department of Labour, *Labour Organizations in Canada*.

Note: Detailed items may not add to totals due to rounding.

Centrale des syndicats démocratiques (CSD). Other unions, notably the Brotherhood of Locomotive Engineers, are not affiliated with any federation or congress. Table 24.1 shows that almost two-thirds of all union members are in national unions, and about one-third in international unions. This represents a reversal of the relative positions occupied by national and international unions as recently as twenty years ago.

Union Goals

In earlier chapters, the objectives or goals of consumers and firms were the key to analyzing and predicting the behaviour or decisions of these groups. If one assumed that consumers wish to maximize utility and that firms seek maximum profits, consumption and production decisions followed logically. The behaviour of unions is more difficult to explain and predict because unions appear to have several objectives, some of which can be in conflict with each other. A general assumption is that unions seek to improve the economic welfare of union members by raising wages, including fringe benefits and working conditions. However, this assumption is too simple to take account of a complex combination of union goals, such as the variety of objectives described in Box 24.1. Priorities among these goals vary, of course, among unions, and over a period of time for any particular union.

Increased Wage Rate   As suggested above, the most common assumption is that unions attempt to raise the wage rate paid to their members. If a union succeeds in doing so, however, it may reduce the number of workers employed by the firm, unless the demand for labour is also increasing.

Increased Total Income of Union Members   Some unions, recognizing that higher wage rates may result in unemployment, argue that they attempt to increase the aggregate income of all union members. Again, this may be possible but only when the demand for labour is inelastic, if there is no substantial increase in demand.

Fringe Benefits and Working Conditions   Particularly when unions have been able to realize recent large increases in wage rates, they may emphasize fringe benefits such as paid holidays, medical and pension benefits, education leave and tuition fees, and so on. Working conditions, including safety devices and equipment, recreational facilities, hours of work, and lighting and ventilation, also tend to receive priority when unions anticipate difficulty in securing large wage gains or have already made such gains.

Work Rules and Job Security   Unions in industries or occupations where technology is changing quickly often bargain on the pace of work and the number of persons employed for a particular job function. In a few cases, this has led to *featherbedding*, or payment for unnecessary

Box 24.1   **Union priority: protect jobs**
By Lorne Slotnick

In 1987, Canada's unions face a basic and unglamorous task — protecting jobs from an onslaught of technological change, deregulation and fierce competition from abroad.

In the steel and auto plants, in the paper mills and on the railways, in the post office and the public service — key areas of collective bargaining this year — workers are worried they might end up among the nearly 10 per cent of Canadians looking for work.

In fact, as Canada's economy has undergone profound changes over the past few years, the prime function of unions has also shifted. In the eyes of both workers and their bosses, unions are increasingly seen mainly as a way of protecting jobs rather than raising wages. . . . Unions will be pushing this year in a variety of ways to restrict employers' freedom to dispense with jobs: some will be looking for outright no-layoff guarantees or curbs on contracting out of work to non-union outsiders; others will be seeking early retirement programs to help preserve the jobs of younger workers, beefed-up seniority rules, retraining schemes, restrictions on the use of part-time workers, and shorter work time; others, fearing that layoffs are inevitable, will be content with better severance pay and longer notice of layoffs.

In return for stronger job security, unions will often have to give up something, and the big trade-off this year may be concessions on the complex web of job classifications and work rules that have been built up over decades and that employers now say hinder their flexibility and efficiency.

. . . Figures compiled by Labour Canada and Queen's University show that, over the past few years, unions have made some significant gains on job security issues such as retraining programs, notice of layoffs, and the right of laid-off workers to "bump" into other jobs.

For example, severance-pay clauses — which make layoffs more expensive for employers and ease the burden for laid-off workers — now apply to 56 per cent of workers covered by major agreements, up from 28 per cent a dozen years ago. More than a quarter of major unionized employers cannot contract out work if doing so leads to layoffs.

Many unions are looking for more, and that is where confrontations could come this year. Strike activity has been low in the past five years, but much of the recent conflict has been over job security.

. . . On the two major railways, for example, unions bargaining for about 65,000 workers find themselves further apart from management than at any time in recent memory. The railways have asked for major concessions, but the unions — which have already lost hundreds of members and face more losses because of deregulation — are bent on improving job security.

"We're not going to the bargaining table giving up things we already have," said Edward Abbot, executive secretary of the Associated Railway Unions, representing about 50,000 of the workers. Two years ago, the unions scored a breakthrough with an agreement that prevents most layoffs for workers with eight years' service. Now the unions want to extend that guarantee to anyone with two years' service, as well as put curbs on contracting out, which Mr. Abbot says has already cost jobs.

. . . Government employees also, despite their popular image as clinging to cushy jobs guaranteed for life, are focussing on job security. They often have less protection than workers in the private sector.

"We're trying to chip away all the time," said Jeff Rose, president of the Canadian Union of Public Employees, bargaining this year for municipal workers in several large cities.

. . . Mr. Rose said CUPE, which is planning a national conference on contracting-out next month, has also been faced with the erosion of full-time jobs by the increasing use of part-timers. One response, he said, is to press for contracts that discourage the use of part-timers, such as overtime rates for part-timers who work more than four hours a shift.

. . . In the federal public service, where contracts expire this year for 150,000 workers, unions face a Government that still wants to trim the ranks, and will be seeking increased protection.

Postal workers, who already have ironclad no-layoff guarantees, are looking for ways to force the Canada Post Corp. to increase jobs by pushing for increased service to the public and for shorter work time. The post office, with more than 60,000 unionized workers, has already begun bargaining with its major unions.

. . . The Canadian Auto Workers—set to begin bargaining this summer for about 60,000 employees of the Big Three automakers—says no-layoff guarantees are an impractical demand in that industry. "The companies have no control over whether people buy the product," says union secretary-treasurer Robert Nickerson. "We know it's impossible; we're not going to try to fool our membership."

Instead, the auto union will be trying to beef up the incomes of the workers who it feels will inevitably be laid off as overcapacity catches up to the auto companies by 1990. The company-financed Supplementary Unemployment Benefits fund in the auto industry now gives workers with 10 years' seniority 95 per cent of their salary for two years after a layoff, but Mr. Nickerson says the union is worried that the fund cannot cope with massive layoffs.

Source: *The Globe and Mail*, 10 January 1987.

work. Featherbedding is evident, for example, in a union requirement that the railways employ locomotive firemen on diesel locomotives when firemen are not required. This situation arose when the railways switched from steam to diesel engines, and the union successfully opposed the displacement of locomotive firemen who previously had stoked the coal-fired steam engines.

Seniority systems are established to protect the jobs of union members with the longest experience in a firm. When lay-offs are required, a seniority system requires that the most recent employees are the first to be laid off.

Grievance procedures also form a part of job security provisions. Arrangements are established whereby any problem or complaint concerning workers can, if necessary, be dealt with at successively higher management levels until a satisfactory solution is reached. If even this fails, the matter is referred to arbitration.

Union Security In addition to seeking improved wages and security for its members, a union is also concerned with its own security. This requires that it preserve its strength by continuing to represent all workers within its potential jurisdiction. Thus there are persistent efforts to organize workers in plants or areas that have not been unionized; another aspect of union security is the need to establish a *union shop* — by requiring that a new employee join the union within a specified period, usually 30 days. This is a compromise between an *open shop*, in which union membership is voluntary, and a *closed shop*, in which employers may hire only persons who have previously joined the union.

Political Goals and Activities Unions also have a number of political goals. Some of these, such as increasing the minimum wage level, are directly associated with labour markets. Other objectives and activities, such as the support some unions have given to the New Democratic Party, are directed to changing more general social conditions.

Union Techniques and Tactics

Unions seek most of these goals in regular negotiations with the management of firms. Techniques other than negotiation are sometimes used, and are a potential threat that management must take into account when replying to union demands.

Strikes An organized strike can be the most effective weapon in gaining a union's objective — but only if the union executive has substantial support from the membership and the financial resources to maintain a strike for a period of up to several months. However, if the management of the firm knows that members doubt the ability of the executive to secure its demands, or that the members' strike pay is meagre, a strike loses much of its potential effectiveness.

Working to Rule and Slowdowns Instead of a strike, or in cases where organized strikes are forbidden, a union may order its members to "work to rule" or to slow down the pace of their work. Working to rule can cause considerable reduction in the normal work flow because workers have generally found methods to circumvent rules that resulted in delays, or because some rules had been ignored. For example, when the postal workers were on a "work to rule" campaign, they set aside mail that was not fully addressed, even when its destination was obvious from the address given. Union members may also organize the use of their sick leave so that a large portion of the employees are absent on particular days. Such tactics can be used by the union to show management the degree of its control over the members, indicating that it could, if it wished, conduct an effective strike.

Picketing   Public sympathy for a union's position in a strike is often sought by publicizing the strike through picketing—carrying signs around the property of the struck firm. The general public and members of other unions making deliveries to the plant or employed in the plant are urged not to cross the picket line, thus denying the firm services beyond those supplied by the union members.

Boycotts   A *primary boycott* consists of urging consumers not to buy the products or services of the struck firm. A *secondary boycott* attempts to put pressure on the struck firm by urging employees and customers of other firms not to handle or buy the product of the struck firm. By boycotting a supermarket, for example, unions associated with meat-packing plants might hope to have more effect than through a primary boycott. Because third-party firms can be harmed by this tactic, secondary boycotts are illegal in some provinces.

Collective Bargaining Procedures

The techniques listed above represent the ultimate weapons available to labour unions. The availability of these tactics, however, is more significant than their actual use: about 95 per cent of all labour contracts or agreements signed during the past decade were settled without resort to such means. Instead, the collective bargaining process has been the predominant method used by unions to gain at least some of their demands. (The two-sided nature of collective bargaining is sometimes overlooked: management also uses the process to gain some of its demands, especially for improving labour productivity.)

Many steps are involved in arriving at a labour contract through collective bargaining. Briefly, they are the following:

- Where there is not a recognized union to represent the employees of a particular firm, one or more unions may send representatives to organize the employees as a union local, or the employees may decide to form their own independent union. If there are two or more unions claiming to have the support of the majority of workers, or if it is not clear that the majority wish to be represented by a union, the provincial Labour Relations Board conducts an election to determine whether any union, or which one, will be *certified to bargain collectively* for the relevant group of workers. A majority of all workers eligible to vote is required before certification can be granted.

- When such certification is given, the accredited union is legally recognized as the exclusive *bargaining agent* for the group of employees it represents, and employers are required to bargain with the certified union.

- Shortly before a *new collective agreement* is to be established, union representatives and management officers meet to review the requests made by both sides. Such items probably include not only wage rates, but also fringe benefits like pensions and health insurance, standard and overtime hours, training programs, work load, seniority rights, grievance procedures, arrangements for technological improvements in the firm, and so on.

- The representatives of the union and management will probably meet many times to discuss these items, perhaps easily reaching agreement on some and spending much time on two or three areas of substantial disagreement. In almost all cases, the two parties are able to negotiate a new agreement. If this is *ratified by a majority of the union members*, it is signed by representatives of both sides and becomes the collective agreement that governs wages, fringe benefits, and labour-management relations in the firm for the period, usually one to three years, specified in the agreement. There will also be provisions forbidding a strike or lockout and for arbitrating problems that arise during this period, as well as for earlier negotiations of a new agreement should unusual conditions arise.

- *If agreement cannot be reached*, the provisions for the next steps vary slightly among the provinces. (Provincial labour legislation governs collective bargaining procedures, with the exception of bargaining in industries under federal jurisdiction — primarily transportation and broadcasting.) Generally, however, a *conciliation officer is appointed* by the provincial Labour Relations Board to meet with each party, in an effort to resolve their differences. About 40 to 60 per cent of collective agreements are reached by the end of this stage.

- When a conciliation officer recognizes that he or she cannot reconcile the dispute, a *conciliation board* is appointed to hear presentations from both parties, to try to mediate their differences, and in any case to make a formal report and recommendation.

- If a conciliation board's report is not acceptable to both parties, the union members can decide by a *vote to strike or to continue bargaining* with management representatives. Should the union choose to strike or should the management decide on a lockout (refuse to admit workers to the plant), a *work stoppage* results. Collective bargaining continues, although often intermittently, until either a settlement is reached or ultimately the union is destroyed or the firm is bankrupt. The latter possibilities occur quite rarely because it is in the interest of both parties to settle at some point, rather than incur the high costs of work stoppage.

Strikes and Arbitration

Although strikes are given considerable publicity in the news media, their importance in terms of days lost during work stoppages is slight. In the 1970s, this averaged less than 0.5 per cent of the total estimated working time of the Canadian labour force, and during the 1980s the number of worker-days lost through labour disputes declined substantially, despite the increasing size of the labour force.

An issue of increasing importance in the collective bargaining process is the *right to strike in essential services*, and especially in the public service. Strikes by postal workers and air traffic controllers, which affect all parts of the country, and by such essential public servants as police and firefighters have led many to argue that strikes by public servants should be forbidden. Strikes in the private sector that also affect the public directly, such as in railroads and shipping, or that cause layoffs in other industries due to material shortages, such as sometimes occur in the automobile industry during a strike in the steel industry, have also led to sharp dispute.

The alternative frequently proposed is *compulsory arbitration*, whereby the decisions are made on subject areas of collective agreements by one or three independent persons appointed by each side. This proposal has been just as frequently rejected, because it could remove the incentive for each party to strive for a negotiated settlement if each believed it would gain more through an arbitration award, and because compulsory arbitration, for example in Australia, has led to illegal or "wildcat" strikes.

For this reason, some provinces have removed the compulsory conciliation stage from the collective bargaining process. Too often, this provision was used by one party to lengthen the negotiations in the hope that the other side would eventually yield.

Union Effects on Labour Markets

Unions are sometimes described as monopoly sellers of labour services. This is not strictly correct, because unions do not have the ability to sell various quantities of labour services at different prices or wage rates. Rather, some unions can affect the wage rate by altering the labour market in various ways. These include directly restricting the labour supply, changing the labour supply by gaining a higher standard wage rate, increasing the demand for labour, and offsetting monopsonistic power in imperfect labour markets.

Restricting Labour Supply

Most labour unions have supported general measures that would restrict the total supply of labour to the economy in order to gain wage increases as the demand for labour increased over time. Thus, some unions have opposed more liberal immigration provisions, and have encouraged compulsory retirement, earlier retirement, and shorter work weeks.

Craft unions have been able to get large firms in important industries such as construction to employ only union craftsmen in such essential trades as bricklaying, carpentry, and plastering. The supply of these services is further restricted by requiring long apprenticeship periods, high initiation fees, and sometimes by setting quotas on the annual number of entrants to the trade. The quantity of labour supplied at any wage is therefore less than it would have been under more competitive conditions.

Effects of supply restriction are illustrated in Figure 24.2a, where the labour supply curve, S, represents the supply that would be available in the absence of a union, and S_1 represents the restricted and more inelas-

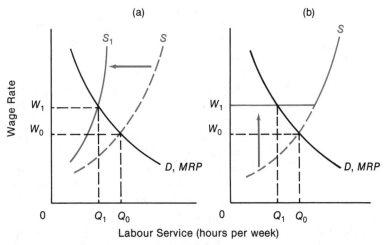

Figure 24.2   Union Effects on Labour Markets
A union that can restrict entrants to an occupation can shift the labour supply curve, for example, to S_1. Given the demand curve, D, this will increase the wage rate to W_1, but reduce the quantity of labour service purchased to Q_1. A union that can impose a higher wage, W_1, on an industry by collective bargaining effectively shifts the supply curve to W_1S. This reduces the quantity of labour service purchased to Q_1.

tic supply resulting from provisions enforced by a craft union. The wage rate under the latter condition is higher, at W_1, and the quantity of labour employed is lower, at Q_1, than would have occurred had supply not been restricted.

Increasing Standard Wage Rates

Industrial unions can try to affect the total supply of labour to the economy by following the approaches listed above, but they cannot restrict entrants to an industry as craft unions do for certain occupations. Instead, industrial unions attempt to get all workers in an industry into the union and then try to obtain a higher standard wage rate. If all workers are unionized, firms cannot obtain workers at a lower wage, and thus must pay the agreed rates. This effectively makes the labour supply curve perfectly elastic or horizontal at the agreed rate, as shown by the solid W_1S curve in Figure 24.2b. If the union has forced the wage upward from W_0, some of the union members will not be rehired. Thus unions are less likely to press for large wage increases where there is an elastic demand for labour. Conversely, a wage increase in cases of highly inelastic labour demand will have proportionately less effect on employment and will increase the aggregate of wages paid to those who remain. In such cases, unions may decide that the increased income more than offsets the unemployment effect.

Increasing the Demand for Labour

Unions that are restrained from pressing for higher wages due to an elastic demand for labour may undertake to shift the labour demand curve outward by assisting employers to improve labour productivity.

Since the demand for labour is derived from the demand for products, unions can also try to increase the latter by urging the public, and especially all union members, to buy only union-made goods, by assisting firms in advertising and other promotional activities, and by lobbying the federal government to maintain tariffs against competing imports.

Although these activities have been particularly characteristic of the industrial unions associated with highly elastic labour demand, all unions engage to some extent in these activities because an increase in labour demand, provided that labour supply does not also increase, leads to an increase in both wages and employment.

Bilateral Monopoly

The three previous cases have dealt with the effects of unions in what are otherwise competitive labour markets. When there are only a few buyers of labour services, and there is a strong union, the condition becomes what is sometimes termed *bilateral monopoly*: the union behaves as if it were a monopoly seller of labour services, and firms that have monopolistic power in the product market tend to be monopsonistic buyers of labour services used mainly in producing those products.

A bilateral monopoly labour market is illustrated in Figure 24.3. This figure reproduces the curves for labour supply, *S*, marginal resource cost, *MRC*, and labour demand, *MRP*, that were shown in Figure 23.2. The monopsonistic employers will, also as indicated in Figure 23.2, want to hire Q_1 units of labour at a wage rate of W_1. But, if the union could actually act as a single seller of labour, it would want to sell the quantity at which its marginal revenue equals its marginal cost. This requires another curve, *M(MRP)*, which is the marginal revenue the union would realize if it sold various quantities of labour priced according to the demand curve it faces, namely the employers' *MRP* curve. (Note that the employers' marginal revenue product is not the union's marginal revenue; rather, the *MRP* curve is the union's average revenue curve.) The union will thus want to "sell" the quantity at which the *M(MRP)* curve intersects its supply curve, since the latter is regarded as its marginal cost. The union would therefore demand a wage of W_2, the wage employers would be willing to pay for Q_2 units of labour. Neither

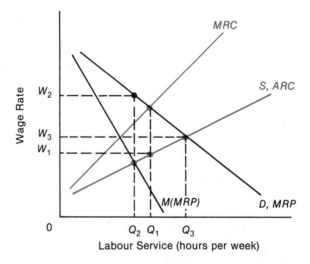

Figure 24.3   Bilateral Monopoly in a Labour Market
In a labour market consisting of one buyer (a monopsonist) and one seller in the form of a labour union, the wage rate is indeterminate. The monopsonist will want to buy Q_1 hours per week, at a wage of W_1. The union's marginal revenue curve, *M(MRP)*, shows the additional revenue associated with each additional unit of labour purchased by the monopsonist. Since the union members' supply curve can be seen as their marginal cost curve, their optimum offering of labour is the quantity at which their supply curve intersects their *M(MRP)* curve, or Q_2. The employer is willing to pay W_2 for quantity Q_2. The actual wage may therefore be between W_1 and W_2; the closer it is to W_3, the closer is the result to what would have occurred under perfect competition.

side, however, has sufficient power to fix its optimum wage level, W_1 for employers, and W_2 for the union. Although the actual outcome cannot be determined by economic analysis, since the agreed wage depends on the relative bargaining power of each side, the bilateral monopoly model can clarify the wage limits within which bargaining takes place.

Economists have expressed some support for the bilateral monopoly situation — or the presence of countervailing powers — since the outcome will be similar to the one that would be determined in a competitive labour market. Suppose collective bargaining results in a wage rate of W_3. This is the rate that would exist at equilibrium in this market in the absence of employer monopsony and union monopoly. (The effect of the employers' monopoly power in the *product* market remains, however, since this is what determines the labour demand curve.) The competitive equilibrium is further approximated with respect to the quantity of labour offered, because once the wage rate is set at W_3, the union will be willing to supply, and employers will be willing to buy, as much as Q_3 units of labour service.

The indeterminacy of the wage rate in bilateral monopoly models of the labour market has led some economists to develop *bargaining theories* of wage determination, which include other economic arguments such as the longer-run costs and benefits to unions and employers of incurring a strike, and non-economic arguments including the degree of political or public support enjoyed by each side in a labour dispute.

Union Impact on Wages

On the basis of the analytical models of union effects on labour markets, one must conclude that unions can raise the wage rate above what it would be in their absence. Indeed, this is the commonly held view, that "unions raise wages". Empirical research to test this view has, however, produced rather inconclusive results. A major reason is that controlled experiments are not possible: one cannot find situations that are precisely the same in all respects except for the absence or presence of a union. Instead, researchers have focused on the wage differences between firms or industries that were or were not unionized. But this approach raises questions about the effect of unions on the wages of non-unionized groups. For example, employers may pay higher wages to non-unionized employees so that these employees will be less inclined to form or join a union.

Ostry and Zaidi, after reviewing the research problems and the evidence for union effects on wages, suggest that:

> At the present time, techniques of analysis and available statistics are probably too crude to enable the researcher to obtain unequivocal results

in relating unionism to the determination of wages or wage structure. For the moment, the verdict one way or another can only be the Scottish "not proven".[1]

A comprehensive evaluation of the evidence for similar research in the United States has led two prominent labour economists to state that:

> It is impossible to measure the true effect of unionism on the wages of unionized workers because we cannot observe what their wages would be in the absence of unionism anywhere else in the economy. Estimates of the difference today between the average union worker's wage and that of the average nonunion worker with the same observable characteristics fall mostly between 10 to 25 percent. Once differences in unmeasured characteristics are accounted for, the estimated wage difference is between 10 and 15 percent.[2]

Labour Legislation in Canada

Federal and Provincial Powers

Labour legislation in Canada varies among the provinces because the provincial governments and the federal government alike have legislative powers in labour affairs. The provincial legislatures have the major jurisdiction, under section 92 of the Constitution Act, 1867, which gives the provinces exclusive power to make laws regarding "property and civil rights in the province". Since contracts between employees and employers are questions of civil rights, the terms and conditions of contracts are therefore regarded as coming under provincial jurisdiction. The federal government's powers in that area are limited to legislation concerning industries that are national, international, or interprovincial in nature, such as transportation and communications, banking, and other industries, such as uranium mining, over which the federal government has direct control.

Labour Relations Acts

Industrial relations legislation dates back to 1907, when the federal government passed the Industrial Disputes Investigation Act, which out-

---

[1] Sylvia Ostry and Mahmood A. Zaidi, *Labour Economics in Canada*, 3rd ed., Toronto: Macmillan, 1979, p. 368.
[2] Daniel S. Hamermesh and Albert Rees, *The Economics of Work and Pay*, 4th ed., New York: Harper & Row, 1988, p. 313.

lawed strikes in public utilities, mining, and railroads until a conciliation board had submitted a report. However, not until the late 1930s
was there general acceptance of the principle that an employer had an
obligation to recognize and bargain with a union representing the
majority of the employees. Legislation embodying this principle was
elaborated in the 1940s to include methods for determining questions of
union representation and appropriate bargaining units, and requiring
negotiation between management and union representatives. Federal
legislation enacted during World War II extended federal jurisdiction
in labour matters, and this set a pattern of legislation that was generally followed by the provinces. Thus there now is an industrial or labour
relations act in each province that provides for the establishment
of a Labour Relations Board and that specifies the conditions for certification of unions and the procedures to be followed in collective
bargaining.

Canada Labour Code

The second major area of labour legislation concerns labour standards
and conditions of employment. The Canada Labour Code, the federal
government's collection of labour legislation, includes, in addition to
the Industrial Relations and Disputes Investigation Act, Acts that
govern minimum wages, hours of work, annual vacations and public
holidays, and discrimination in employment. The federal Employees
Equal Pay Act requires equal pay for equal work for employees of both
sexes. Most of the provinces have Acts dealing with the same questions,
while some provinces also have legislation on additional matters such as
the requirement that employers or employees give notice of termination
of employment and the requirement that employers provide maternity
leave. All provinces have a Workers' Compensation Act providing for
the payment of compensation to a worker or his or her dependents in
case of accident or industrial disease arising from employment. Such
payments are made from a fund established by a levy on all employers.

Review of the Main Points

1. Approximately one-third of all non-agricultural employees in
   Canada belong to labour unions. Craft unions consist of members
   from particular occupations, while industrial unions draw their
   members from specific industries or groups of industries, regardless
   of their occupations.
2. Union organizational structure is based on many local unions, which
   are usually chartered by and affiliated with national or international

unions. These, in turn, are affiliated with national or international federations or congresses.

3. Unions have several goals: to increase the wage rate or the total income of union members, to increase fringe benefits and improve working conditions, to maintain work rules and job security, to maintain the security of the union organization, and to promote particular political goals.

4. To achieve these objectives unions may use one or more of various tactics: strikes, working-to-rule campaigns, slowdowns, picketing, and boycotts, as well as collective bargaining.

5. The collective bargaining process can involve several steps before agreement is reached between union and management representatives. If a union does not exist and two or more unions claim to have the support of the majority of the workers, the provincial Labour Relations Board conducts an election and certifies the successful union as bargaining agent for that group of employees. If the union and management representatives cannot agree on a settlement of the issues presented by each side, in most provinces a conciliation officer appointed by the board attempts to resolve the differences. If this is not possible, a conciliation board attempts mediation and compiles a formal report. If this is unacceptable to either side, the union members can vote to strike or to continue bargaining. If a strike is called, bargaining nevertheless continues until an agreement is reached.

6. Unions can influence the wage rate in several ways: by restricting labour supply, by increasing the basic or standard wage rate in an industry, by increasing the demand for labour, and by offsetting monopsonistic power. This last case is termed "bilateral monopoly", since a union acts as if it were a monopoly seller of labour services to a monopsonistic buyer.

7. Empirical research on the effect of unions on wages has produced rather inconclusive results, because the data are generally not satisfactory for separating the indirect effect of unions on non-unionized firms and industries. However, the available evidence does suggest that unions have increased the wages of their members by a small amount over what the wages would have been in the absence of a union.

8. Labour legislation in Canada is a shared responsibility of the federal and provincial governments, but the federal jurisdiction is limited to those specific industries that it has the power to regulate. Labour Relations Acts in each province have evolved to recognize the rights of employees to organize and to bargain collectively.

9. The Canada Labour Code includes several Acts that govern labour standards and conditions of employment.

Key Concepts and Topics

craft union
industrial union
union goals
featherbedding
seniority
grievance procedures
union shop
open shop
closed shop

primary boycott
secondary boycott
collective bargaining procedures
certification
conciliation
compulsory arbitration
bilateral monopoly
industrial relations legislation

Questions for Review and Discussion

1. Why have labour unions been formed mainly in the blue-collar occupations?
2. What factors determine how high a trade union can push wages without reducing the level of employment?
3. Many unions are opposed to increased mechanization in their industries, yet the existence of strong unions can hasten the rate at which firms mechanize their operations. How can you explain this?
4. Should persons employed in essential services such as police and fire protection have the right to strike? Why?
5. Featherbedding, seniority system, grievance procedure, work rules: what do these terms mean and what effect do you think each has on the efficient use of labour resources?

Sources and Selected Readings

Anderson, J., M. Gunderson, and A. Ponak, eds. *Union-Management Relations in Canada*, 2nd ed. Toronto: Addison-Wesley, 1988.

Anton, Frank R. *Worker Participation: Prescription for Industrial Change.* Calgary: Detselig, 1980.

Craig, Alton W.J. *The System of Industrial Relations in Canada*, 2nd ed., Toronto: Prentice-Hall, 1986.

Ehrenberg, R.G., and R.S. Smith. *Modern Labor Economics: Theory and Public Policy*, 4th ed. Glenview, Ill.: Scott, Foresman, 1991.

Gunderson, Morley, and C. Riddell. *Labour Market Economics: Theory, Evidence and Policy in Canada*, 2nd ed. Toronto: McGraw-Hill Ryerson, 1988.

Hamermesh, Daniel S., and Albert Rees. *The Economics of Work and Pay*, 4th ed. New York: Harper & Row, 1988.

Killingsworth, Mark R. *Labor Supply.* New York: Cambridge University Press, 1983.

Ostry, Sylvia, and Mahmood A. Zaidi. *Labour Economics in Canada*, 3rd ed. Toronto: Macmillan, 1979.

Riddell, Craig, ed. *Adapting to Change: Labour Market Adjustment in Canada.* Toronto: University of Toronto Press, 1985.

_____. *Work and Pay: The Canadian Labour Market.* Toronto: University of Toronto Press, 1985.

_____. *Canadian Labour Relations.* Toronto: University of Toronto Press, 1985.

25 Rent, Interest, and Profit

Rent and Land

Economic Rent and Transfer Earnings

The price for a factor's services is described as having two components: *economic rent* and *transfer earnings*. The meanings of these two terms can be illustrated by referring to the pottery firms constituting the ceramics mug industry. If the firms wish to employ additional potters, they must be willing to pay enough so that the potters will transfer their labour services from other industries.

The minimum payment required to attract resources from other uses is the transfer earnings of the factor.

The total earnings must be at least this amount, but they may also be greater. The reason can be illustrated by Figure 25.1. The supply curve for potters' services is assumed to be upward-sloping, since additional potters can be attracted away from other industries, or into the labour force, only by offering higher wages. Figure 25.1 indicates that if the industry wishes to employ Q_1 potters, it must pay a wage of W_1. Only the last potter hired, however, must be paid W_1 to be attracted into the industry. The other employees will thus be paid more than their transfer earnings because they must be paid the same wage as the last person to be hired. The difference between the transfer earnings for each employee and the actual wage W_1 is a surplus payment that firms could avoid if they could make separate contracts with each employee.

Any payment in addition to the transfer earnings is termed economic rent.

Rent and the Use of Land

The distinction between economic rent and transfer earnings is particularly important in the case of land, because the quantity of land is fixed: land cannot be reproduced or destroyed. (There is one minor

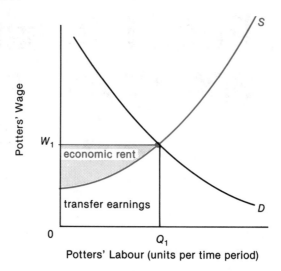

Figure 25.1   Economic Rent and Transfer Earnings
The labour supply curve facing the industry indicates the wage rate it must pay to attract each unit of labour service into the labour force or away from other industries. But all employees will expect, or demand, the same wage rate. Hence, each unit of labour service must be paid W_1, the rate required to attract the last unit. The difference between W_1 and the rate indicated by the supply curve is the economic rent enjoyed by each unit of labour service.

exception to this statement: the quantity of land is reduced when an area is flooded, and increased when an area is drained.) The supply curve for land is therefore considered to be perfectly inelastic in both the short run and long run.

The fixed quantity of land is represented by the vertical supply curve in Figure 25.2. In this case, all possible uses of land — agricultural, recreational, and commercial — are treated together. Similarly, the demand for land is represented as a single demand curve. The use of land is defined here so broadly that no other use for land is possible. Hence there are no transfer earnings associated with the price for using land, since it does not have to be attracted away from some other use. The full price for the use of land is therefore economic rent.

In this general case, land is considered from the point of view of the entire economy. Some land, however, has several uses, while other land may have only one use. The land at the water's edge in many Canadian cities could be used for agricultural, recreational, or residential purposes, as well as for its usual use as the location of warehouses, docks, or offices. This use of land provides a higher marginal revenue product per hectare than if it were used, for example, for agricultural production. Thus, commercial users are willing to pay a higher price for the use of

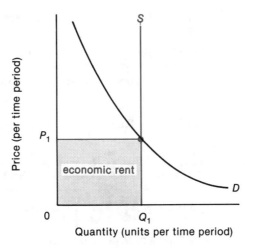

Figure 25.2   Payment for the Use of Land Is Economic Rent
Since the quantity of land available is fixed at Q_1, land has no transfer
earnings. That is, land would be made available for production uses at even
an extremely low price. Payment for the use of land is therefore economic
rent.

the land. The supply curve for commercial land in city centres is therefore highly elastic at low prices, as land is bid away from other uses, but
quite inelastic at higher prices. The price paid for such land *for commercial purposes* therefore has a transfer earnings component, because
a certain (low) price must be paid to attract it away from other uses.

As the demand curve shifts outward, and the price for using commercial land increases, the economic rent component becomes an increasingly large portion of the price. Alternatively, land such as the Halibur-
ton Highlands of Ontario, the Laurentians of Quebec, or Whistler
Mountain in British Columbia can be used for little but recreation.
Even agriculture and forestry are not very profitable in these areas.
The price for using this land therefore has virtually no transfer earnings component, but the economic rent increases annually with the
increasing demand for recreational space.

The above two cases consider land from the perspective of alternative
industries. However, an individual farmer who wants to rent an additional fifty hectares would argue that the price paid for the use of this
land represents only transfer earnings, since this price must be paid
before the landowner will allow this particular farmer, rather than
another farmer, to use the land. From the perspective of the individual
producer, this is correct. The size of the economic rent component
therefore depends on whether one is interested in determining the surplus value associated with the use of a factor being transferred from

another firm or from another industry. From the total economy's perspective, however, the entire price paid for the use of land is economic rent, since land exists: it is available for production at any price. It differs from labour services in that there is a minimum price that must be offered to attract labour into productive processes.

Box 25.1   **Rent and the Value of Land**

Cost of farmland seen keyed to price of grain

By OLIVER BERTIN

Prairie farmland prices will continue to drop in 1983 and 1984, if grain prices stay depressed, says University of Manitoba economist Daryl Kraft.

In a study commissioned by Winnipeg-based United Grain Growers Ltd., Mr. Kraft said the price of farmland could drop by 50 per cent if potential buyers base their offers on the current earning capacity of the land.

"To maintain the bullish investor attitude toward farmland, the earning capacity would have to stay at a level comparable to the price of farmland, but this has not happened," he said. "The price of land has risen more than the income-earning capacity and land price realignment is occurring."

How far the farm-

land price will fall depends on how long sellers can postpone accepting a price below what they were anticipating, he said. If many forced sales occur because of debt consolidation or foreclosure, farmland prices could drop at a record rate.

UGG studies indicate prairie farm incomes will fall by 28 per cent in 1982 from a year ago, because the price of wheat and barley have plummeted on world markets while costs have continued to

rise.

Cash flow has now fallen two years in a row, dropping to 450 per cent of 1971 levels in 1981 and to 375 per cent this year. If these trends continue, the earning capacity of the land may be only 300 per cent of 1971 levels by 1983.

However, the UGG study projected higher farmland prices in the long run because world consumption is growing faster than grain producing capacity, creating upward pressure on grain prices.

It is often thought that the rent on land and buildings is determined by the price of that property. But the reverse is true—namely, that the rental value of a property determines its price. Similarly, the price of farmland depends on its productivity and the value of the crops produced.

Source: *The Globe and Mail*, 10 November 1982.

Recent concern about the private ownership of waterfront land in popular recreational areas provides an example of the economic rent concept applied to public policy. Camping-park operators who lease lakeside land and in turn charge high rates for camping privileges would argue that there is no economic rent or surplus in their prices, because they must pay a high annual rent to the landowner. This high rent, however, is due to the fixed quantity of such land available and the increasing demand for its use. It is therefore sometimes suggested that the economic rent component of the return to this land should be taxed away from the landowner, since the land will be made available for camping purposes as long as the price received covers the transfer earnings, or the return that would be realized from alternative uses such as agricultural production.[1]

Quasi-Rent The use of buildings is distinguished from the use of land because the quantity of land is fixed in the long run but the quantity of buildings is fixed only in the short run. Buildings (or floor space) earn an economic rent due to their inelastic supply in the short run. In the long run, however, some buildings can be demolished or more can be constructed, depending on the expected returns from the use of buildings. The economic rent realized in the short run may thus disappear in the long run; it has thus been termed *quasi-rent* to emphasize its short-term nature.

The concepts of economic rent and quasi-rent are not limited in their application to land and buildings. These rents occur whenever the quantity of a factor is fixed. One of the best-known cases of quasi-rent (although it is seldom recognized as such) occurs in the high prices paid to famous entertainers and sports stars. The available quantity of top-ranking professional hockey players is limited and cannot be changed in the short run. The transfer earnings component of a hockey star's annual salary, for example, might be in the order of $35,000. The balance, amounting to several hundred thousand dollars, is quasi-rent that results from his rare ability as a hockey player and the high marginal revenue product realized by the player's hockey club.

Interest and Capital

Interest is sometimes defined as the price charged or paid for the use of money; it is also defined as the return on capital. The terms "capital" and "money" are sometimes used interchangeably, but an important distinction between them has been made in earlier chapters.

Capital is any means of production that has itself been previously produced, and includes real or tangible items such as plant and equipment, as well as improvements to land such as dams, drainage systems, and paving. A wider concept of capital includes human capital: the improvements to labour due to education, training, and health care.

---

[1] This was the essence of a nineteenth-century proposal that there is only one tax, a tax on land. For an explanation of this argument, see Henry George, *Progress and Poverty*.

Residential housing is also included, because houses are thought of as providing a service over a long period of time, rather than as items produced for immediate consumption. Capital, or real goods that are used directly in the productive process, must be distinguished from financial assets, which represent ownership of, or creditors' claims on, the capital items. A firm's plant and equipment are capital; the stocks and bonds issued by the firm to raise money needed to purchase the plant and equipment are financial assets of the firm's owners and creditors.

A return can be earned both on the use of capital and on the financial assets representing a claim on this capital. However, only if there is a return on capital in terms of real goods and services produced by the capital is it possible for there to be a return on financial assets. A firm that does not use its plant and equipment productively will not be able to pay dividends to its shareholders or interest to its bondholders. A return on financial assets can only be paid out of the returns to real capital items. This is the key relationship between capital and money that is developed in the following sections.

Valuation of Assets

Before turning to the determination of interest rates, it is important to deal with a mistaken impression some people have about what determines the prices of factor services. It is sometimes argued, for example, that land rents are high because the price of land is high. But the statement should be reversed. A particular piece of land may have a high selling price because a high price can be charged for its use.

The value of an asset depends on its yield or net return.

To see why this is so, consider the following example. Suppose a firm is considering the purchase of a piece of equipment that can be leased to other users. What is the maximum price it should pay for the equipment? Assume it knows that the equipment can be leased to earn a net income of $1,000 per year, and that the equipment will be obsolete in 10 years. The income from the equipment over the 10-year period will thus be $10,000. If the firm is to earn a net return on the asset, the equipment's price must be less than $10,000, but how much less? This depends on the opportunity cost of the money used to purchase the equipment, namely, the best alternative rate of return from another asset. If the highest rate of return one could obtain on any other asset is 8 per cent, then one should not purchase the equipment in question unless at least this rate can be realized.

Present Value   The maximum price that will reflect this rate of return requires the calculation of the *present value* of the return earned in each of the future years. At a discount rate (similar to an interest rate) of 8 per cent, the $1,000 earned at the end of the first year is equal to $925.93 (or $1,000 ÷ 1.08) at the present time. (Conversely, $925.93 loaned now at 8 per cent would increase to $1,000 in one year.) The present value of the $1,000 earned on the equipment in the second year is $1,000 ÷ $(1.08)^2$, and so on, for the 10 years the equipment is to be leased. The present value of the sum of the 10 years of annual income from the equipment can be expressed as:

$$PV = \frac{\$1,000}{(1.08)} + \frac{\$1,000}{(1.08)^2} + \frac{\$1,000}{(1.08)^3} + \ldots + \frac{\$1,000}{(1.08)^{10}}$$

A compound interest table will show that *PV* is equal to $6,710.

The present value or capitalized value of an asset is therefore equal to the sum of the present values of the annual income earned by the asset (plus the present value of whatever the asset might be sold for at the end of the period).[2]

Rate of Return This method for calculating the present value of a capital item can also be used to calculate its *internal rate of return*. This is the discount rate that makes the present value of the future stream of net receipts from a capital item equal to its cost. Suppose the equipment in the example above could be purchased for less than $6,710. The rate required to reduce or discount the annual returns to equality with this lower price would be greater than 8 per cent, and thus greater than the opportunity cost of funds used to purchase the equipment. The internal rate of return would thus be greater than the external rate used for evaluations of the proposed capital item.

Investment Decisions The present value calculations provide two approaches for a firm's investment decisions. A firm should purchase a capital item if: (1) its cost is less than the present value of the net returns to the capital item when these are discounted at the best alternative rate of return or the rate on borrowed funds; or (2) the internal rate of return on the capital item is greater than the best alternative rate.

Interest and the Marginal Efficiency of Capital

In the case of capital, the marginal revenue product is related to the total value of the capital item; this is the same as expressing the marginal revenue product as a rate of return on the total value of the item.

[2] The general expression for this formula is $PV = \sum\limits_{1}^{n} \frac{A}{(1 + r)^t}$, where $\sum\limits_{1}^{n}$ represents the sum of n items, and $\frac{A}{(1 + r)^t}$ is the present value of A dollars earned t years hence, when the interest rate is r per cent.

But instead of calling this the marginal rate of return on capital, conventional usage has adopted the shorter term, *marginal efficiency of capital* (*MEC*).

Whether the marginal efficiency of capital declines as more capital is added to an economy depends on whether the additional capital is used for *capital widening* or *capital deepening*. Capital widening occurs when an economy's labour force is increasing in such a way that the use of capital and labour can be increased in constant proportion. Provided that industries have not reached the point of diminishing returns to scale — and this is unlikely for the economy as a whole — the marginal efficiency of capital will remain constant, or even increase where there are increasing returns to scale.

At an advanced state of economic development, however, increases in the economy's capital stock are likely to result in capital deepening: an increase in the proportion of capital to labour. As the capital deepening process continues, the law of diminishing marginal productivity begins to take effect: the marginal physical product of additional capital (or investment) falls, and thus the marginal efficiency of capital also falls.

Figure 25.3 shows the downward-sloping segment of an economy's *MEC* curve: as the capital stock increases, the *MEC* or rate of return on additional capital declines. The existing capital stock in the economy is valued, in this example, at $300 billion: this is shown as a perfectly inelastic supply curve, *S*. The intersection of the *MEC* and *S* curves indicates that the marginal rate of return on capital is 18 per cent.

Suppose that the prevailing rate of interest for business loans is 12 per cent. There will be a strong demand for such loans because firms can earn 18 per cent on each dollar spent for new plant and equipment, but pay only 12 per cent for funds borrowed to purchase these capital assets. As firms increase their borrowing and add to their capital, the increased demand for loans will increase the interest rate on loans, especially if the money supply is constant. At the same time, the marginal efficiency of capital falls with the increasing capital stock. The result may be that the marginal efficiency of capital is equal to the interest rate at 15 per cent. The equilibrium level of investment, or additions to capital, is reached at $350 billion. No further investment will occur unless the *MEC* curve shifts upward or the interest rate falls.

The *MEC* curve will shift upward with improvements in technology. Discoveries of new sources of raw materials and the development of new production techniques and new products usually result in an increased rate of return and additions to capital stock. The rapid improvements in technology in the past few decades, for example, have resulted in a continuing outward shift of the *MEC* curve in most industrial countries. There has thus been a substantial increase in their capital stock, even though interest rates have not fallen. The tendency toward higher inter-

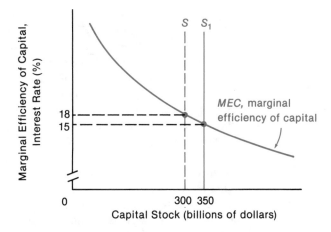

Figure 25.3　Marginal Efficiency of Capital
As an economy's capital stock increases, there is a decline in the rate of
return on additional capital, or the marginal efficiency of capital (*MEC*). An
increase in the capital stock, from $300 to $350 billion in this example, will
occur only if the interest rate is less than 15 per cent; otherwise investors
could not earn a net return on borrowed funds.

est rates in recent years, however, may slow this rate of capital accumulation unless there continue to be substantial improvements in
technology.

　　Changes in the interest rate are influenced by many factors, only one
of which is the demand for loans to finance new plant and equipment.
There is a demand for loans for a number of other purposes: consumers
borrow to finance purchases of consumer goods and residential housing,
and all levels of government borrow both to finance specific projects
such as sewers and roads and to meet budgetary deficits. The supply of
funds available for such borrowers largely depends on the prevailing
monetary policy.

The Structure of Interest Rates

The various interest rates associated with different types of financial
assets are referred to collectively as the *structure of interest rates*. This
may range from 4 to 10 per cent on bank savings accounts, 10 to 15 per
cent on second mortgages, to rates of 25 to 35 per cent on riskier loans.
Maturity and Risk　Variation in interest rates is due to several factors.
One is the *time to maturity* of a loan or bond. For example, the federal
government's 91-day treasury bills normally have a lower interest rate
than its 20-year bonds. (In periods of high interest rates, the shorter-
term bond may have a higher rate than the long-term bond, reflecting

the general expectation that interest rates will soon return to their normal level.) Interest rates vary for loans or bonds of any given length of maturity due to differences in the *risk* associated with each. A 5-year bond issued by the federal government may have an interest rate of 9 per cent, but a bond of the same maturity issued by a provincial government usually has a slightly higher rate, while municipal and corporation bonds carry a still higher rate, reflecting creditors' judgments about the relative degrees of risk, or the ability of borrowers to repay interest and principal, associated with each type of bond.

Security   The *type of collateral or security* provided by a borrower also influences the interest rate charged. Mortgage rates would be somewhat higher were they not secured by houses. These durable, immovable items obviously offer greater security for a creditor than, for example, the signature of a second person who guarantees to repay a loan should the borrower default.

Loan Size   Interest rates also vary with the *size of the loan* and the *number of installment payments*. A small loan requires as much administration and bookkeeping time as a large loan; similarly, monthly repayments require more time than a single annual payment. Since these administrative costs must be covered by the interest payments, the interest rate on a small loan with monthly payments is substantially higher than on a larger loan of equal risk and maturity that requires only one annual payment.

Expected Inflation   Finally, interest rates reflect lenders' previous experience with rising prices and expectations about further *inflation*. The higher the expected rate of inflation, the higher the interest rate lenders will require for any given loan, to avoid the possibility of a loss in real income due to higher future prices of goods and services. A general price increase of 10 per cent in one year, for example, would mean that a loan of $100 would buy only $90 worth of goods and services when it was repaid a year later. In this case, a lender would require an interest rate that was 10 percentage points higher than it would be if no inflation were expected.

Although the differences among interest rates on various types of loans and bonds may change slightly, the entire structure or range of rates tends to move up or down simultaneously as the money supply changes. Thus, one can think of a typical or average interest rate when economic theories are expressed in terms of interest rate. Reference is often made, for example, to the "prime rate", the rate charged by a chartered bank on large loans extended to its regular and least risky borrowers, as an indicator of the general level of interest rates.

Nominal versus Real Rate of Interest   A distinction is frequently made between the *real rate* of interest and the *nominal rate*. The latter is the stated rate on the loan, bond, or bank deposit, while the real rate "corrects" this nominal rate for the prevailing level of inflation. Hence, when inflation is 5 per cent, a nominal rate of 8 per cent results in a real rate of interest of only 3 per cent. The real interest rate for three-month treasury bills is shown for the past four decades in Figure 25.4.

Profit and the Entrepreneur

What Is Profit?

Profit is another term with one meaning in everyday language and a different, specific meaning in economic analysis. In business, profit is sometimes defined as the difference between total revenues and the total direct expenditures for materials, labour, and interest. This definition omits important costs such as the opportunity cost of plant, equipment, and land owned by a firm. For a more accurate measure of profit, these costs should be added to direct or explicit expenditures. When this is done, profit is the difference between total revenue and the total of explicit and implicit costs.

Profit represents the return to entrepreneurial activity, after payment has been made or imputed for all other factors of production.

Figure 25.4   Real Interest Rate for Treasury Bills
The real interest rate is the nominal or actual rate adusted for or reduced by the CPI inflation rate. During the 1950s and 1960s the real rate averaged about 1½ to 2 per cent. There was a negative real rate from 1972 to 1975 when inflation rose suddenly, but it was strongly positive in the 1980s, both when high nominal rates were used to fight inflation in 1981–82 and in the mid-1980s when inflation subsided.

Source: Economic Council of Canada, *Annual Report*, 1983; and *Bank of Canada Review*.

Normal versus Pure Profits   A further distinction is made between *normal profit* and *pure profit*. Normal profit is the minimum profit necessary to retain a firm in a particular industry in the long run. In other words, normal profit is the return to entrepreneurial ability to organize and manage the other factors of production in order to produce a specific commodity. If the return for this activity is insufficient, the entrepreneur will transfer his or her organizational ability to managing a firm in another industry, just as additional units of a factor's service will be made available only at higher prices.

Any profit greater than the normal profit is termed a pure or economic profit. Note the similarity between *economic profit* and *economic rent*. Each is a surplus — an amount greater than that required to attract a factor into a particular use — but economic rent is due only to a fixed or inelastic supply of a factor, whereas economic or pure profit arises because other firms do not enter the industry to reduce the profit realized by each firm.

Risk, Uncertainty, and Profit

Risk   Profit is sometimes described as a reward or return to risk-taking. However, this is only one of the reasons for profits. Moreover, a distinction must be made between *calculable* and *incalculable risks*. Calculable risks are those unfortunate events such as fire and flood which, on the basis of past experience, are certain to happen to some firms, although no one knows which particular firms will be affected in the future. The *probability* that any given firm will experience a fire, flood, death of key personnel, and so on, can be calculated; insurance against loss from such misfortunes can be purchased. Since the insurance premiums are another cost of production to the firm, calculable risks are not the kind of risks that are implied in an explanation of profits.

Uncertainty   *Incalculable or uninsurable risks* are those related to the *uncertainty* of future events. Changes in *economic, political, or social conditions* cannot be predicted on the probabilistic basis used to predict the occurrence of insurable risks. Social conditions may change consumer preferences, for example, with resulting changes in related product prices and wages. Political conditions can open new export markets or close existing ones, or possibly block the import of raw materials from a particular country. Economic conditions can result in substantial changes in fiscal and monetary policies and tariff policies, or in public policies for assisting research and development. Any of these changes can alter a firm's costs and revenues; thus, at any time a firm faces considerable uncertainty about its future profit or loss position. It will of course attempt to predict the changes that will most directly affect its particular operations, but some uncertainty must remain.

Another kind of uncertainty relates not to the economy-wide conditions described above but to the uncertainty associated with particular *innovations*. A new technique, perhaps reflected in more complex equipment, may be expected to reduce production costs. Whether this will actually occur remains uncertain until a firm has made the expenditures to develop and install new equipment. A new product may involve an even greater degree of uncertainty since it may require new machinery and raise special packaging and transportation problems, as well as the uncertainty of consumer acceptance or demand for the product.

Some entrepreneurs will be more willing than others to produce existing commodities or to undertake innovations under higher degrees of uncertainty, and therefore, if conditions are favourable, will realize a pure profit. They may of course incur a substantial loss if their predictions or expectations are seriously inaccurate. The lower the degree of uncertainty, the more entrepreneurs or firms there will be in the industry and, thus, the lower will be profits in the form of a return to accepting uncertainty or uninsurable risks.

Competition, Monopoly, and Profits

The earlier comparison of firms under different market structures emphasizes that any of these firms could realize a pure profit in the short run. Whether such profits were made in the long run, however, depended on the degree of freedom that existed for other firms to enter the industry. Thus profits due to innovation could disappear in the long run, in the absence of patents or other restrictions to entry.

Another reason for the existence of pure profits, therefore, is the variety of barriers preventing a new firm from entering an industry, and thus permitting existing firms to exercise more control over the price of their product. Monopoly profit is sometimes confused with profit due to innovation, because most innovations are protected by patents, a major source of monopoly control. The distinction is important, however, because monopolies or restricted-entry oligopolies are not the sole source of innovation.

Monopoly Profits   The difference between monopoly profit and profit as a return to risk-taking is significant for public policy purposes. "Monopoly profits" is a cliché often used in a manner that implies that all profit attributable to monopolistic conditions is an unnecessary surplus and thus socially undesirable. Under a market system, however, some profit is necessary to encourage innovation that leads to lower costs and improved products. This profit must be viewed separately from the profit due only to barriers against the entry of other firms. When this approach is taken, it becomes clear that public attitutes toward monopoly profits must be reflected in policies to increase competition or to regulate natural monopolies, rather than in policies to simply attack all profits.

One of the advantages often cited for a centrally planned economy, or for public ownership of certain industries, is that under these conditions profit is unnecessary because the state becomes the entrepreneur: profit is not required either to maintain production of given commodities or to serve as an incentive for innovation. In some of the centrally planned economies and in some publicly owned industries, however, it has been necessary to introduce incentive schemes as encouragement for managers to reduce costs and to improve quality.

Review of the Main Points

1. The price for a factor's services may have two components: economic rent and transfer earnings. The latter is the minimum price required to attract the factor away from other uses. Economic rent, the difference between transfer and actual earnings, is due to the fixed quantity available of the factor. Quasi-rent is the surplus earnings realized because the quantity available is fixed in the short run, but not in the long run.

2. Capital includes real or tangible items such as plant, equipment, and residential housing. Financial assets represent ownership of, or creditors' claims on, capital items. The value of an asset depends on its yield or net return.

3. The present value or capitalized value of an asset is equal to the sum of the present value of the annual income earned by the asset, plus the present value of what it might be sold for at the end of the earnings period. The internal rate of return is the rate that makes the present value of the future stream of net receipts from a capital item equal to its cost.

4. A firm should invest in a capital item if the cost of the capital item is less than the present value of the future net returns, or if its internal rate of return is greater than the internal rate on the best alternative project or the interest rate on borrowed funds.

5. The marginal efficiency of capital decreases as an economy's capital stock rises, because increasing the proportion of capital to labour (capital deepening) leads to diminishing marginal productivity of capital.

6. The long-run equilibrium level of the capital stock would be reached when the rate of interest equals the marginal efficiency of capital. As long as technological change continues to shift the *MEC* curve outward, and there is not a long-term rise in interest rates, an economy is not likely to reach the equilibrium level of the capital stock.

7. The structure of interest rates is explained by several factors differentiating loans or bonds: time to maturity; risk; type of collateral; loan size; and expected rate of inflation.

8. Profit, the difference between total revenues and the total of explicit and implicit costs, is the return to entrepreneurial activity. Normal profit is the minimum profit required to retain or attract a firm into an industry. Pure profit is the amount by which total profit exceeds normal profit.

9. Profit is realized by firms that are willing to operate under conditions of uncertainty about general economics, political, and social conditions, and about the consequences of its own innovations. Profit can also be realized, even when there is little general uncertainty and no innovation, when new firms are prevented from entering an industry by barriers such as those described for monopolies and restricted-entry oligopolies.

10. Profits are necessary in a market system to induce entrepreneurs to organize other factors of production in the productive processes, to produce under conditions of uncertainty, and to undertake innovations.

Key Concepts and Topics

transfer earnings	nominal vs. real rate of interest
economic rent	capital widening
quasi-rent	capital deepening
capital	structure of interest rates
present value of assets	time to maturity
internal rate of return	profit
marginal value of assets	risk and uncertainty
marginal efficiency of capital	

Questions for Review and Discussion

1. Suppose that an area of residential land is rezoned for commercial uses. What change, if any, will there be in the economic rent realized on this land? Should any public action be taken concerning changes in economic rent resulting from zoning changes?

2. Why is the interest rate such an important price in the market system?

3. How can one account for the wide range of interest rates that occur at any given time in the economy?

4. "Normal profits, by definition, are enough to keep a firm in a given industry. The government should therefore tax away all profits in excess of normal profits." Do you agree? Why?

Sources and Selected Readings

Barlowe, Raleigh. *Land Resource Economics*, 4th ed. Englewood Cliffs, N.J.: Prentice-Hall, 1985.

Eckert, R.D., and R.H. Leftwich. *The Price System and Resource Allocation*, 10th ed. Hinsdale, Ill.: Dryden Press, 1988.

26 Income Distribution in Canada

Among Canada's basic economic goals is the goal of "an equitable distribution of rising incomes". The Economic Council of Canada noted in its first report that this is a complex objective to pursue, defying simple quantitative measurement. Nevertheless, the Council defined the goal to include at least the elimination of poverty and the reduction of regional income disparities. The problem of poverty is considered later in this chapter, and regional income disparity is the subject of the next chapter.

Income Distribution among Productive Factors

In a pure market system, the economy's output of goods and services would be distributed among the population according to incomes determined solely by the quantity of productive services offered by individuals and the prices of these services. That is, the incomes received would represent purchasing power or claims on the real goods and services available: the more services one could offer or the higher the price of one's service, the more goods and services one could buy. Distribution as it would be determined by a free market system is modified somewhat in a mixed economy by government regulations and direct intervention.

Functional Distribution of Income

The distribution of income according to the basic types of productive factors—land, labour, and capital—is termed the *functional distribution of income*. Statistics for the national income and expenditure accounts are not collected and arranged in a way that shows precisely the share of national income going to each type of factor, but an estimate of these shares can be obtained from the components of Net National Income. Table 26.1 shows an approximation of the functional distribution of income, which treats employee earnings as the return to

Table 26.1

Functional Distribution of Income, Canada, 1990

Payments to Factors	Billions of Dollars	Per Cent of Total
Employee earnings[1]	$383	73
Corporate profits[2]	45	9
Interest[3]	58	11
Income of unincorporated enterprises[4]	40	8
Total (Domestic Income)	$526	100

Source: Statistics Canada, *National Income and Expenditure Accounts.*

Detailed items may not add to totals due to rounding.

[1] Includes wages, salaries, supplementary labour income, military pay and allowances.
[2] Corporate profits before taxes less inventory valuation adjustment.
[3] Interest and miscellaneous investment income, including profits of government enterprises and governments' investment income.
[4] Includes net income of independent professional practitioners, businesses, and farmers.

labour services, and corporate profits, interest, and dividends as the return to capital. Income of unincorporated enterprises (small business and farms) represents a combined return to land, labour, and capital used in these businesses.

The relative share of the national income received by each factor has been fairly stable over a long period of time, with employee earnings representing 68 to 73 per cent of the total income. If one can assume that about one-half of the income of unincorporated enterprises is a return to labour, the labour share of national income has been about 75 per cent.

Personal Distribution of Income

Sources of Personal Income

The functional distribution of income is based on the components of Domestic Income, which also includes income received by corporations and governments but not passed on to individuals. Personal income statistics can be taken instead from a survey of consumers' finances conducted by Statistics Canada. Table 26.2 shows that about 78 per cent of the income of families and individuals is received through *employment or self-employment earnings*. (Some of the latter, however, may be a return to the plant and equipment used by self-employed professionals such as doctors, engineers, and artists.) *Investment income* accounts for 6 per cent, while *transfer payments* represent 11 per cent. The latter include government pension payments, worker's compensation, unemployment insurance benefits, family allowances, and so on.

Size Distribution of Income

Information on the sources of personal income is important in understanding how people obtain their incomes in total, but it does not show how incomes are distributed among the population. The simplest approach, and thus the one that receives the most attention, involves the *size distribution of income: the number of individuals and families at each level of income or in each income group.*

Column 1 of Table 26.3 shows the percentage of families and individuals whose income levels fall within each of several income groups, while column 2 shows the percentage of the total income that is earned by persons within each of the income groups. The percentages shown in each of these columns are accumulated, starting from the lowest income level, so that columns 3 and 4 show most clearly the inequality of income distribution. For example, families and individuals with an income of less than $10,000 in 1989 constituted 9.2 per cent of the population, but they received only 1.5 per cent of the total income. Almost twenty times as much income (29.1 per cent) was received by the 11.4 per cent of the population who were in the income group of $75,000 and over.

Table 26.2

Sources of Income of Families and Unattached Individuals,[1] Canada, 1989

Income Sources	Per Cent of Total
Wages and salaries	72.4
Net self-employment income	5.3
Investment income	6.1
Transfer payments	11.2
Miscellaneous income[2]	4.5
Total	100.0

Source: Statistics Canada, *Income Distributions by Size in Canada.*

[1] Families are groups of individuals sharing common dwelling units and related by blood, marriage or adoption. Unattached individuals are persons living by themselves or rooming in a household where they are not related to other household members.

[2] Includes retirement pensions, annuities, scholarships, alimony and other items not specified or included in other categories.

Table 26.3

Income Distribution by Size, for Families and Unattached Individuals, Canada, 1989

Annual Income	Percentage of Families and Individuals in Income Group (1)	Percentage of Total Income Received by Group (2)	Percentage of Population in This and Lower Groups (3)	Percentage of Income Received by This and Lower Groups (4)
Under 10,000	9.2	1.5	9.2	1.5
10,000–19,999	18.6	6.7	27.8	8.2
20,000–29,999	15.2	9.2	43.0	17.4
30,000–39,999	14.6	12.3	57.6	29.7
40,000–49,999	12.3	13.4	69.9	43.1
50,000–59,999	9.4	12.5	79.3	55.6
60,000–74,999	9.5	15.4	88.8	71.0
75,000 and over	11.4	29.1	100.0	100.0
Total	100.0	100.0		

Source: Statistics Canada, *Income Distributions by Size in Canada.*

Lorenz Curve   The degree of inequality in income distribution is illustrated in Figure 26.1 by a *Lorenz curve*. This shows the extent to which the actual distribution of incomes deviates from perfect equality in income distribution. Since the scales used to show the percentage of families and the percentage of total income are equal, perfect equality in income distribution would be represented by a straight line running out from the origin at a 45° angle to each scale. For example, if 20 per cent of the population received 20 per cent of the total income, this would be shown as point *A* in Figure 26.1. If a further 20 per cent of the population also received a further 20 per cent of the income, this would be shown as point *B*, and so on.

When the information presented in columns 3 and 4 of Table 26.3 is plotted in Figure 26.1, the result is the bowed-out curve below the equal distribution line. Point *C*, for example, shows that the 43 per cent of the population who receive annual incomes of less than $25,000 receive only 17 per cent of the total income.

The degree of income inequality is represented by the size of the area between the equal distribution line and the actual income distribution curve: the smaller the area between the two, the less the income inequality. The Lorenz curves for earlier years have not been plotted in Figure 26.1, because there has been so little change in income distribu-

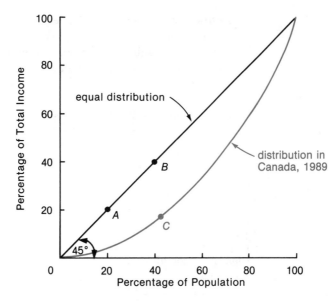

Figure 26.1 Income Distribution in Canada
A Lorenz curve shows the percentage of the total income received by each percentage of the population. The area between the two curves shows the extent to which the actual distribution varies from equal distribution of incomes. Point *A* shows that 20 per cent of the population receives 20 per cent of the income; point *B* shows that 40 per cent of the population receives 40 per cent of the income, and so on along the line of equal income distribution. But point *C*, on the actual distribution curve, shows that 43 per cent of the population receives only 17 per cent of the income.

Source: Table 26.3.

tion during the past two decades that the curves for other years would be almost indistinguishable from the 1989 curve. Table 26.4 shows how little change there was, for example, in the distribution of family income between 1971 and 1989. Although the share received by the highest income families declined slightly (from 40.0 to 39.3 per cent), the gains during the period were in the next-highest income groups rather than in the lower income groups.

Note, however, that *equal* income distribution is not necessarily defined as an *equitable* income distribution. Only if the normative judgment is made that social justice requires everyone to have the same income will these two distributions be the same.

Causes of Income Inequality

There are many causes of income inequality. Combinations of these causes can result in very low incomes for some individuals and families, as the discussion of poverty in the next section shows, while other factors can lead to very high incomes. A few factors can by themselves, however, account for substantial income differences: Figures 26.2 and 26.3 illustrate two of these, age and education.

Table 26.4
Distribution of Family Income in Canada[1]

	Percentage of Total Income Received by Each Fifth of the Population				
	1951	1961	1971	1981	1989
Lowest-income fifth of families	6.1	6.6	5.6	6.4	6.5
Second fifth	12.9	13.4	12.7	12.8	12.6
Third fifth	17.4	18.2	18.0	18.3	17.8
Fourth fifth	22.5	23.4	23.7	24.1	23.8
Highest-income fifth	41.1	38.4	40.0	38.4	39.3
All families	100.0	100.0	100.0	100.0	100.0

Source: Statistics Canada, *Income Distributions by Size in Canada.*

[1] Prior to 1965 only non-farm family income was included, but the change in survey coverage made negligible difference to the relative distributions.

Age   Average incomes rise steadily up to about ages 40 to 45 and then decline almost as quickly to age 65 and over. The increase in incomes is due largely to the experience workers develop in particular jobs or occupations, for which employers are willing to pay a significant premium. By the mid-forties, however, many persons who have been in their jobs for some time have little additional experience to gain, and incomes rise more slowly. This more gradual rise in later years is more than offset, as Figure 26.2 shows, by a tendency for some older workers to withdraw from the labour force and the retirement of most persons at age 65. The lower income at higher ages is also due partly to the lower average level of education of the older population, but even for persons with a specific level of education the average income declines due to the effect of withdrawal from the labour force.

Education   The effect of education on incomes is now widely recognized. Figure 26.3 shows that persons with elementary schooling have about one-half the income received by those with a university degree. Much of the attention given to the effect of education on income, however, has failed to emphasize that other factors are also at work. For example, persons with higher levels of education are more likely to be employed on an annual basis and thus do not face temporary layoffs or as much unemployment as do some other workers.

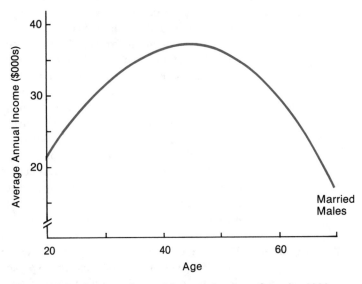

Figure 26.2   Average Annual Income by Age, Canada, 1989
The average annual income varies with age. For example, incomes of
married males rise to a peak at about age 45, and then decline through to
retirement and beyond. The age-earnings profile for females is lower than
for males, but reaches its peak at about the same age level.

Source: Statistics Canada, *Income Distributions by Size in Canada.*

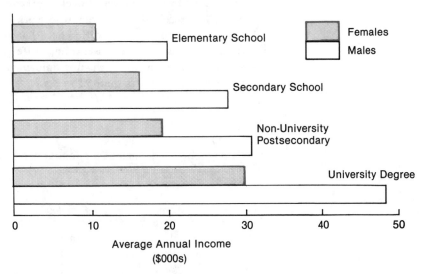

Figure 26.3   Average Annual Income by Education, Canada, 1989
The average annual income for university graduates is almost twice the
income received by secondary school graduates, and about 50 per cent
greater than the average income for other post-secondary graduates.

Source: Statistics Canada, *Income Distributions by Size in Canada.*

Occupation   In a previous chapter, Table 23.1 showed the average employment earnings in broad occupations categories. Much of the variation among occupations is due to education differences: the average education of labourers is lower than the education of managers. But this accounts for only part of the difference in earnings. Other factors such as relative changes in the supply and demand for persons in different occupations can change income differentials fairly quickly: the rapid increase in the number of postsecondary graduates during the 1960s and 1970s, for example, may have narrowed the income difference between professional and clerical occupations. More pronounced narrowing of income differentials will likely occur between manual labour and most other occupations. Other factors, such as degree of responsibility, cost of training, and so on, also explain part of the occupational wage differences.

Weeks Worked   The number of weeks worked per year also explains a large part of earnings differences among occupations. Workers in some occupations, particularly in the managerial and professional categories, are usually employed on an annual basis and are paid for 52 weeks of work. In other occupations, such as farming, logging, and fishing, the work tends to be seasonal and wages are paid for perhaps only 6 or 7 months.

The lower earnings associated with fewer weeks worked, as shown in Table 26.5, would be expected. However, when the average earnings are divided by the number of weeks worked, one finds that lower weekly wages are received by persons who work only part of the year. This accentuates the earnings difference that results from working fewer than 52 weeks. The actual earnings differences shown here, however, are reduced somewhat by the unemployment insurance benefits paid to persons who work less than 52 weeks.

Table 26.5

Earnings by Employment Duration, Canada, 1987

| | Average Earnings from Employment | |
Weeks Worked	Females	Males
49–52	$18,981	$30,633
40–48	11,608	18,503
30–39	9,320	14,561
20–29	5,929	9,539
10–19	4,143	5,258
0– 9	1,416	1,719

Source: Statistics Canada, *Income Distributions by Size in Canada.*

Other Causes Other causes of income inequality are not so easily identified by objective measurement. Individuals and families experience various kinds of fortune or misfortune that accentuate income inequality: some individuals seem to have had the good luck to be "in the right place at the right time", while others have suffered a series of tragedies including accidents, fires, thefts, and so on. Some of these personal and social causes of inequality are considered more fully in the following discussion of poverty.

Redistribution of Income by Transfer Payments

The personal income distribution illustrated in Figure 26.1 is based on gross, or before-tax, incomes. However, these incomes do not reflect the distribution determined by the markets for productive factors, because transfer payments are included in the gross incomes. Without these, the Lorenz curve would be bowed somewhat farther out from the equality line. Table 26.6 summarizes the relative importance of transfer payments in the total income of each group. Families and individuals whose total incomes were between $10,000 and $15,000 in 1989 received 55 per cent of this income as transfer payments. The percentage drops sharply for successively higher income groups, although even the persons in the highest income bracket received some transfer payments — mainly as family allowances. Transfer payments thus increase the share of the total income going to the low-income groups and reduce some of the inequality that would exist in the absence of such government programs as unemployment insurance and welfare assistance.

Table 26.6

Transfer Payment Income of Families and Unattached Individuals, Canada, 1989

Income Class	Transfer Payments as Percentage of Income
Under $10,000	71
$10,000–14,999	55
15,000–19,999	43
20,000–24,999	24
25,000–29,999	20
30,000–39,999	12
40,000–49,999	8
50,000–59,999	6
60,000 and over	4
All persons	11

Source: Statistics Canada, *Income Distributions by Size in Canada.*

Poverty

The elimination of poverty has been specified as an essential step toward equitable income distribution. The Economic Council stated this in clear terms: *We believe that serious poverty should be eliminated in Canada, and that this should be designated as a major national goal.*[1]

Can Poverty Be Measured?

Policies and programs to eliminate poverty, and measures of their effectiveness, require an operational definition of poverty. Although there may be general agreement on the need to overcome poverty, there is some disagreement on what constitutes poverty. It is sometimes defined as a condition in which *individuals or families do not have the means to meet their basic needs*, but any list of basic needs is based on arbitrary judgments. Moreover, the basic needs of families or individuals vary with the specific circumstances of each case.

A second definition of poverty suggests that poverty is a *relative* concept. That is, the elimination of poverty requires more than just the means to sustain life; it includes the notion of a *minimum socially acceptable standard of living*. With a general rise in economic and social well-being, it is argued, the minimum acceptable standard also rises. This definition of the poverty level implies that "the poor will always be with us", at least so long as the minimum standard rises faster than anti-poverty programs can assist those below this rising standard.

A third, somewhat similar, view of poverty is based on the size distribution of income described in the last section. As long as the fifth of the population with the lowest incomes receives such a small share of the economy's total income and the highest-income fifth of the population receives such a large share, *the bottom fifth is said to be in a state of poverty relative to the rest of the population*. In this case an elimination of poverty would require a consensus on a much more difficult question: the most appropriate size distribution of income.

Each of these definitions, however, is concerned only with current income or living standards. Poverty also has a time component, and thus is different from having a low income at any given time. Some persons, notably college students, may have low incomes at one point but have prospects of higher incomes in the near future. This is a substantially different situation from the hopeless cycle of poverty that can perpetuate itself, as described in Box 26.1.

---

[1] Economic Council of Canada, *Fifth Annual Review: The Challenge of Growth and Change*, Ottawa: Queen's Printer, 1968, p. 105.

The Poverty Line

While recognizing the limitations of income measures of poverty, recent reports on poverty have chosen to define poverty, in the absence of other operational measures, in terms of the minimum income believed necessary for meeting basic human needs. Thus the concept of a *poverty line* has been used to measure and describe the magnitude of poverty in Canada.

The poverty lines were determined from a study that showed that, on average, families allocated 39 per cent of their incomes to the basic essentials of food, clothing, and shelter. It was assumed therefore that a family using much more than half its income on such essentials could be described as at or below the poverty level. An arbitrary figure of 59 per cent was chosen as the poverty line — that is, the income level below which families spend at least 59 per cent of their incomes on food, shelter, and clothing. These poverty lines, differentiated by size of area of residence in addition to family size, are shown in Table 26.7.

Characteristics and Causes of Poverty

Just as it is difficult to define poverty, so it is difficult to describe the many features that combine to distinguish the poor from the rest of the population. However, some basic features can be determined by examining the distribution of poverty within selected sections of the population. Table 26.8 compares the *distribution* of poverty with its *incidence*. For example, 9 per cent of families in Ontario are below the poverty line, but 26 per cent of all low-income families are in Ontario.

Table 26.7
Poverty Lines by Family Size, Canada, 1988

Family Size (number of persons)	Poverty Lines[1]
1	$11,867
2	16,087
3	20,446
4	23,540
5	25,720
6	27,917
7 or more	30,028

Source: Statistics Canada, *Income Distributions by Size in Canada.*

[1] As defined by Statistics Canada for cities of 100,000 to 500,000 population.

Over 60 per cent of Canada's poor live in Ontario and Quebec. Apart from the high rate for individuals, the poverty rate was highest among families of two or three. Thirty-nine per cent of the families headed by a woman—usually widowed or divorced—experience poverty. Poverty is not strongly differentiated by age of family heads, although 36 per cent of unattached individuals below the poverty line are 65 or over.

Table 26.8

Incidence and Distribution of Poverty in Canada, 1988

Characteristics	Incidence of Poverty[1]		Distribution of Poverty[2]	
	Families	Individuals	Families	Individuals
	(percentages)			
Size of family		38		100
2	14		38	
3	13		26	
4	9		23	
5 or more	11		12	
Region of residence				
Atlantic provinces	13	40	9	7
Quebec	16	49	35	35
Ontario	9	31	26	28
Prairie provinces	13	36	18	17
British Columbia	12	34	11	14
Place of residence				
Cities	13	40	75	80
Small urban areas	11	36	12	13
Rural areas	9	27	14	7
Sex of family head				
Male	9	30	65	36
Female	39	45	35	64
Age of family head				
24 and under	34	50	11	18
25–34	14	24	27	16
35–44	10	29	22	9
45–54	11	40	12	8
55–64	8	38	13	13
65 and over	13	48	16	36

Source: Statistics Canada, *Income Distributions by Size in Canada.*

[1] Percentage of all families or unattached individuals whose incomes are below the Statistics Canada 1986 poverty lines.
[2] Percentage distribution of low-income families or individuals within the selected characteristic.

Box 26.1 **The Poverty Cycle**

Poverty breeds poverty. A poor individual or family has a high probability of staying poor. Low incomes carry with them high risks of illness; limitations of mobility; limited access to education, information, and training. Poor parents cannot give their children the opportunities for better health and education needed to improve their lot. Lack of motivation, hope and incentive is a more subtle but no less powerful barrier than lack of financial means. Thus the cruel legacy of poverty is passed from parents to children.

Source: *Economic Report of the President*. Washington, D.C.: U.S. Government Printing Office, 1964, pp. 69-70.

Several of the factors used to describe income distribution and the incidence of poverty also constitute an explanation of the causes of poverty. Due to the cyclical, complex process that characterizes the lives of low-income families, the consequences of poverty are not easily separated from its causes. However, one can approach the problem by dealing first with those who are in the labour force but who derive an inadequate income from their work, and then with those who have an inadequate income because they are not in the labour force.

The Working Poor

Individuals' Characteristics About one-half of all individuals and family heads with low incomes are in the labour force, yet are unable to earn an income large enough to lift them above the poverty line. One of the major reasons is *inadequate education and training*. This is frequently the result of growing up in a family that could not provide educational opportunities, or in an area where these were severely limited. Without basic education, a worker lacks the basis for further training, either in technical courses or on the job.

Poor health may compound the problem: a worker may leave school for health reasons, such as respiratory illness, and may then find that the same problem prevents him or her from working at certain jobs or for a full-time week and year.

Inadequate training or *geographical immobility* may constrain a worker from changing to another occupation where seasonal effects and economic fluctuations would permit him or her to work longer periods at a higher hourly or weekly wage rate. *Discrimination* may also bar a worker from a more desirable occupation, especially where his or her skills could be utilized more effectively.

Market power of employers, or the absence of union power among employees, is a serious problem for low-income workers since they tend to work in non-unionized occupations and industries. *Lack of information* about other employment opportunities may also keep workers in low-wage jobs. They cannot afford the time or money to look for other jobs, and many workers are in remote areas where there is little opportunity for learning about jobs elsewhere.

A large portion of the *rural poverty*, and poverty among the self-employed, is associated with farmers who operate farms of inefficient size, on sub-marginal land (rocky, hilly, or poorly drained terrain), without adequate financing for capital needs, and without training in modern agricultural technology and farm management.

Box 26.2   How the Middle Class Creates Poverty

[Note] the middle class orientation of much of our public policy. Consider first our cities, where the majority of the poor live. The central feature of most urban policy has been to accommodate the automobile. This includes massive road building programs into the core, requiring the razing of sites for roads and parking lots. Since the poor are the ones who live adjacent to the core, it is their homes that are removed — typically under the name of urban renewal. Since they can afford only low quality, crowded, and cheap dwellings, they are made worse off by the elimination of the supply of such accommodations, for they must move into newer, higher cost areas that are usually zoned for single family dwelling only.

The same transportation routes permit those with cars to acquire land for housing farther from the city core, and thus subsidize not only their travel cost, but also their housing costs. But with suburbanization based on the automobile, the demand for public transit systems declines, raising the costs of that service to those without cars — again, the poor. In the extreme, public transit is terminated, as in Los Angeles, and the poor become immobilized near the core of the city. When firms also begin to locate at the fringe of the cities because of lower land costs, better transportation, and access to the scarce, more skilled workers who are suburbanites, the poor at the core become pauperized as well as immobilized. Add to this the fact that, as this migration begins to take place from the core to the fringes, the tax base in the inner city declines, forcing decline of the level of much needed social services, and the iron grip of urban poverty grows tighter.

Source: N. H. Lithwick, *Urban Poverty*. Ottawa: Central Mortgage and Housing Corporation, 1971, pp. 54-55.

Economic Conditions   Aside from the individual characteristics of the poor, there is a serious cause of poverty that is external to the individual: the effect of public *economic and social policies*. Fiscal policies, for example, require a choice between unemployment and inflation. When the government chooses to fight inflation by pursuing a contractionary policy, unemployment increases. It tends to have its most direct impact on the kinds of workers who constitute the working poor. Because they usually have no special skills, employers are not reluctant to lay them off, knowing that such workers can be found easily when they are required again. Conversely, an expansionary policy with its attendant inflation reduces the purchasing power of the transfer payments made to both the working and non-working poor, unless such transfer payments are automatically adjusted for changes in the general level of prices.

Other socioeconomic policies, such as the "urban development" process described in Box 26.2, have less obvious but longer-term or permanent effects on the poor. The external effects of such public programs usually receive low consideration because the poor lack either the time or the political skill, or both, to defend their position against the policy-makers.

The Non-Working Poor

The low-income family heads and individuals who are not in the labour force have been termed "the welfare poor". They depend on the welfare system because they have no alternative means of support:

> They are the ones left behind by our economic system — the elderly, the sick, the disabled, and women in charge of families which require their presence in the home . . . . A few others . . . are members of the labour force, but work at jobs which do not pay them enough to live on.[2]

Anti-Poverty Programs and Proposals

Poverty has been identified as a serious national problem for three sets of reasons: moral, social, and economic. Many Canadians realize a moral obligation, on humanitarian grounds, to assist people who are unable to fend for themselves, whether they are in or out of the labour force. The social reasons are somewhat more intangible, involving a concern for social harmony, reducing the hopeless frustration of poverty and its legacy to future generations, and fending off the political strife that could be generated as the poor become more vocal and militant.

The economic burden of poverty, apart from the direct impact on the poor, falls on the rest of the economy in terms of *lost output* and *diverted output*.[3] Lost output is the additional production of goods and services that the economy would have realized had the productive

[2] Special Senate Committee on Poverty, *Poverty in Canada*, p. 31.
[3] These items were suggested by the Economic Council of Canada in its assessment of the costs of poverty as described in its *Sixth Annual Review: Perspective 1975*.

potential of the poor been more effectively developed and utilized. Diverted output refers to the goods and services that could have been produced by the resources required to deal with poverty. Low-income families, for example, usually do not have adequate preventive medical and dental attention and thus may require more remedial care.

Programs to Provide Incomes and Services

The major existing programs for providing income to persons not in the labour force are Old Age Security, the Canada Pension Plan, the Family Allowance Act, and the Canada Assistance Plan. Persons who are in the labour force but who are unemployed are assisted mainly by payments from the Unemployment Insurance Commission.

The *Old Age Security Act* provides for a payment of $326 per month (as of 1989) to all residents over 65 who have been in Canada for at least ten years prior to their application for the payments. A Guaranteed Income Supplement of up to $387 per month for a single person (subject to cost-of-living adjustment) is added to the O.A.S. payments for persons with little or no other income. The G.I.S. payment is reduced by $1 for each $2 of income received from other sources. These rates would provide a single pensioner, as of 1989, with approximately $8,556 annually. This is substantially below the Statistics Canada poverty line for a single person, yet it is estimated that at least 20 per cent of all persons receiving Old Age Security payments had no other source of income.

The *Canada Pension Plan* (or the comparable *Quebec Pension Plan*) provides an annual pension equal to 25 per cent of the recipients' annual earnings (up to a maximum level—$27,700 as of 1989) averaged over the period during which contributions could have been made. The Plan is financed by employee contributions and a matching contribution from the employer.

Family allowances are not specifically a low-income assistance scheme because they are paid regardless of a family's income. However, the payments do supplement the income of low-income families with children: payments are made at a monthly rate of $32.74 per child (in 1989). A province may supplement this amount to vary the payment by age of child or number of children. Moreover, a program has been introduced to provide low-income families with a tax credit in proportion to the number of children.

The *Canada Assistance Plan* (CAP) was introduced in 1966 as the federal government's main program for coordinating the various public welfare programs in each province. All provinces have taken up this option, designing their own programs, for which the federal government pays 50 per cent of the costs.

Recognition that housing accounts for a large share (as much as 50 to 60 per cent) of low-income families' budgets has led the federal government to introduce various programs for low-income housing. The *National Housing Act* provides for subsidies to assist with mortgage and rental payments, and grants for housing rehabilitation. The government's Central Mortgage and Housing Corporation (CMHC) can make low-interest loans for low-rental housing.

An important contribution to the incomes of unemployed persons is made through the payments specified by the federal *Unemployment Insurance Act*. Payments are equal to 60 per cent of the unemployed person's average weekly earnings. The length of time for which payments are made depends on the length of previous employment, with a maximum of 50 weeks.

Proposals for a Guaranteed Annual Income

Welfare assistance systems have long been criticized for their inadequacy, bureaucratic complexity, personal and regional inequity, social stigma, and attitude of charity. An increasingly frequent response to this set of problems is a proposal for a *guaranteed annual income: a guarantee by the federal government that every family or individual would have an income at least equal to some specified amount, often expressed as a function of the related poverty line*. Such a guarantee could be realized in alternative ways. One approach would involve reforming the existing welfare system, but this probably would not solve the administrative difficulties, provincial differences in benefits, and the inadequate assistance for the working poor.

Negative Income Tax

An alternative method for providing guaranteed annual income is based on the introduction of a negative income tax, a government payment to individuals and families whose other income is below the poverty line, but which varies with the amount of this other income.

The specific amounts of the payments would depend on the various components of the formula used in calculating the government contribution: the poverty line established for each group, the fraction of the poverty line income to be guaranteed, and the rate at which the government payment was to be reduced as other income rose.

The operation of a negative income tax in determining the amount of the government payment is illustrated in Table 26.9. Assume that the government guarantees that no family or individual will have an income of less than 50 per cent of the poverty line income level, and that this latter level is set at $20,000 for a family of four. The guaranteed income is therefore $10,000. Assume also that the government payment (the negative tax) is reduced by $500 for every $1,000 of private income. Thus the effective tax rate on private income is 50 per cent. Table 26.9 shows, for example, that a family with no other income receives the full amount of the guaranteed income in the form of a negative tax or government payment. A family with $2,000 in private income has its potential government payment of $10,000 reduced by 50 per cent of its private income and thus receives $9,000. Its total income is therefore $11,000. A family that has private income just equal to the poverty line level receives no government payment. Since the potential payment of $10,000 is reduced by 50 per cent of the private income, the potential payment is reduced to zero at $20,000.

The negative income tax has some significant advantages over the alternative proposals for a guaranteed annual income:

- The scheme is simple to administer: the amount of the government payment is calculated on the basis of income statements submitted to the Department of National Revenue under the existing arrangements for assessing positive income taxes.
- Reduction of the government payment by less than any increase in private income provides a "work incentive". For example, if $10,000 were paid to all families who had other income of up to $10,000, there would be no incentive for the head of a family earning $11,000 to remain at a job. He or she would be better off to earn only $9,900 and collect an additional $10,000 from the government.

Table 26.9

Negative Income Tax Approach to a Guaranteed Annual Income
(for a family of four)

Guaranteed Income Level	Private Income	Negative Tax (Allowance Paid)	Total Income
$10,000	$ 0	$10,000	$10,000
10,000	2,000	9,000	11,000
10,000	4,000	8,000	12,000
10,000	8,000	6,000	14,000
10,000	16,000	2,000	18,000
10,000	20,000	0	20,000

Assumptions: 1. Poverty line for a family of four is $20,000.
2. Guaranteed income is set at 50 per cent of poverty line income.
3. Tax on private income up to poverty line level is 50 per cent.

Similarly, if the government payment were reduced by the full amount of other income, a family head earning $10,000 would have no incentive to continue earning even this low amount since he or she could quit work and receive $10,000 from the government. The fractional reduction of government payments under the negative income tax plan thus provides some financial support, while maintaining an incentive to supplement this by other income. Under most of the existing welfare schemes, the welfare payment is reduced by the full amount of any increase in private income, thus largely removing the incentive to seek earned income unless this can be substantially above the welfare payments level.

- There is universal coverage under the negative income tax scheme: all families or individuals with low incomes receive some financial assistance regardless of the reasons for their low incomes. This point also implies, however, that it may be necessary to set different poverty lines for each region of the country if the costs of living vary significantly by region.

Review of the Main Points

1. Income distribution can be examined in different ways: one is functional distribution, or the distribution among productive factors according to the price and quantity of each general type of factor. The relative share of national income received by each factor category has been fairly stable, with labour receiving about 75 per cent, and the remainder going to capital and land.

2. The size distribution of income, or the number of individuals and families at each level of income, shows that, for example, families and individuals with an income of less than $10,000 in 1989 constituted 9.2 per cent of the population but received only 1.5 per cent of the total income.

3. A Lorenz curve shows the deviation of the actual distribution of incomes from perfect equality in income distribution. The degree of inequality in employment and investment income is reduced by government taxation and expenditures.

4. Equitable income distribution is not easily defined, but it is considered to include at least the elimination of poverty and the reduction of regional income disparities.

5. The causes of income inequality are complex, but some of the basic factors include age, education, occupation, and number of weeks worked per year.

6. Poverty is difficult to define. It has been defined as a condition in which individuals or families do not have the means to meet their basic needs, or do not have a minimum socially acceptable standard of living. A third definition of poverty is the lowest-income

groups' having a very small share of the total income. Similarly, poverty is difficult to measure. The poverty line is based on the income level below which families need to spend somewhat more than half (for example, 60 to 70 per cent) of their incomes on the basic essentials of food, clothing, and shelter.

7. The poverty rate is the percentage of the total group, in different categories, whose incomes fall below the poverty-line income. The poverty rate is highest in Quebec, among families headed by a female, and among persons under age 25. However, the distribution of the poor shows that about 60 per cent live in Ontario or Quebec, and that they are most numerous in the 25 to 34 years age-group.

8. The working poor are not able to earn more for many reasons: inadequate education or training, poor health, geographical immobility, discrimination, market power of employers, lack of employment information, inadequate financing and management training for farm operations, and the adverse effects of several economic and social policies. The non-working poor include persons who are permanently disabled or ill and women who remain at home to care for dependants.

9. Poverty is considered a serious national problem for moral, social, and economic reasons. The latter include the cost of lost output and diverted output associated with poverty. Lost output includes the goods and services that could be produced if the productive potential of the poor were more effectively developed and utilized. Diverted output includes the goods and services that could be produced by the resources required to deal with poverty.

10. Anti-poverty programs include those to improve employment and to provide incomes and services directly to the poor. Programs to provide incomes and services include transfer payments under the Old Age Security and Guaranteed Income Supplement, Canada Pension, and federal-provincial welfare assistance programs.

11. Since welfare assistance programs have not satisfactorily dealt with the low-income problem, a guaranteed annual income has been proposed. This could be provided in various ways; a common proposal involves a negative income tax, whereby the federal government would guarantee persons a minimum income but the government payment would be reduced with increasing levels of income received from other sources.

Key Concepts and Topics

functional income distribution
size distribution of income

Lorenz curve
poverty

poverty line	Old Age Security Act
poverty rate	Canada Pension Plan
incidence of poverty	Canada Assistance Plan
distribution of poverty	National Housing Act
working poor	Unemployment Insurance Act
lost output	guaranteed annual income
diverted output	negative income tax

Questions for Review and Discussion

1. What is the difference between the functional and personal distribution of income? How are these two concepts related?
2. Do you think the existing distribution of income in Canada is equitable? Why? If not, use a Lorenz curve to describe the distribution you believe is equitable. Outline the programs you would advocate to achieve this result. If you think the existing distribution is equitable, what steps must be taken to maintain this distribution?
3. Think of two persons whose incomes you know are quite different. List as many reasons as you can for the difference in their incomes.
4. Develop a definition of poverty without including the general concept of a poverty line as described in this chapter. What difficulties do you encounter in devising such a definition?
5. Can the war against poverty ever be won? Explain. Outline what you believe to be the most effective anti-poverty programs, in light of the data provided on the incidence and distribution of poverty.
6. Some people are in favour of modifying the existing welfare system and increasing the amounts paid, others favour a reduction in welfare payments, while still others favour a negative income tax. Decide which position you favour and outline the arguments supporting your position and opposing the other positions.

Sources and Selected Readings

Economic Council of Canada. *Reflections on Canadian Incomes*. Ottawa: Supply and Services Canada, 1980.

Gillespie, W. Irwin. *In Search of Robin Hood: The Effect of Federal Budgetary Policies During the 1970s on the Distribution of Income in Canada*. Toronto: C. D. Howe Institute, 1978.

Gunderson, Morley. *Economics of Poverty and Income Distribution*. Toronto: Butterworths, 1983.

Osberg, Lars. *Economic Inequality in Canada*. Toronto: Butterworths, 1981.

Ross, David P. *The Working Poor: Wage Earners and the Failure of Income Security Policies*. Ottawa: Canadian Institute for Economic Policy, 1981.

Statistics Canada. *Income Distributions by Size in Canada*. Ottawa: Supply and Services Canada, annual.

Thurow, L. C. *The Zero Sum Society: Distribution and the Possibilities for Economic Change*. New York: Basic Books, 1980.

Vaillancourt, François, et al. *Income Distribution and Economic Security in Canada*. Toronto: University of Toronto Press, 1985.

27 Regional Income Disparity

The narrowing of regional income differences as part of the income distribution goal reflects the national policy of balanced regional development and the sharing by all regions in the results of Canada's economic growth. It is well known in Canada, however, that there are wide differences in the level of economic well-being among the regions or provinces.

Regional Income Differences in Canada

Regional income disparity or inequality can be illustrated in various ways. Table 27.1 shows the average annual incomes of individuals in each major economic region and compares these with the national average. Income differentials of approximately these proportions have persisted for a fairly long time. The Personal Income statistics of the national accounts offer a similar comparison of income differentials since 1951. These, as presented in Figure 27.1, show a continuation of the same general ranking, with Ontario, Alberta, and British Columbia at the top level; Manitoba, Quebec, and Saskatchewan in the middle; and the Atlantic provinces at the lower level; but with a narrowing of the overall inequality of provincial income levels.

These comparisons are based on total personal income including transfer payments. A provincial comparison of earned income per person would show slightly greater differentials, since transfer payments reflect one aspect of the federal government's policies designed to reduce the differentials. Although regional development policies have been directed to parts of all the provinces, major emphasis — as the income differentials would suggest — has been placed on the development of the Atlantic provinces.

Some Causes of Regional Income Disparity

Regional and provincial income disparity has been a basic concern of public policy in Canada for several decades, but there has been remark-

Table 27.1

Regional Income Disparity, Canada, 1989

Region	Annual Income of Individuals	Per cent of National Average
Atlantic provinces	$18,266	81
Quebec	20,904	93
Ontario	24,788	111
Prairie provinces	21,473	96
British Columbia	22,395	100
Canada	22,416	100

Source: Statistics Canada, *Income Distributions by Size in Canada.*

ably little agreement on the basic sources of the problem or on a complete theory of regional economic development.[1] However, some factors that appear to explain much of the regional variation can be identified; these include the relative size and productivity of the labour force in each region, the capital stock and composition of industrial activity, the availability of natural resources, concentration of the population, and proximity to large markets.

Age Composition of the Population

The per capita income of a region is obviously influenced by the size of its labour force relative to its total population. Even if there is a high output per worker in a given region, the income per capita is sharply reduced if the potential labour force is a small fraction of the total population, since each worker is then supporting a number of dependants. In 1979, for example, the Atlantic provinces had the lowest proportion, about 57 per cent, of its population in the working ages of 18 to 64, while Ontario and British Columbia had the highest proportion, 62 per cent.

Labour Force Participation Rate

This rate is defined as the percentage of the population aged 15 and over who are in the labour force. The provincial labour force participation rates roughly parallel the provincial ranking of incomes per capita; in 1988 the participation rate in the Atlantic provinces was 59 per cent, compared with 70 per cent in Ontario and 72 per cent in Alberta. The lower rate reflects a lower participation rate among both men and women in the Atlantic provinces.

[1] For an elaborate treatment of this topic, see Economic Council of Canada, *Living Together: A Study of Regional Disparities.*

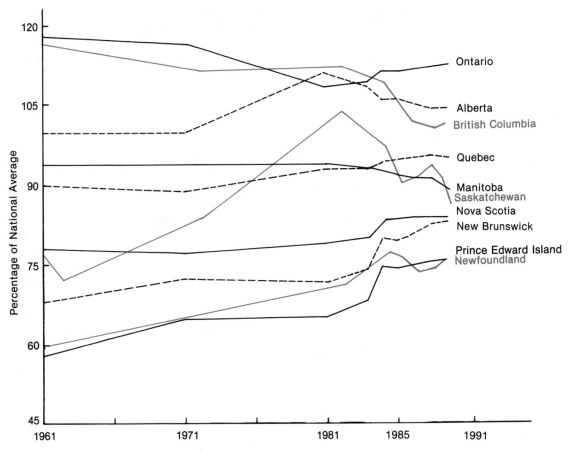

Figure 27.1   Personal Income per Person, by Province
The average personal income per capita is approximately 50 per cent higher
in Ontario than in some of the Atlantic provinces. This disparity has been
narrowed somewhat since the 1950s; however, the ranking has changed
very little over the postwar period.

Source: Department of Finance, *Economic Review*.

Unemployment Rate   Since the labour force includes both the employed and unemployed, a
high unemployment rate can compound the effect of a low participa-
tion rate on per capita incomes. This has been true for the Atlantic
provinces and Quebec, where the average unemployment rates during
1990 were 12.8 and 10.1 per cent respectively, compared with 6.3 per
cent in Ontario. Moreover, the combination of a low participation rate
and a high unemployment rate suggests that some persons who might
have entered the labour force were discouraged from doing so by a
general lack of employment opportunities.

The result of these combined factors (age, participation, unemployment) was that in 1990, for example, only 40 per cent of the Atlantic provinces' population was employed, compared with 48 per cent for the whole country, and 51 per cent in Ontario. The Economic Council has estimated that this fact alone accounts for roughly half of the difference between the per capita income of the Atlantic provinces and the national average.

Level of Education Attainment

The preceding factors in this section are related to the employment rate, but at any given employment rate there may still be considerable variation in personal income per capita due to differences in labour productivity, or the value of output per unit of labour service. The regional variation in earnings per worker shows the same ranking as the personal incomes per capita, with the Atlantic provinces at about 80 per cent of the national average. One important reason for the difference in earned income per worker is the level of education attainment of the labour force in each region. As Table 27.2 indicates, the labour force in Newfoundland, Prince Edward Island, and Quebec has the highest percentage of persons who have completed not more than elementary schooling, while British Columbia has the lowest percentage with only elementary schooling, and Ontario has the highest percentage with a university degree.

Capital Stock

The capital stock of a region can be expected to influence the level of income per worker, because the greater the quantity of physical capital (plant and equipment) associated with a worker, the greater the value the output per worker tends to be. Estimates of the physical capital stock per worker, by province, for 1988, are shown in Table 27.3. These indicate that the capital stock per worker was highest in Western Canada (particularly in Saskatchewan and Alberta) and higher in the Atlantic provinces than in Quebec and Ontario. However, a relatively large capital stock is not enough; it must also be used efficiently. Ontario, for example, had a low capital stock per worker but it had the highest output per worker.

Industrial Composition

Since earnings per worker vary substantially among industries, it is possible that some of the regional variation in income per worker is due to the particular composition or "mix" of industries in each region. It is often suggested that, if more manufacturing firms could be attracted to the Atlantic region, they would directly increase per capita income in that area. However, when the average earnings in each region are standardized according to the industrial composition of the whole country,

Table 27.2

Educational Attainment of the Labour Force by Province, Canada, 1989

Province	Level of Education Completed			
	Elementary (0–8)	*Secondary (1–5)*	*Post-secondary Non-university*	*University Degree*
	percentage of the labour force			
Newfoundland	11	45	34	10
Prince Edward Island	11	55	24	10
Nova Scotia	7	48	31	14
New Brunswick	9	53	28	10
Quebec	11	47	29	13
Ontario	6	55	23	16
Manitoba	8	56	23	13
Saskatchewan	8	58	24	10
Alberta	5	55	27	13
British Columbia	4	56	26	14
Canada	7	53	26	14

Source: Statistics Canada, *The Labour Force.*

Table 27.3

Capital Stock per Worker, by Province, 1988

Province	Net Capital Stock per Worker (percentage of national average)	Province	Net Capital Stock per Worker (percentage of national average)
Newfoundland	138	Manitoba	96
Prince Edward Island	68	Saskatchewan	117
Nova Scotia	91	Alberta	154
New Brunswick	107	British Columbia	109
Quebec	90		
Ontario	86	Canada	100 ($32,236)

Source: Canadian Labour Market and Productivity Centre, *Quarterly Labour Market Productivity Review*, Spring 1990.

there is little effect on the regional variation in earnings. Standardization involves making the assumption that the industrial composition of a region is the same as the composition for the country, and then applying the region's average earnings in each industry to this standard mix of industries. Since this produces little effect, the regional differences in average earnings must be due to different earnings levels for any given industry, rather than to a region's particular industrial composition.

The slight decrease in earnings in the Atlantic provinces when earnings are standardized for industrial composition shows that this region has a more favourable industrial composition than the national average. Attracting mining or manufacturing firms to the Atlantic region would improve average earnings only if those particular firms paid higher wages than other firms in the same industry. But the major reason firms locate in low-wage areas is to take advantage of low wages. If the wage level rose significantly, a firm would likely find it more profitable to locate in central Canada, where it would be closer to large markets and have lower transportation costs.

Other Factors in Regional Income Disparity

Natural Resources   Other factors that appear important in explaining regional income differences affect a region's economy in complex and indirect ways. The discovery of oil in Alberta, for example, and its subsequent impact on the province's economy account for a large share of the higher per capita income in that province. Similarly, British Columbia's forests and the Prairie's wheatlands have conferred natural advantages on these areas that otherwise might have much lower per capita incomes.

Population   The population concentration in central Canada and in the Vancouver area represents both a cause and an effect of higher incomes in those areas. The Economic Council has described the process of population concentration and its relation to economic development as follows:

> Of major importance is the concentration of population in fairly small geographic areas, in which the most efficient production and distribution is more easily achieved. Moreover, once the process of concentration gets underway, similar powerful forces make it of cumulative importance in growth—production can be scaled still more effectively to meet enlarging markets; business services and a versatile labour force are close at hand; new technology is more easily developed and exploited; and advanced management skills and enterprise are more readily attracted. It is on this basis that the concept of the "growth centre" as a necessary focus for regional growth has been widely advanced and accepted.[2]

[2] Economic Council of Canada, *Second Annual Review: Towards Sustained and Balanced Economic Growth*, p. 127. Reproduced with the permission of the Chairman of the Economic Council of Canada, 1991.

Policies and Programs to Reduce Regional Disparity

Public policies designed to reduce the regional income disparity in Canada have tried to reduce the influence of factors causing this disparity, as well as to provide interprovincial income transfers through the federal government. The different policies can be grouped in three categories: income transfers, general stabilization policies, and specific development policies.

Federal-Provincial Fiscal Transfer Payments

The federal government makes payments to some provinces to compensate them for the lower value of their tax bases in the case of different taxes or levies imposed by the provinces. These *equalization payments* for 1988–89 are shown in Table 27.4. Three provinces do not receive equalization payments because their provincial tax bases are so large relative to other provinces. Per capita payments to the other provinces follow roughly the reverse ranking of the per capita personal income shown in Figure 27.1; that is, the lowest income provinces receive the highest equalization payments per capita.

Differentiated Stabilization Policies

One of the limitations on fiscal and monetary policies is the differential impact of these stabilization policies on the different economic regions of Canada. This disparity is evident, for example, in the relative unem-

Table 27.4

Equalization Entitlements under the Federal-Provincial Fiscal Arrangements Act, 1988–89

	Total (millions)	Per Capita		Total (millions)	Per Capita
Newfoundland	$ 859	$1,513	Ontario	$ —	$ —
Prince Edward			Manitoba	720	663
Island	172	1,333	Saskatchewan	347	342
Nova Scotia	800	960	Alberta	—	—
New Brunswick	786	1,101	British Columbia	—	—
Quebec	3,281	494		—	—

Source: Canada Tax Foundation, *The National Finances, 1988–89.*

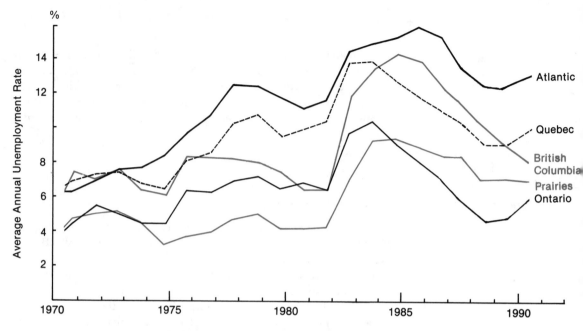

Figure 27.2   Regional Unemployment Rates in Canada
Unemployment rates tend to be highest in the Atlantic provinces and lowest
in Ontario and the Prairie provinces. Although the unemployment rates
generally rise and fall together, the rates tend to show a greater relative
decline in expansionary periods in the low-unemployment regions.

Source: Statistics Canada, *Historical Labour Force Statistics*.

ployment rates of the different regions during periods of economic contraction, compared with the relative rates during economic expansion.
Figure 27.2 shows that, although regional unemployment rates tend to
change in unison with changes in economic conditions, the share of
the total unemployment borne by the high-unemployment areas such as
the Atlantic provinces tends to rise in an expansionary phase. Thus, the
low-income regions do not benefit as much as the high-income regions
from expansionary policies. Furthermore, policies to restrain inflationary pressures in the high-income regions tend to increase the unemployment rates in the low-income regions. Contractionary policies must be
introduced to curtail inflation in the high-income regions before the
unemployment rate has dropped to a satisfactory level in the low-
income regions. There is thus an inherent conflict in determining
national stabilization policies: should the high-income regions be
required to accept a higher rate of inflation so that the low-income
regions can enjoy a further decline in their unemployment rates, or
should inflation be restrained before the unemployment rates have
dropped satisfactorily in the low-income areas?

This dilemma raises the question of whether stabilization policies can be designed to have desirable differential effects on each region. Monetary policy is difficult to implement on a regional basis, because changes in bank reserves and interest rates tend to have similar, although perhaps delayed, effects across the country.

Fiscal policy designed to have differential regional effects would require different tax structures in each region and government expenditure programs related to specific regions. Special tax exemptions and deferrals, for example, have been used to encourage regional relocation of some corporations. Some specific expenditure programs have been introduced to deal directly with regional differences in unemployment rates. Programs such as the Local Employment Assistance Program (LEAP) enabled the federal government to make grants in areas with the highest unemployment rates and to approve applications from persons with a high marginal propensity to consume, thus assuring at least a strong beginning for the multiplier effect of these grants. Nevertheless, the basic dilemma of coping with strong inflationary pressures in some regions while unemployment remains high elsewhere remains a serious problem in Canadian stabilization policies.

Regional Development Policies

Throughout Canada's history, the federal government has undertaken a wide variety of programs specifically intended to stimulate the economic growth of the lower-income regions. The net effect of these programs is difficult to determine, since estimates of how the regional economies would have performed in the absence of programs must be based on crude assumptions. It would appear, however, that reduction of regional income disparity has been slow and slight.

Tariff Policies Canada's protective tariff structure was one of the earliest policies designed to encourage regional development, but the shift of population westward and the declining relative importance of primary industries has frustrated the original intentions of the National Policy. Rather than participating fully in the growth of manufacturing in Canada, the Atlantic provinces, along with the Prairie provinces and British Columbia, have borne the cost of a tariff structure that has increased the real income of Ontario and Quebec. Thus, the tariff policy, which was to have fostered regional development, has instead increased the need for other development policies.

Transportation Policies Another early policy for regional development involved the creation of a national railroad, and later national highways and airline systems, to encourage inter-regional travel and shipping of raw materials and

finished products. Specific attention was given to the problem of transportation costs for producers in the Maritimes in the form of the Maritime Freight Rates Act, which provided for federal subsidies to reduce
freight rates by 30 per cent for trucking and rail shipments moving from
eastern Canada to the central and western areas, plus an additional 20
per cent for virtually all manufactured goods. Prairie grain producers
were also assisted by the Crow's Nest Pass Agreement, which provided
for lower freight rates on grain shipped to the west coast (replaced in
1983 by railway subsidies), and by the construction of the St. Lawrence
Seaway.

Labour Supply   The federal government's labour supply policies were discussed in
Chapter 11. Although these policies are applicable to all regions, the
potential effect of the program is greatest in the low-income regions
where education levels are lowest and labour mobility is essential for
overcoming structural unemployment.

Incentives Policies   A program to encourage the development of population and economic
growth centres in depressed areas was established in 1962 under an Area
Development Agency. Several programs were introduced in succession
in the intervening years. An industrial and regional development program, introduced in 1982, provided for federal grants and loans to
encourage the location and expansion of firms that would increase
employment. This was revised in 1988 to form three regional development agencies to focus on the different requirements of the three tar-
geted regions—Western Canada, Northern Ontario, and the Atlantic
provinces.

Review of the Main Points

1. The average personal or family income differs significantly across
   the major economic regions of Canada, such that the average
   income in Ontario in 1989 was 37 per cent higher than it was in the
   Atlantic provinces.
2. The reasons for regional income disparities include the age composition of the population, the labour force participation rate, the
   unemployment rate, the level of educational attainment, the capital
   stock per capita, and the industrial composition.
3. Other important factors cannot be expressed so precisely; these
   include the indirect effects of important natural resources such as
   forests and petroleum, and the complex effects of population
   concentration on economic growth.
4. Public policies to reduce regional income disparities have included
   income transfers, general stabilization policies, and specific develop-

ment policies. The Federal-Provincial Fiscal Arrangements and Established Programs Financing Act provided for federal equalization payments to some provinces to compensate them for the lower value of their tax bases.

5. It is difficult to design stabilization policies that do not adversely affect one region while benefiting another region, because inflationary pressures tend to develop in the higher-income regions while the unemployment rate is still high in the lower-income regions.

6. Regional development policies have included protective tariffs (which benefited only central Canada), and programs for transportation, labour supply and education, and industrial incentives.

Key Concepts and Topics

regional income disparity
industrial composition
equalization payments

Questions for Review and Discussion

1. Average earnings in Ontario are among the highest in Canada, yet Canada's manufacturing industry is also concentrated in Ontario where labour costs are so high. Why do not more manufacturing firms locate in the lower-wage provinces?

2. It is sometimes suggested that the only way to reduce regional income disparity is to encourage the migration of people from the low-income areas to the high-income areas. What effect would this have on incomes in each area? Would the income change be greater if it were the most educated or least educated people who moved? Who is not likely to migrate in response to a general government offer of financial assistance for migration? Why?

3. If it is not possible to move people to areas where the jobs are, how can businesses be encouraged to move the jobs to areas where the people are? How would a government official weigh the benefits and costs of such a program?

Sources and Selected Readings

Anderson, F.J. *Regional Economic Analysis: A Canadian Perspective*. Toronto: Holt, Rinehart and Winston, 1988.

Auer, L. *Regional Disparities of Productivity and Growth in Canada*. Ottawa: Supply and Services Canada, 1979.

Coffey, Wm. J., and Mario Polèse. *Still Living Together: Recent Trends and Future Directions in Canadian Regional Development*. Montreal: Institute for Research on Public Policy, 1987.

Economic Council of Canada. *Reflections on Canadian Incomes*. Ottawa: Supply and Services Canada, 1980.

Mansell, R.L., et al. *Disparities and Interregional Adjustment*. Toronto: University of Toronto Press, 1985.

Norrie, K., et al. *Federalism and Economic Union in Canada*. Toronto: University of Toronto Press, 1985.

Savoie, Donald J. *The Canadian Economy: A Regional Perspective*. Toronto: Methuen, 1986.

Sitwell, O.F.G., and N.R.M. Selfried. *The Regional Structure of the Canadian Economy*. Toronto: Methuen, 1984.

Statistics Canada. *Income Distributions by Size in Canada*. Ottawa: Supply and Services Canada, annual.

Glossary

ability-to-pay principle States that individuals should be taxed according to their ability to pay, as measured by their income or wealth; sometimes termed the principle of equal sacrifice.

absolute advantage A situation where one agent (nation, firm, or individual) can produce a certain quantity of output with less real resource input than any other agent.

accelerator The effect of a change in consumption, through its effect on investment, on the level of national income.

adjustable peg system An exchange rate system where a government agrees to maintain the price of its currency at a pegged rate, but may gradually adjust this rate.

ad valorem tax A tax that is levied as a percentage of the selling price.

aggregate demand The equilibrium level of national income at each general level of prices.

aggregate expenditure The total spending by all consumers, businesses, governments, and foreign buyers for final goods and services produced in the economy concerned.

aggregate supply The total output of final goods and services that producers would wish to provide at each level of prices for outputs.

appreciation of a currency An increase in the exchange rate of one currency in terms of other currencies.

arbitrage The simultaneous buying and selling of a foreign currency in order to profit from differences in its price in different exchange markets.

arbitration A procedure of collective bargaining whereby the decisions are made on subject areas of the collective agreement by one or three independent persons appointed by each side.

arc elasticity of demand *See* elasticity of demand.

assets Items owned by individuals, firms, or governments.

asymmetry of monetary policy The fact that the Bank of Canada can force a contraction of bank deposits, but can only encourage an expansion.

automatic (built-in) stabilizers Government programs that automatically respond to changes in economic conditions, to offset or stabilize these changes. One example is the increase in unemployment insurance payments that results from an increase in unemployment.

autonomous change in spending A change in aggregate expenditure that is caused by a factor other than a change in national income.

autonomous investment The investment component of aggregate expenditure that is not dependent on the level of national income.

average cost pricing   A pricing scheme, often used by regulatory agencies, whereby the price charged by a monopoly is equal to average total cost at the given level of output.

average fixed cost   The total fixed cost divided by the number of units produced.

average product (of a factor)   The total product divided by the number of units of the variable input used in production.

average propensity to consume   The proportion of total disposable income used for current consumption of goods and services.

average propensity to import   The proportion of total disposable income that is spent on imports.

average propensity to save   The proportion of total disposable income that is saved.

average revenue   Total revenue divided by the number of units sold.

average total cost   The total production cost for a given quantity of output, divided by that quantity or number of units produced.

average variable cost   The total variable cost divided by the number of units produced.

balanced budget   A government budget in which total expenditures are equal to total revenues, resulting in neither a budget surplus nor a deficit.

balanced budget multiplier   A balanced or equal change in taxes and government spending will change national income by the same amount, given that the value of the multiplier is uniform throughout the economy.

balance of payments   The record of all economic transactions between residents of a country and the residents of all foreign countries during one year.

balance of payments surplus   A positive balance of payments, including both the capital and current accounts, but excluding changes in the official international reserves.

balance sheet   A statement of a firm's financial position, showing its assets and liabilities.

balance of trade   The balance on merchandise account; shows the net position for the year with respect to trade in goods.

Bank Rate   The interest rate charged by the Bank of Canada for loans or advances to chartered banks, usually just high enough so that the chartered banks will look to other banks and institutions for the funds required. Set $1/4$ point above the 91-day treasury bill rate.

bank reserves   Assets of the chartered banks in the form of coins, currency notes, and deposits at the Bank of Canada, treasury bills, and overnight loans, held as a specified fraction of demand and notice deposits. *See also* primary reserves and secondary reserves.

barrier to entry   An obstacle that prevents or discourages other firms from entering an industry. Examples are economies of scale, monopolistic ownership or control of unique resources, and patents.

barter   Trade in goods and services in the absence of money or any other widely accepted medium of exchange.

base year   The reference year to which current prices are compared in the calculation of a price index.

basic balance   In the balance of payments, the balance on current account equal (but opposite in sign) to the balance on long-term capital account.

benefit-cost analysis An approach to spending decisions that involves the comparison of the benefits of a project with its cost.

benefits-received principle States that individuals (and corporations) should pay taxes equal to the benefits they receive from government programs.

bilateral monopoly A market structure in which there is only one seller and one buyer of the commodity.

black market The buying and selling of a commodity at a price above the maximum legal price.

bond A written agreement to pay a specified series of interest payments, as well as the face value of the bond, on or before the stated maturity date.

boycott A campaign that consists of urging consumers not to buy the products or services of a particular firm.

break-even point The level of output where total costs equal total revenues, and hence profits are equal to zero.

budget deficit (surplus) A budget in which expenditures are greater than (less than) revenues.

budget line Shows the various combinations of goods and services a consumer may purchase, given the consumer's income and the prices of the commodities.

business cycle The popular term that refers to the somewhat cyclical behaviour of the economy.

Canada Assistance Plan Introduced in 1966, CAP is the federal government's main anti-poverty program, under which it provides 50 per cent of the funding for provincially administered public welfare programs.

Canadian Labour Congress A congress of Canadian unions which acts as a national spokes-agency for labour unions, but has little control over individual unions.

capital Any man-made means of production, including real or tangible items such as plant and equipment, as well as improvements to land such as dams, drainage systems, and paving. A wider concept of capital includes human capital: the improvements to labour due to education, training, and health care.

capital account The category of the International Balance of Payments that accounts for the flows of long-term and short-term capital.

capital consumption allowance In calculating the GDP, the capital consumption allowance accounts for the cost of replacing worn-out or obsolete plant and machinery. *See also* depreciation.

capital deepening An increase in the proportion of capital to labour; occurs at an advanced state of economic development.

capital flows International movements of long-term capital such as direct investment and short-term capital such as bank deposits, as measured in the capital account of the balance of payments.

capital gain A capital gain (or loss) is the difference between the purchase price and selling price of assets such as real estate, common shares, and works of art.

capital widening Occurs when an economy's labour force is increasing in such a way that the use of capital and labour can be increased in constant proportion.

capitalism An economic system characterized by a market economy, and which emphasizes individual ownership of physical capital.

capital-output ratio   The ratio of the value of the capital to the value of the output produced by that capital.

cartel   An arrangement whereby firms agree to establish a central authority which determines the price and output for the industry, tells firms how much each should produce, and regulates marketing by individual firms.

cash reserves (or primary reserves)   The currency and chartered bank deposits at the Bank of Canada held to meet reserve requirements against demand and notice deposits.

central bank   A financial institution established by a government for the regulation and control of credit and currency, in an effort to promote full employment, price stability, and a viable balance of payments. In Canada, the Bank of Canada.

central planning   The main feature of a command economy is central planning, whereby a central authority specifies the total output of each commodity, how much each production unit will produce, and how much of the economy's productive resources will be made available to each unit.

certification   The right granted to a union (by a provincial Labour Relations Board) to bargain on behalf of a group of workers.

ceteris paribus   Latin phrase for "other things being equal"; used to compensate for the inability to control particular variables in the real world.

chartered bank   A private, profit-seeking business that accepts deposits and makes loans and is chartered, or licensed, by Parliament under the Bank Act and regulated by the provisions of this act.

cheque clearing   The process of totalling and transferring the amounts drawn against one bank to be deposited in any of the others. The Canadian Payments Association clears cheques in its clearing houses and advises the Bank of Canada of the net credits or debits so that the Bank can make adjustments to individual banks' deposits.

classical economics   The classical (pre-Keynesian) view of aggregate economic activity which was characterized by the assumption that wages, prices, and interest rates were quite flexible and would move up and down freely with changing economic conditions, thus maintaining equilibrium in all markets.

closed economy   An economy in which there is no international sector, i.e., no imports, exports, or international capital flows.

closed shop   A workplace or union jurisdiction in which employers may hire only persons who have previously joined the union.

collective bargaining   The process by which unions and management arrive at labour contracts outlining wages and working conditions.

collusion   The joint decision-making of firms, particularly concerning the setting or changing of prices.

commercial bank   *See* chartered bank.

commodity   Any item of use to a consumer or producer.

common market   An arrangement between countries for free trade among themselves, free flows of productive resources, namely capital and labour, between members, and a common tariff policy toward non-members. Final stages of development involve greater integration of economic policy.

common stock   Evidence of a share in the ownership of a corporation; entitles the owner to one vote in the affairs of the corporation for every common stock held.

comparative advantage   A country has a comparative advantage in the production of a commodity if it is *relatively* more efficient in the production of that commodity than another. In other words, that commodity has a lower opportunity cost in the country with the comparative advantage. *See also* absolute advantage.

compensating wage differentials Compensating or equalizing wage differentials are those wage differences that compensate workers for the relative disadvantages of their jobs. These differences represent the amounts necessary to attract labour into the less desirable jobs.

Competition Act In Canada, competition legislation is consolidated in the Competition Act, which, among other things, forbids agreements between suppliers that would substantially restrict competition, mergers, and the exercise of monopoly power, and a number of restrictive trade practices.

complementary goods Two goods, *X* and *Y*, are complements if the quantity of *X* demanded decreases when the price of *Y* increases, i.e., their cross-price elasticity of demand is negative.

compulsory arbitration Sometimes used in the hope of averting a strike, when collective bargaining has failed to produce an agreement; decisions on the collective agreement are made by one or three independent persons appointed by each side.

concentration ratio The number of sellers in an industry relative to the market size; usually defined as the percentage of market sales held by the 4 largest firms in the industry, or as the number of firms producing 80 per cent of the industry's output.

conciliation Effort by a Labour Relations Board to resolve the differences between a union and management when their negotiations have broken down.

conditional grant Grants-in-aid made by the federal government to the provinces as their portion of specific cost-sharing programs.

constant dollars To account for inflation in measuring changes in GDP or other accounts over time, comparisons between years must be made in reference to prices in a base year, i.e., in constant purchasing power of a dollar.

constant returns Constant returns or constant costs mean that output and the use of productive factors vary at the same rate.

consumer equilibrium The purchase of two goods such that their marginal rate of substitution is equal to the ratio of their prices.

consumer price index (CPI) The CPI is intended to measure changes in prices of commonly purchased consumer goods and services, and thus, indirectly, the change in purchasing power of consumers' incomes. It compares current prices of commodities generally purchased by consumers with the prices of the same commodities in an earlier base year.

consumer sovereignty The power that consumers have to determine what shall be produced by directing their expenditures to the products they want most.

consumer surplus The difference between the price a consumer is willing to pay for a commodity, and the price actually paid.

consumption The use of goods and services to provide satisfaction.

consumption function The quantitative relationship between consumption (the dependent variable) and income (the independent variable).

cooperative A unique form of corporation, retaining several of the partnership's features, established by a society of individuals to buy or sell commodities cooperatively, according to a set of principles governing the organization.

corporation A firm characterized by the limited liability of its owners or stockholders, and its separate legal identity, as granted by federal or provincial charter.

correlation   Two variables are said to be correlated if they tend to move together, whether in the same direction (positively correlated), or the opposite (negatively correlated).

cost-push inflation   Inflation that occurs because of pressure arising on the supply side of the product markets or factor markets; also called "seller's inflation".

countercyclical policy   Fiscal and monetary policy designed to reduce or to increase aggregate expenditure in order to stabilize the level of national income.

countervailing power   A situation where the economic power of one group is met by that of another, such as in the case of a bilateral monopoly.

craft union   Consists of members from particular occupations, regardless of the firm or industry in which they are employed; the first type of labour organization to emerge.

crawling-peg system   An exchange-rate system where, although each currency has a fixed or pegged value, small changes are allowed to maintain balance of payments equilibrium.

cross elasticity of demand   The percentage change in the quantity demanded of one good divided by, or resulting from, a given percentage change in the price of a different good.

$$E_{XY} = \frac{\Delta Q_X}{\Delta P_Y} \times \frac{(P_1 + P_2)_Y}{(Q_1 + Q_2)_X}$$

crowding out   A jargonistic phrase referring to the displacement of private investment by government borrowing.

crown corporation   A public corporation that enables government to be directly involved in the provision of goods and services, without this activity being subject to day-to-day politics.

currency   The official medium of exchange in a particular country.

current account   The category of the Balance of International Payments that accounts for merchandise trade, services, investment income, and transfers.

current dollars   In comparing GDP over time, when total value of output is expressed in terms of the prices that existed in the year of production, values are said to be stated in current dollars.

customs union   Agreement among countries to remove tariffs against each other's products, and to maintain uniform tariffs against products of other countries.

cyclically balanced budget   A countercyclical fiscal policy, where, as incomes rise, taxes would increase faster than expenditures so that a budget surplus would accumulate to balance budget deficits accumulated when incomes were low. Budgets would thus be balanced over the cycle.

decision lag   The period between the recognition of an economic problem and the time when a policy action is implemented.

decreasing returns   Decreasing returns mean that output increases at a slower rate than the use of productive inputs.

deficit   The amount by which revenues are exceeded by expenditures.

deflation   A decrease in the general price level of consumer goods and services.

deflationary gap   The increase in planned aggregate expenditure required to bring an economy to the full employment level of national income.

demand   The set of quantities of a commodity that would be purchased at various alternative prices, given (or holding constant) all the other conditions that influence purchases of a commodity.

demand deposits Deposits at chartered banks for which the banks do not require advance notice of their withdrawal; these include personal chequing accounts, the current or chequing accounts of businesses, and of provincial and local governments and their agencies.

demand management policy Fiscal and monetary policies designed to change aggregate demand.

demand-pull inflation Inflation that occurs when planned spending at the prevailing price level exceeds the value of goods and services available at the full employment level.

demand shift Changes in demand (as opposed to quantity demanded) that result from changes in consumer income, preferences, or the prices of related commodities.

depreciation Deterioration in the value of plant and machinery through wear and obsolescence. *See also* capital consumption allowance.

depreciation of a currency In a flexible exchange rate system, the decrease in the price of a currency in terms of other currencies.

depression An extended period of decreased economic activity characterized by severe unemployment of both labour and productive capacity.

derived demand The demand for factor services that are useful or desirable only to the extent that they contribute to the production of final products desired by consumers.

devaluation A reduction in the pegged value of the foreign exchange rate.

differentiated products Products that are near substitutes, with only minor differences.

diminishing marginal utility The declining satisfaction from each additional unit of a commodity consumed.

diminishing returns The decrease in total product that occurs as increasing amounts of a variable factor are added to a fixed amount of another factor.

direct foreign investment Ownership of most or all of a firm's physical assets by a foreign individual or firm.

discounting The process of calculating the present value of future annual income from an asset.

discount rate The interest rate used in the process of discounting, i.e., in the calculation of the present value.

discretionary fiscal policy A deliberate effort by the government to achieve not only stable prices and full employment, but also economic growth, favourable income distribution, and equilibrium in the balance of payments, through the appropriate composition and size of its expenditures and tax revenues.

disposable income That portion of personal income that can be used for current consumption or savings, calculated as personal income less personal income taxes.

dissaving Negative saving, i.e., consumption exceeds income.

diverted output In the context of poverty, the goods and services that could be produced by the resources required to deal with poverty. *See* lost output.

dividend Corporate payments to stockholders as a share of the corporation's profits.

division of labour The division of a job into smaller tasks, thus allowing specialization of labour in these smaller tasks. An example is the division of pottery making into the shaping of the clay, fitting handles, glazing, and packing and shipping.

Domestic Income (Net) The total of all incomes earned by the economy's productive factors.

domestic output The total output of final goods and services. It is represented by the 45° line that relates the value of total output to each level of national income.

dumping The selling abroad of a product at a lower price than that in the home market.

durable goods Consumer and producer goods such as refrigerators and lathes that yield a flow of services over a long period of time.

econometrics The analysis of economic phenomena through the use of statistical techniques such as regression analysis.

economic good A good that is scarce; there is not enough of it to provide as much as consumers would want if the good were available at a price of zero. *See* free good, scarcity.

economic growth Increase in an economy's total real output of final goods and services; often adjusted to a per capita basis.

economic (pure) profit Any profit made in excess of the normal profit. *See* normal profit.

economic rent Any payment in addition to the transfer earnings of a factor, i.e., in excess of the minimum payment required to attract resources from other uses.

economies of scale *See* returns to scale.

efficiency A criterion for evaluating economic performance; the use of the minimum amount of resources to produce a given output.

elastic demand Demand elasticity greater than one. That is, a given change in price causes a more than proportional change in the quantity demanded.

elasticity The percentage change in one variable associated with a one per cent change in another variable.

elasticity of demand The price elasticity of demand measures the degree of responsiveness of consumer demand to price changes. The arc elasticity (between two prices) is calculated as

$$E_D = -\frac{\Delta Q}{\Delta P} \times \frac{P_1 + P_2}{Q_1 + Q_2}$$

Point elasticity is calculated for a specific price using the derivatives of calculus. *See also* income elasticity of demand.

elasticity of supply The price elasticity of supply measures the degree of responsiveness of producers to price changes and is calculated as

$$E_S = \frac{\Delta Q}{\Delta P} \times \frac{P_1 + P_2}{Q_1 + Q_2}$$

elastic supply Supply elasticity greater than one.

employment rate The number of persons employed expressed as a percentage of the labour force.

endogenous variable A variable whose value is explained or determined within a model.

Engel curves Curves that show the percentage of income spent for different categories of goods and services at various levels of income.

Engel's Law Engel's observation that the percentage of a consumer's income spent on food usually declined as income increased.

entrepreneur An individual who takes the initiative and the risk in employing and organizing the other factors in a productive process.

equality line The curve representing equal values on the horizontal and vertical axes; forms a 45° angle to the axes when the axes scales are the same.

equalization payments Federal government transfer payments made to provinces to compensate them for the lower value of their tax bases, by comparison with other provinces.

equilibrium national income The income level at which total planned expenditure is equal to actual domestic output or where planned aggregate demand is equal to aggregate supply.

equilibrium price The price at which the quantity demanded is equal to the quantity supplied.

estate tax A tax on property owned at death; paid to government before estate is divided. No longer imposed in Canada.

excess demand The amount by which quantity demanded exceeds quantity supplied, at a given price.

excess reserves In chartered banks, those cash reserves that exceed the reserve requirements on demand and notice deposits.

excess supply The amount by which quantity supplied exceeds quantity demanded, at a given price.

Exchange Fund Account The Government of Canada's foreign exchange reserves account used in official transactions in support of the exchange rate.

excise tax A federal or provincially imposed tax on particular goods such as tobacco products and gasoline.

exclusion principle The idea that defines a pure public good, namely, that it must be impossible to exclude anyone from using or otherwise benefiting from the good.

exogenous variable A variable whose value is determined outside a model, and hence is a given datum to the model in question.

expected yield The expected rate of return on an investment.

explicit costs A firm's direct expenditures of labour services, materials, electricity, transportation, rental of space, etc.

externalities Economic effects of actions of producers and consumers for which no compensation is paid, or economic effects that are not considered in market transactions.

externally held public debt That portion of the public debt held by residents of other countries.

factor of production Something that can make a contribution to producing a good or service. A factor is a stock item, i.e., a stock of potential contributions to production that the factor can provide over a period of time. The contribution made during a period of time is the factor service.

factor services The actual contribution of a productive factor; the flow of the services over a specified period.

fair return The rate of return allowed for a natural monopoly by a regulatory agency. The magnitude of "fair" remains undefined, but economic principles suggest that this should be the opportunity cost of the assets.

featherbedding Payment for unnecessary work, which can result when labour contracts guarantee numbers of employees in an industry where technology and hence labour needs are changing quickly.

federal debt The financial liabilities of the federal government.

federal-provincial transfers Transfer payments from the federal government to the provincial governments.

final good or service A product intended for final consumption, as opposed to an intermediate product that enters the production of another good or service.

financial market A market in which financial assets such as stocks and bonds are traded.

fine-tuning   Small changes in government expenditures or tax revenues designed to counteract small deviations from an anticipated course of economic activity.

firm   An economic unit that organizes and directs the combination of resources in the production of goods and services.

fiscal drag   The effect of automatic or built-in stabilizers such as the progressive income tax in dampening or reducing the effectiveness of discretionary fiscal policy.

fiscal policy   Government expenditure and taxation programs designed to affect aggregate expenditure and hence national income. Fiscal policy can be either automatic or discretionary.

fiscal year   Used for accounting purposes, a fiscal year is any period of twelve months.

fixed cost   A cost that does not vary with changes in quantity of output. Also termed overhead cost, it must be incurred even if the firm produces no output.

fixed (pegged) exchange rate   An exchange rate regime whereby the government agrees to fix the foreign exchange rate at a specified level.

fixed factor   A factor of production whose quantity does not vary with the level of output.

floating (fluctuating) exchange rate   An exchange rate regime whereby the government allows the foreign exchange rate to be determined solely by supply and demand in the foreign exchange market.

floor prices   Minimum prices set by a government for particular products (e.g., agricultural products).

flow   The change in the quantity occurring during a period of time. *See* stock.

foreign exchange market   All buyers and sellers of particular currencies in every country. There is a separate market for each pair of currencies, as a currency can be bought only with another currency.

foreign exchange rate   The price of one currency in terms of another currency.

foreign exchange reserves   Government holdings of foreign exchange and gold used for intervention in the foreign exchange markets.

fractional-reserve banking   A banking system where banks are required to hold cash reserves as a specified fraction of their deposit liabilities.

franchise   The exclusive right to provide a good or service.

freedom of entry   A necessary condition for pure competition, freedom of entry means that nothing would bar or prevent a firm from entering an industry to produce the commodity in question.

free good   A good that exists in sufficient abundance to satisfy everyone's wants, even when no price is charged.

free trade   International trade in the absence of tariffs or other barriers to trade.

free trade area (or association)   A group of countries that has agreed to reduce the tariffs imposed against imports from each of the other countries, usually with the objective of complete removal of these tariffs.

frictional unemployment   Unemployment of those people looking for work who have just left a job or who are just entering or re-entering the labour force.

fringe benefits   Indirect compensation to labour paid by employers. Examples of fringe benefits are paid holidays, medical and pension benefits, and education leave.

full employment   Usually defined as the situation in which everyone aged fifteen or over who is willing and able to work for pay has an income-earning job; can also apply to non-labour factors of production.

full-employment budget A government budget designed so that the tax structure and government expenditure programs would produce a balanced budget at the full employment level.

functional income distribution The share of total income in an economy received by the various factors of production.

gain from trade Increased production that results from specialization in those products in which a country has a comparative advantage.

game theory Formal analysis of strategic behaviour and conflict. There are several applications of game theory to cooperative and non-cooperative economic behaviour, such as oligopoly theory.

GDP price index The number used to convert nominal GDP expressed in current dollars to real GDP expressed in constant dollars; also termed GDP deflator.

GDP gap The difference between the actual GDP and full employment GDP.

general equilibrium A state where all markets are in equilibrium, all products are being produced as efficiently as possible, and each person is realizing as much satisfaction as possible, given the state of technology and the level and distribution of incomes.

gold-exchange standard A foreign exchange regime that evolved earlier in the century when the world was on the gold standard. Smaller countries began to hold the currencies of larger countries, instead of gold, for use in international trade.

gold standard System that governed the financing of foreign trade until the Depression of the 1930s. Countries on the gold standard agreed to fix the price of gold in terms of their own currencies. Since the prices of currencies were fixed in terms of gold, they were also fixed in terms of each other.

good Tangible commodities such as bread, automobiles, and sweaters.

goods and services tax The Canadian version of a value-added tax. A tax is levied on sales at each stage of production, but the producer can claim a refund of the tax paid on inputs.

grievance procedures Arrangements whereby a problem or complaint concerning workers can be dealt with at successively higher management levels until a satisfactory solution is reached.

Gross Domestic Product The value of all final goods and services produced within the geographic boundary of a country. It includes investment income paid to residents of other countries and excludes investment income received from other countries.

gross investment Purchases of new plant and equipment, new residential housing, and real additions to inventories, including the replacement of depreciated and obsolete items.

Gross National Expenditure The market value of all final goods and services produced in a year by the whole economy, but excludes the investment income paid to foreigners and includes the foreign investment income received by Canadian residents.

Gross National Product The GNP uses the factor payments approach to measure the market value of all final goods and services produced in a year by the whole economy, but excludes the foreign investment income adjustment (as for GNE above).

holding company Corporation that produces no goods or services but is established explicitly for the purpose of holding shares in other companies. Canadian examples are Argus Corporation and Power Corporation.

human capital   Improvements to the productivity of human labour, such as education, training, and health care.

hyperinflation   Rapidly accelerating inflation.

impact lag   The lag between the implementation of a policy change and its desired effects; also termed implementation lag.

imperfect competition   Deviations from perfect competition that result from inadequate information, adjustment lags, monopolistic pressures, and market barriers.

implicit cost   The opportunity cost represented by what could be earned through the productive use of factors owned by the firm. Since these costs can only be estimated, implicit costs are also referred to as imputed costs.

import quota   Limitations on the quantity of a good that can be imported.

import substitution   Policies designed to promote the reduction of imports in favour of consumption of domestically produced commodities.

imputed values   These are values that cannot be measured directly and must be estimated, as is the case for some items in the national income accounts.

income-consumption line   The curve showing quantities of a commodity that would be purchased as income varies.

income effect   The effect of a price change on the total purchasing power of a given monetary income.

income elasticity of demand   The percentage change in quantity demanded divided by the percentage change in income. The income elasticity of demand is calculated as

$$E_Y = \frac{\Delta Q}{\Delta Y} \times \frac{Y_1 + Y_2}{Q_1 + Q_2}$$

income line   *See* budget line.

income velocity   *See* velocity of money.

incomes policy   A policy such as wage and price controls designed to reduce cost-push inflation. Such a policy has a set of general targets or objectives concerning changes in wages and prices, as well as a method for inducing voluntary acceptance of these objectives, or a means of enforcing the program.

incremental cost   *See* marginal cost.

indexation   Adjustment of personal tax deductions, exemptions, and "tax brackets"—the taxable income levels at which higher marginal rates are applicable—according to changes in a price index in order to prevent distortion of personal income levels by inflation. More generally, the adjustment of payments such as pension payments and family allowances for general price change.

indifference curve   A curve that represents a distinct level of utility provided by various combinations of two goods.

indifference map   A family of indifference curves for an individual, covering all combinations of two goods.

indifference schedule   Lists of combinations of goods such that each combination provides the same satisfaction to the consumer.

indirect tax   A tax levied on a commodity rather than on individuals or firms.

induced investment   Additional investment that results from an increase in national income.

industrial union   A union whose membership is drawn from specific industries or groups of industries; includes workers in many occupations.

inelastic demand (or supply)   Elasticity is less than one. That is, a change in the price or income leads to a less than proportional change in quantity demanded (or supplied).

infant industry argument　The only economic argument for tariffs, namely, that a tariff could be imposed to protect an industry that appears to be developing a comparative advantage, and that without tariff protection may not survive the initial stage of higher costs associated with low levels of production.

inferior goods　Goods for which the quantity purchased declines as income increases. Such goods have income elasticity less than zero.

inflation　An increase in the general price level. Also defined as a decline in the purchasing power of the dollar or other monetary unit.

inflationary gap　The amount by which planned spending exceeds the spending required for full employment.

injection　Additions to planned aggregate expenditures, or additional planned spending on domestic goods and services at a given level of national income.

innovation　The use of new raw materials, new sources of existing raw materials, new techniques or processes, the development of new products, or improved quality in existing products.

interest rate　The price charged (or paid) for the use of loaned (or borrowed) money.

intermediate goods　Those goods that are partly finished, such as bread flour, and require further processing before they are useful (final goods).

internal rate of return (of an asset)　The rate that makes the present value of the future stream of net receipts from a capital item equal to its cost.

inventories　The available stock of any given good held for production or sale.

inventory adjustment　The equilibrating mechanism of the Keynesian model. The accumulation of undesired inventories is the signal of excess aggregate output, while the response of firms to the inventory change is the means by which equilibrium is achieved.

investment　Purchases of new plant and equipment, new residential housing, and real additions to inventories. *See also* gross investment and net investment.

investment good　A producer good; that is, one to be used in the production process.

invisible　A non-merchandise, intangible commodity, also termed a service.

invisible hand　Adam Smith's metaphor of the price mechanism at work: allocating or guiding resources to the most efficient production of commodities most desired by consumers.

key currency　The prime currency for international transactions; previously this has included the British pound, the United States dollar, the German mark, and recently the Japanese yen.

Keynesian economics　The major macroeconomic theory, as introduced by J. M. Keynes in *The General Theory of Employment, Interest, and Money*, published in 1936. The "Keynesian revolution" consisted of a detailed attack on the classical economists' explanation for the level of employment and output, and Keynes' conclusion that economies could achieve equilibrium at below (or above) full employment, and consequently that government intervention rather than *laissez-faire* was required to move the economy to the full employment level.

kinked demand curve　A model of the behaviour of oligopolistic firms whose products are differentiated. Developed to explain why prices tend to be inflexible, even in the face of changing cost conditions.

labour force　Total number of persons employed and unemployed.

labour force participation rate　The percentage of the potential labour force that is seeking employment, or is in employment, at a given time.

labour productivity   Total output divided by total labour input.

labour supply   The quantity of labour services that will be offered during a specific period at various alternative wage rates.

labour union   An organization of workers with the legal recognition as the representatives of the members in collective bargaining.

laissez-faire   The view that there was no need for government intervention at the aggregate or national levels of economic activity because the economy would function effectively if market forces were allowed to follow a natural course.

land   A factor of production that includes unimproved arable land and other gifts of nature. As a factor, land is characterized by its inelastic supply.

law of demand   The observation that consumers will buy a larger total quantity at a lower average price per unit.

law of diminishing returns   The observation that, given a fixed quantity of one productive factor, the economies realized by the division of labour eventually diminish as increasing quantities of this variable factor are added; more generally, that the continued addition of the variable factor to the fixed factor eventually leads to a decrease in the total product; also called the law of variable proportions.

law of variable proportions   *See* law of diminishing returns.

legal tender   The only currency that, by law, must be accepted for payment of debts.

liability   That which is owed to creditors.

limited liability   Liability limited to the portion of a company and its assets owned by a person.

liquidity preference   The demand for money, as opposed to other financial assets.

liquidity trap   A situation whereby, at very low interest rates, investors will hold exceptionally large quantities of money instead of other assets, thus making monetary policy ineffective; this was the situation during the Great Depression, according to Keynes.

long run   The period of time long enough to enable a firm to alter the quantity produced by altering the quantity of *all* resources used to produce the good, and to make changes in the type of resources used.

Lorenz curve   A curve that shows the extent to which the actual distribution of incomes deviates from perfect equality in personal income distribution.

lost output   In the context of poverty, the goods and services that could be produced if the productive potential of the poor were more effectively developed and utilized. *See* diverted output.

lump-sum tax   A tax of a fixed amount per period, independent of income, sales, or output.

M1   The narrowly defined money supply: currency outside the banks, plus chartered bank demand deposits (excluding Government of Canada deposits).

M2   M1 plus personal savings deposits and non-personal notice deposits.

M3   M2 plus other non-personal fixed-term deposits, plus foreign currency deposits of Canadian residents.

macroeconomics   The study of large segments of the economy, or the whole economy, with emphasis on the broad aggregates of total employment, total output and incomes, total money supply, and so on; from the Greek "macro" meaning "large".

managed float   A foreign exchange regime that involves a floating exchange rate, but with official intervention to maintain the exchange rate within a narrow but unannounced range.

marginal cost The change in total cost associated with the production of each additional unit; also known as incremental cost.

marginal cost pricing Setting the selling price equal to the marginal cost for the given level of output.

marginal efficiency of investment The yield or rate of return on marginal, or additional, investment.

marginal physical product The change in total product associated with each additional or marginal unit of a productive factor; measured in physical terms, that is, in units of output.

marginal productivity The marginal output or revenue obtained from additional units of factor services; the basis for the theory of producer demand for factor services.

marginal propensity to consume The change in consumption associated with additional income.

marginal propensity to import The change in imports associated with additional income.

marginal propensity to save The change in saving associated with additional income.

marginal rate of substitution The quantity of one good that an individual will give up in exchange for one unit of another good, without changing the total satisfaction obtained from the two or more goods consumed.

marginal resource cost The change in the total cost associated with an additional unit of the productive resource.

marginal revenue The change in total revenue associated with the sale of an additional unit of output.

marginal revenue product The change in total revenue associated with each additional unit of the variable factor.

marginal tax rate The tax rate that applies to an additional dollar of income

marginal utility The satisfaction associated with the consumption of an additional unit of a commodity.

market The organized collection of potential buyers and sellers for a specific commodity.

market demand The total demand by all buyers in a market.

market economy An economic system where prices are determined in a separate market for each commodity and factor of production, with these prices in turn determining the answers to each of the basic economic questions.

market failure The failure of the market to produce an outcome that agrees with the currently prevailing notions of social justice, usually a result of imperfect competition or non-market problems such as inequitable income distribution or externalities such as pollution.

market mechanism *See* price mechanism.

market power The ability of a firm or group of firms to influence market price as a result of imperfect competition.

market share The share of an industry's sales held by a particular firm, expressed as a percentage.

market structure The features of a market that contribute to its conduct or behaviour, such as the number of sellers, level of product differentiation, barriers to entry, and firms' control over price.

markup pricing Setting a price that is a specified percentage above the producer's average cost per unit.

median The value that represents the middle value of a sample or population. Half of the values will be greater than the median, while half will be less.

medium of exchange Money; that which is normally used to buy goods and services and is readily accepted by the sellers of these commodities.

merchandise account   That account of the balance of payments that records international transactions of goods, also called the balance of trade.

merger   The acquisition of any control over or interest in the whole or part of one business by another.

microeconomics   The study of individual components of the economy such as the consumer, the firm, and the industry.

minimum wage   The legal minimum hourly wage that can be paid in certain areas, occupations, or industries.

model   An abstraction from the real world that represents a complex set of relationships between important features or variables in an economy. A model often includes a quantitative specification of these relationships.

momentary (or market) period   The period within which the quantity to be supplied has already been produced.

monetarism   A school of economic thought, contrary to the Keynesian school, that the prime economic function of a government is no more than to guarantee a stable growth of the money supply, allowing the economy to function on its own with a stable price level.

monetary policy   The deliberate effort by the government, acting through the monetary authorities (the Bank of Canada), to vary the money supply in order to move the economy toward non-inflationary full employment, and to maintain a viable balance of payments, and the official foreign exchange rate when this is pegged.

monetary rule   The central proposal of monetarists, that the government should allow the money supply to grow at the expected rate of real economic growth.

monetary sector   The interaction of the supply of and demand for money, with its determination of an equilibrium interest rate.

money   Something readily and widely accepted as a medium of exchange for goods and services.

money income   Income measured in terms of current prices; that is, not adjusted by price changes.

money supply   The quantity of money actually held in the economy at any given time, generally defined as coins and paper currency in circulation outside the banks, plus the value of bank deposits. *See also* M1, M2, and M3 for more precise definitions of the money supply.

money wages   The actual wages paid. *See* real wages.

monopolistic competition   The case of a market or industry where there are many small firms selling similar but not identical products.

monopoly   A pure monopoly is a market in which only one firm produces a commodity for which there are no close substitutes.

monopsony   The existence of only one buyer in a market.

moral suasion   Efforts by the Bank of Canada to persuade chartered bank presidents to implement selective or specific monetary policies.

most-favoured nation clause   A component of the General Agreement on Trade and Tariffs for the conduct of international trade, stating that a country may not discriminate between trading partners by imposing a higher tariff against the imports of one country than against another.

multinational corporation   Firms that have plants in a number of countries. Generally these firms are concerned with products where there are increasing opportunities for realizing economies of very large scale.

multiplier   The multiple by which initial changes in spending (or aggregate expenditure) change the level of national income.

national debt *See* public debt.

National Energy Program The energy policy, introduced by the federal government in October 1980, that was intended to decelerate energy consumption, reduce dependence on foreign energy sources, increase Canadian ownership and control, and provide equitable energy prices and revenue sharing.

national union In Canada, a (labour) union independent of foreign-based, international unions.

natural monopoly An industry where a firm's optimum size is so large relative to the market size that only one or two firms can operate efficiently. Common examples include industries providing electricity, natural gas, and telephone communications.

natural rate of unemployment Associated with a vertical, long-run Phillips curve, the natural rate of unemployment is said to be the lowest rate attainable without increasing the rate of inflation. Also termed NAIRU.

near-money The general public's holdings of federal government treasury bills, bonds, and savings bonds; termed near-money because they can be readily sold or redeemed and converted to chequable deposits.

negative income tax A method for providing a guaranteed annual income whereby the government makes payments to individuals and families below the poverty line.

net foreign investment Exports minus imports.

net investment Gross investment minus depreciation.

net worth Total assets minus liabilities.

nominal Values or incomes expressed in terms of current prices; not adjusted for price changes.

non-price competition Includes the use of advertising and emphasis on product style and quality to increase the demand for a firm's product and to make demand less elastic; often a feature of oligopolies.

non-tariff barriers Restrictions on international trade, such as quotas or administrative regulations, that are intended to have effects similar to tariffs in reducing imports.

normal goods Goods for which the income elasticity coefficient is positive; that is, consumption of the good increases as income rises.

normal profit The minimum profit required to retain a firm in the production of a specified commodity, determined by the profit that the firm could realize through its best alternative industry.

normative economics Economics concerned with the way things should or ought to be, as opposed to the way things are.

notice deposit Usually refers to non-chequable savings deposits, termed a notice deposit because the chartered banks have the legal right to require advance notice of withdrawal of funds from the account.

Old Age Security Act An act that provides for monthly payments to all residents over 65 years of age who have been in Canada for at least ten years prior to their application for the benefits. For persons with little or no other income, guaranteed income supplement may be added to these payments.

oligopoly An industry or market with so few firms that the actions of one firm directly affect the decisions of other firms in the industry.

open economy An economy with an international sector, that is, an economy that engages in international trade and capital transactions.

open market operations   The Bank of Canada's buying and selling of securities such as federal government bonds and treasury bills as a technique for managing the money supply.

open shop   A workplace where union membership is voluntary.

opportunity cost   The satisfaction or income forgone by choosing one alternative instead of the next best alternative.

optimum rate of output   The quantity at which the short-run average total cost is at a minimum.

optimum scale of plant   The size at which all economies of scale are realized but diseconomies of large scale have not been incurred.

paradox of thrift   The seeming paradox that while it may be prudent for an individual to save, it may not be prudent for an economy. An increase in saving may reduce consumption and planned aggregate expenditure, and thus national income. Consequently, an intended increase in individual saving may lead to a decrease in aggregate saving.

paradox of value   In attempting to determine what gave a commodity "value", early economists such as Adam Smith noted the seeming contradiction that an item as vital to human life as water commanded a low price, whereas inessential goods such as diamonds were very expensive.

participation rate   *See* labour force participation rate.

partnership   A firm formed by two or more persons who agree to own and operate a single business. Such an agreement usually specifies the contributions each partner will make, as well as shares in profits and losses.

patent   Legal grants of property rights to investors for their inventions. Patent holders are granted exclusive rights to produce their products for a period of 17 years. Alternatively, a patent holder may sell or license his or her rights to another firm.

pegged exchange rate   *See* fixed exchange rates.

perfect competition   A market structure characterized by two key features: (1) Individual firms cannot influence the price of the product in any way; (2) There are no barriers or obstacles preventing new firms from entering the industry or existing firms from leaving it.

perfect price discrimination   *See* price discrimination.

personal disposable income   Personal income minus personal income taxes.

personal income   National income that accrues to individuals, equal to Net Domestic Income, minus undistributed corporate profits and corporate income taxes, plus government transfer payments.

Phillips curve   Curve showing the inverse relationship (trade-off) between inflation and unemployment. Many economists argue that the Phillips curve is vertical in the long run, since any level of inflation can be consistent with full employment in the long run.

piece rate   Payment based on the number of units of output produced by a worker.

planned aggregate expenditure   The total amount that consumers, producers, governments, and foreign purchasers of exports plan or intend to spend for domestic goods and services, at any given level of income.

point elasticity   Elasticity measured at a particular price, or particular point, on the demand curve.

positive economics   Economics concerned with describing and analyzing the way things are, as opposed to the way things ought to be.

poverty   A condition in which individuals or families do not have the income to meet their basic needs, however these needs may be defined.

poverty line A concept used to measure and describe the magnitude of poverty. Technically, a family is defined by Statistics Canada to be at or below the poverty line if it allocates more than 59 per cent of its income to the basic essentials of food, shelter, and clothing.

poverty rate The percentage of the total group in different categories, whose incomes fall below the poverty-line income.

precautionary demand for money Closely related to the transactions demand for money, the precautionary demand is the quantity of money held in order to meet less predictable expenditures.

preferred stock Shares in a corporation that do not give the holder a vote in the general affairs of the corporation but have a stated annual rate of return, a guarantee that this dividend will be paid before dividends are paid on common stocks, and a prior claim against the corporation's assets should it be dissolved.

present value (of an asset) The sum of the discounted (present) values of the annual income earned by the asset, plus the discounted (present) value of whatever the asset might be sold for at the end of the period.

price ceiling The legal maximum price that may be charged for a commodity.

price discrimination The practice of monopolists, or other firms with market power, of charging different prices to different buyers of the same commodity produced under the same cost conditions; perfect price discrimination is charging a different price for each level of output.

price elasticity *See* elasticity of demand.

price floor The legal minimum price that may be charged or paid for a commodity.

price leadership When the largest firm (or acknowledged price-setter) in the industry raises its price, other firms do likewise.

price mechanism The function performed by prices in allocating or guiding resources to the most efficient production of commodities most desired by consumers.

price support programs Government programs, particularly in agriculture, that guarantee producers will receive a specific minimum price per unit for their products.

price-taker A firm that cannot influence the price of the product in any way, but rather faces the price prevailing in the market at any given time.

primary boycott A union tactic that consists of urging consumers not to buy the products or services of the struck firm. *See* secondary boycott.

primary reserves Assets of the chartered banks in the form of deposits at the Bank of Canada and currency in the bank, held as a specified fraction of demand and notice deposits.

prime rate of interest That rate of interest charged by a bank to its preferred, or least risky customers.

product differentiation *See* differentiated products.

production function Shows how a firm's total output changes as additional units of a factor are added to the firm's existing productive factors.

production possibilities boundary (or frontier) A curve that shows the full range of possible maximum combinations of two goods that can be produced with the given resources used in the most efficient manner.

productivity Total output per unit of input.

profit Revenues in excess of costs. Economic or pure profits refer specifically to those returns in excess of all opportunity costs including normal profit. Also, the return to entrepreneurship.

progressive tax A tax that requires higher-income persons to pay a higher percentage of their income in taxes than do low-income persons.

proportional tax   A tax that represents or requires a constant percentage of one's income as that income increases.

protectionism   The tendency for countries to restrict imports and foreign competition from domestic markets.

protective tariff   A tariff implemented for the purpose of sheltering an infant industry from foreign competition. *See also* infant industry argument.

public debt   The total amount owed by all levels of government, principally municipal debentures, provincial bonds, and federal bonds and treasury bills. National or federal debt refers to the debt of the federal government alone.

pure public goods   Commodities for which the consumption by one person does not exclude the consumption by another. Also, goods for which the marginal cost is zero. *See* quasi-public goods.

pure monopoly   *See* monopoly.

quantity theory of money   In its crude form, stated simply that the general price level in the economy would vary directly and proportionately with the stock of money. (This is expressed as $P = kM$, where k is the value of the constant relationship between the general price level, P, and the stock of money, M.)

quasi-public goods   Goods produced collectively due to the high costs of excluding non-contributors, economies of scale, or external benefits; examples include highways, education, and health care. *See* pure public goods.

quasi-rent   Short-run economic rent that may disappear in the long run; quasi-rent forms a large part of a hockey star's salary, for example.

quota   Limitation on the quantity of a good that may be bought, sold, or imported.

rational behaviour   Actions that are expected to lead to one's objectives.

rational expectations   The expectations, particularly about future inflation rates, based on information about current conditions.

rationing   A means of allocating scarce resources, usually implemented by issuing ration coupons, and requiring customers to use both money and ration coupons to buy the quantity available at the legal price.

real income or wage   The actual purchasing power of an income or a wage in terms of goods and services that a worker could receive for his or her labour; the nominal or current income or wage adjusted for price change.

real sector   The national economic activity, expressed in terms of employment, income, and output, while the money supply is held constant.

recession   Less severe than a depression, recession is the common term applied to the "trough" of the business cycle, or a period of low economic growth and high unemployment.

recognition lag   The difference in time between the occurrence of macroeconomic events (such as the beginning of an inflationary period) and the time when corrective action is considered.

regressive tax   A tax that represents or requires a decreasing percentage of one's income as that income rises.

regulatory agency   A government board or commission that regulates prices for specific industries (usually natural monopolies).

relative prices   The numerical ratio of one price to another.

rent   The return to land, or that payment made to the owner of a factor such as land by its user. *See also* economic rent.

replacement cost depreciation   A measure of depreciation based, not on the historical or original cost of the capital good, but rather its current replacement cost.

required reserves   Assets that chartered banks are required to hold as a percentage of their deposit liabilities; classified as either primary or secondary reserves, depending on the nature of the asset.

resale price maintenance   The requirement that manufacturers may impose on the sellers of their products to sell them at no less than a specified price. This practice is illegal in Canada.

reserve ratio   The percentage of deposit liabilities that the chartered banks must hold as reserves. *See also* primary reserves and secondary reserves.

resource allocation   The allocation of limited productive resources to competing uses. In a market economy, the price mechanism governs most resource allocation; in a command economy it is the government that performs this function.

restrictive trade practices   Include price discrimination, loss-leaders, misleading price advertising, and resale price maintenance, and other similar practices forbidden by the Competition Act.

returns to scale   The change in average total cost that can be realized as output relative to inputs with varying plant size. Unlike the law of diminishing returns, returns to scale result from varying the quantities of all factors; no factors are considered fixed.

revaluation of a currency   In a fixed exchange rate regime, the raising of the value of the national currency by monetary authorities.

risk premium   The additional interest or profit to a creditor or entrepreneur to compensate for the risk associated with a particular venture.

saving   Postponed consumption; represents future purchasing power, or the ability to pay for goods and services in the future.

saving function   A function relating the quantity saved to the level of national income.

savings rate   The personal savings rate is the percentage of disposable personal income going to savings, including contributions to registered retirement savings plans.

Say's law   A French economist, Jean-Baptiste Say (1767-1832), proposed the law of conservation of purchasing power: supply creates its own demand.

scarcity   Insufficient quantity of goods and services to satisfy all consumers if no prices were to be charged.

seasonal adjustment   Adjustments made to actual unemployment rates to take account of the fact that the unemployment rate is usually higher in the winter and lower in the summer.

secondary boycott   A union tactic that consists of attempts to put pressure on a struck firm by urging employees and customers of other firms not to handle or buy the product of the struck firm. *See* primary boycott.

secondary reserves   Day-to-day loans and treasury bills held by chartered banks as a certain percentage of their deposit liabilities, as required by the policy of the Bank of Canada.

secular trend   A secular trend refers to the long-run behaviour or value of a variable, as opposed to its cyclical behaviour.

selling costs   Expenditures for sales promotion.

seniority   A worker's length of experience with a given firm.

short run   The period within which it is possible to change the quantity produced by altering the quantity of some productive factors, such as labour and raw materials, but within which it is not possible to alter the quantity of all factors.

shutdown price   The price below which a firm cannot cover its variable costs, and hence must shut down.

single proprietorship   A business or firm wholly owned by one person.

size distribution of income   The number of individuals and families at each level of income or in each income group.

social indicators   A system for measuring or monitoring programs in areas such as health, education, crime prevention, and housing.

special drawing rights (SDRs)   An international fiduciary currency; created and accepted by agreement of International Monetary Fund members, SDRs were to be a replacement for gold as the major medium of international payments.

specific tax   A tax that is levied as an absolute amount to be paid on each unit. *See ad valorem* tax.

speculation   The purchase of foreign currencies, common shares, real estate, or other commodities in the hope of selling them later at a higher price.

speculative demand for money   Money held in bank accounts in order to take advantage of opportune times to buy other financial assets.

spillover effects   The external benefits of a policy, beyond that which was originally intended. *See also* externality.

stabilization policies   Actions by governments to overcome or avoid high levels of inflation and/or unemployment.

stagflation   The popular term for simultaneous unemployment (stagnation) and inflation.

sterilization   Open market operations conducted by the Bank of Canada to counteract (sterilize) the effects of balance of payments surpluses and deficits on the money supply.

stock   The quantity that exists at any particular time. *See* flow.

store of value   The function of money that allows it to represent one's wealth, or the total claim of future goods and services.

structural deficit   The government's budgetary deficit that would exist even if the economy were at full employment with no inflation.

structural unemployment   Unemployment caused by structural changes in the demand for labour, following from changes in the composition of demand for goods and services, and improvements in technology.

structure of interest rates   The various interest rates associated with different types of financial assets (e.g., bank savings accounts, mortgages, and other loans).

subsidy   A payment to a producer to offset part of his or her production costs. The payment may be either a fixed sum or one that varies directly with the quantity produced.

substitute goods   Goods that have a cross-price elasticity greater than zero; that is, when the price of one good increases, consumption of the other good (the substitute) increases.

substitution effect   The effect of a change in relative prices of two goods, leading to a substitution of some of the good that has become relatively cheaper, for some of the good that has become relatively more expensive.

supply   The quantity that would be offered for sale at each of various alternative prices, given all the other conditions that influence a producer's willingness to supply the commodity.

supply shift   A shift of the supply curve that results from a change in prices of inputs or in technology.

supply-side policies   The attempt to reduce inflation by increasing output through influences on aggregate supply conditions.

support price   That price guaranteed to a producer for the purchase of specific products. *See* price support programs.

tacit collusion Implicit collusion; that is, collusion that occurs without formal agreement, such as in the case of price leadership, where firms in a oligopoly follow the price behaviour of an acknowledged price-setter.

take-home pay What is paid to workers, after deductions for income tax, social security and unemployment contributions, and union dues.

tariff A tax on imports, whether *ad valorem* (expressed as a percentage of the price of the good) or *specific* (the amount paid on each unit regardless of price), designed to raise government revenue or protect domestic industry.

tastes All factors other than income and prices that determine a consumer's demand for a commodity.

tax base The total quantity of economic activity subject to taxation, that is, the economic source (for example, sales and income) of tax revenues.

technology All non-price conditions relating to the way in which a commodity is produced.

term deposit A bank deposit that is contracted to remain for a specified period of time.

terms of trade The quantity of one good that will be traded for a given quantity of another good.

theory of the firm The models for behaviour and performance of firms under alternative market structures.

time preference, rate of The measurement of the preference for current consumption over future consumption.

total cost The sum of all costs of production, both fixed and variable, for a given quantity of output.

total product The total quantity produced per time period by the total productive factors of the firm.

total revenue The sum of revenues received from the sale of a good; calculated as the quantity sold multiplied by the price.

transactions demand for money Money held to make routine purchases over a short period of time.

transfer earnings The minimum payment required to attract a resource factor from other uses.

transfer of government deposits Transfers of federal government deposits between the central bank and the chartered banks. These transfers result in changes in chartered bank reserves, and hence in the money supply.

transfer payments Those payments for which no goods or services are provided in exchange, such as family allowances, pensions, and welfare assistance. Private transfer payments are more commonly called gifts.

treasury bill Short-term securities that provide major day-to-day cash needs of the government.

underemployment Situation where persons are employed at jobs requiring less than their highest skills, or for fewer hours than they prefer.

underground economy The transactions that are not included in the national income accounts because there is no report on the total values involved. These include illegal activities, barter, and cash transactions that are not reported on income tax returns.

unemployment Most commonly refers to the inability of those in the labour force to find jobs; also, the underutilization of economic resources.

unemployment rate The number of persons unemployed as a percentage of the total labour force.

union *See* labour union.

union shop   A workplace where a new employee is required to join the union within a specified time period, usually 30 days.

unitary elasticity   Elasticity of demand (or supply) equal to one. Demand such that an increase in price or income leads to a proportional change in quantity demanded.

unlimited liability   Liability such that creditors can claim the proprietors' personal assets—houses, automobiles, and furniture—as well as the business assets, should the proprietorship be unable to meet its financial obligations.

unplanned inventories   Stocks of goods above the planned or desired level of inventory; result when planned aggregate expenditure is less than actual output.

utility   Satisfaction received in consuming a good or service.

value added   Value added to a product at each stage of a process; calculated by subtracting the purchases of intermediate and raw materials from other firms or suppliers from the selling price of the item at that stage.

value-added tax (VAT)   This is a tax levied on the difference between the buying and selling prices of all goods and services at every stage of production or distribution, including the final consumer. *See also* GST.

variable costs   Costs that vary directly (but not necessarily in proportion) with changes in the quantity of output.

velocity of money   Calculated by dividing the GDP, in current dollars, for a given year by the stock of money.

wage and price controls   Government actions to regulate changes in wages and prices, usually limiting wage and price increases in an attempt to combat inflation. *See also* incomes policy.

wages   All forms of payment (direct as well as indirect) for labour services.

wealth effect   The effect on consumption spending of holding highly liquid assets, as opposed to less liquid forms; individuals tend to feel wealthier when they hold more liquid assets, and thus have a higher consumption level.

withdrawal   Reductions in planned aggregate expenditure, or decreases in planned spending on domestic goods and services, at a given income level.

workable competition   Effective competition. A market structure with at least two buyers and two sellers, but preferably more; a mixture of large and small firms; no collusion or coercion among sellers; as much market information as can possibly be made available to buyers and sellers; and no barriers to entry or exit.

Index